The Essential
Garden Design
Workbook

The Essential Garden Design Workbook

Rosemary Alexander

Timber Press

All photographs by Rosemary Alexander except page 136 (bottom left) by Mrs Caroe and page 288 (top left) by Gill Poulter.

All illustrations by Joseph Kent except pages 31, 33, 42, 43, 60, 62, 63, 84, 85, 86, 87, 88, 90, 91, 92, 130, 182, 185, 215, 218, 235, 241, 251, 255 by Carel Lucas and pages 73, 74, 75, 120 by Roger Sweetinburgh.

Mood boards and designs by Rochelle Greayer (page 239); Sarah Haigh (page 219); and Rachel Myers (pages 186 and 233).

Published in 2004 by
Timber Press, Inc.
The Haseltine Building
133 S.W. Second Avenue, Suite 450
Portland, Oregon 97204-3527, U.S.A.
www.timberpress.com
For contact information regarding editorial, marketing, sales, and distribution in the United Kingdom, see www.timberpress.co.uk.

Project Editor Susanne Haines
Design by Dick Malt
Printed through Colorcraft Ltd., Hong Kong

Fourth printing 2006

Library of Congress Cataloging-in-Publication Data

Alexander, Rosemary.
  The essential garden design workbook / by Rosemary Alexander.
      p. cm.
  Includes bibliographical references and index.
  ISBN-13: 978-0-88192-664-4 (flexibind)
  ISBN-10: 0-88192-664-7
  1. Gardens—Design. I. Title.
  SB473.A443 2004
  712'.6—dc22
                                        2004007420

A catalogue record for this book is also available from the British Library.

Contents

Acknowledgements

Writing a design manual is often a partnership, and in this case I was fortunate to be able to draw on a wonderfully supportive team.

Firstly my thanks to Anthony du Gard Pasley, whose vast experience and discerning eye taught me so much in the formative years of The English Gardening School, and who made a great contribution to the original text. My thanks, secondly, to my editor, Anna Mumford, whose encouragement and tenacity greatly improved the book. I am indebted to project editor, Susanne Haines, for her valuable work on the text and to Dick Malt for the excellent design. My thanks also to Joe Kent, Carel Lucas and Roger Sweetinburgh, who were invaluable in providing the line drawings and chapter plans; to Rochelle Greayer for advice on the American perspective; to Rochelle Greayer, Sarah Haigh and Rachel Myers for allowing me to show their plans; to Amanda Crabb for her invaluable and reliable support and for giving some semblance of order to my erratic computer skills; and to Barbara Linton for her patience and experience in dealing with the plans and drawings.

God Almightie first planted a Garden.
And indeed, it is the Purest of Humane pleasure.
It is the Greatest Refreshment to the Spirits of Man.

Francis Bacon

Introduction

What Makes a Well-Designed Garden?

Garden design is all about organizing and shaping spaces, and in this respect it is closely related to architecture. It covers many different elements, from surveying the site and understanding the soil, through to selecting the plants, ornaments and lighting. Because it encompasses so many different disciplines, it is also one of the most complex art forms. But just as someone can be taught how to paint, those new to garden design can be taught how to make a beautiful garden.

This book aims to take you logically through the various stages of replanning a garden. It is a process that begins with assessing the site, the soil and the surroundings and involves everything from surveying to constructing pergolas and terraces, using water and choosing and placing plant material.

To communicate your ideas, you need to be able to present them on paper—this is a very necessary part of the design process, and this book explains what plans need to be drawn up in order to develop your design. Throughout the book, a sequence of model plans for a large suburban garden provides an example of the way a plan for a site is developed through its various stages. You do not need to be artistic to draw up a presentable plan. In this book you will find information about the drawing skills required at the appropriate stages, from an explanation of what drawing materials are needed and how to use them, to drawing a plan to scale, and finally, how to create other back-up or presentation material, such as details, visuals and mood boards.

Choosing the plants is usually the most exciting part of designing a new garden, but it is also the most exacting. Plants have their individual preferences, and it is crucial that you select those that will thrive in your locality. When using plant material, the scene is constantly changing—the shape of plants, their colours and textures all alter as they respond to seasonal changes or as they mature. This book will show you how to choose, combine and arrange plants to provide an ongoing display.

Who Will Use the Garden?

Before starting to plan a garden you need to decide who will use it. It may be you and your family, or perhaps you are making a garden for a friend or neighbour. What do you want to achieve with the new design? Gardens are for people as well as plants, and the space must be comfortable and appropriate for both.

What Makes a Good Garden Designer?

Two qualities are essential—firstly the ability to see things clearly and to understand their intrinsic nature, and secondly the ability to analyze the value of what is seen, identifying good and bad points and deciding how best they may be used or concealed. Once this process is concluded, you will be able to consider your new ideas, experimenting with different themes until you have a workable scheme.

Stages in the Design Process

Designing a garden is a gradual process, and the model plans chart the different stages. The site survey, site inventory and site appraisal are the first drawings made during the research and preparation stages. In researching them and drawing them up you will get to know the advantages and constraints of the site. Concept diagrams illustrate how the site can be reorganized to fulfil your needs.

The design process is then progressed on the drawing board, using the information previously gathered on site. Experimenting with different design themes and relating these to a grid springing from the house will ensure that your new garden sits comfortably within the property.

Gardens are, of course, three-dimensional, and while it is helpful to develop the design initially on a tracing-paper plan, the three-dimensional effects of your ideas must also be considered. The experimental design theme will then probably need considerable amendment before it moves on to the next stage, the preliminary garden layout plan.

From this evolves the final garden layout plan—the most crucial part of your design. The garden will be built to this plan, so it must be accurately drawn to scale, giving details of all hard and soft materials, their dimensions and how they are used.

Although the garden layout plan normally gives a broad indication of planting intentions, often there is not room to detail all the plants, hence the next stage of the design process is to produce an itemized and clearly labelled planting plan.

A planting plan can be used as an inspirational proposal, or as a working document to show where each plant should be placed in the new borders. Sometimes the planting plan is accompanied by an elevation to show the different heights and shapes of plants.

What Will You Achieve by Reading This Book?

By following the process described, you will be well equipped to analyze a site, define its problems and potential, and then develop your ideas into an original and workable design.

Although the book is primarily intended for people wishing to plan or redesign their own garden, the aim is to encourage you to achieve a professional standard in design and presentation. Understanding the design process will also increase your critical appreciation of gardens, and I hope that you will use it to create your own lovely garden.

Chapter 1
Research, Preparation and Design Appraisal

Garden design is a form of art, and just as with painting or music, there are guidelines that, once absorbed, help to make the creative process easier. The most important tools for understanding any form of visual art are our eyes, but often we look but do not see. This chapter provides the basis for design, explaining the various processes that will lead to the eventual layout or plan, taking you logically through the preliminary stages of garden design. It will help you to develop an observant yet practical approach to creating a garden.

Before any planning can begin, it is vital to assess how a garden is going to be used.

A climbing frame for children can be replaced by a pergola (right) when the children have grown up.

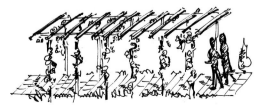

The Garden Owner's Requirements

It is vital that any design for a private garden should satisfy the needs of those who own and use it. If you are designing your own garden you will probably have thought about how you want the garden to function, and the resources, time and skills that you can devote to it, but it is still useful to get this information down on paper. When designing for others you will need to assess what they want and need through sensitive discussion with them. Sometimes they do not know what they want and will hope for your guidance. The garden should reflect not only their needs but also something of their personalities.

By deliberating on site you can also consider the setting. No garden should be conceived in isolation. Every outdoor space, however small or restricted, is part of a larger whole with which it interacts, apparently fitting naturally into its surroundings. It may only extend to the back of neighbouring houses, or it may extend to distant woods and hills. So, in contemplating your garden project it is necessary to look beyond the immediate boundary of the site and decide how to create your own personal paradise within the wider context while still supplying the practical necessities.

Today, with outdoor space an expensive domestic asset, gardens often need to serve as outdoor rooms for eating, cooking, entertaining and so on. Children may use the garden for riding bicycles or for a climbing frame, but as they grow older these needs will change. Try to cater for this by making your proposed design sufficiently flexible to be easily adapted for later changes in use.

Three possible designs for a small, featureless site. The chosen design should reflect the architecture and interior style of the house.

Linking Garden and House

If the garden is directly adjacent to the house, it is important that the two are linked so that they appear to function as one entity. You will need to study the architecture and the interior style of the house to achieve this. Note the type of building materials used to construct the house, and incorporate some of the same materials into the hard landscaping of the garden. Try to carry the colour schemes used inside, and the style of furniture and furnishings, through to the design of the garden. It is often possible to create a subtle, unified effect simply by carefully selecting and painting one or two pieces of garden furniture in the same colour as used inside, or by echoing, in nearby plantings, the colours of furnishing fabrics.

Questions to Ask

There are numerous important points to consider at this early stage concerning how the garden will be used. Start with the broad questions of use and budget:

– What time of day is the garden most used, and by whom?
– Will it be used year-round or only on summer weekends?
– What family and friends may visit?
– How much time and energy will be available for maintenance?

Try to establish a budget for building and planting the garden and for future maintenance. There is no point in creating a high-maintenance garden if there are no resources to look after it. Then consider more specific practical points:

– Is a greenhouse or garden shed required?
– Where will tools, toys and garden furniture be stored?
– Where are dustbins kept, and are they easily accessible for rubbish removal?
– Are compost bins for recycling household waste required?
– Is there parking space for cars, if required, and sufficient room to turn vehicles?
– Is lighting required for security, safety or for simply enjoying the garden in the evening?

Once it has been established how the garden is going to be used, you can consider the aesthetics:

– Is a particular style of garden required?
– Are there any materials that you particularly like or dislike?
– Do you have any preferences for plantings?
– Do you favour a particular colour scheme?

GARDEN OWNER'S CHECKLIST

1. Resident Family Members (including pets)

Name	Age	Hobbies (if relevant)
Dr. A. Williams	45	Love travel; Mediterranean climates
Mrs. E Williams	43	gardens - Both enthuse about La Mortola gardens.
Karen	11	Both children use garden year-round
Peter	9	for wild play. Quote: "It hasn't got any hidden corners to hide in"

2. Existing Problems (visual and functional)

Fences and walls dominate the scene
No views to park - fence blocks view
SIDE BEDS empty except for rose bushes
Front Garden, though small, needs 'more excitement'
     House elevation AB is bare of plants.

3. Positive elements to be retained or enhanced

Trees T1, T3, T5, T6   Brick WALL (good colours + texture)
Garage is v. attractive but cluttered with wall decoration + accessories (hose, light, bird table etc.)
Garage has human scale and a charming roof.

4. Desired Character of site (formal/ informal, etc.)

Informal - a variety of places required - a sense of mystery in places
- to contrast with a sense of openess elsewhere.

5. Favourite Plants (if any)

Exotic, Mediterranean

6. Planting effects
- Emphasis on foliage ✓
- Flowers for cutting - flowers from shrubs preferred
- General all year interest ✓
- Spring interest
- Summer interest
- Autumn interest
- Winter interest ✓ Winter flowering shrubs w/ long lasting flowers - clients emphatic!

7. Favoured materials for hard landscaping
- Brick
- Gravel
- Stone
- Concrete
} Any of these - but watch costs!
- Setts No
- Cobbles No - Client says "I loathe cobbles"
- Timber No
- Iron No

8. Other elements to be included
- Lighting Integrated w/ some flexibility.
- Irrigation ✓
- Furniture ✓ Not "country house", more "Italian café"
- Water ✓ must be ok for wildlife - several small ponds preferred
- Ornaments ✓ A free hand but not to expensive
- Other structures ✓ + not too formal. A vine covered arbour for meals and drinks but "I don't want leaves dangling in our coffee" (height required)

9. Client requirements
- Parking area - soften area near garage
- Sitting area ✓
- Play area ✓ Should invite play + exploration
- Vegetable garden No X
- Herb garden ✓
- Fruit garden - Retain existing trees. Quince + Apricot needed.
- Flowers for the house (cutting garden) X
- Greenhouse X - No tender plants
- Dust bin storage
- Firewood storage X No
- Tool and storage shed - improve
- Compost ✓

10. Budget
- Initial costs   £ 24,000 excluding new shed
- Annual maintenance cost £ 500 - Clients would like maintenance guide

ꞌ Garden Owner's Checklist

As a garden designer, reconciling visual requirements with practical necessities is one of your biggest challenges. These issues need careful assessment from the start, culminating in the checklist, which you will need to refer back to when you begin to design. It is useful to complete a garden owner's checklist to clarify what is actually wanted.

Preceding page: Whether you are designing a garden for yourself, a friend or a client, it is useful to make a checklist of everything that will be required of the garden. You may wish to produce your own list on a computer.

Making a Site Survey

In order to produce an accurate plan of your intentions for the design of the garden, you will need to produce a scale drawing of the site, called a site survey. If you are lucky, there may be an existing ground plan that you can use (even house plans can help by providing the exact location of doors and windows). But usually you will need to measure the site yourself, and in this way you will become much more familiar with the site and at the same time you will have the opportunity to notice all aspects of the garden that need to be considered.

For the survey you will need to locate the house, boundaries and any existing features (good or bad) that are likely to remain unchanged. These will include man-made structures, such as manhole covers, oil tanks and telegraph poles, and existing vegetation, such as mature trees, hedges, shrubs and perennials.

Before any work begins on the garden you must establish the ownership of any boundary walls. You may find, for instance, that the owner is responsible for one wall, an adjacent neighbour for another and a neighbour opposite is responsible for the rear wall. If in doubt, ask your local council at an early stage for advice on ownership and responsibilities.

At this stage it is also important not to make any hasty decisions about removing established plants. On closer examination you may well discover that a particular tree or large shrub has been placed where it is for a specific purpose—for instance, to obscure some eyesore.

"Well, for a start, that borin tree will have to go."

"Ah… I think I may have made a mistake."

Trees and hedges also provide a garden with a sense of maturity, so unless you have a good reason for removing these, try to incorporate them into the new scheme. Some plants, such as herbaceous perennials and shrubs with a fibrous root system (for example, rhododendrons), can be moved and reused quite easily. Others, such as trees and shrubs with stringy roots that do not retain soil (for example, broom), are less likely to survive.

The positions of all of these fixed elements can be measured and plotted on the site survey plan, first as a sketch and then drawn up to scale. At the next stage of the design process, the many other factors that cannot be measured with a tape or ruler are recorded on the plan for the site inventory (see page 60). Following this, an assessment of existing elements and action to be taken is evaluated on the plan for the site appraisal (see page 62). However, it is useful to bear these things in mind when preparing the site survey. They include visual elements such as views and the style of the house, practical matters such as the state of existing plants, and local conditions such as climate, orientation, ambient noise levels and soil type.

You will need the following equipment to make a survey of the site:

- Measuring tape (30 m or 100 ft.)
- Metal skewer
- Flexible metal tape (2–3 m or 6–10 ft.)
- Small plastic spirit level
- Clipboard
- Graph paper (A4 or 8.5 × 11 in.)
- Notebook
- Camera and film
- Trowel
- Small plastic bags, ties and labels
- Torch (flashlight)

And you will need the following equipment to draw up the plan of the survey:

- Drawing board
- Parallel motion rule or T-square
- Set square
- Circle template
- Compasses with beam attachment
- Graph paper (A2 or 17 × 22 in.)
- Tracing paper (A2 or 17 × 22 in.)
- Scale rule (make sure that the scale rule coordinates with the measuring system that you plan to use)

- Masking tape
- Pencils and eraser
- Technical drawing pens
- Felt-tip pens
- Coloured pens

Taking Measurements

You will be using two types of measuring tapes. The flexible, retractable metal tape is straightforward to use and requires no explanation. However, if you have never used the very long 30 m (100 ft.) tape outdoors, you may find it unwieldy and prone to tying itself—and you—up in knots! To avoid this, keep the case under your left arm (if you are right-handed), and pay out, or gather in, with your right hand.

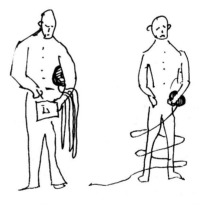

Loop the tape over your arm when walking about, to avoid becoming entangled.

Once you have begun the operation, avoid winding the tape back into the case. Instead, treat the length of tape rather like rope, looping it over your arm. Once you have finished measuring all the dimensions, you can then wipe the moisture and dirt from the tape with a cloth or tissue as you wind in. This method will help keep this expensive piece of equipment in good condition.

A metal skewer, tied to the hook at the end of the tape and anchored into the ground, is useful for securing the tape, particularly if you are surveying on your own. When measuring from a hard surface, you will need to fix the end of the tape with a brick or something similarly heavy and begin to read off any measurements.

If the distances to be measured are longer than your 30 m (100 ft.) tape, you can use a ball of string to set out the line first. The string line can then be measured in stages.

skewer

Where the ground is soft you can use a metal skewer to secure the end of the tape.

tape should lie flat on the ground

make sure the skewer is pushed well into the ground as you will need to pull on the tape

Taking and recording accurate measurements in your garden is quite simple once you know the correct way to proceed. There are three main methods, and often all three need to be used to accurately locate and fix the different elements on the plan. They are baseline measuring (also called running dimensions), offset measuring and triangulation measuring.

Baseline measuring

When measuring up a site accurately, there will be many points that you need to record along one straight line: for example, recording where the doors and windows are located along the front of the house. Rather than measuring from the house edge to the window edge, then shifting the tape and measuring another separate length (which is time-consuming and may cause inaccuracies), align the tape as closely as possible along a fixed line (the baseline—in this

case the exterior wall of the house) and read off each point that needs to be measured. These measurements are sometimes referred to as running dimensions because they are progressive.

Measure the side of a house using baseline measuring.

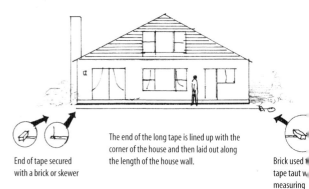

End of tape secured with a brick or skewer

The end of the long tape is lined up with the corner of the house and then laid out along the length of the house wall.

Brick used tape taut w measuring

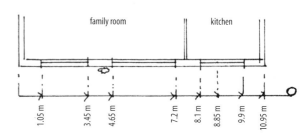

family room   kitchen

1.05 m   3.45 m 4.65 m   7.2 m 8.1 m 8.85 m 9.9 m 10.95 m

Above: Running measurements are used to record the position on the ground plan of such items as doors and windows and the length of the wall.

Below: The information is record on a sketch, drawn freehand on graph paper (not to scale).

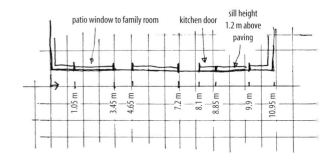

patio window to family room   kitchen door   sill height 1.2 m above paving

1.05 m   3.45 m 4.65 m   7.2 m 8.1 m 8.85 m   9.9 m 10.95 m

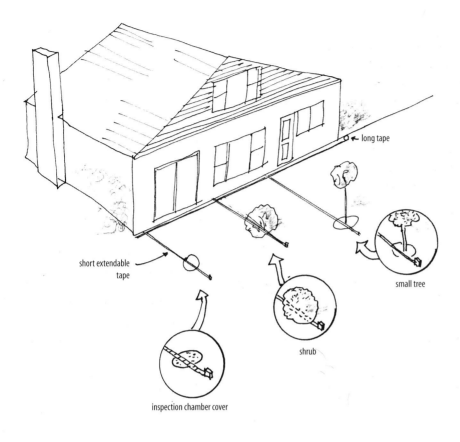

long tape

short extendable tape

inspection chamber cover

shrub

small tree

Take offsets to measure elements close to the house wall.

The long tape, laid against the house wall, is used to measure "how far along" the element occurs, and the shorter tape is used to measure the offset, or "how far out" the element occurs. Manhole covers are particularly important to locate accurately—they will often affect paving patterns around the house.

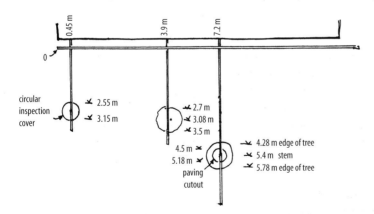

0.45 m   3.9 m   7.2 m

0

circular inspection cover

≮ 2.55 m
≮ 3.15 m

≮ 2.7 m
≮ 3.08 m
≮ 3.5 m

4.5 m ✕
5.18 m ≮

paving cutout

≮ 4.28 m edge of tree
≮ 5.4 m stem
≮ 5.78 m edge of tree

Offset measuring

While measuring from a baseline, you may also wish to take offset measurements to record elements that do not fall on the line itself but are located close to it, such as a manhole cover or a tree near the house wall.

In this case you simply note from the long tape how far along the element is situated and then, placing the rigid tape at right angles to it, record how far out the element occurs.

Triangulation measuring

The triangulation method is used to locate a third point in relation to two known points or an established baseline. Since the starting point for surveying a garden is usually the house, two of the house corners usually act as the two known points from which trees, boundary corners and so forth can be measured. On site you simply measure and note down the distance from each corner of the house to the object (such as a tree). You can then plot the measurements later, using compasses as shown.

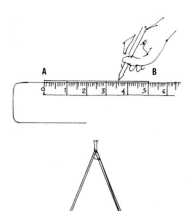

Back in your workplace, using a scale rule (see page 37), draw in the baseline A–B at your chosen scale.

Extend your compasses to the dimension A–C.

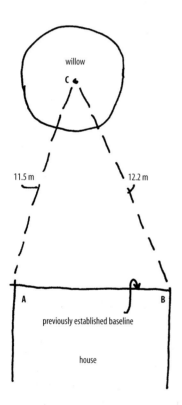

With the metal spike on point A, draw an arc.

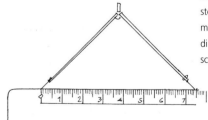

Repeat the previous step for B–C. First measure the dimension on your scale.

When locating a point by triangulation, first you need to establish a baseline (two fixed points or previously located points) from which you can measure. On site, measure the length of the baseline (from point A to point B), then measure from each point to the feature that you are locating (here, the willow tree at point C). Record the measurements of A–C and B–C on a sketch, as shown.

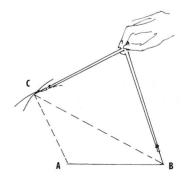

Then draw in an arc. The point at which the arcs cross is the location of point C (the willow tree).

Surveying the Site

Begin by sketching a rough outline plan of the house on A4 (8.5 × 11 in.) graph paper. If the garden is only on one side of the house, you need only sketch that side. Make your sketch as large as possible, leaving some room to write measurements. The graph paper will help you to keep the drawing neat and reasonably proportioned, but do not attempt to draw the house to scale at this point. The sketch of the exterior of the building should include the position of all doors and windows and their direction of opening, as well as elements close to the house, such as drains and manhole covers. If there are any other buildings on the site, such as a garage or shed, you should make sketches of these on separate sheets of paper. These rough sketches will be the drawings on which you note down the dimensions of the buildings. Later they will be drawn to scale on a larger sheet of tracing paper.

Measuring Buildings Using Running Dimensions

Once you have drawn the rough sketch plan you are ready to begin measuring, using running dimensions as described on page 20. It is usually sensible to begin with the house because the walls are generally straight and provide a firm surface for establishing a baseline, but it does not matter if the walls are not straight, or if there are indents or protrusions along its length.

Using a skewer or brick to fix the tape securely to the starting point (usually one corner of the house), pay out the tape along the length of the house as close to the house wall as possible, then lay the reel down on the ground. Go back to the beginning of the tape and read off the position of all corners, doors, windows, taps, drains and so on, along the house wall, and record these neatly. Now plot the running dimensions of the other buildings in the same way.

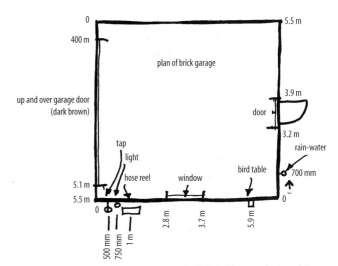

First sketch a rough plan of the buildings on graph paper. Indicate the position of doors and windows and make a note of any items attached to the building that you will need to measure. Then, starting on one side, measure each wall using running measurements and record these neatly on your drawing, as shown.

Measuring Heights and Nearby Features Using Offsets

Use the shorter tape to take offset measurements (see page 21) for the heights of window sills, lights, taps and any irregularities along the line of the building. Start with the house, and then take measurements for any other buildings on the site. Also use offset measurements to locate any nearby features, such as manhole covers.

Measuring More Distant Elements Using Triangulation

When you have completed the house survey, take another piece of graph paper and roughly sketch on it the site boundary by eye. Within this, using triangulation (as described on page 22), draw the house, or house wall, and any other elements that you wish to locate, such as trees, paths and garden buildings.

When you choose a baseline, or two fixed points from which to measure, try to select the longest unobstructed line from which all or most of the area can be seen. For most sites, however, particularly when the house is surrounded by the garden, you will need more than one baseline.

If there is a lot of information, record heights on a separate sketch as shown here. Draw a separate elevation for each side of the building that you need to measure.

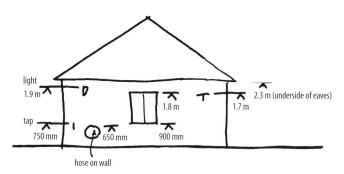

light
1.9 m
tap
750 mm
1.8 m
650 mm
900 mm
1.7 m
2.3 m (underside of eaves)
hose on wall

Elevation of brick garage

stand at a distance and estimate this by comparing it with the height of the garage wall (2.3 m)

2.3 m
this dimension is measurable

Left: You can estimate the height of a roof by photographing the building and scaling off from a print later (see page 27), or by comparing it with a measurable dimension, as shown.

Triangulation is very useful for establishing the position of elements that are not parallel or at right angles to a building, such as paths and boundaries. Before you start to measure, it is helpful to label on the sketch all the points that will need to be located and the known points from which they will be triangulated.

Measuring Heights and Widths of Features

As well as locating the exact position of fences, railings, steps and so on, you will need to record their heights and widths. These measurements can be recorded in detail beside each feature on the sketch plan or separately in a notebook.

It is most important to measure sill heights accurately, particularly if you are intending.to plant up against or close to the house. Your measurements will dictate the size of suitable plants.

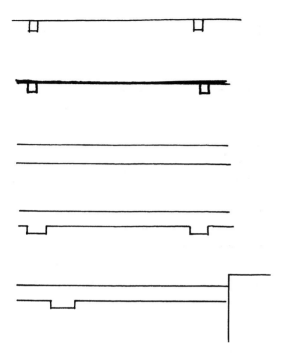

Even a wire fence (which has minimal thickness) will be supported by fence posts, which should be surveyed and recorded on the sketch of the site.

If the posts of a wooden fence are positioned on the garden side, these too should be surveyed and drawn on the correct side of the fence panels.

Walls of any thickness are drawn as a double line, the thickness also being noted on the survey.

If a brick wall is supported by piers or buttresses, these too should be measured and the spacing between them recorded.

Where a wall abuts a building it is important to locate the exact position of the join.

It is incorrect to represent a wall, fence or railing by a single line. When measuring, make sure that you take detailed notes of the width and height of the main supporting posts, plus the width and height of the panels or metal bars between each upright.

In the case of steps you will need to note the sizes of both risers and treads, as well as the number of steps. While taking the dimensions, look also at the state of these features. Are the steps cracked and in need of repair?

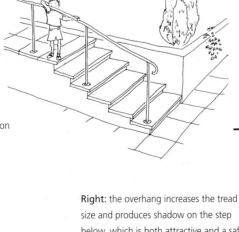

When measuring steps it is important, from a safety aspect, to survey the handrail—both its height and the position of the uprights. Often, as shown here, handrails do not provide a sufficient barrier to prevent small children from slipping through. If you design such a feature you may well be liable if an accident occurs.

Right: the overhang increases the tread size and produces shadow on the step below, which is both attractive and a safety feature, as the cast shadow emphasizes the change in level.

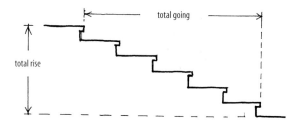

For most formal garden steps, such as these, the dimensions of treads and risers will be the same for every step. Instead of measuring each one individually, you can get an average tread measurement by dividing the total going by the number of treads, and an average riser measurement by dividing the total rise by the number of risers.

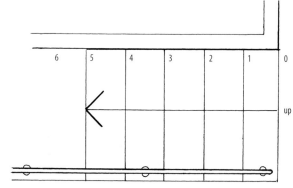

It is useful to number the steps when recording them on the sketch plan.

Estimating Measurements

If a wall is too high to measure with a tape, its height can be estimated. If the wall is made of brick, since an average brick is 75 mm (3 in.) high, the height can be calculated first by counting the number of brick courses, then working out the number of brick courses to 300 mm (1 ft.). Walls made of other materials can be measured against the height of a person, as shown. When checking heights and widths, notice the state of the wall (for instance, whether it has been rebuilt recently), and remember to record these details later on the site inventory.

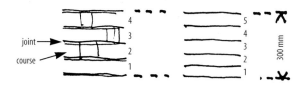

Above: Count the number of brick courses in a typical foot (or 300 mm). Often this is 4 courses, but sometimes slim bricks are used.

Below: There are 12 brick courses in this wall. By dividing by 4 (where there are 4 courses per 300 mm or 1 ft.) the height of the wall can be estimated as 900 mm (3 ft.).

If the wall you want to measure is high, you may find it easier to count the number of brick courses, rather than measure with your tape.

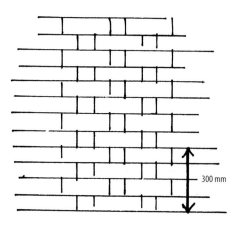

If the wall is not constructed in a material that is convenient to measure (such as brick or cut stone), use a different approach. Photograph a person, a 2 m (6.6 ft.) rod or an extended tape, against it. When the photograph is printed, you will be able to estimate the height surprisingly accurately by scaling off the photograph, using your "unit of measurement" as a reference. Here, the height of the building is approximately five times the height of the person, or 1.8 m (6 ft) x 5 = 9 m (29.5 ft.).

Measuring Trees

If there are any trees on the site that you wish to retain, use triangulation to locate the position of each trunk on the plan. In addition to this measurement you should note the type of tree, the diameter of the trunk, the spread of the tree canopy, the height of the lowest branches and the overall height of the tree. The latter can be estimated by using the height of a person standing near the tree as a unit of measurement (in the same way as for a wall). If there is not enough space for all this information on your plan, record it in a notebook.

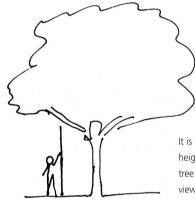

It is often worth measuring the height of the lowest branches of a tree as these may have an effect on views and underplanting.

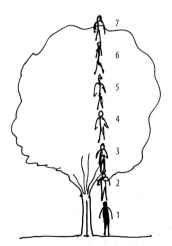

Left: To estimate the height of a tree, place an extended tape against its trunk or ask an assistant to stand next to the tree.

Right: Use running dimensions to record the diameter of the tree canopy, the location of the trunk and its thickness. Always name the tree, if possible, and record its height.

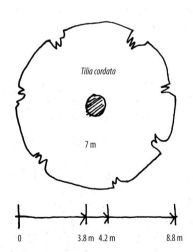

Tilia cordata

7 m

0   3.8 m 4.2 m   8.8 m

When surveying trees, it is important to record the outline form of the tree, particularly of any lower branches that you may wish to remove. Photograph the tree so that you remember the outline shape.

existing tree outline

after removing the lower branches

Measuring Curves

Curving lines that delineate features such as paths, beds or boundaries are measured using offsets taken at regular intervals from a baseline or a triangulation line. When taking offsets you must ensure that the measurements are taken at right angles to the baseline. You may find it useful to use a rectangular object, such as a cardboard box, to make the right angle.

Right: Use a rectangular object, such as a box, to establish a right angle.

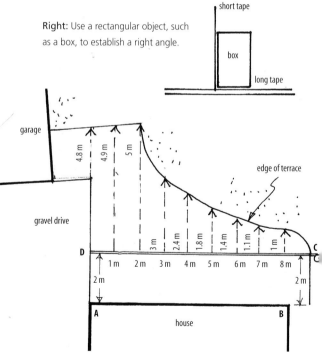

Above: The long tape forms the baseline. Offsets are taken at regular intervals—in this case one-metre intervals using the shorter tape.

Above: Use offset measurements to measure the curve of an existing terrace from a baseline. For accuracy, always try to use a baseline as close to the curve as possible. In this example, offsets are taken from the baseline D–C, established by moving the house baseline, A–B, two metres in the direction of the curve.

Assessing Slopes or Changes in Level

In most gardens there will inevitably be slopes or gradients and areas which to the naked eye look level but which are in fact at odds with each other. It is very important to be aware of any changes of level before working up the design. Squat down as near as possible to the ground in the flat part of the site to get the best view. You may notice that there is a slight slope to one side or another, or that one retaining wall is lower than the one opposite. A change in level or slope can drastically affect the garden layout. Soil may need to be brought in to make up the ground, or the surface may need to be regraded by machine.

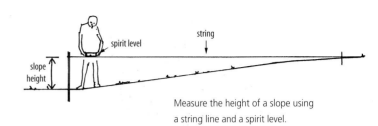

Measure the height of a slope using a string line and a spirit level.

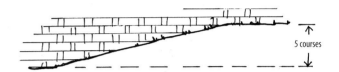

Measure the height of a slope running against a brick wall by counting the brick courses.

Judge the slope of a garden feature by viewing it through a small plastic spirit level. The spirit level must be held directly in front of your eyes, not at an angle. When it is level, you will be able to estimate at what degree the particular feature slopes away from the horizontal. In this case, the ground is level.

By observing the line of the earth against a brick wall, the slope of a garden can be assessed. Brickwork is usually horizontal.

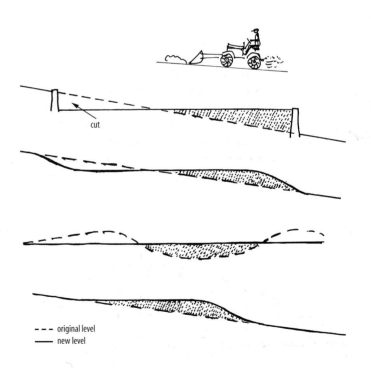

If you intend to create a level area in a sloping garden, the slope must be measured accurately to assess the work required. There are two main ways of levelling an area: by the "cut and fill" method, which involves cutting into the slope and using the "spoil" or removed soil to fill an adjacent area, or by importing soil on to a site.

Drawing a Sketch Plan of the Site Survey

The first stage of drawing up the garden plan brings together on one sketch all the initial surveying information that is recorded about the existing features on the site. It should be kept carefully together with the supporting sketches and notes that you make for future reference.

1. Start by attaching a sheet of graph paper to a clipboard, and—without worrying about scale at this stage—sketch the outline of the house or the part of the house that is adjacent to the garden. Mark the position of any doors and windows, showing the direction in which they open, plus any elements close to the house, such as drains and manhole covers.
2. On the sketch outline, mark the major points, such as the corners of the house, buildings and the main changes of direction in the site boundary, labelling them alphabetically in running order. You can then survey to or from these reference points, and they will be very useful when you come to draw up the survey to scale. If you are using a notebook to record the dimensions, these should tally with the points on the rough sketch plan.
3. Using either imperial or metric dimensions (but not mixing the two), measure one side of the house by laying the long tape along and close to the house wall. Use a skewer or brick to keep the tape in place.
4. Read off the running dimensions and record these accurately on the sketch plan.
5. Keep the long tape in place and use the short rigid tape to record the heights of windowsills, lights, taps and any other relevant features or irregularities along the building line. Add these to the sketch plan.
6. With the long tape still in place, take offsets to measure and record any influencing elements close by, such as manhole covers.
7. If necessary, repeat this exercise around each house wall.
8. On a fresh sheet of graph paper, sketch out the site boundary. Within this, locate and draw in the house (or part of it, as necessary).
9. Using triangulation or offsets, locate and draw in any other influencing elements, such as outbuildings, trees (numbering them T1, T2 and so on, if necessary), paths and planting beds.
10. In a notebook, write down information about each of the trees (using the numbers for identification): the diameter of the trunk, the spread or width of the tree canopy, the height of the lowest branches and the overall height of the tree. This information will be useful later.
11. Measure and record the height and width of walls, fences, gates and the treads and risers of steps in your notebook.
12. Having located the major trees and shrubs, try to name them. This may help you to decide whether or not to keep them in your new design.

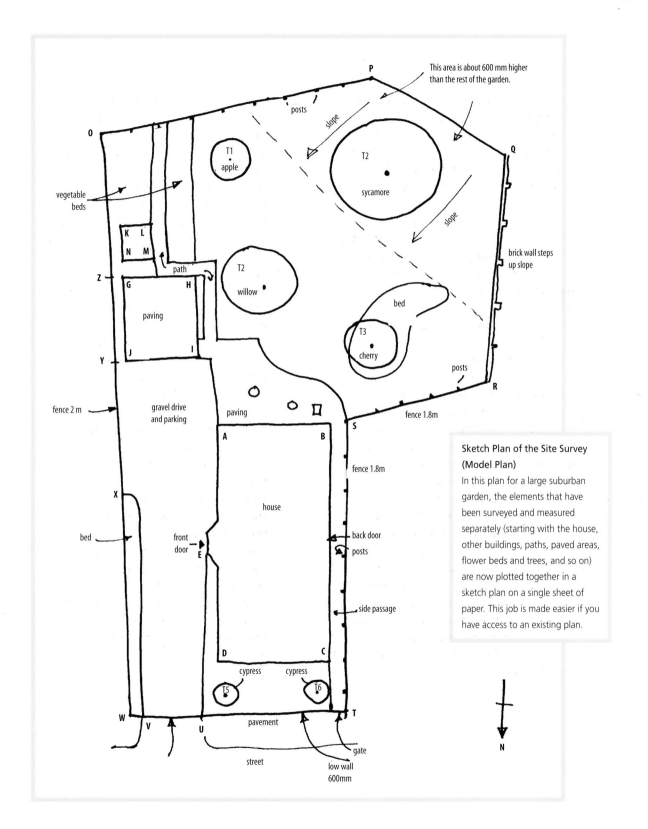

This area is about 600 mm higher than the rest of the garden.

posts

slope

slope

P

O

Q

T1
apple

T2
sycamore

vegetable
beds

brick wall steps
up slope

K L
N M

path

Z

G H

T2
willow

bed

paving

T3
cherry

posts

Y

J I

R

fence 2 m

gravel drive
and parking

paving

fence 1.8m

bed

X

house

fence 1.8m

front
door

E

back door

posts

side passage

D

C

cypress   cypress

T5

T6

W

V

U

T

pavement

street

gate

low wall
600mm

N

Sketch Plan of the Site Survey (Model Plan)

In this plan for a large suburban garden, the elements that have been surveyed and measured separately (starting with the house, other buildings, paths, paved areas, flower beds and trees, and so on) are now plotted together in a sketch plan on a single sheet of paper. This job is made easier if you have access to an existing plan.

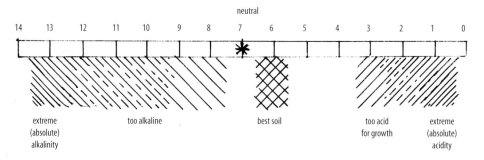

neutral

| 14 | 13 | 12 | 11 | 10 | 9 | 8 | 7 | 6 | 5 | 4 | 3 | 2 | 1 | 0 |

extreme
(absolute)
alkalinity

too alkaline

best soil

too acid
for growth

extreme
(absolute)
acidity

Soil can be tested with a kit to determine the pH factor. The pH scale ranges from 0 to 14, but plants can only tolerate a range from pH 4 to pH 7.5. The consistency of the soil and the type of plants that naturally occur on it are also useful indicators of soil type.

Testing the Soil

It is important to establish what type (or types) of soil you are dealing with and to record your findings on the plan. The acidity or alkalinity of the soil will govern what type of plants can be grown in the garden. This is known as the pH value and usually ranges from 4 (very acid) to 7.5 (very alkaline). A neutral or middle-range soil with a pH value of around 6 will support both types of plants.

Soil varies enormously from area to area. Under trees, for instance, there may be an accumulation of decaying leaf matter, which will render the soil in this area with a more acidic reading or lower pH value than elsewhere. A dry area at the base of a sunny wall may give a different reading with a higher pH. A damp boggy area may give a low pH reading.

You will therefore need to take soil samples (using a trowel, small polythene bags and labels) from several parts of the garden; sample points may include a spot adjacent to the house, under various trees and in existing beds. These samples will be tested later when they have dried (see page 34).

A second test to check the soil structure should be made on the spot at each sample point. Simply take a tablespoonful of soil and rub it between your fingers or squeeze it in the palm of your hand. If it sticks

together or can be squeezed into a largish lump, the soil will be made up of many tiny particles and will be clay. If, instead, the sample disintegrates into sandy, fibrous material, the soil is sandy or peaty. If there is an even balance between the two, you will have the best type of texture—a loam high in organic content. Very poor soil structure will result in poor plant growth, and you may need to consider improving the soil before you plan the planting.

A third test relies on your observation of the vegetation that naturally occurs on the site, and this is dealt with later in this chapter.

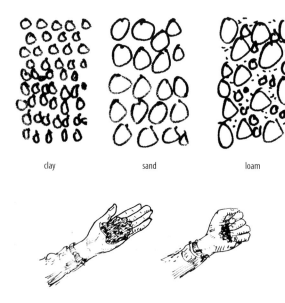

clay   sand   loam

To determine the soil structure, squeeze a soil sample in the palm of your hand—note its consistency and texture.

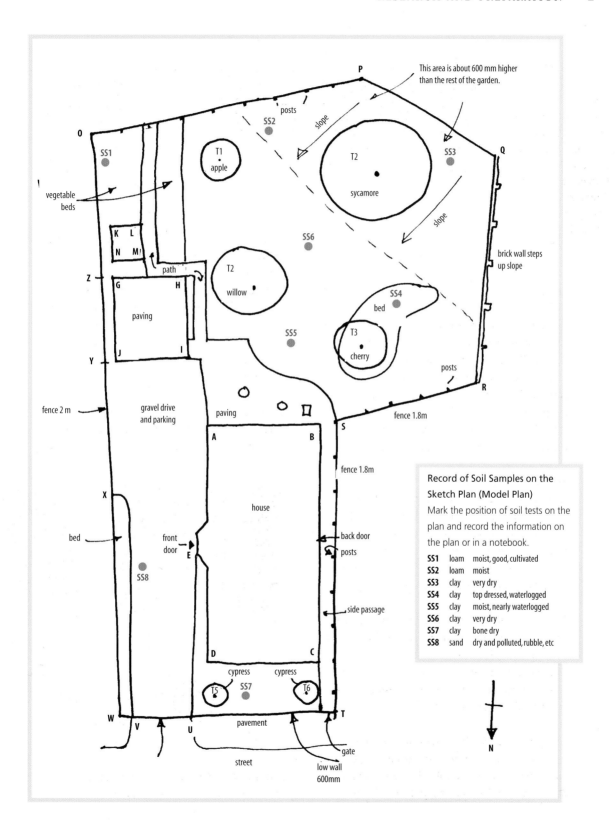

This area is about 600 mm higher than the rest of the garden.

P

posts

SS2

slope

O

SS1

Q

vegetable beds

T1
apple

T2

SS3

sycamore

brick wall steps up slope

slope

K L

N M

SS6

path

Z

G   H

T2

willow

SS4

bed

paving

SS5

T3

cherry

J   I

posts

Y

R

fence 2 m

gravel drive and parking

paving

S

bed

A   B

fence 1.8m

house

Record of Soil Samples on the Sketch Plan (Model Plan)

Mark the position of soil tests on the plan and record the information on the plan or in a notebook.

SS1	loam	moist, good, cultivated
SS2	loam	moist
SS3	clay	very dry
SS4	clay	top dressed, waterlogged
SS5	clay	moist, nearly waterlogged
SS6	clay	very dry
SS7	clay	bone dry
SS8	sand	dry and polluted, rubble, etc

X

front door

back door

posts

E

side passage

SS8

D   C

cypress   cypress

T5   SS7   T6

W   V   U   T

pavement

street

gate

low wall 600mm

N

Collecting Soil Samples

1. Decide where soil tests would be most appropriate and mark these positions on the sketch plan, labelling them SS1 (soil sample 1), SS2, SS3 and so on (see page 33).
2. Take a sample from each by inserting a trowel to approximately 100–150 mm (4–6 in.) below the surface, collecting about a tablespoonful of soil. Deposit this into a polythene bag, and then seal and label the bag in the same way.
3. At the same time, in each chosen position, test the structure of the soil in your hands (as shown on page 32).
4. On returning to your workplace, tip each soil sample onto a separate saucer, then sit each one on top of the labelled polythene bag and allow it to dry out naturally under cover overnight.
5. When completely dry, test the soil using a kit that contains a mixture of dyes which, when added to the soil sample and shaken with water, will change colour according to the pH value. Note your findings carefully (SS1: pH 6.5, SS2: pH 6 and so on) on the sketch plan or in a notebook.

Basic Drawing Skills

Once you have collected all the information you require about a site, you will need to draw up the site survey to scale, creating an accurate representation of the garden that concentrates on the ground plane. Although the garden is rarely seen from this "overhead" view, this survey drawing provides a base plan in which spaces and objects can be rearranged.

You will need some basic drawing skills for this stage of the design process. The plan is drawn on a sheet of tracing paper, the size of which will depend on the size of the garden and the scale to which you draw the plan.

You may produce your work in pencil, or you may wish to use ink drawing pens, which can give a more professional effect, despite a tendency for nibs to clog and lines to smudge. Your work should be kept as clean as possible. Use an eraser to remove lead smears, and a duster, small brush or cloth to remove eraser rubbings. If the sheet is overworked, some lines may become fuzzy, blurred or indistinct. In this case, overlay a second sheet of tracing paper and draw in only the lines that you want to keep. All horizontal lines should be drawn against a T-square or parallel motion rule, and all vertical lines against a set square, held firmly against the horizontal rule. Always keep pencils well sharpened and draw firmly and accurately.

Preparing to Draw the Plan

Set up a drawing board at a comfortable angle. As a backing sheet for your work use a large sheet of graph paper, A1 (22 × 34 in.) or A2 (17 × 22 in.), depending on the size of your drawing board. Use a T-square or parallel motion rule to check that lines are straight, and stick it down with masking tape, depending on the size of the board. On top of the graph paper, tape down a sheet of tracing paper for your plan drawing.

Paper size
A2 (17 × 22 in.) and A3 (11 × 17 in.) papers are a convenient size to work with because they are easier to have printed (as photocopies or dyeline prints) than A1 paper. However, paper size will depend on the size of the site and the scale at which it is to be reproduced.

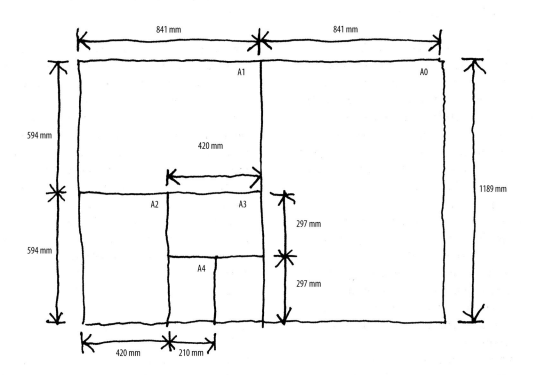

Paper size equivalents

The ISO paper size system is used everywhere except for Canada and the United States. The metric measurements of a range of these "A" sizes are given in the table below. A translation of these measurements into decimal inches is also given, together with equivalent paper sizes that are available in the United States.

ISO	mm	inches	United States	inches
A8	53 × 74	2.07 × 2.91	Business card	2 × 3.5
A7	74 × 105	2.91 × 4.13	3 × 5	3 × 5
A6	105 × 148	4.13 × 5.83	Microfiche	4.13 × 5.83
A5	148 × 210	5.83 × 8.27	5 × 8	5 × 8
A4	210 × 297	8.27 × 11.69	A	8.5 × 11
A3	297 × 420	11.69 × 16.54	B	11 × 17
A2	420 × 594	16.54 × 23.39	C	17 × 22
A1	594 × 841	23.39 × 33.11	D	22 × 34
A0	841 × 1189	33.11 × 46.81	E	34 × 44

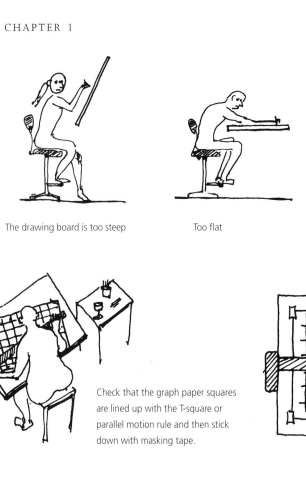

The drawing board is too steep

Too flat

Here the drawing board is set at a comfortable angle

Check that the graph paper squares are lined up with the T-square or parallel motion rule and then stick down with masking tape.

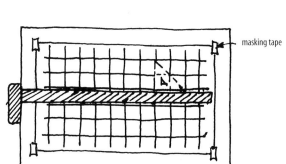

masking tape

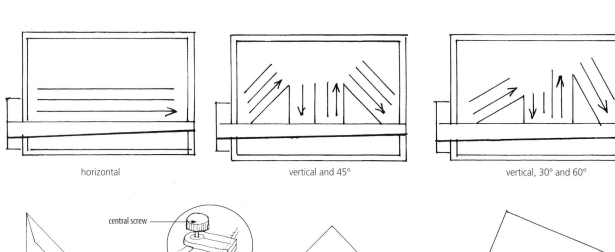

horizontal

vertical and 45°

vertical, 30° and 60°

central screw

An adjustable set square can be set at any pair of angles adding up to 90°.
The central screw that loosens to allow adjustment doubles as a useful handle.

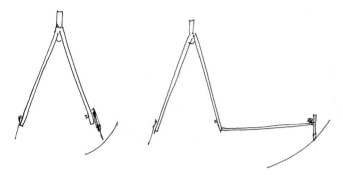

The stretch of a pair of compasses can be extended with a beam attachment arm.

This garden shed is 2 m (6.6 ft.) square; the person, lying down, is 1.8 m (6 ft.) in length. They are shown in plan (from overhead) at a scale of 1:50, 1:100 and 1:200. Notice that reducing to 1:200 makes things of this size too small to be clearly understood.

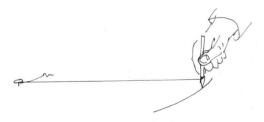

Makeshift compasses can be improvised with a drawing pin, a piece of string and a pencil.

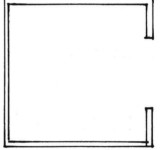

shed

2 m

2 m

1.8 m

Scale of 1:50

Working to Scale

If you have never drawn to scale before, this may seem complicated, but it is really quite simple. A scale rule will do the conversion for you. There are two types: one is triangular in section, the other looks rather like a normal ruler. Both are marked with a range of scales to denote measurements at different proportions, such as 1:1, 1:10, 1:20, 1:50 and so on, which represent different scales. The largest, 1:1, represents a reproduction at the same size as the original (that is, one unit represents one unit of the same size). A ratio of 1:10 (where one unit represents ten units) will give a drawing that is ten times smaller than the actual measurements. The illustrations on this page show how (and why) different scales are appropriate for different situations.

Scale of 1:100

Scale of 1:200

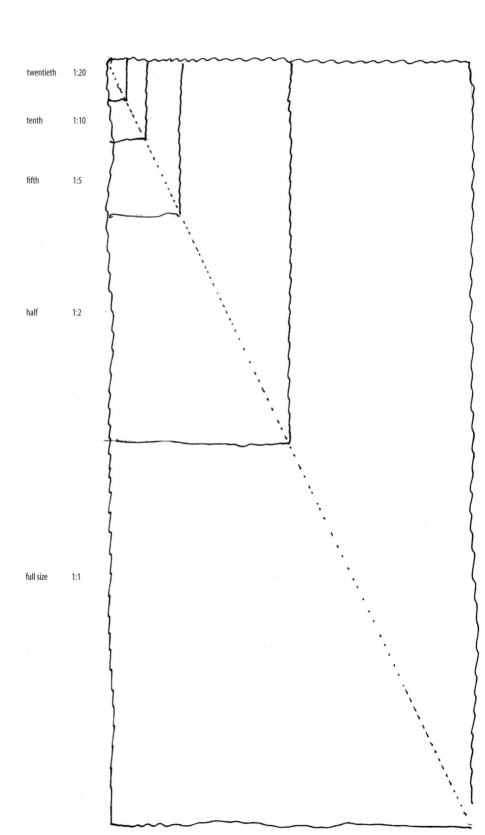

twentieth   1:20

tenth   1:10

fifth   1:5

half   1:2

full size   1:1

At a later stage, when you begin to develop the garden scheme, you may wish to make more detailed drawings of features such as steps, a seat or part of a wall. The outline of a building brick is shown here at different scales.

A full-size drawing (1:1) might occasionally be useful for a detail such as an edge of a step, a moulding or a pool edge.

A half-size drawing (1:2) is a dangerous scale to use as it can easily be confused with a full-size drawing.

A one-fifth (1:5) scale is handy for all sorts of details.

One-tenth (1:10) and one-twentieth (1:20) scales are useful for drawing detailed plans of things like patios, garden rooms or paving.

Practising Drawing to Scale

Before drawing up the plan, practise scaling down the measurements of one room in your house. Select a room that has as many doors or windows along a stretch of wall as possible. You will need drawing equipment (including a scale rule and a pencil) and two measuring tapes.

1. Use a brick to anchor the long tape at one end, and stretch it along the wall, making sure that it lies flat and is not twisted.
2. Record the running dimensions of this baseline, as shown earlier (page 20) to record door and window openings. Mark the starting point as A and the finishing point as B, so that you will know in which direction you are working.
3. Leaving the tape laid down, use the shorter tape to measure the heights of windows and doors and the dimensions of any protruding features, such as bookcases.
4. Set up the drawing board with a parallel motion rule or a T-square and a sheet of tracing paper. Look on the scale rule for the 1:50 scaled measurements and draw in the full length (A–B) of the baseline (and mark the running dimensions). The line you draw will be fifty times smaller than the actual measurement.
5. Repeat at a scale of 1:100.
6. Repeat at a scale of 1:20, provided that it will fit onto the sheet of tracing paper!

Choosing an Appropriate Scale for the Plan

Before you begin to draw up the survey you need to decide what scale you are going to use. The scale should be one that will represent the plan clearly on the sheet of tracing paper you have chosen, at a ratio that will reduce the actual measurements to a size that will make a plan that is easy to handle yet legible. In garden design this is usually either 1:50 or 1:100, or for very large sites, 1:200. A scale of 1:20 might be used for a site such as a small roof garden or terrace. (Later on, as you develop your plan, you may wish to make highly detailed drawings of features and will find that a scale of 1:5 is useful.)

Using the overall measurements of the length and breadth of the site, start with a scale of 1:50, and find the corresponding measurements on the scale rule. Draw up the outline and decide whether it fits the paper you want to use. If not, alter the scale, perhaps to 1:100. The plan can be orientated in any way to fit onto the sheet, but usually the best way is to place the plan so that it reflects the direction from which the garden is normally viewed.

If at a scale of 1:50 or 1:100 the garden will not fit on a sheet of A2 paper and requires A1 size, there is a danger that the site is too ambitious for a first attempt at garden design.

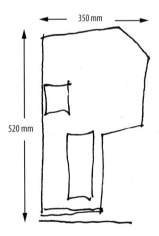

In the model garden plan that we are using, the measurements of the site are 17.5 × 26 m (19 × 28 yd.). At a ratio of 1:50, that gives a measurement of 350 × 520 mm (1.2 × 1.7 ft.). This is a useful starting point for working out the scale of the plan.

A2 sheet

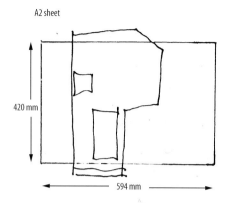

420 mm

594 mm

At a scale of 1:50 the survey, when placed vertically, will not fit onto an A2 sheet.

A1 sheet

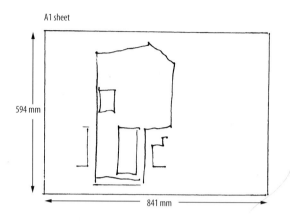

594 mm

841 mm

On a larger paper size, A1, the survey is slightly cramped and there is not adequate space for a border or notes at the top and bottom of the page.

A2 sheet

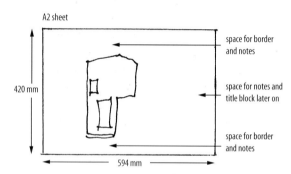

space for border and notes

space for notes and title block later on

420 mm

space for border and notes

594 mm

Left: By reducing the scale to 1:100, there is adequate space for the plan on a sheet of A2 (17 × 22 in.) paper, as well as for information that will be added at a later stage.

Here the plan is drawn on a horizontal axis. The garden owner finds it hard to relate to this plan because he is not used to viewing the garden sideways on.

This is the view that is normally seen from the back of the house, and it is easier to understand as a plan when oriented in this way.

Drawing up the Site Survey to Scale

Watching the site take shape on paper is always an exciting stage in the design process, even if it exposes a few inaccuracies of measurement. It is difficult to be completely accurate when surveying, and a small amount of artistic licence is forgivable! But if your measurements do not seem to work, you may need to return to the site to check the suspect ones. If you are inexperienced, it is very easy to make a mistake in reading dimensions off the tape, and you may not notice the error until you come to draw up the survey to scale. For this, you will need your drawing equipment, together with the sketch plan of the site survey and all your supporting notes and plans.

1. Start by deciding on the size of tracing paper you will use and the scale you will work at. Try a scale of 1:50 or 1:100 to start with and a paper size of A2 or A1. If the garden is very large, you could try a scale of 1:200; if very small, a scale of 1:20. The plan should sit comfortably on the sheet, with enough (but not too much) space for information around it, for labelling and for an information panel on the right-hand side.
2. Decide on the orientation of your plan, and then, using masking tape, stick down a large sheet of tracing paper on the board.
3. Using the sketch site plan and your notes for reference, start to draw up the plan (in pencil) in the same order as you surveyed the site, starting with the house and then the other buildings. As you plot the dimensions, tick them off in your notebook to avoid missing a crucial measurement, which will throw out the whole drawing. (If you want to approach things more gradually, draw up the buildings separately at first.)
4. Now work outwards from the buildings to the boundaries and other more distant features. For points that you triangulated you will need to use compasses (with a beam attachment arm for large dimensions). Refer to page 22 if you need to be reminded of how to plot these measurements.
5. Continue plotting all your measurements until you have covered every dimension.
6. Indicate the various site elements with the appropriate symbols. For trees, show the position of the trunk and the spread of the canopy, and note on the plan the name of the tree and its approximate height.
7. For vertical elements, such as fences, walls and steps, write in their height as well as any relevant design details. Add any useful details to the outlines of the buildings, including door and window openings.
8. When you have finished the drawing, put an arrow in the bottom right-hand corner to indicate the north point direction. In the same corner make a note of the scale to which the plan is drawn. Add any other notes to the plan.
9. The site survey will be used as a basis for the next stage of the garden plan, so keep it safely stored.

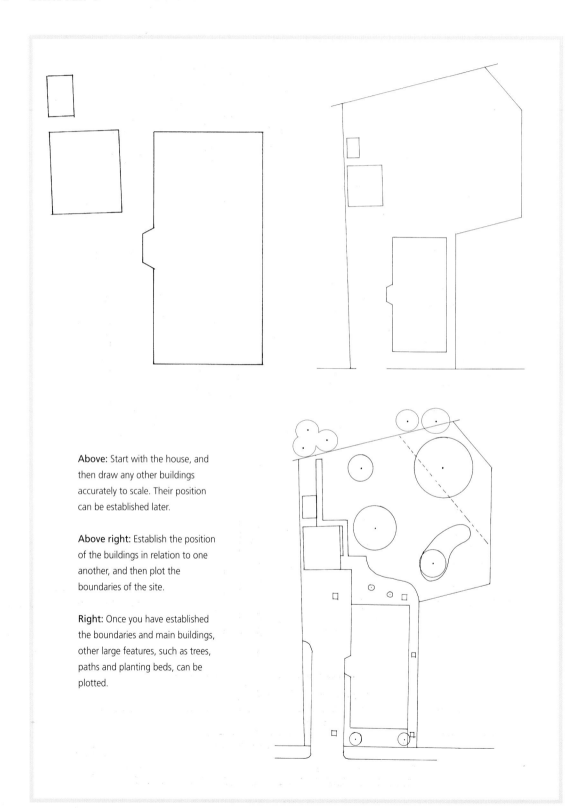

Above: Start with the house, and then draw any other buildings accurately to scale. Their position can be established later.

Above right: Establish the position of the buildings in relation to one another, and then plot the boundaries of the site.

Right: Once you have established the boundaries and main buildings, other large features, such as trees, paths and planting beds, can be plotted.

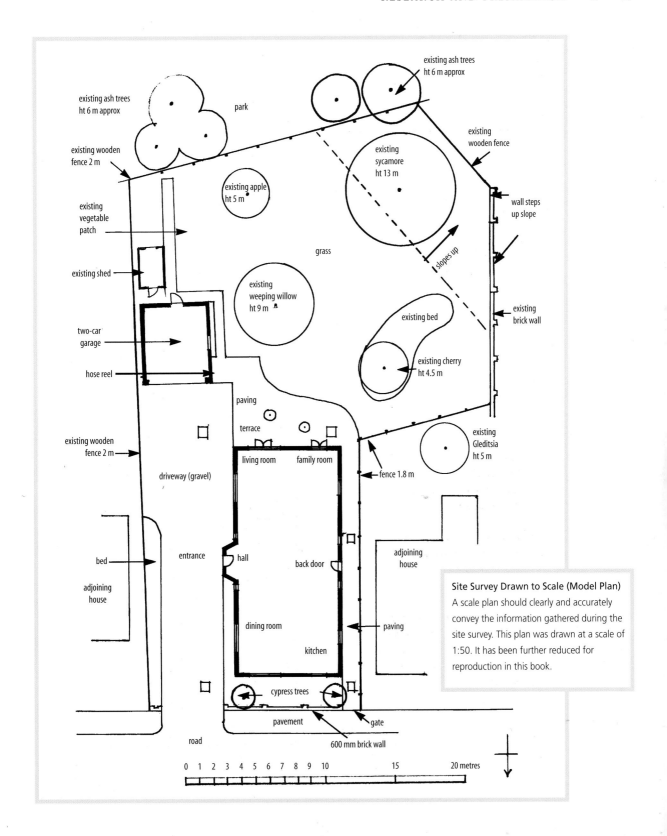

existing ash trees
ht 6 m approx

existing ash trees
ht 6 m approx

park

existing
wooden fence

existing wooden
fence 2 m

existing
sycamore
ht 13 m

existing apple
ht 5 m

wall steps
up slope

existing
vegetable
patch

grass

slopes up

existing shed

existing
weeping willow
ht 9 m

existing
brick wall

two-car
garage

existing bed

hose reel

existing cherry
ht 4.5 m

paving

terrace

existing
Gleditsia
ht 5 m

existing wooden
fence 2 m

living room

family room

fence 1.8 m

driveway (gravel)

bed

entrance

hall

back door

adjoining
house

adjoining
house

paving

Site Survey Drawn to Scale (Model Plan)

dining room

kitchen

A scale plan should clearly and accurately
convey the information gathered during the
site survey. This plan was drawn at a scale of
1:50. It has been further reduced for
reproduction in this book.

cypress trees

pavement

gate

road

600 mm brick wall

0 1 2 3 4 5 6 7 8 9 10   15   20 metres

Site Inventory Checklist

1. Approach to house
Size of street? ... Wide - but only local traffic
Traffic intensity? ... V. Low

2. House
Style and age? ... 1970's detached single family home.
Condition? ... Good
Façade materials? ... Brick and wood siding

3. Outside Services
Location of downpipes? Front left of Garage and front side (right)
Outside lights? (2) - garage   1 at front door
Electric meter? in back garden
Gas meter? ... same
Taps? ... Front side right adjacent to down pipe.

4. Hard Landscaping
Condition and materials of paths? Cement - excellent but generic
        Steps? cement
        Walls? N/A
        Other structures? wood fence w/ gate to back garden.

5. Views from house
To front lhs? ... Neighbours front garden - open
To front rhs? ... Obstructed by garage
To front boundary? bound by side walk
To back lhs? Obstructed by trees
To back rhs? Elevated so can see over privacy fence to neighbours patio
To back boundary? Fence (privacy)

6. Sounds or smells? Neighbours dog barking

7. Microclimate
Orientation? ... North - west
Areas of shade in mid-winter   Entire back garden shaded
        a.m.? ... all day shade
        p.m.?
Areas of shade in the mid-summer. All edges near fences shaded
        a.m.? much of the day
        p.m.? Patio gets full afternoon sun
Prevailing wind direction? From East

8. Level changes
Sloping ground? ... Slopes away from house in front + back.
Areas showing erosion? Tree Roots above ground in front.
Areas showing poor drainage? ... None.
Wall heights? ... 6 foot privacy fence around entire back garden.
Heights of steps? ... 6 steps up to front door

9. Soil
Type? ... Sandy - needs improvement
Depth of topsoil? ... 3 inches

10. Existing Plants
Location? All trees stay. 3 Aspens + 1 maple in front.
Condition? Good except Maple roots exposed in lawn

Recording Information for the Site Inventory: The Checklist

When you have completed drawing up the site survey, the next step is to record the state of the site and make suggestions for improving it. There is so much information to be gathered in this research and preparation phase of the design process that certain points can be easily overlooked. It is helpful, therefore, to refer to a written checklist, or inventory, of existing site conditions such as the one shown here.

The site inventory plan (see page 60) is a factual assessment of everything on the site, from the condition of structures to climatic features, and is prepared as an overlay on the site survey. There will be many reasons, such as cost or lack of access, that will govern what you remove, retain or repair. The site inventory is the first stage in making these decisions.

Photographing the Garden

In addition to surveying and noting facts about the site on your rough sketch plan and scale site survey, there are other steps to be taken before you begin considering the new design. Photographing the garden will allow you to look at the prints away from the garden, where you can be more practical and dispassionate in your feelings towards the site. Photographs also tend to turn up features often overlooked when on site, such as an unattractive light fitting or a badly rendered wall.

Photography provides the most accurate way of recording views (the camera never lies!). Whether you use a digital camera or a film camera, it is very useful to mount prints of the photographs on card (cardboard) and fix them on the wall in your workplace, providing you with a constant aide-mémoire to help you as you work on the project.

The prints can also be used later as a basis for "before" and "after" sketches to show how your intentions will alter the garden (see page 236).

This is often an easier way of getting your ideas across than doing a thumbnail or perspective sketch.

As has already been seen earlier in this chapter, a photograph can also be useful in estimating the height of features in the garden (see page 27).

Making a Photographic Record of the Site

1. Standing in a central position, with your back to the house, pivot round from extreme left to extreme right, taking overlapping shots of the site and its surroundings as viewed from the house (see page 46). A camera that can take wide panoramic shots would be particularly useful for this exercise. You may find that you can get the best views of a small site from an upstairs window.
2. Stand at the opposite end of the garden, and, moving along a line parallel to the house, take overlapping shots of the house.
3. Take photographs of views from and to carefully selected areas of the garden—for instance, where you may site an important feature, or views from a place where you might want to sit.
4. Take close-up photos of any items that you particularly want to record, such as walls, statues, trees, and pergolas, to show their general condition.
5. Have these photographs printed, mount them on card (cardboard), and study them when you need to be reminded of the site.

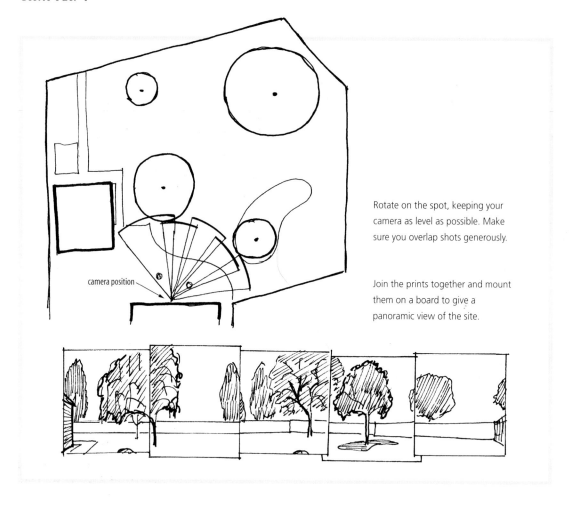

Rotate on the spot, keeping your camera as level as possible. Make sure you overlap shots generously.

Join the prints together and mount them on a board to give a panoramic view of the site.

camera position

The Garden and Its Setting

Planning a garden has much in common with interior decorating and furnishing. There is one subtle difference, however, in that the outdoor room (the garden) is much more influenced by its setting or by what lies immediately beyond its boundary. Just as the surrounding landscape is often visible from the garden, so too will the garden itself exert an influence on its surroundings, sometimes referred to as the Zone of Visual Influence or ZVI. When designing a garden you will need to consider not only what you can see from the site but also how your plans will affect the surroundings and the people passing through. Allow yourself plenty of time to walk around inside and outside the garden to consider how your ideas will affect and relate to the surroundings.

Always consider the safety aspect of your proposals— vigorous thorny climbers, for instance, can be a hazard when overhanging a narrow sidewalk.

Views

First of all, look closely at all the outward views from the garden. Observe and consider the following:

– What are the quality and character of the surroundings?
– Is the pattern of forms, colours and textures created by the combination of man-made features and vegetation?
– Do you like what you see, or is the outlook less than perfect?

If the garden is overlooked, you may want to disguise the boundaries of the garden and create a plan that holds the eye and attention within the site (an "introvert" garden).

Examine each aspect very carefully. Even in the centre of busy, built-up cities there are often glimpses of pleasant views, such as an interesting tree, a cluster of chimney pots or a dramatic skyline, which you can "borrow" to extend the apparent size of your garden (an "extrovert" garden). Every garden appears bigger if the eye is drawn to a viewpoint beyond its boundaries.

An attractive surrounding landscape can be used as a backdrop or inspiration for your new design. You may achieve this by repeating some of the trees, shrubs and materials found in the surrounding landscape, or by echoing the shape of distant features, such as a church spire or roof gable, in your plantings or with clipped topiary. In any outward view it is the shape of the skyline that you will appreciate first. Can you use this line in any way, perhaps by repeating the outline of a curving hill in the shape of a bed or a path? If you can relate your garden to features beyond the boundary, the garden's setting will become part of its overall design.

In most gardens there will be good views to be emphasized or framed up, and less attractive views that require screening. Occasionally, however, a site

Make a note of all good and bad views from your garden, as well as the points from which you may be overlooked.

Your notes on views will help you to decide which to screen and which to frame up or emphasize.

Topiary shapes are inspired by the dominant backdrop of the church and its spire.

The design of a window
can greatly influence the
views of the garden from
the house. An
unobstructed picture
window (right) provides
a full view of the garden
from inside the house.
With a shorter window,
(far right) the view is
slightly reduced, creating
a larger "blind area" just
beneath the window
along the house wall.

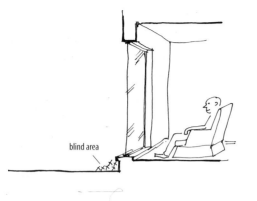

blind area

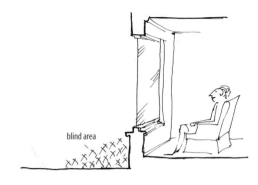

blind area

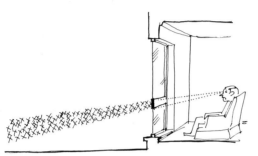

Thick glazing bars or cross-pieces
(above) may affect the view from the
house, particularly from a seated
position. Existing planting around the
house (right) may also block views.

A garden surrounded by
extensive views (left) is
often improved if the
views are broken down
into smaller pictures
(below). Repeating the
curves of distant hills in
the shape of the planting
beds helps to relate the
garden to its setting.

may be surrounded by extensive pleasant views
which, interestingly, provide too much of a good
thing. They will dominate the eye and reduce the
garden to the status of a viewing platform. In these
situations it is wise to break down the view into a
number of carefully composed pictures, framed
by plantings.

Surroundings

From a distance, the colour of roses or the species of shrubs you plant within the garden may not affect the general view. However, a badly placed tree of the wrong type—a purple beech or a striking golden conifer in a very rural setting, for instance—may seriously damage the view over a considerable distance. On the other hand, tree planting of the right type can bring enormous benefits. For example, the rounded shapes of most deciduous trees, and the shadows which they cast, can break up the hard outlines of buildings, reduce the reflected light from cars, windows or pale surfaces and create a woodland impression from a distance, even when the trees are widely spaced.

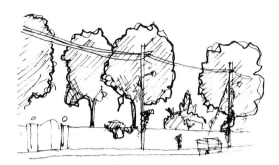

The view from the street has been improved by "losing" the wires against garden trees.

Consider how you can make a positive contribution to the general scene by giving pleasure to those passing by your garden. Even one small tree, cunningly placed, can help to break the monotony of a long treeless street, providing interest as it changes with the seasons and matures over the years.

Trees can soften the hard outlines of buildings, reduce the reflected light from cars, and create a woodland impression from a distance.

The presence of a single tree helps to relieve the monotony of a long row of houses.

Try to think of ways of giving pleasure to people passing by your garden.

When using plants to conceal unattractive features, avoid using unnatural shapes and colour; these will draw attention to themselves and therefore to whatever you are trying to hide. Instead, try to use natural, local plants to harmonize with your surroundings and to blend with, rather than totally obscure, what you are trying to hide. This technique applies equally to town and suburban situations where there are frequently eyesores such as television aerials, drainpipes, fire escapes and ugly buildings from which you would like to distract attention.

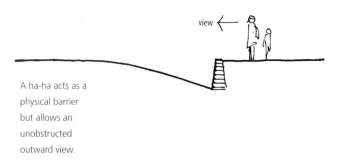

A ha-ha acts as a physical barrier but allows an unobstructed outward view.

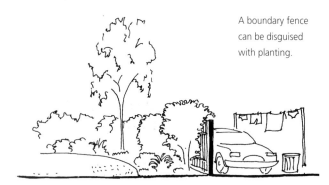

A boundary fence can be disguised with planting.

Boundaries

Generally the boundaries of a garden are fixed and need to be maintained, either for legal reasons, to keep out straying animals or to retain straying children. However, the boundaries do not necessarily need to be seen. They can be concealed with plantings, or they can be sunk, like the eighteenth-century ha-ha (see page 155), to permit an uninterrupted outward view.

If, on the other hand, you wish to emphasize your boundary, then the material used and the general shape must relate to the adjoining house and surroundings so that it is seen as an integral part of the design.

In the country, where the zone of visual influence may extend to the surrounding countryside, boundary planting must be handled very sensitively. Often, the shape and position of the plot is at odds with the general pattern of hills and valleys, woods and fields. By emphasizing these boundaries unduly—for example, with a line of Lombardy poplars or tall conifers—you may create an ugly block that can be seen for miles around.

Left: A garden can be seen from a surprising number of viewpoints.

Right: If you plant your boundaries inappropriately you may spoil the view for miles around.

Sometimes, in order to improve the proportions of an area, an apparent boundary can be built within it while the real boundary line is hidden beyond. Even a small garden can be made to appear more spacious by careful subdivision.

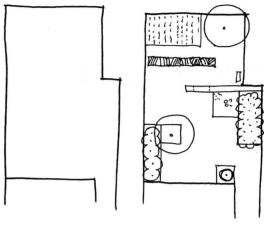

Plan of the existing site   Plan showing proposed design

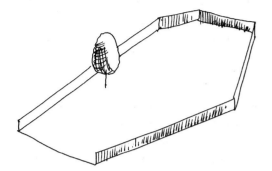

An awkwardly shaped site

Perspective of proposed design

A semi-formal solution

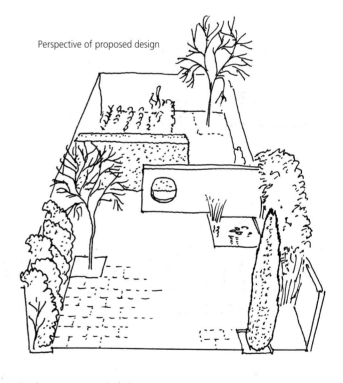

An informal solution

The proportions of awkwardly shaped sites can be improved by disguising the actual boundary and creating apparent boundaries within the space.

An abstract, asymmetric design illustrating the use of artificial boundaries—one of concrete and one of hedging—to subdivide a garden and make it appear larger. Obscuring parts of the side walls with planting further helps the illusion.

Recording Existing Conditions

Weather, orientation and the condition of the land are important factors that influence what can and cannot be achieved in the garden.

Aspect

Aspect, or the orientation of the garden, refers to the direction—north, south, east or west—in which the house or garden faces, which determines how the sun falls on the garden. You will be able to ascertain aspect with a compass or by using a detailed map or street plan on which you can locate the site, and you should mark the north point in the lower right-hand corner of your drawings.

Obviously you will want to make the most of the sunny areas, but the height of the sun will vary according to the seasons and to what is in its path. Estate agents, when showing houses in the depths of winter, will naturally try to emphasize the appeal of any light and sunny rooms. Beware, however, of tall neighbouring trees—you may find quite a changed atmosphere in midsummer when the trees are in leaf.

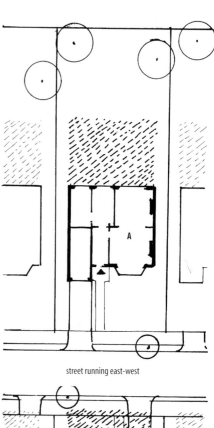

street running east-west

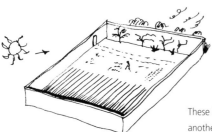

Even in cold climates, many tender Mediterranean plants can flourish on south-facing brick walls in full sun.

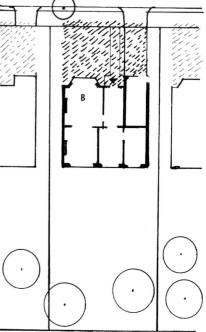

These low-built houses, facing one another across a street, are almost identical. However, because of their orientation, the gardens will feel very different. House A is south facing. This will have a sunny front garden, but the back garden will be shady where adjacent to the house. In contrast, house B will have a shady front garden—but the area adjacent to the house in the back garden will be sunny.

N

The orientation of a garden will affect the kinds of plants that will thrive in it.

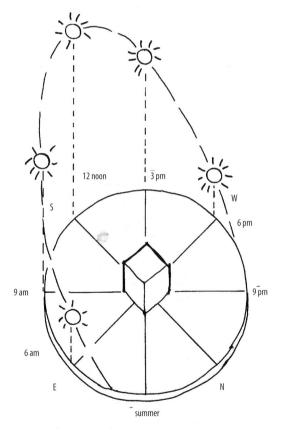

The varied path of the sun in summer and winter.

Shade

Shade can be beneficial. Not everyone likes to bask all day long in blazing sunshine, and the dappled shade cast by trees can often provide relief. Shadows can also create a variety of interesting effects, dependent on the quality of light. For instance, the Italian cypress can be used dramatically in warmer climates such as Italy, where it grows so well, whereas in the variable British climate the bluish light dilutes the shadows and lessens the contrast between light and shade.

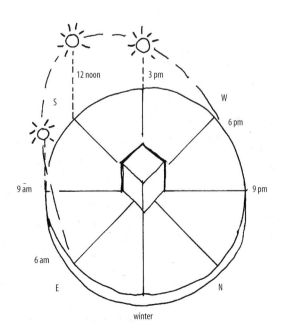

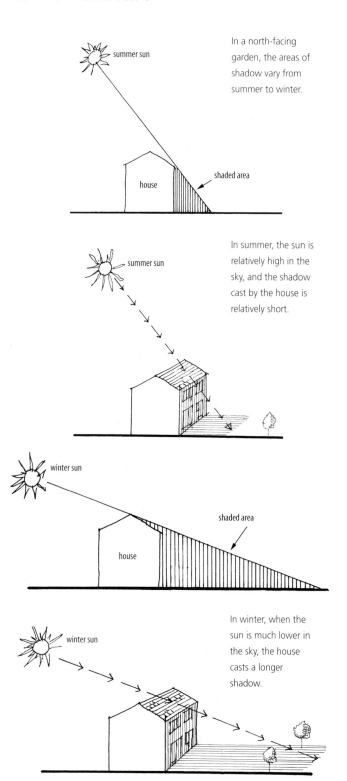

In a north-facing garden, the areas of shadow vary from summer to winter.

summer sun

house

shaded area

In summer, the sun is relatively high in the sky, and the shadow cast by the house is relatively short.

summer sun

winter sun

house

shaded area

In winter, when the sun is much lower in the sky, the house casts a longer shadow.

winter sun

Climate

Climate has a major influence on the character of a site and the way in which a garden is used, and must be borne in mind when planning any new design.

The United States as a whole has a more variable climate than Britain. The hardiness-zone system (see page 271) is based on the average annual minimum temperatures and enables North American gardeners to work out the zone in which they live and then select plants that carry the zone rating of their own region or higher. If you know your microclimate, you have an excellent chance of growing plants rated with a lower zone than your region by planting them in the warmer places in your garden. Heat, wind, rainfall and humidity are other factors affecting the hardiness of plants. If your area tends to hold a snow cover from mid-December until mid-March, you can usually grow plants rated for one zone warmer than is indicated for your region.

In Britain the temperate, maritime climate with occasional extremes such as harsh winters or dry summers makes it possible to grow plants introduced from many parts of the world. Under these cool, damp conditions, grass grows especially well, lawns being recognized as an integral part of the English landscape. However, in both the United States and Britain the regional climate within the country varies enormously. In Britain the north is colder than the south, and the west warmer and wetter than the east; the coastal areas are cooler in summer and warmer in winter. In other countries regional climates will also vary.

The climate has an influence not only on the plants that can be grown but also on the materials that are used locally, and this in turn may influence the style or architecture of the houses in the area. In northern or windswept areas of Britain, stone is readily available, and the houses built of it are able to withstand strong winds. Further south, where the climate is less harsh, brick and timber are more frequently used.

Altitude has a bearing on the climate—higher areas are colder and often exposed to strong winds. The topography of the locality will also affect the amount of rainfall received. Coastal areas may suffer from salt spray but will have a good quality of light.

Wind is among the most damaging factors in a garden, making both plants and people uncomfortable. In Britain the prevailing wind normally comes from the southwest, but it can be unpredictable and may vary according to the surroundings.

Wind Tunnels

In cities, particularly, a garden may be affected by wind tunnels channelling the air through the spaces between high buildings. Building a wall to shield an area from wind is expensive and not necessarily effective: although it may offer some protection on the immediate leeward side, on hitting the ground again wind tends to eddy or swirl around in unexpected directions. As an alternative you can plant a shelterbelt, windbreak or even a hedge, which will filter the wind and reduce its velocity. Use small plants in preference to larger ones so that their roots can get a firm grip in the soil before becoming taller when they may be severely rocked by the wind.

Below right: Structures that allow some air to pass through them, such as hedges, trellis or open-slatted fences, tend to provide more effective windbreaks than solid structures. As shown here, these structures act as filters, allowing some wind to pass through, but greatly reducing its velocity.

Cold air always flows downhill and onto low ground. On a winter morning you can see the effects of this—higher areas may be frost-free while lower levels are still gripped by frost. Buildings, lawns and terraces interrupt the downward flow of air, creating frost pockets, which remain cold for many hours—as uncomfortable for the roots of plants as for people.

Above: A solid barrier, such as a wall, provides some protection from wind on the immediate leeward side, although a lot of pressure is exerted on the barrier on the windward side. Further on, where the wind hits the ground again, it tends to swirl around unexpectedly.

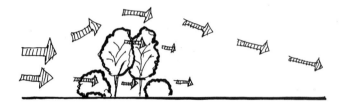

Above: When planting a shelter belt of trees and shrubs, choose a varied mixture of species and heights. The length of the shelter produced on the leeward side will be approximately three times the height of the shelter belt.

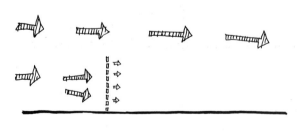

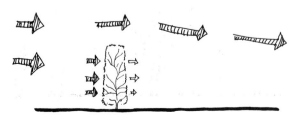

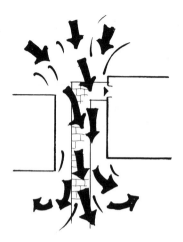

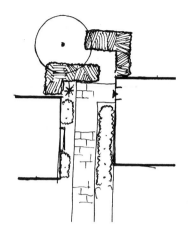

In this typical situation, the wind is channelled through the gap between neighbouring houses, creating an unpleasant wind tunnel effect.

Here, the wind tunnel has been counteracted by the judicious planting of overlapping hedges and a single tree, which work together to filter the wind, reducing its velocity.

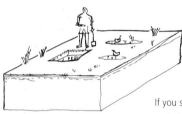

If you suspect poor drainage and/or waterlogging, dig a trial pit.

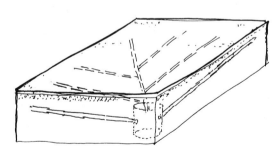

You may need to consider underground soil drainage and a soakaway.

For areas with poor drainage, slope the ground away from the house and away from the centre of the garden into ditches dug either side of the site. Very often the perimeter of the garden will be planted so that any excess water draining into these areas will be absorbed by the soil and plants.

Drainage

Drainage will also have an effect on the site. On sloping sites the rain will drain naturally, whereas on a flat site it may remain for some days, particularly if the soil is compacted or there is no cross-fall to a drainage channel or gulley. A trial pit can be dug to check how quickly the soil drains water away. If waterlogging is a serious problem, a drainage system may be necessary.

Assessing the Soil

You have already taken soil samples from the garden (page 32), and you now need to assess what can or cannot be grown according to the results of the soil tests. As these may well affect the design of your garden, it is important that you understand the advantages or restrictions that the existing soil pH value and the soil structure may impose.

The type of soil in a garden is conditioned by the underlying geology. Both the texture and mineral content of the surface topsoil are derived from the substrata of gravel, clay or rock. The substrata also determine the relative acidity or alkalinity of the soil. The pH factor governs the type of plants that will thrive in your garden. The pH factor under which the widest range of plants can thrive is a fairly neutral pH of 5.7–6.7, but in very acid areas you may find a reading of pH 4, or in very alkaline areas a reading of pH 7.5.

The soil type or pH can often also be recognized by looking at the natural vegetation and identifying "soil indicators", as certain types of plant are known to flourish only on particular types of soil. Rhododendrons and heathers, for instance, will thrive on acid soil, while forms of viburnum or spindle (*Euonymus europaeus*) prefer chalky, alkaline conditions. Extreme degrees of acidity or alkalinity will limit the type of plants that can be grown.

Sandy or peaty soils are often acidic, while heavy clay soil is usually alkaline. Many soils fall between the two and can be classified as neutral.

Soil structure is determined by the size of the particles that make up the soil and by the quantity of accumulated organic matter present in the soil. The layer of soil overlying chalk is often only 75 mm (3 in.) thick. Chalky subsoil is unable to retain moisture and nutrients, so that only shallow-rooted plants that favour a well-drained soil can thrive. Clay soil, often cold and wet, consists of very small, tightly packed particles that stick together and retain moisture for most of the year, only drying out and cracking in prolonged, very hot weather. Sandy or peaty soils, usually warm, are composed of much larger particles, so drainage is quicker and the soil warms up faster. The ideal soil for growing most garden plants is a loam, which consists of a mixture of slightly more sand than clay particles, with a high organic content.

Rushes and reeds indicate wet, poor soil.

Thistles spring up on waste ground and poor soil.

Rhododendrons thrive on acid soil.

Some useful soil indicators:

Viburnum, spindle—chalky, alkaline soil

Heather, lingonberry—dry, acid or peaty soil

Nettle, chickweed—potentially fertile soil

Canterbury bells, catnip (catmint)—chalky or
alkaline soil

Sheep's sorrel—poor, light, dry, acid soil

Foxglove, sandwort—dry, sandy or gravely soil

Paleseed plantain or hoary plantain—dry, hard,
stony, alkaline soil

Barren strawberry or wild strawberry—dry, stony,
barren soil

Furze or gorse or broom—poor, infertile soil

Heath bedstraw—dry, light, acid soil

Silverweed or silvery cinquefoil or goose tansy,
coltsfoot—damp, clay soil

Wild thyme—dry soil

Brooklime, marsh foxtail or water foxtail—wet,
fertile soil

Common butterwort, lesser spearwort—wet,
infertile soil

Goldenrod—wet sand

Legal Considerations

In most countries, active measures are now taken to
protect the countryside and the enjoyment of it.
There are certain legal factors that may affect, or be
affected by, your proposals. These factors, which
include the siting of water points and the removal of
existing trees, must be kept in mind from the outset
to avoid later confusion and expense. You should
always consult the local governing body to confirm
which, if any, of these issues may affect your project.

Conservation Areas or Historic Districts

If the property is in a conservation area, there will be
strict regulations on what you are allowed to do,
including severe pruning or removal of any trees. For
advice, consult your local conservation officer or
county official.

Tree Preservation Orders

In the United Kingdom, a tree preservation order
(TPO) prohibits the removal or cutting down of
trees, and there may be an order on certain trees
within the garden. The local planning authority will
have copies of these TPOs ready for inspection in the
district to which they relate, and they are required to
send copies of these orders to the owners or
occupiers of affected land. Any person who
contravenes a TPO is liable to be prosecuted, and the
High Court may take out an injunction to stop
further disobedience. The authority may also give
consent to the cutting down, topping or lopping of
trees or groups of trees, but this takes time and may
be subject to certain conditions.

Neighbours

The most frequent problems involving neighbours
have to do with overhanging and dangerous trees,
invasive weeds and the right to light.

When tree branches spread over and roots travel
under neighbouring properties, they infringe the right
of the owners to the unrestricted use of their land, so
the neighbour is entitled, as far as the law is
concerned, to cut off the intruding part without
notice, even though this may kill the tree. The owners
or occupiers of the land are also liable to neighbours
and to the public for injuries caused by trees on their
land, only escaping liability if they did not know that
the tree which caused the injury was dangerous.
When it comes to planting, you must ensure that
trees will not outgrow their position and cause
problems in future.

Landowners are not liable to their neighbours if they
allow weeds to grow and the wind to spread their
seeds unless these are "injurious weeds", which
include thistles, dock and ragwort. In this case, the
occupiers of the land may be required to take action
within a definite time to stop the weeds spreading, or
else be prosecuted.

In the United Kingdom, the right to light is a complex issue, the general rule being that nobody is entitled to daylight through their windows unless the landowners or their predecessors have had daylight through their windows for twenty years or more, in which case they will have acquired a right to continue to have a reasonable amount of light as long as the house stands. However, this is a delicate question, and should you envisage interfering with your neighbour's right to light, by building a wall or erecting a building, it would be wise to seek legal advice in your particular region before carrying out any work.

Boundary Ownership

Normally, walls or fences separate small town or village gardens from each other. It is important to establish which boundary is your responsibility—if in doubt, consult your local authority. Disputes regarding dilapidated fences and crumbling walls can easily arise with neighbours, and it is wise to know who is legally responsible for their repair.

Covenant Communities

Covenant communities typically have strict rules about what homeowners in the community can do to the exterior of their homes. When a homeowner buys in an area with a covenant in place, typically all changes to the exterior need to be reviewed by the homeowners association. It is best to find out what is allowed in the community before putting together your design so that you avoid having to change it later.

Preexcavation Responsibilities

In the United States and Australia, it is illegal in most areas to do any excavation without contacting the county or a "call-before-you-dig" clearinghouse service. Services typically include on-site marking of all underground gas, water and electricity pipes and wires as well as providing you with underground network plans. Neglecting to call before excavating can lead to costly disruption to essential services,

injury or death to workers or the general public and heavy financial and legal penalties.

Drawing up the Site Inventory Plan

1. Lay a fresh sheet of tracing paper over the site survey plan.
2. First trace over all the elements shown on the site plan. Referring to your survey notes and the site inventory checklist (see page 44), transfer as much information as you can onto the new drawing using either written descriptions or abstract graphic symbols. Try to use symbols where possible, as they will help to bring your site inventory to life and make it easier to read and refer to later.
3. Make a note of any structural features that you will be retaining, describing the materials used and their general state (for example, worn or newly repaired).
4. Consider existing vegetation, and make a note of any plants that you wish to retain or move in the new design.
5. Using a compass, note the orientation of the site.
6. Observe and note any shadows cast.
7. Record, if possible, and note the direction of prevailing winds.
8. Note areas of good or poor drainage.
9. Note any areas where frost pockets may occur.
10. Note any other features that will affect comfort in the garden.
11. Establish who owns which boundaries, and record this information.
12. Colour (covered in Chapter 5) can help to enhance the plan. For instance, you may wish to use blue arrows to indicate cold winds and yellow stars to represent sunny spots. However, do not apply colour to the tracing paper, as this will not reproduce when copied; instead, have the plan copied first and then colour up the copy.

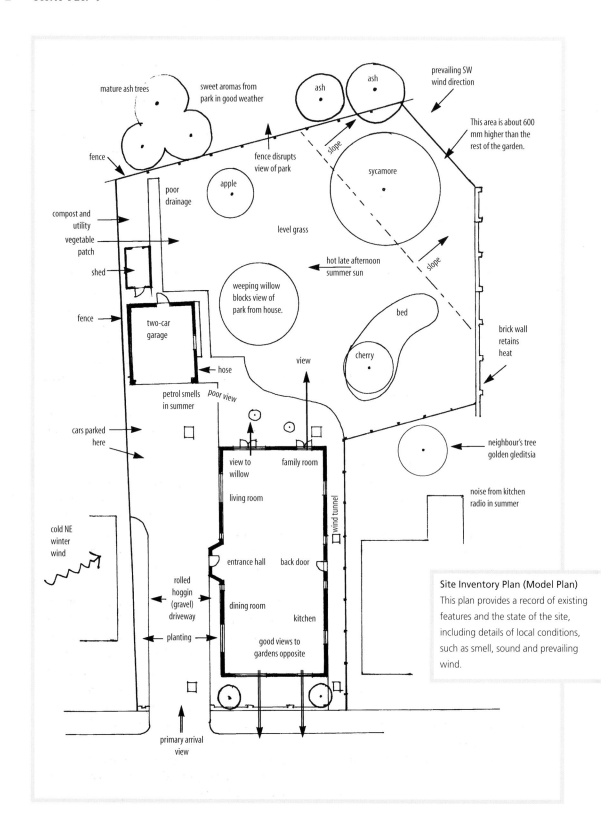

mature ash trees

sweet aromas from park in good weather

ash

ash

prevailing SW wind direction

This area is about 600 mm higher than the rest of the garden.

fence

slope

fence disrupts view of park

poor drainage

apple

sycamore

compost and utility

level grass

vegetable patch

shed

hot late afternoon summer sun

slope

weeping willow blocks view of park from house.

bed

fence

two-car garage

cherry

view

brick wall retains heat

hose

petrol smells in summer

poor view

neighbour's tree golden gleditsia

cars parked here

view to willow

family room

noise from kitchen radio in summer

living room

wind tunnel

cold NE winter wind

entrance hall

back door

rolled hoggin (gravel) driveway

dining room

kitchen

planting

good views to gardens opposite

Site Inventory Plan (Model Plan)

This plan provides a record of existing features and the state of the site, including details of local conditions, such as smell, sound and prevailing wind.

primary arrival view

Drawing up the Site Appraisal

The next stage of the design process involves more thought than the surveying and inventory stages, because, before putting pencil to paper, you will have to take some time to evaluate the importance of the information that you have collected and noted. You will have to ask yourself if the information is relevant and, significantly, whether it presents a problem or offers some potential.

You may, for instance, have recorded on the site inventory the presence of a large tree in the middle of the garden. Now, for the site appraisal, you will have to decide whether the tree presents a problem (for instance, whether it blocks an important view, casts too much shade or is an inappropriate type), or if it offers some potential (it helps to frame the view, provides some privacy or provides a focal point). You will then note down your decision on the site appraisal drawing. For instance, "Large pear tree to remain to provide privacy for new seating area", or simply, "Large pear tree to be integrated into new design".

1. Attach a tracing-paper overlay on the scale drawing of the site survey. Using a pen, work across the plan, annotating it with your well-considered decisions (see page 62) while making the site inventory.
2. Although this overlay is for your own use, practising the habit of writing clearly and evenly will be useful when you are producing later work. Use the T-square or parallel motion rule to keep your remarks running evenly across the sheet.
3. Do not get carried away and lose sight of the particular conditions of the site. Checking back to your appraisal frequently should help you ensure that your design is in keeping with the site conditions.
4. This plan can be used as a tracing-paper overlay on the site survey. If you want to copy it, you will need to trace the outline of the house and boundary and other key features which need to be explained.

Moving Towards the Design Stage

With the research and preparation phase—the site survey, inventory and appraisal—of the design process completed, you should now have a good idea of all the elements that you will need to include in a new design. Referring back to the garden owner's checklist (page 17), you should be able to see at a glance what you have listed as desirable. You may, for instance, have ticked such items as terrace, rose garden, vegetable garden, barbecue area, lawn and shed, all of which will have to be sited somewhere in the design proposals.

At this stage you need to start thinking about where you are going to place each of these items, how much space will be needed to allow for them, and how they are going to function in relation to one another. The site appraisal will help you to decide on positioning, but for every site there will be numerous alternatives.

Where you choose to position various elements will depend both on how you want the items to relate to each other and the constraints of the site. Your site appraisal will be very useful for this. You may, for instance, decide to position a terrace in a particular spot where it is partly shaded by the canopy of an existing tree. Your decision to try out this idea may have been influenced by the comments of the garden users who noted that the terrace, in its existing position, was too hot. With this decision made, you will have to think about what you would like next to the terrace. Would it be suitable to place the lawn

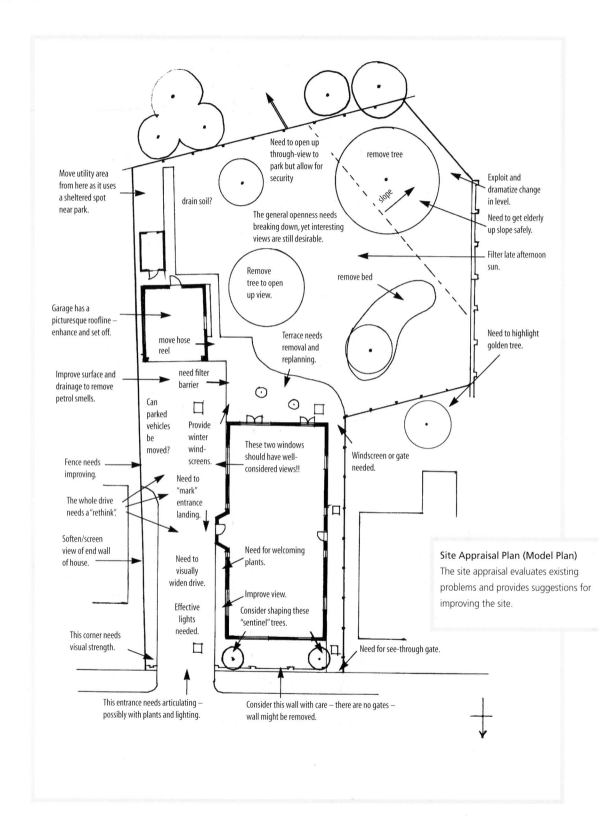

Move utility area from here as it uses a sheltered spot near park.

drain soil?

Need to open up through-view to park but allow for security

remove tree

Exploit and dramatize change in level.

Need to get elderly up slope safely.

slope

The general openness needs breaking down, yet interesting views are still desirable.

Filter late afternoon sun.

Remove tree to open up view.

remove bed

Garage has a picturesque roofline – enhance and set off.

move hose reel

Terrace needs removal and replanning.

Need to highlight golden tree.

Improve surface and drainage to remove petrol smells.

need filter barrier

Can parked vehicles be moved?

Provide winter wind-screens.

These two windows should have well-considered views!!

Windscreen or gate needed.

Fence needs improving.

Need to "mark" entrance landing.

The whole drive needs a "rethink".

Soften/screen view of end wall of house.

Need to visually widen drive.

Need for welcoming plants.

Effective lights needed.

Improve view.

Consider shaping these "sentinel" trees.

This corner needs visual strength.

Need for see-through gate.

This entrance needs articulating – possibly with plants and lighting.

Consider this wall with care – there are no gates – wall might be removed.

Site Appraisal Plan (Model Plan)
The site appraisal evaluates existing problems and provides suggestions for improving the site.

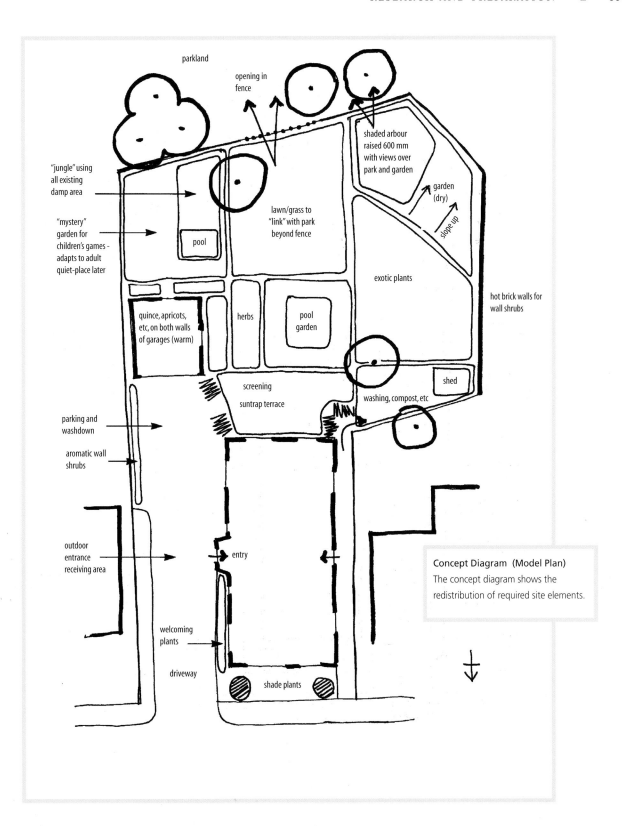

parkland

opening in fence

shaded arbour raised 600 mm with views over park and garden

"jungle" using all existing damp area

garden (dry)

slope up

"mystery" garden for children's games - adapts to adult quiet-place later

lawn/grass to "link" with park beyond fence

pool

exotic plants

quince, apricots, etc, on both walls of garages (warm)

herbs

pool garden

hot brick walls for wall shrubs

shed

screening

suntrap terrace

washing, compost, etc

parking and washdown

aromatic wall shrubs

outdoor entrance receiving area

entry

Concept Diagram (Model Plan)
The concept diagram shows the redistribution of required site elements.

welcoming plants

driveway

shade plants

here, for the children to play football on, or would this perhaps be an ideal position for a pool, which could also be viewed from the sitting room window? If you decide on the pool you will need to think of what will be suitable to go next to it. In this way, you will gradually fill up all the available space.

There are several different ways of approaching the design process, which are fully explored in the next chapter, and which can be developed through theme plans (see page 89). To help you reach beyond preconceived ideas in your approach to garden design, you may wish to try producing concept diagrams.

Drawing Concept Diagrams

1. Attach a sheet of tracing paper as an overlay on the site survey.
2. Referring back to the garden owner's checklist, use felt-tip pens or a technical drawing pen to draw loose shapes or circles to indicate the most suitable position for each of the desired features, such as the lawn, shed or the position for the barbecue.
3. Remember to allow enough space for each area to function comfortably.
4. If possible, each shape should almost touch the next, so that when you have finished, every area in the garden will be allocated to a particular function.
5. By ticking off each element mentioned on the checklist, you can ensure that nothing has been overlooked.
6. There will be many different alternatives for every design, and you should experiment with these diagrams as much as possible. Keep these drawings to refer to when beginning the preliminary garden plan.

Consolidating the Information

If the many issues that have been covered in this chapter are taken into account at the planning stage, the work will progress more speedily and smoothly later. The site survey, site analysis and site appraisal are vital stages in developing a design. If you are asked to design someone else's garden, they will rarely be shown this information and the resulting drawings, but this process should always be undertaken so that you understand the site that you are working with, its limitations and potential. If at a later stage there are queries about how or why you have arrived at your design, you may need to refer back to these notes and drawings.

If you are working for a committee, perhaps for improvements to a communal garden square, or for a public garden, these notes and drawings may be particularly helpful to explain how you have arrived at your solution.

Chapter 2

Developing the Design: Focusing on the Ground Plane

With the research and preparation phase completed, you are now ready to start designing. In this chapter you will prepare a preliminary garden layout plan based on the conclusions you reached through the site survey, site inventory and site appraisal, and your initial planning ideas in the concept diagrams.

The graphic language (the ability to put your ideas on paper) is central to the garden design process. It is used to communicate ideas and solutions and to record information. You may have had no experience with drawing and be daunted by the idea of expressing yourself graphically, but the objective is not to produce beautiful pieces of artwork but simply to communicate your ideas. The basic drawing skills that are needed for working plans (covered in Chapter 1) are developed in this chapter to cover those that are needed to create a garden layout plan.

Approaching the Design Process

When thinking of how to start designing a new garden, it is easy to think in terms of playing with the existing features (for example, enlarging the terrace or widening borders). However, this approach does not properly consider the available space and tends to produce predictable results, which do not really constitute a thorough redesign of the garden.

Approaching things in a different way and starting by creating abstract patterns on paper will inspire a variety of alternative designs for your garden, many of which you may not originally have thought of (just as abstract art is open to different interpretations). Once you have experimented and established how to create patterns of different character, you are ready to redesign your site. The patterns can then be combined with a grid structure, which will lead you to create different design themes based on circles, diagonals or rectangles. These themes can then be translated into gardens by imagining each design as three-dimensional and allocating elements, such as a

terrace or paths, to the spaces created by the themes. The three-dimensional implications of your proposals can then be considered, and the way the mood of a space is affected by the quality of light.

Scale and proportion are examined so that you can relate the scale of the human figure to the much greater scale of the outside world. For instance, the dimensions of garden features such as steps need to be more generous than those usually found inside a house. Surfaces and suitable rigid and loose materials for your hard landscaping are also chosen at this stage. As a general guide, the proportions of one-third or two-thirds of hard landscaping to two-thirds or one-third of soft landscaping (lawn, water and planting) are a comfortable ratio to work to.

Water is a compelling feature that must be included early in the design stage so that it can be integrated with all the other elements, with consideration for the scale of water features in relation to the rest of the design.

Having considered all these factors, you will be ready to examine your previous ideas and refine them, focusing on the horizontal plane of the design (perhaps allowing ample space for a terrace and paths) and enhancing the scheme with some vertical interest, to produce a preliminary garden layout plan.

Drawing Skills for Presentation Plans

The four kinds of plans described in Chapter 1—the site survey, the site inventory, the site appraisal and the concept diagram—are unlikely to be seen by anyone but you, as they are working drawings. However, the next stage—the garden layout plan—should be drawn up on a sheet of tracing paper. This drawing should be neat, clear and well organized so that it can be presented to a client, used by a contractor or simply kept for your own use. This plan will then be reproduced by copying for you to work from at the next stage, and for all subsequent work, giving continuity of the design and the layout of the plan sheet. (Remember that A2 paper is a convenient size to work with, as it is easier to have reproduced as a photocopy or dyeline than a larger size.)

The Plan Sheet

Although preprinted architect's plan sheets are available, for a professional finish it is better to design your own master plan sheet. It should contain the following:

– A "title block", containing the name of the garden owner, your name (as the designer), the title of the drawing and the scale to which it is drawn
– An information panel in which to write additional information to supplement the plan
– A north point to denote orientation
– A scale
– The plan
– A border

The title block, north point and scale should always be located in the bottom right-hand corner of your plan so that this information can be seen at a glance when

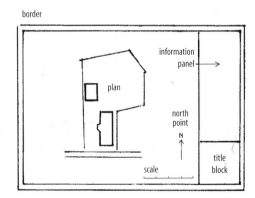

When possible, position your plan so that it reflects your main viewing point of the garden.

the plan is folded. (It might be difficult to open out the plan outdoors in a high wind!) The plan itself should be positioned centrally in the remaining space, allowing sufficient space around it for any labelling or notes.

Designing a Title Block

The dimensions of the title block will be determined by the organization of the information, the size and style of the lettering and the typeface used. The title block should be in proportion to the sheet size but should not exceed a width of 150 mm (6 in.). The following information should be included:

– Printed details giving your name (or company name) as the designer and your logo if you have one, your address, telephone, fax , mobile number and email address (the design can be printed separately and double up as a visiting card)
– The name and/or address of the client or garden owner
– The title of the drawing (for example, garden layout plan, planting plan, visual)
– The scale or scales used
– The date
– A drawing number (any later revisions should have subsequent numbers)
– Any alterations or revisions, numbered accordingly
– "Drawn by [initials only]" (occasionally different people work on the same drawing)
– A disclaimer
– A statement of copyright

The statement of copyright (for example, © RA) protects you as a designer so that your work cannot be used or copied without your permission. If you are designing a garden for a client it is particularly important to include a disclaimer stating that "all dimensions must be checked on site and not scaled from this drawing". This puts the responsibility for checking dimensions for tendering purposes or beginning construction on the contractor. This was

KARENA BATSTONE
GARDEN DESIGN

21 SOMERSET STREET, KINGSDOWN, BRISTOL BS2 8LZ
TELEPHONE/FACSIMILE: (0117) 9441004

Client:

Title:

Scale: Date:

Drawing no: Revisions: Drawn by:

All dimensions must be checked on site and not scaled from this drawing.

© Karena Batstone BSc 2004

An example of a title block

necessary before modern drawing reproduction methods, when drawings were executed on linen, which could stretch and result in inaccurate measurements, but it is still in use as a safeguard.

The title block should have your own logo or style. Choice of lettering or typeface is a personal matter, but simple, clear styles are usually the most effective. The title block can be designed as a separate piece of artwork before being applied to the sheet together with the information panel and border.

Lettering
The lettering on a title block (and for the labelling of the plan) can be produced with stencils or dry-transfer lettering, by hand or by computer. Handwriting is the quickest method for labelling, but it is only suitable if your writing is neat and legible, since lettering is part of the overall visual presentation. Styles of writing vary enormously, and many different styles are acceptable.

The important thing is to aim for consistency of letterform, spacing (between letters, words and lines of lettering) and style. If you are lettering by hand or with stencils, it will help if you use lined paper or lay graph paper under your drawing. Keep the pencil line weight consistent, and work down from the top of the page to avoid smudging.

It is useful to develop a style of lettering that is comfortable for you. Aim to be clear, consistent and legible. Try different techniques, particularly when designing your title block. Practise using stencils, aiming for even letter and word spacing, holding the stencil firmly with one hand against the T-square or parallel motion. It is easier to keep the letters close together than to space them widely at even intervals.

Dry-transfer lettering is usually supplied with spacing guidelines. Again pay special attention to consistency in spacing.

If you have a computer, word processor or typewriter, you may wish to generate text using this equipment. Where possible, try out different sizes and typefaces.

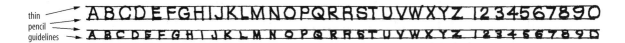

thin pencil guidelines

Above: If you are not using graph paper under the tracing paper sheet, use pencil guidelines to ensure that the letters are all the same height.
Right: You can maintain verticals by using a small set square against your parallel rule.

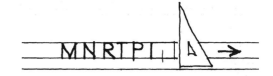

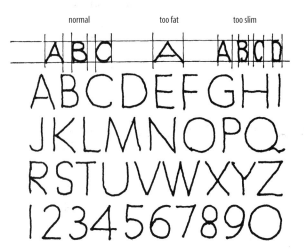

normal   too fat   too slim

typefaces   styles   text sizes
typefaces   *styles*   text sizes
typefaces   **styles**   text sizes
typefaces   STYLES   text sizes

text sizes

text sizes

Left: Oblong proportions result in the most stable lettering.

Above: Computer-generated lettering offers a huge range of styles and sizes.

Remember that the originals will be copied and that some typefaces will reproduce better than others. This is a suitable technique to use for designing a title block, but for labelling, the text will need to be printed, cut out and stuck onto your drawing, and this is a time-consuming process.

Information Panel

This area is usually designed as a vertical extension of the title block. It will eventually contain notes (on design intention and hard landscaping or plant numbers, for example) to supplement your drawings.

Border

Your drawings—the garden layout, planting plans and visuals—will look more professional if a border surrounds the sheet on which they are displayed. This will draw attention to the work in the same way as a frame sets off a painting or a photograph.

A border should be drawn in ink with a technical drawing pen in a fairly thick nib size (0.5 mm or 0.7 mm) around the perimeter of the sheet, approximately 10 mm (0.4 in.) from the outside edge.

Borders may consist of a single straight line, a double line (perhaps with the outer line thicker than the inner

one) or a pattern. A small detail can be used to emphasize each corner. Borders may be drawn by hand or on a computer. Experiment with different effects, remembering that you are aiming for a border design that will enhance, rather than distract from, a plan. A simple, clear design is often the most successful and tends to suit the majority of garden styles.

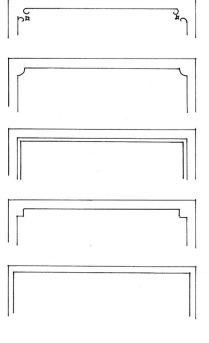

Simple borders are usually the most effective. Fancy or elaborate designs should be used with great care. They may make your design look dated.

Designing the Master Plan Sheet

1. Fix an A2 (17 × 22 in.) sheet of tracing paper with masking tape on a drawing board, making sure that it is accurately aligned.
2. Draw the border with a 0.5 or 0.7 mm pen about 10 mm (0.4 in.) from the edge of the paper.
3. On a separate sheet of tracing paper, design a title block, with logo if desired. Produce this by hand or on a computer and trim around the edges if necessary.
4. Position the title block at the bottom of the right-hand side of the plan sheet (allowing space below it for the scale and north point), using the border as a guideline, and attach it with glue or invisible tape.
5. The space above the title block is for the information panel. Label it "Notes".
6. If you require more than one master plan sheet, you should copy it onto another sheet of tracing paper.

Graphic Symbols

Symbols are used on all plan drawings to represent the objects and elements that occur within the site or are intended to feature in the new design. The symbols should be to scale and can be more or less realistic, depending on the time and budget available to complete the plan. The following pages will review some that you have already encountered in Chapter 1 and introduce you to other graphic symbols that are commonly used in garden design.

Look at garden plans from books and magazines to see how other designers have evolved different symbols to indicate features such as hard-landscaping materials and plants.

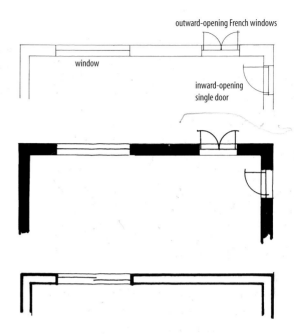

outward-opening French windows

window

inward-opening single door

House walls: when drawing house walls it is important to position doors and windows accurately as these provide key links between the house and garden. House walls have a thickness—usually of around 300 mm (1 ft.)—which should be shown on plan drawings. At a scale of 1:100 or smaller, you can emphasize the house walls by thickening the lines or by filling them in.

Drawing surveys: When drawing a survey, emphasize the house and boundary lines so that these elements are well-defined when the survey is later placed under tracing paper overlays.

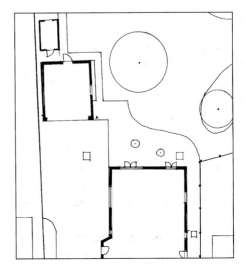

When drawing boundaries such as walls, fences and hedges, always draw the thickness of the boundary to scale.

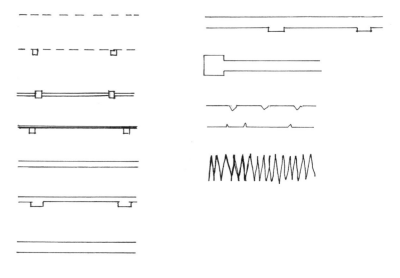

Drawing free-standing walls: The simplest way of drawing a wall is by using a double line and labelling it to indicate the material. If you wish to show more detail, the wall coping for instance, it is only necessary to detail a small section of the wall.

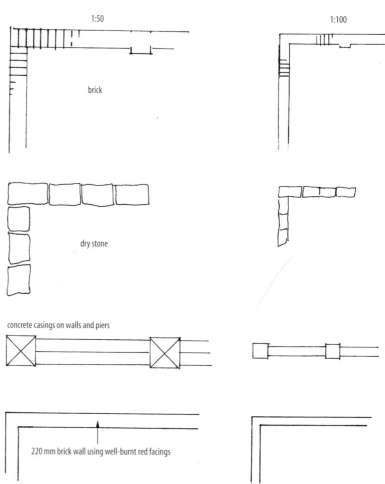

1:50

brick

dry stone

concrete casings on walls and piers

220 mm brick wall using well-burnt red facings

1:100

Paving and ground surfaces:
When drawing an area of paving it is neither necessary nor possible to show every brick and stone. Provide a separate details sheet (at a larger scale) rather than confuse your plan with too much information. Always label each area to clarify the material used and the layout. You may also distinguish between different surfaces by applying colour.

Far left: Water with fountain
Left: Still water

Vertical surfaces: You can give your plan depth—and therefore help the reading of it—if you emphasize all lines representing vertical surfaces, such as those representing tree canopies, free-standing walls, seats, posts, pillars, pergolas and arches (as in the diagram) etc.

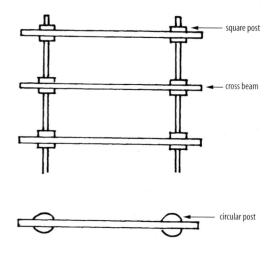

— square post

— cross beam

— circular post

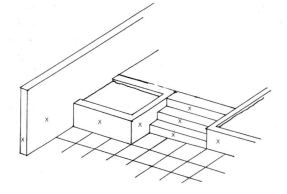

Above: An overview of part of a garden indicating, with crosses, all the vertical surfaces.

Right: A plan drawing of the same part of the garden shows how heavier lines are used to represent all elements with a vertical surface and so clarify the plan. Note how only the outer edge of the retaining wall is emphasized.

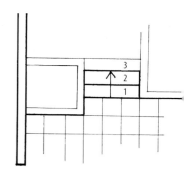

Trees and shrubs: Indicate areas of planting by showing a stylized outline. Plants normally spread out from borders, often overhanging the edge of beds. If you show this overhang (partly concealing the edge of the bed) you will make your plans look more realistic. In Chapter 4, when developing planting plans, you will be shown how to indicate individual plants.

Start with a light guideline circle and locate the centre guideline.

Draw in the main branch structure. Solid branches should taper from thick near the centre to thin near the outside.

Add a few more secondary branches, each one touching the outer circle guideline.

Add many small branches to emphasize the edge.

Simple single circle template outline

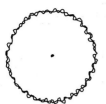

Double wavy line

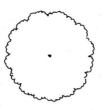

Irregular puffy edge

Bites out of the cookie

The addition of extra lines on one side gives added depth.

Tropical or large-leafed plants

Thin lines may represent leaf ribs.

Always use a circle template guideline for outer edges.

Combine thick and thin lines to provide interest.

Hatch lines to show palm fronds.

Loose squiggles with thick and thin lines.

Conifers

Begin with a series of circles as light guidelines. Vary their size a little.

A simple heavy outline is the fastest method.

Centres may or may not be located.

Loose wavy lines, double or single, are used for outlines.

Conifers

When the larger tree shadow falls onto the top of shrubs, it should be shortened and made with an irregular edge.

Shrub shadows will be proportionately smaller than tree shadows.

To show pyramid tree form, draw a cone-like guideline. The centre line follows the sun direction.

Draw a loose shadow edge.

A quick outline with an uneven edge for an informal hedge.

Box shapes for a trimmed hedge and to define space.

Rounded, smooth edges that show two pen sizes overlapping.

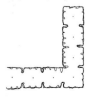

Designing with Patterns and Shapes

Gardens are essentially made up of hard landscaping and plants, but taken at their most abstract they are composed of lines and shapes that make up a pattern. Before getting into too much detail, you must first become aware of shape, line and pattern and how to use them to create gardens of different character and style.

Experimenting with Shapes

In garden design the two most commonly used geometric shapes are the square and the circle, or parts of these two. When we describe a design theme as circular, what we mean is that the circles, or circular shapes, predominate. Circular themes are rarely composed entirely of circles. Similarly, in a rectilinear theme the rectangles, or parts of a rectangle, predominate. These rectangles may originate from using multiples of a square grid. The diagonal theme also employs mainly squares and rectangles, but these are set at an angle to the house or existing terrace to introduce a strong directional element.

Learning how to use and combine shapes to create patterns is the key to producing positive, strong designs. It is worth looking carefully at different shapes and themes to identify the components that are important in their design use.

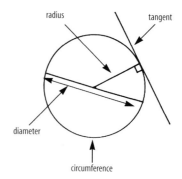

The circle: For designers, the most important parts of a circular shape are its centre, the diameter, the radii, the circumference and the tangent. Each of these is capable of generating different forms.

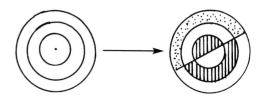

The centre can generate concentric circles

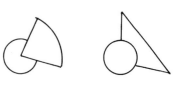

Forms evolved from extended radii

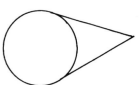

Forms evolved from using tangents

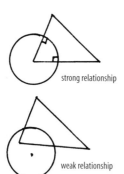

To create strong relationships and avoid awkward angles, lines that meet the circle's circumference should meet it at right angles or tangentially.

strong relationship

weak relationship

The square: The most important components of a square are the sides, the axes, the diagonals and their extensions.

Combining shapes: When combining shapes, try to align the components of one form with those of another (such as a circle combined with a square) to create a strong relationship.

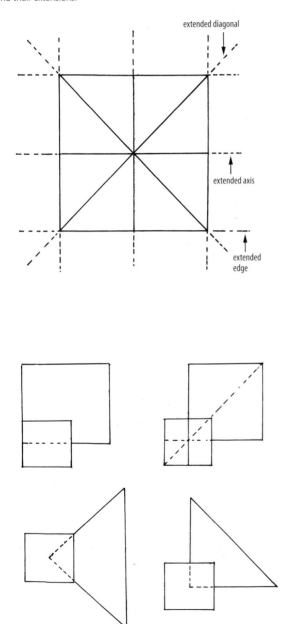

Examples of shapes arising from the square

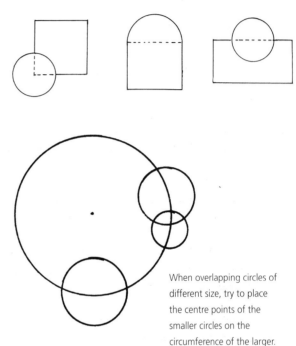

When overlapping circles of different size, try to place the centre points of the smaller circles on the circumference of the larger. If this is not possible, try to ensure that each circle bites substantially into another.

Curvilinear patterns evolve from the outlines of adjoining circles. Often the curved outline of part of one circle will turn, as a reversed curve, into the next circle. Curves should always be generous and appear to flow naturally.

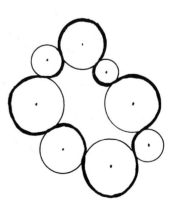

Experimenting with Patterns

A grid is a good starting point for creating patterns. The grid helps to ensure that the shapes created on it relate to one another both in size and through continuity of line. Study the patterns shown here and notice how they differ: some patterns are static, while others are flowing and dynamic. Think about these patterns in relation to a garden—static patterns give a feeling of calm and peacefulness, while dynamic patterns give a sense of drama and excitement. Notice how different shapes have different qualities and how they can be used to give the space a feeling of order, informality or boldness.

Note also how shapes can be directional and used to create optical illusions. For example, lines that run away from the viewer will make an area appear longer, while lines running horizontally will appear to give added breadth.

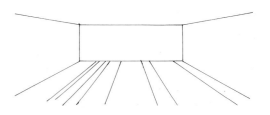

Lines running away from the viewer exaggerate the length of a site.

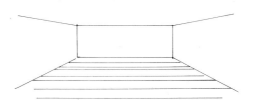

Lines running across a site exaggerate the width.

A grid is a useful starting point for creating patterns.

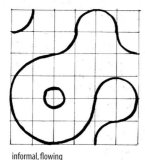

static, symmetrical, ordered

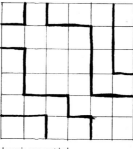

dynamic, asymmetrical

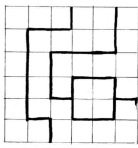

dynamic, combined with a static element (square-shaped area)

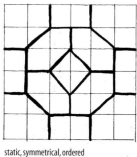

informal, flowing

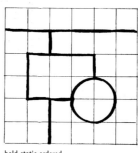

bold, static, ordered

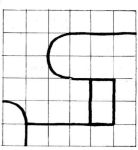

informal

Adding Depth

Shading some areas divides the pattern into positive and negative space, or mass and void. It automatically gives depth to a pattern and should help you to visualize the composition as the ground plan of a garden. Both mass and void are equally important in a design, and it is the interplay between these two that gives a garden its character. Using the informal pattern illustrated here, try to imagine the shaded areas as plantings, for instance, and the areas without shading as grass or paving. Now try reversing the process.

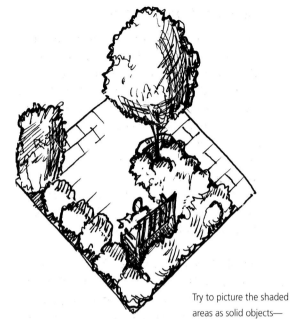

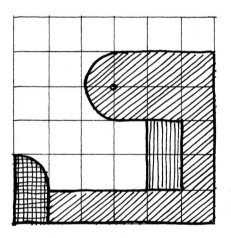

Shading selected areas of a pattern divides it into mass (the shaded part) and void (the unshaded). Experiment with shading different areas of a pattern, then reversing the shading, as shown.

Try to picture the shaded areas as solid objects—planting, benches, raised beds, and so on—and the unshaded areas as representing the garden floor—lawn, paving, or pools, for example.

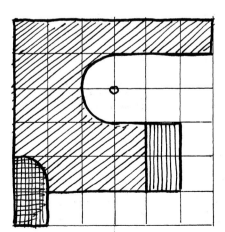

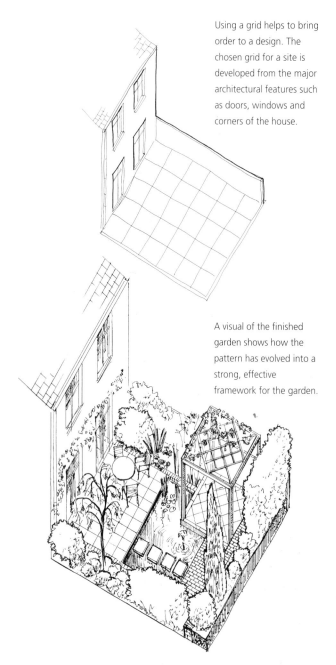

Using a grid helps to bring order to a design. The chosen grid for a site is developed from the major architectural features such as doors, windows and corners of the house.

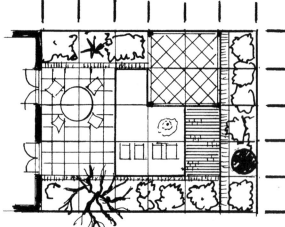

A pattern is drawn up on the grid and developed into a plan

A visual of the finished garden shows how the pattern has evolved into a strong, effective framework for the garden.

and paving, blurring the lines of the pattern, but the underlying framework will still be there, and its presence, even when obscured, will bring a sense of order to the design. Usually, the framework consists mainly of hard landscaping, such as paths, paving, steps and walls. These elements tend to be both more permanent and more expensive than the soft landscaping, or plantings, so the pattern in which the garden is laid out must be effective.

Exploring Patterns and Designs

1. Lay a sheet of tracing paper on top of a sheet of graph paper and stick it down with masking tape.
2. Using the bold graph-paper squares as a guide, draw the outline of six squares—use six major graph-paper squares horizontally and vertically for each outline.
3. Consider the examples shown on page 78 and make up your own patterns, using the information about shapes (on pages 76–77) to give you ideas. Shade in some areas.

Relating Patterns to Gardens

When designing a garden, you are trying to create interesting patterns within the space or site boundary. The shapes created by the pattern will become the framework of the garden. When the garden has matured, the planting may spill over onto the paths

4. Try reversing the shaded and plain areas.

5. Try to assess the character of each pattern, and decide which you prefer. Decide whether it is static or dynamic, formal or informal, historic or contemporary.

6. Consider these patterns in terms of gardens by thinking of the lighter areas as hard landscaping and the shaded areas as plantings.

7. Take a further sheet of tracing paper, lay it over the first and stick it down.

8. Using coloured pencils or felt-tips, try to translate your patterns into gardens. Show paving, pools, lawns, plantings, beds and so on. Repeat with all six patterns.

9. Try to analyze why you like each of them. What does the pattern do? Do you like the ratio of hard landscaping to soft landscaping, or could it be improved?

Creating Grids for Different Sites

All of the patterns given in this chapter have been developed for an isolated abstract space, but gardens are rarely isolated—they are usually connected to houses or other structures which they should relate to and be developed from. The most effective way of relating house to garden is by using a grid that springs from the dominant house lines or major lines of force. By designing the garden on the grid you will automatically link the spaces in the garden to those of the house, providing a connection which will help the garden sit comfortably in its relationship with the house. The most successful garden layout plans are often those in which the designer has used the proportions of the house—the spaces between doors and windows, for instance—to determine a grid for their design. The garden will then appear to have sprung from the property itself, rather than being superimposed upon it.

Where to Start

The first step in developing a grid is to look closely at the façade of the house, using your site survey and any photographs you may have taken on site. Look at prominent outside walls and corners and any protruding bays or indentations, such as extensions or wall buttresses. Which are the most obvious points? Usually the house corners will be the most dominant lines, and an extension of these across the site will form the starting point for the grid. There may also be regularly spaced windows and doors or an existing terrace whose proportions and materials are perfectly acceptable and which you will want to retain. All of these things may influence your grid.

Dividing up the Space

Now look at the dimensions between the dominant site lines to see if they fall into some sort of module. You may find, for instance, that the distance between the house corner and an extension is 2 m (6.6 ft.), the distance from the extension to the next corner is 4 m (13.12 ft.) and the projection of the extension is 2 m (6.6 ft.). In this case a 2 m (6.6 ft.) grid would fit within all three dimensions.

In deciding where to place the horizontal lines of your grid, reexamine the boundary fences, walls, gates or doorways. You may find that there are some prominent points, such as regularly spaced piers on garden walls, or posts on fences, that could be the starting points for your horizontal grid lines. If the boundary demarcation is totally featureless, you can simply subdivide the overall length of the garden.

The Benefits of a Square Grid

Although existing features in your garden may suggest a grid made up of differently sized and shaped rectangles, you are advised to stick to a square grid. When developing design themes later, the square grid will allow you to use circular shapes that could not be superimposed so easily onto a rectangular

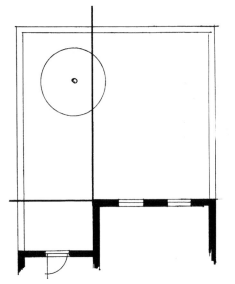

1. Begin the grid by extending the corner lines of the house.

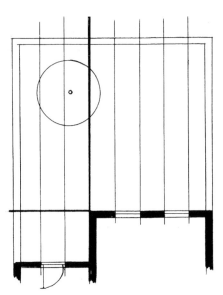

2. Next, use the house facade and the positions of doors, windows or other dominant features to help you divide it into equal divisions, as shown.

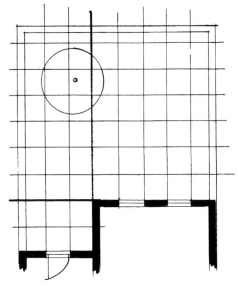

3. Draw in the horizontal grid lines (spaced the same distance apart as the vertical lines) to complete the grid.

In this example, the developed grid fits perfectly with the dimensions of the house and the position of its doors and windows. If your grid proves difficult to fit, try experimenting with moving it up and down or from side to side across the site. You may then find a stronger relationship between all the different elements.

grid. Do not worry if the house and boundaries do not coincide precisely with your grid lines—the grid is a design tool, not a straitjacket.

Grid Size

Your grid can be as large or small as you like, but the golden rule is that the scale of the grid should derive from the mass of the property, which means that if the house is large, the grid must also be large, and vice versa. Too small a grid often results in a fussy and overdesigned garden. Initially, it is usually better to create a larger grid and then subdivide it.

If the front of the house and garden are large, it may be helpful to use a smaller grid in the vicinity of the

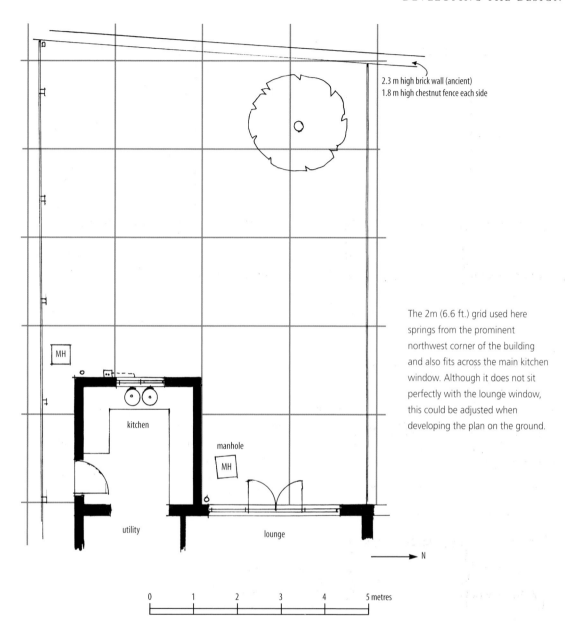

2.3 m high brick wall (ancient)
1.8 m high chestnut fence each side

MH

kitchen

manhole

MH

utility

lounge

N

The 2m (6.6 ft.) grid used here springs from the prominent northwest corner of the building and also fits across the main kitchen window. Although it does not sit perfectly with the lounge window, this could be adjusted when developing the plan on the ground.

0   1   2   3   4   5 metres

house—to unite building and terrace, for instance, or for a more formal area immediately adjacent to the house. The small grid unit can then be enlarged (doubled or even quadrupled) and used to encompass the larger and more distant part of the garden, where using a small grid would result in a fussy, cluttered effect. Any island beds, woodland trees or even areas of rough grass could be

accommodated on this enlarged grid, allowing more generous dimensions while still relating back to the house and the smaller grid.

The examples on pages 86–88 show three different designs for a large country site. In two of them the grid size has been tripled in size; in one, the grid has been doubled.

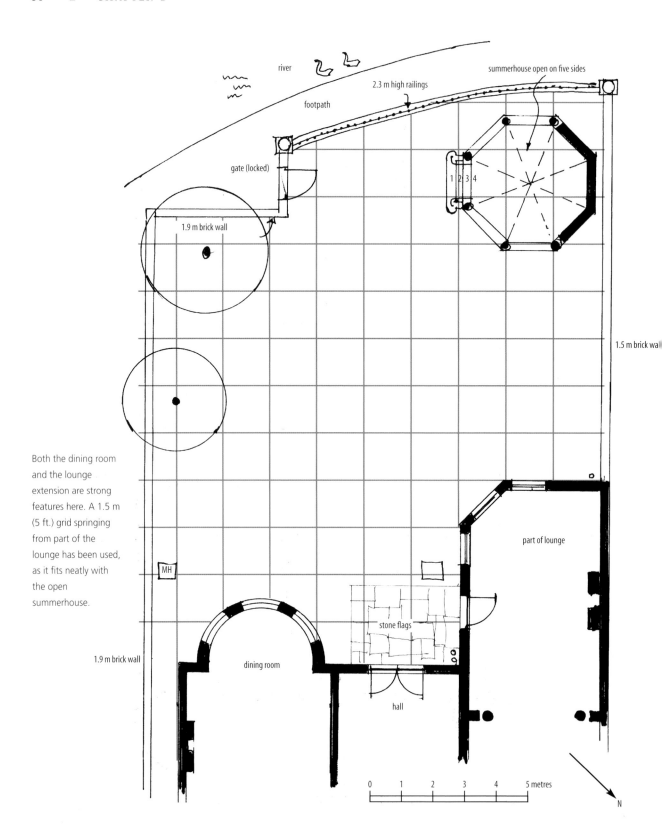

river

summerhouse open on five sides

2.3 m high railings

footpath

gate (locked)

1 2 3 4

1.9 m brick wall

1.5 m brick wall

Both the dining room and the lounge extension are strong features here. A 1.5 m (5 ft.) grid springing from part of the lounge has been used, as it fits neatly with the open summerhouse.

part of lounge

MH

1.9 m brick wall

stone flags

dining room

hall

0   1   2   3   4   5 metres

N

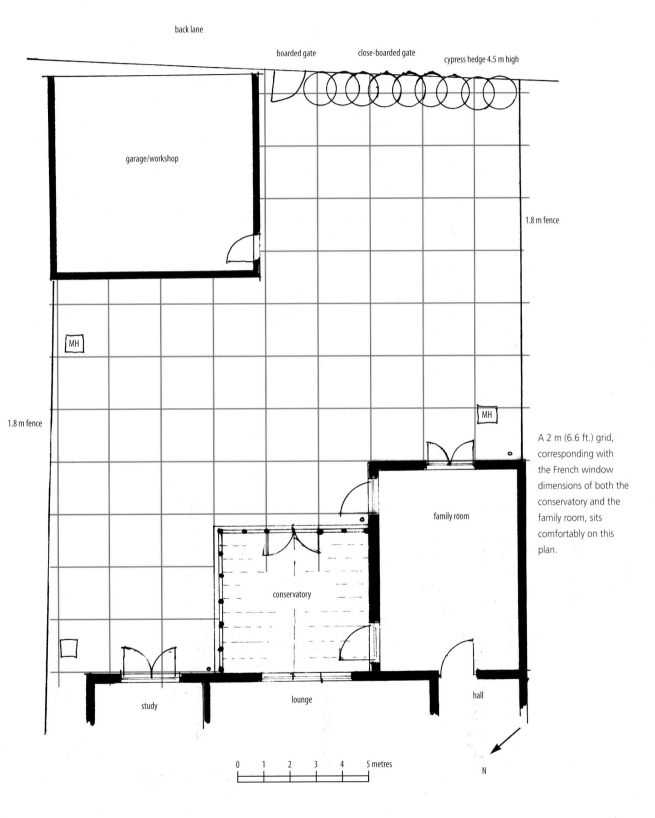

back lane

boarded gate

close-boarded gate

cypress hedge 4.5 m high

garage/workshop

1.8 m fence

MH

MH

1.8 m fence

family room

A 2 m (6.6 ft.) grid, corresponding with the French window dimensions of both the conservatory and the family room, sits comfortably on this plan.

conservatory

study

lounge

hall

0 1 2 3 4 5 metres

N

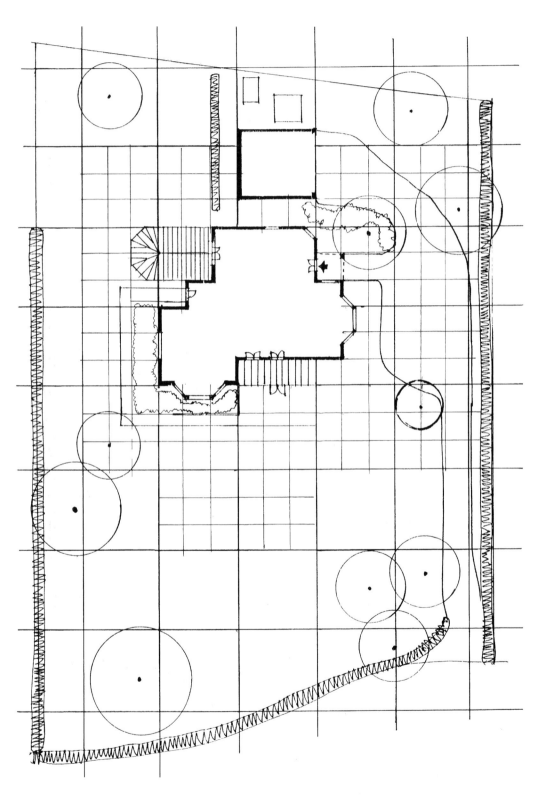

For this large country site a small grid, surrounding the house, has been tripled in size further from the house. Note how the lines of both the small and large grid squares spring from the dimensions of the house.

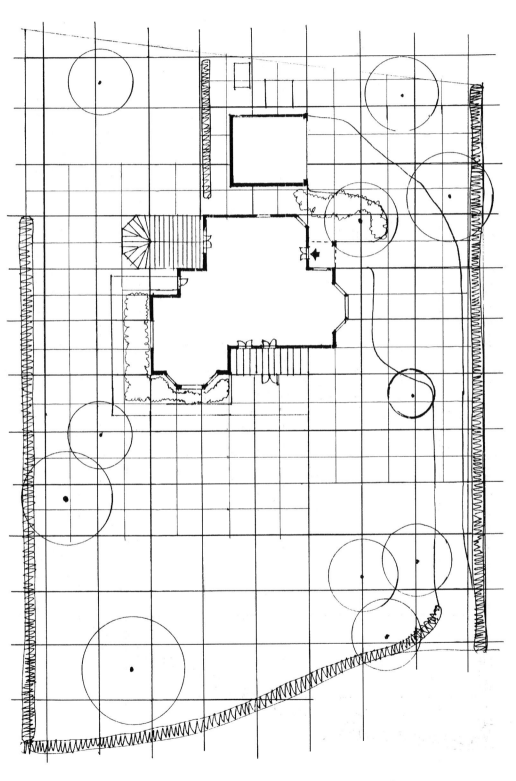

In this example, the grid has been doubled, rather than tripled, in size, further from the house. This solution is less satisfactory because the doubled grid squares do not relate to the dimensions of the house, nor to the scale of existing trees.

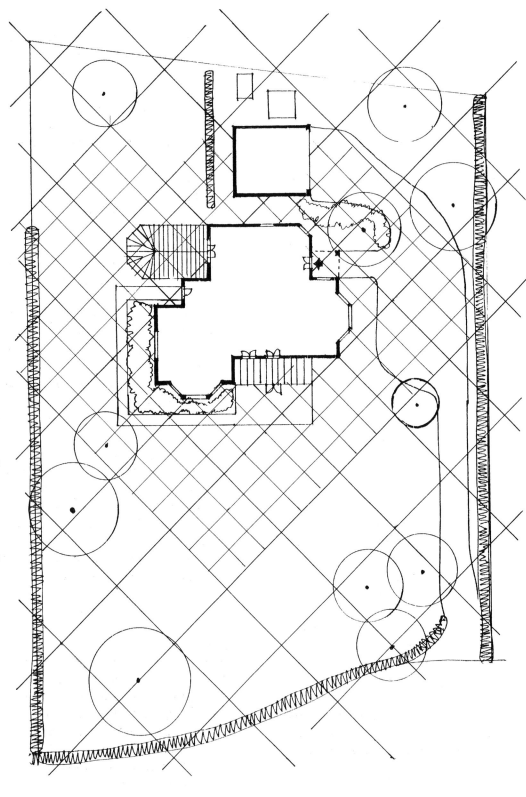

When dividing a garden into different areas, aim for one dominant area on the ground plane, rather than several areas of approximately the same size. By turning the grid, in this diagonal solution, the lawn predominates.

Moving and Turning the Grid

When you are drawing up the grid, extend the lines substantially beyond the site itself so that you can experiment with shifting the grid around and turning it at an angle. You may find that you can create an interesting diagonal effect or a more obvious link between different features.

Once you have become accustomed to designing with this grid system, you will find it easy to work out the grid, and it should prevent such design faults as paths, pergolas or even garden seats not being properly aligned with windows or doorways. When your eye has been trained to observe these alignments, anything out of line or wrongly placed will be a constant source of irritation.

Devising Grids for the Site

1. Stick down a sheet of tracing paper over the site survey. You will draw your grid onto this. A graph-paper backing sheet may be useful as a guide for ruling lines, but do not use this as your grid. The size of the grid will vary with each plan and should stem from the size or proportions of the house and garden.
2. Using the main lines of either house, buildings, doors or windows as a starting point, draw, with your set square and T-square or parallel motion, one vertical and one horizontal line to extend beyond the entire width or length of the site. Try to choose the most prominent points of the building, such as the corners of the house or a protruding bay window.
3. Then, using your scale rule, on the line that offers the most obvious divisions (determined by the features of the house), mark off equal divisions across and beyond the site. Draw these with the T-square, or parallel motion, and set square. Extending the lines beyond the boundaries of the site itself will allow you to move the grid around later.
4. Again using the scale rule and your drawing equipment, draw equally spaced lines, perpendicular to the first lines, across the site to create your grid.
5. Try turning the grid and translating it into areas of hard and soft landscaping by experimenting with moving the grid around first at an angle of, say, forty-five degrees to the house, then at about thirty-three degrees. Try to line up the turned grid lines with something such as the edge of a window or door, or the corner of the house. Does this work better for this particular site?
6. Stick down another sheet of tracing paper, with masking tape, as an overlay on top of the first.
7. Trace over the new grid, drawn at an angle.
8. Now try to work up each plan into areas of hard landscaping (man-made structures) and soft landscaping (plants).
9. Evaluate what you have done. Have you created a formal or informal pattern? Is the pattern balanced and ordered? Is it directional? What illusions, if any, have your lines created? If you crouch down and put your eyes at the same level as your plan, you may see this more easily. You may now have the basis of an exciting new layout.

Theme Plans

There is usually one particular way in which the grid works best and one angle that will work better than others. To help you decide, try experimenting with a design on a rectilinear theme, a circular theme, and a diagonal theme for your garden site. All of these relate back to the shapes and patterns considered

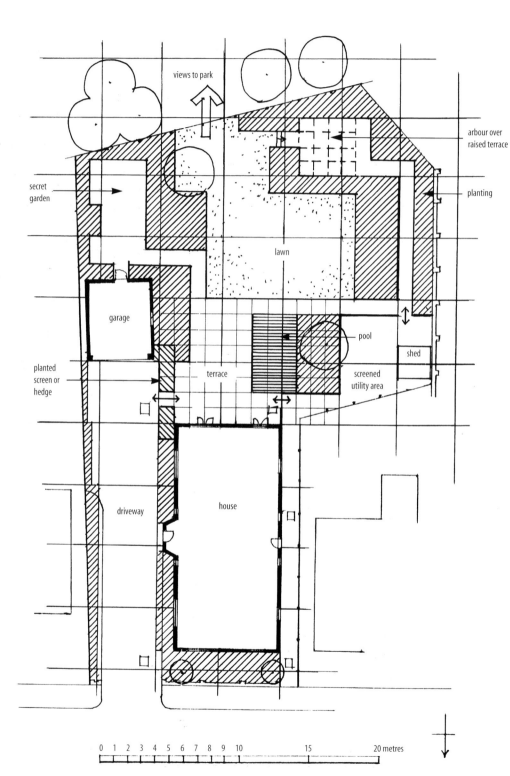

views to park

arbour over
raised terrace

secret
garden

planting

lawn

garage

pool

shed

planted
screen or
hedge

terrace

screened
utility area

driveway

house

Theme Plan 1: A small-scale grid has been used near the house in this model garden plan. Further from the house the grid has been quadrupled in size. In this rectilinear theme plan, the areas have been divided up into rectangles (rather than squares), which give direction to the plan, leading people around a site, as well as directing views through it to the parkland beyond.

0 1 2 3 4 5 6 7 8 9 10   15   20 metres

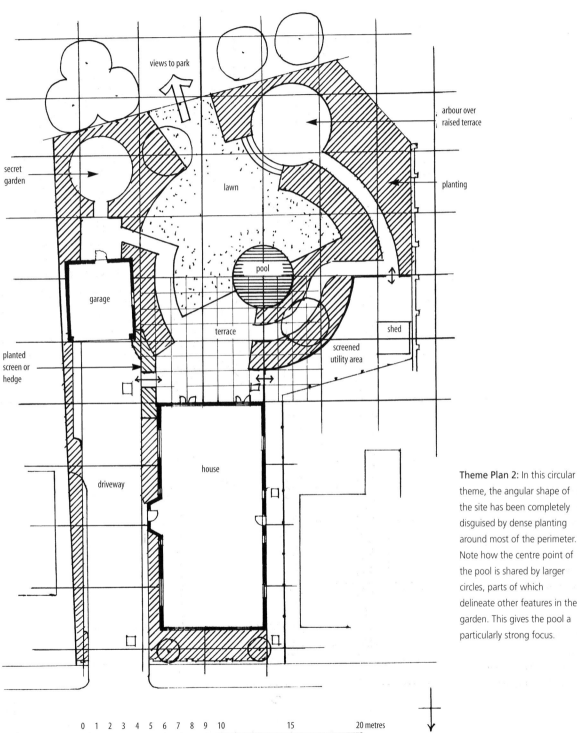

views to park

arbour over
raised terrace

planting

secret
garden

lawn

pool

garage

terrace

shed

screened
utility area

planted
screen or
hedge

house

driveway

0 1 2 3 4 5 6 7 8 9 10   15   20 metres

Theme Plan 2: In this circular theme, the angular shape of the site has been completely disguised by dense planting around most of the perimeter. Note how the centre point of the pool is shared by larger circles, parts of which delineate other features in the garden. This gives the pool a particularly strong focus.

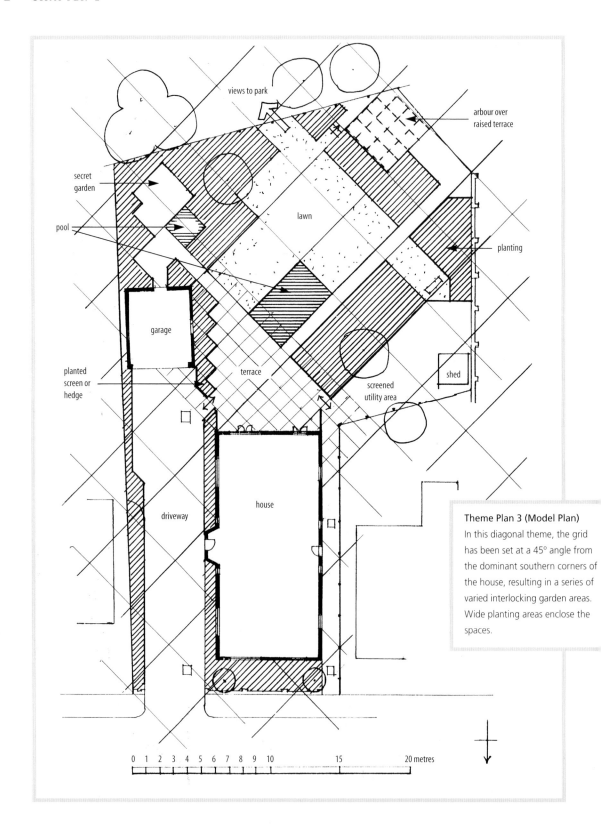

views to park

arbour over
raised terrace

secret
garden

pool

lawn

planting

garage

planted
screen or
hedge

terrace

screened
utility area

shed

house

driveway

Theme Plan 3 (Model Plan)
In this diagonal theme, the grid
has been set at a 45° angle from
the dominant southern corners of
the house, resulting in a series of
varied interlocking garden areas.
Wide planting areas enclose the
spaces.

0 1 2 3 4 5 6 7 8 9 10   15   20 metres

earlier in this chapter. Developing these themes will help you break down any preconceived ideas for the space that you are redesigning and should give rise to completely original concepts for what may previously have been a boring and predictable layout.

It is important to stress that this stage of designing is experimental, and you should allow yourself numerous sheets of tracing paper, stuck down over your survey and grid, to test out different ideas. Do make sure that you have indicated any major existing trees as circles on your survey. Trees may well influence your design, as they cannot be moved, but this also should have shown up on your site inventory and appraisal.

The examples on the previous pages show three different design solutions for the large suburban garden that is the model site for this book. All of the plans suit the outline shape of the site and the style and mass of the house. Each of the design solutions was developed from the same grid. The grid was turned at forty-five degrees for the diagonal design (opposite), and it was this theme that was chosen to be developed into the garden layout plan.

Using the Grid to Direct the Ground Plane

By using the grid to direct your lines, the garden design should work as a balanced whole, mass balancing void, with no leftover corners or weak, wiggly lines. To avoid sharp corners, lines should ideally meet at right angles.

Perhaps the theme you choose might spring from the house itself—a circular theme taken from a curved window, for instance. In general, circles require more space than rectangles, and if the house is obviously rectangular, with straight walls giving a boxed-in effect, it may be overambitious (and alien to the site) to superimpose a circular theme. Examples of successful and unsuccessful designs based on circular and curvilinear shapes for a small rectangular site are shown on the next page.

Drawing up Experimental Theme Plans

1. On your drawing board stick down the site survey plan with masking tape and then place the tracing-paper grid sheet over the plan.
2. Experiment with turning the grid at different angles.
3. Use a further sheet of tracing paper and, with a pencil, trace off any grids that you think may be suitable. (You will probably need to use several sheets of tracing paper until you have achieved setting the grid at an angle that you like.)
4. Now develop your design by using tracing-paper overlays with your chosen grid, and work up (in pencil) the various themes—circular, diagonal and rectilinear.
5. Keep these rough pencil theme plans carefully. You will need to refer to them when you draw up the preliminary garden layout plan (see page 131).

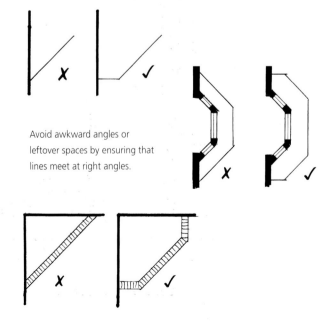

Avoid awkward angles or leftover spaces by ensuring that lines meet at right angles.

Unsuccessful theme plans: In this circular design (right), there is insufficient space to make the transition between the rectangular house and the circles. Each shape seems to collide with the next rather than leading naturally into it. Although the intention is to disguise the rectangular shape of the plot with planting, there is insufficient space around the larger circle to achieve this.
In this small space, the free form curvilinear design (far right) is at odds with the parallel surrounding walls.

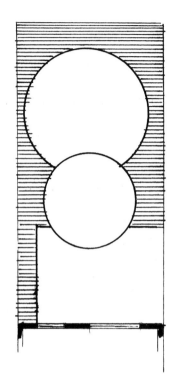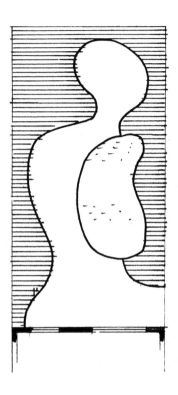

Successful theme plans: In this example (right) a geometry of squares is used. The circle fits into square 1 and although the square disappears, it is strongly implied. Square 2 provides a link between the two main garden rooms, like an ante-room or vestibule.

The strong curve of this design (far right) will be softened as the planting matures, and the sense of space will increase as the walls become obscured. Note how the position of the trees emphasizes the design.

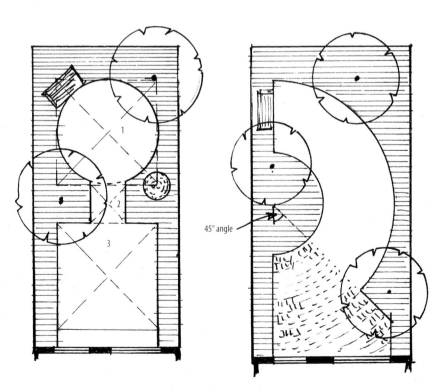

45° angle

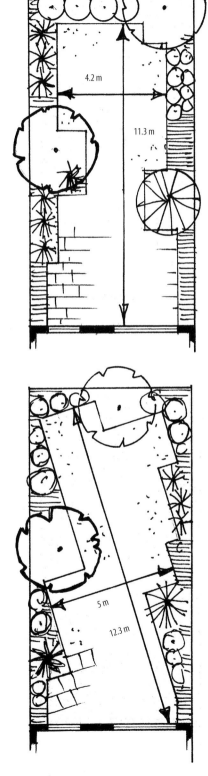

Before making your decision on which theme to adopt, do try turning the grid through forty-five degrees or slanting the plan, perhaps from one corner to the distant opposite corner. This is a very effective method of exploiting the maximum length of the site, as shown in the example on this page, and it was the chosen solution for the model plan (see page 92).

Planning an Outdoor Space

If you find the concept of outdoor space hard to envisage, it may be helpful to think of it as an outdoor room. Just as an indoor room is enclosed by the floor, walls and ceiling, so are outdoor rooms defined by the ground plane (the garden floor), the vertical plane (walls, fences and so on) and the overhead plane (tree canopies, pergolas or anything that interrupts the view of the sky). Within this context, perhaps it is easier to develop an awareness of the three-dimensional effects of mass and void and to consider the effects of light and water in the garden.

Space

It is wrong to think of space, or void, as nothingness: space has character and mood. An enclosed space, for instance, may afford a garden privacy or intimacy, in contrast to an open space, which is essentially outward-looking and may feel insecure.

To increase the apparent length of a site, slant the plan using the angle formed by the longest diagonal.

A garden dominated by mass is enclosed and secluded.

The interplay between mass and void creates the structure of the garden. When void predominates, a garden feels more open and exposed.

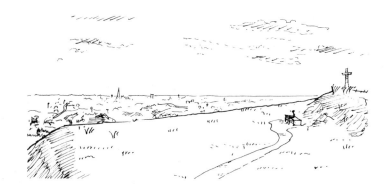

Space is compressed

Space is more open

Space is expanded further still

Above: Using bricks or children's wooden blocks, vary the width between them, as shown, to see how the space is affected when viewed at eye level.

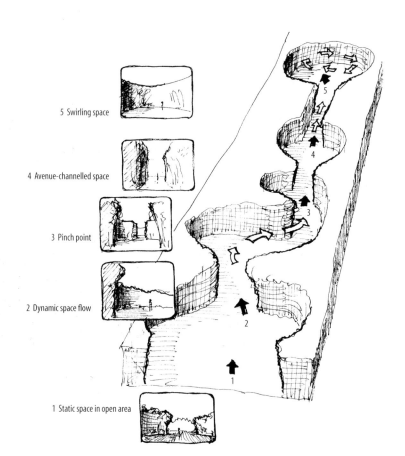

5 Swirling space

4 Avenue-channelled space

3 Pinch point

2 Dynamic space flow

1 Static space in open area

Right: The movement of space is conditioned by the placing of the masses.

Space is not necessarily static but can be made to flow like water. The speed at which it flows can be altered, too. It can move slowly (down a broad drive or around shrub beds to fill a void of lawn) or swiftly (forced down through a narrow path). This apparent movement of space, created by the placing of the masses between which it flows, creates far more excitement and stimulus in the garden than any number of rare plants or bright colours.

Light

The mood of a space is affected by light, and the amount and quality of light entering a garden is affected by the elements placed within or existing close to it. For example, in the growing season a mature tree may completely block sunlight from entering a small garden.

Light Quality and Intensity

We are so used to the presence of daylight that we take it for granted, quite forgetting that its quality and quantity totally control the way in which everything is seen and, therefore, how it should be designed.

The quality of the light varies with latitude. In Britain, even on a bright day, the near distance is tinged with blue and the shadows have no clear definition, while on a sunless day the whole scene lacks clarity, as though it were a slightly smudged pencil sketch. In hotter countries, stronger sunlight makes shadows appear more defined. Temperate gardens tend to need a larger proportion of void to mass, so that enough light can enter the composition. If your garden is in a country where the light is hard and clear, the ratio can be reversed so that there is more dark mass to offset small, brightly lit voids.

In temperate climates, the sun is relatively weak and casts soft, hazy shadows. The low angle of the sun results in long shadows for much of the year.

Lower planting around the perimeter allows more light into the garden.

In tropical climates, on or near to the equator, the sun is strong and bright, casting dense, well-defined shadows. The sun is high in the sky all the year round, producing relatively short shadows.

To increase the amount of shade in the garden, the relative mass is increased by introducing a tall hedge on one boundary and planting umbrella-shaped trees within the garden.

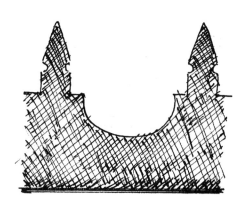

Objects with a well-defined shape or form look most effective when silhouetted by being lit from behind.

Creating Special Effects

When designing a garden it is important to consider the effects that you want to create with light by arranging the masses in a suitable way. The shape of an object (the detail of a wrought-iron gate, for instance) can be emphasized by being silhouetted against a light background. If, on the other hand, the texture of something (such as smooth rocks or gnarled tree trunks) needs emphasizing, the object should be lit from the front, or it should be in sun as opposed to shade.

Looking from dark to light—or, even better, from light through dark to light beyond—adds drama and depth to the view. In temperate climates, where the light conditions may be rather diffuse, it is still possible to create striking effects. The rays of low-level afternoon sun playing through sparsely foliaged trees can cast moving dappled shadows, for instance, and shafts of light can be used to highlight a carefully sited statue.

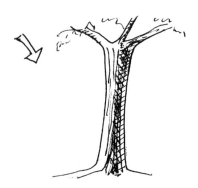

The direction from which an object is lit affects how it is perceived.

Reducing the amount of light before a vista accentuates the scene.

Looking through dark to light.

Looking from light through to light beyond.

Interior and exterior scales differ. External proportions need to be more generous. Indoors, the height of this door looks fine—it is in scale with the interior. Outdoors, the height and the width will be inadequate and out of scale. Note how cramped the door and pergola have become. You need to "scale up" when outdoors.

Scale and Proportion

Scale and proportion are also important factors to bear in mind when thinking about spaces, as without them there can be no harmony of design. Within a built environment, architects create interior living and working spaces that are in scale with the human figure. However, outside, where the sky is the limit, these interior proportions feel meagre and uncomfortable. Outside, the garden designer has to relate the scale of the human figure to the limitless expanse of horizon and sky, requiring the tall verticals of trees or buildings to help balance the horizon. Also, gardens are places for leisure, and they need more ample proportions.

To relate to external scale, steps, paths and openings must be more generous than those found within a building. A useful exercise is to take your flexible tape and measure the steps of your own interior staircase, and then go out to a nearby garden or park and compare these interior measurements with a comfortable flight of outdoor steps. You should find that the stairs indoors—even though they look and feel perfectly comfortable in their more intimate indoor setting—are narrower and steeper than the garden steps.

However, gardens must also relate to the human scale, keeping the human frame and the space it may take up as an integral part of the design. Paths, steps, arbours and sitting areas should be sufficiently generous to be comfortable and intimate, not overgenerous, daunting and empty. Good proportions are the real foundation of the garden.

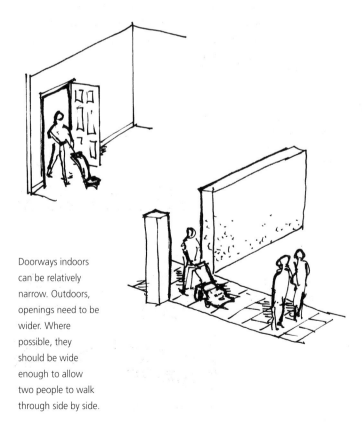

Doorways indoors can be relatively narrow. Outdoors, openings need to be wider. Where possible, they should be wide enough to allow two people to walk through side by side.

Indoors, people adjust to the space they are in and can feel perfectly comfortable sitting very close to one another. Outdoors, if space allows, you may need to double the size of an area used for a similar function to prevent people feeling restricted.

Designing steps for exterior use: Steps based on typical domestic indoor dimensions are inappropriate for outdoor use. Not only will they feel cramped in scale, but they could also be dangerous.

Always scale up steps outdoors by creating wider and deeper treads and reducing the riser height.

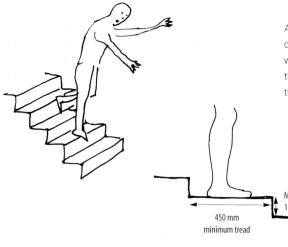

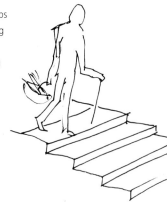

450 mm
minimum tread

Maximum riser
150 mm

Staircases should have plenty of room and frequent generous landings. Above all else, design for safety.

For all sorts of reasons, consider using ramps as an alternative or substitute for steps

Water

If you would like a water feature in your garden, begin by considering the different types before deciding on the form it will take. Water has a seductive, elusive quality that can greatly enhance any setting and, when used effectively, is able to command more attention than any other garden feature. It has the attribute of reflecting light but also has, in the garden layout, a similar strength to a solid structure. If well designed and integrated, a water feature can be a great asset to a garden, but, if used badly, it can be a depressing mistake. Water should be used with discretion, becoming part of the structure of your design. In small gardens, water is best used formally, either in conjunction with a building or as a sculptural feature or fountain. Using water informally, in free-form shapes imitating natural ponds, requires more space. Decide early on which type of water feature you want, and then decide whether it should flow or be static. The safety aspect, particularly for children, is of prime concern—being caged in as a precaution does not enhance any water feature.

Although perhaps the single most magical feature in a garden, water is also the most difficult subject to get right. Once you have decided on your concept, it may be advisable to call in a water specialist who should be able to foresee any potential problems.

Historical Use of Water

Water has been prized in the design of gardens since ancient times. It was used as an integral part of many early Mogul, Persian and Islamic gardens, cooling down the atmosphere, soothing the spirits and giving an additional dimension to a flat landscape.

In Europe during the Renaissance a renewed interest in hydraulics led to a proliferation of water devices, particularly in Italian and French gardens. Fountains had huge jets of water that soared into the air; grottoes had trick water features, which, to the amusement of the host, soaked unsuspecting visitors; cascades tumbled down water staircases; and a series of spouts and rills emitted sounds that imitated music. It was the height of fashion to include an unusual water feature in a garden setting, and wealthy landowners who took pride in their gardens engaged designers with knowledge of modern hydraulics to turn their fantasies into reality.

Although today we accept hydraulic systems, such as pumps, as part of everyday life, there is still huge scope for the imagination when it comes to using water in a garden.

The Qualities of Water

Water awakens the senses. Its movement and reflection provide a feast for the eyes; the range of sounds it produces, from gentle dripping to loud crashing, has the ability to calm or invigorate; and its tactile quality, whether liquid or in the form of ice, is fascinating. When used in a garden it can provide a home for plants and wildlife, colourful swirls of fish and water plants adding to its visual appeal. Water can also enhance the quality of other materials, deepening the colours of mosaic tiles, for instance, or highlighting the smooth surface of river pebbles.

Still water and reflection

The most striking attribute of still water is its power to reflect, thereby doubling the value of any image

A sheet of water used to bring light into a garden.

that falls on its surface. This can be used to great effect in a garden. It can unify a design by bringing together the ground plane, the vertical plane and the overhead plane, and it can create a feeling of space by bringing light into the garden.

To bring out the best of water's reflective quality, it is important to contain the water in a material that is as dark as possible. The reflections on the surface of a swimming pool are usually poor or nonexistent during the day, because the floor and walls are generally pale in colour and can be clearly seen. If, on the other hand, the pool were painted black, the reflected images would be clear, even in cloudy weather, and the interior would be invisible. Of course, this would only apply to ornamental pools—a black swimming pool would be most uninviting.

Being unable to judge the depth of a pool or pond adds a sense of mystery to the feature and has practical advantages as well. Not only does the darkness obscure functional items, such as plant containers and supports for stepping stones, but it also allows the designer to construct a relatively shallow pool, thereby saving on construction expenses.

When thinking about reflections, consider the importance of the water level. As the side of the pool will be reflected in the water, the water level will appear to be lower than it is, reducing the apparent surface area. To maximize the reflective area, you will need to raise the water level as high as possible. In formal pools it should be kept just below the level of the coping stones or edging.

You can experiment with the effect of reflections by placing small objects on a hand mirror.

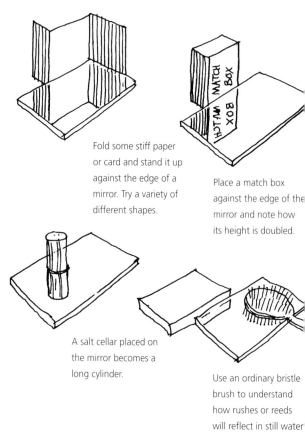

Fold some stiff paper or card and stand it up against the edge of a mirror. Try a variety of different shapes.

Place a match box against the edge of the mirror and note how its height is doubled.

A salt cellar placed on the mirror becomes a long cylinder.

Use an ordinary bristle brush to understand how rushes or reeds will reflect in still water

Colour

If the sun does not fall directly on the surface of the water, the reflected sky appears a more intense blue. This fact can be used to advantage in small town courtyards, where the enhanced colour and light reflected back from the surface of the water can turn a gloomy, dull space into one with vibrant interest.

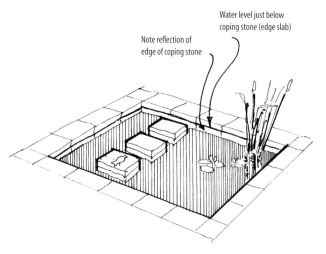

Note reflection of edge of coping stone

Water level just below coping stone (edge slab)

To increase the darkness or depth of colour of the water, dramatize the effect by using dark large-leaved evergreens in the background.

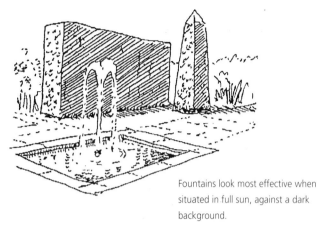

Water as the main feature of a small courtyard enhances the feeling of light and colour.

Movement

Moving water shimmers and sparkles in the light and adds a refreshing quality of sound which is much appreciated in hot countries. Because of the way light dances on moving water, it works best when it is positioned in full sun. Fountains, for instance, are particularly effective when positioned in full sun with a shady background, preferably of dark green plants.

One way in which moving water differs from still water is by the sounds it creates. A small amount—trickling onto rocks in a pool, for instance—can be delicate and musical, whereas a large volume, forced up through the jet of a powerful fountain or cascading over rocks into a pool far below, can produce loud hissing or burbling sounds that bring a sense of excitement to a garden. In an urban setting these sounds can help to reduce outside noise, particularly the distant sounds of traffic or people.

Fountains look most effective when situated in full sun, against a dark background.

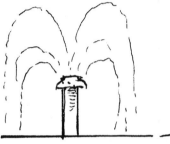

Catalogues may show you perfect spray effects produced by different nozzles but in reality, the tiny holes are easily clogged and the wind can also spoil the effect.

Left: Simple jets are often more effective—the height of the fountain can be easily adjusted at the pump.

Designing with Water

Remember that if you decide to include water in your garden, it is essential that the particular water feature be properly integrated into the design as a whole, complementing existing features as well as proposed hard landscaping and plantings. This applies whether you are creating a new feature or adapting an existing water source, such as a stream or pond.

The need for water and the way it can and should be used varies considerably by region. Stylistically, some water features would be more in keeping with the natural surroundings than others. In Maine, for example, much of the coastal landscape is broken up by the natural effects of rocks and trees, and as a result coastal waters lap gently against the shore. Reflecting this, the design of the Asticou Azalea Garden in Northeast Harbor uses large pieces of granite as stepping stones to continue a path across a stream. In Arizona, mirror-like reflecting pools complement the bold shapes and textures of desert plantings.

In several areas of the United Kingdom, such as Cornwall and the south and west coast of Scotland, where the sea is less threatening, the natural landscape is also used to enhance and soften humankind's intervention. Stone from local quarries is often used for stepping stones used to cross water, giving children the enjoyment of the potential danger of getting wet.

Water in the landscape can also become something of a cultural phenomenon. In the certain parts of the United States, because of high summer temperatures, it is common to have a swimming pool; current trends also include hot tubs as well as lap pools (long, narrow pools for serious swimmers) naturalized by adding waterfalls or streams. In cooler areas, however, pools are often considered a luxury that few people can afford. Pools often take up large portions of the garden and can pose many design challenges.

Climate should be considered when designing any garden water feature. In very hot areas, small amounts of water may be impractical because frequent refilling is required owing to rapid evaporation. Similarly, in very cold winter areas, features should be designed either to accommodate freezing water or to be easy to drain down annually.

National and local water restrictions should also be considered. Bear in mind that pools and water features use a great deal of water, and filling them could be costly or impossible if a drought situation occurs.

Broadly speaking, water features can be divided into those that are formal (and obviously artificial) and those that are informal (either natural or naturalistic and imitating nature). Generally, formal features look better in small urban gardens or positioned close to the house in larger gardens; informal water features are more in keeping with natural landscapes and gardens in rural settings.

Reflections of illuminated foliage near a pool add interest at night.

Formal water features

The size, shape and location of a formal water feature should be determined by existing features. The water feature will be part of the grid so that it relates strongly to all other elements and is an integral part of the design. Unlike informal water features, often elusive or partly concealed, water used in a formal setting tends to make a strong statement.

Formal pools are geometric in shape and do not pretend to look natural. They are constructed of rigid materials, such as concrete (used alone or with a flexible butyl liner) or premoulded resin. Resin pools, although widely available, are rarely satisfactory because you are unlikely to find the exact dimensions of pool that you need. In any case, most of these have overshaped, irregular outlines that emphasize artificiality and do not lend themselves well to formal situations.

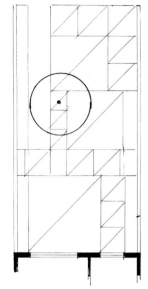

Site survey: A new pool was an important feature for this garden design, and a way had to be found to integrate it successfully on this rectilinear grid. The clients required:

- a pool for reflection and tranquillity
- the garden to look wider
- no steps—they have elderly parents
- space for shrubs
- an existing tree to be retained
- outdoor seating areas.

The garden layout plan (right) shows the solution that was reached, and a visual (opposite page) illustrates the simple, placid oriental mood of the proposed pool.

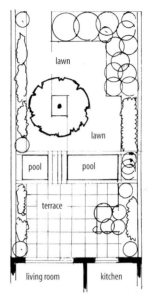

Garden layout plan: The pool runs almost across the width of the garden and separates the terrace from the garden emphatically. It creates a sense of "here"—the terrace—and "there"—the garden beyond.

Linking the two areas is a flat bridge set level and without any steps. It is built of standard "off-the-shelf" precast concrete window lintels. These are thin, inexpensive, and robust. Such lintels are available in a variety of standard lengths. For safety, a handrail with two posts at each end is added.

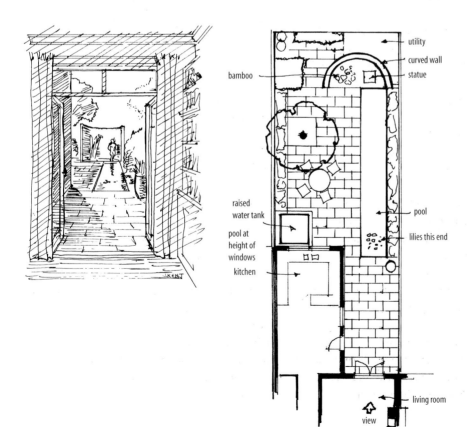

In this example, note how the pool has been made deliberately long and set almost flush with the paving to reduce the foreshortening effect of perspective. Although the pool appears considerably shorter when seen from indoors, the surface of the water will be visible enough to allow a view of the reflection of the statue. The carefully placed water lilies do not obscure the reflection.

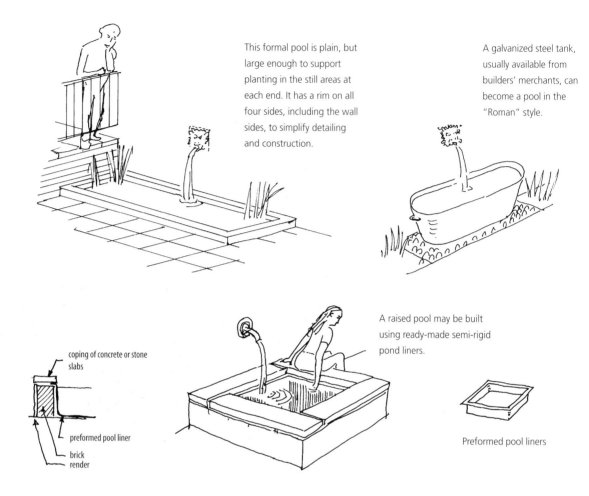

This formal pool is plain, but large enough to support planting in the still areas at each end. It has a rim on all four sides, including the wall sides, to simplify detailing and construction.

A galvanized steel tank, usually available from builders' merchants, can become a pool in the "Roman" style.

A raised pool may be built using ready-made semi-rigid pond liners.

coping of concrete or stone slabs

preformed pool liner

brick
render

Preformed pool liners

Informal water features

If you already have a natural water feature in your garden, you may want to emphasize it and include it in your design. This may involve designing a bridge to cross from one side of a stream to another, changing the direction and movement of the water or providing some waterside plantings. However, a natural water source can also be used to feed a formal water feature, if this style is more appropriate.

When creating a new naturalistic pond, it is essential that you study ponds and lakes in their natural setting. What you are trying to achieve is a pond that looks as if it has always been there. Examine how natural water features have occurred and their effect on the surrounding land, particularly during flooding or drought. A natural source of water may not remain constant. Normally water occupies the lowest part of any site, its surface creating a datum level to which everything else relates. The effect is seldom convincing if ponds are deliberately placed high up or on sloping ground, unless in a natural hollow.

The surrounding contours, too, must be carefully considered, since the edge of the water is in itself a contour line, and if this (or the reflection of the adjoining landform) looks unnatural, the whole feature will be exposed as a fraud. Pay particular attention to the shapes formed by the water, how it flows around or over obstacles and exactly what happens at the edge.

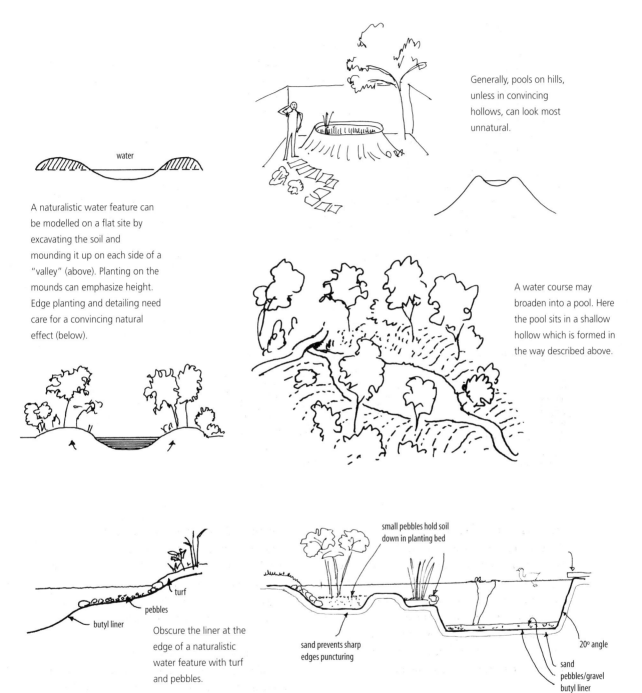

Generally, pools on hills, unless in convincing hollows, can look most unnatural.

A naturalistic water feature can be modelled on a flat site by excavating the soil and mounding it up on each side of a "valley" (above). Planting on the mounds can emphasize height. Edge planting and detailing need care for a convincing natural effect (below).

A water course may broaden into a pool. Here the pool sits in a shallow hollow which is formed in the way described above.

water

turf

pebbles

butyl liner

Obscure the liner at the edge of a naturalistic water feature with turf and pebbles.

small pebbles hold soil down in planting bed

sand prevents sharp edges puncturing

20° angle

sand
pebbles/gravel
butyl liner

With an artificial pond it is generally the point where land meets water that is most difficult to resolve, resulting in unconvincing shorelines of concrete or butyl liner. Generally, the material from which the pond is made should be carried up well beyond the visible edge of the water, at a shallow angle that will allow a marshy zone merging into a shingle beach. The shingle will only be revealed when the water level drops.

Size

Water features should be treated in a similar way to other features in a garden with respect to size. If the garden is very large, the water feature should also be generous. If small, the feature will need to be smaller, reflecting the proportions of the site. However, a pool needs space in which to express itself, and anything under about 2.5 m (8.2 ft.) in length or width may look more like a conspicuous puddle!

From a practical point of view, a small pool is subject to more temperature variation, particularly if shallow, and is more ecologically unstable than a larger body of water, affecting the water clarity and the balance of plant and animal life. The depth of a pool should be proportionate to its surface area—the greater the surface area, the greater the depth required to produce stability. Generally, the minimum depth is about 1 m (3.3 ft.), sufficient to hide the planting baskets of both aquatic and marginal plants placed below the surface, and to allow fish to survive.

Vigorous water plants may need to be kept in check to prevent them obscuring the surface of the water, reducing reflections.

An important point to consider when determining the size of a pool is that planting either in or close to the pool will tend to encroach upon the water area and may reduce it considerably if you are using invasive marginal plants.

If space will not allow for a large pool, there are other options. Where ground space is limited, you can use a wall-mounted fountain. Elaborate lions, dolphin heads or simple metal spouts can allow water to spill into a pool or, if the feature is required to double as a birdbath, first into a shallow bowl. Circular millstones can have a spout that allows water to run over and around them, and lush effects can be achieved by planting moisture-loving plants in deep, damp soil nearby.

A small water feature can double as a bird bath.

Location

The success of a water feature may depend on where it is sited. The position of trees and the aspect and orientation of the site have a bearing on this.

Overhanging trees

Generally it is advisable to site water features away from overhanging trees. In a formal setting, leaves can make the pool look unkempt, and if the pool is not very deep, vegetation collecting at the bottom may turn the water black and result in a proliferation of duck weed over the surface. If a formal pool is to be surrounded by plantings, and particularly if the area is windswept, it is advisable to raise it above ground level to reduce the amount of vegetation blown into the water.

If you intend your pool to provide a home to plant and animal life, beware of siting it near trees with poisonous leaves, berries or seeds, such as yew, holly and laburnum.

Sun and shade

Most plants and animals thrive better in pools that receive sun for at least half a day, preferably more in temperate regions. In hot countries, less would be acceptable. If you only have a shady site, you will not be able to grow water lilies, but a few species of fish, such as golden orfe, are happy in cold water. Mosses and ferns will also thrive in shade.

Directing circulation

Having dwelt on the aesthetic qualities of water, it is worth remembering that water can be used to direct the circulation of people through a garden. Most people will walk around, rather than through, a stretch of water!

Using reflection

Still water can be used to bring light into a garden, but if water is to be used in this way, the pool must be sited so that it catches the available sunshine and reflects it back to an intended part of the garden or house. To achieve this, the level of the water may have to be lowered or raised.

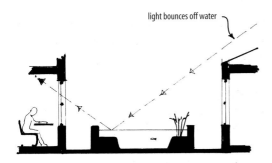

light bounces off water

Reflected light from this large raised pool brightens a downstairs room. As the surface of the water is blown by breezes, ripples are reflected onto the ceiling.

If your intention in using still water is to reflect the surroundings of a garden, consider the angle of the sun. Ideally, as you view the water, the sun should be shining from behind you. If it is shining towards you, the glare it produces may prevent you from seeing any reflections.

Practical Problems

A badly designed water feature may detract from the enjoyment of a garden. Ponds constructed without an overflow pipe may flood and ruin large areas of lawn or plantings, and the entire structure of a pool can be damaged, if not suitably constructed, by harsh weather conditions, such as frost or ice.

In hot countries in particular, a shallow pool of water that is not circulated may attract breeding colonies of mosquitoes or other insects and become smelly and stagnant.

Safety Considerations

Undoubtedly, one of the most important issues in designing a water feature is whether children are likely to use the garden. A young child can drown in as little as 2 cm (1 in.) of water, and all nonswimmers are at risk with deep pools. Ways of increasing safety include covering a formal pool with black-painted metal bars or a steel mesh that can support the weight of an adult, or fencing off a pond or stream. The fence need not be exposed but can be cleverly disguised with plantings. When designing pools, a sheer side is far safer than one with sloping sides at forty-five degrees. At this angle anyone in the water would find it hard to reach and grasp hold of the edge of the pool or to get a foothold from which to get out.

So, when children are young, it is advisable to avoid stretches of water. But if you or the garden owner would like a water feature in the future, do think of how an existing feature may later be adapted inexpensively. A large sandpit, for instance, may be sited and designed for easy conversion. There are

A 45° slope is extremely dangerous—from inside the water it is hard to reach the edge of the pool or to get a foothold from which to get out.

Sheer sides are safer than sloping ones, particularly if they contain a ledge. The ledge can also be used as a shelf for the planting baskets of marginal plants.

A fountain over cobbles provides a child-friendly water feature.

A gradually sloping "beach" is the safest construction for a pool.

many ways of introducing water into a garden without risk to children. You could, for example, create a jet of water that splashes over pebbles. The water would then trickle back through to an underground reservoir and be recirculated with a pump.

Refining Ideas for the Preliminary Garden Layout Plan

When preparing the first stages of the garden layout plan you will be focusing on the ground plane and will need to consider how you will be combining hard landscaping (anything that is man-made, such as paving, paths, walls, arches or buildings) with soft landscaping (soil, grass, water or plant material). At this point it may be wise to refer back to your completed site appraisal and concept diagram (see Chapter 1) and reconsider the following:

– How do your proposals satisfy the recommendations of your appraisal?
– Have you allowed enough space for different activities?
– Are the spaces large enough for people to move about in?
– Have you sited them in appropriate places?

You will probably need to readjust some of your earlier ideas before moving on to make decisions about the horizontal (and later some of the vertical) elements of your layout. The success of your design will depend on how you divide up the garden into these different hard and soft areas and how you link one area with another.

The fashion in twentieth-century gardens was the creation of garden rooms, dividing up the site into a series of interlocking spaces, each with an individual character or style of plantings. This division gives an opportunity for several different types of garden

When refining your ideas for the preliminary garden layout plan, keep referring back to your site appraisal.

within the whole garden and can relate well to the interior proportions of modern houses. Current trends are influenced by television makeovers and the media, and materials such as aluminium and glass have become fashionable.

The Ground Plane or Garden Floor: Horizontal Elements in the Design

The garden floor is perhaps the most important single element in the design. It is the link between house and garden, can be divided up into the appropriate proportions for mass and void and is also usually the most expensive part of the garden to construct. There is a huge and often bewildering choice of materials available, but you must consider whether the material you use will be in keeping with the site and the surroundings. The material must also be suited to the purpose. For instance, heavy and thick stone paving would be inappropriate for the scale of a small circular paved area, and the cost of labour to cut each stone to fit the space would be prohibitive. To keep costs reasonable, the material you choose should be suited to the role it is to perform.

Paved Areas and Terraces

It is often easiest to begin with the paved areas, as this is usually the terrace adjacent to the house, although if the main rooms of the house face away from the direction of the sun it may be necessary to have the terrace, or sitting area, some distance from the house.

The terrace usually provides the major horizontal link between house and garden, the width being at a minimum two-thirds of the height of the house to the level of the eaves. With low buildings, the full height of the house will produce a better proportion. Narrow or small terraces often look meagre, as if there were insufficient paving stones available. They also restrict the amount of seating. Try to leave some space for planting at the foot of the house wall, softening the hard right-angle junction between wall and terrace. Leave enough room for generous planting, rather than having a thin line of plants trying to survive in builders' leftover rubble. Make sure that the soil remains clear of the damp-proof course (DPC).

The terrace should, if possible, be on the same level as the interior floor of the house, but this will depend on the height of the DPC or foundation. Usually the DPC or foundation is at least 150 mm (6 in.) above ground level and can be stepped with the fall of the ground. Ignoring this level (where moisture cannot permeate) by building or banking up soil can lead to problems such as rising damp or flooding. Bugs or termites can also cause premature deterioration of the house structure.

If the finished terrace level is below the interior floor level of the house, try to ensure that the transitional step (or steps) are wide enough to allow a person to stand and adjust to the change of level. If the terrace is above the interior floor level, the steps that lead up to it should be wide. There may even need to be a change of level in the terrace itself, and, if so, you should make this as obvious as possible to avoid accidents. Any terraces or areas of paving in other parts of the garden should be dealt with in the same way as the main terrace.

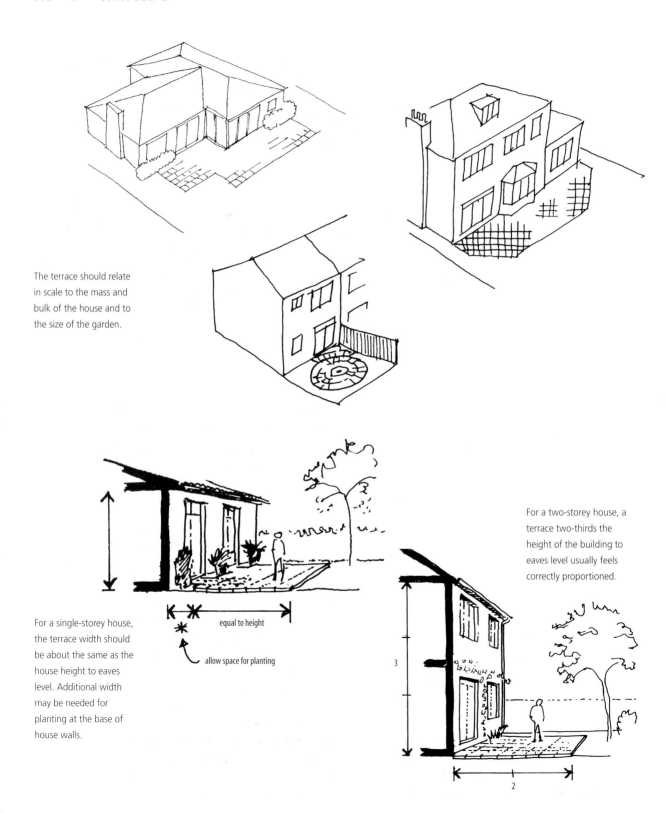

The terrace should relate in scale to the mass and bulk of the house and to the size of the garden.

For a single-storey house, the terrace width should be about the same as the house height to eaves level. Additional width may be needed for planting at the base of house walls.

equal to height

allow space for planting

For a two-storey house, a terrace two-thirds the height of the building to eaves level usually feels correctly proportioned.

3

2

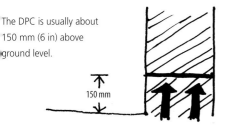

The DPC is usually about 150 mm (6 in) above ground level.

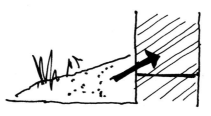

150 mm

The damp proof course is a horizontal layer of impervious material laid in a wall to prevent the damp from rising. Soil piled up above the DPC effectively bridges it, allowing damp to seep inside.

To create a terrace level with the floor indoors without bridging the DPC use a slatted timber deck supported on bricks, with an accessible and ventilated space beneath. This bridges the "trench" between window and terrace.

If a raised terrace is unavoidable, then ample transition space and careful design is essential.

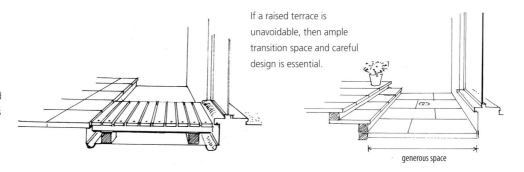

generous space

Any transitional step down from a house should be wide to avoid accidents.

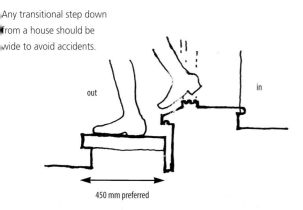

out

in

450 mm preferred

When designing to a grid, remember that this grid can be carried through in the paving pattern, albeit at a smaller scale. This can be particularly effective if your design is on the diagonal, the paving being laid at the same diagonal angle, following the lines of the grid.

Paths

Paths are the arteries of a garden and often lead off and out from the terrace, following grid lines that flow from gateways, doors or windows. Before considering a path, it is important to decide on its exact purpose, since paths leading nowhere (often in a roundabout fashion) always appear ridiculous. Path proportions should relate in scale to other garden features and to the adjoining house, but the following general guidelines may be helpful:

– Always think about who is going to use the path.
– Main paths, perhaps designed to draw people through the garden and allow them to examine views or details of plantings, should, if there is room, be about 1.2–1.5 m (4–5 ft.) in width, to allow two people to stroll in comfort.
– Paths that lead up to the front door of a house should also be generous, as there will often be a group of people approaching or leaving a house together.
– Subsidiary and service paths need be only 1 m (3.3 ft.) or less in width but must avoid sharp curves or right angles which would be inconvenient for wheelbarrows. A service path between a border and hedge needs to take the base of a stepladder safely and should only be about the width of the ladder.

— When designing a path it is vital that it clearly contributes to the overall layout of the garden. There is nothing worse than a path that appears to have been put in as an afterthought to save wear on the grass.

Main paths should allow two people to stroll together in comfort.

1.2–1.5 m

Service paths need not be wide but they should avoid sharp bends and be designed for ease of use.

When designing paths always consider who is going to use them.

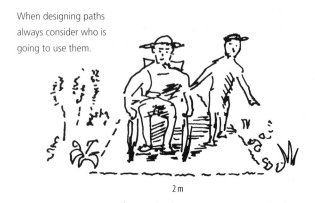

2 m

Allow a generous width for entrance paths, where people tend to congregate.

Lawns and Grassy Areas

You may wish to have a lawn in your garden. It can provide a unifying base, and the shape should be kept simple, without being broken up by island beds, which will only get in the way of the mower. When planning the lawn, think about the type of mowing machine that may be used for cutting it—will it need an electric cable to run it, or space for a turning circle at the end of each strip? Avoid using small areas of grass, as these will be a nuisance to cut or mow.

If you are lucky enough to have the space, a mown grass path running through an area of long grass, bulbs and wildflowers may be desired. This should either be straight or of smooth curves, and it is easiest if the width is the same as the cutting blade of the mower.

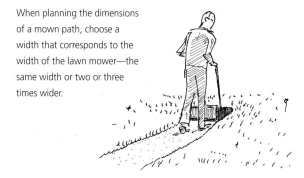

When planning the dimensions of a mown path, choose a width that corresponds to the width of the lawn mower—the same width or two or three times wider.

Planting Areas

As a general rule, these should be as wide as possible, for as plants mature, they tend to take up more space than originally envisaged. Climbers, shrubs, herbaceous plants and bulbs, and perhaps annuals, cannot be effectively combined in a narrow strip at

Most wide borders—particularly mixed or herbaceous borders—need a service path at the back so that the plants at the rear can be easily reached. Where planting is backed by a hedge, leave space for clipping and for the hedge to grow wider.

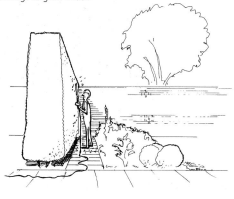

The service path will not be visible when the plants mature.

the base of a wall, where the soil is generally dry and unproductive. An absolute minimum width is usually 1 m (3.3 ft.), but this will only allow space for the spread of one fairly small or upright shrub. A more generous dimension of 2–3 m (6.6–9.8 ft.) will allow you more scope in designing plant groupings.

If the planting area is backed by a hedge, extra space must be allowed not only for the hedge to grow outwards but also for clipping. An additional 1 m (3.3 ft.) may be needed and will allow for a service path along the rear of the border.

Avoid wiggly lines as an edge to your borders. If curves are an integral part of your design, ensure that they are generously shaped. Planting outlines, which are generally soft and irregular, are set off best by strong shapes—a straight line is usually the best foil.

Materials

When developing your preliminary garden layout plan you will need to state where your garden surfaces, structures, ornaments, furniture and so on are to be located. Now you need to be more specific, and for each element you will need to decide on the type of material required and how much space it will take up.

Inspiration and Reference

To help you choose materials, you may want to visit gardens and consult books by leading designers. Perhaps you have read about a garden and admired the detailed construction. Try to identify a style appropriate to your chosen garden and then follow that through with conviction—diluting the idea, to be safe, often shows a lack of confidence that may be apparent in your design. There is no sin in adapting someone else's idea for your own purpose.

Spend some time walking around your locality, looking closely at the materials that have been used and assessing their effect. Notice whether the materials have been used imaginatively, if the workmanship is good and if successful combinations of materials have been used. For future reference, photograph details, make drawings or take measurements.

Visit as many local garden centres and builders' merchants as possible to find out which materials are available in your area. There may be a quarry nearby that could provide local stone at reasonable cost. In order to compare quality, design and the long-term effect of these, make a note of the important points: the cost per unit or per square metre or yard, delivery time and availability, and the dimensions and durability of the materials.

Making Choices

The materials that are available for outdoor use should be considered for their characteristics in both appearance and design use. There are several criteria to think about when selecting materials. They should be functional, easy to maintain, affordable and readily available. They should also complement the overall garden design in style and character and relate to the house and its setting.

Try to restrict yourself to using no more than three different types of hard-landscaping material in a design. More than this tends to look like a sponsored demonstration garden at a flower show or garden festival, where the designer is required to use the manufacturer's materials.

Surfacing

The structural materials used for garden surfaces have different characteristics in terms of wear, appearance and cost. All have their own merits and drawbacks. Some are "loose", such as gravel and bark, some "fluid", such as concrete, and some "rigid", such as paving stones or bricks.

Although each category is considered separately here, different paving elements can be combined to produce interesting variations of colour, texture and pattern. When combining different materials, do ensure that they interlock properly and that any patterns created complement the design of the garden as a whole. From a practical point of view, mixing different materials can help to keep costs down, and from an aesthetic point of view a combination of, say, brick and stone, can relieve an excess of either material.

Loose Surfacing

Loose surfacing consists of materials such as gravel, shingle, small pebbles and bark, that are consolidated but not fixed rigidly into place. They are suitable for areas of any shape. Used for garden surfaces they provide textural interest as well as a weed-suppressing base suitable for walking on. They are comparatively inexpensive and easy to lay, with maintenance consisting only of an occasional raking, weed killing, and replenishing of the top layer. One disadvantage of loose surfacing is that they tend to migrate into neighbouring areas. To prevent this they need to be

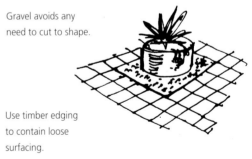

Gravel avoids any need to cut to shape.

Use timber edging to contain loose surfacing.

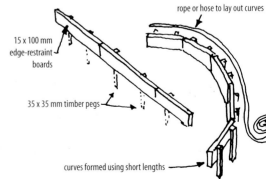

rope or hose to lay out curves

15 x 100 mm edge-restraint boards

35 x 35 mm timber pegs

curves formed using short lengths

properly contained, either with a brick-on-edge strip or by preservative-treated ("tanalized") timber boards secured with wooden pegs. These are not necessary, however, where a gravelled or barked area adjoins a hard surface, such as a stone terrace.

Unless very well consolidated, loose surfacing is not ideal for areas where garden furniture will be placed, or where pushchairs, wheelchairs and wheelbarrows will need access. In addition to being used for surfaces to walk on, loose materials can be used in conjunction with plantings. Plants grown in gravelled areas create an informal, self-seeded look. Gravel and bark can be applied as a mulch to planting beds. Dry stream beds, composed of light-reflecting gravel, are a good alternative to water streams where real water would be impractical or unsafe.

Design use or suitability

Gravel:
- drives and paths
- terraces, particularly when used in combination with other materials, such as brick, stone or timber
- dry stream beds
- traditional and modern settings
- urban and rural situations

Wood and bark chippings:
- paths in rural settings
- children's play areas
- large areas of plantings where maintenance may be a problem

Gravel

Gravel comes in many different colours and textures, depending on the parent rock that produces the chippings. Gravel sizes vary from 20 mm (0.8 in.) coarse-gauge chippings to 3 mm (0.1 in.) fine grit.

Pea shingle (pea gravel) is dredged from the sea and rivers. More rounded in shape than gravel chippings, it provides a softer surface more suited to decorative areas than those subject to hard wear.

When selecting gravel, always try to match any existing stonework, such as garden walls or the façade of a house.

Wood or bark chippings

Chippings can be made up of any type of wood or bark and are supplied in coarse or fine cuts.

Fluid Paving Materials

Fluid paving materials are those that are initially fluid, or paste-like, but which then harden to form a very solid, durable surface. These include in situ or poured concrete and asphalt. Because of their initial fluidity they can be used for areas of any shape.

Design use or suitability

In situ concrete:
- paths or drives
- terraces, particularly when combined with natural materials

Asphalt:
- service paths and drives only

In situ concrete

In situ concrete consists of a mixture of cement, the aggregates sharp sand and stones (known together as ballast) and water. When the water is added, the mixture initially forms a fluid paste, which later sets hard. Concrete mixes can be bought in bags, ready for mixing with water, either by hand or in a motorized mixing machine. For large areas, however, it is more economical to mix the ingredients yourself.

In situ concrete is used extensively in gardens as a base for garden structures such as walls and sheds, but it can also be used as a surface in its own right and indeed is a most underestimated material. It has several benefits:

- It is relatively inexpensive to install.
- If properly exploited, it is capable of considerable variation, both in surface

treatment and by the inclusion of different aggregates.

- Various forms and shapes can be imprinted or stamped onto the concrete while it is still wet, or the aggregate can be exposed by brushing with water and a stiff broom just before the concrete sets.
- Colours can be varied by adding special colouring powders or different sands to the mix.

Most of the drawbacks of in situ concrete arise from its mix and installation. If you require a textured or imprinted surface it is important to experiment first. Similarly, you should experiment with any colour dyes added to the mix. The final colour always looks different when the concrete has dried.

For large expanses of concrete, over 5 m (16.4 ft.) in any direction, expansion joints must be incorporated into the design to avoid the concrete cracking as it settles. These joints, although necessary, can be made to look attractive using materials such as bricks, setts or pressure-treated timber boards. The expansion joints will form an integral part of the paving design and should be carefully selected to complement the rest of the garden.

Asphalt

Asphalt is sold prepacked for direct application to a firm surface, such as concrete or gravel. Preferable in black, it is also available in red and green, and can be textured by adding stone chippings to the surface and rolling them in.

Small-Scale Rigid Paving Materials

Small-scale rigid paving materials, such as bricks, pavers, setts and cobbles, are available in a wide range of styles, finishes and sizes. Because of their small size they can be laid out in a variety of attractive, interlocking patterns to complement the overall design of a garden.

When set in sand, small rigid materials allow free drainage of water through the joints. They are thus ideal to use around proposed or existing trees.

The small unit size of all these materials makes them very labour intensive to lay, and because of this, when used alone they tend to be more suitable for paths than for terraces in the garden. For a terrace, a huge expanse of bricks or setts can look rather cold and severe. It is far better to use these small-scale materials in combination with other materials, such as large slabs, or areas of gravel or lawn.

Fluid paving materials can be used for areas of any shape.

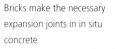

Bricks make the necessary expansion joints in in situ concrete

Bricks laid on loose sand allow water and air to reach the tree roots.

Design use or suitability

All these small-scale materials can be used to create patterns to break up areas of larger-scale materials.

Bricks and pavers:
- rectangular areas of paving or terrace
- to provide a visual link with other brick structures, such as the house
- as edging for lawns and gravelled areas
- as runners for drainage

Granite (or other stone) setts:
- rectangular and circular shapes
- paths and drives
- to create a natural look

Cobbles:
- ornamental areas, such as surrounding the base of an urn
- areas where walking is discouraged (cobbles are uncomfortable to walk on)

Bricks and pavers

Bricks and pavers, small and usually rectangular in shape, are made from both clay and concrete. Generally, bricks are used for walling and pavers for paving, but certain bricks can also be used to pave areas, provided they are guaranteed to withstand frost in cold climates.

Facing or stock bricks, available in a variety of colours and textures, are used to provide an attractive facing to buildings or concrete block walls. Many of these are porous and are unable to withstand severe frost.

Engineering bricks, in a dark greyish blue colour, are very hard-wearing. They are most suitable for edging areas, as their smooth surface makes them rather slippery when wet. They tend to be more expensive than ordinary bricks.

Pavers (sometimes called paviours) are thinner than bricks, more hard-wearing and frost-resistant, and are ideal for paving. Clay pavers usually come in shades

of red, concrete pavers in shades of beige, grey and blue-grey.

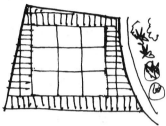

Bricks can be used very effectively in combination with large slab surfaces.

Brick/Block Paving

Stretcher bond: This bond can help draw the eye across a space. It is an excellent bond for pathways. It can also be used for larger areas. When viewed "end on" its character changes. It can be useful used diagonally to "stretch" space.

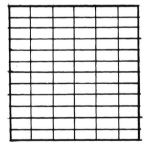

Stack bond: A modern looking pattern. The bricks or blocks do not bond by interlinking. Any settlement in the ground, or poor workmanship, will show. It can be used in small areas to give a spartan or austere mood.

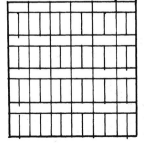

Basket weave and stack bond combination: This has a larger scale. The eye can easily read the bonding. It can be used for paths, terraces and even steps. It requires good setting out.

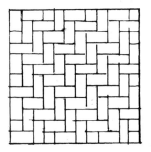

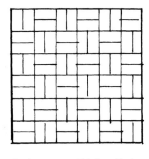

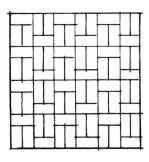

Herringbone: This is a popular bond. It looks good from any angle.

Basket weave: This bond looks identical from either direction.

Basket weave variation

Granite (or other stone) setts

Setts are small blocks, generally $100 \times 100 \times 100$ mm ($4 \times 4 \times 4$ in.) of granite or other hard stone. They have roughened, uneven surfaces. There are now several concrete versions of setts that have a flat face and provide a smoother surface more suitable for walking on.

Cobbles

Cobbles are natural waterworn pebbles about the size and shape of a somewhat flattened goose egg. They can be laid in mortar, either loosely or closely packed together, depending on the effect required.

Granite setts mark out the private gravel drive from the public street, even without gates.

Setts take the wear at an otherwise vulnerable corner of a lawn.

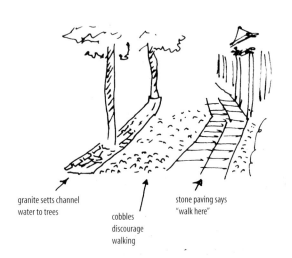

granite setts channel water to trees

cobbles discourage walking

stone paving says "walk here"

Even without a fence, the cobble clearly say "Keep off. Private forecourt".

Use materials to direct circulation.

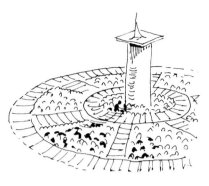

Cobbles easily fill in otherwise awkward shapes.

Cobbles or bricks in gravel form a directional pattern.

Large-Scale Rigid Paving Materials

Large-unit paving materials include stone paving slabs and precast concrete slabs. Both are hard-wearing, easy to lay and are available in a huge variety of colours and surface textures. Generally, a smooth surface is suitable for areas containing furniture, and a rougher, more nonslip surface is suitable for steps or areas surrounding a swimming pool.

Natural stone, even secondhand, is expensive both to purchase and to install and thus, where the budget is limited, should only be used in regularly viewed areas. Many natural stones become very slippery when damp and may be unsuitable for paved areas used by old people or children.

Large slabs can be laid out in a variety of patterns to complement the overall garden design. If using natural stone, a random rectangular or similar layout reduces the amount of cutting required. For an informal look, joints can be left open for planting pockets.

Occasionally, in an old or neglected garden, some paving slabs may be unearthed, perhaps even lurking beneath existing paths or lawns. Where possible, try to use these whole, as breaking them up into smaller sizes tends to spoil their effect. Crazy paving (a mix of paving randomly broken into irregular sizes) should be avoided as it tends to look unprofessional and unfinished and is notoriously difficult to lay effectively.

Design use or suitability

Stone and precast slabs:

- terraces, pathways and drives, either alone or combined with other materials
- as "stepping stones" through gravel, brick or lawn
- with plantings growing through joints for an informal look

Imitation paving

If you select imitation paving, it is important to consider the following:

- Does the colour go right through the material, or is it only applied to the surface? If superficial, the colour will fade with time and exposure, gradually revealing the pure grey concrete beneath.
- How does the material look after it has been laid down for several years? Some types improve with age, perhaps toning down or acquiring moss or lichen. Others are prone to chipping and cracking and remain rather crude looking.
- What does the material look like when wet?
- For paving slabs, is there a good variety of sizes available? Choosing an appropriate size can reduce labour costs considerably. If the slabs are to look natural, perhaps being laid in a random pattern, the more sizes there are, the easier it will be to achieve a convincing effect.
- How easy is it to cut?

Salvaged stone and brick takes time to lay out and time to design because the slabs are all different sizes.

The layout of the paving stones was determined by the sizes of the old slabs available.

Stone flags

Stone flags, possibly the most beautiful of paving materials, come in a wide range of colour tones (in the United Kingdom, the best known is York stone). All stone takes its colour from the geological formation of the locality, which can vary enormously in different areas of a country.

Precast slabs

Precast slabs are available in many shapes and sizes, but all are essentially made of concrete, which is coloured and given textures, sometimes to imitate natural materials, such as stone. Precast slabs are often used as a cheaper alternative to stone. If you want the

slabs to look as much like real stone as possible, buy the slabs in a variety of sizes and lay them in a random rectangular pattern for a natural look.

Timber Decking

Timber decking, or wooden planking, provides an attractive, hard surface. It is very adaptable and easily cut, either to fit a particular area or to be made up into panels. It is suited to both natural and urban designs. In Europe and other temperate countries, the damp climate tends to make it slippery. This can be countered by covering it in wire mesh, although this does spoil the appearance. However, it can be an alternative to stone or brick as a terrace material and is very comfortable on a warm sunny day. It can also provide an inexpensive change of level in a garden.

The timber available for outdoor use is cut from a large variety of trees, either hardwood or softwood. Hardwood is derived from broad-leaved trees, such as beech, teak and oak. It is much more expensive than softwood but does not need to be treated against rot as it has a natural resistance. Softwood comes from coniferous trees, such as pine and larch. With the exception of Western red cedar, which is tolerant to moisture and weathers well, all softwoods must be treated with a preservative to guard against rot and insect attack (such woods are "tanalized" or "pressure-impregnated"). Both hardwoods and softwoods can be stained or painted any colour. If left untreated, hardwoods will age naturally to a pleasant silver-grey colour.

Design use or suitability

Decking:

- terraces, particularly in warm, sunny areas or climates
- balconies
- suitable for a modern design
- useful for creating a unified look incorporating such features as terrace, pergola, built-in seating and barbecues
- looks good in conjunction with water

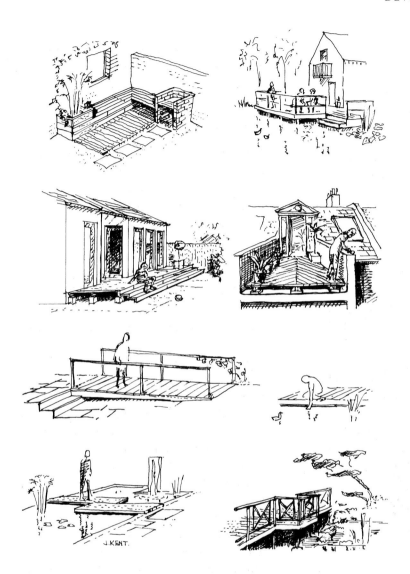

Timber decking is a useful and attractive material which can be used for a wide variety of constructions.

J. KENT.

Grass

Grass is an important surface material in many gardens. Often a lawn forms the largest single area in a design. Grassed areas are generally inexpensive to install when compared with other surfaces, but they do require regular maintenance.

Design use or suitability

Mown grass:
- a soft surface to walk and play on
- a foil for flower borders, paved areas and water
- ideal to use for making curved areas

Rough grass:
- for wild areas of the garden
- to act as a link with surrounding countryside
- a low-maintenance alternative to mown grass

Lawns

There are many different qualities of lawn suitable for different purposes. Immaculate velvety lawns, so typical of elegant English gardens, are usually primarily decorative, laid out in bold shapes to complement the overall garden design or to act as a foil for plantings. They have a fine texture.

If the grass is to be used for a general utility or play area, imperfections are acceptable and inevitable. Coarser grass will take heavier wear, and there are mixtures suitable for many different needs. The better mixtures avoid rye grass, which has flower heads that are resistant to mowing and which forms clumps rather than knitting together laterally. Seed mixtures are also available for growing grass in light shade, although if it is to be used in conjunction with another mix, it is important to make sure they will yield the same shade of green.

Pristine lawns require a considerable amount of maintenance and are unsuitable if subject to heavy wear. Keeping any type of mown lawn short and uniform requires one or two weekly mowings during the growing season.

Rough grass
Rough grass is basically grass left to grow long, only requiring a cut two or three times per year. It can be very attractive, providing a suitable medium for growing bulbs and wildflowers, although it is unsuitable for walking on. If you are growing other plants through it, cutting time is crucial. Bulbs must be left to die down, and wildflowers must be left until after flowering so that their seeds will be distributed. If the ground has been heavily fertilized, the grass, being more aggressive, will grow more quickly and gradually stifle the wildflowers.

Grass is unlikely to thrive in heavily shaded areas and is unsuited to places where mowing would be difficult. Despite the current interest in wildflower meadows, they are difficult to establish, particularly if the ground has previously been well fertilized. Poor, thin soils are preferable.

Edging
Edging is often used decoratively to provide a border around an area, but it also has an important functional role, providing a separation between two areas that would otherwise tend to mingle, such as a

planted area and a gravel path. Most paths require an edging to hold them together and separate them from the soil. If abutting a lawn, the finished level of the edging needs to be below the level of the lawn to allow the mower to skim over unimpeded.

There are many materials that are suitable to use for edging—pressure-treated timber, bricks laid on edge, cobbles, stone or purpose-made Victorian "rope" tiles. Plastic edging should be avoided, as it looks unnatural.

Design use or suitability
Edging:
- to repeat a material used elsewhere and help relate one area to another
- to separate two areas that would otherwise mingle
- to provide a mowing strip, eliminating the need to edge a lawn
- to disguise the edge of a pool liner

Vertical and Overhead Elements

When you have allocated the ground plane surfaces on your preliminary garden layout plan, try lining up the plan at your own eye level, either by crouching down or by bringing the plan up to your eye level. Apart from the areas that you visualize as plantings, the space will still look flat and probably rather boring. Study the three-dimensional aspect of the garden and try to imagine how it might look, then consider how you might interrupt the flatness of the ground plane by introducing vertical and overhead features. Some examples of features you might consider are steps, walls, buildings, arbours, arches, pergolas, statues, pots or urns, seats, trees and large specimen shrubs.

Just think what some verticals could do to this flat site…

Some steps and retaining walls maybe …

…an arbour?

…an arch?

…a tree?

…a statue, a seat, specimen shrubs?

Again, at this stage there is no need to decide exactly what shape or form these features will take, or of what material they will be built. Simply indicate where they will be by writing them in on your plan, trying to keep their proportions on the grid, or on a subdivision of it. Now try again putting yourself on the same eye level as your plan. Can you imagine the difference the verticals make? Even a slight change of level, such as two steps down or up and then back again, can make a garden more interesting. Low retaining walls for planting areas can give, in addition to visual appeal, an area raised up to a sunnier aspect with improved drainage, with the retaining walls sometimes doubling as extra seating, with or without cushions.

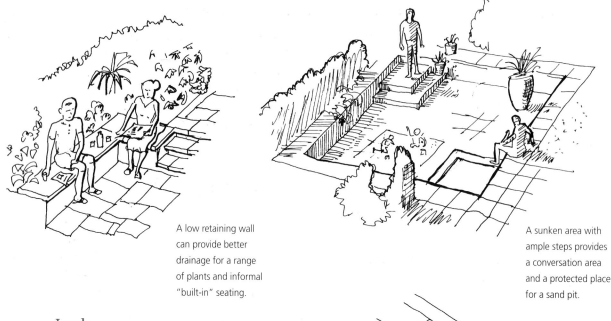

A low retaining wall
can provide better
drainage for a range
of plants and informal
"built-in" seating.

A sunken area with
ample steps provides
a conversation area
and a protected place
for a sand pit.

Levels

Very few gardens are absolutely flat, although they
often appear to be so, and even slight changes of
level, necessitating no more than one or two steps,
can be used to create interest and variety. Although
your garden may be relatively level, there may be the
possibility of steps up or down from the terrace and a
couple more partway along the length of the garden.
If this is the case, try to avoid making the break
halfway along the garden, since 50:50 is not a
comfortable proportion. Dividing the garden up into
thirds is often a better solution.

Steps

Remember that, compared with interiors, the scale
outdoors is greatly increased, and the width of treads
and heights of risers should be as generous as
possible. When designing steps, keep them low, with
the risers at best 100 mm (4 in.) and certainly no
more than 150 mm (6 in.). The treads should be as
wide as possible—450 mm (1.5 ft.), if practicable.
Your steps may need an edging, such as a balustrade
or retaining wall, parts of which can double as a
plinth for pots and containers.

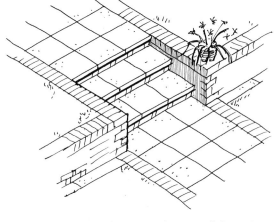

Well-designed steps
with a retaining wall
which doubles as a
plinth for a pot.

Sloping Ground

If there is a slope across the width of the garden, you
must try to correct this, since looking out over a
cross-fall gives a very uneasy feeling, as though the
whole place were sliding downhill. If the fall is slight,
you may be able to correct it by reducing the level on
the upper side and filling in the lower level, with soil
removed from that upper level (see page 29), or just
by filling the lower area with tall, dense plantings.

Ancillary Buildings and Play Equipment

Most gardens contain, or at least require, a certain number of ancillary buildings. Firstly there is the garage, which is frequently already present but may well require concealment or linking back to the house by a wall or hedge. There may also be a garden shed, and perhaps a greenhouse, summerhouse, children's playhouse, space for compost and storage for rubbish bins. All too often these elements are scattered about the place apparently at random.

Completing the garden owner's checklist in Chapter 1 will have helped you to decide if there is a need for any structures that are not already present. Try to group them in a logical way—shed, greenhouse, garage and bin store might well fit together—and allow plenty of working space adjacent to them. Often the rear wall of one building can double for another, saving on space and cost.

A multi-activity children's area has a swing, climbing frame and castle all in a large, ship-shaped sand pit. When designing children's play equipment safety is the priority.

Pivots and Focal Points

Arbours, statues or urns and garden seats can be used to subtly turn a corner, acting as a pivot, or as a focal point to be seen through an arch or pergola. Trees or specimen shrubs, even topiary, can also act as a pivot. The shape of a tree canopy can echo the shape of a pool or provide a positive shape or mass to complement a void.

Stone ball

Traditional focal points include statuary and furniture.

The enclosing wall or hedge must act as a backdrop or foil for whatever is to be seen against it. The various boundaries illustrated here suit many different styles of planting.

	Cottage	Oriental	Mediterranean
	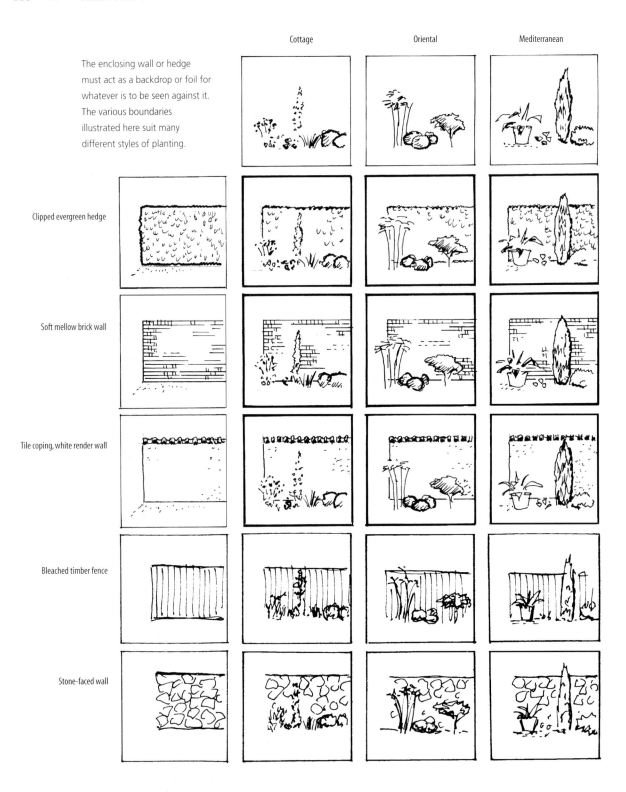		
Clipped evergreen hedge			
Soft mellow brick wall			
Tile coping, white render wall			
Bleached timber fence			
Stone-faced wall			

Boundaries

At this stage in developing the preliminary garden layout plan, the garden boundaries should be considered. In Britain, gardeners tend to enclose their land, to set it physically apart from neighbouring land by constructing or planting a barrier that must be crossed before admission is granted into what is deemed a private area. This custom probably dates from medieval times when protection against a hostile force was necessary, but the habit continues today. In the United States the boundaries are often less defined; sometimes open landscape is marked by a simple and visually unobtrusive fence.

There are many ways to enclose a property, and walls, fences and hedges perform virtually the same function. As the chosen enclosure will often act as a backdrop or foil to the design or planting of the garden, it must be selected to set off whatever is to be seen against it; this is why boundaries need to be considered at this stage.

Boundaries constructed of horizontal wire, or wire mesh, will allow views through them. For best results supporting fence posts should be carefully positioned and obscured where possible.

Gates and Entrances

Access will be required through the enclosure, so a suitable gateway, wide enough for people or for vehicles, will need to be included. Often the most obvious or direct route may not be the best. Offsetting a gate or entrance to gradually reveal, upon approaching, the objective (such as garage or garden shed) is subtle and intriguing, but once again, keep to the grid and do not think about the type or material of the enclosure or entrance at this stage.

When designing the entrances, allow wide enough access for vehicles as well as people.

The Preliminary Garden Layout Plan

The time has come to choose one of the theme plans and to develop your design and commit your ideas to paper. This stage will concentrate on organizing the horizontal plane; the next stage will focus on the vertical and overhead planes.

The garden layout plan is still in an embryo state. In the next chapter, almost inevitably, you will need to adjust your preliminary dimensions to fit all the desired elements and materials into the space.

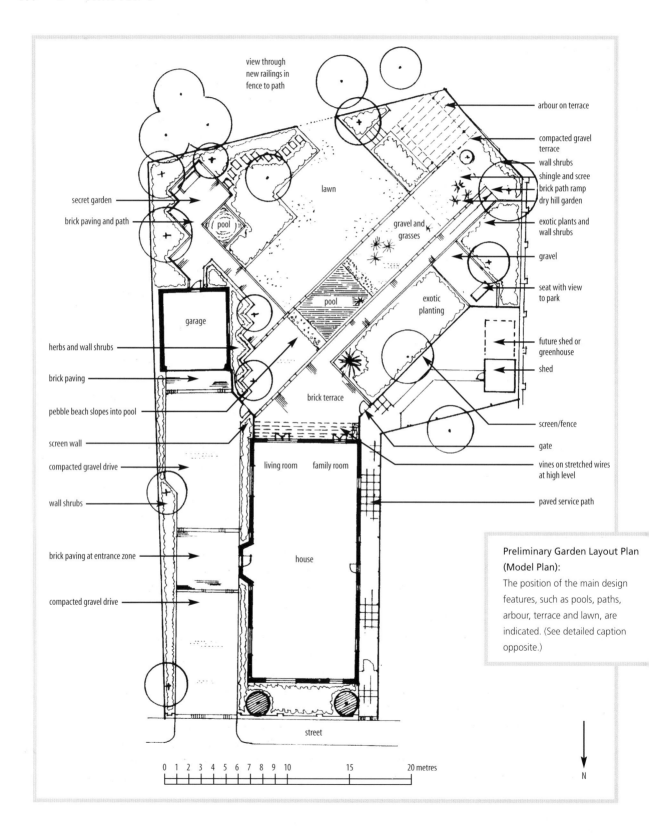

view through
new railings in
fence to path

arbour on terrace

compacted gravel
terrace

wall shrubs

shingle and scree

brick path ramp

dry hill garden

secret garden

brick paving and path

exotic plants and
wall shrubs

lawn

gravel and
grasses

gravel

seat with view
to park

exotic
planting

future shed or
greenhouse

shed

herbs and wall shrubs

brick paving

pebble beach slopes into pool

screen wall

compacted gravel drive

wall shrubs

garage

pool

pool

brick terrace

screen/fence

gate

vines on stretched wires
at high level

paved service path

living room   family room

brick paving at entrance zone

compacted gravel drive

house

**Preliminary Garden Layout Plan
(Model Plan):**

The position of the main design
features, such as pools, paths,
arbour, terrace and lawn, are
indicated. (See detailed caption
opposite.)

street

0 1 2 3 4 5 6 7 8 9 10   15   20 metres

N

Preliminary Garden Layout Plan (Model Plan)

With reference to the garden owner's brief and site appraisal, the following developments have been made:

1. More space has been allowed for planting, and the lawn has been reduced in size.
2. A hill garden runs down the slope into a gravel garden, planted with grasses to give movement and a focus to the centre of the garden.
3. An overhead vine-covered wire arbour has been introduced to provide shade, shelter and intimacy on the south-facing terrace.
4. A path has been infiltrated through the "jungle" shrub belt to lead into the secret garden.
5. The area in front of the French windows has doors "in the wings" to left and right. It can be used as an outdoor theatre for children's shows or musical events at parties.
6. Important trees have been located to improve vistas, provide focal points and give enclosure.

Drawing up the Preliminary Garden Layout Plan

1. Choose your preferred theme plan—circular, diagonal or rectilinear (see pages 90–92). Stick it down onto your drawing board with masking tape.
2. Over this plan, stick down a further sheet of tracing paper.
3. Draw in the outline of your chosen theme plan in pencil, and trace over the house outline and the site boundary. It may also be useful to draw in the grid in pencil as a guide for working it up at a later stage.
4. If necessary, using a sharp pencil, adjust the spaces from your themed plan to ensure

that they are correctly sized and located and that the design works when considered in three dimensions. You will be able to see this more easily if you look at your plan at eye level and try to imagine how it will look when built.

5. When you are satisfied that the design could work, state by writing on the plan which areas are designated for hard landscape and which for plantings (for example, label the lawn, paving, path, pool, planting and so on).
6. Set out your sheet carefully and pay attention to the clarity of your graphics and lettering.
7. Now draw in the north point, either freehand or by using your computer (and cutting and pasting it on the plan). The north point should always be located in the bottom right-hand corner. Remember also to note here the scale to which you are drawing.
8. When you are happy with this draft preliminary plan, lay one of your tracing-paper master plan sheets of an appropriate size over the plan and stick it down with masking tape. Ensure that the draft preliminary garden layout plan is positioned centrally within the area devoted to plans and that it does not encroach on the right-hand area that is reserved for notes and title block.
9. Now start to draw up the finished preliminary plan. Trace off (with a sharp pencil or ink drawing pens) all the horizontal lines on plan, using a T-square or parallel motion, and use a sheet of graph paper as a backing guide. Varying the width of the lines used will make your drawn plan more realistic. Trace the heavier lines first, then the finer lines. If using a pen, decide which pen nib sizes you will use

for each feature and write this down. Use the largest nib (0.5 mm or 0.7 mm) for the largest features: house, boundary wall, tree canopy and so on; use a smaller nib (0.35 mm or 0.5 mm) for paths, steps and other less dominant features.

10. Now trace off all the vertical lines on the plan, holding your set square firmly against the T-square or parallel motion.

11. Use a set square held against the T-square or parallel motion, to trace over all the lines that are at an angle, varying the pen nib size as before.

12. Try to make each area—paving, paths, lawn and so on—look as realistic as possible. Your graphics should communicate your ideas clearly.

13. Indicate areas of soft landscape.

14. Indicate positions of proposed trees and large specimen shrubs, as well as any existing trees to be retained.

15. Write, in clear lettering, what each element or area is. Indicate steps, paths, paving, terrace, pool and so on by writing exactly what it is on the plan. Use the graph paper to guide your lettering.

16. Draw in the title block, remembering to include the north point and the scale to which your plan is drawn. Extend the vertical lines upwards from the outside edges of the title block to become the space for your notes or information panel. (You may wish to use your computer-generated title block here.)

17. Leave your information panel empty at this point.

18. Release the masking tape and hold the drawing up slightly. Check that you have traced off everything necessary from the plan beneath.

19. Undo the masking tape and take the preliminary garden layout drawing, rolled up in a plastic tube or flat in a portfolio case, to a reprographic office to be printed, either as a dyeline print or photocopy. Ask for two copies so that you can colour up the plan at this stage; colouring may help you check on the proportions of hard to soft material—usually one-third hard landscaping to two-thirds plantings, but two-thirds hard landscaping to one-third plantings can work equally well.

20. Keep both the tracing-paper original preliminary garden layout plan and the copies safe to work with in the next steps.

Below: Views of the French countryside surround this garden. Plants within the garden are clipped or "topiarized" to contrast with natural shapes in the distant landscape.

Above: The change of height in this stone house is echoed in the outline shape of the random rectangular stone paving. Softened by drought-tolerant planting in pockets, the generous paving dimensions allow plenty of room for entertaining.

Below: Standard pleached limes soften this entrance courtyard. They also detract from the harsh line of the wall behind—note the box plants at the base of each tree trunk.

Below: A wide, paved terrace is relieved by rectangular beds planted with box. The half-standard evergreen trees provide height and structure.

Above: A garden designer's brief does not always begin with the garden. Here a porch has been added to link the house with the garden. It provides a sheltered place to wait until the door is opened.

Above: The columnar cypress acts as an exclamation mark, drawing the eye to the low-built house. The matt or light-absorbent foliage of the cypress contrasts with the grey or glossy foliage of adjacent plants.

Above: Planters or plant-containers painted the same colour as the front door give structure to this courtyard and help to link it with the house.

Above: The pale green paint used for the door frames and windows of this single-storey house acts as a foil for the dark green foliage that softens the angular lines of the building.

Below: Structural planting emphasizes the entrance to this property. The painted blue doorway is sympathetic to the silver and green foliage tones.

Above: In tune with the mellow stone building, terracotta planters emphasize the curve of the box hedge. In the Italian countryside, cool green foliage is more effective than flower colour.

Above: Two dominant columns of *Cupressus sempervirens* (Italian cypress) unite the vertical façade of the house and the horizontal plane of this formal garden. A built-in seat attracts attention to the mature *Pinus nigra* (Corsican Pine), which is outside the garden boundary.

Above: The herbs in this garden, which was designed by the late Rosemary Verey, are easily accessible from the kitchen. The curved planted beds soften the angular lines of the house.

Above: Planting at the entrance to this country house emphasizes a sense of arrival. The variegated foliage looks cheerful even during the winter and the clipped box and holly are focal points within the planting.

Above: House and entrance-garden are united by a clipped box parterre. The formality of the planting repeats the formal architectural style of the house.

Above: A change of level can easily be achieved with decking. Timber strips need to be placed close together to avoid heels and stones becoming lodged in them.

Above: Hedges and topiary have a strong architectural influence on this space. The lighter foliage of the young mop-head *Robinia* will contrast with the darker green foliage beyond.

Above: A view is often more enticing when glimpsed through an arch. The arch in this yew hedge has been partially castellated.

Above: Hedges are useful, not only as a windbreak, but also to create a series of garden rooms. Here the bright red flowers of the climbing *Nasturtium tropeolum speciosum* contrast well with the texture of the yew hedge and can be easily pulled free at the end of each growing season.

Above: The staggered levels of the timber fence and the covered garden seat set within it help to break what might otherwise have been a harsh line. Multi-stemmed silver birch reduce the impact of the house spire and help to connect house and garden.

Above: A potting shed is cleverly screened by the beech hedge; the offending roof being obscured by the hedge clipped to the same shape.

Above: An example of mass and void, where the lawn flows through the space, held in by the intricate curves of the low box hedge. Planting of foxglove spires, with shrub roses and beech held in by metal tripods, give height to the "mass" of this planting.

Above: During the growing season, this cleverly woven hazel fence merges with the deciduous hawthorn hedge behind. The repetitive detail of the angled finish to the uprights adds to the effect.

Above: An unusual open combination of copper, wood and brick prevent the danger of falling from this raised walkway. Metal is a material easily worked into intricate patterns.

Above: Although closely spaced, the unobtrusive uprights of this fence do not form a threatening barrier. Bamboo or other local materials can be used.

Above: Not strictly a fence, these regular hardwood columns delineate the garden boundary. A similar timber is used for the unusual light-fitting.

Above: The robust lines of this bridge parapet are in keeping with the country setting. Detailing includes wooden plugs as opposed to metal screws which could corrode and stain.

Above: A simple post-and-rail fence defines this field while allowing a view of the wild flowers beyond. Only use oak or a timber treated with preservative. Other untreated wood uprights will eventually rot.

Above: Here, a circular theme is followed in brick and stone with a gravel surround. The use of natural finishes in both the fence and garden furniture enhance the scene.

Above: The circular theme of this show garden is emphasized by the use of stone and copper balls, a small circular "window", and a circular deck with concentric paving pattern.

Above: In this tiny garden room, the apparent "window" is actually mirrored glass, which brings reflected light into the space. The round, painted, upright posts, planted with the fast-growing golden hop, *Humulus aureus*, support overhead timber shading.

Above: Repetition of the vertical accents of the clipped evergreen cypress trees carries the eye through to the view beyond.

Above: A sympathetic planting of *Begonia evansii* and *Helichrysum petiolare* repeat the shades in this terracotta urn.

Above: By placing the larger pot in the foreground, and a much smaller pot behind, the perspective is lengthened.

Above: A colourful planting of the *Tulipa* 'General de Wet' brings out the colour tones of this terracotta urn. Avoid using too many contrasting plants in a pot, especially if the pot is decorative.

Below: A circular scene with cottage flowers bordering a flowering meadow. The wild flowers must be left to seed before the grass is cut.

Above: The mirrored arch helps to break up the length of the wall and brings light into the garden. Flowers and foliage are based on green, yellow, silver and white.

Above: The effect of this border is more dramatic when seen through a dark opening. Shadows and effects of light are often overlooked when considering planting.

Above: Mirrors may be used to bring light into a garden. Here, a mirror has been fitted into the arch and a gate placed in front of it. The gate helps prevent birds flying into the mirror.

Above: An ivy-covered metal frame, hung with a mirrored mobile, gives a view to the countryside beyond. A similar treatment could emphasize any focal point such as a statue or container.

Chapter 3
Finalizing the Garden Layout Plan

We have looked in some detail at how to develop the elements on the ground plane, or garden "floor", to produce a preliminary garden layout plan. We have also already looked briefly at some of the strategic vertical features. In this chapter we will consider more closely how to give a three-dimensional structure to the garden through the selection of vertical and overhead features. Once the practical and visual roles of each feature have been identified, you will be able to determine the form that these features will take, what they will be made of and how they will be built.

While weighing up the advantages and disadvantages of each design choice, you may want to adapt your preliminary garden layout plan to allow for these new features as you work towards finalizing your garden layout plan. You will also need to be more specific about your choice of materials and the precise design of each area or item.

After considering materials used for garden surfaces and structures, garden accessories should be taken into account, reviewing the range of items available for use as garden ornaments, furniture, lighting and children's play equipment. Any garden accessories that you choose should blend in with the rest of your design. You will need to indicate their design—style, size, colour and so on—on your garden layout plan.

While this garden layout may also give a general indication of your planting proposals, detailed planting plans are not usually finalized until the final garden layout plan has been accepted. Frequently at this stage the garden designer (or the client) will change his or her mind and decide to alter the original scheme. As any changes would probably have an effect on the proposed borders, the planting plan is usually carried out as a separate drawing (which is covered in the next chapter).

The Role of the Vertical Plane

Vertical features are a crucial element in all gardens. On entering a garden, perhaps from the house or through a garden gate, the eye needs time to focus on the changed scene. It searches momentarily for a strong vertical feature on which to concentrate while adapting to the new location, adjusting rather like an automatic camera. The vertical feature may be a building, a large pot, a sculpture, or even a striking tree. Without something on which to focus, the eye will wander, and the "picture" may be meaningless. This is particularly true of gardens that rely solely on plants, for they rarely provide that strength of outline. Vertical features are vital in holding the different elements of your design together.

The vertical plane is made up of many different materials, varying from hard, architectural elements, such as buildings, walls, fences and pergolas, to tree trunks, hedges and other shrub masses. All these different components can be used to perform specific roles in garden design.

Enclosing Spaces

Vertical features, such as walls, fences or plants, can be used as physical and visual barriers to delineate where one space ends and another begins, whether defining site boundaries or simply separating one internal space from another. The higher the feature, the smaller the enclosed space will feel.

Directing and Screening Views

The height of the vertical plane affects what can be seen from various points in the garden, directing and screening views within the garden and to the surrounding landscape beyond.

Controlling Exposure

The presence of vertical features will affect the exposure (the amount of sun and wind that a garden receives) by modifying extremes of climate. Walls, fences and hedges and other shrub masses can be placed strategically to act as windbreaks or to provide shade.

Directing Circulation

Vertical features, from low walls to planted areas, can be used to determine the route people will take through the space, in the same sort of way that the presence of water can influence movement through a garden.

Unifying the House, Garden and Surroundings

Vertical features can act as an extension of the house, both through continuing the major lines of the force, such as the house walls, and by the repetition of materials. They can also be designed to unite the house with the surrounding landscape—for instance, by echoing the outline of surrounding buildings or hills.

Aesthetic Contribution

Structural features should be built for a purpose, but there is no reason why they should not be objects of beauty in their own right. In selecting vertical elements, choose from the range of textured and coloured materials to complement your design and help to create the desired character of the garden, but always try to maintain a natural effect. Too many textures and colours can look artificial and self-conscious.

Vertical Features

If you are selecting new vertical features, several factors will help guide your choice. You will need to establish the following:

- The height of the feature
- The space available
- The time scale (a yew hedge, for instance, will require several years' growing time before it can be an effective barrier)
- How the material will integrate with existing features
- The budget allocated for the feature

Existing House Walls

The walls of the house, or of neighbouring houses adjoining a garden, are often the most dominant vertical features in the site, particularly if there are no trees. If the walls are attractive they can be left exposed, and the same type of material can be used in other parts of the garden (for the vertical pillars of an arbour, for instance), helping to unite house and garden.

In some city gardens, particularly small ones, tall house walls can be oppressive. This may be the case where the site is bounded on one or more sides by the walls of neighbouring houses, often consisting of a large expanse of one material, such as brick. One way of "breaking up" or distracting from the expanse is by painting on or adding a "dummy" window or doorway. If you use this trick (or trompe l'oeil) you can enhance the illusion considerably by the careful siting of other garden features, such as a path leading up to the painted doorway. As the wall will probably belong to your neighbour, do ask their permission before beginning any work. To avoid any disputes, all agreements should be put in writing.

Garden Boundaries

Most gardens require some form of vertical boundary to establish the extent of ownership. It may help at

he door and windows are trompe
oeil features. Slightly larger than
e, they reduce the apparent size of
he end wall.

areful planting around a trompe
oeil can help to add credibility to
e illusion.

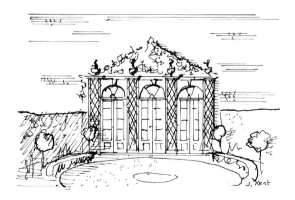

his false "pavilion", on a bare brick
all, is softened by planting.

this point to refer back to your site appraisal. If you
have an existing boundary, you will need to integrate
it into your proposed design. Look carefully around
the perimeter of the garden and consider the
following:

- Does the boundary provide privacy where you
  need it?
- Do you like the materials that have been used,
  and are they in keeping?
- What parts of the boundary, if any, would you
  like to expose or conceal, perhaps to frame or
  to screen particular views?

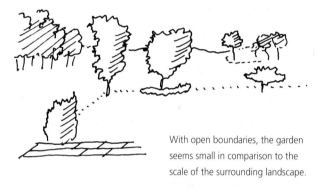

With open boundaries, the garden
seems small in comparison to the
scale of the surrounding landscape.

Entrances and Gateways

First impressions are important, and the entrance to
the garden—or to a garden within the garden—
should always make a clear statement as to what is to
be found within, even if the statement is itself a
deception designed to create an unexpected
revelation. When low gates are needed to exclude
dogs or keep in children, they should make a simple
statement of their purpose and be designed to that
end. Trying to decorate an obviously utilitarian
feature always creates an air of distraction and
unnecessary fuss, with results that can often appear
quite ludicrous.

The material from which the gates are made is
equally important. All too frequently, as soon as an
opening is created, the immediate reaction is to fill it
with a wrought-iron gate, but often this is not the best

Entrances and gateways should be designed to communicate the intended message.

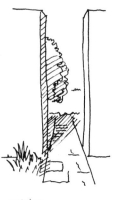

mysterious

domestic, yet mysterious

welcoming

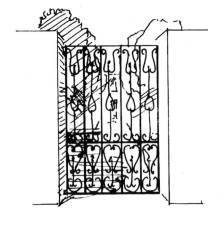

The elaborate ironwork of the gate cannot be seen properly against the background of the garden—a plain, understated backdrop is needed.

A simple pattern of vertical bars allows the house and garden to be viewed through the gate without the risk of visual confusion.

solution. Elaborate wrought or cast iron can only be seen to advantage against a plain background such as sky, grass or water. Anything more complex, such as plantings, or even trees and shadows, immediately sets up confusion between the two images so that neither can be seen properly. In such a situation a simple pattern of vertical bars is the only solution, since it gives an air of proportion and stability to the background detail.

Often, a better solution is to use well-made wooden gates, either constructed of plain uprights set more closely at the bottom than the top (to add visual weight and exclude rabbits or other pests) or entirely solid. There is much to be said for a solid door that reveals nothing until it is opened, since the pleasures of the imagination are often greater than those of reality.

Garden Walls

Walls are the most permanent enclosures used for gardens, and because of their expense, the workmanship involved and the protection they afford, they are often the most treasured. Apart from providing a surface for plants to grow up against, they may also provide warmth and shelter for more tender specimens.

To create an element of surprise, use a solid door which reveals nothing until it is opened.

Walls are often constructed of brick, although stone or even concrete block walls may be appropriate in certain settings.

Walls may also be used as garden dividers and may be freestanding or retaining. It is most important when deciding on garden walls to match, or in some way echo, the colour, texture and style of any existing walls.

The coping (the top course of masonry on a wall) is made up of either the same material as the rest of the wall or a special coping material. A carefully detailed coping course can make an impressive difference to the finish of a wall.

Garden walls can be divided into two types: freestanding and retaining. Freestanding walls can be used both as boundaries and as internal partitions. They can reduce the effects of noise or wind and can screen views. Retaining walls are used to retain or hold back soil, either where there is a change in level or where raised beds are required. The height of a wall will influence the amount of enclosure provided. Consider the following as a general guide:

– Walls higher than eye level, used to form a complete visual and physical barrier, such as boundary walls, should be built to a height of 1.8 m (6 ft.).

The height of a wall determines the amount of enclosure it provides.

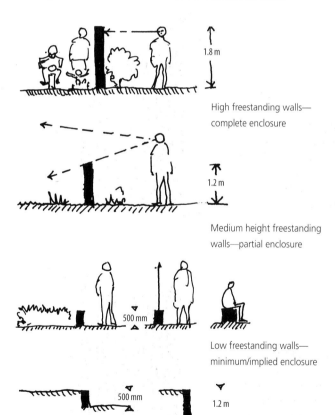

High freestanding walls— complete enclosure

Medium height freestanding walls—partial enclosure

Low freestanding walls— minimum/implied enclosure

Retaining walls—used to hold back soil as well as enclose

- Walls to partially enclose an area, such as a "garden room" or space within the garden, should be 1.2 m (4 ft.) high.
- Low walls acting as a barrier between one space and another, sometimes doubling as extra seating areas or as a base for railings, should be 0.5 m (1.6 ft.) high.
- Retaining walls, used to create changes in level and to hold back soil, may vary in height. A structural engineer should advise on the construction of walls over 0.6 m (2 ft.) in height.

To support the weight of the wall, both freestanding and retaining walls need to be constructed solidly on strong foundations. Retaining walls have an added sideways pressure exerted by the retained soil. The necessity for strong construction is one reason why walls tend to be expensive.

To suit the rest of the garden, walls may be designed in a number of ways—straight or curved, stepped or slanted, rough or smooth, solid or open. A buttressed wall will generate an interesting ground pattern and introduce a sense of rhythm. A smooth-faced boundary used on both sides emphasizes the length and minimizes the width of an enclosure, while one with a rough surface, perhaps allied to slight recesses and projections, will have the reverse effect. A wall of open-work construction, such as a pierced brick screen, allows views to other parts of the garden or its surroundings, whereas a solid wall provides a complete visual barrier.

As well as being used to enclose spaces, walls may be used to support climbers and wall plants or to protect plants from exposure, particularly from wind and sea spray. Brick walls, which retain heat, are often used in temperate climates to protect tender plants.

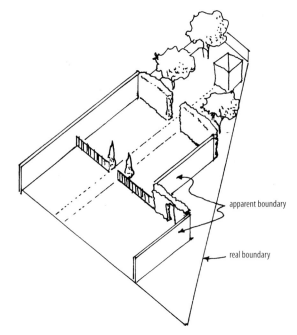

apparent boundary

real boundary

In these four awkwardly shaped sites, false boundaries draw attention away from the real boundaries.

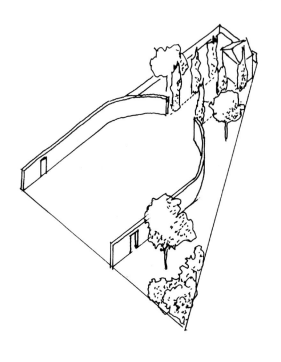

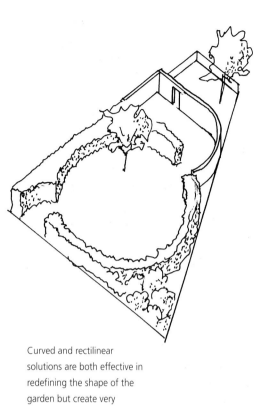

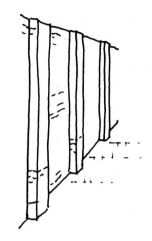

Buttressing can give rhythm
as well as strength to a wall.

Curved and rectilinear
solutions are both effective in
redefining the shape of the
garden but create very
different atmospheres.

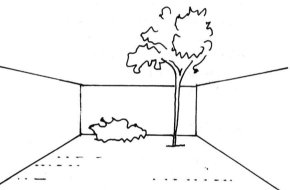

Smooth-faced side walls
emphasize the length of a site.

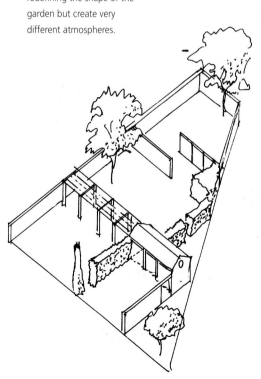

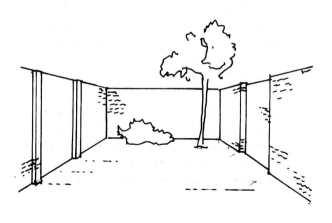

Rough-surfaced side walls
emphasize the width.

Materials

Your choice of materials for important vertical features will have a significant impact on the character of the garden. You may wish to refer to the glossary, which defines many of the materials available.

Walling

Walls can be constructed of many materials, usually stone, brick, concrete or timber. These materials may be used in a variety of designs to complement the design of the garden or, particularly in the case of boundary walls, to blend in with regional styles. When building new walls always try to match their colour and texture to existing structures using, where possible, the best quality material for the purpose. It is much better, for instance, to have a well-made close-board fence, perhaps mounted on a low brick plinth, than to build an insubstantial wall on inadequate foundations that will blow over in the first gale.

Brick

Brick is a very versatile small-scale material for use in garden design. There are many different types of brick available, but if the whole or part of the house or property is built in a particular type of brick, it is usually best to continue with the same type if it is available. This often necessitates seeking out good-quality, clean, secondhand bricks. If the house is not built of brick, introducing a brick pattern within the rest of the material can break up a monotonous space.

Brick walls can vary in thickness and in the pattern in which they are arranged (referred to as the "bond"). Some regions have traditional bond designs, which are often determined by local conditions.

The colour, texture and strength of the brick itself must also be considered. Facing bricks are often used to finish a wall, the interior being made of less

expensive breeze blocks. Engineering bricks, which are darker in colour (from being fired for longer), give greater strength, as they do not absorb as much water. Bricks can have a smooth finish or can be wire cut, with a dragged finish. A coping of weather-resistant bricks, such as engineering bricks, should be used to finish the top of a wall to prevent water from penetrating the walling below.

Brick walls can be finished with a course of bricks on edge, and tiles can be used to create a "lip" or overhang that will help rainwater to drain off without damaging the wall. Compared with stone walls, which can be built to follow the curves of a landscape, brick and concrete block walls are more rigid, although they can be stepped for changes of level.

Stone

Stone will vary according to your region, and your local stone will probably be the most appropriate. If it is limestone or sandstone and can easily be quarried, the stones may be similar enough in size so as to be coursed (with the stones fitting easily together in layers). Other stones, from fields or seashores, will vary in size and can be used in a random fashion. (Since it is illegal to collect stones from some beaches, it is better to buy them from commercial sources.) Traditionally, stone walls were built dry, without mortar to hold them together. If you have a local builder who is skilled in dry-stone walling, this can be very effective, but, as many walls are now constructed from reconstituted stone, mortar jointing is more common. Random stone walls look most authentic when finished with a top course of stones on edge, or stones roughly shaped to an angle (or batter).

Concrete blocks

Concrete block walls, although less beautiful than natural stone or brick walls, are also worth considering because they are considerably cheaper. They may be rendered and brushed, or imprinted in a variety of ways to imitate brick or stone. Alternatively they can be clothed in evergreen climbers. Concrete blocks are usually used to build retaining walls, which can then be faced in natural stone or brick, or rendered.

Steps

Steps that mark changes of level in a garden should be designed with great care so as to be attractive, comfortable and sympathetic in scale and material to the part of the garden in which they are to be sited. Variations in step design are endless, varying from simple straight flights of steps to elegant curving staircases, complete with landings for viewing and highly ornamental balustrades.

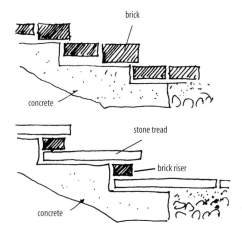

Your choice of materials for steps should be in keeping with the site and meet practical requirements.

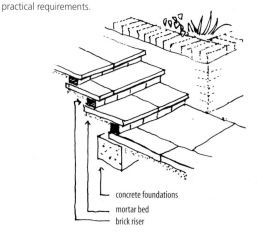

concrete foundations
mortar bed
brick riser

The choice of material to construct steps is diverse. Risers need to be constructed of some solid material, such as stone, brick, concrete or timber, but treads may consist of a loose material, such as gravel or wood chippings. Where growing conditions are right and the stairs will not be subject to heavy wear, grass treads may also be suitable.

Steps may run at right angles or parallel to a change in level. They can change direction as they progress, as in a curving flight of steps, or can change direction partway up the slope, using an intermediate landing. Steps may be recessed, either fully or partially, into a higher level, or project out onto a lower level as a freestanding structure. In the latter case they may need a handrail to provide a safety barrier in the absence of side walls.

When designing steps, consider these points:

– To help you get the proportions of steps right, use the following reliable formula: twice the riser height plus the tread depth should equal 680 mm (2.2 ft.).
– Risers should always be the same height, except in very informal situations, such as when using rocks or tree trunks as steps.
– Avoid exceeding fourteen steps in any one flight without the break of a landing.

Ramps

Usually made out of the same material as steps, ramps are often necessary in a garden, both for easy circulation for the less able and also for ease of movement with a wheelbarrow or mower. If space allows, a ramp can be included within the step area. Crucial in the design of any ramp is the angle of the slope—this should be as gentle as space allows and, for safety, no more than a one-in-twenty slope.

Fences

Fences are generally less costly to build than walls, at least in the short term. They create a more instant enclosure than hedges, and for this reason they are often used to provide temporary as well as permanent enclosures. In the long term they can be more expensive; even if treated with preservative, the base of timber fence uprights are liable to rot and need replacing after eight to ten years.

Fences can be designed in a number of ways to suit the location and purpose. They can be designed and built as a solid structure, or they can be built looser to allow views, light and wind through and to provide a surface for climbing plants to ramble through or over. Whether fences are used for boundaries or for internal divisions, their design should be in keeping with the locality, whether urban or rural. You should take into account both practical and aesthetic considerations:

– What is its function?
– How much will it cost?
– What maintenance will it require?
– Is it well proportioned?
– Is it simple and unfussy?
– Does it reflect the local character?

There are many kinds of fence, but do avoid larchlap, the most frequently used (probably because it is the cheapest), which is made from thin interwoven slats of wood, generally supported by inadequate posts that are 100 mm (4 in.) square. What is cheap to begin with becomes expensive when it has had to be replaced on several occasions, and it is therefore better to pay more at the outset for something reasonably permanent. A closeboard fence of overlapping vertical planks with three, rather than two, arris rails and concrete supports firmly set in the ground is a good choice, since only the lowest board, in contact with the soil, will need replacement.

A well-constructed closeboard fence of pressure-treated timber is far superior to fencing consisting of flimsy panels of interwoven slats.

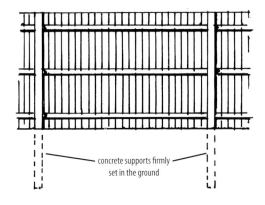

concrete supports firmly set in the ground

It is quite possible, however, to invent fences of your own that can be made to order by a local carpenter. Many kinds of arrangements, where slats or boards are used alternately on both sides of the supporting cross members, can be useful since light and air can pass through to a greater or lesser degree, depending on the spacing. These are particularly appropriate in exposed situations, as they do not present such a solid barrier to the pressure of the wind.

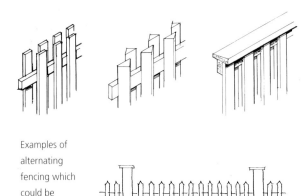

Examples of alternating fencing which could be custom-made to order.

Sometimes a chain-link or galvanized mesh fence, hidden by plantings, may be all that is required, but in this case careful thought must be given to its colour. The "green" generally sold for gardens is an impossible colour, far too artificial to be seen in any natural surroundings—olive, brown or black are better alternatives, being easily camouflaged against the shadow patterns of trees and shrubs.

Timber fencing

Timber can be used both for urban and rural fencing. It is constructed in a huge range of styles and materials, from rustic wattle hurdle and chestnut paling, to elaborately crafted structures with white pickets and finials. In an urban situation, timber looks good stained or painted to blend in with existing features, while in a country setting, fencing should provide a link with natural surroundings. All woodwork must be pressure treated before use. Bamboo fencing can provide an ideal screen for oriental-style gardens.

Metal fencing

Metal fencing is often effective in urban situations, particularly where ironwork has been used locally for railings, street furniture, lighting and so on. Antique wrought-iron railings are sometimes obtainable from an architectural salvage yard, or steel reproductions of old styles can be used. Good-quality ironwork fencing tends to be considerably more expensive than timber fencing, but it is generally more durable. It does, however, require regular painting with bituminous paint to guard against rust.

Trelliswork

Trellis is a type of fencing consisting of a network of crisscrossing wooden slats, or occasionally steel slats, usually attached to a frame. It is manufactured in units of varying sizes and styles but can also be tailor-made to fit the exact dimensions of a site and complement the rest of the design. When choosing trellis for your garden you should first establish the desired degree of visibility through the trellis panels, particularly the size of the aperture between the slats.

Trellis can be used as a decorative feature in its own right (also known as treillage) or simply to provide an inexpensive support for climbing plants. It can therefore be very useful for screening purposes, whether between different parts of the garden or to extend the height of an existing boundary wall. If you intend to cover a trellis in plants, you will need to select panels of strong construction and provide robust supports, such as thick posts concreted into the ground. For extra durability and to prevent the timber rotting, posts can be inserted into a copper tube that is then bedded into concrete. Ensure that the timber has been treated with preservative, and remember that any plants may hamper future maintenance.

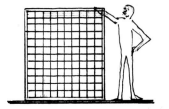 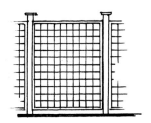

Trellis is usually supplied in panels. To install it, it should be raised slightly off the ground and screwed to supporting posts concreted into the ground.

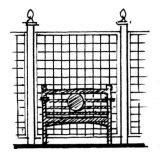 

When designing any fencing or trellis work, it is important to consider where the supporting posts should be sited. Try to position posts either side of a foreground feature, such as a bench—rather than having one post bisecting it.

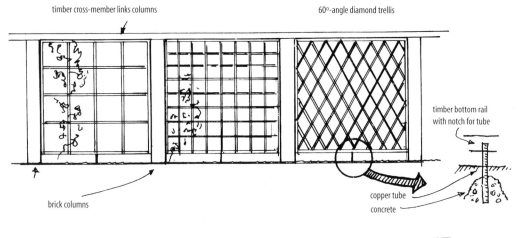

timber cross-member links columns

60°-angle diamond trellis

timber bottom rail with notch for tube

brick columns

copper tube

concrete

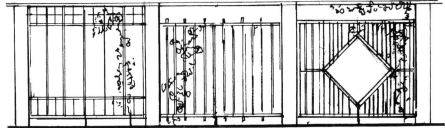

Each of these six trellis infill panels will need its bottom rail supported in the centre—as shown in the detail (above right).

Ha-Has

In a large garden, if you want to create a hidden or unobtrusive division, you could consider using a ha-ha, a ditch-type feature that was popular with many garden designers in England in the eighteenth and nineteenth centuries. Originally used as a device to divide the garden from surrounding parkland to prevent the intrusion of deer or farm stock, a ha-ha is a boundary in which a wall—or sometimes a fence—is sunk in a ditch and is therefore invisible from the garden, while still excluding intruders.

Increased production of iron rails and wire netting led to a decline in the popularity of the ha-ha, but the principle can be adapted for use in modern gardens. Although expensive to construct, a ha-ha need not be very long, the ends of the ditch being concealed and the view framed up by hedges or plantings. If you choose this solution, it is important to create a foreground of plain grass, paving or gravel, since any form of ornament will only distract attention from the view.

As an alternative to trellis panels, simple screens can be constructed out of timber or ironwork. In this contemporary garden the screen acts as a division between two areas, but allows light through to the rear of the garden.

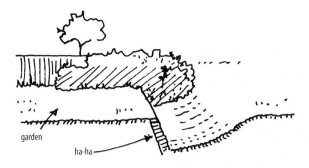

Section through a ha-ha showing the sunken wall and ditch.

The ha-ha prevents livestock from entering the garden

View from the garden over the invisible, sunken ha-ha.

Begin to think about the structural planting in terms of its purpose in the design. Ask yourself the following questions:

– What degree of enclosure is needed?
– How high should it be?
– How much of the year is the planting needed?
– How much space do you have available for establishing the structural planting?

Having considered the practical elements, ask yourself what style of planting would complement the house. If the house is tall and imposing, the plants should also be substantial. If it is long and low, a tall fastigiated (conical or tapering) tree could look out of place.

The height of your proposed border planting may greatly influence the degree to which spaces are enclosed.

Structural Planting: Barriers and Enclosures

The more decorative aspects of planting design will be dealt with in Chapter 4, but at this stage you will need to consider the structural role that plants have to play in the design of your garden, defining spaces and directing views in a similar way to walls and fences. The scope for different kinds of "living" boundaries is enormous, varying from strategically placed trees that imply, rather than dictate, a division of space, to dense, impenetrable hedges.

Year-Round Enclosure

Often a green wall, an extension of the building into the garden, is desired. For this, it is necessary to choose a plant with a neat, close habit of growth which will not only accept being clipped into an architectural shape but will also retain that shape for a full twelve months (since constant clipping is a time-wasting activity). Some shrubs clip neatly and make a good dense hedge but need frequent cutting to keep them in order, while others, such as box and yew, need only a yearly cut.

Where space allows, you may want to consider evergreen hedges that can be left to grow naturally and do not need clipping.

Pleached Trees

Where a tall narrow screen is needed and a hedge would take too long to grow, pleached trees (the branches of which entwine or interlace) are often the answer. In effect, these provide a hedge on stilts. The trees must be pruned every year to keep them neat, and it is best to use types with an even habit of growth, reasonably flexible wood and no thorns.

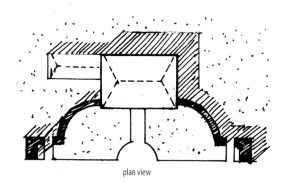

plan view

summer

winter

The hedge acts as "wings" and helps link the house to the surrounding landscape.

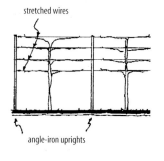

stretched wires

angle-iron uprights

Before planting the trees, a framework must be constructed. Angle iron uprights, drilled to take heavy gauge wires, are concreted into the ground at intervals of 2–2.5 m (6.6–8.2 ft). The wires are then threaded through the holes in the uprights and stretched taut by strainers at the end of the wires.

plan view

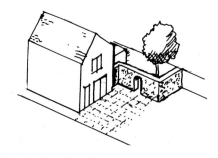

The hedge is used as a green wall to screen the utility area from the garden.

If you are growing them next to a fence 2 m (6.6 ft.) in height, you should use trees with clear 1.75 m (5.7 ft.) stems, above which the lateral branches will spread out in even, entwining rows until the desired height is reached.

Tree Screens

If you require a tall screen and you have the space, you can plant a tree screen. Many are far too large in scale and too greedy to be suitable in most gardens, but some fastigiate (or conical) trees, planted perhaps 1.5 m (5 ft.) apart and lightly trimmed front and back will make a tall screen with a lot less effort than pleaching. Like hedges, trees for pleaching or screening must be planted in very well-prepared ground and be fed and watered regularly.

Backgrounds to Decorative Planting

If the hedge or screen is to provide a background to decorative planting, such as a flower border, it must be light absorbent and recessive in character in order to give a foil to the shapes and colours placed in front of it. Yew is ideal for the purpose since it is dark in colour and has a close matt texture when clipped.

Hedges can be used as a backdrop for decorative planting. A well-chosen hedge will provide a neutral foil to accentuate the colour and shape of the plants.

A screen of deciduous trees can provide an effective barrier in the summer without shading out the garden in the winter.

Fastigiate trees are most suitable for tree screens—they can be planted close together and trimmed to shape.

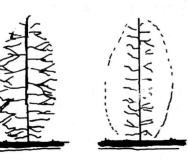

Decorative Divisions

When the hedge is simply making a division of space or concealing some element, such as a vegetable garden, it can be decorative in its own right—perhaps with coloured foliage, flowers or fruit—and of varying degrees of formality. Tapestry hedges, made up of a mixture of different species, such as holly, hawthorn and beech, can be interesting, but as the different species vary in growth rate, clipping can be a problem.

The Role of the Overhead Plane

The overhead plane is created by elements such as pergolas, arbours, tree canopies and umbrellas or awnings. Its main role in the garden is to influence the amount of light entering a space, but it also affects the apparent scale and helps link the garden to the house.

Dramatic shadow lines are created by pergola cross-beams

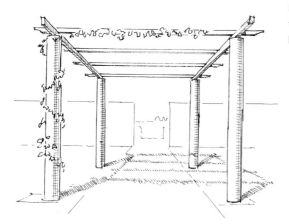

Controlling Light

If your garden is rather gloomy, receiving very little sunlight during the day, you will want to limit any overhead elements as much as possible and place vertical features with great care to avoid shading out what little sunshine the garden receives. If, on the other hand, you have a garden that receives a lot of sunshine, you will need to think carefully where to place the overhead plane so that those using the garden will have some relief from the heat and brightness of the sun at appropriate times of day and year.

Apart from their practical role, overhead features can add greatly to the aesthetics of a garden by creating interesting shadow patterns on the ground, from the dramatic lines cast by pergola crossbeams to the moving, dappled shade of sparsely foliaged trees.

Controlling Scale and Atmosphere

The presence of overhead features greatly influences how we perceive the size or scale of the garden and is thus largely responsible for its atmosphere. The highest overhead plane is, of course, the sky, which is constantly changing. Even the presence of low cloud or mist lowers it and thereby affects the scale and atmosphere of a place.

Overhead features can give a garden atmosphere. This "awning" has been inexpensively created by training a vine through high wires.

If you want to create an intimate atmosphere—in the entertaining area of a garden, for instance—you could lower the overhead plane, with an arbour, perhaps, or a large umbrella. Conversely, if a tall tree creates an oppressive feeling, you can create a more uplifting atmosphere by removing some of the overhanging branches.

Architectural Extension of the House

The overhead plane can be used to link the garden to the house by repeating materials and continuing the line of an indoor ceiling, perhaps in the height of an awning, to provide continuity between the indoor and outdoor space.

The line of the indoor ceiling is repeated in this slatted awning, which gives dappled shade on the terrace area.

A pergola constructed of freestanding metal arches may be made away from the site and simply installed in foundation blocks.

Overhead Features

Pergolas

A pergola is a covered walkway designed to provide shade over a frequently used path during the summer months. It must, by definition, lead from one point to another—from a terrace to a tennis court or summerhouse, for instance. When used correctly it should help to integrate the overall space. The view seen through it should entice one to make the journey, and a focal point such as a tree, statue or urn will help to draw the eye and encourage its use.

For a contemporary house or one of very plain design, uprights of simple steel tubing set in concrete blocks below ground level can be effective, while Victorian and Regency gardens lend themselves to tunnels of wrought-iron hoops to support climbing roses or clematis. It must be remembered, however, that metal structures have to be repainted at intervals, which can be a problem if they are covered with climbers. In hot countries, metal structures may retain heat and burn the plants that are growing on them.

Proportions are important. Ideally the structure should be wider than it is high, or at the very least should form a perfect square—one that is much higher than it is wide always looks uncomfortable, especially when supporting plant growth on top. Pergolas can be constructed in tunnel form, where the arches are set not more than 1 m (3.3 ft.) apart, but usually the spacing of uprights along the length of the pergola is one-quarter more than the spacing across the walk, which is conducive to easy strolling. If the

The urn at the end of the pergola acts as a focal point to entice one through.

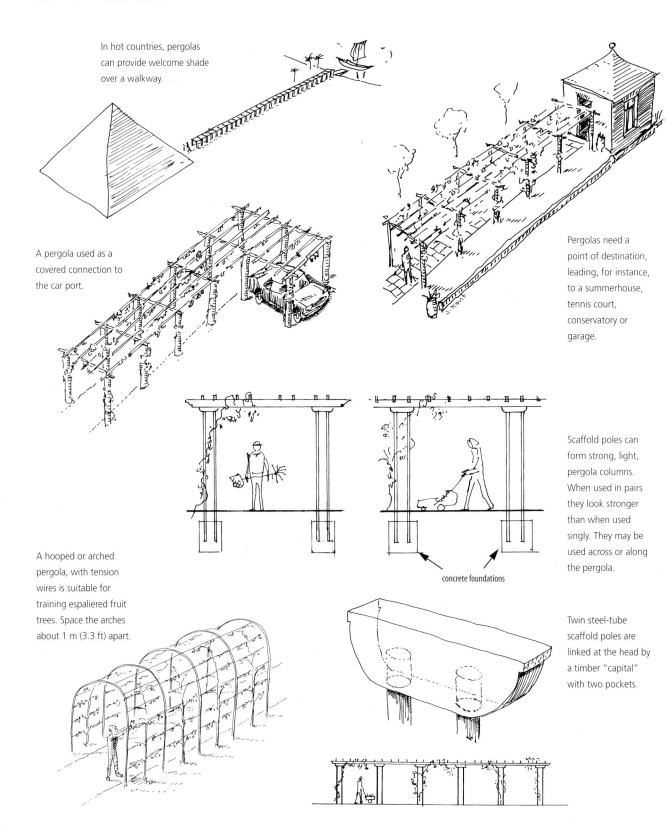

In hot countries, pergolas can provide welcome shade over a walkway.

A pergola used as a covered connection to the car port.

Pergolas need a point of destination, leading, for instance, to a summerhouse, tennis court, conservatory or garage.

Scaffold poles can form strong, light, pergola columns. When used in pairs they look stronger than when used singly. They may be used across or along the pergola.

concrete foundations

A hooped or arched pergola, with tension wires is suitable for training espaliered fruit trees. Space the arches about 1 m (3.3 ft) apart.

Twin steel-tube scaffold poles are linked at the head by a timber "capital" with two pockets.

uprights are particularly large, say 500 mm (1.6 ft.) square, the spacing can be wider, but it must not exceed a reasonable distance for the lengthwise crossbeams. Normally the beams across the path are heavier, making the walk effectively a series of arches, and are linked lengthwise by lighter woodwork over which the plants can scramble. If the pergola or walkway is extensive, it may help to "break" it occasionally by leaving a gap, allowing the user temporary relief from the tunnel-like effect.

Typical defects in pergola construction.

When designing a pergola always ensure adequate width and height.

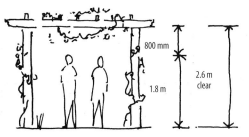

A clear 800 mm (2.6 ft) below the beams allows for trailing and hanging climbers to grow without interfering with people walking underneath.

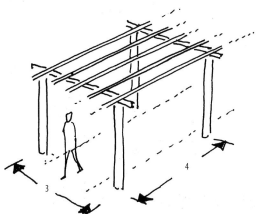

Pergola with robust columns of stone, brick or timber. The spacing of uprights along the length of the pergola is normally one-third more than the spacing across it.

Arbours

An arbour provides shade to a static area, such as a terrace, where one can sit and enjoy some relief from direct sunshine. It should not be confused with a pergola. Again, as it has a strong structural element, the materials used should relate to adjoining buildings and the general style of the garden. For the same reason, the construction must not appear flimsy. The weight and sideways pressure exerted on it by mature climbers can also be considerable.

Arbours may be constructed in a similar way to pergolas, perhaps with back and sides infilled with trellis, or vertical slats, possibly arranged in alternately slatted fashion to give greater protection while still allowing light and air to enter. The roof crossbeams may also be closer together, since shade for sitting needs to be denser than that over a walkway.

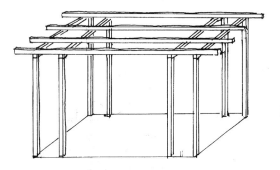

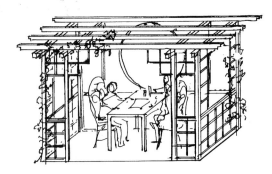

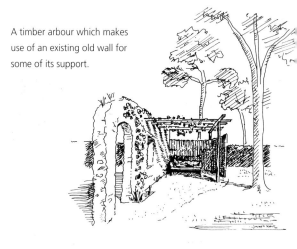

A timber arbour which makes use of an existing old wall for some of its support.

The basic framework for an arbour can be quite straightforward. However, with additional trelliswork and infill panels, it may be modified to suit the owners' needs and their surroundings.

This arbour is created by wires stretched between two buildings. Tensioning turnbuckle wire strainers hold the cable taut. They are available from yacht chandlers and specialist suppliers. The wire can span long distances and support vines.

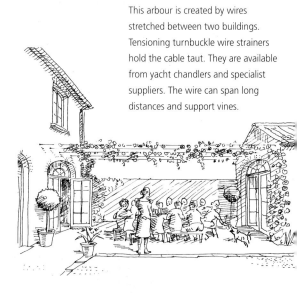

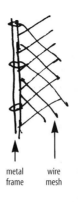

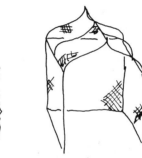

metal   wire
frame   mesh

Arbours can be
constructed out of
mesh stretched
between metal
framing. If desired,
the arbour can be
completely covered
with a suitable
climber, totally
obscuring the metal
framework.

Garden Buildings

A more solid garden building may be required for use
on cold bright days and for protection from wind.
There are many types available commercially, but
before making any decisions, examine the garden
itself. Are there any unused outbuildings which, with
alteration (such as glazed doors, new and larger
windows) might be adapted to suit your purpose?
Such a solution may well be cheaper and more
satisfactory than building or buying something new.

Look into any building proposals carefully, and try to
discover any hidden problems, either of construction
or maintenance, since the superficially attractive may
prove to be badly made and impractical in use. As
with all other elements that make up a total design,
the appearance must suit the style of the garden and
its surroundings.

Disused outbuildings
may be able to be
adapted as garden
rooms.

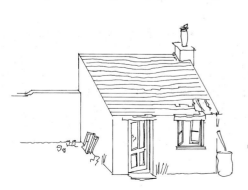

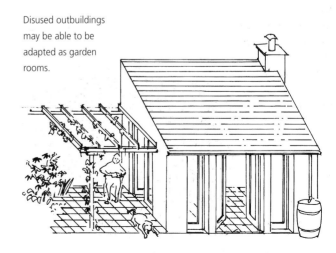

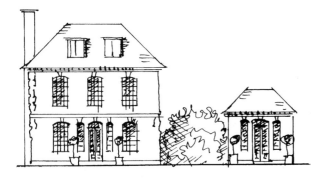

New garden buildings are more successful when they look as though they were built at the same time as the main house.

It may be wiser to adapt an outbuilding than to dispose of it altogether.

Choose the styling of your garden buildings with care. This Chinese-style kiosk looks most odd in this European country garden.

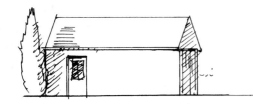

An unwanted garage when removed…

…exposed a neighbouring eyesore.

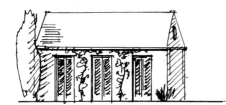

However, it could have been kept and easily adapted for another use.

Trees

The siting of trees in a design is as important as any other element. Trees capture space and, by doing so, shelter a garden and provide it with a sense of security. They should be chosen and positioned with great care.

Before deciding on a particular species you should think carefully about the effects you want to create with different forms, foliage, colours and so on. Consider how a rounded or domed tree, such as a

fastigiate   columnar   rounded   spreading

weeping   picturesque   pyramidal   umbrella-shaped

hawthorn (*Crataegus prunifolia*) or maidenhair tree (*Ginkgo biloba*), might look in the space, then try a tall slim vertical shape, such as a columnar Irish yew (*Taxus baccata* 'Fastigiata'). Each of these will create a different effect, and the outline shape, seen perhaps when leafless in winter, should always be the first consideration. Avoid reaching for your catalogue until this has been decided, or you will be overwhelmed by choice.

The character of a tree varies enormously, depending on whether it is evergreen or deciduous. The colour, size and texture of leaves, trunk and bark; the ultimate height, breadth and growth rate; the density of the canopy and how well the light penetrates through—all of this needs to be taken into account.

The outline shape of a tree is the first thing you should consider when making your selection. Do not forget to anticipate how the ultimate size of a tree will affect the space that it occupies.

Garden Accessories

Once the surfacing and structural elements of a garden have been established, there are many supplementary items, used to furnish the garden and enhance its layout, which need to be finalized. These may be vitally important for making a particular design statement or allowing an area to function in a certain way, or they may simply provide the finishing touches to a design.

Ornaments

If you leave the choosing of ornaments to the end of a project, you may find that there is little left in the budget to do justice to these elements. This is a mistake, because ornaments, if used, should be an integral part of the total scheme; they should be carefully chosen at the same time decisions are made about the hard landscaping so as to complement other features.

What you choose need not be new, elaborate or expensive. Indeed, ornaments and objets d'art that may have been collected over the years will give a garden individual character—similar, perhaps, to the house interior. A simple approach is often best. It is not what you use but how you use it that is important. There may even be old statues or urns already in the garden, which could be restored to create an important focal or talking point.

Large objects, particularly when placed high in relation to normal eye level, give a feeling of drama and aspiration very suited to an extrovert garden, while those that are small or placed below eye level are more appropriate to creating a feeling of introversion in a scheme.

Simply because a garden is small, it does not follow that everything in it must be small—carried to an extreme, this could suggest a garden for dolls rather than humans! A bold feature, well chosen and placed, can give an air of grandeur to even the most modest space, providing that its general character is suitable to the position.

Architectural Salvage

Searching for a particular object can be fun, and over the past few years a number of specialist salvage companies have sprung up, carrying out a thriving trade in old chimney pots, doors, pedestals and so on, recycling the unwanted objects of others. Local auctions, house sales or junk shops can also be worth investigating. Garage sales, car boot sales and flea markets often provide interesting items at a reasonable price.

Chimney pots, with their bold shapes and slender outlines, can look very good either alone or in groups, as can large drainpipes set at varying levels, particularly in a modern garden. Old sinks, complemented with rocks or stones, are now much sought after as planters for a selection of alpine plants.

Old sections of sculptured ornaments from demolished buildings, broken columns and lengths of cornice may find a place in the more romantic garden, perhaps set low amongst the natural sculpture of dramatic foliage.

Reproduction Ornaments

Often easier to obtain are the many reproductions—some excellent, others much less so—of antique ornaments that are widely available. Provided they are cast from fine original pieces, as many of them are, both lead and reconstituted stone items are very satisfactory and, when weathered, almost indistinguishable from the originals. They are, indeed, better in some respects since they have not had to endure a century or two of exposure to the climate, and if they should be stolen they are easily and relatively cheaply replaced.

The new appearance of reconstituted stone items can be tempered by brushing them over with yoghurt (which encourages moss) mixed with soot if a darker colour is desired. Manure water will have much the same effect but is less pleasant to apply.

Reproductions that are cast or moulded in plastic are often finished with crude detailing and so are best avoided.

Natural Objects

Natural objects such as interesting bits of driftwood and sections of tree trunk can look effective if placed in an appropriately wild or naturalistic setting. "Wild" stones and boulders can be bought from garden centres, which is a better option than removing them from environmentally sensitive areas.

Rocks and boulders can look effective in a naturalistic setting

The uniform shape of stone balls is an effective contrast to the informal shapes of plants.

A–Z of Ornamental Ideas

In addition to the more usual types of garden ornament already mentioned, many other items can add a personal touch to your garden. For easy reference, these are listed here in alphabetic order.

Balls and finials are basically ornaments for gateposts, the ends of walls or the corners of buildings. The simplest, and often the best, are variations on the theme of the stone ball, but pineapples and closed urns with lids to keep out the weather can also look attractive. Eagles and heraldic beasts can look pretentious and are best avoided. A finial on a well-designed column can make a striking object and terminate a vista or form the centrepiece of a large circular feature.

Balustrades are used to create a safety barrier at the edges of retaining walls, terraces and steps. Reconstructed stone rails or copings of classical design are easy to purchase, as are cast iron ones. A lighter effect can be achieved by creating your own designs and having them made up in wrought iron by the local blacksmith.

Birdbaths and feeders, providing they are kept clean and constantly supplied with food and water, can bring a lot of life and interest to the garden. Placed in an open position, well away from trees or hedges where cats can lurk, they can be very decorative in themselves, although the design and the material used must accord with the character of the garden. The level should be above the spring of a cat, and there should be a strong overhang to discourage marauding squirrels. Providing water for birds also reduces the risk of them attacking foliage in search of moisture.

Bridges are practical necessities for crossing stretches of water or streams and must be designed primarily for safety. However, their design should also suit the character of the garden, both in style and in scale. Although they can be highly ornamental, especially when reflected in water, bridges tend to look

A simple bridge of two planks, with a balustrade for safety.

ridiculous unless they serve some functional purpose, such as linking one part of a garden to another.

Cisterns made in lead, or occasionally cast iron, were originally used to collect rainwater, for which purpose they are still admirable, and are far more attractive than a plastic water butt. Filled with soil, they are also good for planting, since they allow ample room for the roots of permanent plants. Fibreglass imitations of lead cisterns are available, but these do not weather down to the good matt texture of natural lead.

Old lead cisterns make ideal planters.

Clair-voyées are essentially grilled openings made in the garden boundary, whether wall or hedge, to give a view out onto the countryside beyond. Unless the view is of sky, or a very distant landscape, it is best to have a plain grill in upright wood or metal bars, since any elaborate pattern will tend to clash with whatever detail lies beyond. A squared trellis can be equally effective, and concrete screen-blocks of simple design can look good in a modern garden setting. Sheets of plate glass can been used, but birds may injure themselves trying to fly through these.

Clair-voyées, traditional and contemporary, provide views out to the surrounding landscape.

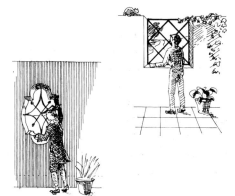

Dovecotes are an interesting addition to a large garden, particularly if stocked with some of the more unusual varieties of doves or pigeons. Since they tend to breed rapidly, it is best not to provide too much accommodation, so that the surplus stock is encouraged to move elsewhere. Like other animals, birds need proper feeding and attention, and they can create problems with their droppings and occasional forays into the kitchen garden.

Flower pots of the ordinary terracotta variety, in various sizes, can be grouped on steps, at the corners of terraces and beside seats to very good effect. Some may contain permanent plants (brought out from the greenhouse or conservatory in the summer), while others can hold bedding plants or lilies that may be exchanged for something else when they have finished blooming. If possible you should try to have a small space where things that are finished, or not yet ready, can wait. Generally speaking, the simplest and most traditional designs are best, but if the pots are to stay year-round, they must be made from frost-proof clay. However practical, plastic pots do not look attractive on display, although they can be placed behind clay pots in large displays, allowing only the plants to be seen.

Mirrors, used with care, can magically extend the apparent size of a small garden, but they should always be set at a slight angle to the viewer—it is disconcerting to suddenly meet oneself face to face! They must also be protected from the weather and be placed so that soil cannot be splashed up onto them. Birds often injure themselves trying to fly through the mirror. To avoid this, a mirror fixed in an arch or doorway can be placed behind a metal gate or frame, making it less attractive to birds and more realistic to the viewer.

Mirrors can be used to give the illusion of extended space. Make sure that they are well sited, and that the edges are obscured.

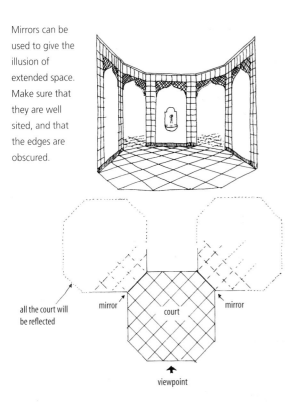

all the court will be reflected

mirror

court

mirror

viewpoint

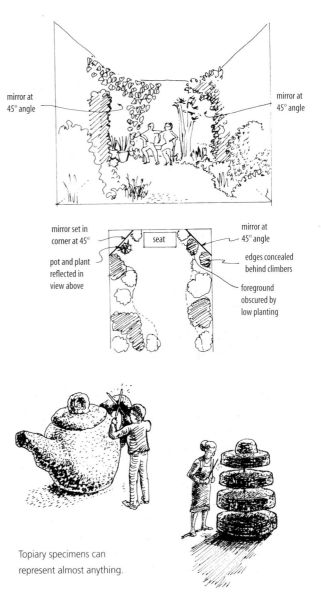

mirror at 45° angle

mirror at 45° angle

mirror set in corner at 45°

seat

mirror at 45° angle

pot and plant reflected in view above

edges concealed behind climbers

foreground obscured by low planting

Sundials, although hardly useful, are both decorative and popular, forming an excellent centrepiece for a formal garden. They range from grand and complex armillary spheres to simple columns topped with a plate and gnomon (the rod or pin that indicates the time by the position of its shadow).

Topiary is essentially living sculpture. Generally made from box or yew, both of which are long lasting but only need a yearly clip, topiary specimens can represent almost anything, the limiting factors being the time they take to grow and the ability of the gardener. It is usually best to grow them through a light frame of bamboo and wire to get the main proportions right and then gradually to add finishing touches as fancy dictates. It must be remembered that however architectural in form, they are still plants and require feeding, watering, and cultivation.

Topiary specimens can represent almost anything.

Treillage (trelliswork) is generally used as a decorative feature to give character and interest to a large blank wall. Since the treillage itself is a feature, any planting against it should be restrained—vigorous climbing plants can quickly obscure the design and destroy the effect (and often the treillage itself, since it tends to be rather fragile). Ready-made treillage is now available in metal and can be fixed to a wall to give a variety of effects.

Treillage can be used to create a false perspective as on the side wall of this terrace.

Trompe l'oeil, the painted scenes meant to trick the eye, have been used to create the illusion of space for many hundreds of years (there are some famously fine examples at Pompeii). A trompe l'oeil scene must be undertaken by a good artist, since a bad painting can completely ruin a garden. Although a wide wall painted with an extensive landscape view can look fine, even a blank archway in the wall of a small garden, painted to show a path to another garden enclosure, can add an extra dimension. The painting should be sited in a place that affords protection from the rain.

A trompe l'oeil can add an extra dimension to a small garden.

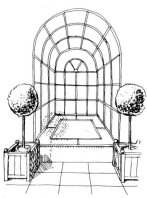

A false perspective is enhanced by the positioning of the topiary balls.

Urns and vases are generally important objects in their own right, the plant material used to fill them being mostly secondary decoration. They may be of stone (or, more frequently, of reconstituted stone), marble, lead, bronze or cast iron, generally standing on plinths to give them greater importance. Flanking steps or doorways, at the end of a walk or along the edge of a terrace, they are invaluable, but the design and material must always match the position. If they are of a material that must be painted, it is best to choose a neutral colour, such as grey, grey-blue or dark bronze-green.

Garden Furniture

For many people, one of the great pleasures of having a garden is that it provides a place to sit outdoors, whether to lounge and relax or to dine. To do this in comfort, garden furniture is essential, and the more inviting the furniture and the view of the garden from it, the more a garden will tend to be used.

As always, you need to think of function first, deciding what is actually needed and where you should position your furniture. Consider the following points:

– Where can the best views of the garden and its surroundings be seen from?
– Would these areas provide an appealing place to sit?
– Who is likely to use this seating, and how many people might use it at the same time?
– What are the dimensions of the terrace? For dining, what type of table will you need, and how many chairs will be required on a regular basis?
– Would an occasional seat, carefully placed at the end of a path (and also acting as a focal point in the design), allow you to enjoy your garden from a specially selected viewpoint?

A bench positioned at the end of a path acts as a focal point and provides a pleasant viewpoint of the garden.

Choosing a design

Once you have established what type of furniture is needed in the garden and where it is going to be placed, you can start to consider the design of each item. There is now a vast range of garden furniture available to suit most styles and budgets. As a general rule, opt for simple, well-made products that blend into the garden—you will be less likely to tire of them in the long run. There are many furniture makers who copy classic designs, such as the Lutyens bench (shown in the illustration below left). Whatever design you choose, make sure that it complements the style of your garden and its surroundings. White plastic patio-style tables and chairs may not look out of place on a yacht or on the balcony of an apartment in Spain or Florida, but they would ruin the carefully planned effect of a cottage garden in a romantic, natural setting.

Permanent or temporary furniture

From a practical point of view, there are basically two types of garden furniture: permanent, which may remain out all year, and temporary, which comes out only when required. Temporary furniture is most useful where space is limited, provided there is somewhere convenient to store it when it is not in use.

Permanent furniture, which needs to be weather-resistant, is usually constructed of materials such as stone, wrought iron, cast iron, timber or plastic. Temporary furniture can be of any material (usually cane, canvas or plastic), as long as it is light enough to be easily transported and stored.

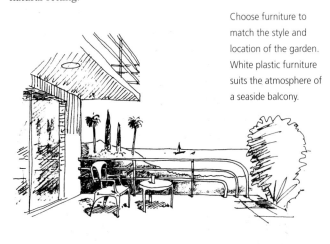

Choose furniture to match the style and location of the garden. White plastic furniture suits the atmosphere of a seaside balcony.

If you intend to move furniture around, choose items that are not too heavy.

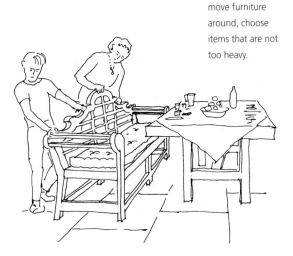

The same furniture in a cottage garden would be out of keeping with the place.

Comfort is another important factor. Many seats, particularly those made of wrought or cast iron, will benefit from the addition of cushions. These should be made out of tough, washable fabric and brought indoors or under cover when not in use.

Some garden seating can be very uncomfortable.

If you already have some old garden furniture that is suitable for your needs, you may consider having it repaired, cleaned up and repainted. This is often preferable to buying newer furniture of inferior craftsmanship. Remember also that you can design your own seating. You do not have to be a master carpenter or stone mason to create simple sawn log seats, suitable for a woodland garden, or to place a slab of stone on two sections of an old column to create a simple bench, ideal perhaps for a small country garden.

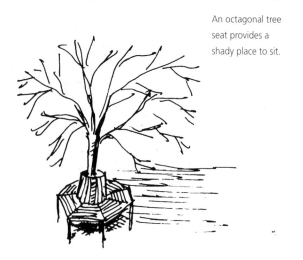

An octagonal tree seat provides a shady place to sit.

For permanent seating, you may also consider furniture that is built in to the hard landscaping of the garden, such as a seat wall or a bench incorporated into a decked area. Built-in seating can be particularly effective where space is limited.

Natural or painted finishes

Hardwood seats generally look best if they are allowed to weather naturally, but if stained or painted, choose a dark, neutral colour such as grey, dark brown, very dark green, or even a deep blue to blend in with the rest of the garden. Ironwork usually looks best painted black. For more striking effects, brighter colours such as orange, yellow or red can look effective, particularly in a contemporary setting. Beware of using white as a colour. Far from being safe and neutral, white is a glaring colour that always demands attention.

The same rules apply to choosing colours for temporary furniture (often of cane or plastic). When selecting canvas chairs or fabric-covered cushions, note that natural canvas will tend to blend in gently with other features, while patterns and stripes are less easily absorbed. If colour is desired, it is usually best kept plain and carefully related to the colours already used in that part of the garden.

Umbrellas

Sometimes, if the garden is in full sun, a large garden umbrella may be needed. The designs modelled on those found in outdoor cafés in Italy are large enough

Umbrellas can provide privacy as well as shade in gardens that are overlooked.

to shade four or six people, giving a feeling of privacy in overlooked town gardens.

Barbecues

Barbecues can be built into a terraced area or may be freestanding. If you would prefer a permanent structure, be very careful about where you site the barbecue. The prevailing wind (and any other freak winds!) can play havoc with the smoke produced, sometimes rendering the terrace unusable while cooking is in process. Freestanding models can be moved out of the wind and are often more practical.

Children's Play Equipment

Children love to play outside, and it is often possible to allocate a particular area of the garden, perhaps visible from the kitchen window, as a play area, always remembering that children soon grow up and that this particular area may need to be reintegrated into the main garden layout in five or ten years' time. A sandpit, for instance, might convert to a pond or water feature when the children are older.

With small, simple items it is better to try to design your own and integrate them into your garden layout plan. An existing tree, provided the branches are sound, might make an exciting climbing frame, or an old garden building could be adapted as a playhouse.

Sandpits

These can give many happy hours of play and are fairly easy to construct out of timber or brick. A sunken square or circular area is often best, and a low surrounding wall of three or four brick courses can double as a seating area. A light, removable or folding wooden cover will help keep the sand clean and prevent it being used by cats and other animals. Sand is readily available from most builders' merchants and may need replacing annually.

Playhouses

An unused garden building, perhaps once a coal shed, may well convert into a playhouse, complete with a scaled down door, door knocker or bell, curtains at the windows, and possibly the children's names or an imaginary house name clearly written outside. Children love to indulge in games of fantasy and will be able to do so in the safety and privacy of their own space.

A children's playhouse is later transformed into a summerhouse.

A sandpit can later be converted to a pool.

Tree houses, swings and ropes

You may be fortunate in having a mature tree that can be adapted as a tree house or as a fixture for a swing or climbing rope, but check that all the branches are sound before proceeding. Sometimes, instead of being removed, a fallen tree can be put to use for climbing games.

A mature tree, adapted as a tree house.

Climbing frames

Climbing frames, complete with swing and slide, can give hours of fun. There are several manufacturers who produce natural timber frames that merge well into a garden layout, but these tend to be expensive. You may, with a little ingenuity, be able to adapt some existing feature to serve the same purpose. Children usually love these custom-made facilities, and they are more fun and easier to live with than the brightly coloured objects usually offered commercially.

Lighting

Most gardens will benefit from some form of lighting, whether for security, to discourage intruders; for access, to define steps and pathways; or for aesthetic effect. Lighting can dramatically enhance a garden at night, highlighting special features, such as a statue, a tree or the texture of ground cover, while allowing other features to recede.

Lighting techniques

The choice of fittings will depend on the effect required but may vary from a single fixture—illuminating a terrace, for instance—to a complex scheme employing many different types of fittings, including uplights, path lights, underwater lights, spotlights and so on. Similar to interior light fittings, garden lights can be a decorative feature in themselves, or they can be discreet and designed to be concealed. When developing a lighting scheme, it is vital to establish early on in the design process how you want your lighting to function. Often, cables will need to be laid and buried during the construction of the garden and certain fittings, such as recessed step lights, installed as part of the building process.

There are several lighting techniques that can be used alone or in combination to create the desired effects. With all types of lighting, use a qualified electrician to install watertight sockets, cables and fixtures, according to the safety regulations in your area. Uplighting is created by placing a light source directly underneath features and is particularly effective when used with shrubs and trees with an interesting internal structure, such as intertwining branches. The effect created is dramatic, especially when used in winter through bare stems and branches.

Spotlighting is used extensively in gardens to highlight the detail of a particular feature, such as an intricately carved urn. For maximum shadow and detail, position the light source to one side of the feature rather than

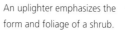

An uplighter emphasizes the form and foliage of a shrub.   Low-level downlighters cast pools of light, accentuating surface texture.

directly in front of it. This form of lighting is most effective when the light source is hidden. When choosing spotlights, note that the spread of the beam will vary, as will the intensity of the light source. Often a pinpoint beam works best because, when correctly positioned, the area lit can be limited to the feature.

Silhouette lighting is a dramatic yet subtle form of lighting used to define the outline shape of features with strong form, such as well-defined plants. The object is lit from behind, usually from below, and the light source is hidden.

Step lighting, built into the supporting wall can be a useful safety feature.

Path lighting and step lighting are usually achieved by using downlighters. These cast pools of light onto the ground, accentuating the surface texture. Path lighting is primarily functional, but it should be carefully designed so that it does not detract too much from other features. When used for entrances and drives, it should be soft and welcoming. Path lighting may be concealed so that it is not apparent during the day, or you can use decorative lights of different design and finishes—often of mushroom or globe shape—that are a feature in their own right. For step lighting, the light source may be attached or built into the supporting wall, the underside of the step or the step itself. For all step lighting a diffuser should be used to direct light downwards onto the tread of each step.

Underwater lighting can bring a pool to life at night. In a still pool, backed by a wall, the flickering shadows cast by the movement of fish can animate the garden in a way that would be impossible during the day. Underwater lighting is also effective for highlighting fountains and waterfalls, especially when used in conjunction with spotlights.

Moonlighting provides an effect that simulates the soft glow of the moon and stars. It is achieved by using several fittings fixed high above the ground, usually in trees, to cast diffuse, dappled light onto the ground below. It is particularly effective in rural gardens where excessive lighting can detract from the enjoyment of the moon and stars.

Security or access lighting

In most countries, elaborate security lighting systems are available, many with built-in sensors activated by body warmth and movement. The sensor does not distinguish between animals and humans, and it can be alarming to find the garden illuminated in the early hours of the morning, even if the intruder is only an innocent cat or fox. These censored systems are easily installed and can be very useful to light up a path from garage to front door or around the house to a rear entrance. The systems can now be purchased from some hardware stores, but an experienced electrician is often needed to fit them to the best advantage. Care must be taken to position the light bulb away from any timbers or other inflammable material.

A simple fixture beside a doorway is often sufficient for both security and ease of access. Try to choose a fitting with clean simple lines in a style suited to the architecture and locality, rather than opting for a utilitarian model. It may take time to find an appropriate fitting, but the wrong lighting can often spoil an otherwise carefully planned scheme. Make sure that lights designed to come on automatically work from both directions.

Think carefully about the positioning of the fitting. It should be neither too high nor too low and should not shine directly into the eyes of anyone approaching.

Unless you need a great deal of light, a fairly low wattage or energy-saving bulb may be all that is necessary.

The advantage of moveable spotlights is that they are easily relocated to take advantage of seasonal changes and plant growth.

One drawback of security lights is that they cannot distinguish between humans and animals.

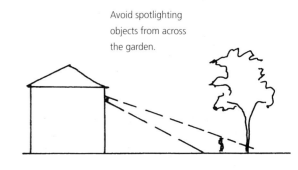

Avoid spotlighting objects from across the garden.

While for security and access lighting it may be essential to have artificial light permanently in place, for aesthetic effects you can create a magical atmosphere by using natural flame from candles, flares or torches. For most outdoor settings, candles will need to be encased in lanterns, which may be of any material—glass, paper, metal and so on—to blend in with the rest of the garden design.

Security lights should be chosen to complement the style of the house and should be positioned with care.

Lighting for aesthetic effect

Gardens can be dramatically enhanced by lighting schemes, but equally, if badly used or overused, artificial lighting can be crude and garish. Moveable spotlights are highly versatile fittings that can be placed anywhere in the garden, provided their cables are long enough. The most useful versions are either mounted on spikes for easy insertion into soil, or incorporate a simple clip for fixing to items above the ground, such as trees and fences. These discreet spotlights, which are normally finished in black, are easily concealed. They can be used for all kinds of lighting effects, from uplighting to silhouette lighting.

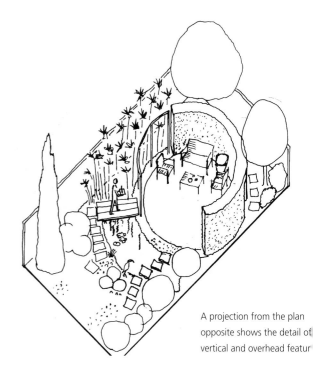

A projection from the plan opposite shows the detail of vertical and overhead featur

Hooded narrow-beam spot-lights throw light down on to the entrance area, the edge pebbles and the armchair.

Uplighters shining through the bamboo grove highlight stems and leaves.

A visual to illustrate the lighting effects proposed in the plan.

Practical Considerations

There are a number of important practical considerations that may influence costs and your choice of materials and accessories. Before making final decisions about the garden layout plan (whether on the horizontal or vertical plane), you need to consider how you will access and prepare the land, whether the soil is in the right condition and how services (such as water and electricity) will be brought onto the site.

Site Access and Clearance

An obvious point, but one frequently overlooked, is how you or the contractor will get into the garden in order to carry out the work. Can the garden only be reached by going through the house? For large items, such as classical columns or mature trees with wide root balls, access simply may not be feasible through the house or a narrow side alley. In towns the only

Designing the lighting for a contemporary garden starts with identifying on the plan which features could be affected. Projection and visuals (see Chapter 5) will help you to imagine how the scheme will work.

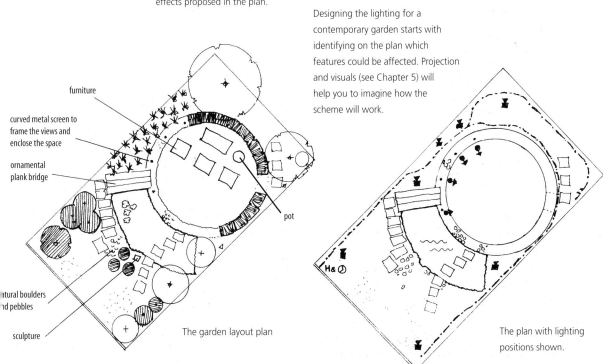

furniture

curved metal screen to frame the views and enclose the space

ornamental plank bridge

pot

natural boulders and pebbles

sculpture

The garden layout plan

The plan with lighting positions shown.

realistic access for large items may be by hired crane over the roof. There may be restrictions on parking, making unloading difficult. It is worth considering access problems early on, as this may have a direct bearing on feasibility and cost.

Normally, before any work can begin, some site clearance is necessary. This will depend on the state of the site and the work proposed. It may mean simply removing a tree or a shrub and applying weed killer, or erecting a temporary protective fence around trees and shrubs that you want to preserve, or it may mean bringing in earth-moving equipment. An area may need to be set aside for a bonfire. This should be in the open to avoid scorching any existing trees, and the local regulations on burning rubbish will need to be investigated.

If heavy machinery is required for site clearance, ensure that access to the site is sufficient.

Build bonfires in open areas to avoid scorching trees.

Soil Preparation

If topsoil is to be removed, this should be done first and the topsoil stacked separately from the subsoil beneath it. If excavating for pools or ponds, ground shaping may be necessary. This will all be done in subsoil, the topsoil only being returned after grading work is finished. The depth of topsoil required depends largely on what is to be grown. Grass or

lawn requires a minimum depth of 50 mm (2 in.), while shrubs need a minimum of 250 mm (10 in.).

Care must be taken to prepare the soil for the planting areas. It should be thoroughly dug over and all pernicious weeds removed or sprayed off. If the soil is impoverished, humus should be incorporated to improve the texture; nutrients may also be needed. The rate of plant growth will be greatly affected by the soil structure, so extra care taken at this stage will pay dividends later.

Drainage and Water

If there is a drainage problem in the garden, there is no point in rebuilding it without first taking some positive action. If the site is waterlogged, a drainage system may need to be installed. When the house was being built or during subsequent levelling and grading, the soil may have been compacted by heavy machinery. It may simply be a question of aerating the soil, or it may be a more serious inherited problem of subsoil dumped over free-draining soil, disguised with only a thin layer of topsoil. The compacted soil may need to be spiked with a fork and have fine grit incorporated to help break it up.

Your builder should be able to advise you on which system to use, and it should be installed early on when the ground work is being prepared, while machinery and access are available.

Soakaways, French drains and tile drainage systems
A soakaway is a hole that can be dug under a damp spot to drain the water off the surface and down into the ground below. The hole should be approximately 1 m (3.3 ft.) square and 1 m deep and filled first with coarse rubble, then with a layer of ash, and finally backfilled with topsoil before replacing the turf.

French drains are steep-sided trenches filled with coarse stone or gravel. They act as water-conducting channels, or temporary drains, which eventually become blocked by a gradual accumulation of silt and soil. French drains are used in preference to open ditches on the sides of paths or driveways to control any seepage.

Tile drainage is a more extensive drainage system, in which clay tile drains are laid underground with the outlet going to a ditch or watercourse. They can be laid in a single line or, for more thorough drainage, in a herringbone pattern. Gradients of the laterals should not be greater than 1:250, with the main drain similarly graded to the outfall. The depth and spacing at which these tile drains should be laid will depend on the type of soil.

Underground tile drainage systems

Tile drainage, laid out in a herringbone pattern

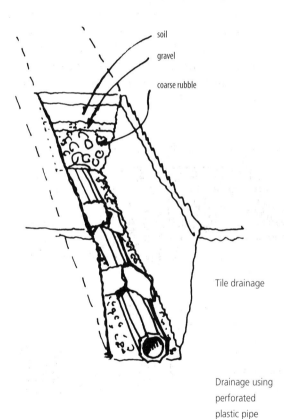

Tile drainage

Drainage using perforated plastic pipe

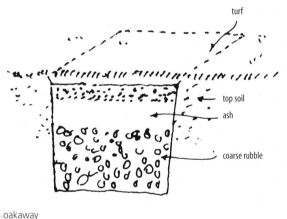

Soakaway

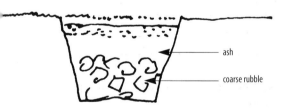

A French drain

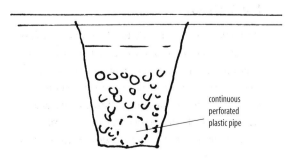

Septic tanks

If your house requires a septic tank for sewage (or an oil tank for fuel), you will need to consider its position with regard to access for vehicles and the route of any pipes leading to and from the tank before you finalize your garden layout design.

Water points and irrigation

Water points should be sited at suitable positions around the garden, perhaps one near the house and another at the opposite end. The pipes for these will need to be tapped into the main supply and will also need to be laid beneath the soil surface.

Ensure that you know where irrigation pipes are situated.

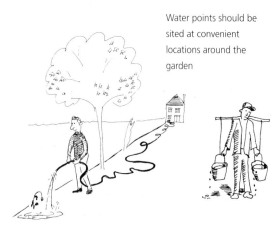

Water points should be sited at convenient locations around the garden

You may also wish to include some form of irrigation, either a surface drip system to moisten soil around plants, or a pop-up underground system that will spray lawns. The latter will need to be installed at the groundwork stage, and it is best to call in an irrigation expert to do the work.

Most plants require regular feeding and watering to help their roots become established and to encourage them to grow quickly. Imagine a prolonged period of hot dry weather during which your plants may need to be watered once or twice daily. Have you included sufficient garden taps, irrigation points or trickle irrigation to give thirsty plants a thorough watering,

or is much time going to be spent carrying a watering can backwards and forwards? Too often this results in the foliage being given a light overhead sprinkling rather than a thorough watering that reaches down to the roots.

To reduce the reliance on watering systems, every garden owner should consider using plants whose water requirements are similar to the natural climate. For areas of minimal moisture or where drought commonly occurs, a more sustainable system such as xeriscaping (using drought-tolerant plants, such as cacti) should be considered.

In areas where monthly rainfall is inconsistent and where you cannot assume that your plants will naturally receive the required water, a sprinkler system should be considered. A system of this type usually involves tapping into the main line. The system will be broken down into zones where you can have a variety of different watering options, perhaps one zone for potted plantings near a terrace, a second zone for the lawn, and a third for the perennial border. These zones are broken up into areas that need the same frequency of watering as well as a similar delivery method (for example, pop-up sprinkler heads, soaker hoses, bubblers or sprays). A central timer will manage all these zones by programmed rotating watering.

Choosing a watering system

The method of irrigation will depend on location, budget and your particular garden. Usually there are irrigation specialists who will be happy to advise and quote on a suitable system, but if your garden is small you may simply need to enquire at a good garden centre to see what is most suitable. There are four main systems to consider.

The first option is water taps, from which you can conveniently fill a watering can or run a hose with a sprinkler attachment. These should be carefully located to be accessible from each part of the garden, not just from the terrace or back door.

Another option is a trickle irrigation system, consisting mainly of a perforated hose that can emit a small amount of water over a prolonged period. Connected to the water taps and coupled with an automatic timer, this will allow you to have watering control even during long absences from your garden. The hose is often black (sometimes made of recycled tyres) and can either be dug in below ground or laid on the soil surface and moved occasionally to give greater coverage.

You may also consider an automatic pop-up irrigation system. This is usually used in gardens with large areas of plants and lawn, often in hot, dry countries.

The fourth option is a system connected to a well within your property. This system is sometimes expensive to install, but the running costs are cheaper. You should seek professional advice locally if you are considering this option.

Electricity

Electricity may also be needed in the garden, either for lighting, for operating water pumps or for running barbecues. The cables to the power points should be protected in armoured casing and marked and buried below the level of the topsoil where they cannot be easily damaged by spades or other tools. Always ask a qualified electrician for advice.

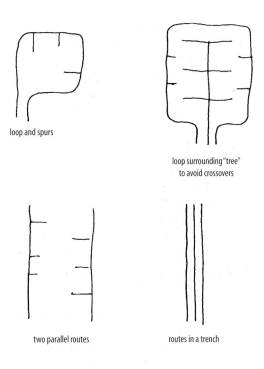

loop and spurs

loop surrounding "tree" to avoid crossovers

two parallel routes

routes in a trench

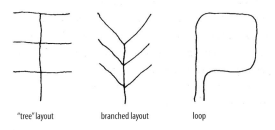

"tree" layout

branched layout

loop

Different layouts for lighting, irrigation and electricity services in a garden.

Finalizing a Scheme for the Final Garden Layout Plan

The suggestions in this chapter are not meant to be comprehensive, and there is always room for the innovative use of different materials in a garden setting. Once you have decided on the precise design of your garden and taken into consideration any practical factors, you are ready to finalize and draw up your garden layout plan. This plan completes the hard-landscaping proposals (both horizontal and vertical) for your garden.

The plan must be accurately drawn so that you will be able to use it in a practical way, both to set out the design on the land and to estimate the materials required for the hard-landscaping elements of the construction. To calculate quantities of materials, measure the area and depth (or volume) of the material, then multiply these figures to find the amount. Alternatively, take the area and depth dimensions to your local builder's merchant and ask them to calculate the required quantity for you.

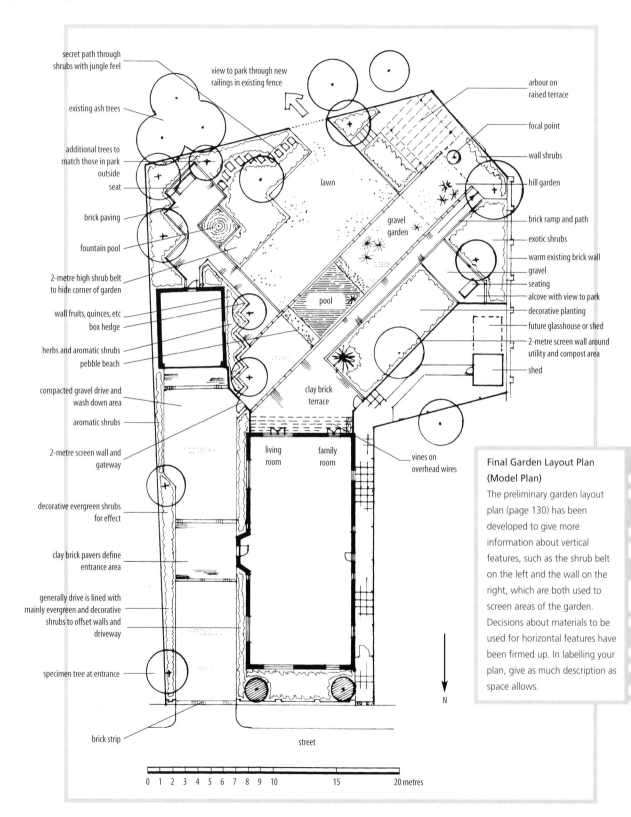

secret path through shrubs with jungle feel

view to park through new railings in existing fence

arbour on raised terrace

existing ash trees

focal point

additional trees to match those in park outside

wall shrubs

seat

hill garden

lawn

brick paving

gravel garden

fountain pool

brick ramp and path

exotic shrubs

2-metre high shrub belt to hide corner of garden

warm existing brick wall

gravel

wall fruits, quinces, etc

seating

box hedge

pool

alcove with view to park

herbs and aromatic shrubs

decorative planting

pebble beach

future glasshouse or shed

compacted gravel drive and wash down area

2-metre screen wall around utility and compost area

aromatic shrubs

clay brick terrace

shed

2-metre screen wall and gateway

living room

family room

vines on overhead wires

decorative evergreen shrubs for effect

clay brick pavers define entrance area

generally drive is lined with mainly evergreen and decorative shrubs to offset walls and driveway

specimen tree at entrance

brick strip

street

N

0 1 2 3 4 5 6 7 8 9 10   15   20 metres

Final Garden Layout Plan (Model Plan)

The preliminary garden layout plan (page 130) has been developed to give more information about vertical features, such as the shrub belt on the left and the wall on the right, which are both used to screen areas of the garden. Decisions about materials to be used for horizontal features have been firmed up. In labelling your plan, give as much description as space allows.

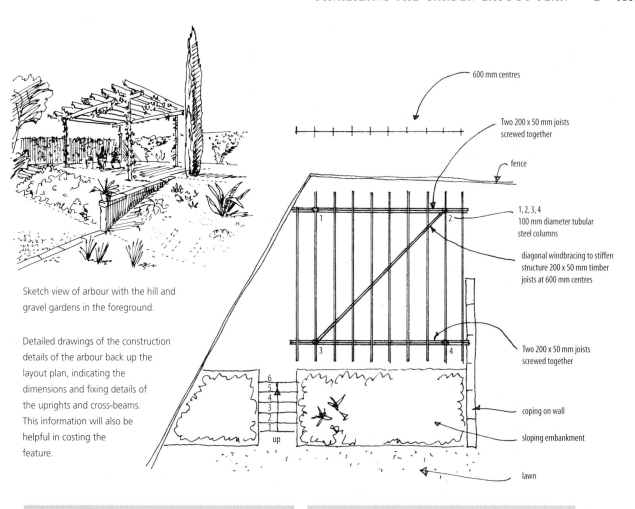

600 mm centres

Two 200 x 50 mm joists
screwed together

fence

1, 2, 3, 4
100 mm diameter tubular
steel columns

diagonal windbracing to stiffen
structure 200 x 50 mm timber
joists at 600 mm centres

Two 200 x 50 mm joists
screwed together

coping on wall

sloping embankment

lawn

Sketch view of arbour with the hill and
gravel gardens in the foreground.

Detailed drawings of the construction
details of the arbour back up the
layout plan, indicating the
dimensions and fixing details of
the uprights and cross-beams.
This information will also be
helpful in costing the
feature.

Drawing up the Final Garden Layout Plan

The garden layout plan may be drawn in pencil
or ink. Technical drawing pens or disposable
fine-line pens will give a more professional
finish, particularly if you vary the line width by
using different nib sizes. Draw the more
important or dominant features such as the
house or the garden boundary with a wider
line, then a thinner line for less dominant items.
If you use a pencil, keep it well sharpened.

1. Fix the preliminary garden layout plan to
   the drawing board, and attach a second
   sheet of tracing paper over it (on which you
   will work up the final garden layout plan).
   Take care with the layout, arranging the
   plan slightly to the left of the sheet, leaving
   enough space above, below and at the sides
   to allow for any notes or labelling. You will
   require an information panel on the right-
   hand side with a title block at the bottom of
   this, together with a north point and scale.

2. Look at the ground plane elements on the
   preliminary plan, starting at the terrace or
   another critical point that links house and
   garden. Decide on your exact choice of
   materials and how you will use them (a
   brick path in a laid basket-weave pattern,

for instance). Are you happy with them, or do they need adjusting?

3. Continue doing the same with paths, steps and any other ground plane elements. If you are content with what you have drawn on your preliminary garden layout plan, you will simply need to trace over the previous drawing. Remember that the idea is to communicate the design or pattern of your ground plan elements, not necessarily to produce a work of art.

4. Now draw up any new ground plane elements individually to scale. Imagine you are looking down on them from overhead, and show the outline shape of the feature as well as the design in which the material is arranged (if appropriate). Indicate the latter by detailing to scale only a small area. If bricks or other materials are too small to be drawn to scale on the plan, you can supplement it with separate detail sheets. Alternatively, you could try to indicate your intentions graphically, possibly by magnifying them in a diagram drawn alongside the plan. If you use this technique, make sure that you number or label your details to key them to the plan so that their positions are instantly identifiable.

5. Next draw in all vertical and overhead elements, beginning with the outer or boundary walls, gradually moving inwards to include any trellis, pergolas, arches and so on. Remember that you are viewing the object from above. Label all vertical features (for example, "Brick wall: 1.8 m in height", "Hardwood trellis, stained dark blue: 1.2 m in height").

6. Draw in the canopies of any existing or proposed trees, and indicate with a cross where they are to be planted. Refer back to page 74 for symbols for these.

7. Provide a short descriptive label for each area of border or planting to indicate your broad intentions (for instance, "Scented mixed border for summer interest").

8. Are there are any elements that need to be shown in more detail, such as a pond or pergola construction? You may not be able to show sufficient detail on your plan drawing, and these should be drawn on a separate sheet. (Make a note of these. Drawing sections and other visuals will be dealt with in Chapter 5.)

9. Once you have completed it, remove the final garden layout plan from the drawing board. The plan will have taken you time to draw and is therefore an important document. Take at least two copies (either dyeline prints or photocopies), and keep the original flat and safely stored—you may need to make amendments to it later if you change your ideas. You may want to colour one of the copies (see page 231) when you have decided on the planting for the garden, which is the next stage in the design process.

10. You should now have an accurate garden layout plan, which can be used either by you for constructing the garden or by the builder to give you a price for the work. The next stage is to decide on the plantings for your new garden.

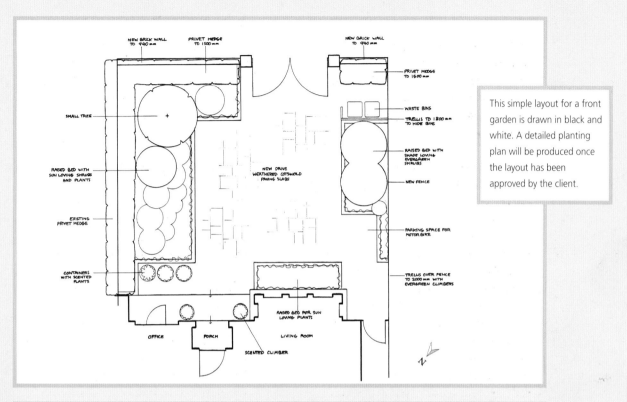

NEW BRICK WALL TO 940 mm

PRIVET HEDGE TO 1500 mm

NEW BRICK WALL TO 940 mm

PRIVET HEDGE TO 1500 mm

WASTE BINS

TRELLIS TO 1800 mm TO HIDE BINS

SMALL TREE

RAISED BED WITH SHADE LOVING EVERGREEN SHRUBS

NEW FENCE

RAISED BED WITH SUN LOVING SHRUBS AND PLANTS

NEW DRIVE WEATHERED COTSWOLD PAVING SLABS

EXISTING PRIVET HEDGE

PARKING SPACE FOR MOTOR BIKE

TRELLIS OVER FENCE TO 2000 mm WITH EVERGREEN CLIMBERS

CONTAINERS WITH SCENTED PLANTS

RAISED BED FOR SUN LOVING PLANTS

OFFICE

PORCH

LIVING ROOM

SCENTED CLIMBER

This simple layout for a front garden is drawn in black and white. A detailed planting plan will be produced once the layout has been approved by the client.

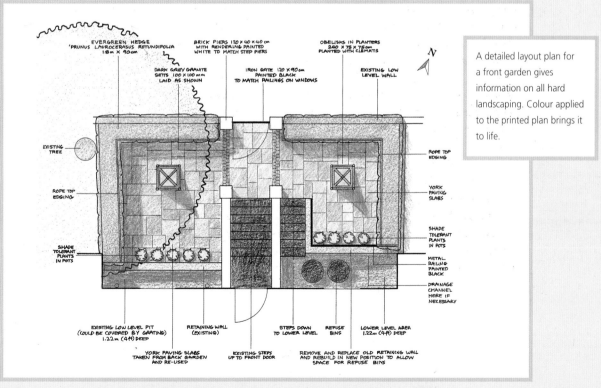

EVERGREEN HEDGE 'PRUNUS LAUROCERASUS ROTUNDIFOLIA' 1.8m X 90cm

BRICK PIERS 120 X 40 X 40 cm WITH RENDERING PAINTED WHITE TO MATCH STEP PIERS

OBELISKS IN PLANTERS 240 X 75 X 75cm PLANTED WITH CLEMATIS

DARK GREY GRANITE SETTS 100 X 100 mm LAID AS SHOWN

IRON GATE 120 X 90cm PAINTED BLACK TO MATCH RAILINGS ON WINDOWS

EXISTING LOW LEVEL WALL

EXISTING TREE

ROPE TOP EDGING

ROPE TOP EDGING

YORK PAVING SLABS

SHADE TOLERANT PLANTS IN POTS

SHADE TOLERANT PLANTS IN POTS

METAL RAILING PAINTED BLACK

DRAINAGE CHANNEL HERE IF NECESSARY

EXISTING LOW LEVEL PIT (COULD BE COVERED BY GRATING) 1.22m (4ft) DEEP

RETAINING WALL (EXISTING)

STEPS DOWN TO LOWER LEVEL

REFUSE BINS

LOWER LEVEL AREA 1.22m (4ft) DEEP

YORK PAVING SLABS TAKEN FROM BACK GARDEN AND RE-USED

EXISTING STEPS UP TO FRONT DOOR

REMOVE AND REPLACE OLD RETAINING WALL AND REBUILD IN NEW POSITION TO ALLOW SPACE FOR REFUSE BINS

A detailed layout plan for a front garden gives information on all hard landscaping. Colour applied to the printed plan brings it to life.

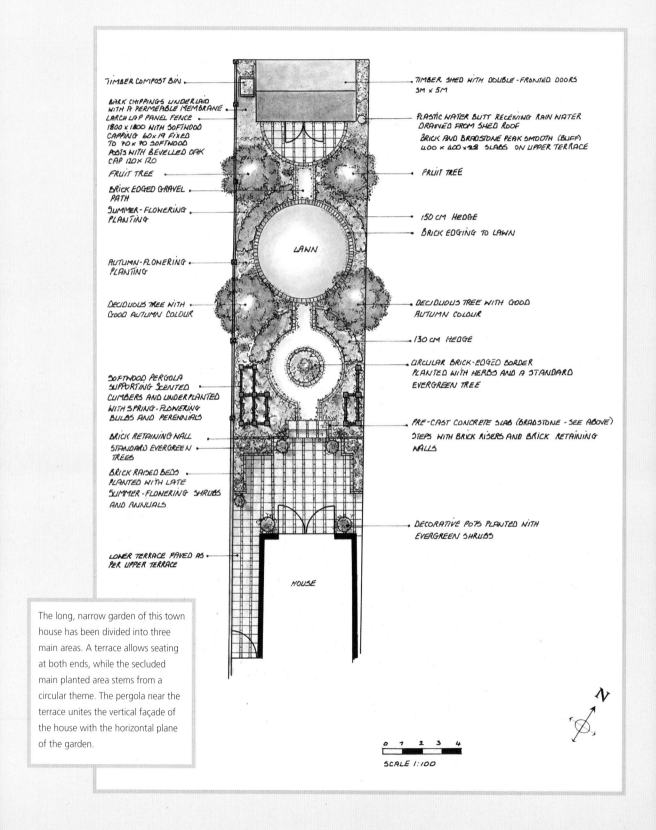

TIMBER COMPOST BIN

BARK CHIPPINGS UNDERLAID
WITH A PERMEABLE MEMBRANE
LARCH LAP PANEL FENCE
1800 × 1800 WITH SOFTWOOD
CAPPING 60×19 FIXED
TO 70×70 SOFTWOOD
POSTS WITH BEVELLED OAK
CAP 120× 120

FRUIT TREE

BRICK EDGED GRAVEL
PATH

SUMMER-FLOWERING
PLANTING

AUTUMN-FLOWERING
PLANTING

DECIDUOUS TREE WITH
GOOD AUTUMN COLOUR

SOFTWOOD PERGOLA
SUPPORTING SCENTED
CLIMBERS AND UNDERPLANTED
WITH SPRING-FLOWERING
BULBS AND PERENNIALS

BRICK RETAINING WALL
STANDARD EVERGREEN
TREES

BRICK RAISED BEDS
PLANTED WITH LATE
SUMMER-FLOWERING SHRUBS
AND ANNUALS.

LOWER TERRACE PAVED AS
PER UPPER TERRACE

TIMBER SHED WITH DOUBLE-FRONTED DOORS
3M × 5M

PLASTIC WATER BUTT RECEIVING RAIN WATER
DRAINED FROM SHED ROOF
BRICK AND BRADSTONE PEAK SMOOTH (BUFF)
400 × 400 ×38 SLABS ON UPPER TERRACE

FRUIT TREE

150 CM HEDGE

BRICK EDGING TO LAWN

DECIDUOUS TREE WITH GOOD
AUTUMN COLOUR

130 CM HEDGE

CIRCULAR BRICK-EDGED BORDER
PLANTED WITH HERBS AND A STANDARD
EVERGREEN TREE

PRE-CAST CONCRETE SLAB (BRADSTONE - SEE ABOVE)
STEPS WITH BRICK RISERS AND BRICK RETAINING
WALLS

DECORATIVE POTS PLANTED WITH
EVERGREEN SHRUBS

LAWN

HOUSE

The long, narrow garden of this town
house has been divided into three
main areas. A terrace allows seating
at both ends, while the secluded
main planted area stems from a
circular theme. The pergola near the
terrace unites the vertical façade of
the house with the horizontal plane
of the garden.

N

0 1 2 3 4

SCALE 1:100

Above: In this garden, the two levels are connected by circular steps, the curve being repeated by the box hedge that surrounds the arum lilies, *Zantedeschia aethiopica*. Round-edged brick columns reinforce the curved theme.

Above: An octagon works well in this change of level. Railway sleepers back-filled with gravel help to unite these steps with the surrounding countryside.

Above: The steps, with generously proportioned treads and risers, take their lead from the dimensions of the terrace and ornamental pool.

Above: Steps and brick wall combine satisfactorily. The height of the risers and widths of the treads make for comfortable going.

Above: Steps can be used to change the direction of a path. The combination of gravel, stone overhang and smaller stone off-cuts blend with the local landscape.

Above: Contemporary and classic materials combine to indicate a strong directional flow. Slate panels (pre-cut to a template), blend with the edging of stone chippings.

Above: A brick path laid in herringbone style is a good foil for the surrounding foliage. Some bricks have been fired for longer than others, resulting in an interesting uneven effect.

Above: Corners are awkward to deal with, and solutions often involve expensive cutting of materials. Here smaller stones are used as an infill to the brick pavers.

Above: The protruding paving stones along either side of the central path make a useful place for standing pots.

Below: Rolled asphalt top dressed with pea shingle (gravel), is separated into a diagonal pattern by bricks laid on edge, harmonizing with the brick edge to the path. The diagonal lines tend to draw the eye forward.

Left: Brick inserts break up this expanse of stone paving. Setting the height of the paving level just below the level of the lawn allows the mower to skim over without damage to the cutting blades.

Left: An inverted man-hole cover is filled with paving stones to give continuity to this terrace.

Below: An unusual way of creating a light fitting. This roofing tile conceals a light bulb, giving a wash effect on the wall.

Above: Here the lights are recessed into the turf so that they will not be damaged by the mower when the grass is cut.

Left: The rounded shapes of plants in this garden are a contrast to the unusual vertical sundial. The different shades of green include both matt and light-reflective foliage.

Below: Use of the overhead plane by means of tree canopy, parasol or pergola, makes a garden feel more secluded.

Above: A low brick wall can double as a seating area and display place for pots. The number of brick courses and the coping used must be carefully considered.

Above: A carved fossil shell sculpture forms an unusual focal point. Set directly on the soil, it is supported from the rear.

Above: Set into cobbles and surrounded by a brick path, this large water sculpture by William Pye relies on its strong shape and colour for visual impact. An internal overflow keeps the water level with the outside rim of the sculpture.

Above: The unusual curved shape of this polished stone bench adds to its tactile quality. Simple timber supports play up the design.

Above: Substantial yet comfortable, this furniture can be left outside all year, provided the timber has been pressure-treated against rotting. The reconstituted stone paving provides both a colour harmony and a level surface.

Above: Garden accessories may be used to complement the planting in a garden. White is a very strong colour in the garden and here it has been introduced by the seat to act as a contrast to the plants.

Above: Searching through architectural salvage yards can yield exciting and original containers. The subtle planting of red tulips with glaucous foliage complements this verdigris metal basin. Holes have been drilled in the base for drainage.

Above: An unusual rush and metal detail accentuates this specimen tree and the nearby woodland planting.

Above: A contemporary arrangement of slate and timber creates an outdoor eating area. The shape of the timber cubes is repeated in the clipped box at the base of the tree.

Above: A pond on two levels gives both sound and reflective qualities to this terraced space. The bright blue chairs are a cheerful contrast with the yellow paint-work, foliage and flowers.

Above: Vertical accents can transform a garden. These clipped yews not only delineate the line of the path, but also link the house to the garden.

Above: Timber, used here for decking, is also used for the uprights to frame both tree and view.

Above: A curved black metal pergola frames this view. The carefully co-ordinated black metal chair frame and marble tabletop add to the luxurious effect.

Above: At the entrance to this garden, an interesting combination of pool and pergola is accentuated by the opening in a curved stone wall.

Chapter 4
Creating a Planting Plan

For many people who are planning a garden, the most exciting and challenging part of the process is choosing the plants. It is not simply a question of going to the local garden centre or nursery and filling up a trolley. Each plant has its own characteristics, situation and soil preferences, and you need to consider how the plants that you want to use will relate to your garden. As every site is different, there is no standard solution.

To design with plants, you need to know them—not just from photographs in a reference book or catalogue or by keeping a plant notebook (see page 259), but most importantly from frequent observation and, if possible, from growing them yourself. However, a collection of plants does not necessarily make a good garden. This chapter gives you guidelines for choosing plants that will create memorable, lasting groupings. Consideration is given to the importance of outline shape and also the texture and patterns of foliage.

Colour can be provided in both foliage and flowers, but flowers are fleeting and subject to seasonal change. Enduring far longer than flowers, foliage is often secondary in consideration to flower colour. A memorable planting scheme usually relies on outline plant shape, texture of leaves, colour of both leaves and flowers, and the relationship between each individual plant and neighbouring plants.

Much effort, time and money may be spent on the garden layout. Now the planting should be planned to harmonize with it and set it off, softening and contrasting with the harsher lines of man-made materials. It is usually the planting that most people remember.

The Role of Planting

You probably associate planting with bringing colour into your garden, which is a perfectly acceptable expectation. However, as plants play many more functional roles, such as providing a garden with structure, colour should not be the first consideration. Examining the different roles planting can play will help you identify your own planting objectives.

Structure and Enclosure

While developing the garden layout plan, you considered certain aspects of the planting, such as using plants to create the garden structure. For instance, you should have decided already which trees to include, and the location and type of any hedges. In shaping the various spaces, these decisions need to be taken early on in the design process because structural planting is as important as hard landscaping.

Plants chosen for structure are usually trees or shrubs which will provide height and bulk throughout the year, but remember that there are also many large herbaceous perennials that can dramatically affect the structure of the garden. Some taller perennials can reach the staggering height of 2 m (6.6 ft.) during the growing season, before dying right back to the ground in winter. Try to think through the effect of seasonal change in relation to the structure and height in your garden. The bare winter appearance will be very different from high summer when the flower-filled borders are at their peak.

There should be sufficient structural planting to enclose and shape each individual space, creating a series of garden "rooms" which can be enjoyed during the different seasons.

Enhancing Hard-Landscape Features

For a garden to read as a unified whole, the plants should work in harmony with the hard-landscaping features. Plants may be used as focal points, such as an ornamental tree at the end of a vista, or a topiary feature drawing attention to an alcove. Plants can also be used to direct movement through a garden, either by forming impenetrable masses or by marking a change in direction.

When choosing plants to function closely with hard structures, they should be of appropriate size, shape and growth potential. Avoid using vigorous plants for quick effect, which may result in narrowed paths, obscured views, and much thinning out later.

Relating the Garden to Its Surroundings

Whether in an urban or rural setting, you can use plants to unite the garden with the landscape beyond. In a country situation a garden can appear to merge with the local landscape by repeating native plants, or their ornamental forms, within the garden. In city gardens the shape of neighbouring buildings can be echoed or contrasted through the selection and arrangement of the plants.

In Chapter 1 the importance of considering a garden's setting to determine its style was emphasized. There are many different styles of planting, or ways of combining plants for different effects. Often, the climate, soil and aspect will rule out inappropriate styles. To take an extreme example, a woodland garden would not be appropriate, or even survive, on an urban rooftop. There are certain styles of planting that, although possible, would be out of character with the house and its surroundings. In a country setting particularly, the view for others may be spoilt if your planting detracts from the surrounding landscape.

Changing Scenes

Plants alter as they mature and adapt to the changing seasons. Just as a bare winter garden may look very different in summer when it is in full flower, a newly planted garden will look very different twenty years later.

One of the greatest challenges of designing with plants is to arrange combinations that create successional interest throughout the year. Seasonal changes can be dramatic, but try to take advantage of this by capturing the energy and rhythm of the seasons in your choice of plants.

Nonvisual Qualities of Plants

Probably the greatest role that plants play in a garden is their visual appeal, particularly when well grouped to provide an appealing arrangement of forms, textures and colours, but they also have other important qualities that should not be overlooked when choosing plants.

Scent

For most gardeners, scent is an important attribute. Some people have a strong sense of smell, and for them, too many contrasting scents in a small space can be disturbing. To the uninitiated it may be assumed that all roses have a scent, but the strength of the scent will vary from plant to plant, and this may affect your selection.

Not all scents are welcome in the garden. While flower blossom often has a sweet or perfumed scent, and leaves and bark may be aromatic, some plants have a strong odour to attract flies, and others have an unpleasant pungent scent. *Salvia sclarea* is nicknamed "hot house maids" or "smelly socks" for a reason.

Sounds

Plants may produce sounds through their movement, such as the rustle of bamboo leaves in a breeze, and through the wildlife that inhabit them, such as the songs of birds attracted to the garden. The bird population can increase rapidly as a garden matures.

Tactile appeal

For children in particular, the enjoyment of touching plants can give great pleasure. Feathery plumes of grasses, silken catkins and rough-textured bark are just a few examples. Other plants, such as the yucca with its spiky leaves, are an obvious deterrent.

Food for the table

Fruit, vegetables, herbs and nuts can make a garden useful as well as pleasurable. Distinguishing between edible and poisonous plants is crucial in designing gardens for young families.

Principles of Planting Design

Plant material can also be used to fulfil particular requirements. Rather than focusing on different kinds of plants, concentrate on their general qualities of scale, form, colour and texture. Try also to sustain plant interest throughout the year, and match plants to your own site conditions while still giving them enough space to develop.

Scale and Proportion

The scale, or outline shape, height and spread of plants that you choose for a particular site can have an enormous influence on the mood of the garden. It is vital to get this right, because if plants are too large, a space may be claustrophobic, and if they are too small, the space may be exposed and unprotected. The scale of the planting should relate to adjoining buildings, to the size of the garden and to the scale of the human figure.

To achieve a sense of harmony in a garden, different groups of plants should relate to, or be in proportion with, one another, both in scale and number. Try to achieve a balanced rhythm of different sizes and effects. If, for instance, you decided to place a large shrub on one side of the garden, you would need to balance this on the other side. An obvious thing to do would be to place another of the same on the other side, but if you wanted to use a smaller type of shrub, one would not be enough to balance the visual weight of the large shrub, so you would have to use several,

perhaps three or five. Odd numbers create a natural effect, while even numbers can be more formal.

In this typical suburban plot, the neighbouring houses are very intrusive.

The same plot with some planting added. The tree helps to enclose the garden and give some privacy, but the other plants are too small, allowing the fences to dominate the scene.

Here, where the scale of the planting has been increased, the atmosphere of the garden is vastly improved. The trees relate well in scale to the size of the house and the shrubs are human-scaled. A good balance of enclosure and openness has been achieved.

If plants are too large in scale for the house, surroundings and size of plot, the garden may feel rather airless and cramped.

To achieve a
sense of balance
in the planting,
one plant, or
group of plants,
must equal the
mass of another.

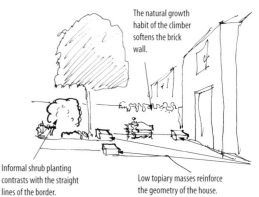

The natural growth
habit of the climber
softens the brick
wall.

Here, a large shrub is
counterbalanced by a
group of smaller shrubs.

Informal shrub planting
contrasts with the straight
lines of the border.

Low topiary masses reinforce
the geometry of the house.

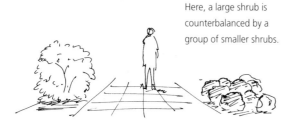

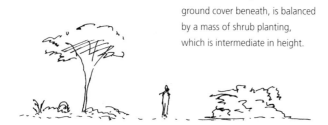

A tall slender tree, with low
ground cover beneath, is balanced
by a mass of shrub planting,
which is intermediate in height.

Within the border, tall
upright forms contrast with
more rounded forms of
different sizes, providing
accents and rhythm to the
composition.

Shape and Form

Once you have established the scale of your planting,
you should consider the shapes and forms for your
plant groupings. At this stage, think about the plant
outline rather than the shape of a particular leaf or
flower. Drawing elevations (projecting your planting
plans onto a vertical plane) is a useful way of trying
out different ideas (see page 212). What you are
aiming for is a group of contrasting forms that
combine together to form a balanced whole, just as if
you were composing a still life grouping for a
painting. For inspiration, observe the garden's
surroundings. Are there any obvious shapes, such as
distant hills or rounded clumps of trees that you may
like to echo or contrast?

Grouping plants

Plan the planting with groups of plants rather than
individual plants. A single iris, for instance, could not
balance a large rounded shrub, but a large group of
irises could do so effectively as the volume, or mass,
would be similar.

Repeating plant groups

When planning the outline form of your planting, be
sure to repeat effects across the garden to relate one
area to another. Repeating plants is one way of
restricting the variety of plants used in a plan, usually
resulting in strong, bold effects as opposed to the
"dot" approach (one of this here, one of that there)
which always looks restless.

Layers of planting

Try to plan the planting in layers, whether horizontally or vertically. Make beds that are large enough to accommodate more than one plant's width, so that plants can be placed in front of, or behind, other plants. This layering effect, where some plants are partly obscured by others, will give your planting depth.

Where space is at a premium and beds are narrow, plants can be layered vertically, similar to the way they sometimes coexist in nature. In a woodland, for example, the plants arrange themselves in several "storeys", with the foliage of large trees at the top, smaller trees and shrubs directly beneath them, and herbaceous plants and bulbs at the bottom. Planting that is planned in this way can occupy the same area of ground for several effects, since both spring and autumn flowering bulbs may be planted between herbaceous plants. Above these, the shrubs and overhanging trees may each have two seasons of interest, enhancing the overall composition.

Imitating the layering of natural plant groups works effectively to create depth in the planting plan.

large trees

small trees
shrubs
herbaceous plants
bulbs

Texture

Texture follows on from deciding on the shape and form of the planting, and is mainly defined by the leaves of a plant. Like fabric, plant leaves have varying qualities of roughness and smoothness, from very coarse to extremely fine, and as many different finishes. Their surfaces may resemble such materials as fur, velvet, suede, sandpaper, leather and plastic. To show off the textural qualities of a plant to greatest effect, contrast it with another of very different texture. In some plants, the underside of the leaf contrasts markedly with the top side.

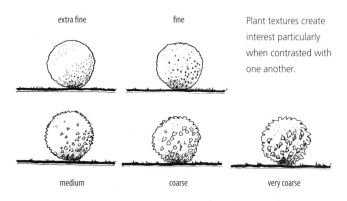

extra fine   fine

Plant textures create interest particularly when contrasted with one another.

medium   coarse   very coarse

Light quality

Texture affects the quality of light reflected or absorbed by a plant. The leaves of some plants are shiny and light-reflective, while others are matt and light-absorbent. A mass of bright glossy leaves can bring life to a dark corner, while a plant with matt leaves may provide a perfect foil for more colourful or decorative subjects.

Experiment with using different textures in your garden, varying the proportion of rough textures with smooth, metallic with furry and so on. It is usually best to allow one texture to predominate, repeating it across the garden to relate one area to another.

Colour

The concept of colour in a garden always seems to be associated with planting, although all hard-landscaping features, such as walls or paving, will also give colour to the overall composition. Although you may prefer a certain colour palette in planting, it may not suit the existing hard-landscape colour. Often it is wiser to consider the backdrop first and then choose your colours to complement or contrast with this.

Spatial tricks

The overall design can be accentuated by using plant colour. For instance, it can be used very effectively to influence perspective. Cool colours, such as pale blues, pale browns, whites and greys, introduced at a distance, will have the effect of lengthening a view, while hot colours, such as strong reds and vivid oranges, clamour for attention and tend to advance towards the viewer. For this reason you should avoid using strong colours in the path of an important view, as the colours will compete with the view and distract attention from it. However, if something needs to be hidden, strong colours will arrest the eye, distracting it from the scene beyond.

Using plant colour to influence perspective

Dark foliage plants "move towards" the viewer.

Light foliage plants "move away" from the viewer.

Dark foliage plants provide an effective background for light foliage plants.

Medium-tone greens can act as a transition between dark and light greens.

Colour from foliage, bark and stems

Although flower colour seems to be most people's primary concern, when you are designing with plants, you should concentrate on more permanent colour, particularly in leaves, bark and stems.

Leaves have a wide range of colours. Within the green range alone there are yellow-greens, grey-greens and glaucous or blue-greens, not to mention purple, crimson and yellow foliage. Leaves may also be variegated or have margins that are a different colour from the main leaf. In some plants the emergent leaves are a fresh pale green, yellow or even pink, but as they mature they dull down. Consider seasonal colour variations as an unexpected asset. Particularly with plants partial to acid soils, autumn leaf colour can vary from bright oranges through vibrant reds to rich purples, and can transform the appearance of the garden towards the end of the growing season when rich, vibrant tones show up the autumn sunlight.

Some plants, particularly certain deciduous trees and shrubs, can have the additional attraction of coloured bark and stems to provide interest in the winter months.

Light

Our perception of colour is affected by light, which is why painters traditionally opt for studios facing north, where the light variation is minimized. As light intensity increases, all colours tend to fade, but stronger hues, such as vivid reds and oranges, retain more brilliance than muted colours, which may be completely "bleached out" by the fierce sunlight typical of tropical countries. In the bluish light of temperate climates, colours are perceived differently—muted colours tend to glow, while stronger colours can look garish. As evening approaches and the sun begins to redden, bright colours tend to be enriched and then deepen to violet and black. Paler colours, particularly white, will continue to glow long after the brighter colours have faded. This effect can be applied to planting in shade. Whites and pale yellows will tend to gleam, while warm reds, greens and blues will become darker.

Adjacent colours

As well as being modified by light, the hue of a colour is affected by its neighbours. When you place one colour next to another, both colours will be affected by each other's presence, and the difference between them will become more exaggerated. This applies not only when colours are seen simultaneously but also when one colour is observed immediately before another. This is why white gardens, filled predominantly with white flowers and grey foliage, appear more intense if approached through an area of hot colour.

Altering mood

Colour affects people in different ways, but in general, reds are associated with warmth and stimulation and blues and greens with coolness and tranquility. You can use these associations creatively to change the perception of a space. For instance, a hot courtyard, on which the sun blazes down, can seem cooler if planted with silvers, cool blues and harsh whites, while a cold, north-facing area can be enlivened by flame, orange, apricot and yellow. In deep shade, however, these strong colours will darken and disappear. You can make a rather sunless area appear brighter with yellow flowers or foliage, much of which will thrive better in shade than in direct sunlight.

Colour themes

The easiest, but nonetheless very effective, way of using colour in planting is one that frequently occurs in nature—to have a mass of one type of plant providing the colour statement at a given time. Far from being boring, the eye often appreciates a rest from being besieged with colour.

Single-colour schemes are particularly effective if used with foliage of a contrasting or complementary colour. Good examples of this technique include yellow flowers or leaves combined with grey foliage, and red flowers with bronze or purple foliage.

An extension of the single colour theme is to use a combination of plants with the same basic colour but subtle variations of hue and intensity. This can be very striking, and there is a tremendous amount of plant material available. For success, try to achieve a balance of deep, medium and pale shades.

Broadly, all flower and foliage colour is based on either blue or yellow. In the blue range are the hard whites, all the bluish pinks, magentas, crimson-reds and purples, as well as the true blues. In the yellow range are warm whites, yellow, orange, orange-pinks (apricot, salmon and the sunset shades) and all the scarlet-reds. If either range is used alone, there will never be a clash, since all the colours derive from a single base. Sometimes a good clash is needed to enliven a space or to stimulate our colour appreciation, preventing a bland effect. Lead up to a clash with an arrangement of less demanding tones, allowing a good stretch of neutral colouring before introducing another clash.

In the fashion trade, colour preferences come and go, and there are similar fashions in planting. To make an occasional very bold statement in your planting, contrast form, texture and colour at the same time. Be careful not to overdo it, however, or the statement will lose impact and become irritating.

Seasonal Changes in Plant Compositions

To achieve well-balanced seasonal effects you need to consider your proposed planting throughout the year. To do this you should observe plants in every season. The effect of spring foliage is just as important as flower colour, berries and autumn leaf colour, while the colour and texture of winter stems and twigs may be a greater asset than the heavy foliage produced by these plants in high summer. To observe plants in intimate detail, there is no substitute for growing them yourself. Even failing to grow them satisfactorily will teach you something about their needs! But if this is impossible, you should at least regularly observe the same plants over the seasons in your local park or botanical garden.

You may find it a challenge to introduce and arrange plants to provide interest throughout the seasons. In some gardens, or in parts of gardens that are only used at certain times of the year, this may not be wanted, but most people will want at least one part of the garden to have some interest in the winter. Avoid scattering little bits of interest throughout the garden; although this may provide something in bloom every month of the year, the overall visual result is rarely effective. Far better to designate a particular season of interest to different areas, so that each area in turn holds the attention, while the remainder of the garden forms a quiet green background, awaiting its moment to perform.

The level of seasonal changes differs throughout the world. Some are very extreme, some almost constant. In temperate areas, there are four clearly defined seasons which, unless the planting is entirely evergreen, present four distinctively different pictures.

Spring effects
In spring, trees and shrubs will be covered in developing foliage, with the branch and twig structure still clearly visible, while herbaceous plants of varying height begin to appear through the ground. In both cases, leaves may predominate and be at their most attractive when young and fresh.

Summer and autumn effects
Summer shows solid outlines of texture, with herbaceous plants gradually becoming taller as the summer progresses. In many gardens, the flowering season is at its peak in late spring to midsummer.

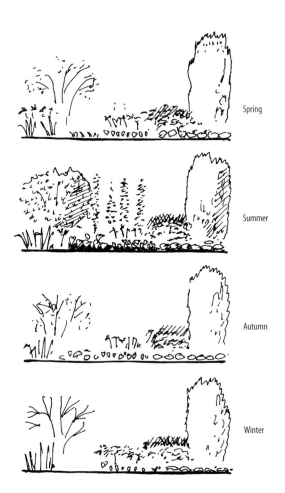

Spring

Summer

Autumn

Winter

Small elevation sketches will help you to consider the effect of the seasons on a planting plan.

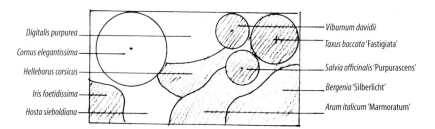

Digitalis purpurea
Cornus elegantissima
Helleborus corsicus
Iris foetidissima
Hosta sieboldiana

Viburnum davidii
Taxus baccata 'Fastigiata'
Salvia officinalis 'Purpurascens'
Bergenia 'Silberlicht'
Arum italicum 'Marmoratum'

Individual plants tend to merge into groups, and it is hard to reconcile the overall abundance with the bare winter scene. From midsummer to late summer, this abundance becomes less interesting, many plants having "gone over" and no longer flowering but still providing greenery in the foliage. By early autumn, interest is rekindled as late-flowering plants come into bloom, often set off against a background of richly coloured autumnal foliage.

Winter effects

Although gardens are mainly dormant in winter, they can still look beautiful. Often this is because the bones of the design, which give a garden its strength, are only revealed as the foliage recedes. Most herbaceous plants and many ground covers will have gone below ground. Trees and certain shrubs will have a skeletal outline, while other more twiggy shrubs will still appear very solid. Evergreen plants will retain their bulk and outline. Plants that appear quite recessive during the other seasons (a light-absorbent conifer, for instance) may now become the dominant feature.

Practical Considerations

Although there are numerous plants to choose from when you are designing a garden, the physical conditions of a site—the soil, aspect, exposure and climate, for instance—will restrict what can be grown in a particular place. Unless your plant knowledge is good, you will need to do some research to check on individual plant preferences.

To understand these individual preferences, try to find out where plants originate, be it Japan, Switzerland or the Mediterranean. By planting them in conditions that are as similar to their natural habitat as possible, they should have an increased chance of thriving. If you cannot offer such conditions, do not try to grow the plant. Lavender, for instance, found in dry, sandy soils in the Mediterranean, would never do well in shady, damp

What is hardy in one area may not be elsewhere.

In a seaside location salt winds can desiccate plants.

Plants must be chosen for their tolerance of given conditions. Many plants can tolerate the fumes and pollution of a traffic-side location.

conditions. In addition to plants that originate in foreign countries, there are many native wildflowers and shrubs that are garden-worthy and may be easier to grow than introduced species. They too need the appropriate type of soil and growing conditions.

Using Existing Plants

You may wish to retain certain existing plants, which can either be moved or kept where they are. Mature small trees or shrubs may need to be root pruned six months prior to the move, and the overall height and spread reduced by a third. Root pruning is achieved by digging around the plant while it is in its existing position, to reduce the spread of the roots. This process encourages the plant to send up new, smaller rootlets that will adapt more readily to the subsequent new position. Reduction of the overall height and spread reduces the amount of energy a plant must use to support its overall size, and as it is smaller, this reduces the likelihood of root damage caused by wind rock.

An existing plant will often look out of proportion in association with newer plants, but with careful pruning to reduce the overall bulk, the plant can be more easily integrated. Existing clumps of herbaceous plants may be split up into several smaller clumps and reused elsewhere in a planting scheme. If you are replanning a mature garden, the kitchen garden could perhaps be used as a temporary holding area, allowing you to dig up the existing plants, line them up in close knit rows and then replant them in new borders later.

Existing clumps of herbaceous perennials may be suitable for dividing.

Plant Spacing

When drawing up a plan of your planting on paper, you will allocate spaces to be occupied by mature plants (a standard approach is to show them at their approximate height and spread after five years). On your planting plan, you will only need to show the spread, but you may also wish to draw an elevation, which will show both height and spread.

A mature shrub may eventually reach 600 mm (2 ft.) in height and 900 mm (3 ft.) in spread, but when first

planted it may take up as little space as 150 × 150 mm (6 × 6 in.). Do not be tempted to overplant the remaining space by placing shrubs too close together. This can quickly lead to overcrowding as the plants grow, resulting in poorly shaped trees and shrubs. Far better to use filler plants that can later be removed as the main plant matures.

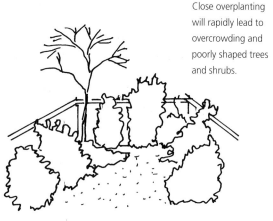

Close overplanting will rapidly lead to overcrowding and poorly shaped trees and shrubs.

Ideal filler candidates include annuals and bulbs, as well as fibrous-rooted shrubs that not only grow quickly but also have a short lifespan. In five years or so, these plants tend to become rather straggly and can easily be removed. In the meantime, the slower-growing, longer-lasting shrubs will gradually fill in the lessened gaps. It is unwise to apply the same system to trees, since quick-growing "filler" trees take too much moisture and nutrients out of the soil. Vigorous ground covers should also be avoided, at least in the first two or three years, as they tend to compete with young shrubs for soil nutrients. Ground cover can always be added later, possibly when the infill shrubs are removed.

Planting Styles

Before you begin drawing up the planting plan, you should reconsider your original ideas for the garden. Now that the hard-landscaping decisions have been made, think how you will complement these with the plantings. Try to imagine that you are walking through the garden—beginning, for instance, at the terrace adjacent to the house—and ask yourself two important questions: What style of planting would be appropriate for each area? What season or seasons would you expect a particular bed to peak or perform at its best?

A clear idea of the style of planting needed to complement the garden layout plan may have evolved while you were working your way through the planning stage. Now you need to translate this style into its essential parts. This stage is rather like painting a picture. It is very difficult to paint something if you do not have a clear idea of what you are trying to paint.

We have already considered how the architectural and interior style should be repeated in the garden design, and you should adopt a similar approach when choosing your plants. House, garden and plants should work together as a unified whole, each enhancing the qualities of the others. In this way it is often the house or the location that will determine the planting style.

First decide whether the style should be formal or informal. Which is most appropriate to the house and its setting? Formal designs are based on straight lines, often with a strict pattern of clipped box or yew outlining geometric shapes of squares, rectangles or circles. An informal design may be based on the more natural lines of gentle curves and meandering paths with plants spilling over the edges.

Formal

Many people feel more comfortable creating a formal garden, reassured by the simplicity of the style. It is still possible, within the strict geometric shapes, to have luxuriant groups of flowing plants set off or framed by the formal scheme to create a romantic effect. The simplicity of a formal design is not only confined to historical associations but also blends well with modern minimalist buildings.

Informal

Informal gardens may imitate the bends and curves of nature, but in nature there is usually a reason for the bend or curve, such as to avoid a tree, large rock or pool. Curves should be generous, allowing you to move around them slowly, and should be emphasized at the widest point by a tree or group of shrubs. Any curves may be created by cutting the border outline around a garden hose laid out on turf. Unless you make your curves generous, not only will they look unnatural and self-conscious but the wiggles will also be emphasized when viewed in perspective from the house.

Romantic

The romantic style is perhaps personified by the cottage garden, often appearing to have a simple and tender charm where roses, honeysuckle and lavender mingle with fruit and vegetables. Our current perception of a cottage garden is a glamorized version of a style that evolved from the need to survive on what could be grown on a small holding. Then and now the planting is insubstantial and only performs for a limited season. Romantic gardens tend to have curves, hidden seating, framed vistas and plants whose scent is seductive or nostalgic.

Natural

Natural gardens, now enjoying a resurgence of popularity, were originally the concept of the Victorian gardener William Robinson. Through the developed world, our current positive movement towards conservation has resulted in a style of wildflower gardening that mimics natural habitats, working with nature and with plants that would occur organically in these conditions.

Japanese

Japanese gardens fall into two distinct categories: the "borrowed" garden, a landscape garden that incorporates distant scenery as part of its design, and the "small courtyard" or "tea" garden, an enclosed space where carefully placed stones, gravel, trees and shrubs combine with lanterns and water basins. Space, illusion and the careful control of natural elements are part of the Japanese culture. They can be very effective in a small space and work well with modern or minimalist buildings.

Modern

Modern-style gardens can be very functional and are an antidote to the traditional English image. These are usually gardens in which Perspex (acrylic plastic), steel tubing or other modern material is used instead of traditional brick or timber. They might incorporate walls painted in strong contemporary colours that combine with plants in complementary or contrasting colours.

Following the Theme

Once you have decided on a style, you can begin to select plants to carry the theme through. Always do this with conviction, keeping in mind the effect that you want to create, rather than allowing yourself to be seduced by some pretty but inappropriate plant that you have just discovered in a catalogue.

Base your decisions on how the garden is going to be used. If it is unlikely that you (or the garden owner) will stroll down to the far end of the garden in winter, think of placing plants for winter interest near the house, where they can be enjoyed from an indoor window on a winter day. Similarly, scented plants should be placed where they will be most appreciated, such as surrounding a paved terrace or on top of a low retaining wall, where the scent will be nearer your nose as you pass.

Creating a Planting Plan

You may intend to plant the garden yourself, or you may ask a contractor or nurseryman to plant it for you, but in either case a detailed planting plan will be necessary. A planting plan is a working drawing—it will be taken onto the site, and each plant will be set out on the soil in the position indicated on the plan. Often this work takes place in the wind or rain, so the planting plan must be clear, legible and easy to understand. Plant names should all be written at the same angle, with spacing and numbers clearly indicated. If the garden is large, several smaller planting plans for small areas are more easily handled than one large sheet.

What to Include

The planting plan is drawn up on a simplified form of the garden layout plan. It shows, using symbols, the planting position and spread of every plant (after about five years' growth) that you intend to include in the garden, labelled with its precise Latin name (genus, species and cultivar or variety), correctly spelt, and the exact number of plants in any grouping. The plan will also include any existing plants, in their original positions or sited elsewhere. In the accompanying plant list, all the plants will be grouped according to category—tree, shrub, climber and so on—and then arranged alphabetically, with the precise number of plants required in each case. Since the objective of compiling a plant list is to enable you to place an order for the plants, it will be appreciated by the supplier or nursery if your list follows the same format as the catalogue pages. Most nursery catalogues categorize plants as follows:

- Trees
- Shrubs
- Climbers
- Roses
- Herbaceous perennials
- Ferns
- Bamboos and grasses

– Bulbs
– Annuals and half-hardies

The plan must be drawn up so that the positions, names and numbers of the plants are clear, legible and easily understood by whoever may be carrying out the planting. With so much information to communicate, it is always quite a challenge to produce a plan that is well labelled. In many text books this problem is circumvented using a key or number system in which, to identify a particular plant or plant grouping, the reader must consult a separate list. This approach is both tedious for whoever is studying the plan and difficult to follow when planting. It is far better to label each plant as near to its symbol as possible, ensuring that label lines do not cross.

The Stages Involved

Begin a rough draft of your planting plan, and try out ideas on a simplified version of your garden layout plan, perhaps also experimenting by drawing elevations to see the effect of contrasting heights. After you have finalized the selection and placement of all the plants you intend to use on a rough sheet, draw up the plan properly on a separate sheet. When all the graphic symbols are in place, carry out your labelling.

The easiest way of working up a planting plan is to start with the largest items (including the trees from the final garden layout plan), then the structural and key planting, working down gradually towards the smallest plants. The stages of planning the planting for a small garden shown in this chapter demonstrate the way the different elements can be built up. These stages are structural planting (including trees), key planting, decorative planting and herbaceous planting.

Structural Planting

Start with the structural plants (mainly trees and shrubs), and try to think through their seasonal effects. Consider the following questions:

– Are there any additional areas where you would like to see some permanent form?
– For these areas, would you like the plant or

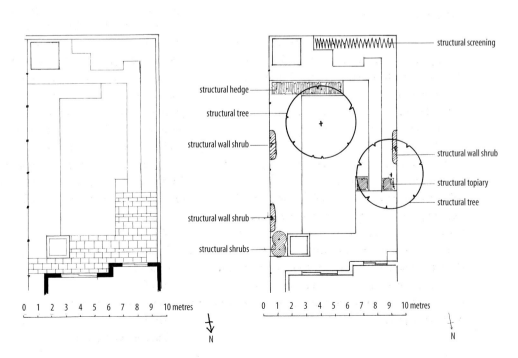

Small garden
A simplified garden layout. The horizontal plane (the garden) and the vertical plane (the house) will be linked once the structural planting is added.

Far right: structural plants (trees and shrubs) are the first to be put in place. The trees and topiary give important vertical emphasis to the space.

structural screening

structural hedge

structural tree

structural wall shrub

structural wall shrub

structural shrubs

structural wall shrub

structural topiary

structural tree

0 1 2 3 4 5 6 7 8 9 10 metres

0 1 2 3 4 5 6 7 8 9 10 metres

N

N

group of plants to be evergreen, or would you prefer a deciduous plant with a twiggy winter outline?

– Think about climbers and wall shrubs. Are there any parts of the garden that require these to emphasize the framework?

While developing the structural planting, remember to repeat plants across the garden diagonally. This repetition will help link one area to another, acting as a foil for the more transitory seasonal or colour groupings. It will also provide continuity and prevent a restless effect.

Try shading in the evergreen plants on the plan. This will remind you to look for a good balance of evergreen and deciduous plants, such as one-third of one type to two-thirds of the other. It will also help you in the next stage to position the more decorative shrubs, whose delicate foliage or pretty flowers may be enhanced against an evergreen backdrop.

Trees, when viewed from a distance, are arresting perpendiculars that link sky, house and garden. Choosing a tree or trees for a garden is always an exciting task; most of us will not plant many trees or see them mature during our lives, so the long-term effect and consequences (of shade, for instance) must be considered.

Trees and shrubs
The difference between a tree and a large shrub is often unclear, but for the most part a tree is a woody plant, evergreen or deciduous, that has had the lower branches removed at an early stage, resulting in a single clear main stem or trunk. A shrub has either several stems, or a main stem with branches along most of its length. The exceptions to this are multistemmed trees, which have two or even three main stems deliberately left for aesthetic effect. These can be very effective on a corner or to give a natural effect, the disadvantage being that as they mature, the leaf canopy becomes heavier and occasionally one of the stems or trunks breaks off, spoiling the effect and

outline shape. Occasionally a large shrub, having outgrown its allotted space, may become too dense, casting heavy shade onto the space beneath the branches. Consider the effect of removing several of the lower branches—this way, the large overgrown shrub may be turned into a tree with a single main stem or trunk.

Using existing trees
There may be existing trees in the garden, perhaps serving the purpose of screening or giving shade. The majority of trees mature slowly, and it may be wiser to improve the outline shape by tree surgery or by judicious thinning or pruning rather than removal or replacement. If the canopy of a mature tree is reduced by carefully removing up to 30 percent of its branches, more light will be admitted, often showing off the tree silhouette better and giving dappled, as opposed to dense, shade. Decisions on which limbs or branches to remove are best made when the tree is in active growth or full leaf, but the actual cutting or tree surgery should be left until growth subsides in late autumn or early winter. The offending branches can be clearly marked with paint and removed later. Dead branches should always be removed to prevent disease, decay, or injury.

Evergreen versus deciduous trees
Deciding between evergreen and deciduous trees may depend on whether something needs to be hidden or screened. Deciduous trees (those that shed their leaves in winter) will only be fully effective while leaves are in full growth. However, even a leafless tree in winter can interrupt and therefore dilute the full impact of what is hidden in summer. The eye will rest on what is in the foreground and often will not stray beyond. A line of deciduous trees can blur the vision of what lies beyond, as well as making it more difficult for neighbours to see into your property. There is usually a wider choice of deciduous trees, but if an evergreen variety is needed, the decision must be based not only on what tree is wanted but also on whether the leaves are glossy and light-reflective or matt and light-absorbent.

Choosing trees

Most trees live fifty to two hundred years or more, so your choice is important and must take into account both short-term and long-term effects. Consider the following points:

- Outline shape or form (for example, rounded, dome, pencil, weeping)
- Classification as deciduous or evergreen (this will depend on the desired effect and whether screening is needed)
- Leaf texture, shape and colour (including

rounded

The size of a tree and its outline shape are significant factors in choosing a tree.

upright or fastigiate

weeping

horizontal

decorative

texture or colour on the underside of foliage and whether the tree is early or late into leaf)
- Flower shape, colour and scent, and the time of flowering
- Berry or hip shape, colour and attractiveness to birds
- Trunk or stem bark type and colour
- Winter silhouette (if the tree is deciduous, this varies enormously)
- Size at maturity (among the most important aspects to consider)

Tree size

Large forest-type trees, such as beech, ash or oak, should only be considered if there is plenty of space and if you or the garden owner are prepared to wait for the trees to mature. If the garden backs onto a beech wood, for instance, a copper beech or a red oak might stand out against the native varieties beyond. Many of these trees will eventually have a spread of 30 m (100 ft.) or more, their intrinsic beauty being in their outline shape. If planted too close to a building or to each other, the effect will be lost. Choose a smaller tree, or group of trees, in preference to lopping off oversized branches and spoiling the outline shape. Large mature trees can be found but are heavy to lift and plant, need support by staking and are expensive.

Medium-sized trees are usually preferable for most gardens and tend to grow more rapidly. With a wide variety to choose from it is particularly important to consider all aspects when making your choice. In a small garden a medium-sized tree must have all the attributes to earn its keep. Try to see mature specimens in a park or botanical garden so that the different features can be compared. Research the origin of the tree to ensure that local conditions are suitable, and bear in mind that trees also have preferences for acid and alkaline conditions. When bulk is needed, perhaps at the end of a drive or to give height at the end of a garden, a group of three, five or more of the same variety will look more natural than a mixed group.

Small ornamental trees are useful when used singly as focal points in smaller gardens and can also be grouped together to give a formal or informal effect.

Buying and ordering trees

It is always wise to inspect a tree before you order or buy. Many trees are raised close together in rows, resulting in a deformed canopy which can take several years, if ever, to regain its classic outline shape. The tree, like many shrubs, may also be pot-bound or suckering from the base of the stem, or from where it has been grafted onto the parent stock. In their formative years all trees need staking to prevent wind rock until the roots spread and grip the soil. It is usually easier to order tree stakes and tree ties to be delivered at the same time.

Shrubs as structural plants

Shrubs must be solid or structural enough in character to form part of the framework of the garden. Flimsy leaves and spasmodic flowers will not give a feeling of permanence and security. Ultimate size must be considered, but a solid effect can be achieved with tall columns of Irish yew, low-clipped balls of box, or other structural plants such as *Mahonia* or *Choisya ternata*. To be effective, structural plants often need to be repeated, either formally as "exclamation marks" through a border or as informal singles or groups. Structural plants usually need to be evergreen to retain their effect.

Use structural plants to emphasize the pattern or shape of your garden layout. A group of five, nine or more low shrubs, all of the same type, can frame the corner of a border or can lead the eye around a circle or curve, acting as a perpetual contrast to the other more ephemeral planting.

Key Planting

Key plants are those that will provide important focal points in your garden, and these need to be identified next. These plants have strongly defined outlines and can be used occasionally or repeatedly for accent.

They will act as strong key elements on which the eye will rest before continuing to take in other plantings. Key plants should stand out from the rest of the plants with some distinctive quality, such as a strongly defined or contrasting shape, texture or colour. Key plants are often also structural, forming a link to the surrounding landscape, or they may act as pivots, emphasizing a change of direction in the hard landscaping.

Small garden

Key planting is added to the structural plants. The strongly defined shapes of these key plants will allow the eye to rest before taking in the other plantings.

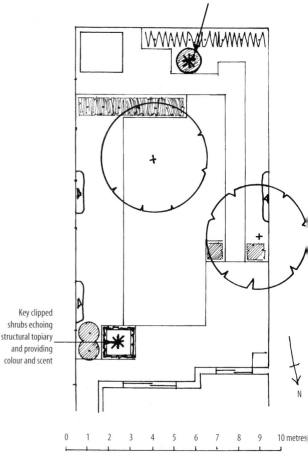

Key shrubs providing strongly defined shape, contrasting with hedges

Key clipped shrubs echoing structural topiary and providing colour and scent

0 1 2 3 4 5 6 7 8 9 10 metres

N

Key plants should be used sparingly in a garden or border. Use too many and they all vie for attention. Consider them like actors or actresses playing a starring role, not to be confused with the rest of the cast or chorus line.

Decorative Planting

Once the structural and key plantings are in place, more decorative elements can be identified. These are composed of shrubs and climbers chosen for a pretty outline or attractive flowers, foliage or berries. Use elevations to help you to visualize your ideas (see next page), bearing in mind the importance of contrasting shape and form, texture and colour.

Decorative plantings give balance and contrast to structural or key plantings and usually only demand attention for a short period of time. In working up your decorative plantings, it is helpful to consider four main points: leaf size, leaf shape, flower colour and time of flowering.

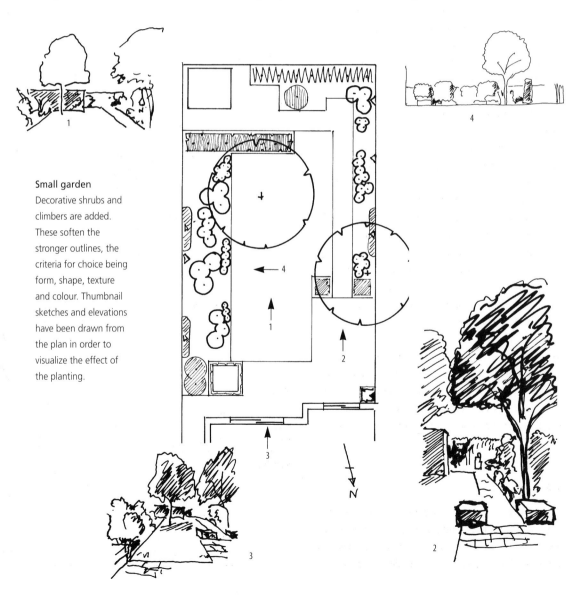

Small garden
Decorative shrubs and climbers are added. These soften the stronger outlines, the criteria for choice being form, shape, texture and colour. Thumbnail sketches and elevations have been drawn from the plan in order to visualize the effect of the planting.

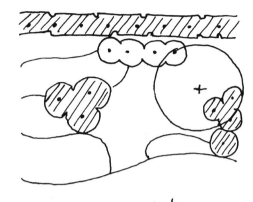

Planting plan

Drawing Elevations: It is helpful to test out planting proposals by using sketch elevations of details of the planting plan. A sketch elevation can be drawn by translating the approximate measurements of the mature plants into an imaginary view of them on the vertical plane. Fully developed elevation or section drawings can be made from the plan (see page 240), and used to supplement the information.

Elevation of a mixed border

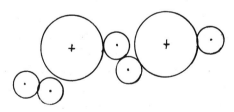

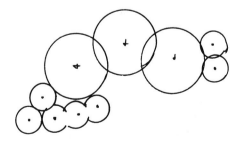

Planting proposal 1: When drawn in elevation, the scheme looked "spotty" and disjointed.

Planting proposal 2: An elevation of a scheme that uses the same plants, but in different numbers and positions, reveals that the massing of the plants is much better balanced.

Roses

For many people, roses epitomize the English gardening style. Since the 1950s there has been a surge of interest in the older roses, mainly brought about by the influence of the English rose-grower Graham Thomas. Through his books and the rose gardens he has created, old roses and their hybrids have replaced many of the hybrid teas and floribundas previously grown. Catalogues list myriad different varieties, seducing you with their names, photographs and descriptions but rarely pointing out their disadvantages.

A distinction should be made between climber and rambler roses. Ramblers are much more vigorous and, as they often reach 9 m (29.5 ft.) or more, are not recommended for house walls, because they would need hard pruning and tying into a framework of wire. They should be grown through trees or to cover an unsightly building; in the wrong place, their long summer growth could be a nuisance.

Climbers have much stiffer stems, larger flowers and smaller trusses than ramblers. Pruning and maintenance is much reduced, as flowers are borne on the framework of mature wood which is more or less permanent. When choosing a climber for a wall, consider the flower colour and how it will look against the stone, brick or other backdrop.

Try to build up a repertoire of reliable and high-performance plants that you are confident about using in your plans. The main points to look for are as follows:

- **Constitution**. For a rose to be worth its keep in any garden it should be healthy, and some are more prone than others to black spot, mildew and other disfiguring ailments.
- **Period of flowering**. Generally roses either flower once, perhaps with a spasmodic later "flush" or occasional flower. In Britain once-flowering roses generally flower in late spring, usually in May or early June, or in summer

from mid-June to the end of July. Other roses have recurrent or repeat flowering, and some flower almost continuously throughout the summer. In the United States the time and period of flowering depend on the area. Several British rose growers have suppliers in the United States.
- **Hips**. Some roses have attractive hips, making them useful in the autumn border or as features in the wild garden.
- **Foliage**. Ranging from glossy green through to glaucous and reddish tones, foliage can be effective even when the flowers have faded.
- **Other uses**. Other useful types of rose are ground cover or procumbent roses, useful near terraces or at the front of a border, and hedging roses, such as *Rosa* 'Fru Dagmar Hastrup', whose flowers turn to colourful hips in autumn provided they are not deadheaded.

Herbaceous Planting

Herbaceous plants are generally, but not always, smaller in scale than the decorative shrub plantings. In a mixed border they look most effective planted in drifts, weaving in and out of structural and decorative shrubs to hold the composition together and provide some movement. Herbaceous plants vary enormously in shape, texture and colour; they can be strikingly architectural or rounded and soft in texture.

Avoid using too many different types of plants, which can result in borders that look restless and unbalanced. To give continuity, repeat certain important groupings. To help you decide which to select from the huge range available, herbaceous plants can be divided into those that give broad-brush effects (long-lasting shrubs and perennials) and those that create fleeting effects (short-season perennials and bulbs which will give flashes of seasonal delight).

Broad-brush effects

Broad-brush plants provide not only large drifts of long-lasting colour but also attractive foliage. Some

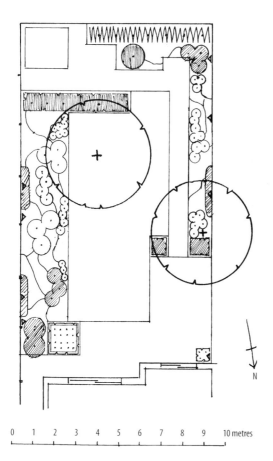

0   1   2   3   4   5   6   7   8   9   10 metres

Small garden: Herbaceous drifts and infill plants have been added. These hold the structural composition together and provide movement.

Fleeting effects

Fleeting effects create occasional interest or highlights that interrupt the longer-lasting broad-brush plants, providing finishing touches that enliven a border or group. They give a flash of seasonal interest and prevent plantings from being monotonous. Bulbs, annuals, half-hardies and short-lived perennials fall into this category and can be divided up seasonally. For example:

- Spring: snowdrops, tulips
- Early summer: lupins, poppies
- Late summer: cannas, tobacco plants (*Nicotiana*), lilies, gladioli
- Autumn: colchicum, cyclamen

Balancing the broad-brush effect with incidents of colour results in an ever-changing seasonal canvas that rarely fails to delight. Even in a small garden, broad-brush plants should be arranged in bold groups of uneven numbers, say five, nine, eleven or fifteen of one plant, giving a more natural and restful effect. Fleeting plants can be used in smaller groups of, say, three or five. Repeat the groups diagonally across the garden, weaving them through structural and key plants until the planting plan fits tightly together rather like a jigsaw, leaving no space, when mature, for uninvited guests such as weeds.

are chosen for their foliage, with any flowers being an incidental extra. The diversity of their outline, colour and texture allows you to counterbalance plants, contrasting spears of iris or crocosmia with the silver filigree of artemisia, for instance, or placing arching blades of grass against the glossy foliage of aconitum or the soft velvet of *Stachys byzantina*. Try to use plants that contrast both in the way they look and their texture. Herbaceous plants should be chosen for their varied outline shapes. Incorporate verticals, such as foxgloves or hollyhocks; horizontals, such as sedums and achilleas; spikes, such as iris or hemerocallis; and mounds, such as agapanthus or *Alchemilla mollis*.

Drawing up the Planting Plan

1. Tape down the final garden layout plan over a graph-paper backing sheet on the drawing board. Tape a fresh sheet of tracing paper over the layout plan, then trace over the house and garden boundaries and any areas that will contain plantings (including containers such as window boxes or pots). Use a sharp pencil or pen (the latter will be easier to read through subsequent sheets of

continues on page 216

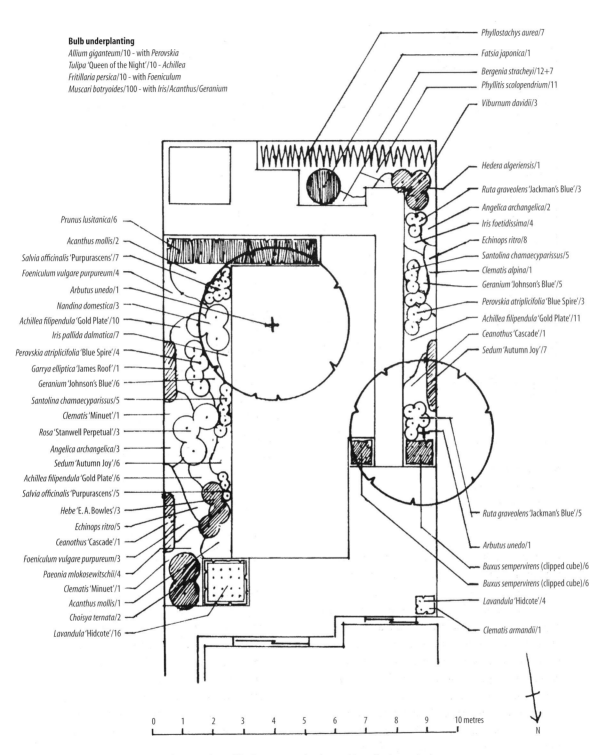

Bulb underplanting
Allium giganteum/10 - with *Perovskia*
Tulipa 'Queen of the Night'/10 - *Achillea*
Fritillaria persica/10 - with *Foeniculum*
Muscari botryoides/100 - with *Iris/Acanthus/Geranium*

Phyllostachys aurea/7
Fatsia japonica/1
Bergenia stracheyi/12+7
Phyllitis scolopendrium/11
Viburnum davidii/3

Hedera algeriensis/1
Ruta graveolens 'Jackman's Blue'/3
Angelica archangelica/2
Iris foetidissima/4
Echinops ritro/8
Santolina chamaecyparissus/5
Clematis alpina/1
Geranium 'Johnson's Blue'/5
Perovskia atriplicifolia 'Blue Spire'/3
Achillea filipendula 'Gold Plate'/11
Ceanothus 'Cascade'/1
Sedum 'Autumn Joy'/7

Prunus lusitanica/6
Acanthus mollis/2
Salvia officinalis 'Purpurascens'/7
Foeniculum vulgare purpureum/4
Arbutus unedo/1
Nandina domestica/3
Achillea filipendula 'Gold Plate'/10
Iris pallida dalmatica/7
Perovskia atriplicifolia 'Blue Spire'/4
Garrya elliptica 'James Roof'/1
Geranium 'Johnson's Blue'/6
Santolina chamaecyparissus/5
Clematis 'Minuet'/1
Rosa 'Stanwell Perpetual'/3
Angelica archangelica/3
Sedum 'Autumn Joy'/6
Achillea filipendula 'Gold Plate'/6
Salvia officinalis 'Purpurascens'/5
Hebe 'E. A. Bowles'/3
Echinops ritro/5
Ceanothus 'Cascade'/1
Foeniculum vulgare purpureum/3
Paeonia mlokosewitschii/4
Clematis 'Minuet'/1
Acanthus mollis/1
Choisya ternata/2
Lavandula 'Hidcote'/16

Ruta graveolens 'Jackman's Blue'/5
Arbutus unedo/1
Buxus sempervirens (clipped cube)/6
Buxus sempervirens (clipped cube)/6
Lavandula 'Hidcote'/4
Clematis armandii/1

0 1 2 3 4 5 6 7 8 9 10 metres

N

Small garden: The planting plan, complete with plant names, planting positions (for trees, shrubs and climbers) and numbers of plants that are required. The numbers of each plant, or how many are in each group, are critical as the same plant may be used in several different positions.

tracing paper). This should be a simplified version of the layout plan; avoid putting in all the detail so that you leave room for the plant details.

2. Remove the garden layout plan from the drawing board, and make sure the newly traced sheet (which will become the planting plan) is firmly stuck down. You will work up the planting plan on this sheet in draft form and transfer it later onto a final sheet of tracing paper.

3. Refer to the site appraisal (see page 62) to remind yourself of existing conditions, such as soil type, aspect and so on, and to help you define the function of different planted areas.

4. Begin the draft plan working in pencil, drawing shapes freehand. Start by drawing in any existing plants that you intend to retain, referring back to the symbols on pages 74–75. Label existing shrubs or groups of herbaceous plants (for example, "Existing *Iris foetidissima*: 4").

5. Now draw in the main structural plants that you require for the plan (some of which will already have been identified on your garden layout plan), stating how many plants you require in each case. When planning a hedge, check a reference book for the recommended spacing between each plant, indicating with a dot the exact planting position of each. Do not forget to include any structural climbers or wall shrubs.

6. Decide on the key plants, then draw them in and label them.

7. Using a blunt pencil, shade in the evergreen plants.

8. Start to develop elevations (see page 212) for each planting area, to help you first contrast shape and form, then texture and colour. You can experiment with different ideas as you develop the plan further.

These elevations can be drawn either on the same sheet of tracing paper, if you have room, or in a notebook. Although they are intended to be experimental, it is important that they are drawn to scale, if only approximately.

9. Use the elevation sketches to help you decide on the decorative plants. Draw these in on the draft plan and label them.

10. Developing the elevations still further, decide on the herbaceous plants, broad-brush or fleeting, that you want for each area, designing these in drifts to flow around and between the structural and decorative planting.

11. When your draft plan is completed, check that you have a good balance of evergreen and deciduous plants, that there is a succession of interest in the garden, that you have repeated groups of plants diagonally across the garden and that the chosen plants are suitable for the site conditions.

12. When content with the draft plan, place it underneath a further sheet of tracing paper and stick it down. You are now ready to draw up the final planting plan on this new sheet. Remember to leave space for your information panel and title block. Your plant list will occupy the information panel. Trace over the draft plan and draw (in pencil or ink) all the plants, using the appropriate symbols. On this same sheet, label each plant (as shown in the examples on pages 215, 218 & 219). Give the full botanical name and, in each case, the number of plants in each group, even if there is only one plant. You may wish to use labels cut from a printout generated by your computer. These look very professional but are also time-consuming to cut out and stick onto the plan.

13. If you have space, your final planting plan could show an elevation. This will need to be titled, showing the view from where it will be seen but there is no need to label the plants themselves, as this information is on the planting plan.

14. At the top of the information panel, before the plant list, it is sometimes helpful to include a note on the reasoning behind your choice of plants, such as the style or colour combination that you are trying to achieve. List the plants according to category (trees, shrubs, climbers and so on), and arrange them in alphabetical order within each category. Give the full botanical name of each plant and the number of plants in each group, even if there is only one plant. When there are several groups of the same plant, they should be subtotalled, as shown on this page and on the planting list of the model plan on page 218. This information should be put onto the information panel, either handwritten or as a printout from your computer in the same style as the rest of the plan.

15. Fill in the title block information, remembering to include the north point and the scale to which you have drawn the plan.

16. After double-checking that you have included all the necessary information, remove the planting plan from the drawing board.

17. Keep the tracing-paper original plan safe. The planting plan will be invaluable both for ordering your plants and for placing them in their allocated positions on the soil. You may need to refer to it at a later stage if any alterations need to be made to the final planting plan. Make at least two copies of it, either dyeline prints or photo-copies. You can add colour to one of these.

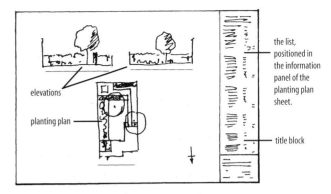

elevations

planting plan

the list, positioned in the information panel of the planting plan sheet.

title block

The completed sheet showing the planting plan, elevations and plant list.

Small garden: The completed plan sheet for this garden includes the planting plan and two elevations. The planting list is positioned in the information panel of the plan sheet, giving the details needed to allow the garden to be planted according to the plan. If space on a plan is limited, use a separate sheet of paper for the plant list.

		QUANTITY	SUBTOTAL
TREES	~~~~~	2	2
	~~	1 + 2	3
	~~	1	1
	TOTAL		6
SHRUBS			
	~~	2 + 4	6
	~~	2	2
	~~	2 + 3	5
	~~	1	1
	TOTAL		14
CLIMBERS			
	~~	2	2
	~~	3	3
	TOTAL		5
HERBACEOUS			
	~~	1	1
	~~	4 + 5	9
	~~	2	2
	~~	5	5
	TOTAL		17
BULBS			
	~~	25	25
	~~	20 + 10 + 10	50
	~~	10	10
	~~	10	10
	TOTAL		95

The plant list

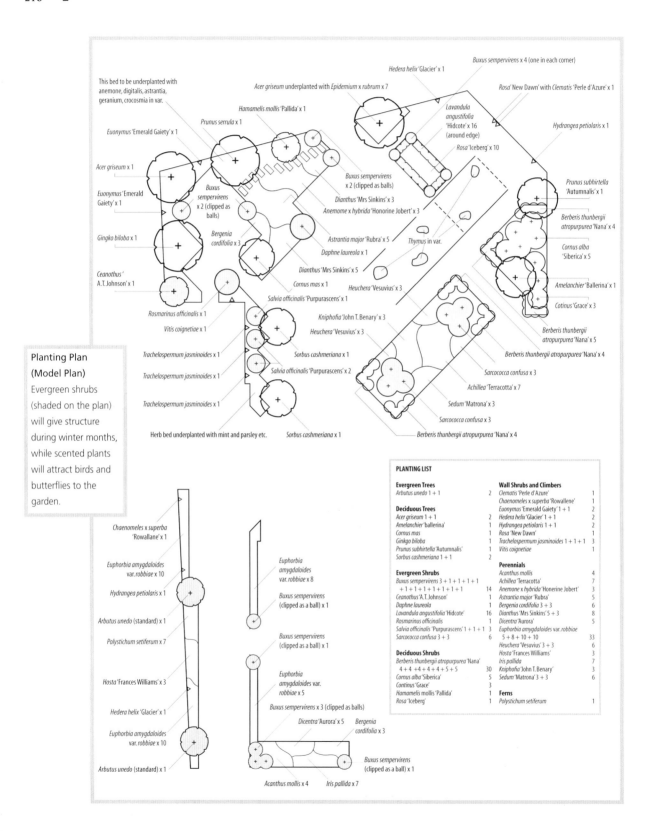

PLANTING LIST

Evergreen Trees	
Arbutus unedo 1 + 1	2

Deciduous Trees	
Acer griseum 1 + 1	2
Amelanchier 'ballerina'	1
Cornus mas	1
Ginkgo biloba	1
Prunus subhirtella 'Autumnalis'	1
Sorbus cashmeriana 1 + 1	2

Evergreen Shrubs	
Buxus sempervirens 3 + 1 + 1 + 1 + 1 + 1 + 1 + 1 + 1 + 1 + 1 + 1 + 1	14
Ceanothus 'A.T. Johnson'	1
Daphne laureola	1
Lavandula angustifolia 'Hidcote'	16
Rosmarinus officinalis	1
Salvia officinalis 'Purpurascens' 1 + 1 + 1	3
Sarcococca confusa 3 + 3	6

Deciduous Shrubs	
Berberis thunbergii atropurpurea 'Nana' 4 + 4 + 4 + 4 + 4 + 5 + 5	30
Cornus alba 'Siberica'	5
Continus 'Grace'	3
Hamamelis mollis 'Pallida'	1
Rosa 'Iceberg'	

Wall Shrubs and Climbers	
Clematis 'Perle d'Azure'	1
Chaenomeles x superba 'Rowallene'	1
Euonymus 'Emerald Gaiety' 1 + 1	2
Hedera helix 'Glacier' 1 + 1	2
Hydrangea petiolaris 1 + 1	2
Rosa 'New Dawn'	1
Trachelospermum jasminoides 1 + 1 + 1	3
Vitis coignetiae	1

Perennials	
Acanthus mollis	4
Achillea 'Terracotta'	7
Anemone x hybrida 'Honerine Jobert'	3
Astrantia major 'Rubra'	5
Bergenia cordifolia 3 + 3	6
Dianthus 'Mrs Sinkins' 5 + 3	8
Dicentra 'Aurora'	5
Euphorbia amygdaloides var. robbiae 5 + 8 + 10 + 10	33
Heuchera 'Vesuvius' 3 + 3	6
Hosta 'Frances Williams'	3
Iris pallida	7
Kniphofia 'John T. Benary'	3
Sedum 'Matrona' 3 + 3	6

Ferns	
Polystichum setiferum	1

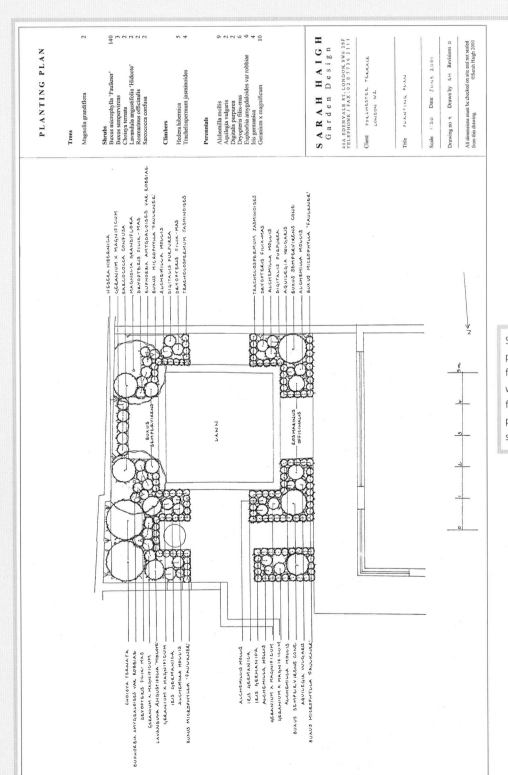

Sculptural evergreens provide a strong framework against which a succession of flowering perennials provide a long season of summer interest.

Above: Instead of being removed, an old tree may be clipped to form a focal point. Without the tree as a vertical feature, this garden would be less interesting.

Above: Clipped box "tables" give structure to this border. The effect can be achieved by using four green box plants, one at each corner, with a single golden box plant in the centre. To clip the central mound, use an upturned hanging basket as a guide.

Above: A yew hedge provides a matt backdrop to the glossy, golden foliage plants. The clipped box balls and yew buttresses define the structure.

Above: Box and clipped Irish yew frame the planting in this traditional rose garden. The fountain provides a central feature as well as a cooling influence.

Above: The muted foliage colours unite with the glaucous foliage of columnar Italian cypress trees. The beech hedge surround is a foil for the rest of the planting.

Above: The deeply veined leaves of the rodgersia, dissected leaves of the fern and cream-edged leaves of the hosta associate well together. The underplanting of *Saxifraga umbrosa* looks attractive at all times of the year.

Above: Provided they are not too rampant, shrubs such as golden privet can act as a host to climbers. Once the flowers have faded, the silvery seed heads of *Clematis tangutica* provide additional autumnal interest.

Above: In this damp and shady border, the strong foliage contrasts of a large-leafed hosta and rodgersia are highlighted by slim blades of the variegated grass *Phalaris arundinacea* 'Picta'. Flower colour is of secondary importance here.

Above: Ferns and hostas are congenial companions, enjoying similar soil and aspect. The intriguingly twisted, white variegated foliage of *Hosta undulata* var. *undulata* draws attention to the change in level.

Above: This waterside planting relies on contrasting shape and texture of foliage as opposed to flower colour.

Above: A circular theme is explored with pool, spouting urn, and circular clipped evergreen oak, *Quercus ilex*. The poolside planting of *Iris pallida* 'Variegata' and *Primula vialli* brings light and colour into the scene.

Above: This garden stream has been designed and planted for a natural effect. The water flows over a series of shallow steps and the small structure above the waterfall acts as a focal point.

Right: Natural water is a bonus to be exploited in any garden. The huge leaves and flowering spikes of *Gunnera manicata* depend on a damp environment to perform well.

Left: This garden follows an English cottage garden theme with roses, delphiniums and foxgloves. Although very pretty, many of these plants have a fleeting flowering season.

Above: The symbolic and studied placement of rocks and trees and absence of colour evoke calm in this Japanese garden.

Above: A "hot colour" border is set off by the red backdrop. Use of these vibrant colours can bring a dark area to life.

Above: The symbolic and studied placement of rocks and trees and absence of colour evoke calm in this Japanese garden.

Above: Summer colour is achieved in this wide border by using perennials; they may need staking, particularly if the site is affected by wind.

Above: The bold-coloured dahlias and cannas act as accents among the gently moving grasses.

Above: A decorative stone urn is framed by blue catmint and the dark red foliage of the *Rosmarinus* 'Rosemary Rose'). The blue tones of *Hosta* 'Halcyon' frame the planting and play up the colour scheme.

Right: The hot colours of red-hot pokers, half-hardy dahlias and cannas are cooled by the surrounding green foliage.

Left: Although the climbing rose that covers this arch has a slightly bluish tone, it is not strong enough to clash with the hot colour planting beyond. Nasturtiums and other annuals mix through the perennial planting.

Above: This two-colour border concentrates on blue and apricot. The spikes of the kniphofia complement the rounded forms of the other plants.

Above: The foliage of the large-leafed ornamental rhubarb, *Rheum palmatum*, and the feathery foliage of the bronze fennel provide a contrast in texture.

Left: Dark red leaves of the smoke bush, *Cotinus coggygria*, are a foil for the orange flowers of *Crocosmia* 'Emily Mackenzie'.

Above: In this courtyard garden, yellow- and white-flowering plants are set off by a clipped box hedge. Topiary in pots adds interest around the pool area.

Above: The large glaucous foliage of *Macleaya* x *kewensis* and the deep red leaves of *Cotinus coggygria* 'Royal Purple' are a foil for the tall spikes of *Eremurus* 'Shelford Hybrids'.

Above: The lower petals of *Monarda* 'Croftway Pink' match the dark purple foliage of *Cotinus coggygria* 'Royal Purple'. These purple tones will contrast later with the sealing wax orange hips of *Rosa moyesii* 'Geranium'.

Above: Spikes of *Eremurus bungei* (*E. stenophyllus*) or fox-tail lily draw the eye to the variety for plants in this border. The rampant deep blue herbaceous *Clematis heracleifolia* needs supporting at an early stage, although it is not a climber.

Right: Although the pale flowers are set off by the dark foliage, the planting is too busy to be effective. The large-leafed hosta in the background will be more evident when some of the taller flowering spikes are removed.

Left: Old-fashioned roses and alliums are a useful partnership. After the flowers have faded, allium heads still look decorative.

Left: The strap-like leaves of the phormium are an effective contrast to the rounded leaves of *Hosta sieboldiana*. Dark foliage and flowers help show up the scented flowers of *Rhododendron luteum*.

Above: A very tactile plant, beloved of children, this grass, *Pennisetum villosum*, stands out against other plants until late autumn.

Above: Flowering grasses bring life and movement to a border in summer and early autumn. These flowerheads create a fountain-like effect but be careful as some grasses are invasive.

Above: Although not hardy except in warmer areas, the glaucous and finely dissected foliage and bronze flower spikes of *Melianthus major* makes a statement in any border. Performing later in the growing season, the foliage will survive until the first frosts.

Above: Easily grown in sunny areas and tolerant of poor but well-drained soil conditions, the architectural *Euphorbia wulfenii* (spurge) is long lasting. When cutting, avoid coming into contact with the latex-like sap—it is a notorious skin irritant.

Above: The elegant pointed pink petals of the lily-flowering tulip *T.* 'China Pink' bring out similar tones in the pink blossoming *Prunus tenella* 'Fire Hill'.

Above: The delicate, dissected foliage of *Acer palmatum* is outstanding in autumn.

Left: Foliage that develops good autumn colour should be included in any garden. Here, the leaves of *Vitis coignetiae* reflect the rust tones of the brick wall.

Chapter 5

Visualizing and Constructing the Design

At the end of the process of creating the garden design and planting plan, you should have a very clear idea of how the garden will look once it is built. However, it may be helpful for both you and others involved to see a further visual or an artist's impression of how the finished work will look. Although flat, two-dimensional plans have their limitations, they can be enhanced with colour or tone to represent light and shadow. Further drawings will explain your intentions and are helpful when read alongside the plan.

Axonometric, or measured, drawings are constructed from the garden layout and planting plan. While working up these drawings, anything you have overlooked (such as the number and width of treads and risers in a flight of steps) will soon become apparent. This is a useful method for double-checking any inaccuracies and will give you an opportunity to fill in any missing details on the garden layout plan.

Drawing sections of a garden will give you a view of the plan that can be investigated at any stage of the work and might be particularly useful when you are developing the preliminary garden plan. Sections and elevations are useful because they help to clarify the vertical elements, but they do not show how all the different planes (the garden floor, walls and any overhead features) work together as a unified whole. For this you need to create three-dimensional drawings, such as an axonometric drawing or photographic overlay.

Photographic overlays are particularly effective because they instantly relate any new proposals to the existing site. In this way they can help to give the new design a credibility that is rarely matched by other visuals, such as artistic impressions, which can have an unreal quality about them.

Once your plans have been agreed on, the site can be prepared, building work can begin, the plants can be brought in and planted, and thoughts can turn to maintenance and future development.

Enhancing the Plan

Some excellent effects can be achieved by applying tone, and it is fun to experiment until you find a method that suits your particular drawings. Colour is enormously helpful in bringing a plan or visuals to life. What you use may well depend on the available media and your time.

Using Colour

When choosing your colours in whatever medium, try to select earthy or natural tones that include a wide range of browns, greens and greys. Much of your hard landscaping will be in shades of brown or grey, and a variety of greens will help you depict variety in your plant selection. A greyish purple can be very useful for shadow effects.

You may already have a range of crayons, felt-tips or watercolours, and perhaps you only need to buy one or two more shades to extend your colour range. It is worth considering several options to see which suits your style.

Colour applied directly onto tracing paper does not usually reprint, so you will need to apply it to a copy of your drawing. It is wise to have two or three copies made so that you can experiment. You may have your work reproduced as a dyeline print or photocopy, choosing a slightly heavier paper, perhaps with a finish or texture that will look effective when coloured. Shiny surfaces can be used, but they do not absorb crayon, felt-tips or watercolours readily. If using watercolours, specialist watercolour paper is recommended, but often the reproduced print lines will not adhere properly to heavier papers. Experiment before making up your mind.

Coloured Crayons or Pencils

These can be anything from a child's set of primary

colours to an extensive artist's range. Some manufacturers supply a good selection in packs of about eight or twelve earthy colours. Alternatively, by selecting your crayons individually you can build up your own range, concentrating mainly on browns, greys and greens, and including yellow, red and blue to enliven the more muted shades.

When applying colour, always try to work in one direction, not pressing too heavily. To obtain an area of regular well-blended lines, a good effect can be achieved by supporting your crayon or pencil against the set square, parallel motion or T-square and moving this gradually down your sheet as you draw a series of lines in one direction. Aim to build up colour intensity gradually rather than applying it heavily when you begin.

Mixing two colours can create a realistic effect. Brown could be used in conjunction with red or yellow to illustrate brick, a light grey and dark grey could be combined to show paving, and a light bluish green and darker green could indicate plants or areas of grass.

Try testing out these mixtures of colour beforehand on a separate sheet of paper. When you like a particular combination, note down the crayon reference numbers so that you will remember them.

Felt-Tip or Marker Pens

These are also available in a wide colour range. Marker pens, with their wider tips, are useful for covering a larger area in a single stroke. They too should be used in a single direction, pushed against the ruler, parallel motion or set square. If the colours are water-soluble they may bleed into each other. Practice is required to apply the colour evenly, and at the end of each stroke it is best to lift the felt-tip to avoid a heavier intensity at one end. If you persevere with this medium you should be able to achieve some good effects.

Watercolours

These can produce delightful effects, but the amount of water used tends to make normal paper buckle, so heavier paper (or watercolour paper) is recommended. Again, take time choosing and mixing your colours, and use a variety of good-quality brushes—perhaps a thick one for covering areas of lawn or paving, a fine one for detailed areas and a short, firm brush for effects such as flowers or shadow. When mixing colours try not to use too much water to avoid making the paper buckle.

Applying Tone and Rendering Texture

A quick and effective way of giving textural interest to a drawing is by producing a rubbing. You simply lay the dyeline print or photocopy of the plan over an embossed surface (sandpaper, an old book cover, a briefcase) and, using a soft pencil, rub over the area of your plan or drawing that you want to give texture.

It is also possible to render onto tracing paper if you are using a thick or good-quality sheet combined with a soft, dark lead pencil, such as 5B. For a drawing on tracing paper, always apply the lead finish to the reverse side so that it does not smudge on the surface. The lead can then be spread, if required, by rubbing it lightly with your finger or a paper tissue. This treatment is particularly effective for shadow effects. If you vary the pressure you can indicate the light direction.

Shadow can be added to a plan to give it a three-dimensional quality and to bring it to life. To achieve this, choose a realistic position for the sun, and determine the length of the shadow by the angle of the sun (as shown on page 234). Lightly mark the areas in pencil that would be cast in shadow, and hatch them with lines.

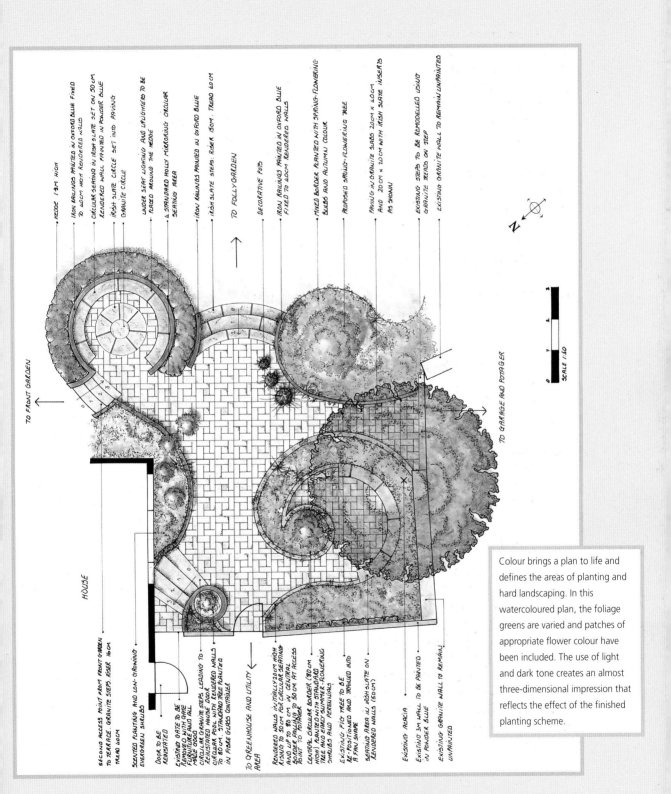

HEDGE 1.2M HIGH

IRON RAILINGS PAINTED IN OXFORD BLUE FIXED TO 60CM HIGH RENDERED WALLS

CIRCULAR SEATING IN IRISH SLATE SET ON 50 CM RENDERED WALL PAINTED IN POLDER BLUE

IRISH SLATE CIRCLE SET INTO PAVING

GRANITE CIRCLE

UNDER SEAT LIGHTING AND UPLIGHTER TO BE PLACED AROUND THE HEDGE

4 STANDARD HOLLY MIRRORING CIRCULAR SEATING AREA

IRON RAILINGS PAINTED IN OXFORD BLUE

IRISH SLATE STEPS RISER 15CM, TREAD 60CM

TO FOLLY GARDEN

DECORATIVE POTS

IRON RAILINGS PAINTED IN OXFORD BLUE FIXED TO 60CM RENDERED WALLS

MIXED BORDER PLANTED WITH SPRING-FLOWERING BULBS AND AUTUMN COLOUR

PROPOSED SPRING-FLOWERING TREE

PAVING IN GRANITE SLABS 20CM x 60CM AND 20CM x 20CM WITH IRISH SLATE INSERTS AS SHOWN

EXISTING STEPS TO BE REMODELLED USING GRANITE TREADS ON STEP

EXISTING GRANITE WALL TO REMAIN UNPAINTED

TO GARKAGE AND POTAGER

TO FRONT GARDEN

HOUSE

SECOND ACCESS POINT FROM FRONT GARDEN

TO TERRACE. GRANITE STEPS, RISER 16CM TREAD 60CM

SCENTED PLANTING AND LOW-GROWING EVERGREEN SHRUBS

DOOR TO BE REINSTATED

EXISTING GATE TO BE REMOVED WITH GATE FURNITURE AND MADE GOOD

CIRCULAR GRANITE STEPS LEADING TO REINSTATED HOUSE DOOR

CIRCULAR POOL WITH RENDERED WALLS TO 80 CM. STANDARD TREE PLANTED IN FIXED GLASS CONTAINER

TO GREENHOUSE AND UTILITY AREA

RENDERED WALLS INITIALLY 120M HIGH RISING TO 30CM FOR CIRCULAR SEATING AND UP TO 80 CM IN CENTRAL BORDER GIVING 50 CM AT ACCESS POINT TO POTAGER

CENTRAL CIRCULAR BORDER (180CM HIGH) PLANTED WITH STANDARD TREE AND EARLY SUMMER-FLOWERING SHRUBS AND PERENNIALS

EXISTING FIG TREE TO BE RE-POSITIONED AND TRAINED INTO A FAN SHAPE

SEATING AREA IN IRISH SLATE ON RENDERED WALLS (50CM)

EXISTING ACACIA

EXISTING 3M WALL TO BE PAINTED IN POLDER BLUE

EXISTING GRANITE WALL TO REMAIN UNPAINTED

SCALE 1:50

N

Colour brings a plan to life and defines the areas of planting and hard landscaping. In this watercoloured plan, the foliage greens are varied and patches of appropriate flower colour have been included. The use of light and dark tone creates an almost three-dimensional impression that reflects the effect of the finished planting scheme.

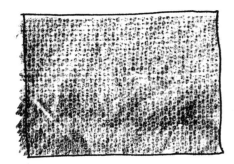

Texture can be created by placing a piece of paper over hardboard, and rubbing over an area with a soft (5B) pencil.

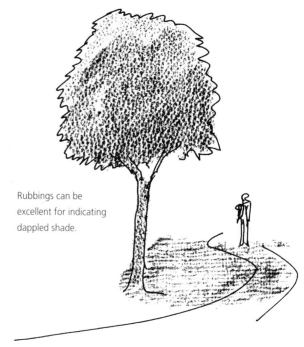

Rubbings can be excellent for indicating dappled shade.

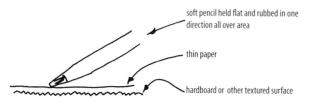

soft pencil held flat and rubbed in one direction all over area

thin paper

hardboard or other textured surface

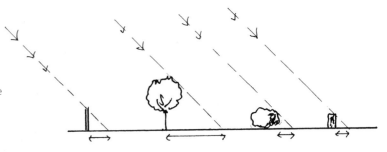

When the sun is shining down at an angle of 45°, the shadow cast by an object is equal in length to its height.

Choose a realistic sun position (shining from the south in the northern hemisphere, the north in the southern hemisphere) and mark the extremities of the shadows in pencil.

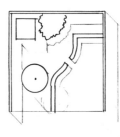

Hatch in the areas in shadow and then remove the pencil construction lines. To complete the drawing, emphasize the outlines of the objects, as shown.

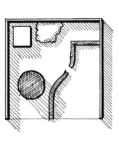

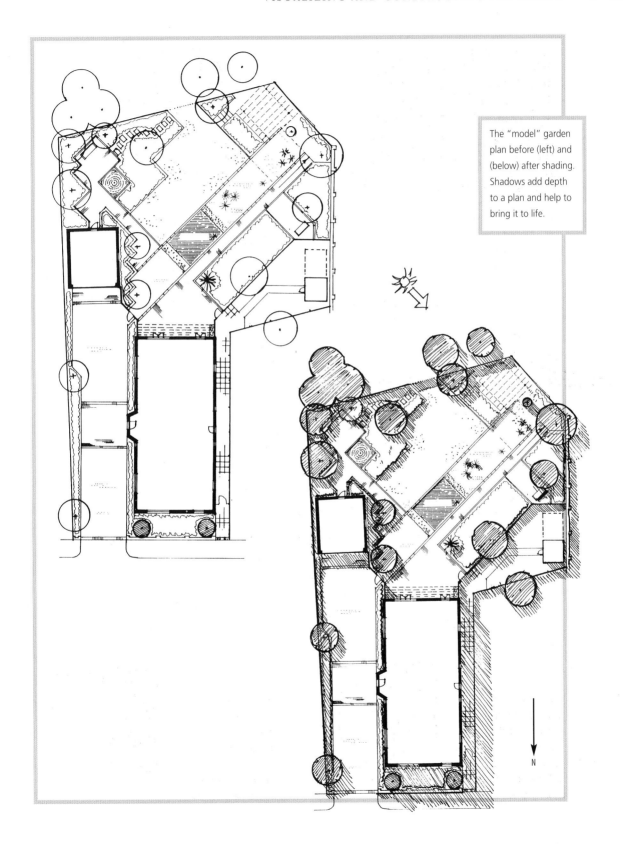

The "model" garden plan before (left) and (below) after shading. Shadows add depth to a plan and help to bring it to life.

N

Using Photographs

Cameras, whether film or digital, are useful working tools. It is worth considering that although computers and digital cameras offer the designer a lot of scope, they do tend to short-cut the hands-on process that will give you closer contact with the actual business of design.

A photographic overlay is a freehand drawing showing proposed changes to a garden. It is created on tracing paper stuck down over an enlarged photograph of the existing site and is a simple and quick method of showing the site before and after the redesign. This type of quick sketch can produce a striking and easily understood impression of your intentions. These drawings are simple to set up, very effective and do not involve creating time-consuming perspective charts. This technique is an easy method of creating perspective drawings of your intended ideas, and, when used earlier in the design process, can be a useful method in helping you to decide which views to frame and which to screen.

Photographic overlays will enable you to "see" proposed views of any area of the garden (from the house to the garden, from the garden back to the house or from the house into the garden beyond, for instance).

A photograph (above) of the existing garden. A scale rule is used to find an approximate scale for the vertical and horizontal features using the measurements taken on site. For example, at the point measured, the brick wall, which is 2.5 m (8 ft.) high, appears at a scale of 1:20. (Further back, where the gate is, the scale will be considerably less.) It is not essential to establish these scales, as you may be able to draw in proposed features by eye, but they can be useful where accuracy is important (for the bench shown in the next drawing, for instance).

Right: The completed overlay showing the proposed new elements, together with the existing items that are being retained.

"Before and after": A sketch on tracing paper laid over the "before" photograph shows the site transformed. Note how the tree in the neighbour's garden has been retained as an integral part of the new design and this shows through the tracing paper.

Creating a Photographic Overlay

1. Study the garden layout plan and choose an area to illustrate. This could be a vertical element, such as a trellis, pergola, arbour, statue, urn, trees, border or even a garden shed. Lawns, paths and pools can also be shown, but as they are on the ground plane, they look less effective.

2. Look at the photographs that you took when doing the site survey (see Chapter 1). Choose the most suitable ones, either a single shot or a panoramic view. If the prints are small, have them enlarged as black-and-white or colour prints, or on a photocopier or scanner.

3. With masking tape, stick the photos down onto the drawing board using the graph-paper backing sheet as a guide to align them.

4. Using a scale rule, try to find an approximate scale for some of the horizontals or verticals in your photographs. These may be, for instance, a brick wall at 2 m (6.6 ft.) high (remember that by counting the number of brick courses, you can arrive at the overall height), a pergola at 3 m (9.8 ft.) high or a garden shed at 3 m (9.8 ft.) high by 6 m (19.7 ft.) wide. Note down the nearest approximate scale.

5. Over each photograph stick down A4 (8.5 × 11 in.) tracing paper.

6. Check back to the layout plan. Note how high and wide the proposed horizontal and vertical elements will be in the area of the photograph—perhaps steps, walls, pergolas and arches.

7. On the tracing-paper overlay, mark the position of the four corners of each photograph. This will help you to position the overlay later, once it has been reproduced.

8. Using a pencil and your chosen scale, pinpoint these dimensions on your tracing-paper overlay.

9. Draw in the proposed elements using a pen and varying the thickness of line to bring the sketch to life.

10. Trace, if you wish, any existing items that are being retained, such as patio doors or trees.

11. Title and date each sheet, and if possible, have it copied either onto tracing paper or onto a clear acetate sheet.

12. With glue, adhesive tape or staples, fix your "after" overlay over the "before" photograph. You will now be able to see the effect of your proposals.

Mood Boards

A mood board can be helpful in identifying the type of mood, style and look you are aiming to achieve in your new garden design. A form of visual stimulus, it is usually a large board covered with images that is designed to represent a mood, atmosphere or feeling. Often used in interior and architectural design, a mood board lends itself well to garden design and can be a very effective tool to explain design ideas.

Although usually used as a presentation tool by the designer, the person for whom the garden is being designed may also prepare a board. This often amounts to a collage of different ideas taken from magazines or journals to show the designer what type of garden they would like to have. A mood board is usually worked up after the garden layout and planting plans are complete and presented with them as an explanatory visual. A mood board can also be used before firming up on the design, as a means of establishing mutual goals between the designer and the garden owner in pictorial form.

A mood board can help to illustrate some proposed planting combinations and to give a sense of the proposed style. For instance, if the new garden is to be formal, the mood board can reflect this by being laid out in a similar manner, whereas an informal design may be better illustrated in a relaxed or contemporary style. It can demonstrate how plant colours and combinations will look together, or it can show how the planting will change with the seasons.

A mood board is constructed by using a selection of pictures cut from magazines and catalogues of objects, colours, plants, paving samples or fabrics that you plan to use in the garden. Generally a large sheet of heavyweight paper or card (cardboard) is used, and the cut-outs are mounted onto this. The size depends on the size of the project, but A2 (17 × 22 in.) is usually the most manageable.

The board should focus on portraying the main elements of the design arranged in a similar layout to your plans and should communicate your design ideas in a visually appealing and representative manner.

Making a Mood Board

You will need heavy-duty coloured card (cardboard) for mounting the main material, lightweight card (cardboard) or foam board for mounting cut-outs, double-sided adhesive tape or spray glue to stick down photographs or cut-out material, a reduced or small-scale plan of the garden, ink drawing pens for lettering and photographs or manufacturers' brochures.

1. Assemble the material that you are going to use, including a copy of the garden layout plan that has been reduced on a photocopier or scanner to a scale that matches the scale of the photographs that you will place around it on your board (usually less than 200 mm [8 in.]). Place the plan centrally on the board.
2. If you are doing the work for a friend or a client, remember to include your title block to ensure that you, as the designer, are credited for your work.
3. Associate areas of the board with areas of the garden. If the garden has only one main area, lay out the samples in the general order of the space. For example, position paving at the bottom of the board, furnishings and planting at the middle and arbours or anything that lies overhead at the top of the board. By grouping things together, you will create a clearer idea than sticking samples randomly over the board.
4. Arrange the photographs around the plan according to where each item is located on the plan. Avoid photographs overhanging the edge of the board, as these will be

damaged when transporting the board. Draw a border and organize the material neatly within in it.

5. The size of the samples should generally reflect how much space the material will take up in reality. For example, avoid filling the board with several photographs of a type of plant if it only occurs once on the plan.

6. By framing some photographs with a border, you increase their importance. Photographs can be stuck to lightweight foam board to add a sense of depth.

7. Use paint swatches to show colours for plantings, walls, furniture and so on.

8. Instead of searching out mood board material for each new occasion, keep a file of high-quality photographs of materials and plants for later use. Avoid torn edges by using a scalpel to cut them cleanly.

9. When you are satisfied with the board layout, use double-sided tape or spray glue to stick the images onto the board.

10. When using natural samples such as sticks, rocks or twigs, be careful not to venture into the world of dollhouse making. Too much novelty will detract from the message you are trying to convey.

The design of this mood board is well balanced. The reduced plan is placed to the left, two atmospheric photographs depict the garden style, a title block is placed to the bottom right of the board, and a range of plant images give colour and interest.

Drawing Sections and Elevations

A section is a scaled drawing of a vertical plane that is constructed from a line that cuts through a plan; it can include the area below ground level if this is needed. Sections are used for two reasons: for a designer to experiment on paper with different spatial compositions, and to supplement the information on a plan, showing details of vertical and overhead elements that cannot be illustrated on a plan drawing. They can be made from any scaled drawing. An elevation is any vertical view of a feature, group of plants or part of the garden, not necessarily along one line (see page 212).

At a chosen cut line (or section line) on the plan, the three-dimensional elements on this line are projected up to scale. Any vertical or overhead features that are close behind this line can also be shown. Some surface detail can be added to bring the drawing to life.

These drawings are quick and easy to complete because, unlike a perspective drawing, all the vertical and overhead elements are shown at their correct scale, no matter how far they are from the cut line. You will probably have drawn your plan at a scale of 1:50 or 1:100, too small a scale to illustrate anything meaningful, such as a change of level, or a pergola. To show enough detail, the scale should be enlarged or doubled, perhaps to 1:20. This will obviously take up more space across the drawing, so instead of showing the whole section across the garden (much of which may be irrelevant), you may prefer to only show a specific area, perhaps one of vertical interest. In this case, mark clearly on the plan where the section begins and ends and indicate your direction of view with arrows.

There is no point in drawing a section unless it is going to show some detail or change of level that cannot be clarified on the plan. Normally, two sections across the garden are enough for a small or average-sized garden, but use as few or as many as needed to explain your intentions. It is crucial that you choose section lines where any major alterations in level, or a reasonable amount of vertical interest, occur. This is usually one line along the length and one line along the width of the garden.

Drawing a Section Through a Garden Layout Plan

1. Study the garden layout plan and consider any changes in level or vertical and overhead features. By twisting the plan around to look at it from all angles, decide where a line can be drawn across the plan, or part of the plan, to show these features.

2. Stick down the garden layout plan, and over this, stick down a fresh sheet of tracing paper. Ensure that the plan is positioned centrally below the tracing paper, and consider the layout of the sheet. You will need to leave room for the title block, but it is unlikely that you will need an information panel on this drawing. Make sure you position the sections suitably on the sheet. It usually looks better to have a longer section nearer the bottom. If you have room, you may wish to include these sections on the garden layout plan instead of on a separate sheet.

3. Mark the beginning and end of the section line on the tracing paper. Is the scale large enough to show sufficient detail, or does it need to be enlarged? If so, you may only have enough space on your sheet to show part of the section line (obviously the area where most of what you need to show occurs).

4. Now draw the section line in pencil across the plan. To do this, use a T-square, parallel motion or, if the section line is at an angle, a set square.

5. Beginning at one end of the section line, progress along this line, projecting vertical

continues on page 243

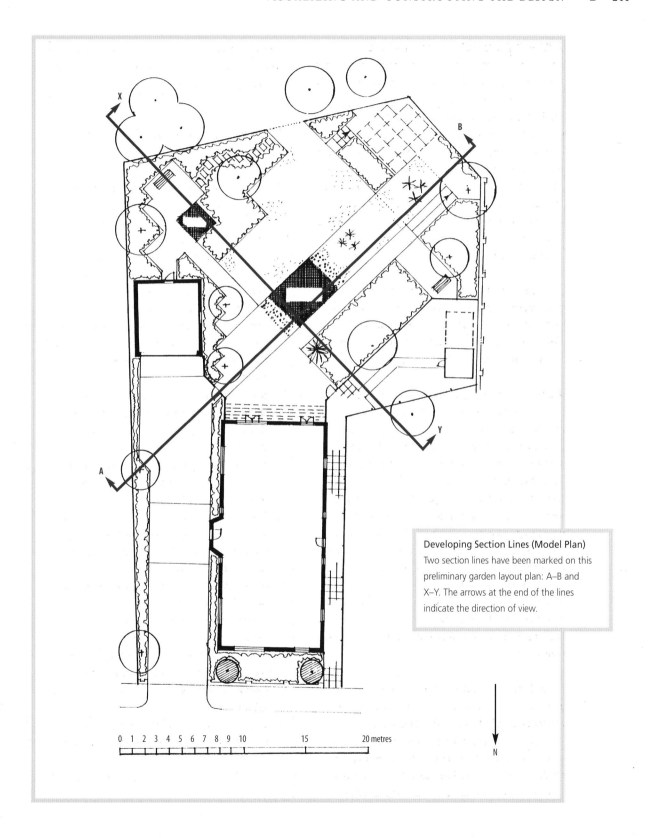

Developing Section Lines (Model Plan)
Two section lines have been marked on this preliminary garden layout plan: A–B and X–Y. The arrows at the end of the lines indicate the direction of view.

0 1 2 3 4 5 6 7 8 9 10   15   20 metres

N

beginning of pool feature   end of pool feature

Draw the section line A–B on a tracing-
paper overlay on the garden plan. Mark
the edges of features that occur on or
very near the line.

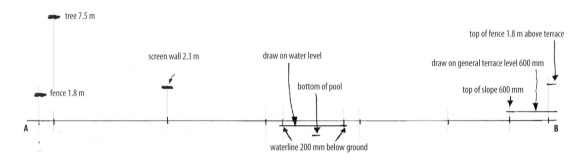

tree 7.5 m

top of fence 1.8 m above terrace

screen wall 2.3 m   draw on water level   draw on general terrace level 600 mm

bottom of pool

fence 1.8 m   top of slope 600 mm   top of slope 600 mm

waterline 200 mm below ground

Establish the height (or depth) of each
feature, and mark this on the tracing
paper in relation to the section line,
keeping all the measurements to the
same scale. Then remove the plan from
the board and continue working on the
section line.

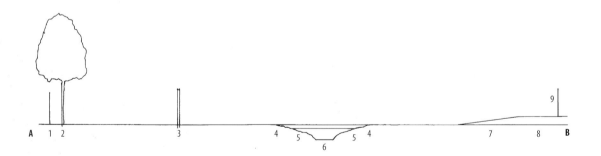

Draw in the outline shapes of the features. The numbers refer to the
features on this plan:
1. Fence—at this scale a single line thickness
2. Tree, with correct spread of canopy (refer back to the plan) and
   height from ground
3. Wall indicated by two parallel lines. Note the section actually passes
   through a gateway

4. Edge details of pool—in this case a pebble "beach"
5. Underwater profiles
6. Bottom of pool
7. Sloping hillside, connected to ground level at top and base
   of slope
8. Terrace level
9. Fence

pencil lines upwards from the edges of any changes in level or any vertical features that are either on or just beyond the section line.

6. Use the measurements noted on the plan or in your notebook and a scale rule to establish the heights of these features, drawing in horizontal lines to indicate the tops and bottoms of the features.

7. Draw in and show some detail of the foreground structures, including the outline form of any planting. If they are not totally obscured by the structures in the foreground, draw in any vertical or overhead features beyond the cut line. If there are any significant trees beyond the boundary of your garden, it is useful to show these as well, as it gives the drawing some scale reference. Write down the measurements if this will help clarify the drawing.

8. Once you have drawn everything in pencil, remove the plan from the drawing board. On a new sheet of tracing paper, trace over the section drawing in pencil or pen. Use a fainter pencil or smaller pen size to indicate more distant features that do not fall exactly on the section line.

9. Adding a person, also drawn to scale, often improves this type of drawing. Remember to add your title block.

10. Remove this section drawing and have it printed. Adding colour to the print may help bring it to life (see page 231).

11. Mark on the garden layout plan where the sections begin and end, indicating this with arrows showing the direction of view. As you will already have had prints made from your original plan, perhaps this can be added to your print.

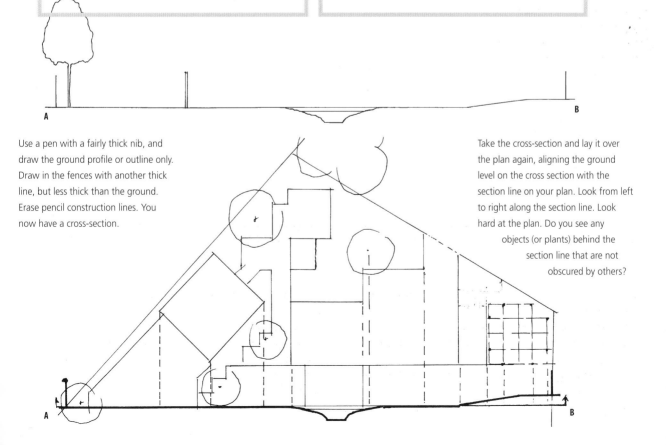

Use a pen with a fairly thick nib, and draw the ground profile or outline only. Draw in the fences with another thick line, but less thick than the ground. Erase pencil construction lines. You now have a cross-section.

Take the cross-section and lay it over the plan again, aligning the ground level on the cross section with the section line on your plan. Look from left to right along the section line. Look hard at the plan. Do you see any objects (or plants) behind the section line that are not obscured by others?

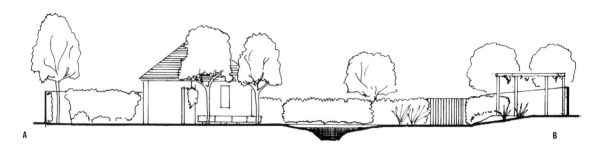

Following the same stages, draw in first
the nearest items, and then those
further away from the section line. The
foreground items may partially obscure
those in the background. You have now
built up a picture of the garden beyond
the actual line of section.

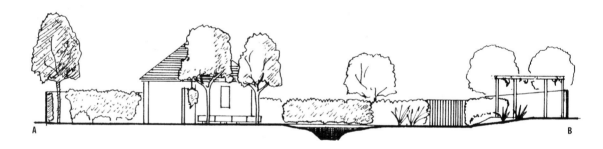

To make the section "read" more
clearly, hatch in any features that fall on
the actual section line, or emphasize
their outline with a thick nib.

Here section X–Y has been developed
in the same way.

Axonometric Projections

An axonometric projection is a type of perspective drawing that creates a three-dimensional impression in which all the planes are described and related to one another. It is relatively easy to set up because it is developed directly from a plan drawing.

An axonometric projection is usually set up by first tilting a garden layout plan, then projecting up the vertical elements, keeping the lines parallel. The plan is usually tilted at forty-five degrees, which produces an angled view of the garden from above, similar to what you would see from the second floor window of a neighbouring house.

If drawing at this angle does not show enough detail (perhaps because the garden design is done on the diagonal), try altering the angles (see below, right). Remember that the angles you choose must add up to 90°.

In axonometric projections, the length, breadth and height of any objects will all be drawn to the same scale, and so the view will look unrealistic and lacking in perspective, although it will be technically correct. As they are essentially technical drawings, they do not depend very heavily on artistic ability for their success. As long as you know the height of any object in the garden (which you will certainly need to know if it is to be built), you should be able to create these drawings without difficulty.

A completed axonometric will show clearly how the different components of a garden—buildings, walls, steps and fences—interrelate. Once mastered, this is a quick and easy method of visualizing your design or checking any construction details.

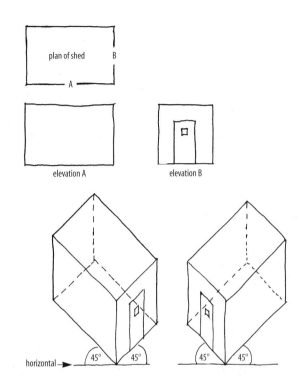

Above: Most guides to drawing axonometric projections will advise using a 45° tilt, as shown by these two alternative views. The advantage of this angle is that you can see both elevations uniformly and without much distortion. However, you can use any angle you wish and should experiment to find the best view.

Below: Experimenting with different angles. Note that the plan (the "floor" of the shed) always remains rectanglar.

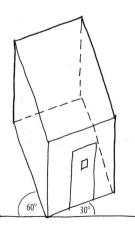

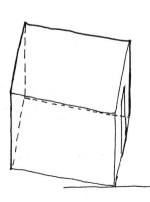

Drawing a Brick in Axonometric Projection

This exercise is designed to help you understand the concept of axonometric projection. The principles can be applied to objects of any size.

1. Set a brick beside you. Measure it and draw this accurately as a plan, at a scale of 1:1 (life size).
2. Using a T-square and set square, draw the plan of your brick at forty-five degrees on your graph-paper backing sheet. Stick this down with masking tape.
3. Using the T-square and set square, draw up the vertical lines. Do this by measuring, with your scale ruler at 1:1, the height of the brick, starting at the lowest level. Mark these points off on each vertical line.
4. Join up each of these points.
5. Rub out any unwanted lines hidden by the mass of the brick.

Drawing a brick in axonometric

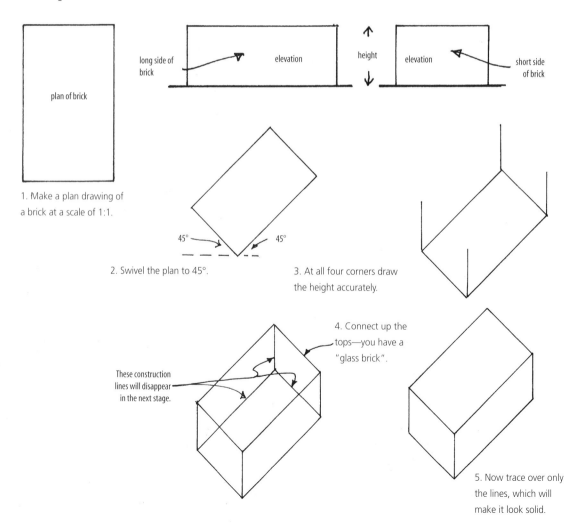

plan of brick

long side of brick

elevation

height

elevation

short side of brick

1. Make a plan drawing of a brick at a scale of 1:1.

45°　45°

2. Swivel the plan to 45°.

3. At all four corners draw the height accurately.

These construction lines will disappear in the next stage.

4. Connect up the tops—you have a "glass brick".

5. Now trace over only the lines, which will make it look solid.

Drawing a Tree in Axonometric Projection

When drawing trees in axonometric projection, use a circle template to construct the drawing of the leaf canopy. The resulting drawing will look something like an egg on a stick, but with a little artistic licence (and the addition of an outline to indicate foliage)

you should be able to make it look more like a tree. Shrubs can be drawn in the same way, but since there is no trunk, the lower circle (representing the bottom of the canopy) is drawn at ground level.

1. Using a pencil, make a plan drawing of the tree width (or spread) as indicated by the circle on the plan. A circle template was used.

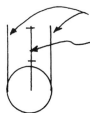

2. Draw vertical lines from the sides and centre. On the central vertical line (which represents the trunk) measure and mark the height of the top and bottom of the canopy.

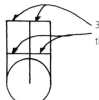

3. Draw lines across to the edges.

4. Slip the circle template up so that the centre is aligned with the height of the bottom of the canopy and draw the lower half of the circle.

When drawing trees and shrubs on an axonometric garden plan or planting scheme, redraw the outline to indicate the character of the foliage.

5. Slip the circle template up to the top and draw another circle (centred on the height of the top of the canopy).

6. The canopy of most trees narrows at the top, so it is likely that you will want to redraw the top with a smaller circle.

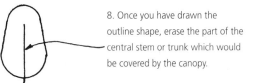

7. Join up the two circular shapes.

8. Once you have drawn the outline shape, erase the part of the central stem or trunk which would be covered by the canopy.

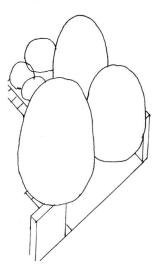

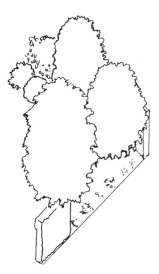

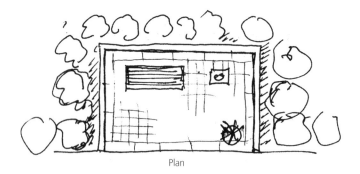

Plan

Elevation

Choosing the Viewpoint

Neither the plan nor the elevation drawing could convey the design of a sheltered alcove within a garden to best effect, so an axonometric projection was constructed. The first attempt was unsatisfactory because the statue is almost entirely concealed. In the second attempt, however, where the chosen viewpoint is from the opposite direction, the statue, and its relationship to the bench and plant, is clearly revealed.

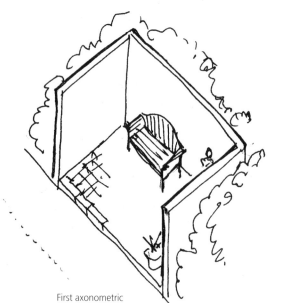

First axonometric

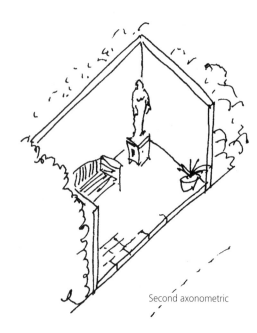

Second axonometric

Raised seating corner

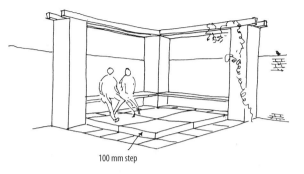

100 mm step

Although it may seem obvious, you need to know the design of every feature of the garden before you draw the axonometric. Thumbnail sketches and details will help. This page shows examples of sketches done before starting the axonometric.

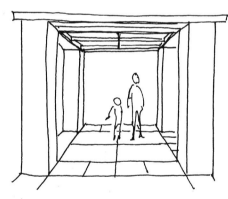

Part of the pergola

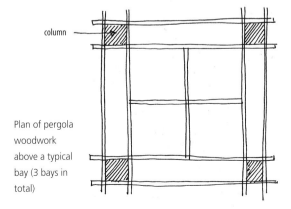

column

Plan of pergola woodwork above a typical bay (3 bays in total)

Drawing an Axonometric Projection from a Garden Layout Plan

1. Using your parallel rule or T-square, and an adjustable set square, fix down the garden layout plan at your chosen angle with, if possible, the lowest level of the garden or the terrace nearest the bottom of the page.

2. Stick a sheet of tracing paper over this. This sheet will contain the draft axonometric plan as it develops.

3. Use the scale rule to measure the vertical lines round the boundaries or exterior of the site, and project up from each corner the height of any structure—building, walls, fence—at these points.

4. Using a set square, join up these points, showing the structure nearest to you as a broken line. This will indicate its presence but allow you to "see through" it on the drawing.

5. Proceed in the same way with the interior of the plan, starting at the lowest level or terrace, which should, if possible, be nearest to you, working up gradually through each construction and change of level. Some more distant features may be hidden behind those in the foreground. At present only show hard landscaping—the plants can be added later. In this drawing, each vertical measurement should be taken from the level of your starting point. If your garden includes several changes of level, it may be easier and quicker, once the first level has been drawn, to slip the tracing-paper overlay up or down to the height of the new level. This will save having to remember to add on, or subtract from, the earlier dimensions each time.

6. All circles on your plan, such as round pools, pots or tables, will appear as the same true

circles in an axonometric. Slip your drawing up or down to the correct height and trace off.

7. When you have finished drawing all the hard landscaping, including pots, pergolas and garden furniture, you may have accumulated so many lines that your drawing is rather confusing. Sometimes it is easier to lay a further sheet of tracing paper over the drawing and trace off only the lines that you actually want.

8. Now draw in the plantings. These can be added to the same sheet or done on an overlay with the two later being combined for the final drawing. Again, begin by moving to the lowest part or terrace of the garden, and locate the planting position of an adjacent tree. Project a vertical line up from the centre point of the trunk to the height of the top of the tree, marking on the trunk where the tree canopy begins. Using that point as the centre, draw a circle to indicate the width or spread of the tree canopy. Normally the tree canopy will narrow at the top of the tree—draw another circle, using the highest point of the

tree as the centre of the circle. Join up the two as shown on page 247. This will leave only a small amount (or none) of the tree trunk showing, and although it may look a little odd, it is correct.

9. Proceed in the same way with other trees and shrubs. Climbers and herbaceous plants are normally indicated by showing an outline of their height and spread. Keep your plant outlines simple, and avoid confusing the drawing with details of stems or leaves.

10. Try to make your axonometric drawing look more natural by softening the outlines of the plants, representing the texture of their foliage.

11. For your final drawing, stick down a fresh sheet of tracing paper over the draft axonometric. Trace over all the relevant lines, adding further lines if necessary to help make the drawing appear as three-dimensional and realistic as possible.

12. Remove your new axonometric drawing and have three copies of it printed so that you can experiment with colouring or rendering techniques.

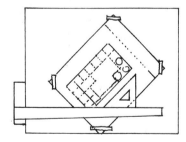
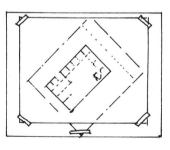
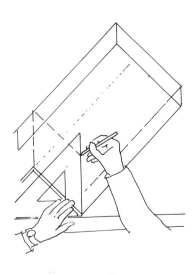

Set up an axonometric projection by attaching the garden plan to the board at 45° (left) and then taping down a tracing paper overlay (right).

Draw verticals after measuring them with a scale rule.

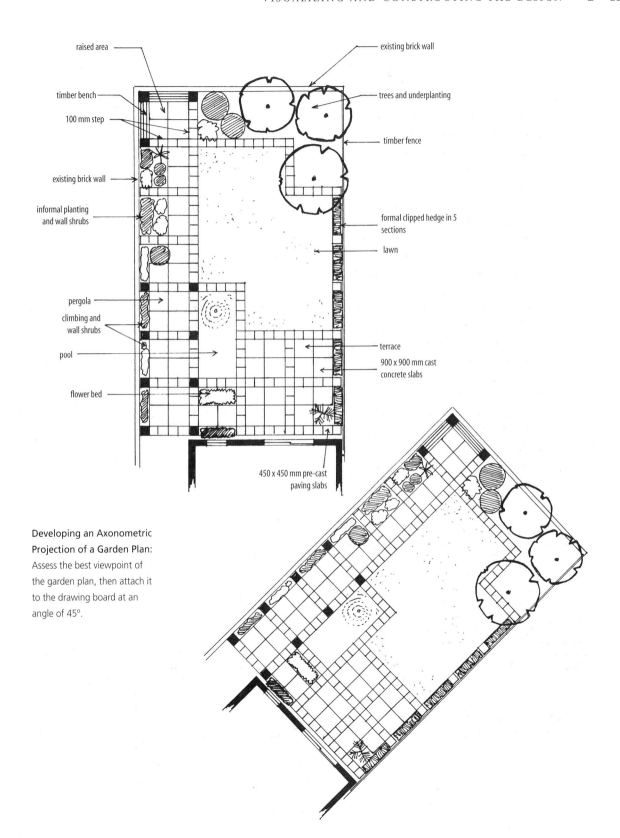

raised area

existing brick wall

timber bench

trees and underplanting

100 mm step

timber fence

existing brick wall

formal clipped hedge in 5 sections

informal planting and wall shrubs

lawn

pergola

climbing and wall shrubs

pool

terrace

900 x 900 mm cast concrete slabs

flower bed

450 x 450 mm pre-cast paving slabs

Developing an Axonometric Projection of a Garden Plan: Assess the best viewpoint of the garden plan, then attach it to the drawing board at an angle of 45°.

On a sheet of tracing paper laid over the
plan, project the boundary walls at each
corner and then connect them.

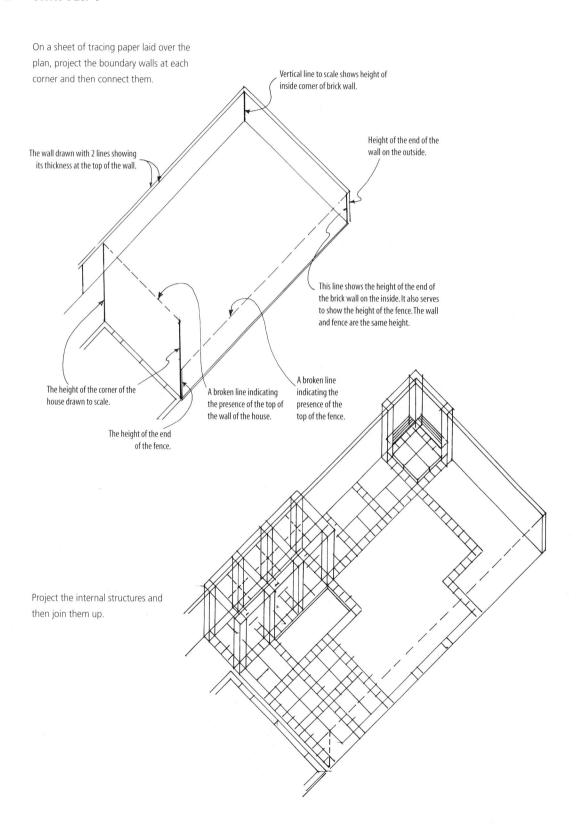

Vertical line to scale shows height of
inside corner of brick wall.

Height of the end of the
wall on the outside.

The wall drawn with 2 lines showing
its thickness at the top of the wall.

This line shows the height of the end of
the brick wall on the inside. It also serves
to show the height of the fence. The wall
and fence are the same height.

The height of the corner of the
house drawn to scale.

A broken line indicating
the presence of the top of
the wall of the house.

A broken line
indicating
the presence of the
top of the fence.

The height of the end
of the fence.

Project the internal structures and
then join them up.

Add the trees and shubs. A further sheet of tracing paper is then laid over the axonometric and it is redrawn omitting all "invisible" lines.

Represent the foliage of the plants in a naturalistic way.

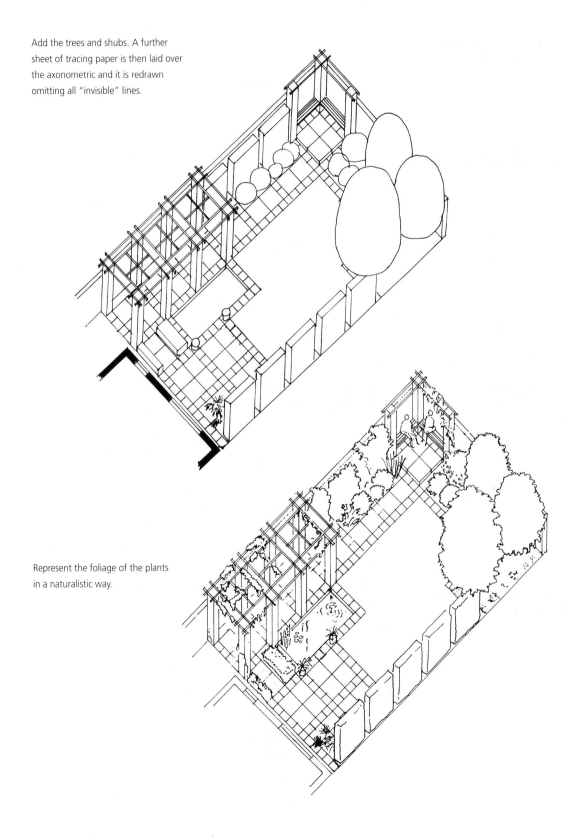

Adding texture and shadow gives the drawing a more solid appearance. This style of rendering is only one of many you can choose from. The light comes from a definite position, casting well-defined shadows. The figures add a sense of scale.

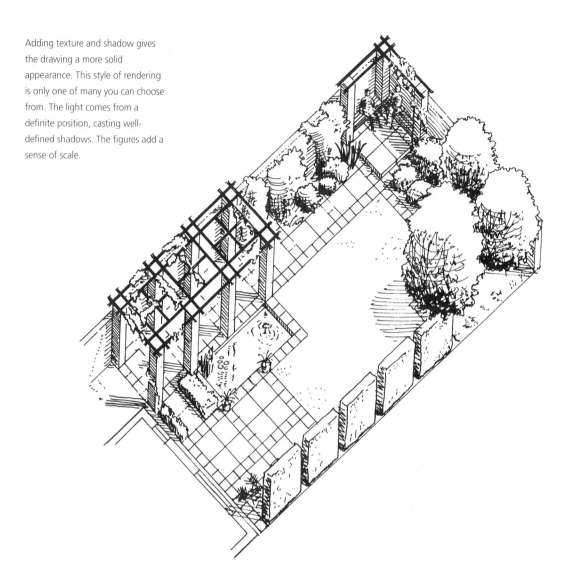

Construction, Planting and Maintenance

How you go about having the garden design built will depend largely on the garden layout plan. If it is an ambitious design that includes new terracing, steps, lawn, pergolas and garden buildings, for instance, it would be wise to hire a contractor. If it involves simply a realignment of existing borders and new plantings, you and your family or friends may be able to carry out most of the work.

Doing the Work Yourself

If you plan to do the construction work yourself it is worth consulting some of the informative do-it-yourself books that are available, which will point out details you might overlook, such as ensuring that the terrace has a cross-fall to a drain or gulley to carry away excess water.

The position of new planting beds can be pegged out in accordance with your garden layout plan. Sometimes it is helpful to mark out the proposed line

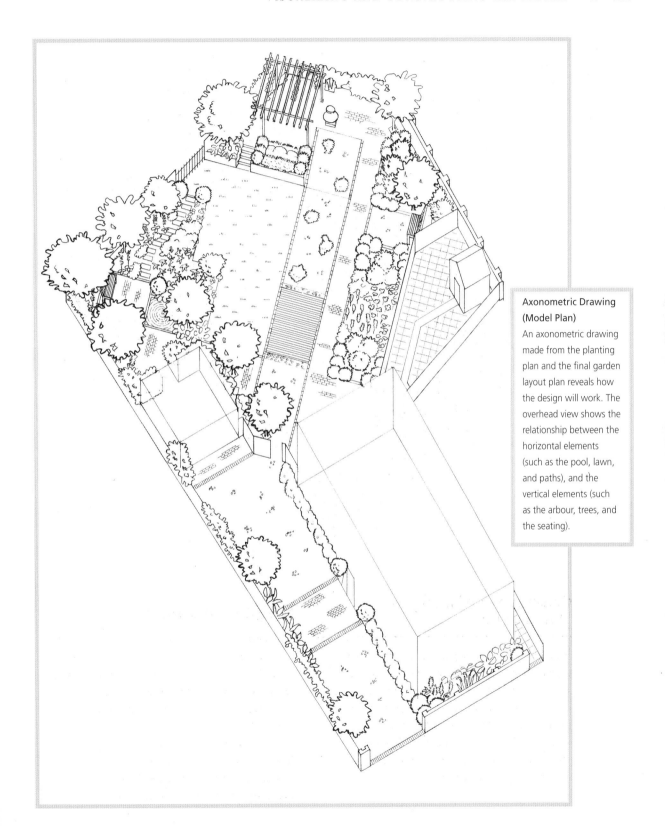

Axonometric Drawing (Model Plan)

An axonometric drawing made from the planting plan and the final garden layout plan reveals how the design will work. The overhead view shows the relationship between the horizontal elements (such as the pool, lawn, and paths), and the vertical elements (such as the arbour, trees, and the seating).

with sand or a length of garden hose, lifting the turf to this guideline.

All areas to be planted must be well dug over and cleared of any perennial weeds, and unless the soil is in good condition, fertilizer and organic material should be incorporated to improve the soil texture and quality. Trees may need staking as protection from wind, and climbers and wall shrubs may need supporting with a framework of wires attached to walls and fences with vine eyes or wall nails.

Hiring and Using a Contractor

If much hard construction work is required, you may wish to bring in outside contractors to build your garden. These may be house builders or a garden construction company who will work to your specifications. Quotations for the work can vary enormously, so try to make sure that they are all quoting for the same work—for the same depth of gravel, the same type of stone, the same foundations and so on. The glossary includes terminology that may be useful in your discussions.

Many professionals write a detailed specification for large or complex sites, but for smaller works it is often best to seek quotations from a contractor who has a reputation for honesty and reliability. Make sure that you read any quotations carefully, comparing like with like, checking that nothing is overlooked.

A good contractor may be able to make alternative suggestions for some of the construction; this may even save you money. Be sure to ask to see examples of previous work before committing yourself, and, if in any doubt, ask the contractor for permission to contact one of his or her clients so that you can discuss reliability, keeping to the budget and other such details. Ask to see and approve samples of any hard-landscape materials before accepting the quotation—economizing on the quality of materials has ruined the carefully planned effect of many gardens. Always try to use the best material you can afford.

Make sure that your contractor is familiar with ground preparation and planting and can supply good-quality plants. Always state, "No substitutes acceptable unless previously agreed", in case your contractor cannot supply your exact order. Most garden construction companies can supply plants at an advantageous price and prefer to quote for the whole job. An alternative is to ask your builder to prepare the borders but to obtain the plants and plant them yourself.

Supplying the Plants

For many designers and clients this is the most exciting part of creating a new garden. But plants vary in size, quality and cost. Obviously, larger plants will be more expensive. They may also take longer to become established, and there may be hidden costs such as bringing them in over the house by crane or requiring a fork-lift truck and manual labour to move them onto the allotted space. For large stock, preparing the planting holes in advance will not only save time but may also prevent deterioration through wind rock or frost. Be sure to have everything needed for planting, such as fertilizer, stakes and ties.

Whether buying through trade or retail, try to obtain all your plants from one source. A retailer may give you a discount for quantity, the plants may be superior, and you may be able to select them personally. If different suppliers are used, the plants may arrive at different times, and you will need to leave space for the later deliveries, which will make it more difficult to place the plants exactly where you want them.

Maintenance and Future Development

After the garden has been built, it will need to be carefully maintained until established, usually over a period of about three years. Sufficient water and nutrients will need to be available for plant growth, and both hard landscaping and plants should be checked twice yearly for repairs or replacements due to weather and general wear and tear. Although in working up your planting plans you will have taken into account the local conditions, there are occasionally unforeseen reasons for certain plants not growing well, and these may need replacing or changing to another variety. As the garden matures and the plants grow, you may wish to make minor alterations to the original concept. Try to keep notes and a photographic record of the different seasonal effects. You may wish to adjust or add to some of your plant groupings, or perhaps experiment with different bulbs or annuals.

No garden is static, and the way your garden matures will largely depend on how well it is looked after, particularly in the early stages.

Your Role as Garden Designer

Designing for a Friend

Once your friends know that you design gardens, it is very likely that they will suggest that you experiment with their gardens. If you are inexperienced, this proposition may sound attractive, but it could lead to dissatisfaction, misunderstanding and a broken friendship. Try to avoid falling into this trap by providing only the plan and the planting plan and suggesting that your friend selects and employs his or her own contractor.

Both you (as the designer) and your friend (as the client) should be present at the meeting with the contractor to discuss the implementation, as only you will have a clear idea of desired finishes, such as, for instance, the pattern of brickwork. Thereafter you have a choice, either to oversee the work on your friend's behalf or to let your friend supervise the work. Although the latter course may not produce such a good finish, it may still be advisable—so much depends on the personalities involved.

Student Designers

There are various ways of beginning in the profession, but at the outset it can be a daunting and lonely experience. Students often begin by working together as a partnership, especially if they have different yet complementary skills. An alternative is to work in an established practice, spending time in the different departments to gain overall experience, or to work in a nursery where you will not only extend your plant knowledge but may also be asked to redesign a customer's garden to accommodate their new plants. A wide range of experience at an early stage is a valuable springboard for the future.

Newly Qualified Professionals

Even if you have trained at a college, accepting your first commission is a daunting prospect. Each job has its own idiosyncrasies, and clients vary in their attitude to a designer. It is essential that a client understands how a designer works and respects his or her professional skills. Most professionals produce a brochure detailing their services—for example, explaining the different stages, such as the garden layout plan, planting plan, visuals, supervision of the work and payment. Some also list and illustrate past work.

As gardens vary in size and complexity, it is usual to quote a daily rate or, for a once-only consultation, an hourly rate. Once you have seen the site and met the client, you should be able to sum up how long it will take you to complete the required stages. After the initial meeting, the client will expect a speedy written reply from you setting out your charges for the work involved, how and when you expect to complete the various stages and what the client can expect for his or her money. You may wish to give options such as supervising the whole job, or perhaps only overseeing at certain agreed stages. Most job relationships that founder do so because the exact responsibilities and expectations were not made clear at the outset. Be sure to put everything in writing, including written agreement to your terms.

Semiprofessional Designers

Many good, often self-taught designers work part-time and have a more casual relationship with their clients. Often these are people well known in their own locality for providing a friendly, reliable local service at a reasonable price, business coming to them largely by word of mouth. Occasionally these designers work in tandem with a contractor or builder who wants someone to draw plans and liaise with the client while the work is carried out. In this case also it is vital that all parties involved know what is expected and when the work will be carried out, although, compared with the professional rules, the service may be more relaxed.

Keeping a Plant Notebook

Acquiring a good working knowledge of plants takes many years. There are so many variables, such as the preferred soil conditions, aspect and time of flowering. If your plant knowledge is good, perhaps you would like to extend it by increasing your repertoire. If plants are a new subject to you, building up your own reference notebook from personal observations will be more useful than looking through catalogues or books, although you will need to refer to these to find out more about each plant. Once you have begun your notebook, you may be surprised at how much you can learn.

Keeping a plant notebook will help you to develop a "palette" or repertoire of plants to use in your designs and planting plans. This will not only extend your plant knowledge but will also develop your skill in combining plants for form, texture, colour and seasonal effects. Try to select a range of reliable plants which you find particularly garden-worthy.

you use them. A garden designer's palette of plants will not necessarily include fashionable or unusual plants, but rather plants that will perform well over a prolonged season, that are easily grown and disease-resistant, and that combine well with other plants. Your aim in preparing a plant notebook is to produce your own reliable planting palette.

For each plant, research information on characteristics, growth rate, propagation and other factors, as shown on the sample sheet (see page 263). Each of your plant sheets should include photographs or drawings of the plant and information on where and when it was seen.

It is useful to divide the information into two sections, the first including your own photographs or drawings and descriptions of individual plants in their specific categories, and the second including information about groups of plants that make effective combinations in specific situations.

Using Plants in Garden Design

Although each plant may have certain outstanding features—form, texture, leaf or flower colour—these can be enhanced by careful grouping to contrast with other companion plants. A shrub, for instance, may well have flowers, berries or autumn leaf colour, and no single perennial herbaceous plant can serve as a complement or contrast to all three. An effective plant grouping might therefore include spring bulbs to accompany the shrub's early spring flowers, an early perennial to show off its foliage and a late-flowering perennial to contrast with its berries. A deep understanding of the special features of each plant and how it harmonizes or contrasts with its neighbours is an important part of getting to know your plants.

In preparing a plant notebook, go further than simply being familiar with a wide range of plants. Be selective and discerning in what you choose and how

Plant Categories

Choose and photograph different plants for each of the categories that is relevant to the garden you are designing. Set out the details of each plant on a plant sheet, and keep this with two photographs of the plant—one taken close up, one taken from a distance. It is useful to note the names of two additional plants that would combine with the plant to form an interesting grouping. Plants can be categorized as follows:

- Native trees and shrubs
- Smaller ornamental trees
- Evergreen shrubs
- Deciduous shrubs
- Conifers
- Plants for hedging and screening
- Climbers
- Wall shrubs

- Shrub roses
- Climbing and rambling roses
- Other roses (floribunda, hybrid tea, ground cover and so forth)
- Early-flowering perennials (up to early summer)
- Late-flowering perennials (midsummer onwards)
- Ground covers
- Bamboos
- Grasses
- Hardy ferns
- Aquatic and bog plants
- Bulbs, corms, tubers and rhizomes
- Annuals, biennials, half-hardies and bedding plants

Plant Information Sheet

Gather together information for each plant based on the list that follows. Use the example opposite as a guide to the level of information to include.

Full Latin name

The name must be accurate and up to date. Use a reliable reference, such the latest edition of the *RHS Plant Finder*. Pay particular attention to the correct use of upper and lower case and single quotes for cultivar names.

Synonym

Give well-known or commonly used alternative Latin name or names, if any.

Common name

Give the name or names the plant is commonly known by.

Origin

For a species, give the geographical origin. For a hybrid or cultivar, note the origin of the parent or parents and the nursery or garden in which the plant originated.

Plant family

This is given in the *RHS Plant Finder*, or use a reliable book which details the plant family.

References

Note the book or books where you found most information on the plant (may be noted in abbreviated form) so that you can refer back later if necessary.

Description

Under "General", identify the category and give a brief summary of the key features of the plant, (for instance, "A vigorous, evergreen shrub with large scented flowers all summer"). Then note the important characteristics of foliage, flower, fruit and stem where these are significant. Technical botanical language is not necessary unless it helps your understanding of various features.

Period of interest

Shade in the chart as appropriate, using coloured pencils.

Form

A simple line drawing of the outline shape of the plant will help you to identify it in the future.

Height and spread

Assuming average growing conditions in your area, state the probable height and spread after a period of approximately five years after planting. This will vary, of course, depending on the sizes of plants available to you. Mature stock or larger plants can usually be supplied but are more expensive and may well take time to adapt to their new location. Smaller plants suffer less from wind rock, which slows down growth by preventing the roots from establishing firmly in the soil.

Cultivation

Give brief details of the various requirements listed. Under soil, include details of moisture and pH requirements.

Plant Information Sheet

Latin name *Anemone* ×*hybrida* 'Honorine Jobert'
Synonym *A. japonica* 'Honorine Jobert' or *A.* ×*hybrida* 'Alba'

Common name Japanese anemone
Plant family Ranunculaceae
Origin Garden origin, sport of hybrid between parents from China and Nepal
References G.S.Thomas, *Perennial Garden Plants*

DESCRIPTION
General Late-flowering hardy perennial, slightly invasive giving a good show of flowers over a long period.
Important characteristics Flowers rounded, pure white with contrasting bunch of yellow stamens, on branching stems that rise well above the foliage.
Leaves rather coarse, three-lobed, pointed, dark green, in clumps. Herbaceous.

	J	F	M	A	M	J	J	A	S	O	N	D
leaf				✓	✓	✓	✓	✓	✓	✓		
flower							✓	✓	✓			
fruit												
stem												
period of interest	J	F	M	A	M	J	J	A	S	O	N	D

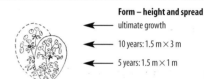

Form – height and spread
ultimate growth
10 years: 1.5 m × 3 m
5 years: 1.5 m × 1 m

CULTIVATION
Soil and moisture Prefers any retentive soil, not too dry; more invasive in light soils.
Aspect Full sun preferred; will tolerate light to moderate shade.
Maintenance and pruning Requires no staking (so useful where labour is limited); cut right down in winter.
Propagation By division of old clumps in spring; or root cuttings taken in dormant season or early spring.
Problems and drawbacks Normally trouble-free, but may take two years to establish.
Hardiness Fully hardy.

DESIGN USE AND ASSOCIATED PLANTING
Useful to give a fresh burst of colour in late summer and into autumn when many plants are looking a little tired. A good plant for a mixed border.

Complementary plants
Aster ×*frikartii* 'Mönch', a good blue-mauve daisy flower for colour contrast at same time of year.
Sedum 'Herbstfreude' (*S.* 'Autumn Joy'), a lower plant with pink flowers and solid fleshy leaves for contrast; grey-green foliage gives interest earlier in season, and dry flower heads in winter.

Alternatives and substitutes
Many cultivars of *A.* ×*hybrida*, mainly in shades of pink, also the original pale pink *A.* ×*hybrida*.
Some good cultivars are: 'Königin Charlotte', large-flowered pink; 'Géante des Blanches', white; 'Margarete', deep pink semi-double. Also forms of *A. hupehensis japonica*, such as 'Bressingham Glow', rosy-red semi-double; 'Prinz Heinrich', pink.

Notes
Hybrid of *A. hupehensis japonica* and *A. vitifolia*, the sport arose c.1858.
The original *A.* ×*hybrida* was raised at the R.H.S. garden, Chiswick, in 1848.

Hardiness

This can be a complex area and will depend on the climate where you live. A plant can be fully hardy, frost-hardy, half-hardy or frost-tender. Find out how low the temperature in your area can reach, then use the chart on page 274 to find your corresponding zone.

Design use and associated planting

This is an important section. Give suggestions of situations where you might use the plant, and try to note two other plants that you believe would associate well with it. Give the reasons for your choice.

Alternative and substitutes

Name a few other plants that are similar to the subject but differ in some significant way, and describe the difference. These may be alternative colours of the same plant, other species of the same genus or plants of different genera that give the same effect in a different situation.

Notes

Add any miscellaneous information, such as notes on propagation, making sure that each sheet represents only one species. A clear system of cross-referencing is helpful. For example, *Taxus baccata* (English yew) could be included under native trees and shrubs, conifers, or plants for hedging and screening. The description of this species would appear in only one section, but a cross-reference could appear in the other sections.

Photographs or drawings

Accompany each master sheet with a separate sheet showing a distant and a close-up photograph of the plant. Beside each illustration give the name of the plant, the date or month when the photograph was taken and the location. A detailed drawing in place of the close-up may teach you more about the habit of the plant.

Plants for a Purpose

It is useful to extend your plant knowledge and to develop your awareness of plants that will look effective when combined. Start by looking at plants, considering good groupings. Confine each of your plant groupings to no more than three to six species, and aim for a wide range of situations in your locality. Choose plants that associate well and that will all grow easily in your specified conditions or tolerate similar conditions. The following are some typical situations:

- Dry shade
- Moist shade
- Dry, sunny situation
- Windy situation
- Shady walls
- Winter interest
- Ornamental stems or bark
- Autumn colour
- Thriving on specific soil conditions, such as lime-free, acidic or chalk
- Thriving by the coast
- Surviving pollution
- Attracting butterflies and bees

Create plant information sheets for these "Plants for a Purpose". Draw an outline elevation to show the shapes of the plants and how they interact. If possible, photograph the groupings, and take rough measurements of the plants and the distances between them to help you understand about spacing and rate of growth. Make a note of the location and the date, and the situation for which the group is intended. Write down the botanical name of each plant, details of features of interest (and the times of year that they occur), and cultivation information. Suggest other plants that might be linked with the plant group, perhaps to extend the season of interest or to continue the theme.

Core Plant List

If your plant knowledge is limited, this list can be used as a basis for making choices for your own plant palette. No plant list can be comprehensive, and most garden designers have their own favourite plants.

If the common name of a plant varies from region to region, only the Latin name is given. Where a variety of a particular plant is not stated, you will need to research the variety most suited to the needs of the garden design.

Structural Planting

Large, Native, Deciduous Trees

These can spread to 30 m (100 ft.).
Betula pendula (silver birch or European white birch)
Carpinus betulus (hornbeam)
Fagus sylvatica (beech)
Fraxinus excelsior (ash)
Quercus robur (oak)

Large, Decorative, Deciduous Trees

Betula varieties (silver birch)
Catalpa bignonioides (Indian bean)
Fagus sylvatica 'Purpurea' (copper beech)
Ginkgo biloba (maidenhair tree)
Liriodendron tulipifera (tulip tree)
Salix babylonica (weeping willow)
Ulmus glabra 'Pendula' (weeping elm)

Fast-Growing Trees

Acer lobelii (maple)
Ailanthus altissima (tree of heaven)
Alnus cordata (Italian alder)
Castanea sativa (sweet chestnut)
Eucalyptus in var. (gum)
Fraxinus excelsior (ash)
Gleditsia triacanthos (honey locust)
Juglans regia (walnut)

Platanus mexicana (plane)
Populus alba (white poplar)
Prunus avium (wild cherry)
Pterocarya fraxinifolia (wing nut)
Robinia pseudoacacia (false acacia or locust)
Salix alba varieties (willow)
Tilia americana (American lime or linden)

Vertical Conifers

Chamaecyparis lawsoniana 'Kilmacurragh'
Chamaecyparis lawsoniana 'Wissellii'
Juniperus scopulorum 'Skyrocket'
Juniperus communis 'Suecica' (Swedish juniper)
Taxus baccata 'Aurea' (golden yew)
Taxus baccata 'Fastigiata' (Irish yew)

Small Trees as Specimens or Focal Points

Betula varieties (birch)
Malus varieties (crab apple)
Prunus varieties (cherry)
Pyrus varieties (pear)
Sorbus varieties (ash or rowan)

Structural Shrubs or Small Trees

Arbutus unedo (strawberry tree)
Arundinaria varieties (bamboo)
Aucuba varieties (laurel)
Berberis thunbergii 'Atropurpurea' (barberry)
Bupleurum fruticosum (shrubby hare's ear)
Buxus sempervirens (box or boxwood)
Camellia varieties.
Choisya ternata (Mexican orange)
Cordyline australis (cabbage palm or cabbage tree)
Eriobotrya japonica (loquat)
Escallonia varieties
Fatsia japonica
Griselinia in var.
Hebe varieties (veronica)
Ilex varieties (holly)
Ilex aquifolium 'Pyramidalis' (holly)
Juniperus communis 'Hibernica' (Irish juniper)

Magnolia grandiflora 'Exmouth' (Exmouth magnolia)
Magnolia grandiflora 'Goliath' (magnolia)
Mahonia ×media 'Charity'
Olearia ×haastii (daisy bush)
Phormium tenax (New Zealand flax)
Photinia
Pittosporum
Rhododendron varieties (rhododendrons and azaleas)
Rhus varieties (sumach)
Sambucus varieties (elderberry)
Taxus baccata (yew)
Viburnum plicatum 'Mariesii'
Yucca

Key Planting

Shrubs as Seasonal Features

Acer varieties (maple)
Amelanchier (service berry)
Berberis (barberry)
Brachyglottis (ragwort)
Buddleja (butterfly bush)
Cornus (dogwood)
Corylopsis
Cotinus (smoke tree)
Daphne pontica (daphne)
Elaeagnus (silverberry)
Genista aetnensis (broom)
Hamamelis (witch hazel)
Hydrangea varieties
Itea ilicifolia (sweetspire)
Lavandula (lavender)
Ligustrum lucidum (privet)
Magnolia ×soulangeana (garden magnolia or
   saucer magnolia)
Magnolia stellata (star magnolia)
Mahonia
Myrtus (myrtle)
Olearia (daisy bush)
Paeonia delavayi (tree peony)
Philadelphus (mock orange)

Rosa (rose)
Rosmarinus varieties (rosemary)
Sarcococca (sweet box)
Skimmia varieties
Tamarix (tamarisk)
Viburnum varieties

Decorative Planting

Deciduous Shrubs (Including Wall Shrubs)

Caryopteris
Ceanothus
Chaenomeles
Cistus
Convolvulus cneorum
Cytisus
Deutzia
Fuchsia
Genista
Halimium
Lavandula
Lavatera
Spiraea
Syringa
Viburnum
Weigela

Decorative Climbers

Clematis
Cobaea
Hedera
Hydrangea anomala subsp. *petiolaris*
Lathyrus
Lonicera
Parthenocissus
Passiflora
Rhodochiton
Rosa
Solanum
Trachelospermum

Tropaeolum
Vitis
Wisteria

Rounded Plants

Berberis thunbergii 'Atropurpurea Nana'
Buxus
Genista hispanica
Hebe varieties
Lavandula angustifolia 'Hidcote'
Ruta graveolens
Santolina
Teucrium

Grasses

Arundo donax (giant reed)
Calamagrostis ×acutiflora 'Karl Foerster'
Carex elata 'Aurea' (Bowles' golden sedge)
Deschampsia cespitosa (tufted hair grass)
Festuca amethystina (sheep's fescue)
Festuca glauca (blue fescue)
Hakonêchloa macra
Helictotrichon sempervirens (blue oat grass)
Milium effusum 'Aureum' (Bowles' golden grass)
Miscanthus sinsensis (Chinese silver grass)
Molinia (purple moor grass)
Panicum virigatum (switch grass)
Pennisetum alopecuroides (fountain grass)
Stipa tenuifolia

Herbaceous Planting

Broad-Brush Herbaceous Perennials

Achillea
Aconitum
Agapanthus
Alchemilla mollis
Anemone japonica
Anthemis punctata

Artemisia
Aster
Astrantia
Bergenia
Campanula
Crocosmia
Dianthus
Diascia
Dicentra
Digitalis
Epilobium
Eryngium
Euphorbia
Geranium
Hemerocallis
Hosta
Iris
Kniphofia
Lobelia
Macleaya
Nepeta
Oenothera
Paeonia
Penstemon
Persicaria
Rodgersia
Romneya coulteri
Ruta graveolens
Salvia
Sedum
Sisyrinchium striatum
Thalictrum
Veratrum
Zauschneria californica

Plants with Fleeting Effects

(B) after the plant name denotes a bulbous plant.

Allium (B)
Alstroemeria
Amaryllis (B)
Anemone blanda (B)
Canna (half-hardy in Britain)

Chionodoxa (B)

Colchicum (B)

Cosmos

Crocus (B)

Cyclamen (B)

Dahlia (half-hardy in Britain)

Digitalis

Felicia

Fritillaria (B)

Galanthus (B)

Galtonia (B)

Gladiolus (B)

Hedychium (half-hardy in Britain)

Helichrysum

Lilium (B)

Lupinus

Malva moschata

Muscari (B)

Narcissus (B)

Nectaroscordum (B)

Nerine (B)

Nicotiana

Osteospermum

Papaver

Phlox

Pulsatilla

Ricinus (half-hardy in Britain)

Salvia

Scilla (B)

Tulipa (B)

Verbena

Viola

Plant Hardiness Zones

In the United Kingdom, plant hardiness is generally described in terms of relative hardiness. A plant can be fully hardy, frost-hardy, half-hardy or frost-tender. In other parts of the world, however, hardiness is often more complex because of the wide variety of climates. Often, plant hardiness zones are used. These zones are a guide to help you know which plants will grow where you live.

United States and Canada

Based on weather records throughout North America, temperature zones have been created and mapped (see page 274). The United States Department of Agriculture (USDA) hardiness zone map (this 1990 version is based on weather records from 1974 to 1986) is generally considered the standard measure of plant hardiness throughout much of the United States. The Canadian government's agriculture department has issued a similar map for Canada. The USDA map divides North America into eleven hardiness zones. Zone 1 is the coldest, zone 11 the warmest, comprising a tropical area found only in Hawaii and southernmost Florida. Generally, the colder zones are found at higher latitudes and higher elevations.

If you live outside North America, you can roughly translate the USDA hardiness zones by finding out how low the temperatures reach in your area and then using the chart on page 274 to find your corresponding zone.

The Problem with Plant Hardiness Zones

The average minimum temperature is not the only factor in figuring out whether a plant will survive in your garden. Soil types, rainfall, daytime temperatures, day length, wind, humidity and heat also play roles. For example, although Austin, Texas, and Portland, Oregon, are both in zone 8, the local climates are dramatically different. Even within a city,

a street or a spot protected by a warm wall in your own garden, there may be microclimates that affect how plants grow. The zones are a good starting point, but you still need to determine for yourself what will and won't work in your garden.

Sunset and American Horticultural Society Maps

Gardeners in the western United States often use a twenty-four-zone climate system created forty years ago by *Sunset* magazine. The *Sunset* zone maps, which cover thirteen western states, are much more precise than the USDA map, since they factor in not only minimum winter temperatures but also summer highs, lengths of growing seasons, humidity and rainfall patterns, to provide a more accurate picture of what will grow there. If you live in the western United States you'll find that nurseries, garden centres and other western gardeners usually refer to the *Sunset* climate zones rather than the USDA plant hardiness zones.

The American Horticultural Society (AHS) Plant Heat-Zone Map aims to tell gardeners if a plant cannot survive in a place, based on the high temperatures in the area rather than the cold temperatures. There is currently an effort to mark all plants with not just the USDA and Sunset zones but also the AHS heat zones.

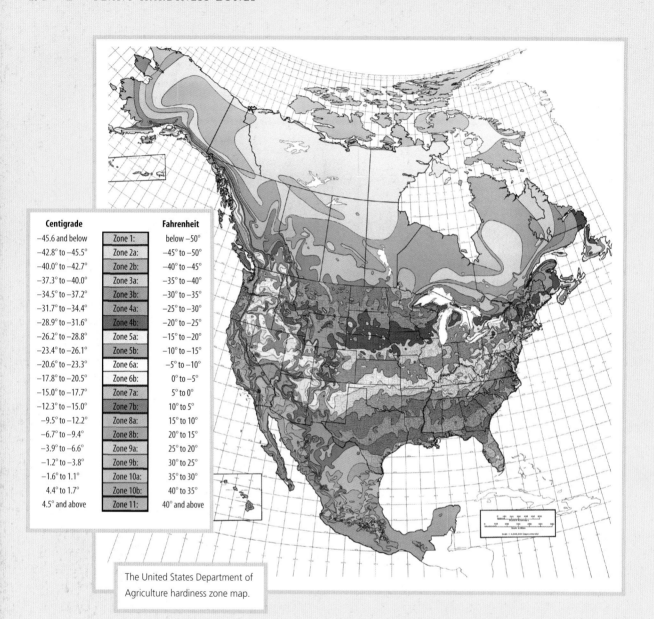

Centigrade		Fahrenheit
−45.6 and below	Zone 1:	below −50°
−42.8° to −45.5°	Zone 2a:	−45° to −50°
−40.0° to −42.7°	Zone 2b:	−40° to −45°
−37.3° to −40.0°	Zone 3a:	−35° to −40°
−34.5° to −37.2°	Zone 3b:	−30° to −35°
−31.7° to −34.4°	Zone 4a:	−25° to −30°
−28.9° to −31.6°	Zone 4b:	−20° to −25°
−26.2° to −28.8°	Zone 5a:	−15° to −20°
−23.4° to −26.1°	Zone 5b:	−10° to −15°
−20.6° to −23.3°	Zone 6a:	−5° to −10°
−17.8° to −20.5°	Zone 6b:	0° to −5°
−15.0° to −17.7°	Zone 7a:	5° to 0°
−12.3° to −15.0°	Zone 7b:	10° to 5°
−9.5° to −12.2°	Zone 8a:	15° to 10°
−6.7° to −9.4°	Zone 8b:	20° to 15°
−3.9° to −6.6°	Zone 9a:	25° to 20°
−1.2° to −3.8°	Zone 9b:	30° to 25°
−1.6° to 1.1°	Zone 10a:	35° to 30°
4.4° to 1.7°	Zone 10b:	40° to 35°
4.5° and above	Zone 11:	40° and above

The United States Department of
Agriculture hardiness zone map.

Glossary

Aggregate Small stone content of a given mixture.

Ashlar A facing of dressed stone blocks on a backing wall of brick, rough stone or concrete block.

Automatic valve A valve which can be remotely operated. The remote operation method may be electrical (the most common) or hydraulic. Automatic valves are commonly used as "control valves" for irrigation systems.

Ball valve A valve which controls the water by means of a rotating ball with a hole through the centre. When the hole is aligned with the water flow, the water moves freely through the valve with almost no friction loss. When the ball is rotated so that the hole is not aligned, the flow is completely shut off. Ball valves are used primarily as isolation valves. They tend to be very reliable and trouble-free, but ball valves as a group tend to require more effort to turn on and off than other valves. For largest pipes, butterfly valves are usually used rather than ball valves.

Ballast A mixture of sand and stone aggregate. Usually associated with the mixture used for making concrete.

Balustrade A complete railing system consisting of a top handrail supported by balusters (which sometimes rest on a bottom rail).

Batter The angle of a wall where it is made to lean inwards from the perpendicular.

Belt course A continuous horizontal course of flat stones marking a division in the wall plane.

Bentonite A natural clay product commonly used for a soil sealant in ponds. When hydrated, the bentonite granules swell into the voids surrounding soil particles, creating a tough watertight seal.

Blinding A layer of sand laid to cover sharp edges of stone, such as over a hardcore base, or when laying a liner for a pool.

Bond The way in which bricks or stone are laid to give structural strength.

Brick on edge A brick laid with the thin stretcher face uppermost, as when used as a trim to an edging or as a coping to a wall.

Brushed finish A textured finish obtained by brushing with a coarse rotary-type wire brush.

Brushed aggregate Concrete, the surface of which has been brushed before setting (when "green") to expose the selected stone aggregate to give a textured finish. Also referred to as exposed aggregate.

Bull nose The convex rounding of a stone member, such as a stair tread.

Bush-hammered finish A textured finish made by a pounding action.

Cement The medium used as the binding agent in mortar or concrete.

Chat-sawn finish A finish featuring irregular, uneven markings.

Concrete A mixture made up of cement, sharp sand and aggregate (usually gravel stone). The sand and stone are often referred to as ballast.

Controller A timer used to turn an automatic irrigation system on and off. Controllers range from very simple to extremely sophisticated computer systems that utilize modems, cell phones or radios and allow two-way communication between the controller and the units being controlled (valves, metres, weather stations, soil moisture and sensors, for example).

Coping The top course of a wall, usually made of brick, stone or concrete, designed to prevent water from seeping into the body of the wall.

Coursed Describes stone or brick laid in a particular pattern.

Cubic feet A measurement of liquid quantity, often used by water companies in the United States. A cubic foot is 1 foot long, 1 foot wide and 1 foot deep.

Curbing Slabs and blocks of stone bordering streets, walks and so forth.

Damp-proof course (DPC) A course laid near the base of a wall to prevent moisture rising within the wall. It can consist of a number of courses of high-density engineering bricks, two courses of overlapping tiles or a layer of bitumen-impregnated strip. Where there is a poured concrete foundation this can also be referred to as the "top of foundation".

Design pressure The pressure at which a specific piece of irrigation equipment is designed to operate.

Drip irrigation Any type of irrigation that applies water to the soil very slowly. Drip irrigation tends to be the most efficient irrigation technology in terms of both water and energy use.

Drip system An irrigation system that uses drip irrigation.

Dry-mix A mixture of sand and cement without any water added, sometimes used when laying brick or slab paving.

Emitter A small device, also known as a dripper, that controls the flow going to the soil during drip irrigation. Emitters come in many different flow rates and styles.

Fall The slight slope created to carry water off hard surfaces to prevent flooding and puddling. The fall, also referred to as the slope or grade, is directed towards open soil areas or specially sited drains and gullies.

Finish A surface treatment. Stones may be finished in a variety of ways. In general, smooth finishes emphasize colour and veining, while rough finishes subdue veining and markings.

Flagstone Thin slabs of stone used for flagging or paving walks, driveways, patios and so forth, generally consisting of fine-grained sandstone, bluestone, quartzite or slate, although other stones may be used.

Flamed finish A rough finish developed with intense heat.

Footing The load-bearing (underground) substructure of a wall—for example, with a wall, the excavated trench, foundation and lower courses.

Gallons per minute (GPM) A measurement of water flow primarily used in the United States.

Gauging A grinding process that results in the uniform thickness of all pieces of material to be used together.

Gravity flow A water system that relies on gravity to provide the pressure required to deliver the water. Consists of a water source located at a higher elevation than the water delivery points.

Ground-water table The level at any given time of the water travelling through the soil. It varies according to the soil conditions and the time of year.

Gulley A shallow channel that carries away surface water. Sometimes used as another name for a drain, a gulley may also be known as a swale.

Hardcore A mixture of broken brick or stone used to create a firm base on which to lay concrete foundations, paving and so on. It should not include any soil or traces of vegetation. Can also be referred to as base course, bedding or sub grade.

Head to head Said of sprinklers spaced so that the water from one sprinkler throws all the way to the next sprinkler. Most sprinklers are designed to give the best performance when this kind of spacing is used.

Hoggin A mixture of gravel and clay used as the binding agent in gravel paths and driveways.

Honed finish A dull finish without reflections.

Hydro-zone An area of an irrigation system in which all the factors that influence the watering schedule are similar. Typical factors to be considered would be the type of plants, the precipitation rate of sprinklers or emitters, solar radiation, wind, soil type and slope.

In situ Constructed on site in the position shown. For example, a concrete wall is created in situ by pouring liquid concrete into a "form" using timber shuttering.

Liner A waterproof layer used to create water features ranging from small pools to lakes. This can be a variety of materials, including clay and sheeting made of butyl or PVC.

Litres per minute A metric measurement of water flow used worldwide.

Mainline The pipes going from the water source to the control valves.

Mortar A mixture of soft sand and cement used for walling, paving and so forth. Sometimes referred to as cement.

Natural cleft Stones formed in layers in the ground. When stones are cleaved or separated along a natural seam, the remaining surface is referred to as a natural cleft surface.

Nozzle The part of a sprinkler that the water comes out of. Usually a nozzle is carefully engineered to assure a good spray pattern. In most cases the nozzle is removable so that is can be easily cleaned or replaced. With plastic nozzles, replacement is generally preferred over cleaning, as small scratches in the plastic can cause big problems with water distribution uniformity.

Operating pressure The pressure at which a device or irrigation system is designed to operate. There can be "optimum operating pressure", "minimum operating pressure", "maximum operating pressure" and "operating pressure range".

Paver A "shin" brick specially manufactured for brick paving. It can also be used as a facing on walls.

Planed timber Timber that has been cut to a nominal size with a saw and has a rough finish. Also referred to as sawn timber or rough-sawn lumber, this timber can be planed or sanded for a smooth finish. Timber sizes are quoted in sawn sizes unless otherwise stated. For example, after planing, it is "F4S" (Finished Four Sides): 50 × 100 mm (2 × 4 in.) is the rough-sawn dimension, but the actual piece of wood measures 37 × 87 mm (1.5 × 3.4 in.).

Polished finish A shiny finish with sharp reflections. This is the smoothest finish available, resulting in a high lustre (gloss).

Pop-up sprinkler head A sprinkler head that retracts below ground level when it is not operating.

Precipitation rate A measurement of water application, given in the depth of water applied to the soil—in other words, the depth that the water would be if it did not run off or soak into the soil. In the United States, precipitation rates are measured in inches per hour. In metric countries, they are measured in mm per hour.

Pressure gauge A device used to measure water pressure. The best pressure gauges are "liquid filled"; however, most inexpensive gauges work well enough for irrigation use.

Pump A device that increases water pressure or moves water.

PVC Polyvinyl chloride, a type of plastic used to make pond liners and water pipe. PVC is available in several colours. Purple indicates unclean or wastewater.

Quoins Stones at the external corner or edge of a wall emphasized by size, projection, rustication or by a different finish.

Random course Paving laid so that the roughly shaped stones are in a random pattern instead of in coursed lines. Various sizes of square paving can be laid in a random pattern, such as when using slate or York stone paving.

Riprap Irregular, broken and randomly sized pieces of rock used for facing abutments and fills. Stones are thrown together without order to form a foundation, breakwater or sustaining wall.

Rise The height of stone (generally in veneer) or the vertical dimension between two successive steps.

Rock-face finish Also referred to as a pitch-face finish, this convex finish is similar to a split-face finish except that the face of the stone is given line and plane, producing a bold appearance that is considered to more closely resemble natural stone.

Sharp sand A sand that is washed to remove the silt content, used mostly for concrete and rendering. It is coarser, larger-grained, and lighter in colour than soft sand.

Slab A lengthwise cut of a large quarry block of stone, approximately 1.5×2.4 m (5×8 ft.).

Smooth finish A softened effect created by a saw, grinder or planer.

Snapped edge A style, also known as quarry cut or broken edge, that usually involves a natural breaking of stone either by hand or machine. The break should be at right angles to the top and bottom surface.

Soft sand A very fine sand with a relatively high silt content, often referred to as building sand and used to make mortar for brickwork.

Spall A stone fragment that has split or broken off the face of a stone, either by the force of a blow or through weathering. Sizes may vary from chip size to large stones. Spalls are primarily used for taking up large voids in rough rubble or mosaic patterns.

Split-face finish Also referred to as a sawed-bed finish, this finish is concave or convex, usually sawed on the stone bed and split by hand or machine so that the face of the stone exhibits the natural quarry texture.

Sprinkler A device that distributes water over a given area for irrigation.

Stretcher and header The different faces of a brick. The stretcher is the long face, either when seen as the narrow side in walling or when laid on edge, or the wider face when laid flat in paving. The header is the small, end face of the brick.

Thermal finish A coarse finish created by applying a mechanically controlled flame to a surface.

Tread A flat stone or surface used as the top walking surface on a step.

Valve A device used to control the flow of water. Isolation valves are used to shut water off for repairs. Control valves turn water on and off to the individual circuits of sprinklers or drip emitters. Check valves allow water to flow in only one direction. Master valves are located at the water source and turn water on and off for the entire irrigation system when not in use.

Veneer Any decorative facing material which is not meant to be load-bearing.

Recommended Reading

You may wish to extend your understanding and skills in garden design through further reading on the subject. The books on these lists include both American and British titles. If a title is out of print, it is often possible to find a copy in a secondhand bookstore.

History

Barlow Rogers, Elizabeth. 2001. *Landscape Design: A Cultural and Architectural History*. New York: Harry N. Abrams.

Hobhouse, Penelope. 2002. *The Story of Gardening*. London: Dorling Kindersley.

Otis, Denise. 2002. *Ground for Pleasure: Four Centuries of the American Garden*. New York: Harry N. Abrams.

Quest-Ritson, Charles. 1996. *The English Garden Abroad*. London: Penguin.

Design and Inspiration

Brookes, John. 2002. *Garden Masterclass*. New York: Dorling Kindersley.

Dickey, Page. 2003. *Breaking Ground: Portraits of Ten Garden Designers*. New York: Artisan.

Dixon, Trisha. 1998. *The Vision of Edna Walling*. Hawthorn, Victoria: Bloomings. Australia and New Zealand only.

Hayward, Gordon. 2003. *Your House, Your Garden: A Foolproof Approach to Garden Design*. New York: W. W. Norton.

Strong, Roy. 1989. *A Small Garden Designer's Handbook*. Boston: Little, Brown.

Strong, Roy. 1995. *Successful Small Gardens: New Designs for Time-Conscious Gardeners*. New York: Rizzoli.

Trulove, James Grayson, ed. 1998. *The New American Garden: Innovations in Residential Landscape Architecture: Sixty Case Studies*. New York: Watson-Guptill.

Verey, Rosemary. 1989. *Classic Garden Design: How to Adapt and Re-create Garden Features of the Past*. New York: Random House.

Drawing

Alexander, Rosemary, and Karena Batstone. 1996. *A Handbook for Garden Designers*. London: Ward Lock.

Reid, Grant W. 2002. *Landscape Graphics: Plan, Section, and Perspective Drawing and Landscape Spaces*. New York: Watson-Guptill.

Hard Landscaping

In addition to any of the collection of *Sunset* and *Ortho* books:

Archer-Wills, Anthony. 2002. *The Water Gardener: A Complete Guide to Designing, Constructing and Planting Water Features*. New York: Todtri.

Blanc, Alan. 1996. *Landscape Construction and Detailing*. New York: McGraw-Hill.

Van Sweden, James. 2003. *Architecture in the Garden*. New York: Random House.

Plants

Beales, Peter. 1997. *Classic Roses*. London: Harvill.

Brickell, Christopher, and Trevor Cole, eds. 2002. *American Horticultural Society Encyclopedia of Plants and Flowers: The Definitive Practical Guide*. New York: Dorling Kindersley.

Davis, Brian. 1987. *The Gardener's Illustrated Encyclopedia of Trees and Shrubs: A Guide to More Than 2000 Varieties*. Emmaus, Pennsylvania: Rodale.

Dorling Kindersley. 2000. *American Horticultural Society Great Plant Guide*. New York: Dorling Kindersley.

Hillier Nurseries. 2002. *Hillier Manual of Trees and Shrubs*. Ed. John Hillier. Newton Abbot, England: David & Charles.

Phillips, Roger, and Martyn E. Rix. 1988. *Roses*. London: Pan.

Phillips, Roger, and Martyn E. Rix. 1989. *Bulbs*. Ed. Brian Mathew. London: Pan.

Phillips, Roger, and Martyn E. Rix. 2002. *Perennials: The Definitive Reference with over 2500 Photographs*. Toronto: Firefly.

Royal Horticultural Society. 2004. *RHS Plant Finder 2004—2005*. London: Dorling Kindersley. For British use only; reprinted annually.

Stuart Thomas, Graham. 1992. *Ornamental Shrubs, Climbers and Bamboos: Excluding Roses and Rhododendrons*. Portland, Oregon: Sagapress.

Stuart Thomas, Graham. 1993. *Perennial Garden Plants, or, The Modern Florilegium*. London: Orion.

Planting

DiSabato-Aust, Tracy. 1998. *The Well-Tended Perennial Garden: Planting and Pruning Techniques*. Portland, Oregon: Timber Press.

Hunningher, Erica. 2002. *Gardens of Inspiration*. New York: Dorling Kindersley.

Johnson, Arthur T. 1972. *Plant Names Simplified: Their Pronunciation, Derivation and Meaning*. Bromyard, Herefordshire: Landsman's Bookshop.

Lord, Tony. 1999. *Designing with Roses*. North Pomfret, Vermont: Trafalgar Square.

Quest-Ritson, Charles. 2003. *Royal Horticultural Society Encyclopedia of Roses*. London: Dorling Kindersley.

Tettoni, Luca Inveruizzi, and William Warren. 2001. *Balinese Gardens*. Boston: Tuttle.

Toogood, Alan. 1991. *The Hillier Guide to Connoisseur's Plants*. Portland, Oregon: Timber Press.

Warren, William. 2000. *The Tropical Garden*. London: Thames & Hudson.

Irrigation

Smith, Stephen W. 1996. *Landscape Irrigation: Design and Management*. New York: John Wiley & Sons.

Lighting

Lennox Moyer, Janet. 1992. *The Landscape Lighting Book*. New York: John Wiley & Sons.

Raine, John. 2001. *Garden Lighting*. San Diego, California: Laurel Glen.

Index

THE CONFESSORS' CLUB

Jack Fredrickson

This first world edition published 2015
in Great Britain and the USA by
SEVERN HOUSE PUBLISHERS LTD of
19 Cedar Road, Sutton, Surrey, England, SM2 5DA.
Trade paperback edition first published 2015 in Great
Britain and the USA by SEVERN HOUSE PUBLISHERS LTD.

British Library Cataloguing in Publication Data

Fredrickson, Jack author.
  The confessors' club. – (A Dek Elstrom mystery)
  1. Elstrom, Dek (Fictitious character)–Fiction.
  2. Private investigators–Illinois–Chicago–Fiction.
  3. Serial murder investigation–Fiction. 4. Detective and
  mystery stories.
  I. Title II. Series
  813.6-dc23

ISBN-13: 978-0-7278-8488-6 (cased)
ISBN-13: 978-1-84751-594-0 (trade paper)
ISBN-13: 978-1-78010-645-8 (e-book)

Typeset by Palimpsest Book Production Ltd.,
Falkirk, Stirlingshire, Scotland.
Printed digitally in the USA.

For Jack R. Fredrickson

My guide, my dad

ACKNOWLEDGMENTS

The whole gang – Patrick Riley, Missy Lyda, Eric Frisch, Mary Anne Bigane and Joe Bigane – slogged through the early drafts of this one, criticizing, counseling, supporting. As always, I'm grateful.

Thanks, too, to the ever-patient Sara Porter of Severn House for managing this book, and me, with grace and aplomb.

First, and last, thank you, Susan. Again. For it all.

The gold Rolex Day-Date on his wrist had cost eleven thousand dollars. It was still keeping perfect time, but that would be expected. It was water resistant to a depth far greater than the shallows at the marsh end of the small lake. And it had been engineered to run on the faintest of movements: the gentle lapping of the water through the rushes was more than enough to engage the self-winding mechanism. It was a gentleman's wristwatch, designed for a man who need make only subtle gestures – a wealthy man, a man of nuance.

He had dressed well. His gray gabardine trousers were of the finest wool, light for the warming spring. His white shirt was cut to precise specification, sent over from Jermyn Street in London. His shoes were English as well, lace-up brogues polished by a houseman to a high gloss.

His attire had not fared as well as the wristwatch. The press had gone from the trousers and soft, milky flesh protruded where the water reeds had abraded the wool. The shirt was now a putrid green, mucked by the moss at the shore. And the shoes had puckered and blistered, since even the finest of leathers, no matter how well oiled, are not meant to withstand even partial submersion.

His face, of course, had suffered the worst of it. The part of the forehead closest to the bullet hole had gone, nibbled away in tiny bites by the sunny fish and microscopic urchins that worked the shore of the small lake.

His eyes, though, still commanded. They remained as clear and direct as they'd been in life, demanding that notice be taken, witness be made, to the truth of the horror they had seen.

ONE

Amanda called me two days before what would have been our fifth wedding anniversary.

'Happy almost anniver—' I said, before I slammed my mouth shut on words that bubbled up from nowhere. I hoped.

My remembering had caught her off guard, too. 'Dek, how sweet of you,' she said, after an awkward beat. Then, 'I'd like to have dinner.'

We hadn't spoken in months. 'Surely not to celebrate?' I asked.

'Our divorce?' She managed a little laugh. 'Of course not.'

'I'm good all next week, after Monday.'

'Business has come back so well you're not available until then?'

I hesitated for an awkward moment of my own. 'I'm headed out of town.'

'Not business, then,' she said.

'A mini-vacation.'

'Today?' She knew I'd never taken a vacation in my life.

'Not for a couple of days.'

She paused, then said, 'How about tonight? It's important.'

I paused too, but only for a second. 'I'll pick you up. You're still on Chicago's tony Lake Shore Drive?'

'Did you get shock absorbers yet?'

'They diminish the aged Jeep experience.'

'I'll meet you at Petterino's,' she said. 'Afterwards, we'll go to the theater. My subscription tickets are for tonight.'

It was going to be like old times, for whatever reason.

'A play afterward?' I managed. 'Surely you remember that's over my head.'

'See you at Petterino's at six.' Her voice softened. 'And Dek?'

'Ma'am?'

'Little is over your head.'

Little was over Jenny's head as well, though her calling ten minutes after I'd clicked off with Amanda could only have been coincidence.

'I can't wait to show you Fisherman's Wharf,' she said.

It was going to be our first time together since she had taken the San Francisco television job eight months earlier. They'd been long months, those eight, and we were set to celebrate the wonder of making our new relationship work at such a long distance.

'Picturesque, is it?'

'Just your cup of Twinkies,' she said.

'Real and authentic, old-time San Francisco?'

'You can get a picture of Elvis on black velvet to hang above your table saw.'

'Black velvet would also nicely complement the white plastic of the lawn chairs,' I said, of the turret's first-floor conversational grouping. 'I'm also in need of a really wide refrigerator magnet, maybe of the Golden Gate Bridge.' The avocado-colored refrigerator I'd found in an alley was rusting from the inside out, and I was looking to slow the loss of semi-cold air.

'I've got four days off, time enough to take care of all your needs.' She laughed, hanging up, leaving me with the promise of unspoken naughtiness.

And grateful that I hadn't had the chance to tell her I was having dinner with my ex-wife that evening.

TWO

I've always suspected that a malevolent chicken farmer designed the Goodman Theater complex in downtown Chicago. It's set up like a poultry processing plant. Petterino's is on the corner, a high-glitz restaurant of hooded table candles and deeply cushioned chairs. Good food, big prices. Petterino's is for the plumping and the plucking.

The theater connects through an interior doorway so that patrons, overfed and softly sweating, can be shepherded straight to their seats without being aroused by fresh outside air. Amanda always insisted that the Goodman offers mainstream productions, but to me the plays were confusing. And that, I used to say, is the point. Dulled by overeating at Petterino's, staggering straight into the dim plush of the theater, folks are further numbed by droning actors saying things that make no sense. The audience slips from stupor into sleep; it's the poultry man's intent. The Goodman is for the lulling.

Two hours later, the audience is jolted awake by the smattering of applause at the final curtain. Groggy, now disoriented by the sudden noise and lights, they're herded across the street to the garage, where they're made to wait in lines to pay a credit card machine that mumbles nonsensical instructions in an adenoidal, digitized voice, then funneled into other lines for a chance to push their way into one of the two overcrowded elevators. By the time they reach their cars, they're dripping sweat, their eyes bright with the need for escape. But the final chaos is yet to come. The automobile exit lanes all merge into one, and the flow quickly becomes choked, an impacted drain, backed up all the way to the roof. Trapped, frantic at the stoppage, the drivers whimper and slap at their horns, but the sudden, overwhelming noise only enrages them further. Control vanishes; it's every chicken for himself. They gun their engines, aim recklessly at imagined hair-width gaps in the line. Fenders crumple, voices scream. It is at this moment that they welcome death. The garage is for the slaughter.

And somewhere, unseen, the poultry farmer laughs.

To me, it is not amazing that people pay great sums to do this. What shocks is that they subscribe to do it several times a year.

Petterino's was crowded with pre-show diners. Amanda, now one of Chicago's wealthiest socialites, had been provided a quiet table in the corner. As she'd said on the phone, she wanted to talk.

I hadn't seen her since I'd dropped her into the welcoming arms of her father, his small army of heavily armed security men and, pacing in front of them all like a silvered peacock, her impeccably attired, suitably affluent new beau.

She looked magnificent as always, in dark slacks, a cream blouse and the garnet pendant I'd given her for her birthday.

I, in my blue blazer and the least wrinkled of my khaki pants, looked like a used office furniture salesman.

We ordered drinks and proceeded carefully. 'How's business?' she asked.

A scandal, stemming from a false accusation, had trashed my

business and our marriage. The business was resurrecting, though slowly.

'Two more old insurance company clients are using me again to verify accident information. It's not much, but it's a foot on the road to hope.'

'And the turret?' she asked. We were stilted, awkwardly catching up, but there was something else in her voice. Hesitation. She was stalling, not yet ready to tell me why she'd called.

'I've finished hanging the kitchen cabinets and am awaiting only the funds for new appliances. Now I'm up on the third floor.'

'The master bedroom,' she said. It had never been ours. We'd lived in her multi-million-dollar home in Crystal Waters, a gated community, before my career, our marriage, and then her neighborhood had blown up.

The bed, though, had been ours. She hadn't wanted it, but I'd not been willing to give up. I'd hauled it from her house before it had been reduced to rubble.

'I've built a closet,' I said, with as much pride as another man might say of a new Ferrari.

She sent a bemused glance toward the wrinkles in my blue button-down shirt.

'I don't as yet have hangers,' I said.

She smiled. 'Of course.'

'Any day now, some hotshot commodities trader is going to drive by, see my five-story limestone cylinder, and buy it for millions. The turret is my other foot on the road to hope.'

Her smile tightened. I'd slipped, seemingly into pettiness. Richard Rudolph, her silver-haired new beau, was a wealthy commodities trader, and precisely the sort of hotshot I was trying to snare.

'You are well, you and Mr Rudolph?' I asked of the hotshot, trying for casual. It had been some time since my friend Leo Brumsky had reported seeing their picture in the papers, always at some appropriately charitable event. I'd supposed that at some point, Leo had decided I didn't need to stay current on such news.

'He's in Russia – new opportunities,' she said, perhaps a little too quickly. Then, 'Jennifer Gale, the newswoman?' Her gaze was direct, her eyes unblinking.

We were catching up more pointedly now. 'How could you know . . .?'

'Your photo ran in the papers too, Dek. Some journalism awards dinner. She's as lovely in print as she is on television.'

Jennifer Gale had been a features reporter for Channel 8 in Chicago until she'd been offered newsier television opportunities in San Francisco. With me, though, she was Jenny Galecki, a sweet, solidly Polish girl struggling to mix celebrity and ambition with feelings for me. For eight months, we'd managed to stay involved, telephonically. And now I was about to head to San Francisco.

'She is lovely, yes,' I said.

For a moment, we let silence shelter us. We'd moved on, some.

I veered away, asked about her work. She'd given up teaching at the Art Institute to establish philanthropies in her father's name. Wendell Phelps, head of Chicago's largest electric utility, had come to regret being an indifferent parent, and had offered Amanda the chance to do really good things with really big money. It was an offer she did not refuse.

'He's moving me into operations. I'm day-to-day electricity now, Dek. I liaise with every city and town on our grid, building relationships. Philanthropy hasn't been on the agenda for several months.'

'He's prepping you for great responsibilities.'

'All of a sudden, he's in a rush.'

'He's the major shareholder. It's prudent to bring his only child into the family business. Lots of investment to protect.'

Our waitress came with drinks – a Manhattan for her; a first-ever, low-carb beer for me. As in old times, we ordered the everything-but-the-kitchen-sink salads that had long been one of the prides of Petterino's.

She stirred her drink for a long minute, and I took a pull from the bottle of de-carbed beer. It tasted like it had been run through something alive, perhaps hooved, to get the carbohydrates out.

She removed the cocktail stick, its cherry still impaled, and set it on the napkin. 'I've told my father to hire you,' she said.

'Whoa,' I said, understanding why she'd played too long with her drink. I set down the bottle of carb-less beer residue. 'Me, work for your father?'

Wendell Phelps was no admirer of mine. We'd never talked face-to-face, but we'd argued plenty on the phone after his daughter had been abducted. His arrogance, along with my stupidity, had almost gotten her killed.

'Actually we've discussed it several times. No, that's wrong. I've brought it up several times.'

'What, exactly?'

'He's hired bodyguards.'

'A deranged shareholder or some nut pissed about his electric bill?'

'He won't say.'

'The business pages say he's taking heat because of all the service outages. The governor and the mayor are pushing him for equipment upgrades, but the big shareholders don't want him to spend the money. It's a real tussle.'

I reached for the low-carb but quickly stopped my hand; drinking more might stick the taste to my tongue permanently. 'I also heard his stock price dropped. People have lost money. Maybe some cranky shareholder got wiped out.'

'He said it was nothing like that.'

'What then?'

She shook her head. 'He won't say, other than he hired an investigator to take care of it. The man found out nothing, apparently. My father looks old, Dek; old and afraid and weak.'

'Could that have something to do with his new wife?' Long a widower, Wendell's recent marriage lingered only briefly on the society pages before descending into the gossip blogs. The most charitable of them said the bride was charmingly eccentric.

'You're wondering whether she's driven him into becoming delusional? I don't think so. His fear is real.'

'Cops?'

'He hasn't gone to them.'

'What is it with rich people, so afraid of going to the police?' A bomb-wielding extortionist had assaulted the mega-rich home-owners in Crystal Waters, yet none of her neighbors wanted to call the cops. At least not until people started getting blown up.

'He said he'd talk to you.'

'Because if he didn't, you'd hire me yourself, and then he'd lose control of what I learned?'

She smiled a little. 'Of course.'

'No doubt he pointed out I'm a lightweight as far as investigators go, that I research records for lawyers, chase down accident information for insurance companies. I don't do life or death.'

'You did, for me.'

'I got you kidnapped.'

'Talk to him, Dek. Reassure me he's having some sort of small mental lapse. Tell me he's just feeling too many ordinary pressures.'

I smiled then, too, because ultimately that was what I always did with Amanda. Our salads came, and we smiled through them as well. Our awkwardness was disappearing.

After the play, she told me I'd slept through another magnificent performance. That was too close to old times, too.

THREE

Wendell Phelps's house, stone clad and slate roofed, loomed high, a dark fortress on the bluffs above Lake Michigan. To the south, the Chicago skyline was a blur in the gloom of the late March sky, as though it were a backdrop painted pale and inconsequential to make the magnificent mansion stand out even more. Down below, past the closely mowed lawn and the terrace of tightly trimmed yews, the lake lapped at the edge of the raked beach, gray and vaguely restless.

One of the doors in the five-car garage was open, exposing the tail end of what I knew was Wendell's old black Mercedes and, alongside it, the lighter-colored fender of something inexpensively American, likely belonging to a live-in housekeeper. I drove past the garage and stopped behind a dark brown Nissan pickup truck.

A young woman in her early twenties, wearing a brown sweatshirt that matched the truck, was picking shredded yellow flowers out of the concrete urns at the base of the front steps. Large money bought that; fresh flowers before spring. I got out of the Jeep and smiled at the girl, one tradesperson to another.

'Pigs,' she said, jamming the ruined blooms into a paper yardwaste bag.

'Ah, but they pay the bills,' I said, and walked up the stairs to the massive walnut door.

Amanda told me once that state senators, mayors and business leaders had been summoned to this house, but the only visitor who'd not been made to wait at the door like a pizza driver was the mop-headed former governor of Illinois, now doing prison time out west. Go figure, she'd said, laughing.

An unremarkable man answered the door. Not tall, not short; not dark haired, not blond; not young and certainly not old. Right down to the faint gray stripes in his bland blue suit, he was indistinct, an average man, a medium all around. The best ones are like that: mediums all around. They don't get noticed in a crowd. Only the slight bulge in his suit, under the left arm, gave him away. He was one of the bodyguards Amanda had mentioned, and he was packing.

I showed him my driver's license. 'Dek Elstrom to see Mr Phelps.'

'You're expected.' He pulled the door open all the way.

The foyer was dark, lit only by four small wall sconces. It was only after I'd followed him halfway across what seemed like a football field of black-and-white tile that I realized the walls were paneled in walnut as thick as the front door. That the head of Chicago's largest electric company was wasting none of the company product at home might have come from frugality. Or it could have come from fear.

The bodyguard knocked on a door, stepped aside, and motioned for me to enter. I went into a library as dim as the foyer. The curtains were drawn. The only light came from a yellow glass lamp on the desk in front of the curtains.

'Mr Elstrom,' Wendell Phelps said, rising from behind the lamp.

I'd seen his face in the business news and, of course, in the oil portrait I'd cut to make a Halloween mask in the last drunken days of my marriage. Those pictures were of a younger and more relaxed man. As he came closer, I saw lines deeper than any sixty-three-year-old should have. He wore golf clothes – yellow slacks to match the lamp, and a green knit shirt with a crocodile on it – as though he were about to go hit a bucket of balls in his foyer. The croc's mouth was open, which fit with what I knew of Wendell Phelps.

'Mr Phelps,' I said.

We sat on opposing sofas without shaking hands. A tan envelope lay on the low plank table between us. The only other thing on the table was a small framed photograph of a little girl holding a blue balloon. The picture might have been of Amanda, but it was too small to tell in such dim light.

'What has Amanda told you?' he asked.

'She said you hired bodyguards, one of which I saw for myself, and that you retained an investigator, who learned nothing.'

'We speak in confidence, you and I? You do not report back to Amanda?'

'So long as you're the client, and not her.'

He frowned at the reminder of his daughter's threat, and pushed the tan envelope an inch toward me. 'There have already been three murders.' His hand shook a little as he lifted it from the envelope.

There were three letter-sized sheets in the envelope. I held them up to catch the faint light from the desk. They were photocopies of obituaries from the *Chicago Tribune*, the big, quarter-page kind that ran with photographs when someone important died. Each of the three dead men had been prominent in Chicago business. The first had died of a heart attack the previous October, the second from cancer two months later, in December. The most recent had been the victim of a hit-and-run in February, just the month before. None of the obituaries implied murder. I slipped the three sheets back into the envelope and set it on the table.

'They were murdered,' he said.

'Did your investigator tell you this, or is this a hunch?'

'That man was ineffective, and I try never to rely on hunches.'

'Two deaths from illness, the third from a hit-and-run. Not the stuff of foul play.'

'They were CEOs of major corporations.'

His eyes seemed steady; his focus appeared good. Yet he seemed to be speaking gibbered paranoia.

'CEOs die just like ordinary people,' I said.

'They were murdered,' he said again.

'Because they were CEOs?'

'Don't patronize me, Elstrom.' He turned around to look at the heavy curtains. A thin sliver of light, half the width of a pencil,

shone where the two fabric panels did not quite meet. He got up
and went to pull them together.

'Yes,' he said, remaining by the curtains as though worried
they'd open again on their own. 'I believe they were killed because
they were CEOs.'

I stood then, and walked to the desk. Another tiny picture frame
had caught my eye. 'For what motive?' I asked, picking up the
photo.

It was the same as the one on the plank table: a little girl holding
a blue balloon. I wondered whether it was the only childhood
photo he had of Amanda.

'I'm hiring you to find that out,' he said.

'To keep your daughter from nosing into it?'

'She need not worry about this.'

'A plot to kill major business executives would surely interest
the brass of the Chicago Police Department. They'll investigate
for free.'

'A man with my links to the business community would lose
credibility if such accusations were seen as unsubstantiated, or
worse, just plain crazy. The effect on my shareholders would be
disastrous. Gather sufficient information, Elstrom, and then I'll go
to the police.'

He handed me a folded check from the pocket of his golf shirt.
It was for two thousand dollars.

It was too big a retainer to indulge what seemed like a rich
man's delusion, and it was more than I'd made in the last two
months. I put the check in my pocket.

He reached to pinch the seam in the curtains, though no light
was coming through. Whatever the man's tensions were, they were
very real to him. I took the manila envelope and showed myself
out into the hall. The Medium Man was waiting, and together we
made footstep echoes across the marble to the front door.

The flower girl had almost finished replacing the shredded
yellow blossoms with vibrant, dark red blooms. I winked at her
as I came down the concrete stairs.

She frowned. 'Pigs,' she said.

FOUR

The Bohemian's offices are on the top floor of a ten-story rehabbed yellow brick factory on the west side of Chicago. The ancient wrought-iron elevator doors opened right into the reception area. Earnest-looking bond and stock-fund sales-people, wearing good suits and carrying thin attachés, sat on the green leather wing chairs and sofas, studying the proposals they were about to pitch to the Bohemian's staff of financial advisors. I crossed the red oriental carpet to the black walnut reception desk.

'Dek Elstrom, wondering if I might have a moment of Mr Chernek's time.'

The receptionist was new, a tanned brunette at least a decade shy of murmuring the word 'Botox.' She flashed a perfect white smile. 'Do you have an appointment, Mr Elstrom?'

I shook my head. 'If you would just ask?'

'Certainly, sir.' She pushed a button on her telephone console and said my name with a question mark into the thin mouthpiece of her headset.

Behind me, I thought I heard the uneasy shifting of good wool. The tailored suits had sensed a sudden intrusion of polyester. Though my blue blazer, with but the merest hint of mustard on the left cuff, had a forty-five per cent wool content, a blend is a blend, and was as out of place in that reception area as a bongo drummer at a chamber recital. Even the grandfather clock in the corner seemed to stop ticking, anticipating my swift dispatch.

Buffy, the Bohemian's frozen-faced, helmet-haired assistant, materialized in less than a minute to hold the door open for me. And a woman in one of the green leather chairs behind me sighed.

In a different life, I couldn't have gotten into Anton Chernek's offices to wash the windows. He's an advisor – a *consigliere* to Chicago's most prominent families, the ones whose names adorn the city's museums and parks, endow its philanthropies, and attend its most fashionable events. I imagined his financial counseling was straightforward enough – the usual recommendations on blue-chip stocks, bonds, mutual funds and such – but it's his role as the go-to guy for other, touchier concerns that defines his real value to the city's ruling elite. When a problem arises that cannot be handled traditionally – a divorce arising from the gamier appetites of human behavior; a scion caught cheating at a prestigious university; an embezzlement within a family firm – the rich summon the Bohemian. He is wise and he is discreet. He makes problems go away quietly, with smiling assurances, packets of cash and, if need be, swift retribution.

We first met when he accompanied Amanda's lawyers to our divorce settlement conference. He'd liked that I'd brought no lawyer and no demands. Months later, he hired me to uncover who'd begun blowing up houses in Amanda's gated community. The case got more gnarly when Chernek was accused of embezzling from his clients. The charge was false, but he was publicly humiliated, and that cost him most of his staff and, for a time, many of his clients.

I knew about false accusations, so I didn't pile on. I kept on reporting to him as though nothing had happened. He never forgot that, or the fact that I never hit him up for freebie financial advice about how to manage the 250 dollars I'd rat-holed in a passbook savings account.

'*Vuh-lo-dek*,' he boomed from behind his carved desk, stretching the two syllables into three. I'm named for my grandfather, a handle that charmed the Bohemian the first time we met. He's been the only one. Not even an animal used to extract carbohydrates from beer should be named Vlodek.

I sat in one of the burgundy leather guest chairs. The Bohemian was around sixty, and a big man, just shy of my six feet two. Today he wore a pale yellow, spread-collar shirt with a figured navy tie that perfectly matched the color of the custom coat hanging on his antique mahogany coat rack. His teeth gleamed; his tan glowed. Not a single combed-back silver hair was out of place.

'You're prospering, Anton,' I said.

'Times are fine, Vlodek. And you?'

'Improving.' I handed him Wendell Phelps's tan envelope. 'I'm interested in these three men.'

He removed the photocopies. He might well have been on

retainer with the men whose obituaries he was now reading, but his face betrayed nothing. The Bohemian respected confidences, even with the dead.

'Fine businessmen, in the heavy cream,' he said, looking up. 'Right up at the top with your ex-father-in-law.' He leaned forward slightly. 'Why do their deaths interest you?'

'A client is wondering if anything about those deaths was overlooked.'

He nodded, respecting my need to maintain confidentiality. 'How may I help?'

'How well did you know these men?'

He eased back in his chair. 'Two of them quite well. The third, Grant Carson, the one who got killed by a car last month, I'd met only at social functions.'

'Have there been rumors about their deaths?'

'None that I've heard. It was no surprise that Benno Barberi died of a heart attack last October. His friends knew he had a bad heart,' he said. 'Jim Whitman's death last December came after a long illness, also as the *Tribune* said. That's true enough, as far as it goes, but technically his was a suicide. Jim was dying, and he swallowed all his painkillers at one time. The papers had the decency not to print that, though it's widely known. As for Carson's hit-and-run, you'll have to check with the police. They haven't found the driver, but I don't believe they saw it as anything other than a tragic accident.' He slipped the papers back into the envelope. 'How is Wendell Phelps, Vlodek?' His smile had become sly, venturing a guess about who had hired me.

I gave back just enough of a grin to keep him wondering. 'How many men in Chicago are like these three?'

'Of their stature in business? Off the top of my head, I'd say perhaps fifty.'

'May I have a list?'

The Bohemian's eyes worked to get behind my own. 'You'll keep me apprised?' Meaning that I'd alert him to anyone I thought might be in trouble. Client safety was always his major concern.

'Of course.' It was a necessary quid pro quo.

'I'll email names,' he said.

FIVE

T raffic was backed up solid on the outbound expressway. No matter the years of supposed improvements, the Eisenhower is almost always a crawl. In my darker moments, I let myself think a secret cabal of oil and communications executives engineered it that way, to trap drivers into burning up expensive gallons of gasoline while raging on their phones, burning up cell-plan minutes. Like my Goodman Theater imaginings, it's baloney – a poor man's cranky fantasy and flimsy as a cobweb – but ever since the Jeep's radio got boosted, it's given my mind something to mull when I'm stuck on the Ike.

I wondered if that sort of paranoia got notched up inside Wendell Phelps. The *Tribune* had seen nothing suspicious in the deaths of Barberi and Whitman, nor had they reported Carson's death as anything more sinister than a typical hit-and-run. More calming was the Bohemian's ear. It was finely tuned, and he kept it pressed to the ground, yet nothing about the three deaths had tripped his sensors. Likely enough, Wendell Phelps had given me nothing more than a dark delusion, except his came with the money to pursue it. Me, I had to get stuck in traffic, sucking auto exhaust, to indulge mine.

I got back to Rivertown as the dying sun began turning the turret's rough limestone blocks into a hundred soft shades of yellow, orange, and red. My narrow five story cylinder is always beautiful at sunset, with its shadows and fiery colors, marked hard here and there with the black stripes of the slit windows, but it can be melancholy then as well, a slim monument in dying light to a dead man's dead dream. The turret was my grandfather's fantasy. A small-time bootlegger with big-time plans, he built it as the first of four that were to connect with stone walls to form a grand castle on the bank of the Willahock River. The one turret was all he got built. He died broke, leaving behind only a corner of his dream.

I walked down to the river to count leaves. When I'd moved to the turret on the first of a November several years before, out of money and out of hope, the spindly purple ash growing alongside the water had already turned its expected autumn purple color and seemed healthy enough. The next July, after a normal spring, it suddenly shed its leaves. By then, that summer had already gone bad. My records research business was struggling to survive and I was trapped in a seemingly hopeless bomb and extortion case that I could not puzzle through. I took the hollow clacking noise the dying ash's branches made, in the wind, in the night, as one more sign the world wasn't spinning right.

I didn't need new signs of bad times. When the next new spring came and the other trees along the Willahock began budding and my ash still resembled nothing but upright kindling, I went out with a pole saw. Better to cut it down than to suffer its death rattle in the night any longer.

I started at the top, sawing and pulling, until all of its brittle upper branches lay on the ground. But as I reset the ladder to cut off one of its two main limbs, I spotted the tiniest tendril of green, no longer than an inchworm, protruding from the bark. I don't know trees but I know trying, and I left that ash as I'd butchered it: a dinosaur-sized wishbone, thrust upright in defiance against the sky.

Several years had passed since then, and it was still slow going for me, and for the ash. Yet once again, in this new spring, the tree was unfurling tiny new leaves like little flags of hope. It was only the end of March, too soon to know how many would come, but I kept count as I had in previous springs, as an act of faith. That night, a fresh sprout brought the new spring's total up to twenty-six.

I take my positive omens wherever I can find them.

I spent two hours on the Internet that evening and found nothing to counter what the *Trib* and the Bohemian's ear had concluded. There had been nothing premeditated about the deaths of Benno Barberi, Jim Whitman or Grant Carson. Still, I planned to give the deaths a long, last mull on the plane west to San Francisco the next day, before calling Wendell to tell him I'd be refunding almost all of his money. Though with that, painfully, would go my hopes to replace my leaking refrigerator.

I took a flashlight into the kitchen, laid it in the refrigerator, shut the door and turned off the lights. A pinpoint sparkled next to where the handle was coming loose; air was leaking out there. As I'd told Jenny, such a small rust-through would be easily contained by a Golden Gate Bridge refrigerator magnet.

Happy times – seeing Jenny, and acquiring a magnet – seemed just around the corner as I reclined in the electric-blue La-Z-Boy, also salvaged from an alley, to watch the start of the ten o'clock news.

And then the Bohemian called.

His voice did not resonate with its usual optimism. 'I started on the list of names at six o'clock. It was fairly straightforward to establish who our prominent businesspeople are, and I was done by seven o'clock. There are forty-six,' he said, then paused. 'No,' he corrected, 'there *were* forty-six, before the three deaths.'

'This afternoon you guessed fifty. Pretty close, Anton.'

'Life is not so much about numbers as it is about percentages, Vlodek. That's why the three deaths are troubling.'

I shifted the La-Z-Boy to full upright and silenced the four-inch television balanced on my lap. 'Percentages?'

'Three is too many.'

'Two of the three were men in their sixties, and ill,' I said. 'The third was fifty-five, not that it matters, and the victim of a hit-and-run. All three deaths seem easily explainable.'

'Remember the heavy cream?'

'You said all three were among the top fifty business people in Chicago.'

'I misspoke. I meant to use the term more narrowly, to define Barberi, Whitman and Carson as being among the very top of the city's leaders, in the heaviest of the cream, so to speak.'

'I don't understand.'

'I just told you there were forty-six top-flight business leaders in Chicago, right?'

'With Barberi, Whitman, and Carson among them.'

'The forty-six was a simple ranking of business prominence. I then filtered that list to include only those individuals prominent in civic, political and charitable endeavors as well.'

'Only those are in the heavy cream,' I said.

'Exactly. I got down to sixteen names.'

'Of which three are now dead?'

'That's troubling. Nineteen per cent of the most influential people in Chicago – three of only sixteen – died in the last four months. Mathematically, that's beyond reason.'

Anton Chernek never indulged false alarm. He was too level-headed, too grounded. And almost always too well informed.

'I'll say again, Anton: two were older and ill. The third, Carson, got whacked by a passing car.'

'Yes, and I was inclined to accept it as an anomaly, an explainable oddity.'

'Exactly—'

He cut me off. 'Arthur Lamm has gone missing.'

'Arthur Lamm, as in head of Lamm Enterprises?' Lamm headed a conglomerate of real estate sales, management, and insurance brokerages. He was very prominent: a political player and a close friend of the mayor. There was no doubt he was in the heavy cream.

'A vice-president of his insurance company told me he's not called in for four days. Do you see what this means?'

I barely heard his voice. My mind was forming the word that I knew he wanted.

'Vlodek?' he asked after a minute.

'Percentages,' I said, giving it to him.

'Arthur's only fifty-one and, from all accounts, he's in peak condition. A marathoner, in fact. If he's met a bad end, he increases your list to four out of sixteen.'

'That's twenty-five per cent.'

He murmured something about emailing me his list of names in the morning and hung up.

I needed fresher air in which to think. I went outside to sit on the bench by the river. A small speck lay on the ground, almost colorless in the pale white light of the lamp along the crumbling asphalt river walk.

It was one of the would-be leaves from the purple ash, curled up, stillborn and dry.

Sometimes I don't like omens at all.

SIX

I woke at five-thirty in the morning, remembering the Bohemian's anxiety about percentages too much to go back to sleep. I put on jeans, a sweatshirt and my Nikes and, stepping around the duffel that lay on the floor, still to be packed for California, I went downstairs.

The Bohemian wasn't having a good night either. He'd emailed me his list two hours earlier.

I printed his list, put on my pea coat and took a travel mug of yesterday's cold coffee up the stairs and then the ladders to the fifth floor and the roof. I like to believe I think best on top of the turret. Even when I don't, the dawn likely as not serves up a spectacular sunrise, and that's a good enough reason to go up on any roof at the end of the dark. I leaned against the balustrade, sipped coffee and looked out across the spit of land at Rivertown, waiting for the cold caffeine and the chilled, pre-dawn air to rouse me from a sleep that never much was.

The town was softly shutting down. The tonks along Thompson Avenue were switching off their flickering neon lights, discharging their last, hardiest customers into the night. The slow-walking girls who smiled into the headlights of the slow-cruising gentlemen were shuffling away too, alone at last. And from somewhere down by the river, the sound of shattering glass rose above the rasping staccato of automobile tires hitting the rub strips on the tollway; a trembling hand had let go of an empty pint. Rivertown was twitching itself to sleep.

The thin hint of orange rising over Lake Michigan was bright enough to read what the Bohemian had sent. He'd drawn a simple grid, labeled it 'H.C.' for Heavy Cream – a wit, that Bohemian, even when troubled. On the left side of the sheet he'd listed the sixteen primo shakers of Chicago in alphabetical order. Across the page he'd made columns for the criteria he'd used to select them: business affiliations, political access, social and civic relationships. He'd assigned letter grades for each person, for each category, like a report card. Almost all of the boxes were filled with an 'A.'

All but two on the list were men. The Bohemian's Chicago, that world of vast money coupled to political and social influence, was still very much a boys' club. The names seemed vaguely familiar in the way that names captioned under society news photographs often seem familiar. Yet if asked, I couldn't have said what most of the primos in the heavy cream had done to achieve their prominence. My own world existed farther down, in the muck stuck to the bottom of what was Chicagoland.

The Bohemian had put asterisks next to the names of Barberi, Carson and Whitman. In the middle of the page, next to the name of the missing Arthur Lamm, he'd first drawn a question mark, then added an asterisk.

Asterisk meant death. It was those four asterisks, those four names out of sixteen, which had kept the Bohemian up in the night.

It was the fifth person on the list, four lines below Arthur Lamm's, who had put me in a trick bag: Wendell Phelps. For that, I now hated the son of a bitch even more than before.

My history with the man was limited. I'd called Wendell's office right after Amanda and I married, thinking it reasonable to intro- duce myself as the man who'd wed the daughter he hadn't seen in years – and maybe become a hero to my new wife, by effecting a reconciliation between the two.

I never got past the secretary to his secretary. No matter, I thought; there would be time to try again later.

There wasn't. I was soon implicated in a fake evidence scheme, having erroneously authenticated cleverly doctored checks in a high-profile insurance fraud trial. My name flashed dark across the front pages of Chicago's newspapers, there not for the notoriety of the trial, or my sloppiness, but because I was Wendell Phelps's son-in-law. I was soon found to be innocent, but I was guilty of being stupid – and of being Wendell's son-in-law. The publicity vaporized my credibility and killed my records research business. Unmoored, I poured alcohol on my self-pity. I blamed Wendell for my notoriety and found that so satisfying that, with the logic of someone totally lost to alcohol, I spread that blame to Amanda for being my link to him. No matter that she'd been estranged from her father for years. In my twisted, liquored logic, she was a most convenient target, and that was enough for me.

It was too much for Amanda. She filed for divorce and I got flushed out of her gated community – appropriately enough, on Halloween – unmasked as a fool.

I crawled back to Rivertown, the town I thought I'd escaped years before, and into the rat-infested turret I'd inherited from another failed man, my grandfather. Amanda fled to Europe, because she had no good place to go either. As I sobered up, I blamed Wendell Phelps for that, too. No matter that I'd trashed his daughter's life; he could have descended from his executive suite to help undo the damage I'd done.

Amanda and Wendell later reconciled, so much so that he enticed Amanda to quit her jobs writing art books and teaching at the Art Institute to join his utilities conglomerate.

He and I had never had need for reconciling anything. We were done, and that was fine for us both.

Except now he was bringing new breath to old furies. If I misplayed his case, investigated what were delusions too seriously, the press might get wind of it and trigger his public humiliation. Worse, if the Bohemian's fears of percentages were accurate and there really was a murderer out there, targeting Wendell and his ilk, my misplaying the case could get people killed.

Damn the man, Wendell Phelps.

By now, the glow of sunrise had risen above the massive dark shapes of Chicago to touch the top of the turret. Mine is the tallest building in Rivertown, a modest attainment in a town of abandoned factories, huddled bungalows and deserted storefronts. The only grand building in town, a city hall of long terraces, expansive private offices and tiny public rooms, was still in the darkness behind me. It, too, had been built of my grandfather's limestone, but later, by corrupt city managers who saw no shame in seizing most of his widow's land and all of its great pile of unused stone blocks. But those lizards couldn't take the sun, nor change the fact that it always lit the turret first every day. I took satisfaction in that.

I crossed the roof to look down at the river. The sunrise would soon light the butchered, two-limbed ash, causing it to cast a dark, jagged 'V' west along the river path. The shadow would look like a giant, crooked-fingered hex, a Greek *moutza* of contempt, thrust directly at Rivertown's corrupt city hall. I took satisfaction in that, too.

Likely enough, there would be no satisfaction in the direction I was now heading.

Damn the man, Wendell Phelps.

SEVEN

N ews of Arthur Lamm's disappearance had not yet hit the Internet, so I searched for more information on Grant Carson's hit-and-run, the most recent of the deaths in the heavy cream. There was plenty of speculation over the impact his passing would have on his international conglomerate, but there were very few facts surrounding the hit-and-run, and no suspicion that his death had been premeditated murder.

On a day in early February, just after midnight, Grant Carson had pulled his Lincoln Town Car sharply to a curb, got out and was struck by a passing car. He was thrown twenty feet and died instantly. The police noted that by all appearances it had been an accident: Carson had stepped out of his car without checking for oncoming traffic; a car had struck him. Panicked, the driver sped away. The police were seeking anyone who might have witnessed the accident.

I phoned a dozen of my insurance company contacts to learn who'd carried policies on Carson's life. I wasn't interested in beneficiary information; I was hoping an insurance company's private investigation had yielded more than the few facts the cops had released. It was the kind of work I used to do often, before I got tangled up in scandal. I struck gold nowhere, but got promises that others would ask around.

By now it was eight o'clock in the morning in California. I called Jenny. 'I've got a job,' I said.

'A trip-canceling job?'

'More like a trip-rescheduling job.'

'It's life or death, this case?'

'I'm fearing that.'

'What aren't you telling me?' Her newswoman's antennae had picked up words I'd not used.

'Amanda's father is the client.'

'And Amanda – she's involved, too?'

'Only to have steered me to her father. I'm working for him.'

'We were going to have such an amazing four days,' she said, dropping her voice.

'I know.'

'An amazingly lustful four days,' she said, whispering now.

'Oh, how I'd hoped . . .' I said.

'Oh, how I hope you'd hoped,' she whispered one last time, and hung up.

Mercifully, in the next instant I got a call to change the direction of my thwarted naughty thoughts. It was from Gaylord Rikk. He worked for one of Carson's insurers.

'What's your interest?' he asked.

'One of Carson's rich friends asked me to follow up to see if anything new has been uncovered,' I said, trying for casual.

'Ask the cops.'

'I will. What's the status of your investigation?'

'There is none. We've closed our file.'

'So soon?'

'It's been over a month. The police have no leads.'

'The area where Carson got hit is upscale, full of nightlife. It was only midnight. Surely someone saw something.'

'Only midnight,' Rikk agreed, 'in a late-night district that's full of Starbucks, young bucks and sweet girls.'

'Nobody was headed home after a late last purple cocktail or out walking a designer dog?'

He gave me the sort of long sigh one gives an idiot. 'Remember a few years ago, some young woman hit a homeless guy with her car, knocked him up over her hood and half through the windshield?'

'Everyone remembers that.'

'She drove all the way home with the guy stuck, head first, through her windshield. That was at midnight, too, when there were other cars on the road and people out walking. She pulled into her garage with the poor bastard still alive, his head and upper body leaking fluids into her car. He pleaded with her to get him help. Nope. She left him as he was and went into the house – though at the trial she assured the judge she did come out several times to apologize profusely to the guy for ruining his day, or whatever.'

It was the kind of thing I thought about, up on the roof in the middle of the night. 'The guy finally bled out.'

'The point is that she drove through town with the guy's ass sticking out of her windshield, and nobody reported anything. She got caught only when she asked a few friends over to help remove the body. It was one of them who called the cops.'

'Was is mechanical difficulty that forced Carson to the curb, or was he drunk?'

'Neither. No mechanical problems, other than a right front wheel bent from hitting the curb. His blood alcohol was under the limit. He wasn't drunk.'

'You think he was forced over?'

'And got out mad to confront another driver who'd stopped, or just to inspect his car for damage? Possible scenarios, both of them.'

'Why get out at all? If his car was not drivable, why not call AAA or someone else for help?'

'We don't know. He had a cell phone. He didn't use it.'

'What about paint from the car that hit Carson?'

'No sample was recovered from his body or the smashed-back driver's door. Don't trust what you see on TV. Paint doesn't always transfer. Plus, the point of impact could have been glass or stainless or chrome-plated steel, or the car could have had one of those front-end bra things.'

'One of those vinyl covers yuppies used to put on the fronts of their BMWs to protect against stone dings?'

'You still see one, now and again,' he said, 'though most everybody knows they do their own damage, flapping against the paint. All I'm saying is there are all sorts of reasons why paint doesn't transfer.'

'The cops played it by the book, sent out alerts to body shops?'

'Ideally, but there again, those bulletins work mostly on television. Hit-and-run drivers are ordinary people who freak out. They panic, stick the car in the garage and don't open the door for anything. After a day or two of dry puking and no sleep, they get the idea to dump the car in a bad neighborhood with its keys in the ignition and report it stolen. It almost always works; the car gets boosted and stripped. Hit-and-run cars never get brought to legitimate body shops.'

'Where did Carson have dinner?'

'Somewhere north, I suppose, near where he was killed. He lives up that way, in Lincoln Park. The payout's being processed, Elstrom. The case is dead.'

I called the Bohemian. 'Any news on Arthur Lamm?'

'Perhaps there's been much ado about nothing. He has a camp somewhere up in the piney woods of Wisconsin. He does the real outdoors stuff: small boat, small tent, eating what he catches swimming in the water or crawling on the ground.' The Bohemian's tone of disgust made it sound like Lamm dined on roadkill. 'Anyway, Arthur has some guy who stops in from time to time to check on the place. He said one of Arthur's boats is missing.'

'Meaning Lamm is off somewhere camping.'

He offered up a chuckle that sounded forced. 'I might be imagining evil everywhere, in my old age.'

I asked if he could put me close to people who knew Barberi and Whitman.

'I'm not just imagining, Vlodek?'

'I like to be thorough.'

'I'll call you back.'

He did, in fifteen minutes. 'Anne Barberi is at home. You can go right over.'

'You told her what I'm looking into?'

'Here's the odd part: I didn't have time. She interrupted, saying she'd receive you immediately. She's anxious to talk.'

EIGHT

Anne Barberi lived at the Stanford Arms, a tall, upscale gray brick-and-granite building across from the Lincoln Park Zoo. While the upper floors surely provided magnificent vistas of

Lake Michigan, I imagined the lower apartments occasionally offered troubling views of coupling chimpanzees, and suspected that those units were equipped with electrified, fast-closing drapes. Even when living the good life along Chicago's Gold Coast, the rich had to be vigilant.

A parking valet leaning against a Mercedes straightened up with a pained look on his face, likely soured by the clatter of my arrival. I thought about pulling in to give him a closer blast of my rusted exhaust, but the thrill wouldn't have been worth the parking charge. I drove on, found a spot on a street four blocks over, and hoofed back.

The lobby was enormous, dark and deserted except for two potted palms and two potted elderly ladies, slumped in peach-colored velvet wing chairs, sipping fruited whiskies. The oily-haired man behind the oak reception counter scanned my khakis, blue button-down shirt and blazer like he was looking for resale shop tags.

'Dek Elstrom to see Mrs Barberi,' I said to the oiled man.

'Photo identification, sir?'

I gave him my driver's license. As he studied it, and then me, the corners of his mouth turned down, as if he were wondering whether the blue shirt in the photo was the same one I was wearing. Such was wealth, I wanted to tell him. Even I didn't know; I had three.

'A moment, sir,' the man said, handing back my license. He picked up the phone, tapped three digits and said my name. Nodding, he hung up. 'Mrs Barberi is expecting you.'

I turned and almost ran into a burly fellow who had noiselessly slipped up behind me.

'Mr Reeves will show you to the elevator,' the oiled man said.

He meant Mr Reeves would show me only to the elevator, and nowhere else. We walked to the farthest of the three sets of polished brass elevator doors and Mr Reeves pressed the button. I stepped in and the doors closed before I could ask which floor was Anne Barberi's.

There was no need. The elevator panel had only one button, and it was not numbered. After a short whir and the merest tug of gravity, the doors opened directly into a rose-colored, marble-floored foyer. A gray-haired woman wearing a lavender knit suit stood waiting. Likely enough, she hadn't strung the jumbo pearls around her wrinkled neck from a kit.

'I'm Anne Barberi,' she said, extending a hand that was as firm and in command as her voice. I followed her to a small sitting room. She sat on a hardwood ladder-back chair; I sat on a rock hard, brocaded settee. Freshly cut yellow flowers sat just as stiff between us, on a black-lacquered table.

'Mr Chernek tells me you have questions concerning my husband's death,' she said.

'I'm afraid they're not very specific.'

'At whose behest are you conducting your inquiry?'

I'd considered inventing a lie, but decided simply to stonewall to protect Wendell's identity. Truths are always easier to remember than lies. 'One of your husband's associates,' I said.

'Within Barberi Holdings?'

'No.'

'Fair enough, for now.' She folded her hands in her lap.

'I understand Mr Barberi had a long history of heart disease,' I said.

'For twenty years, he'd been careful, monitoring his cholesterol, exercising under supervision, watching his diet. At work, he chose very able assistants, young men and women who could shoulder much of the stress. My husband was cautious with his heart, Mr Elstrom, which is why I am interested in what you are doing.'

'I'm merely gathering facts, for now.'

She studied me for a moment, realized I wasn't going to offer more, and went on. 'As I said, Benno kept a tight lid on the pressures of his job. Until the night he died, when he lost control. He came home from a dinner furious, literally trembling because he was so upset. I tried to get him to sit and tell me what had happened, but he would not. He went into his study, and a few minutes later, I heard him shouting into the phone.' She looked down at her hands. She'd clenched them so tight the knuckles had whitened. Pulling them apart, she looked up. 'I found him in there the next morning, slumped over his desk.'

'Do you have any idea who he'd called?'

'I assumed one of his subordinates, but I really don't know.'

'No one thought to question what set him off?'

'Come to think of it, no.'

'Can we find out?'

'Surely you're not sensing something deliberate, are you?'

'I like to check everything out.'

'His secretary might be able to help.' She reached for the phone next to the vase and dialed a number. 'Anne, Joan. Fine, fine,' she said, brushing away the obligatory questions about her well-being. 'I've asked a friend, a Mr Elstrom, to find out something for me. I want to know with whom Benno was speaking on the phone, the night he died. It was about some matter that upset him greatly.' She paused to listen, then said, 'I'll tell Mr Elstrom you'll call him to set up an appointment.' She read the number from the business card I'd given her, then hung up.

'Joan was Benno's secretary for years,' she said. 'She knows things she'll never tell me, but she's always been loyal to Benno. And unlike me, she did think to inquire with whom Benno was speaking the night he passed away. He'd set up a conference call with two of his subordinates. She'll make them available to you.'

She walked me into the foyer and pushed the elevator button. 'It was not like Benno to allow himself to become so upset, Mr Elstrom. I won't ask again what you're pursuing, but I expect the courtesy of a report when you're done.'

I said I'd tell her what I could, when I could. As I stepped into the elevator, it seemed likeliest that Benno Barberi had simply lost control as accidentally as had the driver of the freak passing car that had smacked Grant Carson. But as the elevator descended, I imagined I heard the Bohemian's voice intermingled in the soft whine of the motor, whispering urgently about the certainty of percentages. And by the time the door opened, I almost knocked over the burly Mr Reeves in my haste to get out. I hurried across the tomb-like foyer, silent except for the ancient ladies gently snoring beside their drained whiskies, and out into the daylight.

I called the Bohemian from the sidewalk. 'Any luck on getting someone close to Whitman to talk to me?'

'He was a widower. I left a message, and your cell number, for his daughter, Debbie Goring.'

'She'll call soon?'

'My God, Vlodek, do I detect urgency?'

'I don't know.'

'You've seen Anne Barberi?'

'I just left her.'

'And?'

'Call Debbie Goring again.'

NINE

I was stuck waiting for the Bohemian to set up a call from
Whitman's daughter, Debbie Goring. I could do it pacing the
planks at the turret, or I could indulge in the illusion of exercise
at the Rivertown Heath Center. I chose illusion.

The health center is a stained, yellowish brick pile that used to
be a YMCA, back when young people came to work in Rivertown's
factories and needed rooms, and running was considered exercise
instead of a means of fleeing the police. Nowadays, the health
center still has a running track and exercise equipment, and it still
offers rooms, though now the equipment is rusted and the rooms
are occupied by down-and-out drinkers working only half-heartedly
to stay alive.

I knew those foul-smelling, dimly lit rooms. After being flushed,
drunk, out of Amanda's gated community, I spent the night at the
health center, as vacant-eyed as any of the grizzlies who puddled
the upstairs halls. Waking the next morning in a room still damp
from the pine-scented cleaner used to mask the death of its previous
occupant, I looked up and recognized rock bottom. I moved into
the turret, clear-eyed for the first time in weeks, and began inching
my way back to life.

I still come to the health club. The exercise doesn't hurt, and
the sting of pine-scented cleaner in my eyes and nose is a fine
reminder not to slip that far again.

I eased over the potholes and parked in my usual spot next to
the doorless Buick. As always, the lot was empty except for a
half-dozen thumpers – high-school-age toughs in training – leaning
against the husks of several other abandoned cars. I made a show
of leaving my door unlocked. There was no sense in making them
rip the duct tape from my plastic side curtains only to see that the

seats had already been slashed and the radio boosted from the dash.

Downstairs, I changed into my red shorts and blue Cubs T-shirt quietly, pretending not to disturb the towel attendant pretending to sleep at the counter. Authentically, he was even drooling on the short pile of stained towels. Nobody minded; nobody dared use them. As with the Jeep, I left my locker door unlocked. The attendant need not dull his bolt cutters only to see I'd not left my wallet or keys inside.

Normally, raucous laughter from the exercise floor echoed down into the stairwell – chatter from the men in their sixties and seventies, retired from jobs that no longer existed, who came not to exercise but to laugh and sigh and share old stories. Not so today. The stairs to the exercise floor were eerily silent.

I understood when I got to the top. The regulars were all there – Dusty, Nick, Frankie and the others – roosting as usual on the rusted fitness machines like crows on felled trees. But that day, nobody was joking. They were staring across the exercise floor.

'Purr,' Dusty said softly.

'Doo,' Frankie murmured, almost worshipfully.

The others nodded, staring, just as transfixed as Dusty and Frankie. Big, yellow-toothed grins split their wrinkled faces.

Across the floor was a woman. She was no ordinary woman. She was a big woman, a jaw-droppingly huge woman, the biggest woman I'd ever seen. She was at least six-foot eight and three hundred pounds, but she packed no fat. Every ounce of her was perfectly proportioned, solid and muscular. And she was beautiful, with golden skin and long, dark hair. She was stretching and bending with the grace of a tiny ballerina, curving her body in such lazy, perfectly fluid motions that I could only imagine what long-smoldering embers were being fanned into a full blaze in the minds of the exercise room regulars.

She turned, so that her back was towards us.

'Purr,' Dusty said.

'Doo,' Frankie added.

The Amazonian goddess wore black collegiate exercise shorts, emblazoned with the university's name in yellow letters across the rump. Those kind of printed shorts are designed with a gap in the middle letters, to allow the fabric in the center to curve into the cleft of the buttocks, yet still be read as one word. But her shorts, probably a man's double extra-large, were stretched so taut that the name read as two distinct words: 'PUR' and 'DUE'.

I left the old men to the frenzy of their imaginations and ran laps.

Amanda called my cell phone that evening. 'Still in town?'

'Yes.'

'Is that worrisome?'

'Tying up little loose ends, is all.'

'My father said you stopped by.'

'Yesterday.'

'How come you didn't then call right away to say he's delusional?'

'I'm trying to be thorough, dot my "t"s, cross my "i"s.'

'Don't dodge with cheap humor.'

'I report to your father, not to you.'

She took a breath. 'You think there's something to his fears?'

'Probably not.'

'Now I am worried.'

'Don't be. There are just a couple of wrinkles I want to check out.'

'*Wrinkles?*'

Too late, I realized she remembered my hot word. A wrinkle was my slang for something troubling enough to require being checked thoroughly.

I tried to joke. 'The older I get the more I'm like an aging beauty queen. Even the smallest wrinkles demand more attention than they're worth.'

She let it go because she knew I wouldn't say more. We tried other, smaller talk but it was stilted, like the stuff of two people passing time, sharing a cab. After another moment, I invented an excuse to get off the phone. She didn't try to find an excuse to stop me.

I supposed that, too, was a wrinkle.

TEN

Benno Barberi's secretary called just before nine the next morning. I'd been up since five, varnishing wood trim for the third-floor closet and thinking about men dead in the heavy cream. She asked if I could meet with Barberi's two assistants at one o'clock. I said that was convenient. She said fine.

Barberi Holdings, Inc. was headquartered north of Chicago, in a concrete building sunk low, like a bunker, into the rolling close-cut grass alongside the Tri-State Toll Road. The interior was just as hard – concrete walls and a blue quarry tile floor. The receptionist took my name and motioned me to wait on one of the immense, curved white leather sofas. As I sat, my left blazer sleeve grazed the sofa cushion. And stuck. I tugged it free and turned it for a look. A smashed drop of varnish sparkled next to the spot of yellow mustard I'd forgotten to rub off.

I draped my sticky left arm high on the back of the sofa and used my right hand to leaf through a *Forbes* magazine. The issue featured the 400 wealthiest people on the planet. Their brief biographies were disappointing. None of them had made their fortunes rehabbing architectural oddities.

A young man named Brad came for me after five minutes. He wore a blue suit and had an impeccable haircut. He brought me to a small conference room where another young man, this one named Jason, stood waiting. He also looked to have recently visited Brad's barber. His blue suit was the identical shade of Brad's, as was my blazer. But mine, I guessed, was the only one sporting a shiny speck of varnish and the merest blush of yellow mustard.

We sat at the round table and Brad began. 'We understand Mrs Barberi is interested in the problem we discussed with Mr Barberi the night he died?'

'She told me her husband took great care to control stress, yet that evening he came home very upset about something. She thinks that triggered his fatal heart attack.'

Jason spoke. 'Mr Barberi called me at home; I conferenced in

Brad. Mr Barberi was worried someone was making a play for equity in the company's stock.'

'Isn't Barberi Holdings a publicly traded company?' I asked. 'Can't anyone buy its stock?'

Jason's gaze had dropped to the sleeve of my blazer. He'd spotted the varnish, or perhaps the mustard. For a second he seemed to struggle to raise his eyes to focus again on my face. 'How technical do you want me to be?'

'A short answer will do.'

'Yes, BH is a publicly held corporation. Anyone can buy its stock. The night Mr Barberi died, he learned that a company he'd never heard of had acquired an insurance policy on his life. He was afraid the insurance payout would be used to acquire BH stock when he died.'

'And gain control of the company?'

'Hardly.' Jason's eyes had begun to stray again, down to my sleeve, but he stopped them cold and looked back up. 'It would take many, many such insurance policies for that. Still, it was an agitation, and he wanted us to look into the matter.'

'Look into what, exactly?'

'He wanted us to find out who had taken out the policy.'

'Even though such an individual could do no damage?'

Jason looked at Brad. Brad shook his head. 'It's complicated,' Jason said.

'You're thinking I won't understand business talk?' I said, too fast. It was the Rivertown chip that occasionally throbs on my shoulder, reacting to two condescending, over-barbered MBAs. I smiled like I was making a little joke, to cover it.

'Anyone who acquires stock can have a voice at the annual shareholders' meeting,' Jason said. 'Someone who owns a large block can have a louder voice, and that can be disruptive.'

Brad cleared his throat. 'It's pointless, now.'

'Because Mr Barberi is dead?'

Brad nodded.

'Mrs Barberi will not be pleased if I come back empty-handed, so I'll ask again: Did you look into the company that took out the policy on Barberi?'

Jason said, 'As Brad said, it was pointless. Mr Barberi was dead.'

They both stood up. They were concerned about their own futures, not the king. The king was dead; long live the king. And I was an inconsequential interloper with varnish and mustard on his jacket. They walked me to the lobby, went through the charade of telling me to call anytime with more questions, and breezed me out into the sunshine.

Before getting into the Jeep, I took off my blazer to lay it on the back seat to dry. As I opened the door, I happened to look back at the building. Brad, or perhaps it was Jason, was standing in one of the windows at the side of the lobby, watching me.

Or perhaps it was neither, but another well-barbered MBA, taking an innocent look outside. The place must have been lousy with them.

Then again, that was probably just Rivertown talking.

ELEVEN

There were two messages from Wendell on my cell phone. I returned neither. I hadn't learned enough to dismiss his suspicions outright, or enough to interest any cop.

I called the Bohemian. 'Arthur Lamm?'

'No news might be good news, if he's simply out in the woods, eating insects. Debbie Goring?'

'No news is irritating news. She hasn't called.' Then, 'How common is it for a company to insure the life of the CEO of another company?'

'It's done sometimes when a shareholder makes a big investment in the CEO's company. The loss of a chief executive can be catastrophic to the investment, hence the insurance policy.'

'Is the CEO, whose life is being insured, notified when a policy is taken out on him?'

'Almost certainly, because medical history and perhaps even an actual physical will be required. Plus, CEOs are always in touch with their big shareholders. They need their support at shareholder meetings. Where are you going with this, Vlodek?'

'I have no idea.'

'Do you want me to call Debbie Goring again?'

'No. Give me her address. I'll stop by.'

Debbie Goring lived in Prospect Park, a few miles east of O'Hare airport. Hers was a beige bi-level in an older mix of ranch houses and other bi-levels.

A green Ford Taurus station wagon with its tailgate up was parked in her driveway. A short, squarish, dark-haired woman in blue Levis and a plain black T-shirt was pulling grocery bags out of the back of the car. The T-shirt wasn't long enough to cover the death's head skull tattoo on her lower spine. I parked the Jeep in the street and walked up.

'Debbie Goring?' I said.

She straightened up, a grocery bag in each arm, and turned around. Most of her was in her early forties, but the skin around her eyes was deeply wrinkled, as though she'd spent sixty years squinting distrustfully at the world.

'Unless you're from the Illinois Lottery, bringing a check for a million dollars, she's not home.' Her voice was raspy from too many cigarettes.

'I'm Dek Elstrom,' I said. 'I'm not from the lottery.'

'No shit,' she said.

'An associate of mine, Anton Chernek—'

She cut me off. 'I've gotten Chernek's messages. I'm not interested in talking to any more insurance bastards.'

'I'm not an insurance bastard.'

'What then?'

'A freelance bastard, with questions about your father's death. Can I help with the bags?'

She hefted the bags closer to her chest and started to walk towards the front door. Tops of four cereal boxes – two Cheerios, two Cinnamon Toast Crunch – protruded out of the brown bags. Oats and sugar seemed a sensible mix; she must have been a sensible woman. 'Adios,' she called over her shoulder.

'I'm serious about investigating your father's death.'

She stopped and turned around, hugging the bags. 'For who?'

'I can't tell you, but it's not for an insurance company.'

She lifted her chin. 'My father was murdered.'

I held out my arms for one of the grocery bags.

She shook her head. 'There's another bag in the car, and two gallons of milk. And slam the back lid.'

I went back for the bag and the gallons, closed the tailgate and followed her to the front door.

She led me through a living room that smelled faintly of old cigarette smoke. Pictures in gold frames of her with two young boys were on a spinet piano against the wall. 'My boys are six and ten,' she said as we walked into the kitchen. I set the milk and the last of the groceries on the counter and stood by the door as she put them away.

Without asking if I wanted any, she poured coffee into two yellow mugs, nuked them for twenty seconds and, after turning on the kitchen exhaust fan, brought them to the table. She lit a Camel from a crumpled pack and dropped the match in a cheap black plastic ashtray. 'When I heard Chernek's messages on my answering machine, I thought, "I'm not doing this crap anymore."'

'What crap?'

'Trying to get deaf people to listen.'

'About your father being murdered?'

She blew smoke towards the exhaust fan. 'I was in an abusive marriage, Mr Elstrom. My husband took off, leaving me dead broke. My father bought me this house, so I would have a place to raise my sons. He was a very wealthy man, but he expected me to make my own way in the world.'

'Yet he bought you this house,' I said.

'He drew the line at his grandsons doing without.' She took a long pull on the Camel. 'My father had pancreatic cancer; he knew he was dying for quite a while. He had plenty of time to get his affairs in order. He'd arranged for his stocks to be donated to various charitable causes in which he was involved, and had just finished cataloguing his art collection for museums. That, too, is set to be donated.'

'Nothing for you?'

'Not true.' Her face was defiant. 'Insurance was for me. He told me he had a two-million-dollar life insurance policy, naming me as sole beneficiary.'

'He died from painkillers,' I said.

Her eyes tightened, daring me to say the word.

'Suicide,' I said.

She stubbed out her cigarette. 'No payout for suicide.'

'Bad pain can make anyone desperate for relief.'

'I was his only child. We didn't get along great, but he adored his grandsons. If he'd been in the kind of pain where he needed to end his life, he would have changed his other bequests to make sure I got money for my sons.'

'Still, sometimes pain—'

'Please,' she said, lighting another Camel. 'His pain was being managed. He went to the office every day, kept up his schedule. For him to come home and swallow a bottle of pills is too much to believe.'

'What do you know about the day he died?'

'I was told he got to the office about ten in the morning, looked at his mail, and went out to lunch with his attorney. He had nothing pressing because, by this time, my father had shifted his responsibilities to others within the firm. Like I said, he had plenty of time to take care of things.'

'Time enough to make sure there would be money for his grandsons.'

'You got it. After lunch, he talked briefly to a few of his managers about small things and was driven home about three o'clock.'

'Your father had a chauffeur?'

'A hired driver was on standby for the last months, in case his pills made him woozy.'

'And when he got home that day?'

'He took a nap. According to Mrs Johnson, his housekeeper, he got up at six, watched the news as he got dressed to go out to one of his dinners. He left about seven.'

'Do you know where he went?'

'No.'

'What time did he get home?'

'Eleven-thirty, according to Mrs Johnson. And then he went into his study and died, still in his evening clothes.'

'Not in bed?' It was a wrinkle. I'd always assumed pill swallowers laid down, for the wait.

She'd caught the question behind my eyes. 'At his desk,' she said, a little too loudly.

'There was no note?'

'A pill bottle in his pocket doesn't have to mean suicide,' she said. 'He didn't even pause to take off his suit jacket, if the bullshit is to be believed.'

'A medical examiner must have conducted an investigation.'

She stabbed the ashtray with the Camel. 'Haven't you been listening? What the hell kind of person sits at his damned desk, writes no note, and swallows pills knowing his adored grandsons won't get one damned dime?'

I asked if she knew the name of Whitman's chauffer.

'We can get it from Mrs Johnson.' She looked at the clock on the wall. 'I have to pick up my boys from school,' she said. 'Be here tomorrow morning at eleven. I'll take you to her. She'll tell you about my father and my boys.'

At the front door, she said, 'I'll give you a hundred thousand dollars if you can prove it wasn't suicide.'

'I already have a client,' I said, ethical purity spilling from my mouth like gospel washed in Listerine.

'So you said. And just who the hell is that?'

I shrugged.

She smiled, softening the wrinkles at her eyes. 'Tomorrow morning, eleven o'clock. Mrs Johnson will tell you.'

I walked to the Jeep morally intact, true to my first responsibility, my client Wendell Phelps.

And all the way to Rivertown, I fantasized about what I could do with a hundred grand.

TWELVE

The next morning, before heading off to meet Debbie Goring, I drove across Thompson Avenue to Leo Brumsky's house. Leo has been my friend since grammar school. He is brilliant, and eccentric. He makes upwards of five hundred thousand dollars a year authenticating items for the big auction houses in New York, Chicago and LA; he drives Porsche roadsters that get jettisoned at the ten-thousand-mile mark; he wears designer suits when he must, and he dates a beautiful research librarian who is younger and taller but has the same genius IQ. All that could fit him into a rare, high social niche except he lives with his mother in her brown brick bungalow. He has an aversion to anything smelling of social snobbery, and buys his casual clothes at the Discount Den, a place where thirty bucks acquires a whole outfit, so long as one is not picky about color, style or size. Since Leo is barely five feet six inches tall, and weighs a spare one-forty, his casual attire is invariably several sizes too big, and makes him look like a malnourished dwarf with an oversized pale bald head, wearing someone else's clothes.

He is the smartest person I know, but more importantly that morning, Leo knew the art market in Chicago. Likely enough, he knew of Jim Whitman.

I noticed the black BMW as soon as I pulled away from the turret. It was parked on the short road that leads from my street to the dingy string of honky-tonks, hock shops and liquor stores that is Thompson Avenue. It was one of the smaller BMWs, the sort junior pretenders drive until they can afford one of the more dramatic models.

A car parked on the stub road was no oddity after dark; lots of johns looking to enjoy fast, last-of-the-night bargains often linger in that exact spot. Never, though, had I seen a car parked there in sunlight.

Odder still was the speed with which the driver's head slid from view, as if it belonged to someone who did not want to be seen watching me.

I did not continue on toward Leo's. I swung left on Thompson and headed east toward Chicago. The BMW appeared in the rear-view mirror two times, hanging far back, but by the time I got to the health center lot and parked next to the doorless Buick, it seemed to be gone.

Still, to be certain, I went straight into the exercise room. It was too early for Dusty and Frankie and the rest of the regulars to be roosting; too early for the Amazonian Pur Due to be stretching her magnificent bulk as well. Except for one poor soul in stained street clothes sleeping on the barbell press bench, I was alone. I walked to the window that looked out over Thompson Avenue and watched for fifteen minutes. No black BMW came into sight. I gave it up and motored over to Leo's.

His yellow Porsche roadster was parked out at the curb, meaning not only that he was home but that likely he'd already been out. And that might mean, if the fates had properly aligned, that he'd been to the Polish bakery.

I walked up the cement stairs. One of the front windows was open a crack, and the sound of people stage-whispering lustful things came through the screen. I pushed the doorbell button twice, trying to time it between the moans coming from Ma Brumsky's softly erotic cable television program.

'Yah?' the old woman's voice shouted above the fast breathing.

'It's Dek, Mrs Brumsky,' I yelled.

'Who?'

'Dek Elstrom!' I screamed. Leo's mother has known me ever since her son brought me home, like a stray cat, in seventh grade.

She thumped the floor with her cane, almost in time with the thumping coming from the television. Leo's office is in the basement. 'Leo, the UPS man is here,' she yelled above the TV voices.

A moment later, the sound of footfalls came through the window screen, the front door opened and an assault of bright colors appeared behind the screen door. Today's rayon Hawaiian shirt was a medley of chartreuse palm fronds and yellow parrots. It was shiny and huge and hung in folds down his scrawny chest, sagging the parrots into something more closely resembling snakes.

'You working for UPS now?' Leo grinned.

'You've been to the bakery?'

'Nothing wrong with your sniffer.' He opened the door and stuck his head out. 'And it's warm enough for the stoop,' he said, and disappeared back into the dark of the bungalow.

He came out a moment later with a long white waxed bag and two cups of coffee in scratched porcelain mugs. The mugs had been scratched even before Ma Brumsky swiped them from the lunch counter at Walgreen's. When we were twelve, Leo had told me, proudly, that all of his mother's plates, cups and silverware came from Walgreen's. I told him I'd figured that out already, since everything had 'Walgreen's' etched on its handles or imprinted into its porcelain. I didn't mention what he had yet to figure out, that Ma had swiped it all on lunch breaks when she worked downtown, before he was born. Nobody wants to think of his mother staggering away from a drug store lunch counter with a purse full of dirty dinnerware.

Leo knelt so I could take a mug, and then sat down. He slid an end of the raspberry coffee cake out of the bag, pulled a steak knife from the front pocket of blue knit pants that coordinated not at all with the blinding chartreuse rayon, and cut me a slice.

'This coffee cake cost more than your shirt,' I said, eyeing the half-sleeve that drooped almost to his wrist. It wasn't even good chartreuse. It reminded me of stomach contents, perhaps de-carbed.

'I should hope so,' he said. 'I wouldn't put a shirt like this in my mouth.'

For a minute, we ate coffee cake and looked at the row of brown bungalows across the street, every one identical to his, like we'd done a thousand times since we were kids.

'I drove by your place yesterday afternoon,' he said, carving me another slice. 'The Jeep was gone, and the turret was locked up as it should have been, since you're supposed to be in San Francisco, indulging fancies with the luscious Jennifer Gale.'

'I'm working on a job,' I said.

'Must be important, if you dusted off Jenny.'

'Wendell Phelps.'

Leo raised his eyebrows. Most of the time, the dark fur above his brown eyes languishes in boredom. But when he laughs, or his enormous intellect charges at something, his eyebrows come alive and cavort like crazed caterpillars across the pale skin of his forehead. The caterpillars danced with abandon now, frenzied with curiosity.

'Yes, I finally spoke to the great man, face to face.' I cut myself a third piece of coffee cake. Chicago is known for its wind; one must maintain ballast.

'He called you?'

'Amanda was the one who called.'

'You cancelled Jenny for Amanda?' He liked Amanda and he'd liked us together just as much as he now liked the prospect of Jenny and me together.

'Postponed, not cancelled.'

'I haven't seen Amanda in the papers lately, with that commodities trader, Rudolph,' he said.

'She didn't seem to want to talk about him, other than to say he's in Russia, investigating opportunities.'

'Did you mention Jenny?'

'I didn't need to. Amanda had seen the photo of us at that network correspondents' dinner.'

'The one where you're wearing that cheap, too-small rented tux?' He laughed.

'I should have tried it on at the rental place. Anyway, Amanda and I are strictly business now.'

'Where did you meet her? Someplace dimly lit?' The eyebrows waited, poised high on his forehead.

'Petterino's, and then the Goodman for a play.'

'Just like old times.'

'Wendell thinks somebody is trying to kill him.'

'Jeez.'

'Amanda is hoping her father is simply stressed, imagining things.'

'But you don't.' He didn't ask it; he said it. Since we were kids, Leo could see into my head like he was looking through glass.

I told him about Grant Carson's hit-and-run and Benno Barberi's fatal heart attack. 'You've heard of these guys?' I asked.

'I recognize the names. Movers and shakers, for sure, though I'm not solid on what they moved and shook.'

'Then there's Jim Whitman.' I eyed the coffee cake, thinking it wouldn't take running but a few laps to justify an incredibly tiny small fourth piece.

'I knew Jim.'

'Actually, he's why I'm here.' I removed a three-inch width, fully intending to get back to the health center soon.

'No doubt,' he said, watching me heft the wide new slice.

'How well did you know Whitman?' I asked through the pastry.

'I helped value some of the paintings he was going to leave to museums.' Leo's eyebrows began to move, restless with a new thought. 'His death wasn't understandable?'

'He went out for the evening, came back, sat at his desk at home and up-ended a bottle of painkillers. It was understandable to the medical examiner, given Whitman's terminal condition.'

'But?' Leo at his most terse is Leo at his most probing.

'His daughter doesn't buy it. His suicide nullified an insurance payout to her, money intended to provide for his beloved grandchildren.'

'I remember Jim mentioning his grandchildren. He was very

proud of them. And, for a man facing death, he seemed very businesslike, very much in control.'

'Suicide that nulls provision for his adored grandchildren doesn't sound businesslike.'

'How much?'

'Two million to her.'

'No. I meant how much did Whitman's daughter offer you to prove her father's death was no suicide?' His lips started to tremble with the beginnings of a smile.

'I told her I already have a client.'

The grin widened into a smile that split his lips.

'Damn it, Leo.'

He smiled broadly, exposing eight hundred big white teeth. 'How much?'

'A hundred thousand.'

'All wrapped up around a case involving Amanda.' He raised his scratched Walgreen's mug, satisfied.

'I love quandaries and ethical dilemmas,' he said.

THIRTEEN

Debbie Goring was leaning against the back fender of her Taurus, smoking, when I got there at eleven. She looked to be wearing the same blue jeans, but her T-shirt that day was orange and had a Harley Davidson logo on the front. She took a slow look at the silver tape curling off the Jeep's top and side curtains like a spinster's hairdo gone wild in an electric storm, flicked the cigarette butt into the street and said she'd drive. I took no offense.

Ten minutes later, we pulled into old streets lined with big trees and what used to be considered substantial houses. Used to be – because the teardown phenomenon was now changing the definition of substantial in Deer Run, her father's town. On every block, at least one huge new house hulked across an entire lot, dwarfing its neighbors.

'Teardowns are big here,' she said, braking as a flatbed truck ahead stopped to unload a bulldozer. 'Any property worth less than five hundred thousand gets pushed over to build something for a couple million or more.'

'That would buy an entire block of houses where I live,' I said.

She backed into a drive and turned the Taurus around. 'People want to live here, for the charm of an old town, but they don't want the modesty of an old house. Better to knock it down, they think, and put up something flashier and bigger in the middle of all that old charm.' She shook her head. 'You should see these new places at night. They've got lights everywhere – under the eaves, on the railings, beneath the shrubs. After dark, some of these streets look to have a whole bunch of starships landing.' She shot me a sly grin. 'All that need for showiness makes me wonder if there's something wrong with their personal parts.'

She stopped in front of a Spanish-style stucco two-story home with a red tile roof, across the street from the Deer Run Country Club. It was a nice enough house, but not the kind of place I'd been expecting for a multi-millionaire. My respect for Jim Whitman went up a level.

I looked at her.

'Sure to fetch a half-million as a teardown, if Mrs Johnson sells,' she said, getting out.

'The housekeeper inherited his house?'

'While his grandchildren got nothing.'

We walked up to the front door and she rang the bell. A minute later the door was opened by a trim older woman in gray pants and a black sweater. The woman smiled.

'Hello, Mrs Johnson.' Debbie's voice had turned soft and I wondered if the butch rasp she'd been using, talking to me, was an act for when she felt threatened. She introduced me to the housekeeper and we walked into a cool central hall.

The living room had a brown glazed tile floor and mission-style, black metal windows. Lighter rectangles on the beige stucco walls showed where pictures had recently been removed. Several cartons were stacked in the corner. We sat on wide, well-worn, nubby fabric chairs.

'Forgive the mess,' Mrs Johnson said to Debbie. 'I'm boxing up the last of the bequests he left to the museums.' She said it almost apologetically.

'Thank you for seeing us,' Debbie said.

Mrs Johnson reached to squeeze Debbie's wrist, and turned to me. 'I understand you're going to help with the insurance.'

I nodded. It saved me from explaining I had another client who was seeing murder. 'The day Mr Whitman died, he came home in the middle of the afternoon, took a nap, then watched the evening news as he dressed to go out?'

'Yes,' Mrs Johnson said.

'How were his spirits?'

'The usual, no worse. Mr Whitman tried not to let his troubles show.'

'Did he appear to be in pain?'

She pursed her lips, thinking back. 'No. His pills seemed to be working as always.'

'What time did he go out?'

'At seven. Mr McClain, his driver, came by early and we had coffee in the kitchen while Mr Whitman finished getting ready.'

'Do you remember where Mr Whitman went that night?'

'I'm sure it's written in his appointment book. Is it important?'

'I like to get all the details.'

'Let's find out, then.' She stood up and Debbie and I followed her down the narrow stucco hall to a small study lined with bookshelves. The Spanish motif of the rest of the house had been continued in the carved mahogany desk and the tooled red leather reading chair.

'I've thrown nothing of your father's away,' Mrs Johnson said to Debbie as she picked up a blue leather planner from the desk. She opened the book, flipped the pages to the back. She stopped at December thirteenth. It had been a Tuesday.

I looked over her shoulder. 'What is "C"?' I asked.

She shook her head. 'I don't know. Mr Whitman abbreviated everything,' she said, slowly fanning a few more pages so I could see.

The pages were filled in with one- and two-letter abbreviations. For someone dying, James Whitman was a busy man.

'Most of them I can decipher,' she said, looking down at the book, 'but "C" has me puzzled.'

'His driver would know where he took him.'

'Of course, especially since that was the night Mr Whitman died,' Mrs Johnson said.

We went back to sit in the living room.

'How did Mr Whitman seem when he came home later that evening?'

'Very fatigued, but he tired easily, the last few weeks. I was putting away some things in the hall closet when I heard the car pull up. I'd been listening for him because he was out later than usual. I looked out, saw him get out of a different car—'

'A different car?'

'Mr McClain usually drove a black Cadillac, but that night he brought Mr Whitman home in a tan-colored car,' she said. 'When Mr Whitman came in, I asked him if he needed anything. He said he was tired and was going to get something in his study and then go to bed. I said goodnight and went upstairs.' She pulled a tissue from the pocket in her pants.

'Do you have a card for Mr McClain?'

'I have his telephone number memorized,' she said, reciting it. I wrote it down and asked, 'You were the one who found him?'

'The next morning. He was always an early riser, even at the end. I made coffee, and brought a cup for him to the study. It was then . . .' Her voice trailed off as she touched the tissue to her eye.

It was all so eerily similar. Anne Barberi had also found her husband dead in his study the morning following a night out.

'What medication, exactly, was Mr Whitman taking?' I asked.

She glanced at Debbie, then back at me. 'You mean, what did he use to end his life?'

'Yes.'

'Gendarin. I'll get it for you.' She got up and left the room.

Debbie turned to me. 'Why is the kind of pills important?'

'It's only a detail for now, nothing more.'

The sound of a cabinet door opening and closing came from upstairs, and then Mrs Johnson came back into the room and handed me an orange vial. 'Gendarin, as I said.'

The vial was full. The label said it contained twenty-eight pills, to be taken one every twelve hours. It was a fourteen-day supply.

'These haven't been touched.' According to the label, the prescription bottle had been filled a little less than two weeks before Whitman died.

'This wasn't the vial they found in his pocket,' Mrs Johnson said. 'This was to be the new supply. He always reordered when he opened a new vial. That way, he always had a full two weeks in reserve, which I kept upstairs.'

'This was the only Gendarin he kept in reserve?'

'It's a controlled narcotic. They won't let you buy too much. I was to pick up a new refill when he began taking pills from this one.'

Something about what she'd just said flickered in the dark attic of my mind and disappeared.

'He carried the current vial he was using?' I asked instead.

'Always. The police made much of the vial they found in his pocket, but I told them he didn't want to risk being someplace without his pills.'

'He occasionally took extras, when the pain got severe?'

'Not that I know of. Carrying the pills was mostly a precaution.'

'Do you know where that vial is now?'

'I imagine the ambulance people took it.'

Debbie leaned forward in her chair. 'My father would not have left me without insurance.'

'Of course not,' Mrs Johnson said, shifting to look right at me. 'Mr Whitman was a meticulous person. He had his insurance man over here several times in the last year, going over this and that. He wanted to make sure everything was in order.'

The room went quiet. Both women leaned forward, attentive, anticipating, as though I might pop out a theory that would correct everything. I had no theories. I stood up. Debbie Goring and Mrs Johnson exchanged glances, then got up too.

At the front door, Mrs Johnson said, 'I feel so bad, Debbie. Your father left me a wonderful bequest. I don't have to work again if I don't want to. But you . . .' She reached for her tissue.

'It's all right, Mrs Johnson,' Debbie said. 'Elstrom here is going to set things straight.'

I didn't look at either of them as I walked to Debbie's station wagon and got in.

Debbie got in a second later, started the car and we pulled away. Lighting a cigarette, she spoke in the same small voice she'd used in front of Mrs Johnson. 'That didn't help, did it?'

'I don't know,' I said. I seemed to be saying that a lot lately.

'You won't help me?' she asked, her voice rasping now.

'I don't know how, yet.'

We drove the rest of the way in silence. She pulled into her driveway and we got out.

'I'll call his driver,' I said over the roof of her car, but it was to her back. She was already walking away.

FOURTEEN

The main drag through Deer Run was noisy with traffic. I pulled into a cemetery, parked next to a granite Civil War sentry who looked like he might welcome company, and called the chauffeur's number. Robert McClain answered on the first ring. He sounded eager for company, too, but said he played bridge until three o'clock. I told him I'd see him then.

I hadn't eaten since the modest half of a long coffee cake at Leo's. I drove into Deer Run's business district, hunting for a fast-food restaurant with the right kind of windows. I got lucky right away. A storefront across from the train station was papered with window banners advertising chili dogs, half-pound hamburgers and cheese fries. The promise showed in the sharpness of the red letters on the white signs. They were not sharp. They were blurred. I cut the engine and got out to make sure. Right off I spotted a fly stuck to the inside of the window, proof enough that the faintly fuzzy signs weren't the result of sloppy brush work. The blur came from the glass. I went in.

Kings, Kentuckys and Macs are never my first choice because their windows are invariably spotless. The joints I seek have glass made opaque by the inside air. If the windows are filmy with grease, the chef is using properly fatty meat and real lard – sure signs he's not cooking to some bland, committee-crafted, offend-no-one formula. I see it as my obligation to support such efforts by visiting those grease blots as frequently as I can, for they are highly flammable and regularly explode into black smoke.

I ordered a hot dog, onion rings and a Diet Coke and took them to a Formica counter to look at the blur of the world outside. My first bites validated my greasy window theory once again. The hot dog was properly slippery, topped with pickle, tomatoes, peppers, mustard, chopped onions, dill salt and absolutely no trace of catsup. The rings were strong, sure to delight for the rest of the afternoon. And the Diet Coke . . . well, the Diet Coke, like every diet soft drink, was there simply to dissolve calories.

I puzzled again over my earlier sense that I'd missed something when Mrs Johnson talked about Whitman's pills. And in a moment, I had it: Whitman had been about to crack open the reserve vial of pills she'd showed us. That meant his current supply, the one they found in his pocket, should have been almost depleted if he'd been taking his pills in the dosage prescribed.

I swallowed the last bit of hot dog and turned around to ask where the police station was. The man behind the counter shrugged and said something in Spanish to the woman who'd taken my order. 'Three blocks up the street,' she said. 'It's in the basement of City Hall, opposite the park.'

I stepped almost lightly outside, sure of my wisdom in selecting a hot dog and onion rings for lunch. Like an automobile, my brain functions best when it's freshly greased.

I decided to hoof the three blocks. Crossing the first street, I spotted a junior-grade black BMW parked down the side street, just like the one that had tailed me for a time earlier that morning. I continued on to the middle of the next block, and stopped as if to look in a store window. No black BMW or well-barbered head on feet had followed.

Deer Run's city hall was red brick and white pillars. Walking down to the police department in the basement set the onion rings to barking. I slid three breath tapes into my mouth. The tapes were generic; I get them at the Discount Den in Rivertown, at the same place I get the duct tape to mend the rips in the Jeep's top and Leo gets his shiny Hawaiian shirts and fluorescent pants. I aimed a test breath at the painted yellow block wall before opening the metal door at the bottom. Nothing peeled. Encouraged, I went in.

'I'd like to talk to someone about Jim Whitman's death,' I said to the desk sergeant.

He scooted his chair back a yard, making me wonder if the Discount Den's breath tapes were as unreliable as the duct tape that curled from the Jeep every time it rained. I slipped my hand surreptitiously into my pocket and thumbed loose another tape.

'Your business?' he asked, looking off to my right where, perhaps, there was better air.

I held out a card. It says I do insurance investigations. He scooted forward, grabbed it, and again retreated fast. I slipped the new tape into my mouth.

He frowned as he studied the card. 'I thought you insurance guys closed your file.'

'I'm just filling in a couple of blanks.'

The sergeant swiveled around. 'Finch, get the Whitman file,' he yelled to the empty hallway behind him. Turning back, he motioned for me to sit by the door, on the plastic chair farthest from his desk.

Officer Finch came out in five minutes. He was young, maybe twenty-five, and carried a brown accordion file. 'How may I help you, sir?' he asked.

'I'd like to know how much Gendarin Jim Whitman swallowed the night he died.'

Finch looked to the desk sergeant, who nodded. Finch took a sheet of paper from the file and said, 'Approximately twelve hundred milligrams. It was enough to send him to the moon twice.'

'You're sure it was Gendarin?'

Finch took out a clear plastic bag. Inside was an orange pill bottle identical to the one Mrs Johnson had showed me. It rattled as he held it up to read the label. 'Gendarin,' he said.

'May I?' I asked.

'So long as you leave it inside the plastic bag,' he said, and handed it to me.

The pill bottle rattled again as I held the bag up to the light. 'There are still pills in there,' I said, like I was surprised.

'Two,' Finch said.

'This vial was found in Whitman's suit jacket?'

'Yes.'

I read the label through the bag. Just like the reserve supply Mrs Johnson had showed me, this vial had contained twenty-eight pills, eighty milligrams each, prescribed at two a day. It had been filled almost a month before Whitman died. That made sense, calendar-wise. It had been kept in reserve for two weeks before

Whitman had begun taking pills from it, at the prescribed rate of two a day, not quite two weeks before he died.

Which meant the vial I was now holding should have contained but a few pills, the end of a two-week supply.

Which meant it could not have contained enough pills to kill him.

'You're sure the medical examiner found twelve hundred milligrams of this stuff in Whitman's system?' I asked.

'Approximately.'

'Isn't it odd that two pills remain inside this vial?'

'Whitman would have known just a few would do the trick.'

I gave him the arithmetic. 'Fifteen pills were needed to put twelve hundred milligrams in his system.'

'OK,' the desk sergeant said slowly, not comprehending where I was heading.

'That's over half a vial. His reserve supply at home was untouched.'

'What are you saying?'

I rattled the vial in the plastic bag. 'He took pills from this vial exactly on schedule, two a day. Where did Whitman get fifteen pills to swallow all at once?'

Finch grabbed the bag back. 'From this—'

'No,' I cut in. 'There weren't enough left in there.'

The desk sergeant cocked his head, motioning Finch to leave. 'You'll have to check with the medical examiner,' he said to me.

I gave it up, and walked up the stairs. I took a long look through the window in the door before going out. I saw no black BMW or sharply barbered MBA outside, but I'd just seen plenty inside.

I crossed the street to a drug store and bought a pack of Listerine breath tapes. They were stronger than my generics, and got rid of the taste of onions right away.

But they didn't mask the bile that had risen in my throat.

FIFTEEN

Robert McClain was in the parking lot behind his dark brick apartment building, dry wiping a shiny black Cadillac Seville. He looked old enough to have been driving when roads were made of dirt.

'I like to be ready, in case I get a call,' he said, smiling.

I asked him about Jim Whitman.

'Working for Mr Whitman was a real pleasure,' he said. 'Most fellows would have insisted on a younger driver, but not Mr Whitman. He was always real polite and regular, always sat up front with me. He tipped really well.'

'Do you remember the night he died?'

'Like yesterday. I knew he was ill – he was straightforward about it – but he didn't act like a man about to kill himself.'

'His spirits were good?'

'Considering what he was facing, yes. As usual, he talked about his grandchildren all the way into the city.'

'You picked him up about seven?'

McClain nodded. 'Went in, had a spot of coffee with Mrs Johnson while Mr Whitman was getting ready.'

'Do you remember where you took him?'

'Corner of Michigan and Walton, downtown.'

'I meant which restaurant.'

'No restaurant. Dropped him at the same corner, as usual.'

'You'd taken him there before?'

'Every few weeks. He never did say where exactly he was going from there.'

'And you picked him up later at that same corner?'

'Not that night. He called to say he was catching another way home.'

'You didn't bring him home in a tan-colored car?'

'This baby's all I got,' he said, touching the gleaming hood of the black Cadillac.

'Was it usual for him to find another way home from there?'

'He'd never done it before. Every other time, I picked him up at ten o'clock sharp. He'd be standing on that same corner, waiting.' He picked up his rag, worked at an imagined spot. 'That was the last time I drove anybody.'

'Business slow?'

'I'm old, and I look it. The agency's got younger drivers.'

There was nothing left to say. I left him in the late-afternoon sun, polishing a future that likely had disappeared.

I busied myself cutting the last of the closet trim that evening. I needed simple work requiring clear and logical steps while my mind stumbled about in the fog surrounding Jim Whitman's pills.

For a time, it worked. The cutting, sanding and staining were calming, easy steps in an understandable sequence. But then, well into the evening, it came time for varnishing. Varnishing, done right, requires care: one pass, no over-brushing. Be too fast, and a spot can get overlooked.

And that's what happened with the cops looking at Jim Whitman's death. They'd missed a big spot: they hadn't accounted for his pills. He couldn't have used his current two-week prescription to kill himself because there had been too few remaining. And he hadn't tapped his reserve vial because it was untouched. He had to have gotten his fatal batch of fifteen pills from a third source.

Unless he hadn't. Someone else could have slipped Gendarin into his meal or his drink, knowing that the excess in his blood-stream wouldn't be questioned because it was the pain medication he was already taking. It would have been assumed that Whitman used his own supply to overdose himself.

What I couldn't see was the logic in risking the murder of an already dying man.

The vague thoughts and the pungent smell of the varnish finally made me woozy. I walked down to the river to sit on the bench and breathe in the cold March air. Behind me, the jukes in the tonks along Thompson Avenue were beating out big bass notes, primitive drums summoning tribe members to return. I almost envied those in that dark carnival. They were sure of what they were seeking: a simple tingle from some booze, a few laughs, a rub of rented flesh.

Perhaps it had been that simple for Jim Whitman, that last night. Maybe he'd finished a good meal, enjoyed a few drinks, had a few laughs being driven home by a friend . . . and realized things would never get any better than they were that evening. Maybe he'd rat-holed a stash of Gendarin for just such a time, and asked himself, on the spur of that moment: Why not? Why not check out with a belly full of good steak and good Scotch, and the sound of a laugh still resonating in the back of his throat? Why not?

Except for the grandchildren he'd left without a nickel.

The dim light from the lamp along the riverwalk made a tiny shadow on the ground just beyond my feet. It was another still-born ash leaf, curled and dried on the grass. I looked up at the tree. There was not enough light to see for sure, but I knew in my throat that no new leaves had appeared that day.

I took out my pocket calendar and recorded that loss, too.

SIXTEEN

Two men in loose-fitting gray suits, one carrying a square carton, the other something the size of a wrapped painting, came out of the Whitman house the next morning, heading toward the black Ford Expedition parked at the curb. They stopped when they saw me pull up. The one with the painting gestured at someone in the big SUV, and a third man, also in a suit, got out from the driver's door. All three stood motionless, watching me. I couldn't see the guns, but I knew they had them. Whatever Jim Whitman had bequeathed, it was worth enough to merit three guards.

Mrs Johnson had followed the two men out of the house, saw them tense and stop on the front walk. She turned to look where they were looking. I waved out the Jeep's open side curtain. She squinted, recognized my face. 'We're almost done,' she called. And the world righted itself. The men carrying the box and the painting resumed walking toward the SUV, the driver got back inside, and I settled back to wait.

Ten minutes later, Mrs Johnson followed the armed men out

with the last of the cartons, and watched them drive away. She came over to the Jeep. 'You can't imagine how relieved I am that those things are on their way to the Museum of Contemporary Art,' she said. 'The house has an alarm, but I've not been comfortable there, alone with all those valuable pieces.'

'They'll be exhibited soon?' I asked as we went up the front walk.

'The curator said they'll be catalogued, then stored. In a year, maybe less, they'll be rotated into exhibition.'

'How valuable are the pieces?'

'Millions,' she said, as we entered the house. 'Mr Whitman was a plain man, not the usual patron of the arts. Those pieces were recommended as investments. From what I understand, he profited quite handsomely from their purchase.'

'Yet not even one was left to Debbie.'

The distress on her face seemed genuine. 'Wealthy fathers can be especially difficult on young daughters. And Debbie, as you might imagine, was very strong-willed. But Mr Whitman cared for his daughter, and adored his grandsons.'

'You find it odd that he left them nothing?'

'It's impossible to believe. And now you've come back because you're wondering where he got the pills, haven't you?'

'Yes, and I'd like to see his calendar again. You're certain there was only one bottle of Gendarin in reserve?'

'Certain as I can be. As I said, Mr Whitman wanted to keep more on hand, in case the pain got worse, but his doctor wouldn't go for it. Federally regulated narcotics are so very tightly dispensed.'

'Could he have set aside a pill or two from each refill, to build up an extra supply?'

'That's very doubtful. He truly needed those pills, and skipping one would mean going twelve full hours in pain. And yes, Mr Elstrom,' she said, 'I told that to the police, but they didn't seem interested.'

'Any more thoughts on where Mr Whitman might have gone that last night?'

'Mr McClain was no help?'

'He dropped off Mr Whitman on North Michigan Avenue. Someone else drove him home.'

'In that tan car I saw.'

'Any idea whose it was?'

'Only thing I know it was tan, and it was a Buick.'

'You know cars well enough to spot a Buick?'

'Goodness, no. All cars look the same to me these days, like jelly beans. It's just that when I was young, Buicks had those holes . . .' She stopped, searching for the words.

'Like portholes, on the sides of the car?'

'That's it. Imagine Buick still doing those holes, only smaller, after all these years.'

We went into Whitman's study. She picked up the calendar from the desk and handed it to me. I opened it to the page for December 13, the day he died, and looked again at the half-dozen entries. His first appointment was for lunch, at eleven-thirty. Other names were penciled in, beginning at one, ending at two-thirty. After that, the calendar was blank until the 'C' entry, scrawled across the lines for the evening. I pointed to it.

'As I told you last time, I don't know that one,' she said. 'After you and Debbie left, I flipped back a few months. There are other entries just like it.'

'McClain said the same thing. He dropped Whitman at the same intersection, Michigan at Walton, every few weeks.'

'You think he got the Gendarin there?'

'I can't understand why he'd need to. He had enough in reserve here to kill himself.'

'I went through the whole house, Mr Elstrom. I found no third vial, no trace he'd hidden more Gendarin.' She studied my face. 'You came back because you're thinking what I'm thinking.'

'Two pills remaining in the vial in his jacket, as there should have been? Full reserve supply upstairs, as there should have been? Leaving us to accept he'd gone to the bother of obtaining the pills he needed to kill himself elsewhere, when he didn't need to? Yes, I'm having a problem understanding why he'd go to that trouble.'

'He didn't commit suicide, did he, Mr Elstrom?'

'I can't prove that.'

'Why would someone risk killing him? Why not simply wait?'

'Did he have enemies?'

'Business adversaries, perhaps, though Mr Whitman was not ruthless, not someone who took unfair advantage.'

I started turning back the calendar pages. 'I need to know where he went that evening.'

The appointments looked to have been written by two different people. Most were in a feminine hand. 'Did you make most of these entries?'

'His secretary made those,' she said. 'The ones that are barely legible, like that 'C' for the night Mr Whitman died, he wrote himself.'

Almost every page had an abbreviation for an evening appointment. I started pointing randomly to different evening entries.

'Y?'

'YMCA of Metropolitan Chicago, usually a dinner meeting for the directors, every three months.'

'MP?'

'Millennium Park, the new park on Michigan Avenue. He donated one hundred thousand dollars.'

I came to another 'C' entry, two months earlier, in October.

'That's one of the others I found,' Mrs Johnson said.

Again it was simple and cryptic, scrawled across the lines for evening appointments. Beside me, Mrs Johnson shook her head, offering nothing. I turned back more pages. There were 'C' entries in August, June, April and February.

'Did he keep another desk diary at his office?' I asked.

'This was the only one; he carried it back and forth in his briefcase.'

'Maybe the prior year's book has more information?'

'His secretary kept his old diaries,' she said, picking up the phone. Then, while she was dialing, 'Why would someone murder an already dying man?'

There was no answering that.

SEVENTEEN

Whitman Industries occupied four floors in a high-rise office building just north of the Chicago River. Jim Whitman's former secretary, a trim, efficient woman in her mid-fifties, came to the lobby carrying two blue leather desk calendars identical to the one I'd brought from Whitman's house. We sat in a secluded corner next to a plant.

I opened the calendar I'd brought to December 13, the night Whitman died. 'Do you know what this is?' I asked, pointing to the 'C.'

'I wondered about those,' she said. 'I wrote most of the appointments in his book, and knew almost all of the ones he entered. But those "C"s . . .' She shook her head. 'I never asked, of course.'

'Were there many?'

'Several a year.' She opened one of the calendars she'd brought, the book for the year before last. Turning the pages, she made notes on a small pad. When she was finished, she said, 'The year before last, he attended 'C' meetings on February tenth, April thirteenth, June eighth, August tenth, October twelfth, and then December fourteenth. They seem to have been regular enough, all on Tuesdays.' She handed me the list.

'How about the year before that?'

She opened the other book she'd brought, the one for the third year going back, and, turning the pages, read off the dates so I could write them down. 'Regular thing,' she said, when she was done. 'Tuesdays, every other month.'

'You have no idea where he spent those evenings?'

'No.'

'How did he seem, his last day here?'

'For a man whose life was being cut short – a strong, powerful man who had to give up control of an empire he had constructed?' Her lips tightened, then relaxed. 'Actually, he seemed in remarkably good humor that day. He met with several people, dictated a few letters, mostly apologies for matters he could not attend to personally, and left around three o'clock.'

'Did he keep any extra medication in his office?' I asked.

'You mean pills to kill himself?'

'Yes,' I said.

'I went through his office thoroughly. There was no trace of pills.'

I had no doubt she'd searched immediately, looking to destroy any evidence Whitman had taken a deliberate overdose.

'You wouldn't tell me if there were,' I said.

'I find it difficult to believe he killed himself. In any event, there was no trace of an extra supply in his office.'

I believed her like I believed Mrs Johnson. Whitman had no extra pills.

And that was enough for Wendell Phelps to call the cops.

I called his private cell phone number as soon as I got outside. 'I've got something for you to take to the police. Jim Whitman loved his grandsons, and would have known his suicide would null the insurance policy he'd left for their well-being.'

Wendell said nothing for a moment, and then asked, in a surprisingly weak voice, 'Insurance?'

'He had a two-million-dollar life policy, benefitting his grandsons. Death by suicide nulled it.'

Again he paused. 'Perhaps there were other policies . . .' He let the question trail away.

'If there were, his daughter, Debbie, does not know of them. She got nothing for the care of her kids. You have enough to go to the police, Wendell.'

'The cops will say he was a sick man. Pain doesn't make for high lucidity.'

'He was lucid enough to arrange his other bequests.'

'That proves nothing,' he said, his voice stronger, almost combative.

'Then try this: I can't find the source of the pills he supposedly took. He had plenty at home, but he didn't touch those. If he took his own life, he used pills from a secret stash.'

'Cops will say a secret stash was easy to create.'

'He could have been fed those pills. Murdered, as you suspect.'

'Jim Whitman was dying, damn it. There was no motive for murder. Cops will laugh.'

'Why fight me on this, Wendell? You suspected right away your friends were being murdered.'

'I overreacted.'

'The night Whitman died, he went downtown to a place that begins with a "C." He went there every two months, always on a Tuesday. He was secretive about it. He had his driver drop him nearby, but never directly at the destination.'

He chuckled, but it sounded forced. 'Whitman was a widower. Maybe he went down there to visit a lady friend he didn't want anyone to know about. Hell, she could have been a high-priced hooker.'

'His regular driver didn't come back for him the night he died. Someone else drove him home, somebody in a light-colored Buick.'

'This is all you've got?' He exhaled disgust into the phone. 'There are thousands of Buicks in this town, like there are thousands of places that begin with the letter "C." I'll get back to you if I want you to continue.'

'Go to the cops,' I said, but I was talking to dead air. He'd hung up.

Wendell had become too argumentative. He'd swatted away every red flag I'd waved. For a man who'd been so certain his fellow tycoons were being murdered, a man who'd been frightened enough to stand by his curtains to make sure they didn't open even an inch, his behavior had transformed suddenly from fear to aggressiveness.

The day was breezy and sunny and good for a walk to mull my new confusion. I headed over to Michigan Avenue, where Jim Whitman had spent the last evening of his life.

Measured by glitz and geography, North Michigan Avenue is the middle sparkler in a three-diamond necklace, approximately equidistant from Rodeo Drive in California and Fifth Avenue in New York. Amanda and I used to walk the grand boulevard when we were new to each other. I was charmed by the way she'd look through the store windows for customers who'd mastered a certain curve to their backs and the oh-so-slight rise to their eyebrows that feigned unconcern to the ridiculous prices of the baubles they were inspecting. 'Arch,' the beautiful girl who'd grown up so rich used to call such false posturing. On North Michigan Avenue, Amanda said, life started and ended with false attitude.

I'd brought Wendell validation of his worries, at least about Jim Whitman. He should have pressed me to find out more. Instead he'd dusted me off with impatience and anger. And arch.

I got to Walton Street, where Whitman had been let off. It was one of the grandest intersections in the city, anchored on the northeast by the Drake Hotel. Upscale shops fanned out from the other three corners, lots of vogue for lots of arch. In the distance, past Lake Shore Drive, Lake Michigan rippled blue and calm, already dotted with the first of the season's sailboats.

I stepped close to the curb to see better in all four directions. I wasn't expecting anything obvious like a neon sign flashing a big orange 'C' or a raven-haired dame in a black dress slit to her hip, blowing C-shaped smoke rings from an upper-story window. I would have settled for even the tiniest of mental nudges, but I didn't even get that. All I saw were sun-washed storefronts and restaurants offering subtlety at non-subtle prices, and not one had a name that began with a 'C.'

I turned right, walked east on East Walton Place, toward the lake, then reversed, and came west all the way to State Street. I passed the Drake, shiny new storefronts and old three-story graystones – some housing fashionable boutiques and trendy bars, others housing those who hung out in the fashionable boutiques and trendy bars. It was a rich, hip, ever-evolving neighborhood, but mostly it was young, and a seemingly unlikely place for Jim Whitman to visit six times a year. I got back to the Jeep no smarter than when I'd left it and considerably less employed.

I drove south toward the expressway. Michigan Avenue across the bridge is a different place. Gone is the sunny glitz of the boulevard to the north. Michigan Avenue south of the river is dark. The buildings lining its west side are tall and close to the street and shut out the sun from the sidewalk early as it heads away from the lake. There are no strolling swells swinging little boutique bags south of the river, just art students and secretaries, store clerks and podiatrists; people hustling with their heads down just to stay even. And there are pigeons, often dozens of them, strutting and worse on the sidewalk. There is no pretense on Michigan Avenue, south of the river. There is no arch.

But there is often chaos. Unfamiliar drivers heading southbound are often made crazy trying to find the expressway; the signs pointing the way are small and placed too far down. Only at the last moment do the uninitiated comprehend that a left turn is needed to make the right-hand curve to the expressway. And then they swerve, panicked, across several lanes of traffic.

That's what happened that afternoon. The driver in front of me shot across my bow, barely missing my front bumper.

I didn't hit the horn; I didn't raise a fist or a finger. I didn't even remind myself to stay mellow, that this was normal road life Michigan Avenue, south of the river.

I did none of those things because the sight of the car veering in front of me seemed to demand more than that, like I was supposed to focus on what I'd just seen. It was an ordinary enough car – light-colored, beige or tan, swerving in the same stupid way that I'd seen a hundred times before. Yet somehow this car, at this time, seemed very much to matter.

I replayed the image over and over in my mind as I drove back to Rivertown, but I could make no sense of why the image nagged.

Just like I couldn't make sense of Wendell's arch behavior.

EIGHTEEN

I'd just stepped into the turret when a slow ripping creak sounded loud from upstairs. I ran up the wrought iron, knowing, and shot into the kitchen to see for sure.

The turret's craggy, curved limestone walls make for interesting architecture, but they play hell with converting the place into a residence. Hanging anything onto them is a true nightmare. One of the kitchen cabinets I'd just hung was coming loose. I'd arrived home just in time to pull it safely from the wall before it crashed to the floor.

I changed into my rehabbing clothes, which look only marginally worse than my dress duds, and spent the next few hours re-anchoring the cabinet to the wall. By the time I got it to hang right, it was well past dusk, and Amanda had called three times. I'd dodged each call, knowing she must have spoken with her father, and now she wanted truths from me. I didn't want to worry her by saying I suspected Jim Whitman had likely been murdered, and that Wendell didn't want me to learn any more about it.

I walked across what one day might be a hall, and sat at the card table I use as a desk. My cheesy, giveaway black vinyl calendar was nothing like Jim Whitman's leather-bound desk diaries. Though mine was dressed up in gold like Whitman's, instead of mono-grammed initials, mine sported an air-freight company's logo of an emaciated bird. And where his provided an entire lined page for each day, mine offered a stingy small page for an entire month – space enough, the air freight company must have concluded, for people who don't have much going on in their lives. Certainly they'd been right about me. Save for the leaf counts of the ash by the river, and the few hours I'd invoiced so far that spring, my pages were mostly empty.

I switched on my computer, typed in my billable hours for Wendell's final invoice, wrote a check to refund the balance on his retainer, and printed out two copies of the invoice. One went with the check into an envelope addressed to Wendell. The other was for me. Opening the case folder, I saw again the photocopy of Benno Barberi's obituary.

This time, though, the date of his death the previous autumn danced on the paper like it was lit by a strobe: October 11.

I grabbed the notes I'd made just that day. Jim Whitman had scrawled a 'C' in his calendar across the same Tuesday evening Benno Barberi had come home, furious, to die.

I spilled the rest of the file onto the card table, pawing for the newspaper article about Grant Carson's hit-and-run. My hands shook as I read it. He'd been killed on February 15th. It had been a Wednesday, but very early in the morning.

My cell phone rang again. I glanced over. It was Amanda. I let it ring.

I read all the obituaries again, double-checking the dates with my vinyl calendar to be sure. There was no doubt. Benno Barberi, Jim Whitman and Grant Carson had all died on, or just an hour or two following, the second Tuesday of an even-numbered month.

I got out of the chair and went up the stairs to the third floor. I wanted a sweatshirt.

Suddenly, I was cold.

NINETEEN

I called Anne Barberi at eight-thirty sharp the next morning.

'No, I can't remember where Benno went that evening,' she said. 'He attended so many dinners.'

'Who has your husband's appointments calendar?'

'His secretary, I would imagine.'

'Can you arrange for me to look at his appointment books for last year and the year before?'

'What have you learned, Mr Elstrom?'

'I'm casting a wide net, trying to gather as much information as I can.'

'What do you suspect?'

'I'll tell you when what I suspect becomes what I believe. For now, tell me, was your husband taking much medication?'

'Of course; several prescriptions. You're wondering why they were ineffective, that last night?'

I was wondering if they'd been too effective, for a killer, but I couldn't dare say that yet. 'Sort of,' I said instead. 'Can you arrange for me to talk to his primary physician?'

'As part of that mysterious wide-net business?'

'Yes.'

'Benno's doctor is a close friend. I'll have him call you.'

And he did, fifteen minutes later. 'What's this about, Elstrom?'

'Was Benno Barberi taking any medication that, in larger than prescribed doses, could have killed him?'

The doctor paused, as he must have often, in this modern era of high-buck medical malpractice suits. And then he evaded. 'Aspirin, taken in large doses, can kill you.'

'Could Barberi have overdosed?'

'The cause of his death was obvious to the EMTs: massive heart attack.'

'He wasn't autopsied?'

'No need.'

'If there were sufficient grounds, can he be autopsied now?'

'Elstrom, you're inferring something untoward? The EMTs would have noticed anything suspicious about Benno's death, as would the emergency room personnel who pronounced him dead.'

'Maybe they didn't probe because his heart condition was well documented.'

'My God, man; you're insinuating he was deliberately overdosed?'

'For now, it's something to rule out.'

'Who would benefit from his death? I don't believe Benno had any enemies.'

There was no answering that yet, just as there seemed to be no
reason to overdose Jim Whitman, a dying man.

'I need your support to exhume Benno Barberi,' I said.

'Summon divine intervention instead. Benno was cremated and
his ashes were scattered off his boat in Lake Michigan.'

Benno Barberi's former secretary called twenty minutes after the
doctor slammed down his phone. She was as crisp and as efficient
as she'd been the first time we'd spoken. She told me I could come
anytime. I left immediately.

She was waiting in the lobby. She was an austere but attractive
brunette in her late thirties. If she'd been briefed by Barberi's two
sharply barbered assistants about my first visit, she didn't show
it. Certainly she did not glance down to see if any varnish or
mustard remained on my blazer sleeve.

We went to the same small conference room where I'd met Jason
and Brad. Two red leather appointment books sat on the small table.

'I recorded all of Mr Barberi's appointments,' she said. 'What
are you looking for?'

'Symmetry,' I said.

'I'm afraid I don't understand,' she said, 'but that's not necessary. Where shall we start?'

'The day and evening of his fatal heart attack.'

She opened one of the books and started turning pages. 'That
would be October eleventh,' she said, stopping at the page. She
turned the book around so I could see.

The page was crammed with entries, beginning at seven-thirty
in the morning and ending with a notation at five-thirty that read:
'Emerson.' Nothing was posted for the evening.

'What's Emerson?' I asked.

'Emerson is a fitness trainer. Three times a week, Mr Barberi
took light exercise, as prescribed by his physician.'

I pulled out my note pad. 'Where's the health club?' I asked.

She smiled. 'In the basement here. Mr Emerson is on staff for
our senior executives.'

'Of course,' I said, like I had the lifestyle that would have presumed
that. I pointed to the bottom of the calendar page. 'There's nothing
written for the evening, yet his wife told me he'd gone out to dinner.'

'I wondered about that.' She looked down at the book. 'He

didn't tell me of a dinner engagement, and that was a rarity. His evenings were as busy as his days, and he expected me to keep track of his after-hours obligations as well.'

I started turning the pages backwards. She was right; every one of his evenings, Monday through Saturday, had a notation penned in her handwriting. I didn't find a blank, working-day evening until I'd gone back to August 9.

It, too, had been the second Tuesday of the month.

I turned the book to show her. 'Nothing here, either.'

'I guess he forgot to tell me his plans then, as well.'

I continued backwards through the book quickly, growing more certain. And all were there. Or rather, they were not: The evenings of the second Tuesdays in June, April and February had been left blank. I picked up the calendar for the preceding year. It was the same. Benno Barberi had listed no evening appointments for any second Tuesday in February, April, June, August, October or December for two years.

Second Tuesdays, even-numbered months. I closed the second calendar and stood up.

'Did you find what you were looking for?'

'I don't—'

'I know: you don't know.' Her smile was tight and telling. She knew I'd spotted something.

I could only smile back. She walked me downstairs to the fitness center in the basement. Rudy Emerson, dressed in gray sweats, could have been forty or sixty, and looked like he'd never gotten outside a Twinkie in his life.

He remembered his last session with Benno Barberi. 'Of course I knew about his heart. Like always, there was no unusual exertion that day. I started him with easy stretching exercises, we moved to the light weights, and finished with more stretching. Thirty minutes, easy does it. He left here feeling good, looking good.'

'Looking good?' I asked.

'Same suit, but a fresh shirt and a different tie.'

'He sounded good, too? No disorientation, no signs of physical distress?'

'Whatever he ate that night might have killed him, but I guarantee it wasn't the exercise he got here.'

'He didn't happen to mention where he was headed?'

Rudy Emerson shook his head. 'Not for a heart attack, that's for sure.'

Barberi's secretary left me in the lobby. Walking out, I had the thought to turn around and look back. Like the last time I'd left Barberi Holdings, I caught sight of a young man in a dark suit watching me. It could have been Brad; it could have been Jason; it could have been someone else, similarly barbered. Whoever he was, he must have caught sight of me looking back, because he quickly moved from sight.

The Rivertown chip pressed down a little on my shoulder, suggesting a little show. I took a leisurely stroll down the rows of the cars parked in the lot.

There were six of the junior-grade black BMWs, each identical to the one that had tailed me at least twice.

A tailing car need not be driven by a killer, I told myself.

Nor did it need be driven by an innocent, either.

I spent a showy moment in front of each car's license plate, writing its number in the little spiral notebook I always carry. Then, back in the Jeep, I checked my cell phone before I started the car, wanting whoever might still be watching to think I was running the plate numbers I'd just written down. And maybe later I'd get a cop friend to do just that. For now, I had other things to think about.

Amanda had left fresh, furious messages, demanding to know why I had not returned any of her calls. Leo offered to buy lunch. And the Bohemian had asked me to call right away. I thumbed his number.

There was no booming 'Vlodek' to begin the conversation, but there was a chuckle, of sorts. 'Arthur Lamm is still missing,' he said.

'You don't sound worried.'

'Perhaps because his absence has become even more explainable. The IRS began investigating him last fall.'

'For what?'

'Unreported income from insurance irregularities.'

'Insurance? I thought the guy was in real estate.'

'Arthur might have the longest tentacles of those in the heavy cream. He acts as a broker, selling large office buildings. Then he negotiates to become its property manager. To top it all off, he gets the property owner to buy the building's insurance from his agency.'

'An IRS investigation wouldn't make a guy like Lamm run into the woods,' I said.

'Of course, unless his battery of high-priced attorneys told him to get lost until they could work something out with the Feds.'

'Or unless he committed big-time fraud?' I asked. 'Such things can attract long prison sentences. In which case, he wouldn't run off into the woods of Wisconsin. He'd flee the country, go someplace where he can't be extradited.'

'Look, we already know his rowboat and fishing gear are all gone, and that his cottage is on a string of lakes,' the Bohemian said. 'I suppose we could see something clandestine in that. I guess it's possible he could have headed north to Canada, and from there gone overseas.'

'Or he's staged things, leaving a false trail to buy time to leave the country another way.'

'This might be of interest to some of his associates,' the Bohemian said. 'Those in the heavy cream often cross-invest in each other's companies.'

'You want me to look more deeply into it?'

'I want you to be ready.'

TWENTY

Rikk, at Carson's life insurance carrier, sounded half asleep when he picked up the phone.

'Did anybody identify where Carson went, his last night?' I asked.

He yawned, quite audibly. 'You're killing me, Elstrom. You already asked that. Our concern starts at the moment he got smacked. Dinner doesn't matter.'

'Didn't your investigator ask, anyway?'

'Maybe; probably; I don't know. How does knowing where he ate help us?'

'You never know,' I invented. 'Maybe he was fed something that disoriented him, made him step out in front of traffic.'

'And we could sue the restaurant or his dinner companions to recover our payout? You think he was murdered? For what purpose?'

'I don't know,' I said.

'You're reaching.' He yawned, and added, 'As well as holding back.'

'I'm wondering if someone was with Carson, in the car.' I said, thinking specifically of the man in the tan Buick who drove Whitman home.

'Listen, Elstrom, asking these questions helps us only if the passenger was wealthy, had a hand in forcing Carson in front of the kill car, and we could sue to recover. We discussed all this. Vehicular homicides are too chancy. There are better ways to kill.'

'That's what any right-thinking person would think. That's what makes it a clever way to murder.'

'Give me a motive.'

'I don't have one.'

'There were no witnesses, remember? Even if you found a motive, we can't prove anything.'

'At least find out where Carson went, before he got killed.'

'If I call our investigator, will you leave me alone?'

'If you will also check Grant Carson's appointment books for the last two years, to see if he went to that same place on the second Tuesday evenings of every even-numbered month.'

That woke him up. 'What the hell do you know that you're not telling me?' he shouted.

'Help me here, Rikk.'

'How can I rationalize asking for his calendars?'

'With creativity.'

'You're nuts, Elstrom,' he said, and hung up.

I called Leo after I'd gotten on the tollway, southbound. 'You said you're buying lunch?'

'Yes, but I'm dieting.'

Leo's metabolism runs as fast as his intellect. There'd been no change in his 140 pounds since high school. 'You're porking up?' I asked anyway.

'A pound and a half since Christmas.'

'I can achieve that with a lone raspberry Danish.'

'So I noticed on my front stoop, very recently. See you at Kutz's.'

I'd saved the worst call for last. I thumbed on my cell phone directory and clicked Amanda's number. 'Hey, sorry I haven't been returning your calls,' I said. 'I've been swamped . . .'

Her voice was barely audible in the headset I'd bought cheap at the Discount Den. Then again, I was surrounded by trucks.

'I can't hear you,' I yelled, speeding up to get clear of the trucks.

'Do you miss me?' she shouted.

'Like there'll be no tomorrow, Amanda,' I screamed, joking, at last getting free of the trucks.

'Jenny,' the voice yelled, horribly clear. 'Jenny Galecki.'

'Ah,' I said, hearing too perfectly. For sure, jackasses should not be issued speed-dial features, or thumbs, or headsets. Or mouths.

'Talking with Amanda, are we?' she asked.

'It's that case involving her father that I told you about,' I said, fighting the urge to say I wasn't lying.

'Did you get my little package?' There was frost in the words that I couldn't blame on the cheap headset.

'Package? No.'

'I sent you a little something, to keep you thinking of me. It seemed funny at the time.' She clicked off.

In the eight months since Jenny went west, we sometimes went weeks without speaking. Still, an hour didn't pass where I didn't think of her, hoping an hour hadn't passed where she hadn't thought of me. And somehow San Francisco seemed closer.

Now I'd messed things for sure by fumbling my mention of Amanda. San Francisco felt like it had moved to another continent.

The phone rang again as I got off the tollway. 'Listen, Jenny—'

'Damn you, Elstrom,' Gaylord Rikk corrected. It had only been twenty minutes since we'd spoken. I ripped the headset off and pressed the phone to my ear, in clear violation of Illinois law.

'That seems to have already happened.'

'I got intrigued, but only because I'm bored. In some disgusting way, you liven up my dreary existence.'

'You've got something?' I asked.

'It only took two phone calls. Turns out our people did ask where Carson had gone, the night he was killed. No one seemed to know, not his wife or his secretary, and we dropped it because it didn't seem relevant. So . . .' He lingered in silent smugness, waiting.

'So?' I asked, accepting the cue.

He dropped his voice, a secret agent for sure. 'I called Carson's secretary, saying I was tidying up the last of our paperwork, and needed to know where he'd been that night. She said she already told the police she didn't know, which I knew.'

'And?' I asked, anxious. He'd learned something.

'Nothing,' he said.

'You struck out?'

'No, I mean Carson had nothing written on his calendar for that evening.'

'I don't suppose—'

'I caught your drift earlier,' he said. 'I schmoozed. Carson's secretary had his appointment books, five years' worth, right at her desk.'

'And?'

'Nothing was written in for any of those Tuesday evenings.'

'You're sure?'

'Why do you sound so excited?'

'I'll tell you in a minute.'

'His secretary thought it was unusual because he was always busy at night. But she double-checked because I was so persuasive. Nothing had been penciled in for any of those evenings. And that, to her, is inconceivable.'

It was inconceivable to me as well, almost.

'Tell me how this is going to help me sue the beneficiary, Elstrom,' he said.

'Who is the beneficiary?'

'I can't divulge the entity.'

'Entity? The beneficiary wasn't family?'

'I'm sure Carson had multiple policies. We only carried one of them, and the beneficiary wasn't family. It was an organization, a company. Tell me how you're going to help us.'

I told him I'd call him when I learned more, and clicked him away, but not before I heard him swear.

I swore, too, at the bulb flickering stronger in the back of my brain. Grant Carson had been careful to make no notation of where he'd been off to, those Tuesday nights. As had Benno Barberi. Jim Whitman had noted them in his appointment books only with the letter 'C.' Whatever those three men had been doing, they were doing it secretly, and they were doing it together.

Right down to getting killed, one after the other.

TWENTY-ONE

I skidded to a dusty stop across the few stones left on Kutz's gravel lot with what I thought was considerable élan.

Leo was waiting in his Porsche. The top was down, but he'd parked in the shade under the overpass, and he wore an oversized red straw hat that, even without its tightly knotted blue chinstrap, would have looked ridiculous. Thought it was months before the burning rays of summer, Leo was careful; his pale skin burns like an infant's.

'So elegant, your driving finesse,' he said.

'I know the words to that bit of music you're listening to,' I said, through the newly exposed rip in my side curtain. Another curl of Discount Den duct tape had let go on the tollway.

'They're called lyrics, you boor, but Jobim didn't use them in this song.'

He was listening to a piece of Brazilian bossa nova that, for once, I recognized. I didn't know its name, but it was smooth and flowing and getting a lot of play as background in a television laxative commercial.

'No more pressure,' I began singing, warbling with the same solemnity as the singer on TV.

He sighed, shut off the player, and got out of the car.

We walked up to the peeling wood trailer. Young Kutz glowered at us through the tiny order window. Young Kutz is young in name only; he's on the wrong side of eighty, and had been glowering from his trailer long before Leo and I started coming in grammar school.

'Hiya, Mr Kutz,' Leo said.

'What's it today, twerp?'

Leo stretched up to his full five foot six inches so he could line his eyes along the counter. 'The usual six pups, cheese fries, and Big Swallow root beer, of course.'

'I thought you were dieting,' I said.

'The trick is to chew slowly, thereby atomizing all the fat calories before swallowing.'

'For sure you'll drop that nettlesome pound and a half.' I added my one dog and small diet to his order, gave Leo eight singles – Kutz's prices were an outrage, given the quality of the food – and went around to the back of the trailer.

The lunch rush was over and empty picnic tables were everywhere. The snow was long gone, and it hadn't rained at all in March, yet incredibly, I found a table that was almost half free of pigeon droppings.

Leo noticed when he came with the food. 'Partially dropless – nice,' he said, setting down the flimsy tray of hotdogs, fries and drinks with a careful, soft sliding motion of his hands and forearms. Kutz uses ultra-thin plastic trays because they're likely to flex and be dropped, resulting in re-orders as well as queasy pigeons, which then results in excessively spotted tables.

As always, we ate silently for the first minutes, savoring the truck exhaust drifting down from the overpass mingling with the steam we imagined might be rising from our barely lukewarm hot dogs. They were the exact smells of our youth, nostalgia at its purest. Rumor had it Kutz had never changed the hot dog water in all the years he worked the trailer. No need, he'd supposedly once said: grease floats and ends up on the product, to be consumed by customers or pigeons – depending. That meant the hot dogs Leo and I were now eating might have been cooked in part of the very water Kutz used when we were kids. Nostalgia doesn't get any purer than that.

'You may now tap the power of my formidable brain,' Leo said, after his third hot dog. 'How's the case?'

I told him that Barberi, Whitman and Carson had all died on, or right after, the second Tuesdays of even-numbered months.

He slammed the brakes on the sagging cheese fry he was about to propel into his mouth. When I dare eat Kutz's cheese fries,

I use a plastic spoon because the yellowish substance he says is cheese quickly dissolves potato fiber, rendering them too limp for me to hold. Not Leo. He regards Kutz's cheese fries as among life's worthiest adversaries, and while still in high school, mastered the art of arcing them into his mouth with his fingers. He says it's a matter of wrist speed and pride.

Now, all that was forgotten. The cheese fry slid from his fingers to drop, with a soft, gelatinous slap, back into its cardboard tray. 'What have you made of that?'

'Each of the three men took pains to obscure their whereabouts those nights.' I told him of the 'C' notations in Whitman's desk diary.

'They were together, at this "C" place,' he said.

'Until they started dying, one by one.'

'What's premeditated and sinister in a heart attack, an understandable suicide and a random hit-and-run?'

'What if the first and second deaths came from administered overdoses, and the hit and run was deliberate? Barberi came home highly agitated over some insurance concern, but he'd learned to handle stress. A dose of something might have sent his heart into overdrive, but we'll never know; he was cremated. We do know Whitman ingested too many pills, and right now we know there was no good reason for him to go outside his home to get them. If Whitman was murdered, then it's likely Carson was murdered too, pushed in front of an oncoming car.'

'To what end?'

'I don't know.'

'Does Wendell have any thoughts on motive?'

'He fired me.'

The eyebrows came together and stuck, shocked. 'Surely not for a lack of progress.'

'His whole attitude has changed. Instead of being intrigued by my suspicions, Wendell became combative and swatted every one of them away.'

'What did he say about those mysterious "C" notations in Whitman's calendar?'

'No curiosity there, either.'

'He knows what they mean,' he said.

'He spent those Tuesday evenings with Barberi, Whitman and Carson,' I said, 'and I'll bet he knows who drove Whitman home.'

'You've gotten too close,' Leo said.

'Yes.'

'What's next?' he asked.

'Arthur Lamm.'

Leo shook his head, confused. 'The real-estate biggie?'

'He's gone missing, though it might be because the IRS is investigating him.' I told him what the Bohemian had learned.

'What if he didn't take off?'

'Then twenty-five per cent of the biggest shots in Chicago have just been murdered.'

TWENTY-TWO

'**M**y father fired you.' Amanda spoke slowly over the phone, each word precise, distinct, and under control. I knew that control. She was furious.

'Apparently.'

'He told me you'd made no progress, you'd pocketed his two-thousand-dollar retainer without doing anything but mewing around a little bit, and dusted him off by telling him to go to the police.'

'Mewing? Like a cat? He said I was mewing?'

'Don't evade. What is he up to?'

'Actually, I've made out a check for his refund.'

'Don't parse my words, either. What's all this about: the body-guards, the secrecy? Is his life in danger?'

I'd had an inspiration, driving home from Kutz's. 'I want to deliver the refund in person. I'm certain he won't take my call, or see me at his office.'

'You want me to set up a confrontation without telling me what's going on?'

'He's still my client.'

'I ask again: is his life in danger?'

'Get me in front of him, Amanda. If I learn he's in real trouble, I will violate his trust and tell you.'

It was enough, for the moment. She said she'd get back to me.

I crossed the second floor, headed to see how my freshly re-hung cabinet was faring, when the lid on the front door mail slot clanked. I'd installed one that was extra-large, anticipating improved times, but even the junk mailers didn't yet think me worthy. Today though, my mail slot clanked. Mail had come. I clanked, too, beating down the wrought-iron stairs.

It was Jenny's small something, sent in a padded envelope. I ripped it open. An untied purple bowtie was inside, with a note that read, 'It's not so much the look that's sought, but rather the demonstration of proficiency.'

It was a nudge, aimed with a joke, and so quintessentially, marvelously Jenny.

I'd never tied a bowtie. That was the laugh, and the nudge, because she knew I'd wrestle with learning to tie the thing, and think of her every second I was doing it. And I would, along with thinking about my aborted trip to San Francisco and the phone call I'd fumbled just a few hours earlier.

I took my bowtie upstairs. The cabinet I'd straightened was listing. Not much, just a few degrees, and surely no more than the smoke stacks on the *Titanic* had tipped in the first minutes following its collision with the iceberg. I set down the tie and spent the next hour trying to correct the cabinet, but no amount of shimming, leveling, and shaving got it to hang right.

Amanda called. 'We're having barbecue tonight with my father, at five.'

'That's early,' I said.

'With the pig lady,' she said. It was rough, especially for Amanda.

'You mean his wife?'

'Second wife,' she said.

I knew that, of course. It had been in the papers. Wendell, a long-time widower, had married after Amanda and I divorced.

'You'll have time to tell me everything as we drive up there,' she said. 'Everything.'

Amanda was waiting beneath the portico of her lakeside condominium building. She wore exquisitely fitted jeans and a burgundy top that didn't pull all the fire from her eyes. She flashed the rest of it at me as she slid onto the passenger's seat. 'I don't like cagy.'

'For the time being, I have to respect your father's confidence,' I said as I pulled onto Lake Shore Drive.

She gave my invariable khakis and blue shirt the usual quick glance, but lingered at my neck. Her voice softened. 'A bow tie, and purple?'

'Shock and awe.' It had taken me an hour practicing with downloaded instructions to achieve the partially crumpled mess around my neck.

'You want my father to be shocked and awed by your tie, or by what you're going to say?'

I didn't want to say I'd worn the tie to keep reminding myself of who'd sent it, and I didn't want to tell her of the accusations I was going to lay on Wendell, so I said nothing.

She fingered the wires sticking out of the hole in the dashboard where the radio had been. 'You used to have a Mercedes,' she said.

'Bought used,' I said.

'And such very nice clothes.'

'Fortunes wane.'

'Perhaps, but you gave your clothes away, right after we split up. Including that nice camel-hair sport coat I bought you for your birthday . . .' Her voice trailed off.

It was old detritus, and it was accurate. And it was useful, because it beat discussing what her father hadn't told me about Barberi, Whitman and Carson.

'I'd gotten to living a little too fancy,' I said. 'Jettisoning the duds and the car seemed a reasonable way to simplify my life.'

'Along with going to live in a turret?'

'You are demeaning my castle?'

'You have to admit, there's something monastic about your life . . . the turret, the lack of variety in clothing, this . . .' She bent back one of the wires sticking out from the dash, and turned to me. 'Was I part of all your clutter, Dek? Was I too fancy?'

'Too fancy?' I repeated, startled. 'You've never been too fancy, Amanda.'

It might have been from the rapid turns in the road, but she'd leaned closer before shifting away. 'Your new bow tie is a promising addition to your wardrobe,' she said. 'What prompted you to buy it?'

'It was a gift . . .' I stopped, though my abrupt silence spilled the rest of it.

'Ah . . . the newswoman.' Then, 'What are you going to ask my father?' she asked, leaning more toward her door and safer talk.

Or more dangerous, depending. 'I'm going to ask him about Wendell Phelps.'

She turned to look at me. 'What the hell?'

'I'm going to ask him if he fired his previous investigator using the same baloney he gave me.'

I told her I wanted to talk to Wendell before I said anything more, and we fell into silence as she mulled, and I mulled, things each of us didn't understand about Wendell and perhaps, less than fleetingly, about ourselves. I tried to fill the quiet by shifting more than was necessary, working through the rush-hour traffic up Lake Shore Drive to Sheridan Road, through Evanston, Wilmette, and Winnetka. With every mile, the homes got grander and set back farther from the road. By the time we got to Lake Forest, most of the estates were invisible.

I turned right onto Red Leaf Road and followed it as it curved along the shore of Lake Michigan. As I rounded the last turn, brake lights flashed ahead as cars slowed to turn through Wendell's stone pillars.

Amanda inhaled sharply. 'He didn't tell me he was having a party. I'm wearing jeans, for God's sake.'

'Nice jeans, though,' I said. 'And of course, I'm wearing a purple bow tie.'

She didn't laugh.

We passed a bush that looked like it had been ripped in half.

'Pigs,' she said. Earlier, she'd referred to her father's new wife as a pig lady, but now, apparently, she was including Wendell in her contempt.

I followed a black Mercedes sedan into the long driveway and coasted to a stop. Four more dark Mercedes were ahead of the one in front of us. At the head of the line, several blue-jacketed parking valets were waiting for a uniformed security guard to check invitations. It took ten minutes for the guard to get to us.

Amanda leaned across me and spoke through the rip in my side curtain. 'I'm Amanda Phelps. I've brought a guest.'

I found myself holding my breath. Her body weight, so easily pressed against me, felt like the best of our old times.

The private cop's list of invited guests had small photos alongside the names. He peered in at her. 'I'm sorry, Ms Phelps, we don't have your guest listed.'

'I'm Mr Phelps's daughter. That's sufficient.'

The private cop looked a little too long at the gray primed section behind the driver's side door before asking for my driver's license. Amanda had to straighten up so I could reach for my wallet. I handed out my license, and the guard stepped back to speak into his two-way radio.

'Obviously I didn't tell my father you'd be coming along,' she said to me.

I gestured toward the guard reporting my arrival. 'There goes my shock and awe.'

'Maybe not. My father hasn't yet seen your purple bow tie.'

Behind us, expensive automobile engines revved loud and impatient. Finally, the radio crackled and the guard motioned for one of the valets to come over. 'Thank you,' the private cop said, handing back my license.

'Don't let anybody paint over that primer,' I told the valet as I got out, pointing at the gray patch behind the driver's door. He nodded gravely, probably thinking it was a sign of great wealth to have the confidence to drive up in such a heap, particularly wearing a purple bow tie.

A big man was waiting for us by the front walk, his suit coat bulging from a gun. He motioned for Amanda and me to follow him along the flagstone path around the south side of the house. Wendell had sent him out fast when he learned Amanda had brought a most unwanted guest.

A huge red-and-white striped tent had been set up on the lawn. A four-piece combo was playing gentle jazz on the stone terrace as a hundred people, holding champagne flutes, swayed to the music and made appropriate rich people noises. The unseasonably warm weather had held, and the men wore pastel jackets, the women, pastel dresses. All the guests seemed to be tanned, from Palm Beach or Palm Springs or wherever the palms were where they wintered when Chicago got slushy. I supposed I stood out, because I don't get tanned until summer, and even then it comes mottled with spots of white wherever bits of caulk and paint had blocked the sun from my skin.

I looked around for Wendell. Three more men in ill-fitting, too-square suits stood fairly close together at one end of the terrace. Wendell stood in the approximate middle of them, talking with a small group of people. I started to head over but the big man blocked my way. 'Mr Phelps is busy.'

'Not for his daughter,' Amanda said.

'Mr Phelps suggested later,' the big man said.

Wendell had allowed me in, only to box me in.

Amanda was about to head for her father when a bell sounded from a few hundred feet away. The jazz group stopped playing in mid-riff.

'Delores's new baby,' a woman with impossibly white teeth said to Amanda. Delores was the name of Wendell's second wife.

The crowd began to move as a herd toward the far side of the lawn. I looked toward the tent. Wendell had gone.

I grabbed two flutes of champagne from a passing waiter. 'Delores's new baby?' I whispered to Amanda, handing her one. 'You've become a half-sister?'

I'd expected a glare. Instead, Amanda gave me a faint smile and we followed the crowd.

TWENTY-THREE

Only the waves crashing onto the beach below sounded as we moved, hushed like congregants summoned to a secret sunset ceremony, through a tall grass prairie preserve and into a dense tunnel of arched trees that shrouded the path in almost complete darkness. We emerged fifty yards later into a clearing where the last of the day's sun shone again. Some of those ahead of us had apparently participated in such gatherings before, and were forming a broad semicircle facing a lit-up, miniature stone cottage.

A large woman stood in front of the tiny rock house. Her closely cropped dark hair was streaked with gray, and she wore

a loose-flowing, multi-hued robe that, in the backlighting from
the little windows behind her, made her look like a pagan priestess
afire with the setting sun. She held a champagne flute in her right
hand, and the end of a leash in the other. I stepped around the
people in front to see more clearly. The other end of the leash
was attached to a pig.

It was not the sort of small pink pig seen on farms, destined to
become bacon. This pig was larger, with brown and white spots,
and looked to weigh two hundred pounds.

The woman in the robe raised her champagne. 'Welcome
Jasmine, everybody,' she shouted to the sky.

Everyone raised their glasses.

As I raised my champagne, I snuck a glance at Amanda. She
was looking directly back at me, her own flute raised, but not
toward the pig. She was toasting my ignorance. 'My new half-
sister,' she mouthed above the muffled applause, the best the crowd
could do while holding champagne.   —

After a few last claps, and several more shouts of 'Welcome,
Jasmine,' the group began to disperse in the direction of the path
back to the food and stronger booze. The homage had ended. I
turned to follow, when Amanda stepped up and seized my hand.

'No, Vlodek,' she said. It was the first time she'd ever used my
given name. 'You must meet Delores, the woman at the center of
my father's not-quite-rational universe.'

Her fingernails dug into my palm as she half tugged me to the
small group of people clustered around the woman in robes. As
we got closer to the cottage, I noticed that the thick Plexiglas
windows were deeply scratched and smeared milky, no doubt from
snouts.

Just then, the rubber door swung outward and, to the faint strains
of classical music playing inside, another pig lumbered out, this
one pure black and half the size of the leashed Jasmine. I glimpsed
straw on the floor of the rock cottage before the rubber door
slapped shut.

Delores spotted Amanda standing at the edge of the little group.
The way the two women stiffened simultaneously said it all.
Amanda put her arm under my elbow and marched me forward.

'Amanda,' Delores Phelps said.

'Delores.'

People to the left of us stepped back, to make room for the pig that had come from the cottage.

'Peter!' Delores Phelps cried, holding out her champagne flute low enough for the new arrival, the black pig, to insert his tongue. 'Peter just loves Dom Perignon,' Delores said.

Several in the small cluster murmured approvingly, and Peter the pig grunted, a low, long snorting sound, likely in agreement.

Delores turned to me. 'And you are Mr Rudolph, Amanda's most successful young man?'

'Not young, nor successful, nor Mr Rudolph. I'm Dek Elstrom.'

'We're divorced,' Amanda said, of me.

'I believe I did hear something about that,' Delores said. 'Lovely tie, Mr Elstrom.'

Peter nudged Delores for more Dom Perignon.

'Peter is so attached to his mommy, aren't you, Peter?' Delores cooed, lowering her flute to give him another taste. 'Peter is a Vietnamese potbellied pig,' she said. 'He used to sleep in his own bedroom, just down the hall from ours, but after he outgrew his bassinet, he started coming into our bedroom.' She stopped, noticing the look on my face. 'He was mostly potty trained, of course, but still, he did have his accidents.' She bent down again to nuzzle the pig's hairy ear. 'So we built him his own little cottage, and got him some brothers and sisters.' She straightened up and nodded to the pig at the other end of the leash. 'Jasmine's our newest, a Kunekune from New Zealand.'

I looked at my empty champagne flute, simply because I couldn't think of what to say.

Delores noticed, and held out her own flute, swishing the little in the bottom that Peter had not licked out.

I shook my head. 'Thank you, no.' I took a quick look around for Amanda, but she'd disappeared. Only the bodyguard remained.

'It was lovely meeting you,' I told Delores Phelps.

'Likewise, I'm sure.'

'You, too,' I said to the guard, but he made no move to step away. We walked back to the mansion, me in front, him a close two steps behind.

Amanda was talking to her father on the terrace. 'What have you been telling my daughter, Elstrom?' he asked, when I walked up.

'That you've not been forthcoming, and nothing else.'

'We'll discuss your ignorance privately.' Then, to Amanda, 'Just he and I, my dear.'

'I'm part of this,' she said.

'I'll explain later,' he said.

For a moment he stood silent, I stood silent, and she glared. Finally, she shrugged and walked away.

Wendell led us across the lawn, a small parade with him in the lead, me in the middle, and three body guards bringing up the rear. We entered the house through a side door and passed a laundry room with a porcelain-topped table for folding clothes and a kitchen fitted out, wall-to-wall, with stainless steel. A right turn down another hall brought us to the passage that led to his study door. We didn't go in. The three guards moved up close behind me as Wendell continued marching us through the long dark foyer to the front of the house.

'What are you hiding, Wendell?' I asked the back of his head.

He opened the front door. 'Why call the police?'

'I didn't call any cops.'

He stepped back, and two of the three guards came up on either side of me. I took the hint. I pressed Wendell's refund check onto the guard at my right, and stepped outside. The door slammed.

A valet had been alerted to bring up the Jeep. I got in and drove through the gates. I pulled over fifty yards from the house and called Amanda. Her phone went automatically to voice mail. I didn't leave a message because by then I noticed the glint of a familiar bumper parked just past a copse of trees alongside the road ahead. I started up, motored past without looking directly at the driver. It didn't take long to be sure. The car, a black junior-grade BMW, pulled out and stayed far back at every turn, from Lake Forest all the way south and into Evanston.

I found the sort of cul-de-sac I was looking for just before I got to the outskirts of Chicago. I turned in, spun around fast, and was waiting for him when he eased into the cul-de-sac. He slammed on his brakes but he was too late; I'd pulled sideways to block him in. I jumped out of my car.

His window was open, and so was his collar. I reached in and grabbed it.

It was Jason, or Brad. I couldn't tell because they'd been so similarly barbered.

'Tell Mrs Barberi that I'll report when I'm ready,' I shouted. 'And tell yourself that if I see you again, I'll break your snout.'

As I got back into the Jeep and drove away, I realized I'd misspoken. I'd meant to say nose, not snout.

It had been that sort of day.

TWENTY-FOUR

The fellow flashing a badge early the next afternoon had to be one of the cops Wendell accused me of calling. He didn't look like a cop. Blond and fresh-faced, he wore a gray herringbone sport coat, charcoal slacks, a white shirt and a blue-striped tie. Right down to his highly polished burgundy penny loafers, he looked bound for the Ivy League, Princeton perhaps. He said his name was Delmar. I asked if that was a first name or a last name. He said his first name was Delray.

'Delray Delmar?'

'I figured a guy named Vlodek would understand.'

'Like we were joined at the hip.' I invited him in.

'Nifty,' he said, looking around the bare limestone room. First-time visitors are always impressed with the craggy, curved limestone walls and the beamed wood ceiling, though typically they offer up more than one word of architectural praise.

I motioned for us to sit in the two white plastic chairs. Except for those, two cans of varnish and my table saw, the first floor is unfurnished.

'I know how it is, starting out,' he said.

I was old enough to be his father, almost. Mature enough, certainly, to control my temper.

'I'm saving up for furniture, too,' he added after another beat, as if that helped.

I fought the urge to ask if he'd like some chocolate milk. He might have said yes, and I didn't have any. Milk. Or chocolate. So I stayed silent, and stared at the knot of his striped tie.

He cleared his throat. 'You were hired by Mr Wendell Phelps to investigate the recent deaths of three prominent businessmen?'

He was asking two troublesome questions. He wanted me to confirm the identity of a client, something I wouldn't do. And he was asking me to admit to running an investigation, terminology I had to tiptoe around, because 'investigate' is a touchy verb in official Illinois. Investigators – private detectives – are required to be licensed, and that in turn requires law enforcement experience or a law degree. I had neither. But there's a loophole, as there usually is in Illinois laws: a person can operate as an investigator if he's working for a lawyer. It's a gray line, but it's a mile wide. I knew several lawyers, including the Bohemian, who would cover for me if I ever got in trouble. Still, I like to dodge the word 'investigate.'

'Did Wendell Phelps tell you that?' I said, instead of answering.

'I got your name from Debbie Goring, who was delighted to talk to me. It didn't take much Internet research to learn that you nibble at investigating. I also learned you are Mr Phelps's son-in-law.'

'Former son-in-law,' I said.

'Mr Phelps is a friend to many powerful people, including Arthur Lamm,' he said, floating the name while watching my eyes.

The kid had a contact in the IRS. 'I went to see Mr Phelps,' he went on. 'One of his guards said he wasn't home. So now I've come to see you.'

'I'm a records researcher,' I told the lad. 'Mostly I work for insurance companies, though I chase down information for law firms as well.'

'And for Wendell Phelps?'

'I agree with Debbie Goring. I'm troubled by where Jim Whitman got the pills to kill himself.'

'I believe you're also bothered by the timing of the deaths of Benno Barberi and Grant Carson because they, like Jim Whitman, died on or just after the second Tuesdays of even-numbered months.' Young Delray Delmar had also talked to Barberi's and Carson's secretaries.

'Therefore,' he went on, 'you've probably deduced that the three dead men spent those Tuesday evenings together.'

I liked the way he applied the word 'deduced' to my thinking. It made me sound like something other than a schlump who couldn't hang a kitchen cabinet straight.

'By Jove, Holmes, it's an interesting puzzle,' I said.

'Work with me, Mr Elstrom. I'm not interested in Wendell Phelps. You can continue to protect Mr Phelps and perhaps help Debbie Goring. She might even part with some large dollars if you help her gain insurance money.'

'Who are you really interested in?'

He leaned forward. 'Arthur Lamm. What do you know about him?'

'If he's not gone fishing, then he's gone missing,' I said, rhythmically.

'I think he's on the run,' he said.

'From the IRS?' I asked.

'Surely from them, but I'm wondering if he's running from something more. I want to question him about those deaths. Do you know where he might be?'

'No. Do you think he killed Whitman and Carson?'

'All I think right now is he travels in the same circles as the dead men and now he's disappeared.'

'Do you think he's part of that Tuesday evening group?' I asked.

'He's wealthy enough. Do you have any idea where they hold their get-togethers?'

'No idea.' It was true enough. All I had was the letter 'C,' and I wasn't going to share that without Wendell's permission.

'Somewhere north of the Chicago River, on the Gold Coast?' he asked.

'Because that's where Grant Carson was killed?' I shook my head. 'Are you in Homicide?'

'Special Projects.'

'I've never heard of it. How many are in that department?'

'Just me.'

'Why isn't Homicide looking into this?'

'Not enough heat yet.' Delray grinned. 'My boss respects un-official inquiries from powerful men.'

'Someone asked your boss to look into Arthur Lamm?'

'You got it.' He stood up. 'I'm going to take apart Grant Carson's hit-and-run, because it's the freshest death. I'm looking at Whitman, too, because his daughter, and you, can't figure where he got those extra pills or even why he would have bothered. I'm saving Benno Barberi for last, because frankly, I see nothing in his death that suggests murder.'

'And Arthur Lamm?'

'I'm interested in him most of all.' We walked outside. 'Keep me informed, and I'll do likewise. I'll even put in good words to Debbie Goring, help you get a reward. But we do things my way.'

'Who's your rabbi?' In Chicago-speak, a rabbi is a clout guy, somebody connected, a person who can take care of getting whatever a kid in a striped tie needed.

Grinning, he said, 'The deputy chief,' and got into his car.

As I watched him drive away in his long black cop sedan, I saw a young, brash, arrogant guy who knew how to get clouted into a job. He was ambitious, and he had power behind him. He'd be relentless; he'd learn things.

Some of which would lead him straight to Wendell Phelps and whatever he was hiding.

TWENTY-FIVE

The cell number Wendell had given me no longer worked. It must have been a disposable, discarded like me.

I mulled, but not for long. I owed Amanda an explanation for last night, and a warning about the cop who was likely to complicate her father's life.

I called her cell phone six times in three hours and left no messages. She answered the seventh, angrily.

'You dumped me,' she said.

'Your father had me thrown out.'

'He said you stormed off.'

'He accused me of calling the cops. One was just here.'

'Why would you call the cops?'

'I didn't. You know I'd never rat out a client . . .' I paused, a hypocrite, about to do just that. 'It must have been someone else in the heavy cream who called—'

'*The heavy cream?*' she interrupted, almost shouting with impatience.

'They're the people who have risen to the very top, people like your father, who run Chicago. One of them must have gotten scared and called the Chicago police. Delray Delmar, a pup but earnest, caught the case, and came round to ask what I knew.'

'Scared by what?'

'Your father told you nothing last night?'

'Only that you blew up and left. I tried to press him. He mumbled something about talking later and walked away. For the next hour, he kept himself surrounded by others. Obviously he was avoiding me, so I got one of the guards to drive me home.' She paused for a moment, then said, 'You could have waited out on the street, you know.'

'I called you from outside, but your phone was switched off. Then I realized I'd been followed. It was safest to leave you with your father's guards.'

'You're scaring me. Who was following you?'

'Benno Barberi's widow put a tail on me. She knows I'm chasing the case and doesn't want to wait for information. I put a stop to it.'

'Is Mrs Barberi frightened like my father? Benno died last year from a heart attack.'

'Did you know Jim Whitman, or Grant Carson?'

'Benno Barberi died of a heart attack, right?'

'All signs point to that.'

'And Mr Whitman and Mr Carson . . .?' She stopped, understanding. 'This is why my father hired bodyguards? He sees something sinister in their deaths?'

'Yes.'

'But Mr Whitman technically died of natural causes, though he may have swallowed too many pain killers. Mr Carson was hit by a car.'

'There are wrinkles surrounding each death.'

'I ask now for the third time: is my father in danger?'

'He'll be in less danger if he tells the cops what he knows. Do you know Arthur Lamm?'

'Don't change the subject.'

'I'm not.'

'Arthur is my father's closest friend,' she said. 'He handles our corporate insurance, and my father has invested in a couple of Arthur's real-estate ventures. Is Arthur in danger, too?'

'He's dropped from sight. He might have gone camping, or he might be evading the IRS.'

'I heard a rumor about the IRS investigation, but Arthur wouldn't run from that. He's got lawyers and accountants to take care of such things. If he's not around, it's because he's gone camping . . . Right, Dek?'

'I'd like to be sure he's gone camping.'

'You believe my father's not delusional, that someone's out to kill the men in the . . . whatever.'

'Heavy cream,' I said, supplying the words. 'Wendell won't tell me what he knows. Young officer Delmar has better resources than mine, and he'll find out what that is.'

'This can't be real,' she said, but she said she'd talk to her father.

On the stoop, outside his bungalow, Leo went straight for a vein. 'You, pass for a rich guy?' He laughed.

'Just for a night, maybe two. I'll breeze up to Lamm's fishing camp and see if I can sniff out his whereabouts.'

'Because you think that's something Lamm's friends, family, Wendell's previous investigator, the IRS, and most especially your new young cop friend haven't been sharp enough to consider doing themselves?'

'Because I don't know what to think.'

'Your cop is OK with you pursuing this on your own?'

'I promised I'd report anything I find out.'

'Meaning you'll report anything that doesn't incriminate Wendell.'

'I'm sure he understands.'

A sly grin lit Leo's face. 'Merely driving my car won't pass you as rich enough to be a friend of Lamm's,' he said. 'You've got to have the threads, too.' He touched the hem of his tropical shirt like he was caressing imperial silk. 'Red parrots and yellow flowers on blue rayon are the true signs of affluence. They make you look wealthy enough to not give a damn.'

'I want to look like I own the Porsche, not like I stole it.'

He sighed and handed over the keys.

TWENTY-SIX

Two hours north of Milwaukee, the concrete highway softened into rippling blacktop and the barns began fading from freshly painted reds to chalking shades of rose. An hour north of that, the blacktop crumbled and so had some of the barns. Every few miles, I spotted one lying in a bleached gray pile across an abandoned field. Bent Lake was one more hour up. I arrived just before sunset.

It was a one-block town, anchored at the front by a Dairy Queen and the remains of a gas station. The DQ's parking lot was empty, though the red-and-white wood hut was lit up bright with yellow bug lights and looked ready for commerce.

The gas station across the street did not. Its pumps had been pulled and the only visible reminder of its heritage was an oval blue-and-white Pure Oil sign creaking from rusty chains on a pole. The young man working inside on an old truck didn't jerk up, startled, as I passed by, so I assumed the town was accustomed to some degree of traffic.

I drove slowly past storefronts that were boarded up. The only light came from a Budweiser sign in a tavern window in the middle of the block.

A cluster of old, clapboard motel cottages was curled at the far end. Its sign read: 'Loons' Rest. Rooms $30.' The paint on the sign was fresher by a couple of decades than the white flakes peeling off the cottages. A new, shiny blue Ford F-150 pickup truck with a big chrome radiator and pimp lights on its roof was the only vehicle in the lot.

'Forty dollars for the night,' the woman behind the counter said as I jangled the bells above the door, coming in. She was wrinkled and her skin and hair were colored almost the same gray as the collapsed barns I'd passed, south of town.

'The sign outside says thirty.'

'Them's off-season rates.'

I cocked a thumb at the window looking out at the parking lot, empty except for the truck and the Porsche. 'Hasn't snowmobiling season just ended?'

'You from Illinois?'

'Does that matter?'

'I like to know how our clientele finds us.' She smiled, showing me where she needed dental work.

'In desperation,' I wanted to say but didn't. Loons' Rest was the only place around, it was getting dark, and it wasn't hard to imagine insects the size of antelope roaming the deserted old town. I pulled out my Visa card.

'No credit; cash,' she said.

'American currency OK?' I asked as I peeled off four tens.

'That'll be forty-four with tax,' she said.

I added four singles. 'Do you know where Arthur Lamm's place is?'

'Never heard of him.'

'Thank you,' I said.

'Illinoyance,' she muttered.

'Cheesehead,' I said, but only after I'd stepped outside and banged the door shut on the woman and the jangling bells.

It was all so very adult.

My room smelled of the same strong pine cleaner the Rivertown Health Center sloshed about when a tenant expired, and I wondered whether the weak, twenty-six-watt bulb hanging from the stained tile ceiling was meant to conceal as well. Even in the dim light, the knots on the knotty pine paneling appeared troublesome, and I thought it best not to look at them closely, for fear some weren't knots at all but rather shoe-heel marks on top of cockroach splats.

A tufted orange spread covered the mattress, and a disconnected gold pay box for a long-gone Magic Fingers electric bed massager was screwed to the headboard. It never boded well when the Magic Fingers fled a town. For sure I would only stay one night.

I sat on the bed to check my cell phone for messages. It had not rung. The reason was not that there had been no calls or texts. My display showed that no bars of service were available.

I left my duffel tightly zipped on the bed – in case any of the knots jumped off the wall paneling, frisky – and went out into the dusk. Across the street, several teenagers were running along the sidewalk, yelling as they raked broom handles under the ribs of the corrugated metal awnings of the vacant stores. The racket was deafening, reverberating along the deserted street as though monkeys were banging on pans. Every few seconds, shadowy things dropped from beneath the awnings, which set the teens to waving flashlights, jumping up and down, screaming and laughing with delight.

It made no sense. 'What are you doing?' I called across the street.

They stopped and stared at me. 'Stomping bats, a course,' one young girl, pretty in denim and a pale yellow jacket, yelled back.

'A course,' I shouted back. There were worse places to grow up in than Rivertown, I supposed.

I stepped into the center of the street, reasoning that bat splatter was less likely out there than on the sidewalks, and walked down to the neon Budweiser light. Three men in flannel shirts sat at the bar inside, jawing with a bartender who had a red beard.

'Can I get something to eat here?' I asked.

'Pickled eggs which I prepare special myself, and Slim Jims,' Red Beard said. 'Anything fancier, you got to go to the DQ.'

I told him I needed fancier, and would be back for a brew after I'd eaten.

The Dairy Queen's parking lot was still empty, since the town's evening merriment remained underway beneath the metal awnings at the other end of the block. Inside the hut, a teenaged boy and girl were pressed together as tight as a double-dip of soft-serve ice cream jammed hard in a cake cone. The girl saw me appear in the glow of the yellow bug lights and broke the clinch. So long as I only wanted a hamburger, they could serve me dinner, she allowed. I asked what if I wanted two? That froze her face until I said I was making a joke. They both smiled then, sort of, though I suspected they'd discuss it later. No matter. Two hamburgers soon appeared, and I ate them with fries and a chocolate shake at a picnic table facing the road, so I could watch the cars that passed by. There were none. Afterward, I gave them back their plastic tray and walked down to the tavern.

The three flannel shirts and Red Beard stopped talking when I came in. I ordered a beer.

'Up here for some early fishing?' the bartender asked, skimming the head off the beer.

'At Arthur Lamm's camp. Know him?'

The six eyes above the three flannel shirts turned to look at me directly.

'I don't think he's around,' the bartender said.

I put on my confused face which, in truth, is never far away. 'I came up from Chicago a day early. I hope I didn't get the date mixed up.'

'Lamm's car is there, but no one has seen him,' the bartender said.

'Does anyone know where he's gone?'

'Herman says Lamm's off camping. It's caused a ruckus. You guys from Illinois . . .' The bartender's lower lip curled down, following the thought that was dropping away.

I bought beers for the men at the bar, the bartender, and another for myself. It set me back four bucks, not counting the single I left on the counter. It made everyone more talkative.

'Us guys from Illinois, you were saying?' I asked.

'Cops,' the bartender said.

'There was only the one,' said one of the flannel shirts – his was red.

'Young sonofabitch,' said the man next to him. His flannel was green.

'What was he asking?'

'I didn't actually talk to him. I just heard he was up from Chicago, asking for Lamm.'

'Nobody knows exactly where Lamm is, and that includes Herman,' the third man at the bar said, speaking for the first time. His flannel shirt was plaid, half red, half green, which I supposed made him an excellent arbiter for the other two. 'And if Herman's been drinking, he wouldn't have noticed Lamm being abducted in an alien spaceship.'

'Herman works for Lamm?' I asked.

'Supposedly he takes care of Lamm's camp,' Green Flannel said, 'but Herman Canty's never done a lick of work in his life. Herman's what you call an opportunist. He latches on to things.'

'Like Wanda, over at Loons',' Red Flannel said. 'Latched on to that some long time ago.'

'Rockin' the cot, God help him,' Green Flannel said.

That got the three flannels and the bartender laughing.

'She even lets him stay nights, sometimes, when his sister throws him out,' Red Flannel said.

'Not all nights. She's not all dumb,' the bartender said. 'She knows Herman for what he is.'

'A damned user,' Red Flannel said. 'Strikes at every opportunity.'

'This Canty, he latched on to Lamm as well?' I asked.

'Big time,' Green Flannel said. 'Sooner than later, you'll see a new blue F-One Fifty over to Loons'. That's Herman's truck. No one can figure out what he done for it, being as he's never been useful.'

'That truck come out of Chicago, according to the license plate frame,' Green Flannel said. 'He didn't buy it up here.'

'Either somebody died, leaving him an inheritance,' the plaid man said, 'or he's got Mr Lamm paying him way too large for watching his camp.'

The bartender was giving me a long look. 'You say you're a friend of Lamm's, yet you didn't call ahead to say you were coming up?'

'I'm more like an insurance client,' I said, 'but you're right. It's been a couple of months since he invited me. I should have checked before I drove up.'

'Cell phones don't always work up here, anyway,' the bartender said, shrugging. 'We're just yakking; nobody up here knows Lamm. He's certainly been too good to set foot in here.' He gestured at the murky shapes in the cloudy jar on the bar, as if to suggest that the eggs should have been reason enough to lure Lamm in. As if to warn me to not suffer the same loss, he slid the jar closer to me.

I resisted, saying it might incite the milk shake resting heavily on the hamburgers in my stomach, and asked for directions to Lamm's camp.

The bartender drew a map on a cocktail napkin. 'Mind that rickety old bridge on County M. It's a one-laner. Hit it wrong, you'll end up wet. And dead.'

I told them that if Lamm had indeed disappeared, I might want to speak to the sheriff. That got me another cocktail napkin map, and I left them to their pickled eggs and their flannel.

Outside, I envied their flannel. The night had turned frigid, and my pea coat was in Leo's Porsche. I hurried down the center of the street, deserted now, squinting for glints on the dark pavement. Nothing sparkled, freshly splattered, and I got to Loons' with shoes as dry as when I'd set out.

The inside of my cabin was as cold as the air outside. I spent five minutes looking for a thermostat before I realized that the cabin simply had no heat. I took a fast shower with what little lukewarm water could be coaxed from the pipes, dried myself with a towel that had a fist-sized hole in its center, bundled back into my clothes and pea coat, and slipped into bed.

I thought, then, of the newness of Jenny, waiting to warm me in San Francisco. And I thought of Amanda, and the easy, familiar way she'd warmed me, leaning against me in the Jeep, outside her father's house.

I tried to push those thoughts away, finding it easier to think about what I didn't understand about Arthur Lamm, the dead men in the heavy cream, and the frigid air inside the cabin. It wasn't until the middle of the night that I was finally able to shiver and shake myself to sleep.

TWENTY-SEVEN

'I'm in real need of caffeine,' I said to gray-skinned Wanda as I looked around the motel office for the coffee maker. It was six-thirty the next morning.

'DQ,' she said.

I pasted on the best smile I could offer to such a creature. 'You don't have coffee for guests?'

'DQ does egg sandwiches. You could have a whole breakfast.'

'With ice cream, just the thing for a cold morning.' I turned for the door.

'You checking out?'

'I'll be gone by the end of the morning. Check-out is noon?'

'Eight-thirty in season.'

I looked out the window. The Porsche was the only car parked on the gravel lot.

'I imagine you need to hustle to get rooms ready for the next onslaught of visitors,' I said.

'Eight-thirty,' she said.

'I'll leave the key in the room for when you come to make sure I didn't steal either the towel or the hole in the middle of it.'

'Illinoyance,' she muttered as I went outside.

'Cheesehead,' I muttered back, but likely she hadn't heard me, since I'd already slammed the door.

A truck shot from a parking space down the street and sped away. The truck was shiny and blue and I was fairly certain it was the one I'd seen in Loons' lot the previous evening, which meant it belonged to Herman Canty, Lamm's caretaker. If the rumors were true, that he spent his nights at the frigid Loons' Rest, curled beside the gray-faced Wanda, the man was entitled to whatever haste he needed to get away.

I drove down to the DQ. It was closed, though the sign said it was supposed to have opened at six, almost an hour earlier. I wasn't going to wait for someone to show up. I was anxious to speed out of that town, too. Besides, risking a launch of coffee in Leo's meticulously maintained Porsche, as I so often did in my Jeep, was unthinkable. I drove on.

Fifteen minutes later, in the sheriff's office, I regretted not waiting at the DQ. A massive caffeine-withdrawal headache had blossomed, and was pulsing along in perfect rhythm with the slow, doubting drone of the deputy sitting with his feet up on a brown steel desk.

'Tell me again why you're interested in Mr Lamm.' The man's tan shirt was stretched taut across his ample stomach, as though he'd often visited the DQ in Bent Lake.

'He invited me up for some fishing.'

His face was too red, too early in the year, to have come from the sun, and I guessed that his shirt might have been tightened more from beer than soft-serve ice cream. He craned his neck to look outside the window at the Porsche. 'Don't see gear,' he said, like he could see inside the trunk along with being able to smell a lie.

'Arthur said I could use his.'

The deputy sighed and shifted in the chair. 'Nobody seems to know where Mr Lamm has gotten himself to. People from his office in Chicago called up to report him missing. I sent two guys out for a day in a boat, and even hired a Cessna for an hour, but we found no sight of him. Then that damned fool Herman Canty up and says Lamm likes to go camping around this time of year. Wish to hell he'd spoke up before we hired a plane.'

'Lamm's family says it's normal for him to be camping for so long?'

'He's divorced, no kids. Ex-wife's out in California, and doesn't much give a damn. She got an annuity out of him instead of monthly income.'

'I heard a Chicago cop was up here looking for him.'

'Some kid, I heard, but he didn't bother to check in with me.'

'Lamm doesn't have a cell phone?'

'I tried. His was switched off.'

'How would I find Herman Canty?'

'Hard to say, especially now that he's getting about in that fancy new truck.' The deputy tilted forward to sit upright. 'You want to ask him about fishing?'

'I want to ask him about Lamm.'

'Herman will tell you Lamm's out fishing for muskies,' he said. 'Ever fish for muskies?'

'No.'

'Then what are you fishing for up here, Mr Elstrom?' he asked.

'Something I can sink a hook into, I suppose,' I said, and left.

TWENTY-EIGHT

I followed the bartender's napkin map down roads designated with alphabet letters to junctions with roads marked with other letters, and finally came to the bridge on County M that the bartender had warned me about. It was a rickety, single-lane contraption of bleached wood and rusted brackets that looked to be spanning the narrow frothing river below more from habit than any lingering structural integrity. The bartender said the knee-high side rails were loose and the whole thing suffered dry rot. I took his concern seriously, and eased forward in first gear. Even barely crawling, the old planks shifted and rattled loudly, like I was disturbing old bones.

A fire lane had been cut into the woods one mile farther on. A half-mile after that, an eight-inch white board, with 'Lamm' written on it, was nailed to a tree beside two narrow clay ruts heading into the trees. I followed them to a clearing.

Herman Canty's shiny blue pickup truck was parked beside a dark Mercedes 500 series sedan made opaque from a rain-pocked mixture of dirt and bird droppings. I parked the Porsche and got out.

The log cottage facing the lake looked right for a rich man wanting to pass as poor. The timbers were splotched with moss, the black tarpaper roof was curling at the bottom, and green paint was flaking off the door and window facing the parking area. There was no lawn, just weeds in abundance, some two feet tall.

Capping the rusticity of the entire enterprise was a privy set far enough into the woods to provide splendid opportunities, while enthroned, for the intimate study of thousands of insects. I would have visited such a privy only under extreme distress, and then at warp speed.

The Mercedes was locked. I'd just begun rubbing the grime off the driver's window when a man stepped out of the cottage. He was lean, tall and grizzled with unkempt gray hair and a week's worth of unshaved beard stubble. Without doubt, he was tough enough to get through every word of the entire Sunday *New York Times* in the privy in the woods. Assuming, of course, that the man knew how to read.

'Herman?' I asked.

'Yep.'

'I came up to see Mr Lamm, but I understand he's not here.'

'Yep.'

'People from his Chicago office reported him missing?'

'Yep.'

For sure, the man must have enjoyed old cowboy movies.

'You told the sheriff there's no need for worry because Arthur takes off sometimes, for days on end, to go camping and fishing?'

He said nothing.

'That's a yep?'

'Yep,' he said. 'His business friends called me over at Loons'. Told them the same thing.'

'You didn't know he'd come up until you saw his car? You didn't actually see him?'

He stared off into the woods. 'Mr Lamm likes to take off, is all.'

I looked past him, toward the lake. An orange rowboat, barely floating above the waterline, was tied to a collapsing dock. 'Lamm's boat is still there.'

'Huh?'

'How can Lamm be off camping if his boat is still here?'

He blinked rapidly and licked his lips. After a minute, he said, 'He has two.'

'Mind if I look around?'

There was nothing friendly about the way he was now looking at me. 'What are you doing here, mister?'

'Arthur told me to come up any time for the fishing.'

Herman spat into the clay. 'Sure he did.'

I started walking toward the lake. Herman bird-dogged me from ten paces behind like he was worried I was going to make off with one of the trees.

When I got to the dock, I pointed at the boat. Barely two inches rode above the water. 'You're sure Arthur took a boat like this one?'

'Yep.'

'Must have bailed it out first.'

He spat again. 'I imagine.'

'Why didn't he bail out this one while he was at it?'

Herman shrugged. 'He only needed the one.'

'You're the caretaker here, right?'

'I look after things.'

'Why haven't you bailed out the boat?'

He looked away again.

'When Arthur gets back, tell him I came up to drop a few worms,' I said. I felt his eyes on me all the way to the Porsche. I hadn't bothered to give him a name. More importantly, he hadn't bothered to ask for one, as though he never expected to talk to Lamm again.

I drove the half-mile to the fire lane and pulled far enough into the leafless trees to hope the Porsche would be hidden from the road. The day had warmed. I left my pea coat in the car and doubled back through the woods. I wanted another look at Lamm's camp without Herman's breath misting the back of my neck. I got within sight of the privy when the sound of a loud engine came rumbling low along County M.

The woods hid the vehicle, but I guessed it was a truck, shiny and new and blue. Herman Canty, the man who'd made sure I'd left Lamm's clearing knowing nothing more than when I arrived, was driving slowly, maybe searching into the trees to make sure I had gone.

I held my breath, straining to hear any easing of his gas pedal. The engine loped on, low and steady. He didn't slow at the fire lane and, in another minute, the big-barreled exhaust had gone.

I ran the last yards through the trees and down to the shore. I could see no other cottages or clearings at Lamm's end of the lake, no places where someone could see me prowling around. Several channels split the shoreline across the lake, leading to other lakes.

I stepped onto the narrow dock. The orange rowboat shifted uneasily in the water. The next rain, even if it was light, would drop it to the bottom of the shallows.

I went up to the cottage. It had three windows at the front, facing the lake. The middle one was unlatched. I slid it open and slipped through.

There was one big room, furnished simply with two vinyl sofas, a couple of sturdy wood rockers, a table and four straight-back wood chairs. Two gray metal-frame cots were folded up in the corner. I imagined the sofas would pull out for extra sleeping. A small, butane cook stove stood next to a large, wood-burning heat stove. Burned-down candle stubs stuck in glass ash trays were set beside two lanterns on a shelf above the back window. There was no refrigerator because there was no electricity; a dented green metal cooler rested in the corner, ready for ice or chilled water from the lake.

I went back out the window and down to the shore. The almost-submerged orange wood boat still nagged. Unless it had a hole in it, Lamm should have bailed it when he was emptying the other. Or Herman, simply because that should have been his responsibility.

Unless neither of them expected Lamm would ever come back.

I bent to look closer at the boat.

Something zipped like a bug into the water five feet from my arm. In the fraction of the instant I needed to think it was an insect, rifle fire exploded the stillness around me. A second bullet zipped even closer, not two feet away.

I dove into the murk of the lake.

TWENTY-NINE

I hit muck in an instant. I was too close to shore, too easy a target for a man with a gun.

I clawed blindly at the spongy decay, grabbing madly to pull myself down and away. The water was ink, thick with the sediment I'd stirred up, slimy in my nose, gritty in my eyes. The saw-edged weeds scratched at my face and ripped at my hands as I tugged at them, one handful after another, to get deeper, farther from shore.

My lungs begged for air, but death was a gunshot waiting at the surface. The water was deeper now, clearer. I let go of the cutting weeds and began breast-stroking through the frigid water to stay down, fighting my lungs, counting, ten more strokes, then nine and five and then no more. I lunged up for air, my eyes shut for the crack of gunfire, the burn of a bullet.

No explosion came. No burn, no pain. I gulped air, dropped back under.

Ten new strokes, and ten more, then up again, gasping, pawing at my face to clear my eyes. Lamm's cottage was two hundred yards away.

My jeans and shoes were lead, tugging me down. I let them pull me under, and breast-stroked below the surface toward the center of the lake until I could do no more, and came up to look. The brown log cottage was lost in the blur of the trees at the shoreline. I made wide circles with my arms, staying up, watching for movement. Nothing moved at the shore.

A thousand iced daggers pricked deep into my legs. My strength had gone; my shoes were dragging weights. I needed to untie them and let them fall away but, barefoot, I wouldn't have a chance of outrunning anyone in the woods.

A thought struck, so perfect that I hugged it like I was hugging life: *A killer would have killed.* I'd been a plump target at the shore and then swimming the first yards away. Anyone close could have easily put bullets into me. But there had been no more gunshots after the first two.

It had been some fool hunter, sure. I was way up north in the land of the gun-toting free, where everybody got armed at birth and shooting wild was a part of life. Hell, by now my hunter was probably a mile away, resting on a termite-infested log for a mid-morning bite of bratwurst and cheddar, perhaps even lifting an ear flap on his plaid cap to scratch his pointed head and wonder why he never hit anything.

Damned fool hunter. Damned fool me.

I'd panicked over nothing.

Cramps hit, great contorting pulsations that dug into my legs with iron fingers. I dropped under the water, doubled over to knead my knuckles into my right leg, then my left. The cramps dug back deeper, relentless in the frigid water.

Damned fool me. I was going to drown if I didn't get out of the water.

I kicked for the trees, flailing my arms at the water as the great electric curls of pain wrapped tighter and tighter around my calves. My hands as well began to cramp, too weak to do anything but slap at the water. Swallowing water, I went down.

Incredibly, a foot grazed the bottom. I pushed up, saw sky, disbelieving. I was still yards from shore, but I'd touched bottom. I wanted to laugh, for the mercy of it. I screamed instead. From the cramps twisting deep into my legs.

I half dog-paddled, half-stumbled to the narrow ribbon of slick moss at the shore and crawled out on my belly. I collapsed face down on to the mud, shivering, sucking in the cool musk of the shore with ragged breaths.

And cursing. I swore at everyone I could think of. I cursed wedge-headed, cheese-worshipping, damned-fool inbred hunters. And their mothers. And the women who ran places like Loons' Rest. And their broom-beating, bat-stomping offspring.

I cursed Arthur Lamm, who might simply have been off camping. I cursed the lead-headed Herman Canty, stoic Northwoodsman, for not telling me anything definitive.

But mostly, I cursed myself. I'd almost died, not from gunshot, but from drowning in stupid panic.

A branch hung low above my head. I reached up and pulled myself up to stand. My legs wobbled and then calmed under my weight. Breathing came easier. After a moment I dared to let go of the branch, and bent to retie my shoe laces, loosened and slimed by ten thousand years of decayed plants and fish.

I started into the trees. The damp rotting carpet of last year's leaves muffled my footfalls as I pushed my legs to move quicker. My hunter might still be in the woods, about to spray a last few thousand rounds into the trees before heading home.

Even stumbling fast, whole swarms of stinging insects found me, chilled wet meat, pulsing with blood – a smorgasbord of lake muck and sweat served up in a thick residue of fear. I didn't slow to learn if they were mosquitoes, flies or gnats. They all stung like they were on steroids. Everything liked to hunt up in those piney woods.

Sooner than I hoped, I caught a shimmer of bright yellow through a thinning in the trees. Leo's Porsche, designed for the autobahn, hunkered low on the scraped clay of the fire lane, as out of place in those woods as I was. I dipped my hand into the pocket of my jeans, came out with the keys. Water dribbled from the little electronic remote. I ran up to the edge of the fire lane.

And stopped.

The sloped nose of the sleek German car was too close to the ground. The right front tire was flat. As was the rear tire. I backed deeper into the dark shelter of the woods and dropped behind a massive oak, to think, to understand.

Two tires, flat, immobilizing the Porsche.

Someone wanted me trapped, defenseless, in the woods.

THIRTY

My cell phone was in the glove box, and not worth the risk of a sprint to get it, even if it did work in that particular patch of woods. It wouldn't do any good anyway; the Porsche would never make the crawl out of the woods on flat tires.

I needed to run – run through the trees, run up the fire lane to the road, to the town. But a small part of my brain knew to beg to be rational. A man of the woods, used to tracking running prey in dark places, would expect that. He'd be waiting.

I scrambled to my feet and ran the other way, down to the lake. Every whisper of the wind came cold like the breath of a mad man with a gun; every creak of a dry limb the snick of a sliding rifle bolt; every snap of a twig the first crack of sudden gunfire. I got to the water and ran along the shoreline until it broke to feed the river. The water was rushing too fast to cross there. Only one direction remained now.

I ran up the bank of the river, to the rocks below the rickety bridge, and crept up to the edge of the road. It seemed deserted in both directions, but that's what he'd want me to think.

There was no choice. I pounded onto the rotting planks, my footfalls jouncing loud on the loose timbers. If my shooter was within a half a mile, he'd know exactly where I was.

I got across in an instant, ducked into the woods and got snagged by a barky vine lying like a snake beneath the blanket of rotting leaves. I crashed down hard. Then, pushing up, dazed, I started to run only to get tripped again. Up once more, my legs were now too weak. I could only stagger from tree to tree in a kind of palsied shimmy, dodging vines when I could, falling when I couldn't. Sweat burned my eyes. Horseflies, bigger than I'd ever seen, bit at my cheeks and my neck. Sometimes I swatted at them, my hand coming away bloody. Mostly I just let them bite. I had no strength.

Somehow, I kept moving. An hour and a half later, I got to the used-to-be gas station across from the Dairy Queen.

Both service bay doors were open. A man wearing dark blue coveralls straightened up from the front bumper of a rusting green Chrysler minivan to eyeball the blood, dirt and bits of bark and leaf shreds that clung to my skin and wet clothes.

'Jesus, mister,' he said. He was young, in his early twenties.

'I had an accident,' I said.

'I guessed that already,' he said, grinning.

'I've got a car with flat tires in one of the fire lanes off County M. I need you to go out and fix the tires.'

He cleared his throat. I would have too, if I'd been confronted with someone bloody and slimed head to toe with lake muck and compost. 'Is the car in the water?'

'No.'

'Then how did you get so—?'

I took out my wallet, extracted the bills, damp and stuck together like a thin sheaf of steamed cabbage, and peeled off a fifty. I laid it on the van's fender. 'It's real money, just wet.'

He looked at the limp bill, then back at me. 'How many tires are punctured?'

'I don't know. I'd gone for a walk. When I came back to the car, at least two of the tires were flat.' I peeled off another fifty, pasted it next to the first one. 'Do you have a gun?'

'I hunt,' he said.

'The second fifty is for you to bring it along.'

He looked at my clothes and then at the two fifties, and then he shrugged. A hundred was a hundred, no matter that it was offered by a crazy man demanding he bring along a gun. He unpeeled the two fifties, went into the office, and came back with a shotgun. We got into his dented, powder-blue tow truck.

'You up here on vacation?' he asked as we rumbled down the road.

'I came to see Arthur Lamm.'

He laughed. 'I guess everybody knows him, leastways his car. Drives a hundred thousand dollars' worth of Mercedes Benz.'

'Seen him lately?'

He shook his head. 'There's a story going around that someone in Chicago reported him missing to the sheriff, but Herman Canty says that's nuts, that Lamm's just gone camping. On the other hand, that Mercedes has supposedly been sitting idle, collecting bird drops, out at Lamm's camp for quite some time.'

'Do you know Herman well?'

'Nobody knows Herman well, except maybe Wanda at Loons' Rest.'

'Herman drives a nice new truck.'

'Noticed that, huh?' he asked, a wide grin on his face. 'Herman ain't never worked much, yet here he is, driving an expensive machine. Somebody must have died for him to afford a rig like that.'

He came to a full stop at the bridge on County M. Shifting into low, he eased the truck onto the timber planks like he was rolling it onto eggs. 'One of those fifties is for risking this bridge,' he said, as the loose old wood shuddered beneath us.

We got to the fire lane a couple of minutes later and bounced up to the Porsche.

'I'll be damned.' The tow driver made a show of looking at me with new respect. 'I'm sorry, mister; I didn't figure you for a Porsche.'

I picked a fleck of leaf off my shirt and flicked it out the window. 'Understandable,' I said.

I stayed in the truck when he got out. He walked over to the driver's side rear wheel and squatted down. Pulling out a pocket knife, he picked at something stuck to the side of the tire, then got up, and moved around the car, bending to flick at each tire with his knife.

He came back to my side of the truck, smiling. 'No need for my gun.' He opened his palm, showing me four bits of twigs. 'You been pranked, is all. All four tires. Kids jammed these into your valves to let the air out. I'll have you on your way in no time at all.'

He started the compressor on the truck bed and uncoiled a long hose. Moving around the Porsche, he inflated each of the tires.

I got out, but had to lean quickly against the door. My legs were still rubber.

He gestured at my filthy wet clothes. 'Be a shame to sit like that in such a nice car.'

'I'm going back to the Loons' Rest to get cleaned up.'

'I probably owe you some change, mister,' he said, coiling the hose. 'This wasn't a hundred-dollar job.'

'It was a bargain,' I said, as much for the company of his gun as it was to fix my tires.

'Fair enough, then,' he said, climbing into his truck.

I led us out of the woods and we drove back to town. As he turned into his old station, I gave him a wave and continued down to Loons'. The parking lot was just as empty as when I'd checked out that morning. I grabbed my duffel from the trunk.

Wanda frowned as the bells inside the door danced.

'I need to get cleaned up. I'll pay for another night, though I'll only be a half-hour.'

'We're full up.'

I stared at her for a couple of seconds before I pointed a finger at the empty parking lot outside. 'There's nobody here.'

'They're out sightseeing.' She looked away from me, and out the window at the parking lot. She wasn't just being deliberately rude; there was something in her eyes. Fear, maybe.

'And I suppose it's your friend Herman leading them around, in that new pickup truck I've been seeing absolutely everywhere?'

She kept looking out the window, as though waiting for someone to pull in. 'Full up,' she said.

It had been no kid with twigs and a gun back in those woods. It had been Herman. I was being warned.

'Tell that son of a bitch I'll see him again,' I said at the door. It was true enough.

THIRTY-ONE

I drove several hours, almost to Milwaukee, before my subconscious quit tensing for bullets whizzing past my ear.

An enormous truck stop just north of the city had showers and a dour-looking cashier who expressed no surprise when I asked to use the showers. I rewarded him with a much fresher smelling me when I emerged in changed clothes, looking and smelling like the Porsche driver I might have been, had I learned more lucrative career skills. I bought paper towels, leather cleaner, carpet shampoo and, as a particularly elegant touch, a three-pack of little air fresheners that looked like flattened pine trees and smelled like urinal cakes. I scrubbed and patted and daubed the driver's side of the Porsche's interior in the parking lot. An hour later, satisfied that the car's interior would heal, given time, air and prayer, I took my little three-pine forest on the road.

I called Delray Delmar's cell phone when I got to the Illinois state line. There was truck noise in his background. I had to shout to ask him where he was.

'In my office,' he yelled. 'Lousy office. Trucks outside. Let's meet tonight.' He named a restaurant we both knew, five miles southwest of Rivertown.

I would have shouted back that any place at all would have
been fine, so long as it wasn't in Wisconsin, but I didn't have the
strength.

Since it was dark when I set out from the turret, I figured I could
head over to Leo's, leave his keys under the mat and switch the
Porsche for my Jeep unnoticed before I went to the restaurant. I'd
gone over the interior once more after I got back to the turret,
even rubbed the three little pine trees together to release more of
the fresh, Wisconsin urinal cake smell before throwing them out.
As a provenance specialist for high-end auction houses, Leo made
his living searching for small inconsistencies, but I was hoping
that he wouldn't go into the car until the next day, when the carpet
might be dry and the lingering scent of the tiny flat pines had
eradicated any last lake muck smell. I parked the Porsche in front
of his mother's bungalow, found my own key under the Jeep's
mat, and was gone like a bandit in less than thirty seconds.

The notion that I'd pulled off the switch unnoticed lasted barely
fifteen minutes.

'Did a bear pee in my Porsche?' Leo demanded when I answered
my phone.

'Does it smell like a bear peed in your Porsche?' I countered,
trying to sound offended.

'My car looks and smells like a bus station men's room. The
floor is wet and it stinks of urinal cakes.'

'There you have it, then,' I offered, smooth as greased glass.
'Bears don't use bus station restrooms, even in Wisconsin.'

'What the hell are you talking about?' was all he could finally
sputter, and even that took a number of seconds.

By then I'd gotten to the restaurant, a dark, beef and brew place.
I told him I'd call him tomorrow, and added he ought to lock the
Porsche's doors, in case any bears had followed me south.

'Nasty bites,' Delray observed as I slid into the booth in the corner
farthest from the door.

I'd daubed clear ointment every place that itched, and I glistened
like the sidewalks of Bent Lake at nightfall. 'Wisconsin offers
more than just cheese,' I said.

Our waitress came and we ordered beer and cheeseburgers. As

she started to walk away, I called out, telling her to hold the cheddar. I'd had enough of the notion of that.

Delray grinned. 'What did Wisconsin offer you, exactly?'

'No more than you learned up there,' I said, testing to see how much he'd reveal.

His expression didn't change. 'Tell me anyway.'

I told him about Arthur Lamm's car, seemingly abandoned at his camp; Herman and his shiny new truck; an orange row boat that should have been bailed out; the Porsche's deliberately deflated tires. And I told him about getting shot at.

'Shot at, but not getting shot?' he asked.

'I've come to realize the difference.'

'You were being run off.'

'It worked.'

'I'll bet. But it was a cheesy way of doing it . . .'

I groaned.

'Forgive the pun,' he said. 'You're guessing the shooter was Herman?'

'He was nearby.'

Our burgers came. Delray squirted a massive glob of yellow mustard on his fries, as I remembered kids did in high school. 'The question is why Herman wanted to run you off,' he said.

'So I wouldn't find Arthur Lamm.'

'Maybe, or maybe not,' he said, playing with a smile.

'Herman Canty need not have worried,' I said, not understanding. 'Too many lakes; too many trees. Even with an army and a fleet of boats searching for him, Lamm might be able to stay hidden up there for years, if he didn't go to Canada.'

'Think harder. Go back a little, consider what else Herman might have been up to.'

'After Lamm's Chicago people called, the sheriff started looking him. It was Herman who remembered Lamm always went camping this time of—' I stopped, remembering a thought I'd had, talking with the Bohemian.

'Do you see?' Delray asked.

'Herman established that Lamm is up there, when perhaps he's not up there at all.'

'Herman wasn't afraid of what you'd find, but rather what you wouldn't find.'

'No Lamm,' I said.

'Exactly. Herman could have driven the Mercedes up there, let it sit until Lamm's people in Chicago thought to report him missing, at which time Herman says it's all a false alarm, that Lamm's out camping on one of the million lakes around there.'

'When in reality, Lamm didn't go up there at all,' I said.

'The truck's the proof,' he said.

'The truck's the pay. Herman got rewarded with a shiny new truck.'

'I've been reassigned,' he said. 'It's part of my training. I'm now working drug investigations on the North Side.'

'Who takes over this case?'

'I've passed my file on to Homicide, but there's no heat on it. They don't see the deaths as murders. They won't follow up.' He reached into his jacket pocket for a white envelope. 'I've now got access to snitch money. In this case, twelve hundred dollars.' He slid the envelope across the table. 'Use it to work confidentially. Report only to me. Find Arthur Lamm. He travels in the same circles as did the dead men. He's got to be the key to everything.'

As perhaps was Wendell, but Delray had the decency to leave that unsaid.

'You didn't go back far enough with Whitman's calendars,' Delray went on. 'I had his secretary pull two more of his appointment calendars. Four years ago, Whitman wrote "C. Club" on two of those special Tuesday nights.'

'That's not much more help.'

He nudged the envelope closer to me. 'Check it out.'

'Is it legal, you paying me?'

'Requisitioning money for one purpose, and using it for another?' He laughed. 'Hardly, but as far as you're concerned, it's expense reimbursement. You don't know I've been reassigned.'

'If I can prove Jim Whitman was killed, and not a suicide, I'll be a rich man.'

'So Debbie Goring said. This money will help you find that out quicker.'

'What's in this for you, if you've been transferred?'

'I'll be seen as riding in on a white horse to save Chicago's most prominent people. My career will be made.'

I admired the kid's candor, but I suspected he was holding something back. 'What aren't you telling me about Arthur Lamm?'

'Nothing. He's disappeared, and he hasn't shown up dead. For now, that's enough to make him a suspect.'

'Why would he kill?'

'Let's find him and ask.'

'And we do that by first finding the C. Club?'

'It's our only lead.'

The kid had a point.

We ate our burgers and talked of Chicago politics. When we got up to leave, I pushed the envelope back toward him. Technically, or maybe not, Wendell was still my client, and Amanda was my first obligation. I couldn't split my allegiances.

I told him Debbie Goring was going to make me rich.

It seemed reasonable at the time.

THIRTY-TWO

I trolled the Internet the next morning for anything that smacked of a 'C. Club' in Chicago and its surrounds. Google spit up a thousand organizations such as the University of Chicago Alumni Association and a curling club that met in the northern suburbs to sweep brooms fast on ice. None looked like they needed to meet in secret.

I then widened my search by including all organizations that began with the letter 'C.' Eleven thousand names popped up, including a women's rugby club in England and an outfit claiming to own the world's largest catsup bottle. Narrowing these down to only those in Chicago didn't help.

Finally, I searched the public donor lists of Chicago's premier civic, charitable and social organizations. Barberi, Whitman, Carson, Lamm and Wendell Phelps had all supported the Union League, the Standard, the Boys' Clubs of Chicago, the Metropolitan YMCA and a dozen others. It was to be expected. They'd traveled in the same do-gooding circles. I switched off my computer. Delray's lead had been a bust.

I knew a Fed in the city. He didn't think much of me because
we had history, but I called him anyway and asked my question.
He said he could give me five minutes of his time, in precisely
one hour, but only in person, in his lobby. He wanted me to fight
traffic to ask a question which he might or might not answer. That
was understandable, too. Time does not heal all wounds.

I thought about bumpers to bumpers and the impossibility of
making it downtown in one hour, which was probably his intent,
and I hustled to take the train. As it clattered along, I looked out
the window, remembering when Leo and I were in high school
and rode downtown, headed for un-chewable, two-dollar steak
lunches served up with a spotted, hard potato and a piece of toast
smeared with something the approximate color of butter. We'd
cracked wise on those rides, at the colors and sizes of the clothes
hanging on the lines behind the three-flats, sharing our stunted,
sophomoric witticisms with those other passengers who'd not
thought to bring earplugs, ear buds or whole buckets of water in
which to submerge their heads.

I saw no clotheslines on this trip; basement dryers must be
everywhere by now. Nonetheless, my faith in adolescent boys
remained. They'd always ride trains, and they'd always find ways
to embarrass themselves in public.

Agent Till's offices were on Canal Street. He was an investigator
at Alcohol, Tobacco and Firearms. He'd threatened to prosecute
me one autumn for withholding information he considered vital
to wrapping up a case. He'd been half right – I was withholding
– but the information wasn't crucial. The case closed fine without
it. Still, we both knew he'd been charitable in letting me skate
unpunished.

He came down to the lobby, walked to the granite bench by the
window where I was sitting. He was a short, wiry man in his fifties
with the wizened, creased face and hunched shoulders of a career
investigator. Every time I'd seen him in the past, he'd been wearing
a brown suit. Today was no different.

'Five minutes,' he said, by way of an opening pleasantry. He
remained standing.

'You appear to be brimming with good health.' The last time
I'd seen him, he'd complained about the healthy food his wife was
forcing upon him.

'Cut the crap.'

I stood up so I'd be taller than he was. 'I need information.'

'Me, too,' he said, still touchy about that previous autumn.

'Have you heard anything about an investigation of Arthur Lamm?'

'The insurance guy?'

'Yes.'

He shook his head. 'ATF is not investigating him.'

'I think the IRS is.'

'I wouldn't know about them.'

'Could you find out what's going on, and where they think he is?'

'Sure.'

'*Will* you find out?'

'Will you tell me what I've wanted to know for too many years?' he asked.

'The case is closed.'

'It doesn't matter.'

'No,' I said.

He smiled and suggested I do something that, were it even physiologically possible, I would never do in the lobby of a government building, particularly on a bench by a window where passersby could see.

Chuckling, he walked past the guard and disappeared into an elevator, and I headed back to a train not due to depart for another hour.

THIRTY-THREE

The outbound train was a midday plodder that stopped at every crossing on its way west. I could have used the time to review what I'd learned about the men in the heavy cream – the three who died, the fourth who'd gone missing, and the fifth, my ex-father-in-law, whose evasiveness clung to everything, blurring it like thick, black smoke – except I'd learned nothing. So mostly, I looked out the window and let my mind drift back to old times, when laundry was hung on lines and semi-chewable steaks could be served up with rock-hard potatoes and yellowed toast for two bucks.

A black Chevrolet Impala, the kind of car Federal agents drive, was parked a few yards past the turret. There was nobody inside. It didn't matter; I knew who it was. Such a car parked outside my turret was like old times, too.

I headed into the kitchen to rummage in the cardboard box where I keep my dry food. For lunch, I had the choice between Cinnamon Toast Crunch, which I usually ate dry, or peanut butter, which I usually ate sticky. Sparks of culinary creativity, borne of financial deprivation, fired into my skull. I put two scoops of peanut butter into a plastic cup, shook in ten of the little sugared cereal squares, grabbed a plastic spoon, and went down to the river.

ATF Agent Till, who'd just given me a bum's rush downtown, had beaten me back to the turret and was sitting on the bench. A brown lunch bag was beside him. He was throwing scraps of a sandwich at a duck.

It was no surprise that he'd remembered the way. He'd come around often, frequently and futilely, when I'd been recuperating from the lacerations and burns I'd suffered in the explosion Till was investigating. I hadn't wanted to talk, for fear of incriminating those who didn't deserve incrimination. Amanda and a friendly doctor kept him away from me, citing my need to heal.

That did not deter Till. For two weeks, he came every day at noon, to sit on the bench and throw bits of his lunch at the ducks, and to threaten me with his relentless presence. New cases finally forced him to give it up, and he quit coming around.

I sat next to him on the bench and ate the first of my peanut-buttered Cinnamon Toast squares.

The sandwich Till was tearing had little green tendrils poking out from under the bits of wholewheat bread. Each time Till tossed a piece, the duck would circle it, floating in the water. The river was calm that afternoon, barely moving. Bits of sandwich surrounded the duck.

'The duck isn't eating, Till,' I said, after a moment.

'He's waiting for the green things to wash off.'

'What are they?'

'Alfalfa sprouts. My wife says they're good for arthritis.' He ripped off another piece and tossed it at the duck.

'Are you going to throw away your whole lunch?'

'It's called recycling. I throw this into the water, the duck eats it, and converts it to something better: duck shit.'

'But the duck's not eating.'

'Then it's going to get arthritis.'

'And you?'

'I stopped for two chili dogs on the way here.'

'Ah,' I said. I spooned up more peanut butter and Cinnamon Toast Crunch.

'What are you eating?' Till asked after a time.

'What's available.'

'Ah,' Till said.

We sat silently on the bench until all of Till's sandwich lay floating around the duck. Then he folded up his brown bag, put it in the jacket pocket of his brown suit, and stood up.

'Are you going to tell me what I want to know?' he asked, of that long-ago explosion.

'No,' I said.

'Arthur Lamm is in big-time trouble,' he said. 'He took customer deposits from an escrow account holding insurance premiums.'

'Embezzling?'

'Absolutely. Sometimes clients pay their premiums to an insurance brokerage agency. That agency is supposed to put the money into a reserve account for forwarding to the insurance company. Lamm tapped the keg for personal expenses like upkeep on his mansion and beauty treatments for his lady friends, replenishing it with new escrow payments as they came in. The IRS also likes him for giving freebie insurance to his heavyweight pals in Chicago and for not returning client overpayments. They're getting indictments ready.'

'Sounds like reason enough for Lamm to run.'

'Lamm's on the lam.' He laughed, delighted by his wit. 'He hasn't been seen for some time.'

'Isn't the IRS out looking for him?'

'They need warrants first.'

'You found all that out awfully fast,' I said.

'Only took one phone call. I did it in the car, between chili dogs.'

'Thank you.'

'That tree's dead,' he said, looking up at the ash.

'Not yet,' I said.

'Soon,' he said, and walked away.

THIRTY-FOUR

'Your information was correct,' I told the Bohemian. 'Arthur Lamm is being investigated by the IRS. He might be running.'

He sighed into the phone. 'That's good news of a sort, if it means he's hiding out and not dead, a fourth prominent man killed. Fears of a murderous conspiracy are unfounded?'

'I don't know.'

'Your client knows, though, doesn't he?' By now I was sure he'd guessed that I'd been hired by Wendell Phelps.

'Debbie Goring promised me five per cent of any insurance she collects if I can prove her father was not a suicide,' I said.

'You won't tell me your client's name?'

'No.'

'Any chance of helping Debbie collect?'

'Only if I can prove someone else gave her father an overdose.'

'So we *are* back to imagining conspiracy?'

'You're familiar with very private, exclusive organizations?'

'Some,' he said, evading now himself.

'I'm interested in something called a "C. Club". It meets on the second Tuesdays of even-numbered months.'

'That's very specific.' He paused so I could tell him why I was asking.

I didn't. I waited.

'I've never heard of it,' he said finally.

'Perhaps you could contact a few friends.'

'My God, Vlodek; I can't call around and ask whether they belong to some secret organization.'

'Barberi, Whitman and Carson each died on, or immediately following, one of those secret-meeting Tuesdays.'

'This is for real?'

'Real as death, Anton.'

'Then I shall try,' he said.

The Bohemian called back early that evening. 'No one admits knowing anything of a "C. Club." More interestingly, two gentlemen whom I know very well, and who are ordinarily very voluble, actually blew me off by saying they had to take important incoming calls.'

'Dodging you?'

'These are men who talk confidentially to me about all sorts of things,' he said, still sounding shocked, 'but they clammed up, almost rudely, when I mentioned your club.'

'I'm striking nerves.'

'What's going on, Vlodek?'

'Fear. Where is Arthur Lamm's primary office?'

'He runs everything out of his insurance brokerage.' He gave me the address.

Lamm's insurance brokerage was in a three-story building in Oak Brook, several towns of better income west of Rivertown. I got there at eight o'clock. Since it was Friday night, only a handful of cars remained in the parking lot. The back vestibule door was locked, but a woman was coming out.

There was a FedEx box outside, next to the door. I opened the supply compartment, pulled out an empty envelope, and pretended to fill out the label. The woman came out, in too much of a hurry to notice I'd used my shoe to stop the door from closing behind her. I slipped inside and went to the directory by the elevators. Lamm's insurance agency was on the top floor.

My gut wanted the cover of the stairs, but my brain took the elevator because it reasoned I'd look more like I belonged if I rode up. Executives coming back for evening work don't use stairs; they're too tired from spending long days being executives.

The top floor hall was empty, except for filled black plastic garbage bags piled outside several of the offices. Luckier still, Lamm's office was one of them, and his doors were propped open by a metal cart filled with cleaning aerosols, more black bags and rags. I tucked the FedEx envelope under my arm and stepped inside, clever as hell.

A vacuum cleaner was running close by, off to my left. I walked away from the noise, towards the row of offices in the back.

The vacuum cleaner stopped. Footsteps approached from behind, padding softly on the lush carpet. I turned to smile, executive-like.

The vacuuming man wore dark blue trousers and thick-soled black shoes. The pale blue oval on his white shirt said his name was Bill.

I held up the FedEx envelope. 'I forgot to leave this for Mr Lamm's secretary.'

He smiled and went back to the vacuum.

It was that simple.

The doors to the private offices had names lettered in black on their glass sidelights. Lamm's was in the corner. Seemingly studying the FedEx envelope, I bumped up against the knob. It was locked. The glint of a square silver dead bolt showed in the gap between the door and the jamb, too solid for a credit card to pop.

I sat behind the L-shaped secretarial desk closest to Lamm's office, took my pen from my pocket and a yellow Post-it from the pad next to the phone, and pretended to write a note. I stopped to shake the pen like it was out of ink. It was more clever subterfuge, an excuse to riffle the top of the desk. There were phone directories, a dozen folders filled with insurance applications and a file of local restaurant takeout menus, but there were no pens on the desk. And there was no appointment book.

I opened desk drawers, one by one. There were files and note pads, envelopes and paperclips, but there was no appointment diary inside the desk either. There was, however, a pen. I used it to pretend to finish the note on the Post-it, stuck it to the FedEx envelope, and turned it upside down so the cleaning person, Bill, wouldn't see I'd written nothing. Lamm's secretary would throw out the FedEx envelope the next morning, thinking only that somebody had accidentally dropped it on her desk.

It had been a long shot, amateurish, and hadn't yielded a thing about where Arthur Lamm spent six Tuesday nights a year. Nonetheless, I left his insurance agency warmed by the self-satisfied glow of a truly daring and clever sleuth.

THIRTY-FIVE

A t seven-thirty the next morning I was lying in bed, admiring my half-built closet from across the room, when someone began banging on my door. I slipped on jeans and a sweat-shirt and hustled down the stairs barefoot.

Two men in dark suits and even darker neckwear stood outside. The older one, about my age, held up a glossy plastic card. Next to his picture were the letters 'IRS.'

'Can you come with us, Mr Elstrom?' he asked.

'It's Saturday morning,' I said, almost giddy with admiration for Agent Till. He'd moved quickly to get his contacts at the IRS to meet with me about Arthur Lamm, even though it was the weekend. I ran upstairs, put on shoes, grabbed my pea coat and was out to their sedan in less than three minutes, ready to be enlightened.

The agents who'd been sent to drive me were close-mouthed. Heading to the expressway, I got only grunts in response to my questions. It was understandable; they were errand boys. Till must have arranged for me to meet with an agent-in-charge. I leaned back and looked out the window.

Halfway into the city, I spotted a tagger high up beneath one of the overpasses. Graffiti artists work silently and anonymously, usually too high up to ever be noticed. Perhaps like a killer preying in the heavy cream.

We got off at Wacker Drive, drove another few blocks and stopped in front of a black glass office building. The agent riding as a passenger got out, opened my door and walked me past the two uniformed guards in the lobby to the bank of elevators. We rode up to the eighteenth floor and went into a conference room that had no pictures on the wall.

'I'll be outside the door,' the agent said.

'I'm delighted to wait,' I said.

The building's ventilation system wasn't on, probably since it was Saturday, and the conference room was humid and stuffy.

Faintly gasping for air, left to stare at walls that had no pictures, anyone with even the mildest sense of claustrophobia would cop to lying on a tax return, just to get out of that room.

Five minutes later, the door opened and in walked two thin men, one in his thirties, one in his fifties. The younger man set a cardboard tray of three cups of black coffee on the table and sat down. He moved one of the cups toward me.

The fifty-something-year-old had a disc in his hand and a mix of patience and distaste on his face. 'My name's Krantz,' he said, walking to a gray metal cart in the corner that held a player and a television. He turned on the television, slipped the disc into the player, and pushed the play button.

The video had been shot from a ceiling-mounted camera in the hall outside Lamm's brokerage. A man wearing khaki pants and a blue button-down shirt, clutching a blue-and-white Federal Express envelope, came down the corridor and stopped at the open glass door of the insurance agency. Taking a slow, guilty look around to be sure the camera recorded that he was up to no good, he stepped inside.

Another camera then recorded the man stopping to cock his head, listening, before turning to mouth silent words to someone out of the picture, undoubtedly a man wearing a white cleaning supervisor's shirt with a name patch that read 'Bill.' After a minute, the cunning blue-shirted intruder smiled, obviously relieved. His shoulders relaxed, and he moved into the general office.

A third camera recorded the blue-shirted man approaching the private offices. He moved jerkily, like an overly medicated person trying not to collapse in a tea room. After pausing several times to take more furtive looks around, he finally bumped to a stop against a door. He pawed the doorknob. The knob didn't turn; the door was locked.

The man walked to the nearest secretarial desk and sat down to write a note on a yellow Post-it. Shaking his own pen as though it had run dry, he picked through the items on the desk, pretending to be looking for another pen but clearly looking for something else. Finding nothing of interest, he opened the desk drawers and, after a prolonged search, came out with a blue ballpoint pen. He made writing motions on the Post-it and stuck the note to the FedEx envelope. The camera was high-resolution, and recorded that the Post-it was blank; the man had written nothing on it. The man turned the FedEx envelope upside down on the desk and sauntered away, a moronic smirk on his face. The screen went blank.

There had been no sound accompanying the video. Clown music, especially if accompanied by a chorus of honking squeeze horns and an uproarious laugh track, would surely have made the video a contender in any short comic film contest.

Krantz turned off the television, sat down and sighed. 'Our man followed you down to the first floor and identified you from your license plates.'

'Bill, the man operating the vacuum cleaner?'

'Actually, his real name is Roger.'

I gestured at the now blank screen. 'You don't see that kind of cleverness very often, do you?'

'Sadly, no,' Krantz said, looking truly mournful. 'If criminals were that inept, we'd have them all behind bars in a matter of weeks.'

He leaned back in his chair and made a come-to gesture with his hands. 'Tell us.'

I had to offer something, having been caught by Feds. 'I think Arthur Lamm is connected to three murders.'

I told him everything I knew, minus any mention of Delray and Wendell. By the time I finished, some of the lazy contempt in their eyes had gone.

'You think Lamm's a killer?' Krantz asked.

'I can't see a motive for that, but I think he might know plenty.'

'You're working for Whitman's daughter?' Krantz asked.

Debbie Goring had become a superb justification for my snooping around, especially useful in keeping Wendell's name out of the questioning. 'She promised me five per cent of her father's insurance proceeds if I can prove his death wasn't a suicide.'

'How will Lamm's appointment book shed light on that?'

'Each of the murdered men was secretive about where he went on the last night of his life. Lamm traveled in their same circles. His calendar might show exactly where they all went.'

Krantz looked at the younger agent, who then got up and left the room. Turning back to me, he said, 'You really think Lamm killed those other three men?'

'That, or he's another victim. What can you tell me about your investigation?'

'Not a damned thing,' he said.

'But you do have men looking for him?' I asked.

'We don't have enough to arrest Lamm yet.' Krantz stood up and opened the conference room door. 'No more illegal entering, Mr Elstrom.'

THIRTY-SIX

Down in the lobby, I realized I'd hustled out of the turret without grabbing my wallet or cell phone. I thought about calling up to Krantz, demanding a ride home, but his demeanor suggested he didn't consider us to be pals. One of the guards in the lobby let me use the desk phone to call Leo's cell.

I hoped this was one of the mornings he'd slept at Endora's, because her condo was close by. She is young and beautiful and his time with her is not to be interrupted, especially by someone who had recently trashed his Porsche and then slipped away without explanation. But this was no ordinary morning.

He answered on the third ring. 'This had better involve my winning a lottery.' His voice was scratchy with sleep.

'Even better. It's your friend for life, abducted this morning by the IRS, now stranded downtown with no money in his jeans and a real hungry expression on his face.' I gave him the address. 'Come pick me up, buy me breakfast, and drive me home.'

He said he would. Or at least that's what I hoped he might have said after he swore and clicked me away. I didn't know for sure until he roared up forty-five minutes later.

'Do not speak,' he said as I slid in. Beard stubble smudged his pale face.

I started to do just that.

He held up a hand for silence. 'And do not rest your shoes on the carpet. Someone disgusting fouled the interior of this fine machine, and clumsily attempted to clean it himself. I shampooed it myself last evening, but it's still damp.'

'I'll pay for a proper detailing—'

'And leave your window down. The whole car smells like an over-treated urinal.'

'I told you: I'll pay—'

'Exactly how much money are you packing these days?'

'I have potential.'

He downshifted, turning onto LaSalle Street. 'Tell me when we get to Min's and I've had coffee.'

Greasy spoon, spotted vest; no term can do proper justice to Min's Café. No words can accurately describe the impact the fat-cat pols and business types who've warmed Min's plywood and pink vinyl booths have had on Chicago, nor can words convey the artery-clogging magnificence Min piles onto her chipped green plates. In a town renowned for its massacres, from Fort Dearborn through St Valentine's, to the latest gang shoot-outs in public parks, Min's entrees have felled more crooks, saints and just plain ordinary folks than any gun-wielding hoodlums or gang bangers ever have. It was an appropriate place to discuss murder. We took a booth under a paint-by-number picture of a forest and ordered Eggs Bud.

Leo held me off until he finished his first mug of coffee. After the waitress came by with a refill, he took another sip and said, 'Now talk.'

'I got picked up on video tape illegally entering Arthur Lamm's office.'

His eyebrows tangoed at my foolishness. 'What the hell were you doing there?'

'Hoping for a peek at his appointment book.'

'You fiddled with locks . . .?'

'The door was open.'

'And inside was a federal crew with video cameras?' He grinned, lighting the morning with a thousand bright teeth. Dumb was dumb.

Before I could answer, our Eggs Bud came. Bud had been the grill man at Min's for ten years. His masterpiece was four over-easy eggs piled atop two English muffins, slathered with sausage, melted cheddar and mushroom gravy the thickness of porridge. Bud died young. No one wondered why.

Leo smacked his considerable lips, lifted a dripping forkful and asked, 'So, you passed yourself off as prospecting for that five per cent Debbie Goring will give you?'

I nodded. 'I said I think Arthur Lamm attended those secret Tuesday night get-togethers.'

'As a killer, or as a victim?'

'I think Lamm's alive,' I said.

'Why do you think that?'

'Because I think that's why Wendell fired me. I think Wendell is covering up for Lamm.'

'How much of this have you told Amanda?'

'She knows her father is withholding.'

'How is it, being close to Amanda again?' he asked, a little too gently.

'We're getting along,' I said. For now, that's all I would allow aloud.

'And Jenny?'

I gave him what I could manage in the way of a grin. 'We're getting along, too.'

'What's next?' he asked.

'Finish my Eggs Bud.'

'And then?'

'Wait for inspiration.'

He sighed.

THIRTY-SEVEN

My wait for inspiration wasn't long.

The younger agent who'd sat wordlessly with us in the IRS conference room, before Krantz sent him out for something, stopped by before noon. He opened a large white envelope and took out a sheaf of photocopied calendar pages. 'All we have is this year's. We think he destroyed the previous ones.'

It was Lamm's calendar. I flipped through the sheets. 'He's got the same notation for each of those second Tuesdays,' I said. '"Sixty-six."'

'As you can see by his other entries, he noted all his appointments with numbers, sometimes followed by a letter or two.'

'Abbreviations for addresses?'

'We think so. Lamm didn't use a driver. He drove himself around. Those entries were the properties he visited. On those second Tuesdays, his last stop was always a place with a number sixty-six street address. It's meaningless and irrelevant to our investigation, but Special Agent Krantz thought you'd appreciate a first-hand look.'

He held out his hand, I gave him back his copies, then he said, 'Mind giving me a quick tour of one more floor? I've never been inside something like this.'

It surprised me. Unlike most first-time visitors, he'd paid no attention to the craggy walls. 'Sure,' I said, and led him up to the second floor.

'That cabinet isn't quite level,' he said in the kitchen. He was looking at the one that had been vexing me for days.

'I'll get it right,' I said.

He stepped out into the large area that would one day be something more specific, like a living room or a study or maybe both.

'This is your office?' he asked, walking up to the card table where I keep my computer.

'Things are simple here,' I said.

He touched the torn vinyl covering on the card table, smiled, and said, 'I'd best be going.'

I don't remember whether it was Albert Einstein, Thomas Edison or Bozo the Clown who said genius was one per cent inspiration and ninety-nine per cent perspiration. I'm guessing it was Bozo, because he had to stomp around in huge shoes, something sure to make him sweat like crazy. Stomping around, sweating, was all I could think to do next, though mercifully I wouldn't have to do it in two-foot-long floppy red footwear.

I drove to the corner of Michigan and Walton in Chicago, where Jim Whitman had been dropped off that last evening of his life. I parked the Jeep two blocks over, just off State Street, and headed west on foot. State Street is the dividing line for east and west addresses, and I figured Arthur Lamm's number sixty-six would be a block or two east or west of it, and similarly, only a block or two north or south, since it had to be within easy walking distance for Whitman, a dying man.

North of Walton, I walked east and west along Maple, Elm, and finally Division Street. There were four properties numbered with a sixty-six address: a Thai restaurant, an adult bookstore, a day spa and a private, three-story graystone residence.

I turned around and walked the streets south of Walton. There were only two properties numbered sixty-six down there. Both were three-story graystone homes.

I'd seen nothing, but I knew somebody who might know somebody who knew more. I walked west to Bughouse Square. Its real name is Washington Square Park, but to generations of Chicagoans it's always been Bughouse Square, the place where soapbox orators used to stand on crates to rant about the inequities of the day, real or imagined. For decades it was a welcoming place for activists, lunatics and those who simply liked to watch.

Then the neighborhood went upscale, like so many in Chicago. Some of the old graystones were renovated, but more were bulldozed to make way for concrete towers of condominiums, beige and bland inside and out. Sadly, Bughouse Square became gentrified along with everything else. Its worn, grassy expanse was professionally landscaped and cut with diagonal concrete walks, its loonies chased away to AM talk radio where they wouldn't have to stand on boxes – or for that matter, even wear pants – to orate.

Fortunately, the Newberry Library, across the street from the north of the square, remained untouched. I sat on one of the new benches the city had installed for trendy ladies and well-clipped dogs to share with homeless people and looked up at the fine old building.

I called Endora's cell phone. 'Who do you know that's a wiz on finding obscure private clubs in Chicago?'

'Me, of course. I have access to wonderful computers.'

'I know it's Saturday, but would you care to swing over to the Newberry?'

'I'm already there.'

Her office faced the park. 'Look out your window,' I said, waving.

'I see.' She laughed and said she'd meet me in the third-floor reading room in fifteen minutes.

I tell Leo that the reason Endora adores him can be fathomable only to aliens from more twisted civilizations. She is in her early thirties and has magna cum laude degrees in history and anthropology that she'd financed by modeling upscale clothing in national women's magazines. At graduation, she'd turned down longer contracts with the big New York agencies to work at the Newberry. Beautiful, brilliant and quirky, Endora was devoted to two things: the study and preservation of historical documents, and Leo.

That she loved Leo pleased me immensely.

That she worked at the Newberry assured me that occasionally there is perfect symmetry in the universe. For the Newberry Library, too, is quirky. It was planned on a promise of funding in the 1880s by a Mr Newberry, one of the richest men in Chicago. Unfortunately, before ground for the new library could be broken, Newberry died on board a ship en route to Italy. His traveling companions persuaded the captain not to deep-six the influential Newberry, as was the custom then for on-board expirations, but instead to preserve him in a barrel of whiskey. And so it went. Newberry completed his journey, to Italy and back to America, bobbing in a cask. In fact, even returned to Chicago, Newberry never left his barrel. He was rolled up the hill to Graceland Cemetery and buried in it, pickled and, by then, undoubtedly puckered.

Newberry's heirs squabbled over honoring his commitment to build the new library. Compromise was reached: exactly half of the library would be built. And so it became. Its front and sides are ornate, built of fine stone exactly as planned, but the detailing along its sides ends abruptly, like an ornately frosted rectangular cake sliced smack down the center. The upper cornice work stops crudely, and the back of the building is walled with the cheapest common bricks. Half was half.

Such rudeness aside, there is nothing half-finished about the Newberry's resources. It is renowned for its collections of arcane history, especially about Chicago.

The third-floor reading room is a great old hall of golden oak, arched windows and massive tables lit by pull-chain, green glass lamps. It is a sturdy, safe place. I pulled out a book of old maps of Europe, brought it to a table, and looked at ancient geographies while I waited.

Ten minutes later, a hand lightly touched my shoulder. Endora wore her usual dark, concealing work clothes. Her hair was pulled back in a severe bun, and she wore no makeup. Even dressed so sternly, she was lovely, and I had no doubt that many of her male colleagues spent much time each day imagining what naughtiness with Endora might be like.

'What's up?' she whispered, sitting down.

I handed her the piece of paper on which I'd written the addresses of the buildings I'd just checked out. 'What information do you have about these locations?'

'For ownership or tax records?'

'I'm trying to find a private club.'

We went to one of the computer kiosks where she typed in a query. A moment later, she keyed in another question, and a couple of minutes after that, she motioned for me to follow her out into the hall.

'There might have been such a club, a hundred years ago, at Sixty-six West Delaware, though I can find no current description of it. There's someone else who may know more, and he's in today, too.'

We went through the double doors leading to the private offices. At the end of the corridor, Endora knocked on the wall next to an open door, and leaned in to speak to someone inside. After a second, she stepped back and motioned for me to go in ahead of her. 'Mickey Rosen, Dek Elstrom,' she said.

The office was the size of a utility closet. It was crammed with bookshelves, a small metal desk and a tiny old man seated on a swivel chair. Mickey Rosen was at least eighty-five, and dressed in a pilling orange polyester sweater and maroon pants. He stuck out a small, leathery hand. 'Any male friend of Endora's is an enemy of mine,' he said, leering up at her.

'Dek's got a question about properties around here,' Endora said. 'Specifically, private clubs, with street addresses numbered sixty—'

'Stop!' Mickey held up a liver-spotted hand to silence her, then moved it to his forehead like a psychic. He closed his eyes as a big grin split his face, exposing yellowed teeth. 'Nobody say anything. I'll divine what your friend wants to know.'

I glanced at Endora. She looked stricken.

I cleared my throat. 'Mr Rosen, all I'm looking—'

He moved his hand from his forehead, opened his eyes, and finished my sentence. 'You're looking for an organization of influential people that meets only six times a year, does so secretly, is named with a word that begins with a "C" and has a street number of sixty-six.'

He dropped his hand and looked at Endora. Satisfied with her look of stunned admiration, he asked her, 'Will you sleep with me now?'

'No.' She laughed.

'Just as well,' he sighed. 'My heart beats best in boredom.' He turned to me and winked. 'Do you know a man named Small?'

I shook my head.

'Certainly there's nothing small about him. A heavy man, heavy breather, destined for a coronary event,' he said. 'Anyway, this Mr Small came to see me. Edward, I think he said his name was, or Edwin.' Mickey shook his head. 'He too wanted to know about a property around here numbered sixty-six.'

'How recently?'

'Late February, or maybe the beginning of March.'

'Was he a cop?'

'He didn't show a badge.'

Small might have been the investigator Wendell had hired. 'Were you able to help him?'

Mickey Rosen smiled. 'The Confessors' Club,' he said.

THIRTY-EIGHT

Sixty-six West Delaware was one of the graystones I'd seen south of Walton, an old, narrow, three-story with high steps leading to a black-painted front door. It was in the middle of a mix of residences, boutiques and bars.

I didn't spot any security cameras outside, but some might have been mounted inside the windows. Remembering my obviousness at Lamm's office, I didn't linger, and ducked into a bar directly across the street instead. It was one of those places that catered to the slim, hip, wanting to be noticed. Its front wall was almost all glass, so that people inside could be admired from outside, and people out on the sidewalk could be admired from inside. But all that admiring was for later, after it got dark. Now the bar was almost empty. I stood at a high table close to the window, ordered coffee, and pretended to be slim and hip, but really wishing I had a doughnut to go with the coffee.

I called Delray's cell phone. 'I'm in a bar across from the C. Club,' I said to his voice messaging, right after the beep.

He called right back. 'Where?'

'State and Delaware.'

'What is it?'

'Apparently, a club inside a private residence. How soon can you get a warrant?'

'Any sign of activity?'

'You mean Lamm, puttering about, freshening the lawn for spring? I've seen no one.'

He told me he'd be there soon. I told him I'd wait. By now it was getting dark, and the slim and the hip were beginning to descend on the intersection in slim, hip droves.

There was a restaurant across the intersection trying to pass as a fifties diner. The counter waitress was a cutie done up all in pink, right down to the bubble gum she was chewing with an open mouth. I sat on one of the red vinyl stools, slapped a roll of Tums on the counter and ordered a chili cheeseburger, chili fries and chocolate malt. She gave me an admiring glance, recognizing me as a serious contender who knew to bring antacids to a grease pit.

The chili burger and fries had *cojones*, the malt was too thick to go through the straw and the music was quintessential rockabilly, made long ago by men who'd married prepubescent cousins. I took my time, savoring the malted milk and inbred rock and roll, until seven-thirty when Delray showed up at the corner across the street.

He was dressed in a black silk shirt, black trousers, black silk sport coat and black shoes. Subtract the gelled stuff he slathered on his hair, add two hundred pounds, a beard, and fifty years, and he could have been Orson Welles. Except not dead.

He studied me as I crossed the street like he was checking out a Salvation Army mannequin. 'Is there a story behind you never wearing anything but a blue button-down shirt and khakis?' he asked.

'Not much of one,' I said. 'Where's your team?'

'I'm not assigned to this case anymore, remember? Second, there's no Chicago PD warrant out for Lamm. And third, it's Saturday night.'

'So you're not going inside?' I asked.

He grinned. 'You said it's a residence?'

I knew that sort of grin, and knew that I'd be protected, being in the company of a cop.

'Let's go clubbing,' I said. By now the sidewalks were teeming with people younger than me and older than Delray.

I took him to the bar I'd been in earlier. The guy sitting outside, on a stool, didn't give me a second glance but asked Delray for identification. Delray flashed his open wallet, and we went in to stand in the crush by the window. We shouted an order for long necks to a young girl with really blonde hair.

'Where is it?' Delray leaned to ask, after the girl had brought us the beer.

'Sip slowly,' I said. 'Anticipation is everything.'

'Then tell me about why you wear only blue shirts and khakis.'

'I got in some trouble, had to sell stuff to pay legal bills. It was strangely liberating, and I found I enjoyed it. What I couldn't sell I gave away, including most of my clothes.'

'I read up on you. You were all over the front page of the *Chicago Tribune* for a couple of days before you got cleared.'

'Yes, but I was not cleared on page one. My honor was restored right below notice of a sewer bond recall, well inside the paper where my former clients didn't notice.'

'*C'est le monde,*' he said. Then added, 'That's French for "that's the world."'

'My *monde* is taking a long time getting straight.' I nodded towards the three-story graystone across the street. A single lamp with a multi-colored Tiffany-type shade had been switched on behind the sheer curtains on the first floor. The second and third floors were dark.

Puzzlement furrowed his forehead.

'The Confessors' Club,' I said.

He looked past the throng on the sidewalk. A slow smile had formed on his face.

'It's been there since 1896,' I said professorially. 'It started as a leisure club for the elite gentlemen of the city: dinner, whiskey, underage prostitutes, the kind of place influential men could enjoy basic Victorian debauchery. I doubt the underage prostitutes visit anymore, but I'm guessing that on the second Tuesday of every second month, there's good food and good booze to be had inside, as well as sanctuary for the richest men in town to relax among their kindred.'

'"Confessors?"'

'Supposedly, the club was formed so that its all-important members could relax and say anything – confess anything – and know it would be kept in the strictest confidence.'

Delray waved to the blonde girl for more beer. 'How did you track this down?'

'Sheer, dogged digging through accounts of old Chicago,' I said. I couldn't tell him about the private investigator who'd beat me to the Newberry without implicating Wendell Phelps.

Our second beers came, and as we drank, Delray leaned back, studying me.

'What?' I asked.

'Have you reported anything to Debbie Goring?'

I told him the thought had crossed my mind, but I hadn't done anything about it.

He asked me for Debbie Goring's number and thumbed it into his cell phone. 'Ms Goring? Officer Delmar, with the Chicago police. I'm calling to tell you that Dek Elstrom is being very useful in our examination of the circumstances surrounding your father's death.' He paused, listening. 'Yes, ma'am, though I can't discuss progress yet. No guarantees, but if anything comes of this, you can thank Dek Elstrom. He's a very diligent man.' Another pause, and then, 'Of course we'll stay in touch.' He clicked off, and looked at me with raised eyebrows.

'You're a stand-up guy, Delray. Thanks.'

'With that five per cent from her, you could buy new clothes,' he said.

'And you can be a star in Homicide.'

'Screw Homicide. I'm headed higher than that.'

It was eight-thirty. By now, people choked the sidewalk, bobbing laughing heads. 'The neighborhood is as loud as it's going to get,' I said.

He nodded, agreeing. 'The neighbors must shut their ears to everything.'

'We'll keep our bottles.'

'Why?'

'People look away from wandering drunks.'

We carried our beers outside. April was just beginning, and the young men and women chattering on the sidewalk wore leather appropriate for the evening's soft chill. We crossed to the other side only when I was sure we were out of camera range of anything that might be mounted at the front of Sixty-six West Delaware. We continued down, turned up the side street and walked into the alley that ran behind the Confessors' Club.

'Here's where these bottles come in especially handy,' I said. 'We can't nose around during the day – too many business types and smart young mothers pushing imported prams can see us. But at night, the streets belong to people like you, Delray, hip as hell.'

'And the alleys?'

'After dark, exclusively the territory of the young hip male. No one wants to watch a well-dressed young man, carrying a beer, duck into an alley, for fear they'll hear the splash of his relief.'

We stopped when we got to the chain-link fence at the back of number sixty-six. All the rear windows were dark, but a low-watt bulb shone above the back door. There was no way of telling if there were any rearward mounted cameras.

'Second thoughts?' he asked.

I set my almost full bottle next to the fence and raised the metal latch on the gate. 'I'm with a cop. If anybody comes along, just flash your badge.'

'No chance. I don't have a warrant.'

I pushed open the gate anyway, and we crossed to the shadows at the back of the house. There were basement windows on either side of the door. I started to kneel at the one to the right.

The bulb went dark above my head. Delray had unscrewed it.

The basement window was locked tight. As I straightened up, I heard something jangling. Delray had pulled out what looked like a ring of loose wires.

'A cop with lock picks?'

He didn't answer as he bent to the lock. Almost instantly, the tumblers let go with a short, loud click. He pushed open the door. For a moment, we stayed outside, listening for any sounds from within. But all I could hear was my heart.

He turned and pressed the lock picks into my hand.

'I don't want these,' I whispered.

'They go in your pocket. If we're caught, I can help us more if I don't have them.'

It wasn't a good place for spirited debate. My fingers clenched the slender metal picks and jammed them in my pocket.

I stepped inside.

THIRTY-NINE

The darkness of the house was cleaved, front to back, by the soft reds, greens and yellows spilling into the other end of the long central hallway. The Tiffany lamp I'd seen behind the sheer curtains in the front window was the only light burning on the first floor.

I stopped just inside the back door, straining for the sound of a muffled footfall or the sharp intake of a breath. All that came back was the blood beating in my ears, and the smells of a hundred years of cigar smoke, grilled meat, whiskey. And secrets.

Delray pressed up close behind me. 'Basement,' he whispered. I felt rather than saw him pat his inside jacket pocket. He'd come armed.

The door was against my left shoulder. I stepped away.

He tapped my right hand with slim, cool metal. I closed my fingers around a small flashlight. Lock picks, a gun, and now a flashlight – Delray had come a real scout, fully prepared.

'Keep it low,' he whispered, meaning I should descend into the basement first.

'But you're armed,' I whispered back. Surely proper police protocol demanded that the cop go first.

'Best I stay up here, in case someone comes,' he said low, stepping back.

That did nothing to calm the blood rushing loud in my ears,

but I supposed it made sense. Any threat was likely to come from someone on the first or upper floors.

I turned the knob, swung open the door. Cool, dank air rushed out as though from a long-sealed crypt. I reached inside, feeling for a rail. There was only cold plaster.

Steadying myself with my left arm against the wall, and holding the flashlight with my right, I stepped down onto the stairs. A slightly lighter gray haze lay like a thin fog on the basement floor, streetlight washing in through a basement window. Ten steps down, I got to the concrete floor. Enough light came in from the two side windows to show spindly shapes against the walls, but the center of the basement was pure darkness, as though something hulking was resting there, sucking up the light.

I stayed at the base of the stairs and switched on the flashlight, aimed at the floor. The black mass in the center was an enormous old boiler, hot water pipes extending from it like tentacles from a giant squid. The shapes along the wall were a shovel, a rake, and an old-fashioned, reel-type push lawnmower, manufactured in a time when engines to cut grass had not yet been imagined.

I'd seen enough; there was nothing alarming there. I hurried softly back up the stairs, pressed the flashlight into Delray's hand. He could lead into the next dark place. He had the gun.

I followed close behind as he moved to the open door to the kitchen, just ahead on the right. An old white porcelain sink counter, tinged a ghostly blue from the moonlight coming through the back window, took up most of one wall; on another was an ancient, chipped eight-burner gas stove. Dented, dulled pots hung like steel moons from an overhead rack. The only modern presence in the cramped room, a small refrigerator, was jammed into a corner, an interloper in a kitchen outfitted when ice was kept in a box.

By now my ears had acclimated to the old house's rattling and pulsing every time a car or, even louder, a motorcycle passed by. My eyes, too, were now comfortable in the gloom. I made out ornate, curved shapes of electric light sconces, dark now, set high above the deep grooves in old wainscot paneling along the hall.

Delray stopped a few steps down the hall. A sliver of light ran up the wall on the left. It came from the center seam of a pair of closed pocket doors. I pressed my ear against one of them, but heard nothing above the noises from outside.

'Open the door,' he whispered. His hand moved to the inside of his jacket.

I placed my fingertips at the seam and, when he nodded, slid open the rightmost door.

It was a dining room, lit stronger by the same reds, yellows and greens that were spilling into the hall. Another set of pocket doors had been opened directly into the tiny front parlor. The colored glass Tiffany lamp I'd seen from across the street sat behind the sheer curtains on a mahogany claw-footed table, plugged to a timer. Two red plush settees were set on either side of it.

'Stay away from those parlor doors,' Delray said softly, close to my ear. 'We don't want to make shadows that can be seen through the front window.'

In contrast to the small parlor, the dining room was huge, and almost completely taken up by a long oak table surrounded by more than two-dozen high-backed oak chairs. The whole first floor was meant for dining and drinking.

Delray moved around me, and I followed him into the room.

'Let's have a look at a couple of those,' he whispered, pointing up. Two long rows of tankards hung from rails on the paneling.

It seemed an odd thing to be interested in, but I pulled two off their pegs and held them in the glow coming from the parlor. The mugs were heavy pewter, dented, and old. Each was etched with a different number: I was holding numbers seven and eight. I started to hand one to him. He shook his head. 'How many do you count?'

I set the two mugs on the table and looked up to count the pegs. 'Thirty, all told.'

'Same number as the chairs,' he said softly.

'Thirty members,' I whispered.

He motioned for me to back out into the hall. I started to reach for the two mugs I'd left on the table.

'Go on out. I'll put them back,' he said. He came out a few seconds later.

I crossed the hall, opened a door to a tiny washroom that contained a toilet and a porcelain pedestal sink. A cloakroom was cut in next to it, partially under the stairs. There was no rod, no hangers, just rows of brass hooks on three walls, set high and far enough apart for the sorts of broad coats that would have been worn in 1896.

I started to cross the hall, to take another peek into the parlor, but Delray grabbed my upper arm. 'Remember the front window,' he whispered.

I stepped back, pointed to the staircase. He nodded. I started up first.

Pressing myself against the wall to minimize any creaking, I climbed four steps, stopped, and held my breath to listen. I heard only the sounds of automobiles and motorcycles. Almost certainly, we were alone in the old house. Delray came up behind me and we continued up to the second floor.

A blush of moonlight backlit the gauzy fabric at the rear window, but most of the hall was in absolute darkness. The smell of cigar smoke, mingled with must and old wood, was strong, like below. The air moved next to me as Delray reached into his pocket. A second later the pencil beam of his flashlight broke the darkness at the floor.

It was enough to see the five doors that lined the old corridor. Each was partially open – for ventilation, I supposed.

Motioning me to stay behind him, Delray moved to the closest door. Easing it open with his shoulder, he stepped in quickly and stabbed low at the darkness with his pencil beam. It was the size of a small bedroom, no doubt once shared with prostitutes. Now it was furnished for relaxed conversation, with two pairings of red leather wing chairs, each with its own smoking table and glass ash tray, facing each other. There was no closet for someone to hide in. The graystone was built when clothes were kept in armoires.

Delray stepped back out of the room. One by one, he moved on to the others, nudging their doors with his shoulder, then sweeping his light beam fast and low, searching for feet and legs, arms and guns. All were furnished with chairs, tables and ashtrays, except for the last one, which was a bathroom.

At the staircase to the third floor, he whispered, 'Go back and pull the doors almost closed, the way they were.' He watched from the stairs until I'd closed each door to its previous position, and then we continued up.

The street noise was barely audible at the third-floor landing. We stopped to listen anyway, this time just for a few seconds.

There were only three doors on the third floor. Two were ajar, like those below. The third door was closed tight.

I stood aside as he nudged the first of the slightly open doors. It revealed a small attic of exposed wall studs and roof rafters, empty except for an iron bedstead leaning against one wall and a dusty, galvanized bucket. The other partially open door led to a bedroom furnished with an iron bedstead like the one in the attic, a painted wood dresser, and a metal night table. There was no mattress. It must have been a servant's room, unused for a hundred years.

Delray again raised his hand to the inside of his sport coat, stepped back, and motioned for me to open the closed door. He hadn't yet drawn his gun and the thought that he was readying himself now made me nervous that he'd sensed something I had not. I twisted the knob.

The door was locked. I held out his picks. Handing me his pencil-beam, he worked the old lock open in an instant. We traded picks for flashlight and again his hand moved closer to his gun.

I turned the knob and pushed too hard. The door flew open, banging loudly into the side wall.

'Shit,' Delray muttered, stabbing his light into the room. He inhaled sharply, in surprise.

Only a table sat in the center of the small room. On it were four large, professional quality digital recorders. Thin wires ran from each of them to holes in the floor, likely down to microphones placed throughout the house.

Delray raised his forefinger to his lips, but I already knew. The recorders could have been sound activated.

He swept the flashlight beam swiftly across them, looking for any glow of LEDs or other signs that they'd been triggered by the sound of the door I'd just slammed into the wall. But the machines were still; they'd all been switched off.

The recorders had been labeled: BR1, BR2, BR3 and BR4. I had the inane thought, then, that even when bugging the former second-floor bedrooms, tradition required the eavesdropper to behave as a gentleman. The washroom had not been wired.

'Let's get out of here,' Delray said, snapping off his flashlight.

We padded down the two flights of stairs and through the hall to the rear door. I opened the door and was about to step out when he whispered he should go first, in case anyone was waiting. He

stepped outside and I pushed the button lock on the door and
pulled it closed behind me.

We didn't say anything as we walked down the alley and around
the corner.

'Coffee?' I asked, after we'd crossed Delaware.

'Booze,' he said.

FORTY

T here was a bar in a boutique hotel two blocks east of State
Street. It was empty except for a bartender watching a
television sitcom and two dozen chrome bowls of peanuts.
Delray bought us squat tumblers of whiskey and ice, and though
the place was deserted, carried them to the plush chairs in the
back. I followed with two of the bowls of peanuts.

'Paranoid about being seen committing a crime?' I asked when
we sat down, trying a joke.

He took a long sip of his whiskey. 'I have to admit, it's not my
favorite thing to do.'

I took my own deep sip. Never before had the cold fire of
whiskey tasted so good.

'I'm getting used to it.'

'What do you mean?' he asked.

'I got caught on a surveillance video last night; Lamm's office.
I had to tell some of what I knew.'

His face tensed as I told him about my morning at the movies
with the IRS. 'You're sure you didn't mention me?'

'Positive.'

He relaxed back into his chair. 'How close are they to finding
Lamm?'

'We weren't sharing confidences. The conversation was mostly
about me, looking stupid, though one of Krantz's men stopped by
later with Lamm's appointments calendar. Lamm went to an
address numbered sixty-six on those same Tuesday nights. That's
how I zeroed in on the clubhouse.'

'The question is: who set up the recorders?'

'Think about the purpose of those recorders,' I said. 'Likely someone was hoping to grab stock tips, or other insider information, by bugging the conversations going on in those private rooms.'

'That doesn't rule out any of them,' Delray said. 'They all would have had access to the clubhouse.'

'Along the way, whoever bugged the rooms also learned who was vulnerable, health-wise, who had a condition or an illness.'

Delray leaned forward. 'Benno Barberi's heart condition,' he said, seeing where I was headed.

'And Jim Whitman's cancer.'

'Insurance,' he said.

'Barberi came home from the Confessors' Club agitated that some anonymous someone had insured his life,' I said. 'Jim Whitman's daughter had a different insurance concern: there was none that insured suicide.'

'Unless?' he asked, grinning, certain now.

'Unless there was,' I said. 'Someone wrote a policy on Whitman's life that Whitman knew nothing about.'

'Like with Barberi?'

'And like the policy taken out on Grant Carson that named some anonymous entity as beneficiary.' I raised my glass in salute. 'Insurance motives, three times over: Barberi, Whitman and Carson.'

'Arthur Lamm.'

'Arthur Lamm, the insurance man,' I said. 'He owned his own brokerage. He could fake his own medical exams, write his own policies, name his own beneficiaries. Smooth.'

'Why risk murder? Lamm's one of the wealthiest men in the city. Why dose Whitman with Gendarin at the December Confessors' Club when all he had to do was wait to collect on the policy he wrote on the man's life? And why risk pushing Carson out of a car?' He swirled the ice cubes in his glass. His whiskey had gone.

I had no answer for that. I went to the bar and bought us another round. It was the first time I'd had a second drink since I'd been tossed out of Amanda's gated community one sodden Halloween a few years earlier. That Halloween, though, I'd had a lot more than two whiskies.

'How do we find Lamm?' he asked when I came back.

'Let Homicide find him. You've got enough to get them interested.'

'Recording machines discovered during an illegal search? They'll freak.'

'Tell them to start by squeezing Canty. You do remember Canty, up in Wisconsin?' Delray had to be the cop from Chicago the flannel shirts in the bar had told me about.

Delray grinned. 'Yep,' he mimicked.

'Canty had to be the accomplice Lamm needed to kill Carson.'

He shook his head. 'It isn't enough to get Homicide involved.'

'Then call Krantz, tell him you've got a hunch Lamm and the three dead men are linked to that graystone. They don't need to know we went in. They'll get search warrants; you'll still be the hero.'

'No,' he said, staring into his drink. 'I want to find Lamm myself.'

'Career and ambition?'

'Having a rabbi means I have to work doubly hard to prove myself.' He looked up. 'You've got to squeeze Wendell Phelps about Arthur Lamm. Phelps might know where Lamm is hiding.'

I had no illusions about keeping Wendell out of the investigation forever. Sooner or later, Delray or another cop would tumble on to the fact that Wendell had hired a private investigator to nose into the killings before he hired me to do the same thing. They'd pull out all the stops on Wendell, then, and squeeze out everything he knew.

But that time had not yet come. 'That kills the deal for me, Delray,' I said. 'You wreck Wendell Phelps, you wreck me.'

'Because of loyalty to your ex-wife?'

'I put her in the newspapers once. I'm not going to do it again. I'll call Krantz, give him a heads-up on the graystone.'

He stared at me for a long minute, judging whether I'd carry out the threat. He knew as well as I that the Feds always trumped local cops. They'd chase Delray and the homicide cops right off the case.

'OK; no Phelps and no IRS, for now,' he said, backing down. 'I'll go to Homicide, but my way, and on my time schedule.'

'You don't have a schedule anymore.'

'What do you mean?'

'Arthur Lamm might have another insurance policy we know nothing about. He might kill again.' I took a last sip to finish my whiskey and stood up. 'You've got seventy-two hours before the Confessors' Club meets again,' I said.

FORTY-ONE

Sunday went calmly before it went to hell.

I awoke late that morning, well rested from knowing that Delray Delmar had alerted homicide cops to the links between Arthur Lamm and the deaths of Whitman and Carson. I had no doubt they'd be all over the Confessors' Club on Tuesday, to stop whatever killing was meant to go down.

And by the early afternoon, I'd achieved success with my troublesome tilting kitchen cabinet at last. I'd loosened every screw, re-shimmed, and re-tightened to get it to hang perfectly straight and level.

Even the butchered ash seemed to stand victorious, out the window, a headless man with both of his arms raised in triumph.

So I was feeling good, sipping coffee and more than occasionally sneaking admiring glances at my perfectly aligned cabinet, when Debbie Goring called.

'Elstrom, you son of a bitch,' she said, sounding almost jovial as she exhaled smoky carcinogens into her mouthpiece. 'Guess what?'

Surely she was phoning about Delray's call, trumpeting my worthiness, but I waited so she could say it and I could act pleasantly surprised.

'I just opened yesterday's mail,' she went on. 'Know what was in it?'

'Not a clue.'

'A cashier's check for a hundred thousand dollars.'

'From whom?' I asked.

'Come on, Elstrom. No need to be coy.'

'Doesn't the check show the remitter?'

'No.'

'It wasn't because of me.'

'A deal's a deal. You shook some big bucks loose. I owe you five per cent, five grand.'

'Hold the dough. It wasn't my work. There's no clue who sent it?'

'One of my father's rich friends, someone you made feel guilty. Stop by and pick up your check. Oh, and Elstrom?'

'Yes?'

'That cop who called me last night? Total unnecessary, pal. I'm good for paying you a commission on everything I get. I got faith that more is coming for both of us, Elstrom. You and the cops will prove my father was murdered.'

A faint squeak came from across the would-be kitchen. I spun around. And froze. The cabinet I'd just tightened so perfectly was starting to tilt.

'Keep plugging, Elstrom; there's big money—'

The cabinet gave up a mighty screech, a horrible, wood-ripping sound, and let go from the wall. I dropped the phone and ran but I did not get there in time. It slammed to the floor and split into a dozen pieces.

Some seconds later, I thought to pick up the phone from the floor and put it back to my ear. Debbie had hung up.

Coherent thoughts about anything in that kitchen were out of the question. I left the cabinet kindling on the floor and went across the hall to my computer and the numbing diversion of the Internet. I started off by Googling hardware sites, searching for miraculous advances in wall-mounting technology. Nothing wondrous appeared. I'd used the right anchors; they just hadn't been right enough.

My mind wandered, then, to Wendell and what sort of investigator he'd hired before he hired me. As I expected, Edward Small was a common name, and there were many of them. A toymaker, a guy who studied earthworms, and another who offered to repair Disney collectibles were just some of those listed. There was no mention of any being a private investigator.

I thought back. Mickey Rosen at the Newberry had said the first name could have been Edwin. I keyed in the new first name, found three different salesmen, an antique car enthusiast, four college professors, and at least two Rotarians – though in different parts of the country – and still no private detective.

I wanted coffee, but not bad enough to face the carnage in the kitchen. I typed in a new first name – Eugene – to delay getting up. My computer screen lit up with listings of lurid stories from the *Chicago Tribune* and the *Chicago Sun-Times*, dating back only several weeks, to the beginning of March.

Eugene Small had been murdered.

The *Tribune*'s website tersely summarized: 'Eugene Small, a local private detective, was found shot to death in an alley on Chicago's north side. His wristwatch and wallet were missing, leading Chicago police to theorize that Small had been robbed.'

Plenty of people get killed in Chicago: dope distributors arguing over deals; gang bangers fighting for turf; addicts slumped too far into a fix; and kids, lots of kids, and other just plain folks dropped by drooling morons shooting wild, not aiming so much as looking to simply make a cry in the night. The robbery and death of a private dick didn't need to mean anything.

Unless it came from the Confessors' Club.

Delray could find out more. I called but got his voice mail. I figured he was still huddled with Homicide. I left a lie for a message, saying I'd known Small from another case, had just heard of his death, and wanted him to find out what he could.

The Internet gave me Small's business address. Being Sunday, mid-morning, I breezed into the Chicago Loop in twenty minutes.

South Wabash struggles to find the sun even more than South Michigan Avenue, one block to the east. Tall buildings still smudged from Chicago's sootiest days a century earlier line both sides of the narrow street, and the elevated train that gave the Loop its name runs high on rusting old scaffolding down its center, casting the pavement in ever changing grids of shadow. Even at midday, when the sun is directly overhead, South Wabash Avenue is perpetually in gloom.

It is a street of ancient enterprises. Second- and third-generation diamond merchants, beef restaurateurs, and seedy clothing merchants operate behind dark doorways. Eugene Small's building was a rickety old warren of tiny offices, catty-corner and down from what used to be Marshall Field's before Macy's bought it, cluttering its aisles and dimming its lights.

The door to the faded gilt lobby was open. The directory on the wall just past a small pharmacy said Small's office was on the fifth floor. I pressed the elevator button, unsure whether the rumbling I then heard came from the elevator or a train passing high on the tracks outside. I waited for a few minutes, then gave it up and took the stairs.

The fifth floor was hushed. Everybody was at home for the weekend. My footsteps slapped loud and alone at green-and-black tiles dulled by too few waxings and too many decades of shuffling feet. The lettering on the frosted glass door panels was old and chipped and hard to read; no lights burned behind them. Another elevated train rumbled outside, shutting out the sound of my foot-falls. And then it had gone and the building went silent again.

'Small Detective Agency' was lettered on a door halfway down. The office to the right advertised loans for people who had no credit; the glass on the door to the left was blank.

I remembered how easy it had been for Delray to pop the lock at the Confessors' Club, and realized I'd forgotten to give him back his picks. They wouldn't have done me any good even if I'd thought to bring them. I was strictly zero-tech when it came to illicit entering; all I was packing that morning was a Visa card.

Nothing clicked as I pressed the card between the door and the jamb. I didn't even turn the knob. The door simply swung open.

FORTY-TWO

I bent to look at the jamb. Orange chewing gum had been pressed into the recess to prevent the bolt from sliding shut. Someone wanted easy access for a return visit.

Small's desk was old scratched oak, littered with papers, a Starbucks cup, and a tipped over Dunkin' Donuts box. The green vinyl on the desk chair was cracked; the red vinyl visitor's chair held an old blue IBM Selectric typewriter. A half-dozen cardboard file boxes lay in a ragged row on the floor near the wall.

I sat at the desk. The green desk chair had been dished by a substantial man, and groaned as I reached to move away the Starbucks cup that still stank of the cream, dried now, that Small must have used to keep his weight and cholesterol up. One doughnut remained in the tipped Dunkin' twelve-pack. It was sprinkled with coconut and somewhat intact, missing one human-sized bite and a few hundred smaller rodent nicks. Probably a few mice or rats were anticipating coming back to finish it, as had Eugene Small, I supposed.

The papers scattered next to the black phone were copies of invoices sent to furniture stores and used-car dealerships. Someone had pawed through them.

I re-sorted them into numerical order, reading as I went. Eugene Small had been a small-time repo man, grabbing back patio furniture and reclining chairs when he couldn't get work repossessing cars. The invoices charged flat rates, three hundred for a car, fifty for a sofa, and twenty-five for a patio set.

One invoice was missing from the sequence. Judging by the dates of the invoices preceding and succeeding, it had been dated around the first of March, a few days before Small was killed. It seemed likely that the man who'd jammed gum into the office door lock thought that particular invoice was worth taking.

There was nothing in the desk drawers except a stapler, a full box of red-capped ballpoint pens boosted from an Econo-lodge, and a small pad of note paper with a trucking company logo on it.

I scooted the chair to the ragged row of file cartons. Most of the folders had been used several times, their tabs erased and re-lettered in pencil. That they'd been jammed roughly into the cardboard boxes might have meant simply that Small was a slob, except they were not in alphabetical order. Likely they'd been hurriedly searched and jammed back by someone who knew Small was never again going to return to his office.

There was no file for the Confessors' Club, no file for Arthur Lamm or any of the dead men. Most especially, there was no file for Wendell Phelps. I felt no relief at that. I was certain Small was the detective Wendell had hired. Whoever had searched Small's office knew that now, too.

I stood up, went to the closet. Four wire hangers dangled empty on a rod. An enormous pilled polyester cardigan sweater hung on a fifth. It smelled of gin and sweat and, like the worn, reused files in the cardboard boxes and the empty desk, was another marker of a guy who'd haunted the poorer alleys of town, grabbing back unpaid-for used cars and discount furniture.

A guy who might have stepped out of his league and into the path of someone killing in the heavy cream.

I'd seen enough of nothing to be sure I'd seen enough. The office had been looted.

I paused at the desk on the way to the door. I don't like creatures that scurry, and saw no point in making their dinner easy. I dropped the foul smelling Starbucks cup and the remains of the coconut doughnut into the trash basket and was about to toss in the stained, crumb-littered paper desk-top calendar when I noticed its corners. The top sheet, January's, was blank – nothing had been written on it. But the pad's corners were creased from being turned up. I shook the candy sprinkles into the wastebasket and flipped to February's page.

For a big man, Eugene Small wrote tiny; the little numbers and initials scribbled inside the squares beneath the coffee rings were almost indecipherable. Only the dollar sign at the top of the sheet was big. He'd retraced it so many times that the tip of his black ballpoint had cut through the paper. I flipped to the next page.

He'd filled the first days of March with tiny numbers and initials, too. They stopped on March 8. Small had been killed the next day.

Many of the initials matched the Bohemian's list of those in the heavy cream. One pair of initials – A.L. – appeared most of all. Arthur Lamm.

Something rustled inside the closet. It was feeding time at the rat ranch. I grabbed the desk calendar and left.

I called Delray when I got outside but again got his voice mail. 'Eugene Small's office was tossed,' I said. There was more to say, but I'd say it when he called me back.

Small's intruder, likely his killer, had missed something important.

FORTY-THREE

I studied the calendar for an hour back at the turret, and then I called Leo.

'I've broken and entered twice more since we last spoke,' I said.

He groaned. 'As skillfully as you did at Arthur Lamm's agency?'

'Even stealthier.' I told him about Arthur Lamm, and the recording equipment Delray and I had found at the Confessors' Club. And then I told him about Eugene Small.

'You think Small got killed because he was working for Wendell?' he asked.

'Everything else the man did was small-time repo, not worth being killed over. I need you to look at something of significance.'

He said he was headed downtown to Endora's, but always liked being delayed for significance. He told me to come right over.

Light showed from the window of his basement office. I tapped the glass six times with the toe of my shoe – three taps, a pause, then three more, our code since seventh grade – and went to sit on the front steps. He came to open the door a minute later, wearing a huge blaze-orange T-shirt with a black deer head on it, the sort a 300-pound hunter would wear on a warm autumn day. Pressing his index finger to his lips to let me know Ma was still asleep – Saturday night was late-night dirty-movie night on her favorite cable channel, and she often didn't stagger to bed until almost dawn – he led me through the front room to the kitchen.

Leo poured coffee into Walgreen's mugs and we sat at the kitchen table. I placed Eugene Small's calendar between us and flipped past the blank January sheet to February, littered with small markings and the enormous dollar sign, traced and retraced, at the top. I pointed to a small, almost microscopic 'W.P.,' with an equally small huge dollar amount written next to it: '$5,900.' I told Leo of the one invoice copy that was missing from the small pile on Small's desk.

He laid his finger on the tiny markings. 'These are Eugene Small's billable hours?'

'And surveillance record.'

'You think the missing invoice was Small's copy of one he sent to Wendell for fifty-nine hundred?'

'It's a good guess.'

'Why would someone want to take the invoice?'

I pointed again to the most obvious mark on February's page, the enormous dollar sign inked over and again, so obsessively that the pen had almost torn through the page. 'I'm worried someone else besides Small sees big bucks in going after Wendell.'

'Blackmail, over what Small learned about the Confessors' Club?'

I could only nod.

Leo picked up the calendar. 'Let's put this under better light before we draw too many stupid conclusions.'

We tiptoed down the basement stairs, not speaking as we passed the cartons of Leo's old school books, the spindly little plastic tree they stuck on the television at Christmas, and the model train tracks we'd screwed on green-painted plywood when we were kids.

His office didn't have a door, just a roughed-in opening to unpainted drywall, bare concrete and mismatched filing cabinets in black, gray, tan and orange. He set the planner upside down on the light table and pulled over the long-armed Luxo magnifying light.

'Sale stickers,' he said, pointing to two little red tags stuck to the cardboard back. 'One for four dollars, then one for two dollars.'

'As I said, Small was a repo man who grabbed furniture and cars. He didn't need such a large calendar until the very end of January, or perhaps the beginning of February, when he had to keep track of lots of pairs of initials, and lots of billable hours for Wendell. By then, calendars were on sale.'

'Excellent, for such a modest mind,' he said. He turned the calendar right side up and began examining February's sheet through the magnifying lens of the Luxo. I sat in the sprung over-stuffed chair that had been his father's favorite up to the moment he'd died in it. For all his flippancy, for all his finger-clicking, hipster mannerisms and outrageous clothes, Leo Brumsky was recognized as one of the best ferrets in the country when it came to examining historical documents and pieces of art.

He worked slowly, examining each inch of the February sheet, saying nothing. After thirty minutes, he switched to a stronger lens on the Luxo and bent down again. 'Who's R.B.?' he finally asked, straightening up after he'd spent another twenty minutes on the marked-up quarter of the March page. 'Those initials appear most frequently, always appended to other initials.'

'Look at which sets of initials they're always closest to.'

'A.L.'s. I already noticed. Arthur Lamm?'

'I'm thinking Small hired R.B. to tail Lamm so that Small could tail the others.'

He switched off the Luxo. 'If Small indeed worked for Wendell, then only two people know what Small learned,' he said.

'R.B,' I said, because it was easiest.

'And Wendell Phelps,' he said.

FORTY-FOUR

I called Wendell's home as I pulled away from Leo's. The woman who answered had a Latin accent. She said he wasn't home.

'Call him on his cell phone. This is urgent.'

'He not to be disturbed.'

'Delores, then. Is she home?'

'She with her pigs.' She pronounced it 'peegs.'

'I need to talk to Wendell now.'

'No.'

'You're going to lose your job.' It was the cheapest of false threats, and remarkably ineffective. She hung up on me.

I called Amanda. 'I need to speak to your father.'

'What's going on? What have you learned?'

'A couple of small things.'

Her voice got scared in an instant. 'What small things?'

'Damn it, Amanda. Your father is still my client.'

'He's playing golf.'

'Where?'

'Crest Hills, north of the city. I think he teed off at ten o'clock. He switches his phone off when he's out there, so your best bet is to catch him in the bar, afterward.'

She started to ask a question. I told her I had to run.

Better she worried about what I didn't say than about what I did.

I'd passed by Crest Hills Country Club several times in the past, seen the colorfully clad players driving slowly in electric carts as their white-uniformed caddies followed on foot. Though the golf bags were in the carts, I supposed course rules required that every player be tended by someone to replant the huge chunks of turf that golfers launch when flailing at such little balls, though the folks hustling behind might be better termed gardeners rather than caddies. I'd heard it cost half a million dollars to join Crest Hills, plus tens of thousands more each year for dues and fees. If I'm ever that rich, I'll go dig holes for free in a prairie somewhere, and spend the money instead on employing a world-class pastry chef.

I drove through the stone arches and parked in the lot adjacent to the white stucco clubhouse. The bar, a room of dark paneling with a wall of glass facing the course, was in back. Wendell sat at a table with three other men who were all drinking clear drinks made with sparkling cubes of ice and slices of preternaturally green lime. He wore a lavender shirt and pale blue trousers, and had a yellow bucket hat tilted back on his head. His colorful clothes and sun-pinked skin combined to remind me of an Easter egg.

Oddly, I got right to him. There were no security men hulking anywhere in sight.

'Mr Elstrom,' he said, frowning but not surprised. One of his secretaries, or even Amanda, must have given him a heads-up that I'd be rolling in. He didn't stand, or extend his hand.

The other three men at the table were also dressed in country-club pastels. Together, the entire foursome suggested a giant basket of jovial, decorated eggs. They turned to Wendell, expecting to be introduced. Wendell said nothing.

'Dek Elstrom,' I said to them. 'I'm here to repossess Mr Phelps's car.'

That popped Wendell from his chair to grab my elbow and hustle me outside through a service door.

'Was that necessary?' Most satisfyingly, his face had gotten darker under the pink.

'Tell me about the Confessors' Club.'

'I don't know that club.'

'How about you and I have a glance at your day planner? If you attended other engagements on the second Tuesdays of even-numbered months, I'll back off.'

The red beneath the pink darkened even more.

'Or you can tell me about Eugene Small,' I went on, after he said nothing.

'Ineffective,' he said.

'Particularly now that he's dead?'

I watched his face, looking for change, but it stayed tight, in control. He knew.

'Small's office got tossed,' I said. 'If it wasn't you, then someone else took one of the invoices he sent to clients. I think that person also took a file. I'm guessing both had your name on them.'

Surprise hit his face, but it could have been shock, or fear. He said nothing.

'Do you understand, Wendell? Someone has now linked you to Small, and what he knew. Maybe what he knew got him killed. Maybe it will get you killed.'

'Let this alone,' he said.

'Where are your guards? I breezed right in.'

'Unnecessary.'

'Unnecessary because you now know your friend Arthur Lamm's been behind the killings? Or unnecessary because he's gone into hiding?'

'Don't be a fool,' he said, but his voice was wavering.

'Did you send Whitman's daughter that anonymous hundred grand from guilt, or are you hoping she'll drop her interest in her father's murder?'

'You're fired, Elstrom,' he said, starting to turn.

'You already did that. When did you first suspect Lamm was behind the killings?'

His back stiffened as he headed toward the clubhouse.

'The cops have discovered that third floor,' I called after him.

He stopped cold and turned, confusion on his face now. 'What the hell are you talking about?'

'The room with all the recording equipment, in the house on Delaware Street. Were you listening, too?'

The pink had drained away from his face. I'd gut-punched him with something he didn't know. He headed into the clubhouse, walking jerky-legged, like he'd just torn a ligament. Or ten.

I let him go. He was no ordinary ex-client. He was Amanda's father.

I walked back to the Jeep. For a time I sat behind the wheel, drained too. And wishing that somehow I'd managed to fly to San Francisco, and lost my cell phone on the way, before Amanda had ever thought to call me about her father.

Time passed. Then, ten or fifteen minutes later, loud laughter came from the portico of the clubhouse. Wendell's three fellow colorful eggs were coming out. He lagged several paces behind them, shuffling like a ninety-year-old man. He reached in his pocket, came out with keys and fingered a remote lock.

His car chirped and flashed its headlights.

I knew Wendell drove a vintage Mercedes. Not today. The car he got into wasn't expensive. It was a medium-priced sedan, the kind of car that retirees, merchants and countless thousands of other ordinary people drive.

It was older and tan, the one I'd seen in Wendell's garage the day I'd first gone up to speak with him. The kind of car that had swerved in front of me on South Michigan Avenue, wanting to trigger that memory.

The kind with holes on the side, the kind Mrs Johnson had seen Jim Whitman coming home in the night he'd been murdered. A Buick.

Wendell Phelps had driven Jim Whitman home the night Whitman was murdered.

FORTY-FIVE

Monday: the day before the Confessors' Club was to reconvene.

I woke at six, light on sleep but heavy with what I knew should be done.

I should pull photos of Buicks with portholes from the Internet and forward them to Mrs Johnson to identify – for me to then forward to the police – the precise model and year of car that had driven Whitman home. The cops would then run a list of all such Buicks, in tan, registered in the Chicagoland area. Even if the car was titled to some corporate entity, some enterprising young cop – perhaps Delray, perhaps not – would probe deeper, and link Wendell to the Buick, and from there to Jim Whitman.

This I did not do.

I should call Delray again, in hope of getting him and not his voice mail, to tell him of a mysterious associate of Small's whose initials were R.B., someone who might know important things about the secret meetings of the men in the heavy cream. It was a useful lead, one that should be tracked down before the cops converged to watch the Confessors meet the following night.

This, at least, I tried to do, several times, but each time I got Delray's voice mail. Finally, I called the main number of the Chicago Police Department. 'Delray Delmar, please.'

'Which department?' a woman said.

'Special Projects.'

She hesitated, then said, 'Hold please.'

She came back on a moment later. 'We have no department named Special Projects.'

'He reports to the deputy chief.'

'You mean deputy superintendent?'

'Sure.'

'Which one?'

'There's more than one?'

'Of course.'

'I don't know.'

'Hold please.' This time she didn't come back for three minutes. 'Officer Delmar is in Traffic, but he's on leave.'

She transferred me to Traffic, and I asked the crusty voice that answered how I could contact Delray.

'You a friend?'

'Yes.'

'You're a friend, and you don't know he's on leave?'

A thousand charged needles began prickling the top of my head, thinking he'd been hurt. 'What's he on leave for?'

'Look, pal, if you're a friend, ask the family.' There was a question now in his cop voice. He hung up.

I called the main police number again, asked to be transferred to Traffic. Luckily a different voice, young and female, answered. 'I'm from Haggarty and Dunn, jams and jellies out of Napa, California?' I said. 'Someone, a Mr Delray Delmar, gave this phone number when he placed an order. I can't read the delivery instructions. What time will he be in?'

'This has to do with police work?'

'No, ma'am. This has to do with a gift he wants to send.'

'We don't give out home phone numbers.'

'I should leave a message with you?'

'What the hell, call St Agnes in Chicago.'

None of it made sense. Delray had said nothing about working in Traffic; he'd just been reassigned to Narcotics on the north side. More troubling, he was now in the hospital. And that might have meant he hadn't tipped Homicide about the upcoming meeting at the Confessors' Club.

A new spring storm had raged up suddenly outside. I ran out to the Jeep through rain drops hurling down as big as nickels. The Eisenhower was the most direct route to St Agnes, but the sewers built to drain the expressway were collapsing, like so many in Chicago, and had begun clogging up, stopping traffic in monstrous puddles whenever it rained. I sped as best as I could through the side streets, blowing through stop signs, running the red lights. It took an hour to make what should have been a thirty-minute trip.

The kindly lady at the hospital's front desk said it was too soon for visiting hours. I asked for Delray's room number, said I wanted to send him flowers. She smiled and said he was in 518, and that he was fortunate to have such a considerate friend.

I went out the main door, came back in through the hall from Emergency, and took the elevator up.

A pushcart holding breakfast plates under stainless steel covers was outside 518. Above it, the slip-in name holder by the door read 'Delmar, D.' I peeked in. The bed closest to the door was empty. A woman in a yellow uniform was by the window bed, taking a plate from a rolling table. The occupant of the bed was concealed behind the curtain. I smiled at her when she came out. She didn't smile back. I went in.

'Delray—' I began, but stopped when I got past the curtain. The man in the hospital bed eating scrambled eggs was at least fifty years old, and had gray hair.

'Sorry; wrong room,' I said, and started to back out.

'I'm Delray,' he said in a surprisingly robust voice.

I moved forward to the edge of the curtain. 'Delray Delmar?'

He nodded.

'Chicago police?'

'Twenty-eight years,' he said.

'I'm looking for your son.' There was nothing else to think.

The man set down his fork. 'No son; just two daughters. What's this about?'

I turned and walked out of the room. At the nurses' station, I said I was the old man's nephew in as steady a voice as I could manage. 'I just learned about my uncle's condition. How long has he been here?'

The nurse checked a chart. 'His bypass surgery was last week, but there were complications. His lungs started—'

'He's lucid?'

'Of course. No problems with that . . .'

I walked away before she could finish, on legs that felt like they weren't mine.

Outside St Agnes, the rain had stopped, but the sky had gotten even darker, as if it too knew that hell was coming to Delaware Street tomorrow and that all the notecards I'd made in my head had been reshuffled and thrown into the wind. The air felt too heavy to breathe. I walked across the street to the garage and leaned against a cold concrete column. Delray Delmar, the boy cop, was no cop. The kid was a fraud and maybe a killer.

I called the IRS. A sweet voice said Krantz wasn't in. I asked if I could speak with anybody who was working on the Arthur Lamm case. Sweet Voice said she couldn't confirm which cases the IRS was working on. I said bullshit. She asked if I would leave a number and I said I damned well would, that the matter was extremely urgent.

I hurried to the Jeep, but made it only a block before the sky opened up again. The earlier rain had filled the sewers. The new downpour was now turning the streets to rivers, the intersections to lakes. Worse, every form of road cholesterol had come out to clog my way, from distracted, pokey drivers too intent on cell phones to the truly timid, frozen by the deluge and waiting, I supposed, for a white-bearded man in robes to part the waters and show them the way to the ark. I swore at every damned one of them, cut up an alley, across another, and finally got free several blocks later.

I pulled into a gas station and called the IRS again. This time I insisted on speaking with someone who worked directly with Krantz. A man took the call, said Krantz was in Washington. Hell was coming down, I told him; Krantz had to call me. The man said Krantz was in meetings.

'There's a murderer out there, maybe two!' I yelled. I hung up, realizing I'd sounded too deranged to warrant pulling Krantz out of any meeting.

The rain had slowed to a drizzle by the time I got back to the turret. I walked down to the river, to have one last think at what seemed to be my only remaining option.

The Willahock agreed. It was angry, kicking up white spray over the banks and onto the crumbling riverwalk. Lightning lit the sky to the west, promising another storm, and the wind snapped hard at the two-armed ash. The ground around the tree was littered with young, green leaves, dead now forever. I didn't need the leaves to tell me the world had turned into a dark tempest, and that the kid cop imposter, and Arthur Lamm and his caretaker, Canty – and R.B., whoever he was – were swirling right in the middle of its dark heart. It was four-thirty. Barely twenty-four hours remained before the Confessors were set to meet the next evening, when another of them might be killed. And Agent Krantz, the only person I could hope to trust, was too busy in meetings to call me.

I phoned the bastard who'd trashed my life.

'John Keller,' the voice said.

'This is Dek Elstrom.'

He gave me a contemptuous sigh. 'Listen, Elstrom, you gotta put this behind—'

I cut him off. 'I'm not drunk this time, calling to rant about how you shafted me in your columns. I've got a story, maybe the biggest story you'll ever get. It's ideal for you, Keller, because I can't prove any of it. You're going to have to go with speculation.

But you like that, Keller. All I ask is that you lead with it in tomorrow's column – "details to follow," your usual crap.'

'I'll listen,' he said.

'You better do more than that, or people are going to die.'

FORTY-SIX

Tuesday morning. Confessors' Club day.

All night, one storm after another had thundered through Rivertown, pounding the ground, roiling the river. I wouldn't have slept much anyway, not the night before the Confessors were to gather.

I got out of bed at six, finally, because there was no reason not to. I started coffee, slipped into my yellow rain poncho and stepped out into the downpour. In the faint light of the streetlamps, Rivertown looked like it had been shaken by a furious giant. The ground was littered everywhere with branches, and several trees were down in front of city hall. Rivertown, being Rivertown, would not field a city crew to clear the streets until well past noon. The lizard in charge of municipal services owned one of the tonks on Thompson Avenue, and spent most nights until dawn drinking deeply from his own inventory.

I pushed the end of a spindly limb off the Jeep's hood, and then ran across the spit of land and Thompson Avenue to buy an *Argus-Observer* from the blue box in front of the Jiffy Lube. Ducking beneath the eave below the sign advertising full lubrications, it struck me, because my mind so often speeds in unnecessary directions, that full lubrications were the essence of Rivertown. During the day, cash greased the palms of the town's fathers to ease sticky zoning violations or troublesome brushes with what passed for the law in Rivertown. At night, cash bought lubrication of an entirely different sort, from the sweet-smelling women who worked the darker patches along Thompson Avenue. I gave a mental nod to the red-and-white sign lit bright in the rain; it was a perfect beacon for the town.

I flipped the paper open to 'Keller's Korner' only long enough to be sure he'd led with my words, then tucked it under my poncho and ran back to the turret. The coffee was ready. I caffeinated my travel mug and read what I had wrought.

Keller had headlined his column with his typical hysteria: 'FEDS AND CHICAGO PD COVER UP SECRET BLACKMAIL MURDER CLUB.' The smaller print below continued in his usual breathlessness: 'According to the agent of a well-known local businessman, a secret blackmail and murder society has been operating in the city for over a century. In the past six months, several prominent Chicagoans have been snuffed out after attending meetings in the society's secret headquarters in a graystone off the Mag Mile. And just one month ago, a private detective who discovered recording machines set up for high-stakes blackmail and worse in the ancient den was killed before he could spill what he knew. Still to be fathomed: another club member, a prominent insurance man with big-big connections to the very top-ola, has gone missing while CPD dithers and Federal boys bungle. Details to follow.'

'Details to follow,' was Keller's signature tag line, and since there were rarely any details to begin with, almost none ever would follow. He was a master at frenzied innuendo, a jester at journalistic integrity. He'd distorted what little I'd given him, used only words that would sizzle in print. He'd not named the Confessors' Club or its precise location, nor the Federal agency that was involved, the supposed murder victims, or Lamm. He'd written nothing of substance, and he'd done it as magnificently as I'd hoped. Now it was time for tens of thousands of Chicagoans to read 'Keller's Korner' online or in print, and without realizing it, they'd begin to fill in the blanks themselves. Newsreaders abhor vacuums, and in talking the story up in office corridors, over store counters and on the phone from their homes or their cars, they'd add their own little suppositions that they were sure to be true. And by noon, a hundred versions of the story would have spread to half the people in town. It was Keller's particular genius, setting roaring fires with so few tiny twigs.

I knew, because I'd been burned by those same flames. 'POWER SON-IN-LAW DETECTIVE WHINES HE WAS DUPED TO CONSPIRE' had been my bold print when Keller ridiculed me as a stupid schlep that conspired to falsify evidence. That I'd been stupid was true. That I'd conspired was false. But I was the son-in-law of Wendell Phelps, a major Chicagoan, and that got me the big ink. No matter that I'd never met Wendell, no matter that I'd been fooled by some very expert forging. No matter even that the charges against me were piled thick to obscure some very sloppy prosecution. None of that saw print in 'Keller's Korner.' My details to follow, in the form of a full exoneration, never had followed in Keller's column, and only in tiny print in the back pages of Chicago's other newspapers.

I walked to the window. Lightning lit the Willahock, heaving and frothing in the storm. Amid a hundred lesser fallen branches, the butchered ash stood as though raging in the rain, angrily thrusting its two contorted, rain-slicked limbs at city hall. I had the hope that other, more human limbs were being contorted farther to the east, in the city. By now, someone at the IRS had read Keller, and had called Krantz in Washington, and I wondered if Krantz would order that I be run downtown for some extended, repetitive questioning, if only as retribution in advance for the ridicule his snail-paced investigation was soon to receive. The Chicago police would be slower. They'd have to play catch-up, frantically call the various Federal offices in Chicago to find the agency that knew who'd made them look stupid. I had no doubt that when they rang the IRS, Krantz's crew would cough me up in a heartbeat, understanding that the Chicago cops needed their piece of me, too.

So be it. What mattered was that Keller's words would render the Confessors' Club toxic to its members. No one would dare go there that evening for fear of Feds, cops and killers. And in the coming days, other reporters, more conscientious than Keller, would dig. The names of the Confessors would be revealed, the house on Delaware would be pictured, and the graystone nest would be poisoned for all time. Nobody would ever return. Nobody would ever again be killed because of what had been recorded there.

Or so I thought, that morning.

FORTY-SEVEN

The first response I got wasn't from Krantz's men, pounding on my door. It was Wendell calling, and he was smoked.

'What the hell are you doing, Elstrom?'

'Your name isn't in the column. Neither is mine.'

'You should have checked with me first.'

'You walked away from me, remember?' I paused, then said, 'What was Jim Whitman doing in your car on the last night of his life?'

He ignored the questions. 'Somebody at the IRS or the Chicago police is going to track this to you, and then to me.'

'Too late; the IRS already knows me. That's why I can't talk long. I want to be available to make sure they get the spelling of your name right.'

'You're a son of a bitch, Elstrom.'

'Tell me how deep you're in with Arthur Lamm.' I needed to tell him more, that there was a cop imposter also chasing Lamm, but he didn't give me the chance. He hung up.

It was time to make the call I'd been dreading, but she called me before I could punch in her number. 'The acquisitions committee is meeting at the Art Institute all day,' Amanda said, her voice amazingly calm. 'Dinner tonight at five, on the cheap, at the Corner Bakery across the street?'

Even now, after the dust from our divorce had long since settled, she had the power to charm and transfix me, no matter the turmoil. I supposed that would never change.

I went into the would-be kitchen for more coffee. The cabinet that had fallen lay now in pieces on the makeshift counter. It had taken me hours to tap it apart. I'd salvaged what I could, but still it needed new structure. I'd considered scrapping it, making a new cabinet from scratch. But there are times when starting over seems unwise.

Krantz finally called. 'Care to have lunch?' he asked, though his tone made it clear I had no choice.

'I thought you were tied up in meetings in Washington, discussing ways to harass innocent taxpayers.'

'I'd like to say I flew back first thing after hearing about your friend Keller's column. But the truth is, I'd already landed at O'Hare when I got the news.' He named a Chinese restaurant close to his office and told me to be there at one.

I took a noon train that got me to the restaurant at the tail end of the lunch rush. Krantz was waiting at a table in the corner. A copy of the *Argus-Observer* lay on the table, opened to Keller's page.

I set my rolled peace offering on another chair and sat down. 'No muscle with handcuffs?'

Krantz peered through his reading glasses at the newspaper. 'I love this: "Federal boys bungle."'

'I knew you wouldn't be upset.'

'About you broadsiding a federal investigation, blowing us wide open before we could assemble all our facts?'

'You're not identified.'

He looked over his glasses like I was some sort of exhibit. 'Actually, I suppose I'm pleased. You've speeded things up. As we speak, I have an agent in a judge's chambers. It won't take long to get warrants now.'

'Warrants for what?'

'To search the so-called Confessors' Club at Sixty-six Delaware.'

He'd referred to it by name. 'You knew about it?'

'Of course. Arthur Lamm writes the property insurance for it, and collects a rather sizable management fee for its maintenance. We've known, too, that they gather on the second Tuesdays of even-numbered months. But until now, that's been no cause to go inside and search.'

'Tonight's a second Tuesday.'

'Your reason for going to Keller was to protect your father-in-law?' he asked.

'Ex-father-in-law,' I corrected, 'but no, he's not involved. I did it to make sure nobody got killed tonight.'

'We'll be watching the place to make sure,' he said, 'along with the Chicago PD.'

'The word's out?'

'Maybe not about everything,' he said. 'A private detective was murdered?'

'Eugene Small, hired to do surveillance on the members.'

I had the sense Krantz already knew about Small, like he knew all about the Confessors' Club.

I took the thin roll of paper I'd brought and put it on the table. 'Small's desk calendar. It details the dates, hours and initials of his surveillance targets.'

'How did you get it?'

'Someone dropped it on my doorstep, anonymously.'

Krantz frowned. 'Who hired Small?'

I looked around for a waitress, any waitress, to let me veer away from the questioning by ordering lunch. Only one was in sight, and she was coming toward us carrying two small brown bags.

'I already ordered for us.' He leaned forward across the table. 'Same guy who hired you?' he repeated.

'I don't know who hired Small.'

'I'm going to interview your client as soon as I can.'

'Debbie Goring?'

'Don't be a smart-ass. You're in this because Wendell Phelps hired you. Phelps is a prominent guy. So is his business partner, Arthur Lamm.'

'Not business partner, Krantz. Wendell invested in a couple of real-estate ventures with Lamm. Rich guys do that. To them, it's just playing Monopoly.'

'I've only just started looking, Elstrom. I'll learn more.'

I told him about Delray Delmar, the young cop imposter.

He didn't seem all that surprised, but I supposed by then he wasn't surprised at any of my fumblings.

When I finished, he asked, 'The supposed cop really told you, with a straight face, that his name was Delray Delmar? Wasn't that enough to tip you the guy was a fraud?'

The waitress stopped at our table and set down the two bags. 'To go, so you don't starve,' Krantz said, smiling.

FORTY-EIGHT

I understood the moment I stepped out to the sidewalk. Two Chicago police detectives sitting in a dark sedan waved badges, motioning me over.

The driver gave a smiling Krantz a thumbs-up as he walked away with his little bag of lunch. He'd saved them the legwork of finding Keller's source, even reeled me in by summoning me downtown. Such was his revenge for my calling Keller.

'Mind if I check out your IDs?' I asked the two cops, giving them what I hoped was the intelligent smile of someone newly smart about such precautions.

'Might be a good idea, considering,' said the cop behind the steering wheel, showing me his wallet ID. His name was Pawlowski. The cop riding shotgun was Wood.

I moved a few steps away and called the Chicago police main number. In seconds I received emailed photos of Pawlowski and Wood. I walked back to the car.

'So now tell us,' Pawlowski said, gesturing with his thumb at the back passenger door.

I told them just about all of it, in the car, by the curb, excepting anything about Wendell.

When I finished, Wood sniffed the air. 'We're missing lunch,' he said to Pawlowski.

'You need to work with our artist,' Pawlowski said. 'As we drive, you can give us a better description of this Delray Delmar.'

Wood turned his bulk to look at me sitting in back.

'Chinese,' I said, handing my brown bag forward. Wood opened it, took out the chopsticks, and began eating sweet-and-sour chicken from the white container. He was remarkably agile with the sticks, dropping little as we hit potholes that likely wouldn't be repaired for months, since most tax money, by court decree, was now being given over to replenish the city's looted pension accounts.

I described Delray's thin build and boyish looks for Pawlowski.

'A damned preppie?' Pawlowski asked.

'Right down to his polished Weejun loafers.'

'You ever see other cops dressed like that?'

I couldn't see Pawlowski's tie, but Wood's had a fish on it, right below a fresh speck of sweet-and-sour sauce. 'I took Delray to be typical of your fine fashion expertise.'

Pawlowski glanced at the chewing Wood. Cops have heard most things, from fools, at least twice.

As we headed south across the Congress expressway, I asked, 'How did you two happen to catch this case?'

'Lots of people caught this case. You made us all look stupid.' Pawlowski stopped the car at a nondescript office building a block down from Buddy Guy's blues club. I used to go there, back when I was young, cool and financially stable, and had to look elsewhere to find the blues.

'This is a police station?'

'We're using a freelance sketch artist. Ours got cut back to part-time.'

We got out, went through a tiny, brown-painted lobby to a door marked 'Art School of Chicago.' Adjacent to it was a door marked 'Hair Salon School of Chicago.'

'Budgets,' Pawlowski said.

Looking sorrowful, Wood dropped the empty white food container in an open trash barrel, wiped his hands on his pants, and pushed open the door. The foyer had been converted into a break room, and we took a moment to select those scuffed orange plastic chairs that contained the smallest residues of dried colas.

'I'm still not understanding the fuss about these Tuesdays, and Barberi, Whitman and Carson,' Wood said. 'Heart attack, self-administered overdose, hit-and-run.'

'All three men died after getting together on second Tuesdays,' I said. 'That can't be coincidence.'

'You're saying where?' Wood asked.

I hadn't yet mentioned the Confessors' Club by name, though I figured by now everyone in law enforcement knew it, since Krantz had said it at lunch. He'd also said there would be a heavy police presence there that evening.

'An old graystone at Sixty-six West Delaware,' I said, to be sure. 'You need to have people there tonight.'

'This private dick you mentioned – Small?' Wood asked. 'Who hired him to watch these rich guys?'

'I have no idea,' I said, 'You should send a guy up to sweat information out of Lamm's caretaker, a guy named Herman Canty.'

'And this young punk cop imposter, the one you're going to help us draw a picture of, who hired him?'

'I think Small did. Then the kid started working for himself.'

'He's a killer, this kid?'

'He could have killed Small.'

'Why?'

'To get Small out of the way, so he could shake down someone, likely Arthur Lamm.'

'The kid tricked you into finding this Delaware Street meeting place?' Wood grinned.

'Only the outside. I tricked him back by not finding out much else.'

Pawlowski shifted on his chair, fixed me with the beady eye they teach at police school. 'What's Wendell Phelps, your father-in-law, going to tell us?'

For sure Krantz had passed along Wendell's name. I gave Pawlowski my own beady eye back, the one I practice in the mirror. 'Ex-father-in-law,' I corrected.

'Come on, Elstrom.' Pawlowski smiled. 'What's Wendell Phelps going to tell us?'

'Same thing he tells everybody: his daughter is well-rid of me,' I said.

FORTY-NINE

The sketch artist, an instructor at the art school, finished a passable cartoon of Delray at four-thirty. Pawlowski and Wood took it and disappeared out the door without offering to give me a ride. I didn't object. The Corner Bakery, where I was to meet Amanda, was just a few blocks away.

Jenny had called while I'd been inside. I returned her call once I got out.

'A huge story is coming out of Chicago,' she said, right off. 'A secret society in a creepy old mansion, and dead rich guys exactly like your father-in-law.'

'Ex-father-in-law,' I corrected.

'Is this the case you're working?' she asked fast, still in a rush.

'I blew the whistle.'

'You didn't call me?'

'You're in San Francisco.'

'This story is going national.'

'Conflicting obligations,' I said. 'Old father-in-law.'

'Ex-father-in-law,' she corrected, laughing.

We were well. I told her everything, on deep background.

'And Amanda? You're protecting her, too?' she asked, when I was done.

'Of course.'

'Are you wearing the purple bow tie I sent you?'

'Not at this moment, but I'll put it on when I get back to the turret.'

She said she had to take another call and that we were not done.

'I hope so,' I said.

I walked north. I wanted to feel good. I'd rung the alarm bell, alerted everybody to the danger up on Delaware Street. Cops would soon mobilize there, and every one of the Confessors, wherever they were, would be on guard from now on. Arthur Lamm might be on even greater guard, too, though for different reasons. I still couldn't fathom why that exceedingly rich man would resort to killing for insurance money, if indeed he had. But that was for cop minds to determine, not mine.

With luck, too, the investigations would prove that Jim Whitman had been fed pills. And that might make Debbie Goring the recipient of some insurance proceeds, at last.

And some of that might trickle down on me, but it would feel like dirty rain. Wendell was playing too tight with Lamm. He'd driven Whitman home an hour or so before he died; he'd hired a private detective who'd gotten killed. Wendell's secrets put a darkness over everything, and that might well envelope his daughter. Damn the man, Wendell Phelps.

Keller called. 'I'm going to make you a star, Elstrom.'

'I'm tapped out. You've gotten everything I'm going to give you.'

'Who came knocking after this morning's column?'

'Ours was a one-shot deal. We're done.'

'You're sure you won't need me again?'

'You'll always bite at anything sleazy.'

'The Chicago police?'

'And the IRS,' I said, folding like a paper tent.

'Give me the agent-in-charge.'

'Krantz.'

'What's with Wendell Phelps, your father-in-law?'

'Ex-father-in-law,' I corrected, 'and he's not involved.'

'Wendell's involved; his daughter Amanda is involved.' He laughed, though it was more like a cackle.

'You're a bastard, Keller.'

'Details to follow,' he said, and hung up.

Amanda was waiting in the Corner Bakery at what had been our favorite table, farthest from the window counter, before we got married. She'd gotten me a roast beef sandwich on a jalapeño roll, a Diet Coke and a brownie – my dinner of choice, back in the day.

A copy of the morning's *Argus-Observer*, opened to Keller's column as Krantz's had been at lunch, lay on the table next to her salad.

'This unnamed "agent for a prominent businessman" is you?' she asked as I sat down. Her voice was calm.

'Should I eat the brownie first in case I have to run?'

She didn't smile.

'You've talked to your father?' I asked.

'Mostly he apologized for being absent when I was growing up.'

I touched the newspaper with my forefinger. 'Your father is furious with me, but I had to sound an alarm before someone else died.'

'That club.'

'It needs to be exposed.'

'My father has placed all voting authority of his common and preferred stock in my name. Worse, he's begun transferring owner-ship of the stock itself to me as well. He says it's in accordance with some tax plan his accountants and attorneys had long been planning to put in place, but I don't believe him. He's acting like a man about to die.'

I looked again at Keller's column lying open, a battlefield I'd strung with landmines that even I couldn't see. 'It's going to come out that your father is a friend of Lamm's.'

'I figured Arthur was Keller's "insurance biggie." How exactly is my father involved?'

'I think your father belongs to what's known as the Confessors' Club, a group of wealthy, influential men. I think he hired Eugene Small to tail some of the other club members because he was afraid some of them were being targeted, like Barberi, Whitman and Carson had been. When Small got killed, your father got truly scared. He hired bodyguards. You noticed that anxiety, and pressured him to hire me. He agreed because he still wanted answers, and he could control my investigation. When he realized that Lamm, his closest friend, might be behind the killings, he fired me.'

'My father went along with murder, Dek?' The words came out of her mouth dry and hoarse.

'I'm pretty sure your father drove Whitman home the night he died, which might not mean anything other than it was an act of a friend. I'm also pretty sure your father sent Debbie Goring a hundred thousand dollars anonymously, because she'd gotten none of her father's life insurance.' I tried a smile. 'That seems like the act of a friend, too.'

She turned to look at a family at the next table. The little girl was putting a potato chip in her father's hand.

'I don't understand any of this,' she said. 'What now?'

'We hunker down and let the investigations run their course.'

She leaned back, pulled a tissue out of her purse, and dabbed at her eyes. 'My father and I were estranged, and then we were not . . . I wonder if I know him.'

She didn't ask any more questions, and I didn't offer any more speculation. We ate a little, and talked of other things a little, and then she took a cab to her condo, and I hoofed it to the train station.

And both of us headed away remembering when our evenings didn't end that way and we understood so very much more than we did that night.

FIFTY

D reading that Keller had done a follow-up mentioning Wendell or Amanda by name, I hustled out early the next morning to get the day's *Argus-Observer*. But I did not go out early enough.

I'd just grabbed a paper from the box in front of the Jiffy Lube when two vans with local television logos pulled up in front of the turret. Keller could have identified me in the paper I was holding, or Krantz – or any number of angry Chicago cops – could have made calls. What was certain was that television vans had rolled up. I was now in the light and the circus was about to begin.

Going back directly meant video. I walked a half-mile down on Thompson Avenue, crossed, and came up the river path. The turret has only one door and it faces my stub of a street, so the short stretch around to the front required a sprint. Key in hand, I charged like Teddy Roosevelt up San Juan Hill, unlocked the door and ducked inside before the news folks even thought to set down their lattes.

Angry hands began beating on my door as I climbed the stairs to my would-be office. The red light on my answering machine was flashing. Another light glowed constant: though I'd only been gone an hour, the recording tape had already maxed out. I listened to the first few messages. All were the same. Television and print reporters from as far away as Minnesota were requesting phone interviews. I left the machine full, so it couldn't record any more.

By now the incessant banging on my timbered door had taken on an arrhythmic, irritating quality that set my circular metal stairs, loose at points, to ringing in an unsympathetic vibration that pulsed through my head like an infected tooth.

I have a large gray plastic wastebasket. It is thin, and tall, and rectangular. I used it to catch leaks before I got the roof fixed. I ran into the kitchen, filled it with cold water, and added a long spritz of dishwashing soap for color and bubbles. Forcing away any thoughts of restraint, I cranked open the slit window directly above the entry.

Though lousy for admitting light, my windows are medievally correct for raining down liquids like boiling oil on marauding pillagers. And also, I hoped, for sudsy water. I upended the wastebasket out the window. The frigid soapy water cascaded magnificently down onto the door-bangers, bringing forth much yelling and swearing. The pounding stopped. It had been the minor gesture of an immature mind, and I retreated from the window a satisfied child.

I scanned Keller's column and saw no mention of the Confessors' Club. The day's new allegations concerned short-pours by crooked concrete contractors at a city park. Typical Keller: yesterday's news was yesterday's news. He'd flung a grenade and moved on. Details to follow.

Not so the websites of Chicago's main daily newspapers. All offered up new details, including speculation from unnamed law enforcement types that I was Keller's unnamed agent, recaps of my involvement in the phony-check trial years before, and brief mentions of my marriage to Amanda Phelps, daughter of Wendell Phelps, a wealthy Chicagoan.

None of the reporters had dug deep enough to mention the Confessors' Club by name. Nor were there any references to Delray Delmar, though I supposed Krantz and the Chicago police were keeping a lid on him in the hopes of grabbing him, unawares.

All the reports did note that Agent Krantz of the IRS would be holding a press conference at noon, to discuss matters that bore on the case.

It would be a good day to not answer the phone or look out the window. I put sandpaper into the block, Robert Johnson into the ancient CD player, and worked on rebuilding my most trouble-some kitchen cabinet.

An hour later, a car horn sounded outside. Three blasts, a pause, and three more. It was the secret staccato from seventh grade.

I peeked out the window. Leo and Endora had gotten out of his Porsche and were making their way through a cluster of the now seven news people thrusting microphones and aiming video cameras. Leo wore a black suit, black shirt, white tie and a cream fedora, and looked like a perfect miniature of a twenties-era gang-ster. Endora, much taller, was dressed as a flapper, in a pale blue beaded shift and a red cloche hat. Each of them carried a carton filled with groceries.

I ran down the stairs, ringing the metal. No one bringing food has to wait at the door of my turret. I unlocked it, eased it open a crack.

'Now,' I yelled, tugging the door open all the way.

Leo and Endora ran at the door, laughing. Endora came through, but Leo paused at the threshold. 'Not only did Elstrom grab the Lindbergh baby,' he yelled out, 'but he killed Archduke Ferdinand to start World War One. And I have it on good authority that he's personally responsible for the last two earthquakes that hit California.'

I pulled him in and slammed the door on the shouting news people.

Endora, still laughing at the theater of it, handed me her carton. It was filled with celery, carrots, apples and oranges, bottles of fruit juice, a head of lettuce, and some low-sodium microwavable meals. 'It was my idea to bring you food, since we knew you'd be hunkering down. It was Leo's idea to dress up.'

'Good thing we'd gone to a costume party last fall,' he said, setting his carton on the floor. He'd brought Twinkies, Oreos, Ho Hos, peanut butter and Cinnamon Toast Crunch, and several two-liter bottles of Diet Coke. He is my friend.

'I'll get us coffee,' I said.

'Laced with sawdust?' Leo blew at the dust mites floating in the narrow beams of sunlight crisscrossing the room. 'No. We only drink bathtub gin,' he said, still in character, 'and we don't even have time for that. Endora has to be at work, and I've got a plane to catch.'

They moved toward the door.

'Ready?' I asked.

'Twenty-three skidoo,' Leo shouted, and out they went.

I slammed the door shut behind them and ran up the stairs to watch from the window above the entry. Leo marched towards his Porsche with his arms outstretched like a pint-sized southern governor. He held the car door open for Endora, the perfect moll, who paused to curtsy before getting in. Grinning, Leo went around, got behind the wheel, and drove them away with a loud blast of exhaust.

FIFTY-ONE

Semi-reclined in the electric-blue La-Z-Boy, the micro-television resting on my lap, I was ready. My hands balanced coffee, a stick of celery and a two-pack of Twinkies. It was exactly noon, the time Krantz was to hold his televised news conference.

Krantz apparently wasn't ready. He was late.

The WGN noontime anchor, a trim fellow with a tanned face that likely had never been smeared with a Ho Ho, began to ad-lib to fill time.

'While we wait, we have some . . . ahem . . .' He lit his tan-toned face with a slightly trembling, professionally whitened smile, as though he were about to be overcome by something momentous. '. . . rather bizarre footage, shot earlier this morning outside the residence of one of the people allegedly involved in the newly unfolding secret club mystery.' He nodded at some unseen technician, and the screen switched to tape.

A videocam zoomed in on the window that was opening above the newsmen beating on the turret's door. My face materialized from out of the gloom, pale as Marley's ghost, followed by my hands, then arms, all struggling to tip a thin but obviously heavy wastebasket down at the ground below.

'Vlodek Elstrom,' Tan-tone narrated, 'allegedly a source cited by John Keller in his newspaper column yesterday, apparently took offense to some news people seeking to interview him this morning . . .' Tan-tone paused to let the video carry the spectacle.

On the screen, my arms swiveled to upend the gray plastic wastebasket.

'Whereupon, as you can see, well . . .' Tan-tone chuckled softly, professionally overcome by the ludicrousness of what was unfolding.

The water came. Soapy and glistening, it gushed down in a torrent of a million sparkling colors, drenching the two dark-suited reporters and setting them to jumping up and down and shaking their fists up at the window over their heads.

The usually stern voice of Tan-tone dissolved into perfectly modulated laughter, and was joined by the guffaws of his always jocular sportscaster and the station's newest weather sweetie, a hip Latina. Normally the little news-at-noon band offered fake laughs at the end of the show, to leave their viewers happy despite the murders and war deaths they'd just reported. There was nothing fake about the howls that day. Real tears of laughter were running down their cheeks. I would have laughed too, if it hadn't been me on the screen, starring as the perfect jackass.

'Let's . . . replay . . . that . . .' the almost hysterical voice of Tan-tone managed. But the screen cut abruptly to a shot of Agent Krantz standing at a podium, and I was saved.

'I have a statement, and then I will take questions,' Krantz began, adjusting his reading glasses. 'Approximately four months ago, we began investigating allegations of accounting irregularities at the Lamm All-Risk Insurance Company. Based upon the information we obtained during this careful and thorough investigation, we have now issued warrants for the arrest of Mr Arthur Lamm, charging him with failure to maintain mandated premium accounts, use of premium balances for personal expenditures, illegal reimbursement of political donations, providing illegal discounts, and falsifying policy applications. Other charges may follow.' He took off his reading glasses and attempted to smile. 'If there are any questions, I will be happy to take them now.'

He'd just announced charges for the sorts of business irregularities that never headlined the news and said nothing about what had drawn the reporters: the killings coming out of the graystone on Delaware.

Everybody shouted at once. 'Is Arthur Lamm connected to the secret society?'

'The so-called Confessors' Club?' Krantz asked.

'Confessors' Club?' several people yelled. The name was new to them.

For a moment, Krantz appeared flustered. 'It's what some people call it, I've heard. Mr Lamm's brokerage carried the insurance on the property.'

'That's the only relationship?'

'We believe he also managed the maintenance of the property.'

'Come on, Krantz; this isn't important enough to hold a press conference.'

Krantz shrugged.

'Lamm ran this Confessors' Club?'

Krantz shrugged again.

'Where is Lamm now?'

'As I said, we have issued warrants for his arrest,' Krantz said.

'You're not interested in the deaths of the businessmen and the private eye?' the well-creased political reporter for the local ABC affiliate shouted.

The room went quiet as everyone strained to hear.

Krantz's face acted confused. 'Chicago homicides are never our purview.'

'You're saying you're only investigating Arthur Lamm for income tax?'

'We're the Internal Revenue Service. That's our job.'

'And in this matter, you're only interested in Arthur Lamm?' someone shouted.

'Well . . .' Krantz said slowly, as coy as a young girl in gingham being asked on a first date. 'There is another individual.'

'Give us a name, Krantz.'

'I'll only say that he is a business partner of Lamm's. We're not ready to name him at this time.'

And there it was, squeeze theater, performed for an audience of one: me. Krantz would go public with Wendell's name, and innuendo, unless I got more cooperative.

The shouting got louder. The press was ravenous for the new name and was yelling for more angles into the Confessors' Club.

'Ladies and gentlemen,' Krantz yelled, 'you are asking me questions about murders.' He flashed a humorless smile, tossed out a quick 'Thank you very much' and strode abruptly from the podium.

He'd completed his mission artfully. He'd used a bland statement about the ongoing IRS investigation to limit its responsibility to income-tax issues only. The IRS should not be blamed for any lack of progress in a murder case.

And he'd called out the name: the Confessors' Club.

He was the only one who'd used it.

He'd used the name, too, during our lunch at the Chinese restaurant. I supposed that needed to mean nothing. Krantz was way out in front of Pawlowski and Wood and all the Chicago cops who hadn't yet known the name. He'd been investigating Arthur Lamm for months.

Still, I wondered how Krantz had learned the name. He'd used it so easily, so familiarly, at our aborted lunch. He'd known its members met on the second Tuesdays of even-numbered months. He seemed to have known about Eugene Small, and about Delray Delmar, too.

He'd been investigating for months, I told myself again.

Still . . .

I thought then of how promptly Krantz had dispatched one of his agents to the turret with copies of Lamm's appointments calendar. And the agent's almost dutiful request to see a little more of the turret, and how I'd shown him the second floor, the floor where I worked at a card table, the floor where I did most of my talking on the phone.

I pushed myself out of the La-Z-Boy and went to feel under the card table.

It was just a little bump, a tiny piece of plastic no bigger than a nickel stuck to the underside. I left it alone.

The agent had also gone into the kitchen. The second little bump was stuck beneath a cabinet. I spent the next hour searching the second floor. I found no more.

Two bumps; two bugs. Krantz had been listening to what I'd said on the phone, mostly talking to Leo, but also to Amanda and Debbie Goring. I hadn't said it much, but I'd said it enough: The Confessors' Club, second Tuesdays, even-numbered months. No doubt I'd said other things, too.

I wanted to run down to the river and drown the little bugs, but that would tip Krantz that he'd been discovered, and might prompt him to pick me up to sweat me harder. Better to leave his bugs alone, so Krantz would leave me alone, in hopes he'd hear more.

I thought about spending the afternoon working in the kitchen, trying to soothe my nerves with working wood. But I didn't have the calm for that.

I called Gaylord Rikk from outside.

FIFTY-TWO

'You said you were going to help us recapture our payout,' he said.

'I've got a new lead, but I have to know where the money went.'

'I've been reading between the lines in the papers, Elstrom, and watching television. You're thick in the middle of everything, yet you tell me nothing.'

'Did Arthur Lamm write the policy on Carson?'

'Lamm's agency is huge. He writes a lot of the people we insure. Give me other names, so I can see if we got screwed over with them, too, and maybe I'll tell you a little more about Carson's policy.'

'Benno Barberi, James Whitman.'

I heard his fingers typing at a keyboard. 'No go on both.'

Lamm had spread the policies around, to avoid attracting attention. 'The check on Carson has gone out?'

'Some days ago.'

'Who was the beneficiary?'

'A guy from Chicago PD called just an hour ago, asking the same thing.'

'The police, and not the IRS?'

'The police. Now you. The IRS will be next. Sometimes it takes the Feds longer, is all.'

'Did the cop leave a name?'

'Come to think, no,' he said. 'Just some guy, younger.'

'You knew to stonewall him, didn't you, Gaylord? You didn't give him the beneficiary?'

'I told him that information was confidential, like I'm telling you. He said he'd get a subpoena over, but I'm doubtful.'

'He was no cop, but maybe you already figured that.'

'Damn right I did, just like I'm trying to figure your motives this very moment. Why do you need the name of the Carson beneficiary?' he asked.

'I want to see who's collected on running Carson down. You'd look dumb, Gaylord, if you blew a chance to recover the payout.'

'Meaning what?'

'Meaning you let an opportunity slip by to stop the Carson check.'

'We're an insurance company. We can't go grabbing back checks because there's an insinuation of a crime.'

'Not even from the killer?'

'Oh, hell, Elstrom, I don't want to know anything more,' he said, speaking fast now. 'It was a two-million-dollar term life policy, payable to a Second Securities Corporation.' He gave me an address on North Milwaukee Avenue in Chicago.

'Thank you, Gaylord.'

'Up yours,' he said.

Jenny called me as I headed to that north part of the city.

'Though a most interesting story out of Chicago has gone national,' she said, 'and I've been on intimate terms with the man at the center of it . . .' She faked a cough. 'And I've been anticipating becoming even more intimate . . .' She let her voice trail away.

'I'll tell you almost all of what's new,' I said, and did.

'What about Wendell Phelps?'

'I don't know the truth about Wendell.'

'Do you know your truth about Amanda?' She wasn't asking about the case.

'I think so,' I said, but it might have been after a hesitation.

'You're still coming to San Francisco?'

'Soon,' I said, but I wondered how long it would take to know the truth about that as well.

FIFTY-THREE

I blew past the place twice before I saw the tiny numbers. They were tarnished, almost invisible on a dark brick building wedged between a dry cleaner's and a quick loan place that had gone out of business. I parked around the corner on a residential side street and walked back.

A rusting bracket looked to have once held a barber pole, and the front window next to it had been filled in with glass blocks. The front door was full glass except for the mail slot cut into the metal scuff plate at the bottom. There was no name anywhere, or anything else that made it look like the legitimate recipient of a two-million-dollar insurance payout. I went in.

A young girl, nineteen or twenty, was talking to a glitter-encrusted cell phone that lay on a small wood desk. She was chewing spearmint gum and painting the nails on her right hand with silver glitter that matched the phone, the sequins on her black sweater and the sparkle of the silver studs piercing her ears, nose, and one cheek. Even her dark hair had been dusted with silvery specks. I didn't imagine all that sparkle was problematic during the day, but come nightfall, any driver catching her million glints in his headlights would likely be blinded and driven off the road.

She had no computer, no typewriter, no papers, and no desk phone. The walls were also blank, except for a closed door in the wall behind her.

Her thick eyelashes rose and then sagged, probably from their own caked weight, as I sat on a ripped vinyl chair and smiled.

'I'll call you back, Arnold,' she said, releasing more spearmint into the air. Mindful of her wet nails, she touched a button on her cell phone with only the tip of a glistening little finger.

'Can I help you, sir?'

'I'm here to see Mr Lamm.'

'I'm sorry. We have no . . .' She'd already forgotten the name.

'Lamm.'

'Like in "Mary Had A Little—?"' She ground harder at the spearmint gum, working the thought.

'No. L–A–M–M.'

She shook her head, confused. As she did, she caught sight of her wet right nails, still suspended like pincers splayed up in the air. She laid them down carefully, nails up, on the surface of her desk.

I replaced my smile with an officious frown. 'This is Second Securities Corporation?'

'Just a minute.' With her left forefinger, she hooked open the center drawer of her desk, read something, and said, 'Yes, this is Second Securities Corporation.'

'I'm with the Department of Verification,' I said, trying to intone like Tan-tone did on the news at noon. 'My office set up an appointment with Mr Lamm.'

'I'm sorry, sir—'

'Sorry won't cut it.' I stood to loom over the poor girl. 'If Lamm thinks he can avoid this, he is sadly mistaken.'

'I don't know Mr Lamm,' she said, her chair scraping back on the tile floor as I made for the door behind her.

The faintest of foul smells came as I reached to turn the door knob. It was locked.

'What's back there?'

'A garage full of rats, I'm thinking. Some alive, some dead.' Her voice, frightened, had shot up an octave.

'Where's Lamm?' I demanded, louder than was necessary.

A tear began descending in a black rivulet. 'I don't know any kind of lamb. My ma never cooked it. I'm just supposed to sit here and take in the mail and not look at it and put it in the desk.' She tugged at a right-side drawer handle, mindless now of her wet nails, and pulled it open. It was stuffed with flyers and catalogues. 'Somebody comes by at night to pick it up.'

I reached past her, grabbed a handful. All of it looked to be junk: grocery flyers, ads for cosmetic dentists, sales at a tire discounter. There were no first-class business envelopes in the pile.

'This looks like more than a day's worth,' I said, handing it back.

She took it, sniffling. 'They must be on vacation. They haven't been by for a few days.'

'I have to get in back,' I said.

My cell phone rang. I pulled it out.

'Dek?' It was Amanda. Her voice was high pitched, almost shrill. 'An Agent Krantz—'

'Department of Verification,' I said officiously, for the glitter girl's benefit.

'Dek, he says—'

'Hold please,' I said, cutting her off again. I nodded curtly to the glitter girl and started for the front door. 'Tell Lamm I'll be back. He can't hide forever.'

'Tell him yourself,' she sniffled behind me. 'I haven't been paid in over a week, and I don't need this shit.'

I strode out, pompous and erect, a bully. And sure of the obvious: Second Securities was a front, a mail drop, a place set up only to receive an insurance payout.

I clicked Amanda back on. 'Sorry; I was role playing.'

'An Agent Krantz just phoned . . .' More words came, but they were muffled, indistinct, lost to the traffic rumbling along Milwaukee Avenue.

'Yell, Amanda,' I shouted.

'He says my father's going to jail!' she screamed.

FIFTY-FOUR

Amanda's condo tower is for the very rich. She'd called down to the guards in the lobby, and one of them whisked me right into an elevator. Amanda was waiting for me in the hallway outside her door.

'I just don't know what's going on,' she said, 'but I figured I better get away from the office in case Krantz showed up.'

'Your father is stonewalling everybody.'

'But why?'

'Arthur Lamm is his best friend?'

She nodded.

'I just came from Second Securities, a mail drop Lamm set up to receive insurance payouts like the Carson check. There was a girl there, a receptionist, who doesn't do anything except wait for the mail and put it in a desk drawer. I don't like the set-up; it's crooked. I'll go back after dark for a more thorough look around.'

'You think this has to do with my father?'

'I think I'd like to know how close he is to Arthur Lamm.'

'Let's go to Second Securities now,' she said.

'The girl will still be there. I'll go alone, tonight.'

I didn't want Amanda along. My mind, or rather my nose, had slipped back to that noxious smell coming from behind the locked door at Second Securities. It could have been rats. It could have been something else.

She stood up, grabbed her purse and her cell phone. 'I have a plan for her.'

There was no mistaking the resolution on her face.

'Good deal,' I said.

Thirty minutes later I sat in the Jeep, waiting. I'd parked at the edge of a drugstore lot, mostly hidden but angled for a good view of Second Securities across the street. Amanda had gotten out a block away, so she could walk up to the drugstore alone.

Amanda came out of the drugstore. With her back turned to the building across the street, she stopped at the trash receptacle on the sidewalk to thumb off the price stickers before dropping the lipsticks into the small case she'd brought. When she was done, she turned and, without a glance at me, crossed Milwaukee Avenue. It wasn't a sophisticated plan, but we didn't have time for sophistication: she was selling cosmetics, door-to-door, and anxious to hire an assistant, even a gum-chewing, glittered-up assistant, right on the spot.

She pulled the door handle at Second Securities, and stopped. It was locked. She pressed close against the glass to peer in and began knocking. After a moment she started to turn away, but as she did her purse fell out of her hand, spilling its contents against the door. Making a gesture of disgust, she knelt down, her back to the side-walk, the street, and me. She took an incredibly long time to pick up her things. Finally she stood up, and walked down Milwaukee. I started the Jeep and followed her around to a side street.

'Nobody home,' she said, getting in. She was perspiring lightly.

'Let's drive around, check for a back door.' I started to pull away from the curb.

She held her hand out. 'We'll use the front door, like we were invited.'

I hit the brakes. In her hand was a key.

'I got lucky,' she said. 'I saw the key through the glass, lying on the floor. There's a mail slot at the bottom of the door. It took me forever to fish it out.'

'I scared the girl away,' I said.

'Enough for her to drop the key back inside the mail slot before she took off.'

'You wait in the Jeep while I go inside.'

'We'll go together,' she said.

'Let's check around back first.' I drove around to the alley. There was a dented, gray steel garage door at the rear of Second Securities. I jumped out quickly and gave the handle a tug. The door was locked from the inside.

'Likely enough, the garage is full of rats,' I said as I got back in the Jeep.

'I don't care. We're going in together,' she said.

Remembering what had appeared to be a solid interior door leading to the garage in back, I drove to a Home Depot we'd passed a mile down Milwaukee Avenue and bought a short jimmy bar, a sixteen-ounce claw hammer and, after a second's consideration, a pair of thin work gloves for her, a pair of thicker yellow rubber gloves for me. I wasn't only thinking fingerprints; I was recalling smell.

I parked on the side street. Amanda put the Home Depot things in her purse and we marched up to Second Securities like we had an appointment. A turn of the glitter girl's key and we were in.

The place still smelled of her spearmint chewing gum and cheap perfume, but the other smell – the dead smell – had grown stronger in the hours that the place had been shut up.

Amanda sniffed the air. 'What is that?' she whispered.

'Rats, as I told you,' I said. After a moment's hesitation, I switched on the overhead fluorescents and pointed to the desk. 'Sit at the desk like you belong and search every inch inside for an envelope with a check in it, even behind the drawers. Try to keep your hands out of sight because I want you to keep your gloves on. If anybody comes in, say your friend asked you to fill in for the day.'

I didn't expect Amanda would find anything; Lamm would have grabbed the Carson check by now. But I wanted her away from whatever wasn't right in back.

I took the hammer, gloves and pry bar from her purse.

'Maybe I should first go with you, to the back, to help you . . .' She stopped as I shook my head. She didn't want to follow that smell, not really. She put on the thin gloves I'd bought for her.

I pulled on my own gloves and went to the door.

I slipped the jimmy bar between the door and the jamb, just above the lock, and struck it with the hammer. The solid-core door splintered around the lock at the fourth blow, releasing the scent of hell.

Behind me, Amanda caught her breath. 'Oh, Dek, that's not rats.'

I pushed open the ruined door. Enough light filtered in from the office to show a car shape at the center of the garage. I found the light switch and closed the door behind me. The overhead fluorescent fixture buzzed, sputtered and caught.

The car was several years old, a small, white two-door Ford made faintly green by the fluorescent light. It was filthy, except for the crumpled front fender that was strangely dulled.

I walked up to it. Fine scratches crisscrossed the damaged fender. Someone had flattened the car's finish with steel wool. Likely, I thought, to remove Grant Carson's blood.

The car's doors were locked, and it had no license plates, no temporary dealer tag or windshield parking stickers. It could have been bought for cash in a bad neighborhood, or simply stolen.

The garage was stuffy and hot from being closed up. Trying to breathe in only through my mouth, I pressed against the glass to look inside. The interior appeared empty. Whatever was fouling the air wasn't coming from the passenger compartment.

I turned away from the car and swung the hammer backwards, exploding the driver's side window into a million tiny green-edged bits. I opened the door and was brushing some of the glass off the seat when Amanda stepped into the garage. She'd heard the shattering glass.

'Dek?'

'Go back. If anybody comes, keep them in front.'

She didn't argue.

The dead smell was worse inside the car. A key was in the ignition. I took it out and went around to the back. The key didn't work the trunk. I leaned back into the car, replaced the key in the ignition, and searched beneath the seats, under the floor mats and in the glove box. There was no second key, nor any interior trunk release.

I slid out. The trunk seam was narrow. Jimmying the bar into it only slightly bent the lid. I'd have to go in through the back seat to see what was dead in the trunk.

I climbed in behind the driver's seat and began hacking at the back of the rear seat with the claw end of the hammer. The vinyl upholstery came away in chunks, still attached to its foam padding. The rank smell of death came at me stronger with each new blow, sticking thick in my throat and nose. I whacked faster at the seat back; I wouldn't be able to stay in the car much longer.

The last of the upholstered seatback tore away, but the metal springs behind it wouldn't budge. They'd been fastened tight with a pneumatic wrench on an assembly line.

I swung blindly at the rear shelf now, crazed by the ever stronger foulness rising from the trunk. The fiberboard dented and at last split apart. I ripped at the pieces, threw them out of the car, and reached down into the trunk.

I touched cold metal, ribbed and hard. Reaching past it, I found something just as cold, but not quite as hard, wrapped in thick plastic. My gut twisted. It was what I knew I'd find. Rigor.

I pulled my hand back, felt again the cold metal. It was a case of some sort, wedged between the seat back and the corpse. I found the handle and tugged it through the hole where the rear shelf had been. It was an aluminum metal briefcase. I dropped it on the front passenger seat and stuck my hand back into the hole.

I was sure I was touching death, perhaps days old. I felt along its shape, found a shoulder, and then the curve of an arm locked in place, unyielding. And a knee, tucked up under the chest.

I wanted to run, get free from the stench, the death. But I had to know. For myself. For Amanda, more.

I sunk the teeth of the hammer's claw into the plastic shrouding the death, ripping it. The purest fumes of hell came at me, searing my nose, constricting my throat, pulling up bile. I held my breath, afraid I'd vomit. I found a belt and followed fabric – denim, wool or cotton; I couldn't tell through the yellow gloves – past a dead hip to the small raised square that I was hoping to find. A wallet in a back pocket. An answer.

I eased it out with my fingers, backed out of the car, and dropped it on the hood. I poked it open with my index finger. The driver's license was in a plastic window.

Herman Canty, PO Box 12, Bent Lake, Wisconsin.

The body exhaled behind me, a soft sound of gas escaping through the rips I'd made in the plastic. I grabbed the metal case from the front passenger seat, left the wallet behind, and ran to the ruined door that led to the office.

FIFTY-FIVE

'Oh, hell,' Amanda said after we'd sped down the first mile of Milwaukee Avenue. 'I forgot to leave the key.' She looked stricken at the thought we'd have to drive back and slip the key through the slot in the door.

After the briefest glance at the cash inside the metal case, we'd fled Second Securities unnerved, sick from the smell of death, barely able to remember to lock the door behind us.

'Put it in the ashtray,' I said. 'I'll get rid of it later.'

'Why did we take all that money?' she asked, gesturing at the metal case I'd tossed in back. Her hands shook as she dropped the key in the ashtray.

'To see who comes after it.' It was all I could think to say. I had no plan that involved grabbing cash. I hadn't expected it would be there. 'Canty must have been Lamm's partner in running down Grant Carson. Lamm must have killed him to silence him for all time, then left the money with the corpse, thinking it would be safest there, while he went north to tidy up a last detail.'

'What last detail?'

'Canty's girlfriend, Wanda. Lamm must be thinking Canty told her some things. Do you know how to block your number when you make a call?'

'Sure,' she said.

'Get the number of the sheriff's department near Bent Lake.

Leave an anonymous tip that Wanda over at Loons' Rest might be in trouble.'

It only took her a couple of minutes. Then she asked, 'I still don't understand: if Arthur needs money badly enough to kill for it, why risk leaving it in that garage?'

'Guys like Lamm and your father, they don't fly commercial, right?'

'Lear jets, chartered out of Midway Airport,' she said.

'Then Second Securities is the safest short-term place he knows. Nobody knows about it except Rikk at the insurance company . . .' I let the thought trail away.

'Dek?'

'And anybody else he might have told. He swore he didn't tell Delray when he called, posing as a cop. But you never know.'

'Does that matter?'

I thought for a moment, and said, 'I don't think so. Delray's got to be thinking the check was picked up and cashed somewhere. I'm pretty sure the only person who's going to be shocked at Second Securities is Arthur Lamm, when he comes back. He'll be light the two million dollars he needs for fleeing in a corporate jet.'

'Are you going to tell Krantz to keep watch for Arthur to show up at Second Securities?'

'I owe your father more than that. We're going to tell him about the money we just found. That ought to make him talk about his friend Arthur.'

'And then?'

'We find a way to give it to the cops without implicating your father.'

'Damn it,' she said. 'I wish my father didn't get rid of his security detail. Too much cash is being tossed around.'

'He believes he has nothing to fear from his old friend Arthur.'

'I'm going to call my father when we get back to my apartment.'

We drove in silence for another five minutes, until she told me to pull over in front of a discount men's clothing store.

'My treat,' she said. I stunk of the death I'd found in the small battered Ford, and I'd torn one knee of my khakis, ripping my way into the car trunk. She was out with a bag in five minutes, and we were back on our way.

Upstairs in her condo, she handed me the bag.

'Ah, new duds,' I said.

'But the same you,' she said. 'Cheap khakis, de rigueur blue button-down shirt in cotton polyester, socks and underwear. Thirty-six fifty for the whole outfit. Once you've showered, you'll smell and look like new.' She forced a nervous laugh, but she was firing on all pistons, in control. 'Guest bath is waiting. While you're showering, I'll call my father, see if we can meet him in an hour or so.' She handed me a paper bag for the clothes I was wearing. 'Incinerator chute is outside, in the hall.'

Shampoo and soap were in the shower; I needed nothing. Yet previous lives occasionally demand a fast indulgence. Inside the medicine cabinet were wrapped bars of soap, two fresh tubes of toothpaste, a sealed toothbrush, and nothing else. Most especially, there was no man's razor, shaving cream, or deodorant.

She'd mentioned Richard Rudolph, socially impeccable silver-haired hedge fund manager and investor, only in passing, saying he was in Russia, doing a deal. I'd mentioned Jenny the same way, just as reluctantly and also only in passing. I'd supposed our vagueness was normal, an offering of respect for the past and probably nothing more.

Now, in her guest bathroom, surrounded by her soaps, her linens, things didn't feel so firmly rooted in the past.

I opened the linen closet, looking for a towel, and got a soft jolt. An inch of familiar red and blue striped terry showed bright behind the stack of white towels. I pushed the towels to one side and was sure. It was the robe she'd bought me right after we married. That she'd kept it wanted to set off too many conflicting thoughts, and I showered trying not to think about any of them.

I emerged twenty minutes later, studiously scrubbed, garbed in fresh polyester and smelling swell. I dropped my paper bag of clothes into the incinerator chute down the hall, came back, and went into the kitchen. She'd made us coffee, and set cups on the kitchen table.

'My father is in meetings,' she said.

'I'll leave the two million here,' I said. 'You've got all the building security it needs.'

We drank the coffee, then she walked me to the door and told me she'd call as soon as she heard from her father.

FIFTY-SIX

Amanda didn't call, and I fiddled away all of the next morning and the earliest part of the afternoon on the Internet. News sites everywhere had seized upon the graystone they were all now calling the Confessors' Club, used only six times a year for the secret meetings of wealthy men. Facts were in short supply, so many of the reports offered Keller-like speculations of wild drunkenness, sexual debauchery, political manipulations and, of course, murderous plotting. It seemed that the farther the news organization was from Chicago, the wilder was the prose it used on its website.

Close to home, the reporting was more responsible. The *Tribune*'s site ran a story about the IRS investigating Lamm next to a history of the Confessors' Club, leaving no doubt that the two stories were related. The IRS story reported the likelihood that Lamm had high-tailed it out of Chicago to escape his impending indictment. Unnamed federal authorities, Krantz or one of his subordinates, said that the search for him had shifted to Sarasota, Florida, where Lamm had another home, and to a small, unnamed Caribbean country, where he might have transferred funds.

The Confessors' Club article was historical, and featured a photograph, taken around 1900, captioned as being the only one known to ever have been taken of its members. It showed thirty men, in high collars and walrus mustaches, sitting stiffly at the long dining-room table, staring unsmiling into a camera that must have been set up in the parlor. The story noted that no record had been found of the club ever participating in civic or charitable endeavors, despite the prominence of its members, and seemed to have always conducted its activities in secret.

There were short sidebar biographies of Barberi, Whitman and Carson, noting that the deaths, though still presumed to have resulted from natural causes, excepting Carson's, were being re-examined as part of the Lamm and Confessors' Club investigations.

No site mentioned Delray Delmar, or offered the police artist's sketch of Delray I'd been hauled in to help create. The lid was still tight on the cop imposter. I supposed it didn't much matter. It was the other stuff that was big news, and no real news at all.

Amanda called at two-thirty, but not with news that we were to meet with Wendell. Her words were perfectly precise with rage. 'The man from the IRS is now here at my home. He's the one who called yesterday. He says his name is Krantz. I'm wondering if you might stop by.'

'What's he saying?'

'Sleazy innuendo that I'd rather you heard first-hand.' Undoubtedly Krantz was within hearing distance.

I told her I'd get there in a hurry, and I did. She was waiting out in the hall. We shared a brief hug and I followed her inside.

Agent Krantz was standing in the center, looking tiredly at the framings on the wall. If he knew art, he recognized the names on the oils. If he didn't, chances were he at least recognized the bold signatures on the big Manet and the small Renoir. And if he didn't know a Manet from a Monet, like me before I met Amanda, he still would have guessed from the heavy security in the building that he was staring at big-dollar art.

'Ms Phelps has been educating me about light and brush strokes, and backgrounds and shadows and colors,' he said to me, instead of saying hello. He turned to Amanda. 'May we proceed now, Ms Phelps?'

Amanda ignored him and smiled at me. It was a smile that could have cut steel. 'I asked Secret Agent Krantz if—'

'That's *Special* Agent—' Krantz cut in.

'Whatever.' Amanda changed her smile to a glare. 'I asked this *man* if he wouldn't mind waiting until you got here, Dek. I didn't want you to miss one word of his slimy accusations.'

'Now wait . . .' Krantz started to protest again, but Amanda had already turned to go into the kitchen. Krantz and I followed and sat at the table. It was the one she'd had at her multi-million-dollar house at Crystal Waters before it blew up – cheap pine, poorly enameled, and chipped from years of use. If Krantz took any meaning in being led from fine art to sit at a garage sale table, he didn't show it. Coffee that smelled fresh came from a high-end

Braun maker on the counter. Amanda, an able gameswoman when angry, sat down without offering to pour us any.

Krantz took a long breath, which only built more tension in the room, and began. 'I stopped by to ask Ms Phelps if she knew where her father was. Ms Phelps told me that she did not. I asked her if she knew about her father's business relationship with Arthur Lamm. Ms Phelps said she wanted you here. I've just spent thirty-eight minutes learning things I do not need to know about fine art.'

Amanda cut in before I could answer. 'Secret Agent Krantz is implying all sorts of things—'

'That's *Special*—'

'Wendell is missing?' I asked Krantz.

'My father often travels on business,' Amanda cut in.

'According to his housekeeper,' Krantz said, 'he never went into the office this morning. He threw clothes in an overnight bag and left about eight o'clock, telling her he'd be gone for one or two days.'

'Secret Agent Krantz is implying my father fled town rather than speak to him.'

'I was to interview Mr Phelps this afternoon at his office,' Krantz said. 'When I got there, I was told he'd left. Ms Phelps confirms she hasn't seen him today.'

'He's only been gone for a few hours. Our offices are on different floors,' Amanda said.

'When did you set up the appointment?' I asked.

'Day before yesterday, Tuesday.'

Tuesday, Confessors' Club day.

'You talked to him directly, to set up the appointment?' I said.

'It took a while to get past all the secretaries, but yes.'

'How did he sound?'

'Unappreciative.'

'How about today? Did you speak to his wife?' I asked.

'Apparently his wife didn't see him leave. She was home at the time, but off . . .' He paused to look at Amanda, perhaps afraid she'd come across the table at him if he used the wrong words.

'Tending pigs,' Amanda said.

'Exactly,' Krantz said, wincing only a little. 'I only spoke to the housekeeper.'

'Secret Agent Krantz is implying that my father took off to avoid being questioned,' Amanda said.

Krantz sighed. 'I merely informed him of his responsibilities when we spoke, day before yesterday. We're not much interested in this so-called Confessors' Club, the murders that were supposedly set in motion there, or even why your fingerprints are everywhere inside, Elstrom.'

I started to say something, offer up some lie about why I'd failed to mention I'd been inside the graystone, but he waved it away. 'The Chicago police are pursuing all that, Elstrom. I want to interview Mr Phelps because of his shared business interests with Mr Arthur Lamm.'

'My father serves on many boards,' Amanda said. 'And he bought shares in some of Arthur's real-estate ventures.'

'Your father bought half of Lamm's insurance brokerage last fall.'

Shock widened Amanda's eyes. It linked Wendell to the insurance agency's enormous IRS problems. Worse, though Amanda couldn't realize it yet, it tied her father to any killings Lamm might have done.

I rested my hand lightly on her wrist. 'Buying into an insurance agency doesn't link Wendell to any of Lamm's alleged frauds.'

'For Christ's sake.' Amanda stood up and walked out of the kitchen. A moment later, a door closed down the hall.

Krantz looked at me across the chipped table. 'As I've been saying, we've been investigating Lamm for all sorts of tax law violations. It's not hard to imagine he was also instrumental in the deaths of James Whitman and Grant Carson, but that's for the cops. Our focus is on income tax evasion, and that must include Wendell Phelps, because he owns half of Arthur Lamm's brokerage.'

'But you said Wendell only recently bought into the agency.'

'Phelps is tight with Lamm, damn it. He owns half of his insurance brokerage, belongs to the same secret club. Lamm has gone missing. So has Wendell Phelps. Even if Phelps is completely innocent, Lamm is dragging him down. Phelps can help himself if he tells us what he knows.' He leaned back in the chair. 'As can you, Elstrom.'

'Meaning what?'

'That Confessors' Club on Delaware Street.'

'How is it you knew its name before anyone else?'

'We've been investigating Lamm's activities for months,' he said, lying, with an impressively straight face.

'Maybe you should have tipped the cops about that club. Maybe you could have saved lives.'

'Maybe you should explain what you were doing inside.'

'I went in with a guy I thought was a cop.'

'Where the hell is Phelps?'

'I don't know.'

'Where's the supposed cop?'

'*Supposed?*'

'Maybe he doesn't exist,' Krantz said.

'Why don't you get the cops to release the sketch I helped their artist develop?'

'They're touchy about someone passing as one of their own. They think people will end up not talking to any of them.'

Delray had gone to Wendell's house, but I didn't want to bring Wendell any closer into this conversation. 'The kid posing as Delray Delmar is real. Whitman's daughter spoke with him,' I offered instead.

'Your fingerprints were on pewter mugs left on the dining-room table in that graystone.'

'Delmar had me take them off a wall rack. He left them out so they'd be printed.'

'CPD also pulled your prints off a lot of doors.'

'Delray was careful to leave no fingerprints of his own. He was setting me up to become a fall guy, someone to pin everything on.'

'Why?'

'Maybe to use as leverage, to get me to do something.'

'What?'

'I have no idea.'

Amanda came back into the kitchen, but stood facing the coffee maker, as though waiting for Krantz to leave before she poured herself a cup.

Krantz stood up. 'Encouraging Wendell Phelps to come forward will deflect some of the glare off you, Elstrom, and help your father, Ms Phelps.'

I walked him out because the set of Amanda's back showed she wouldn't turn around to look at him.

At the door, Krantz looked at his watch. 'I'm thinking twenty-four hours.'

'Until?'

'Until I ask the Chicago police to pick you up for questioning. They can lose records long enough to sweat you for forty-eight hours if I tell them you're withholding information in their murder investigation.'

'That's crap.'

'That's notoriety for your ex-wife, and legal fees you can't afford.' He stepped out into the corridor. 'Play tough with me, Elstrom, and there'll be "details to follow," to quote your favorite columnist.'

I slammed the door as he walked, whistling, to the elevator.

'You left us to call Lake Forest?' I asked, coming back to the kitchen.

'My father raced out of there this morning with a suitcase, just as Krantz said. No one's heard from him since. Delores is frantic.'

'Did he leave by cab?'

'No. He drove himself.' She took coffee cups from a cabinet and was about to pour coffee when suddenly she shook her head. She set down the coffee pot and reached over to the counter for a corked bottle of Shiraz.

'In that tan Buick?'

She spun around. 'Why shouldn't my father give Jim Whitman a ride home? They were friends. They served on boards together.'

'As I said before, giving Whitman a ride home the night he died doesn't mean your father killed him.'

'My father was better friends with Arthur,' she said, her voice quieting.

'I don't like your father buying into Lamm's insurance brokerage.'

'Arthur must have really needed money.' She smacked the bottle hard as she started to fill one of the coffee cups. 'Where's my father?'

'No wine for me,' I said. 'I'm driving.'

She looked up, startled. 'Where?'

'The only place I'm thinking your father would need to take a suitcase.'

'Bent Lake,' she said.

FIFTY-SEVEN

My first run north, by borrowed Porsche, had been a breath-taking mix of German engineering, fast speeds and precise, road-hugging turns. I'd had time, and something of a plan.

Now I was clattering to upper Wisconsin in an aged Jeep Wrangler that shook and trembled in perfect accompaniment to the fear and confusion playing tag in my gut.

I'd lied to Amanda. I had no belief that Wendell was innocent of anything. He and Lamm were friends, going way back. Some sense of loyalty, or just as possibly some sense of greed, might well have gotten Wendell to fold himself into whatever Lamm was up to, including buying into the scams Lamm was running from his insurance brokerage.

I could only blunder around blind. I'd ask around town to see if anyone had seen Wendell, or Lamm. I'd confront Wanda, the hostile girlfriend of the dead Canty, or at least see if the sheriff's department had protected her from Lamm.

Only as a last resort would I come up on Lamm's camp to see if he, or Wendell, was there.

Amanda demanded two things before I left her apartment. The first was that I take the two-million-dollar Carson payout along to Bent Lake, for no other reason than Arthur Lamm wanted it and it might be leverage, somehow, in keeping her father safe.

Her second stipulation was simpler: if any danger arose, I was to call Krantz.

I phoned when I got to within an hour of Bent Lake. She answered on the first ring.

'No word from my father,' she said.

I told her I might lose cell phone contact in a few miles, hung up, and went back to hoping Wendell wasn't involved up to his neck in whatever Lamm was doing.

I got to Bent Lake later than the last time. It was now pitch black. The used-to-be service station was closed, its concrete island, shorn of pumps, looking like a casket vault left low and forgotten in the shadows. Of more interest was the phone booth next to the service bays. It had been awhile since I'd seen one, but then again, it had been awhile since I'd been any place where cell phone reception was considered so unpredictable.

Like last time, though, the Dairy Queen across the street was bright with lights and lust, and the same carb-swelled high school lovers were framed, embracing, in the order window beneath the yellow bug lights. Such was their intensity that neither looked up as I drove by.

I passed by the neon Budweiser sign beckoning in the middle of the block and pulled to a stop in the gravel lot of Loons' Rest. As I'd feared, it was dark. But there was a note handwritten on lined tablet paper taped to the inside of the front window. 'Closed for a while,' it read. 'Off for New Adventures.'

I drove back to the gas station, parked in the dark next to the pay phone, and took the aluminum case for a walk to the bar down the block. My footsteps echoed off the deserted store fronts, loud and alone, though I imagined the Bent Lake Children's Club would soon come to fill the evening air with joyous sounds of beating brooms and stomping feet. It felt like a night for death all around.

The same three flannel shirts were perched at the bar, talking with the bartender. All four remembered me. In appreciation, I slapped a five-spot on the bar and bought short beers for the house.

'Come back for more excitement?' the beard behind the bar asked. I wondered whether he knew I'd been shot at during my last visit, or was just being witty. I played it like he was a comedian.

'The excitement's already started,' I said. 'There's a note taped at Loons' saying it's closed.'

'Wanda and Herman took off,' the bartender said.

The faces above the flannel shirts nodded in agreement.

'Who would know where they went?'

'Who would want to?' the bartender asked.

The flannel shirts laughed.

'I don't suppose Arthur Lamm's been by?'

The bartender shook his head.

'How about this guy, drives a tan Buick?' I set an Internet photo of Wendell Phelps on the bar.

The bartender's eyes narrowed. No longer was I some fisherman pal of Lamm's. Now I was a guy asking too many questions.

I laid another five on the bar for a second round, and tapped the photo. 'This is my girlfriend's father. He's a friend of Lamm's, too. I think he came up here looking for him.'

The bartender relaxed, and they all shook their heads. The second five-dollar bill disappeared, and more beer was poured.

I put the photo back in my pocket. 'I'm afraid I know the answer to this, but is there a place I can stay for the night?'

'Yep,' the bartender said. 'Chicago.'

That brought outright guffaws from the gents in the flannel.

'How about the ski lodge?' Red Flannel asked.

'Closed by now, I think,' Green Flannel said.

'No place within thirty miles, mister,' the bartender said. He poured me another beer, set it next to the second I hadn't yet touched. 'On the house. Just kidding about the Chicago part.'

'No offense taken,' I said, and took a sociable sip of one of the beers in front of me. 'You're sure there's nobody watching Loons' for Wanda, someone who might rent me a room?'

'Like I said, she ain't got nobody,' the bartender said, 'exceptin' Herman.'

'Best I get looking for a room elsewhere,' I said, getting off my stool.

'What you got in that metal case, mister?' one of the flannel shirts at the end of the bar asked as I started towards the door.

'Two million in cash,' I said.

It dropped them. They were howling as I walked out.

FIFTY-EIGHT

I went back to the Jeep. Across the street, past the bug bulbs and the greasy plastic of the order window, the young man stared deeply into the girl's eyes as his hand rustled at the pulled-out hem of her DQ blouse. I envied him his youth and his certainty that miracles could be touched so simply.

I drove to the sheriff's office. A different deputy was on duty.

'I'm looking for this man, Wendell Phelps, drives a tan Buick.' I handed him the Internet photo of Wendell.

'Who might you be?'

'His son-in-law. If you need to verify, you can call his daughter.'

He shook his head. 'What was he doing up here?'

'Looking for Arthur Lamm.'

'Man, that Lamm must be in some big-time trouble. Federal guys called about him a couple of days ago. Likewise a Chicago cop, all of them wanting us to look around. I went to his place myself. Lamm wasn't there.'

'I heard his car is there,' I said, like I didn't know.

'Damn shame, a fine Mercedes taking bird doo, tree sap and stuck bugs.'

I held up Wendell's picture again. 'Any chance you or the sheriff could run out to Lamm's place with me tomorrow, take another look for this guy?'

'Your father-in-law is law enforcement?'

'He's just a friend of Lamm's.'

'He got Alzheimer's?'

'No.'

'Then no can do. There's just me, another deputy, and the sheriff. We got plenty to keep us busy, busting up bar fights and scraping drunked-up teenagers off the roads, without looking for Chicago people who might be up here, visiting friends.'

At the door, I turned back to look at him. 'I was hoping to stay in Bent Lake, but I heard the woman who runs the motel might have run off with Lamm's caretaker, some guy named Herman.' I tried to make it sound easy, like I was just making conversation.

The deputy grinned. 'Don't that beat all? They been rocking the cot back of Loons' office for damn near ten years. Now, all of a sudden, they get the urge to see the world? Don't know a thing about it, mister.'

'You don't suppose they're in trouble?'

'Am I missing something? I thought you were up here looking for your father-in-law.'

'Where's the nearest place to sleep up here?'

'This is a dead time, too late for snowmobilers, too early for summer people. Lots of places closed.'

'How about the ski lodge?'

'Oh, they're always closed up by this time of year. Best you call around, if you can get your phone to work.' He was done providing information.

It was dark like it never got in Rivertown, except inside closets. I drove back to Bent Lake along deserted roads, unchallenged by anything except an occasional stop sign and hundreds of pairs of eyes, low to the ground, watching me from the edges of my headlight beams like I was dinner.

Bent Lake had become a veritable festival of beacons since I'd left for the sheriff's office. White lights swarmed along the sidewalk like frenzied giant fireflies. The young broom beaters were out with flashlights, aiming up, then after a little jig, down at the soles of their boots, to admire what they'd turned to goo.

I nosed the Jeep back into the darkness alongside the gas station and found, by jockeying the Jeep around a little, that I could raise enough service bars to use my cell phone. I called Amanda.

'Anything?'

'Nothing.'

'I haven't found anyone who's seen your father, which I'm hoping means he didn't come up here. I'll have a good look around tomorrow.' I gave her the number of the pay phone. 'In case my cell phone gives up from weak reception, I'll hear the pay phone from the Jeep.'

'That's not the number at the motel?' she asked.

'I'm sleeping in the car, next to a pay phone. Wanda is not here.'

'Dead?'

'Not so anyone has noticed. She left a note taped to the window, implying she's run off with Herman.'

'Is that town safe?'

I glanced down the street, at the white lights of flashlights crisscrossing up into the canopies. 'This place is so quiet, the teenagers bring out brooms at night, just for something to do.'

'Just be careful,' she said, too distracted by worry to tell me I must be exaggerating, and hung up.

Romeo and Juliet separated when I materialized into the DQ's yellow light. Juliet came to the order window, hurriedly jamming her wrinkled blouse into her jeans.

I showed her the picture of Wendell Phelps, said he drove a tan

Buick. She shook her head twice. Romeo came to the window and shook his head, too. They were earnest and nice and so focused on each other that they wouldn't have noticed Attila the Hun thundering by with his herd of marauders.

I had two burgers, fries and a chocolate shake at the picnic table, and left weighted sufficiently to withstand even the fiercest of windstorms, should one arise. I climbed in the Jeep and fell asleep more easily than I would have thought, beside the aluminum case that, until recently, had shared its nights with a dead man.

Despite a thunderstorm that rolled in, I slept almost until six the next morning, when my cell phone beeped with a text message: *Still got my picks?*

FIFTY-NINE

For sure, the guy had brass in his pants.

Delray? I typed.

He messaged back instantly: *good name as any*

Who are you?

u took

Turn yourself in.

u only 1

I don't understand, I texted, but of course I did. Either Delray was working with Lamm, or he'd found out about Second Securities on his own, perhaps through Rikk. No matter; he'd known to go to Second Securities, to look for cash. But what he'd found was a splintered door, a trashed Ford, and the realization that, with my extensive insurance company contacts, I'd gotten the address of the Carson beneficiary, and beaten him to the money. I shivered, realizing we must have missed each other by only a few hours.

u bring, he wrote.

Bring what? I texted, still playing dumb.

we trade

For what? I wrote, like I didn't know.

wp

And there it was. Likely enough, Wendell had driven right into his own abduction.

I'll have to call Wendell, I texted.

noon bl will tell u where then

I don't understand, I wrote again.

wp not where u think

I need more time.

He didn't respond. He had gone.

I called Amanda.

'Delray's in it with Lamm. They've got your father.'

She inhaled sharply. 'How do you know?'

'Delray just texted me. They want to trade your father for the payout, up here at noon.'

She paused, thinking. 'We should call Krantz?'

'They've anticipated that. Delray wrote that your father's not where I think he is, meaning not at Lamm's camp. Since there's two of them, they can operate from two locations.'

'What do we do?'

'We've got a big advantage. They don't know I'm already up here. That buys us six hours, time enough for me to sneak out to Lamm's camp, to see who's around before I call the sheriff.'

For a minute, only the rain made a sound. 'You're sure this is the best way?'

'If I knew that, I wouldn't have spent the night sleeping in a leaking Jeep in the rain.'

SIXTY

A faded brown Chevy Malibu pulled into the DQ and parked next to the overhang above the restrooms. I needed that overhang, too, and I needed hot coffee. I drove across the street, wondering what the hell I was doing, considering a new kind of insurance.

A fiftyish woman with stringy blonde hair dangling limp from her scalp and an unfiltered cigarette dangling just as limp from her mouth got out of the Malibu and ran for the door as I pulled up, covering her mouth so the rain wouldn't extinguish her smoke. I backed up as close as I could to the overhang.

I got out when the inside lights came on and jumped over the growing puddles to the order window and tapped on the plastic. She nodded and slid open the window, offering up the smell of old grease and new cigarette smoke. I ordered coffee and eggs on muffins. I wasn't hungry, but I needed to get her away from the window long enough to work at the back of the Jeep. She told me in a hoarse voice that the griddle wasn't warm yet. I said I could wait, and went around to the side, first to the Jeep, then, after five minutes, to the men's room. It was puddled too, though I did not linger to determine whether that had resulted from the rain. Fresh from a cold water rinse of my face – there was no soap – I went back to the order window. My coffee was sitting outside on the counter, cooling in the downpour. I took the cup to the picnic table under the side eave, sat, and watched the red clay beside the cement slab dissolve and run toward the road.

'Up here fishing?' the woman rasped through the screen.

I went to press as close as I could to the window, out of the rain. 'I came up here looking for a guy who came up here looking for a guy.'

'Huh?'

I showed her Wendell's picture. 'Have you seen this man?'

'He was here,' she said, lighting a fresh unfiltered Camel. It was the same brand Debbie Goring used to hoarsen her own voice.

'You saw him?'

'Yesterday. I worked a long shift.'

'He drove a tan car?'

She nodded. 'Parked right where you did, ordered coffee.'

'At night?'

'Huh?'

'He came in at night?'

She exhaled smoke. 'I don't work nights. Teenagers work that shift because they like to screw when things are slow.'

'Afternoon, then?' That would have fit, time-wise. Krantz had said Wendell packed a bag at eight in the morning.

The Camel hung limp from the edge of her mouth, confused.

'The man came in the afternoon?' I repeated.

'About three o'clock. Not that I mind a little screwing.' The

Camel was rising between her lips. Her eyebrows had risen, too. Her hair, though, stayed limp.

'This man, did he say where he was headed?'

'I don't expect much,' she added, after giving me a head-to-toe look.

I had to look away. 'Anything you remember will help,' I said to the clapboards next to the order window.

She pointed down Main Street in the direction of the road to Arthur Lamm's fishing camp. 'He gave me a five-dollar bill, told me to keep the change, and shot out of here like his britches were on fire.'

I nodded. It was not hard to fathom.

She went to pull my two egg muffins off the grill. She wrapped them in paper, slid them through the little window. I gave her a five-dollar bill, and told her to keep the change because I was no slouch either.

She said I owed another buck seventy-five.

SIXTY-ONE

T he rain came down in sheets of gray glass beads, dissolving my headlight beams into mist and blurring the trees alongside the road into seamless dark curtains. Every few seconds, great jagged spears of lightning gave me enough of a snapshot of the narrow gravel road ahead to speed forward another hundred yards before everything went dark again, and I had to drop back to my snail's safe crawl.

So it went, for an hour, until a fresh flash of lighting lit the tall, narrow Tinker Toy shape coming out of the gray. The rickety bridge was twenty feet ahead. I downshifted to first gear, unzipped the driver's curtain so I could see to orient myself with the left side rail, and eased onto the old wood. Lightning flashed again, bringing a huge stutter clap of thunder that shook the ancient span like loose sticks. The rail next to me swayed in the sudden light. It was barely a dozen feet above white caps frothing in roiling water. The river was rising.

Ice needles blew in through the open curtain, stinging my face as I watched the rail to my left. It was the only way I knew to drive straight. But drift too close and I could catch a front tire, knock the left side loose and plunge over the side. Drift too far the other away, I might hit the right rail, and drop off that side.

Lightning flashed; I was halfway over. I squeezed the steering wheel tight and, holding my breath, punched the car forward. After what seemed like an hour, my tires crunched gravel. I'd made it across.

Still, I dared speed up only when lightning cracked to give me a view. Finally, at what seemed like the twentieth flash of lightning, or perhaps the hundredth, the fire lane appeared for an instant. I stopped, downshifted into the ultra-low gear that off-road Jeep crazies use to assault steep hills, and waited. At the next flash of lightning I gunned the Jeep down into the slush of a gulley and up through the gap in the trees, and cut the engine as the woods darkened again into invisibility. I could only hope I'd pulled far enough in to conceal the Jeep from the road.

I found my black knit hat under the passenger's seat, but left behind the yellow poncho. Yellow would light me up like neon every time lightning flared. Telling myself that courage can only be strengthened by adversity, I stepped out into the rain.

There was a thick tree fifteen paces directly perpendicular to the Jeep's right front wheel. The soft loamy compost at its base went deep enough to easily bury the aluminum case. I pulled back the loam, dropped the case, and covered it with wet leaves. By now my khakis and shirt were soaked clear through with freshly strengthened courage.

Though the rain was beating harder, louder, the woods felt suspended beneath the din, as if every living thing within it – every bird, every squirrel, every insect – was holding its breath in fear of what was about to happen.

I ran to Lamm's camp. My footfalls barely sounded above the rain invading the trees, but to my ears now every twig snapped like a gunshot, every breath called out as loud as a shout.

The Mercedes rested in its same place, still filthy with its fuzzy carpet of sap, pine needles and a thousand pats of green-white bird guano. But here and there the hard rain was loosening the crusted blanket into spots of bubbling paste that had begun to run down the sides of the car in dirty little rivulets, like the car had become something evil, molting, shedding its skin.

There were no other cars there, no tan Buick. The clearing and the back of the cottage appeared deserted, yet something flashed bright in the gloom, down by the water. Staying inside the trees, I moved to the shore. An orange rowboat with an outboard motor attached to its stern bobbed high, despite the rain, at the end of Lamm's dock. I edged closer to see into the water. The barely floating boat I'd bent to look at last time, the instant before I'd been shot at, had gone. Canty had said it had been a second boat. I hadn't believed it then; I didn't believe it now. There'd been no other boat. Someone had bailed out the one I'd seen earlier, attached an outboard motor, and used it to go off somewhere.

'We're gonna be rich!' a man screamed in a strange, singsong voice from inside the cabin.

I crouched, and moved back deeper into the woods. I knew the voice. It was Delray Delmar, no doubt yelling at Wendell.

I pulled out my cell phone to dial 911. There were no bars. No service.

I backed farther into the woods. Still no bars.

I did the minutes in my head. Fifteen to run back to the Jeep, maybe forty-five minutes to make it through the storm either to the sheriff's department or to the pay phone in Bent Lake. No matter which way I chose, the sheriff might not get there for two hours.

Still, the cops would arrive well before noon, when Delray told me I had to be up in Bent Lake.

'Son of a bitch!' Delray screamed.

I turned to run back into the woods, to the Jeep.

A bolt of lightning lit the dark sky, and a second later, thunder shook the ground.

A gunshot fired.

I turned around, charged the back door, twisted the knob and shouldered it open.

And got clubbed on the back of the neck with a million-pound bat.

SIXTY-TWO

I came to on my belly, trussed like a hog. My wrists were tied together behind my back with rope that was then crisscrossed down to tug up my ankles before it was knotted behind my knees. A blanket was thrown over my head. I could barely breathe through the suffocating wool. I couldn't see a thing.

'Dek Elstrom to the rescue.' The unnaturally high voice giggled faintly.

'You're a shit, Delray,' I said to the floor.

'You've brought treasure?' His voice was skittish, insanely wrong.

'Wendell Phelps.'

'The money, honey,' Delray sang.

'Wendell,' I called into the floor.

In an instant, a steel rod, likely the barrel of a gun, was jammed through the wool into the center of my neck. It surprised me. I thought Delray was across the room.

I didn't resist, concentrating instead on keeping my body loose. There was play – an inch, maybe two – in the rope. Tugging would only tighten the loops around my wrists and ankles.

He pressed down on the big knot. Pain like I'd never known shot through my shoulders and legs as they were drawn closer together. I shut my eyes, and tried to focus on sucking more air through the wool.

'The money!' Delray screamed, so seemingly distant. Strangely, he'd said nothing about me arriving hours early.

'Wendell!' I shouted. 'Tell me where he is, and I'll tell you where I've got the money.'

He pressed harder on the knot, ripping new pain into my shoulders, knees and legs. But there had been a lag for just a fraction of a second. For sure there was play in the rope.

'The money,' he called out in that faraway voice.

'Wen—'

A gun fired just above my ear, shattering glass somewhere and filling my head with thunder.

I yelled fast, for surely Delray had gone insane. 'Follow the road to town, go into the fire lane. My Jeep's there. I buried the case at the base of a tree, fifteen paces perpendicular to the right front wheel.'

'See?' Delray shouted from far away. 'All is good!'

Footsteps, loud in heavy boots, thudded across the plank floor. The door creaked open.

The gun fired twice, something thudded, and the door slammed shut.

The thud, I was sure, was the sound of a body falling. Wendell.

'Damn you to hell, Delray; damn you to hell,' I managed, in little more than a whisper, beneath the wool. 'Damn you too, Wendell; damn you as well.'

I had to get away. Delray would come back to kill. Ten, fifteen minutes was all he'd need to get to the Jeep, walk off the paces, paw through the leaves and find the metal case. He'd check it and he'd come back, wild-eyed and furious, eager to torture. He'd want everything, and then he'd want me dead.

'Delray!' I shouted, to be sure.

No answer. He was gone. I was alone, but only for a few minutes more.

I tried to roll up onto my side, to shake away the suffocating blanket. Pain tore at my shoulders as the weight of my legs tried to tug them from their sockets. I teetered up for only an instant before I fell back on my belly, still covered by the blanket, and now even more desperate for air. I counted one, counted two, and lunged again. This time, I made it up on my side and held. The blanket fell away.

He was slumped against the front door. Laying on the floor, all I could see were his pants, his shoes. And the fresh blood puddling back toward the center of the room.

I took in a breath, and another. Another precious minute had gone, maybe two. Delray was pacing off the steps to the tree by now.

I flexed my shoulders back. Daggers shot deep into my back and arms, but the rope slipped an inch. I flexed again and my legs dropped another inch. I raised them back up, as tight to my back as the pain would let me. It was enough. The rope slacked enough to get my thumbs inside the loop around my wrists.

My mind flitted to the dark fury that would be contorting

Delray's face when he returned. I bit at my lip, pushed the image away, and kept working my thumbs. They were numb, unfeeling stubs, but somehow the cord around my left wrist loosened even more, and then my left hand slipped free. I pulled the cord from my right wrist, and then from my legs. I almost wept.

I rolled onto my knees and started to stand. Too soon. I fell back. I crawled across the room.

The body had two gunshots: one to the head, one to the heart, leaking red on the floor.

Not Wendell.

Delray Delmar looked back at me through dead eyes.

SIXTY-THREE

There was no time to make sense of it, only to get away. Surely Lamm – for it had to be Lamm; Wendell wouldn't hunt me – was coming back with hellfire in his eyes. By now he knew what I'd done.

I staggered out the front door on trembling legs, braced for the sudden bark of a gun, the cold fire of a bullet tearing into my skin. Incredibly, nothing sounded in the now softly falling rain. I still had a minute, maybe more. I looked back. The Mercedes was still parked there; he'd gone through the woods. I hobbled down to the water and into the trees, for it would be the fastest way back to the Jeep. I could only hope to spot him and drop down before he saw me; he had the gun.

I stumbled into a jog along the shore. When Lamm returned to the cabin and saw I'd escaped, he'd race back to the Jeep. He'd run better than me, quicker. I had to get to the fire lane first.

Sooner than I dared hope, the red of the Jeep appeared faintly through the gray of the rain. I dropped to the sodden ground and crawled the last few yards to see.

To my left, the fire lane stretched clear back to County M. It was lined thick enough with trees to hide anyone waiting to squeeze a few shots into the Jeep. But Lamm couldn't be there. He'd be racing back to the cabin.

I moved forward a few yards, enough to see that the leaves had been clawed from the base of the tree. Lamm had found the aluminum case. He would have opened it, to be certain.

He would have seen.

I ran for the Jeep, holding the ignition key in front of me like a sword. Jumping in behind the wheel, I fired the engine and ground the gears, shifting loudly into reverse. The Jeep slammed back into a tree, killing the engine.

I spun around to look. The spare tire was pressed too hard against the tree. I jumped out; I had to know. The spare was still solid on its bracket. Back in, I restarted the engine, and shot up the fire lane and onto the gravel of County M. My tires grabbed at the stones, spraying them back into the wheel wells, rat-a-tat, like machine-gun fire that must have been loud a mile away.

Though the rain had slackened, County M was even more blurred now with fog, and Lamm was somewhere close by, in the murk of it, enraged, with a gun. There was no time for caution. I sped into the gray, foot hard on the gas, arms rigid, not daring to use my headlamps for fear of giving him lights to shoot at, wherever he was.

I'd gone only a few hundred yards when headlamps rose up faint out of the mist at the side of the road ahead, like some dim-eyed primordial beast trying to claw itself free from a steaming swamp. I slowed as the car in front teetered up at an angle, its fang-like grill aimed at the sky, shaking and rumbling before its front end dropped, its wheels caught, and it lurched forward, kicking back dark spray like it was venting its own entrails. It fish-tailed for an instant, straightened and took off down the road.

It was a tan car with dark, tinted windows. A Buick.

Lamm, in Wendell's car. Or Wendell himself.

I pressed down on the accelerator and switched on my head-lights. He was going to damned well see my face.

Red brake lights flashed for an instant; he'd spotted my headlamps.

He sped up, surging and sliding on the gravel, fighting to keep the car straight, speeding forward. I pressed down harder on my own accelerator. Jeeps aren't worth much on highways. They vibrate like blenders, chuck and skitter at the smallest bumps and potholes. But shifted into four-wheel drive, on the loose marbles of County M, the Jeep charged straight forward like it was on rails.

The distance between us closed; three hundred feet, two hundred feet, then a hundred. From somewhere close by, I heard a man yelling. Only in the next second did I realize it was me.

Fifty feet separated us when the Buick's window powered down. A pistol came out, wavered, then steadied, pointing backward at me. It might have fired, I couldn't tell. We were speeding through gray mist, and I was deaf to everything except the gravel blasting up beneath the Jeep and the rain beating on my hood and vinyl top.

His tapped his brakes, slowing for a steadier shot. I dropped back a few yards and tucked in directly behind him. The gun recoiled once, and again. No starbursts appeared on my windshield; no glass exploded. I was in his blind spot. He sped up. We raced on.

County M dipped us into low-lying thick fog for an instant, and then the road rose up. And when it did, the black, spindly one-lane wooden bridge filled the soft rain in his headlights. His gun wavered, firing back at me. He wasn't looking ahead.

His brake lights flashed. He'd turned and seen the frail timbers rushing towards him, but it was too late. He hit the right edge of the bridge at thirty miles an hour. The Buick reared up like a frightened horse, then slammed down hard on the loose planks and inched forward, its still-spinning front wheels tugging him tighter against the right side rail.

Some faint part of my brain shouted to slam on my own brakes: I was charging a one-lane bridge that was already filled with a car. There was no room.

But I, too, had gone insane, at least a little. I needed vengeance. I had to see the eyes of the man who'd trussed me like a pig, the man who'd just tried to shoot me. And he had to see mine.

I aimed for the narrowing space between Wendell's Buick and the rickety rail to my left. He had to go over the right side, to crash on the boulders below.

I hit him on his left rear fender, sending up a thousand sparks as the Jeep tore into the Buick. I tugged the steering wheel all the way to the right and pressed harder on the accelerator, grinding the Jeep further up into his car. The sagging side rail only a foot to my left was too frail to prevent my own plunge to a wet death on the boulders below.

It was no matter. I fed the Jeep's engine more gas; he had to die. But my wheels wouldn't move. The Jeep and the Buick were pinned between the uprights at the entrance to the bridge, trapped together like they were welded.

The Buick groaned as it shifted forward. His right front wheel dropped off the right side of the bridge. He turned to look back over his shoulder at me, wide-eyed and frantic.

It was Herman Canty, and he was seeing the Devil and his own death reflecting off my eyes.

He pulled at his shift lever, struggling to raise it into reverse. Lurching backward would be his only escape.

The whine of my engine was deafening, the stench of my spinning tires acrid in the rain. The Buick slid forward another foot. He let go of his steering wheel, turned for something on the seat.

The gun.

I tugged harder at my steering wheel. Only another foot or two would send him off the bridge, but the Jeep's wheels were spinning uselessly. I shifted into ultra-low, the mountain-climbing gear, and let out the clutch. The Jeep shuddered for an instant, and then began grinding slowly forward, one inch, then two, pushing the Buick farther off the edge.

Wood snapped, not loud, but almost gently, and the right side rail beyond his windshield fell away.

Canty didn't see. His hand had come out with the gun. I ducked down below the plastic passenger curtain, keeping my right foot on the gas pedal, my left above the brake, tugging the steering wheel hard to the right to keep grinding into the Buick. A shot ripped through the plastic curtain, another sparked off the roll bar above my head.

And then the Jeep lurched forward several sickening feet. I slammed on the brake and pulled myself up, terrified I was about to plunge over the right side.

The nose of the Buick had slipped all the way off the bridge and was angling slightly downward toward the rocks in the river below. The frail wood uprights to either side of the teetering car were snapping away almost lazily, one after the other, as the Buick was slowly being tugged off the bridge by its own gathering momentum.

Canty had dropped his gun and was scrambling to push himself out of the driver's side window. His eyes locked on mine, pleading, begging.

A great new scream of ripping wood filled the air and the entire right side of the bridge fell away. The Buick's nose went down after it, the car's trunk rising now like the stern of the *Titanic*, gently, almost beautifully. The Buick creaked, and settled backward, its left rear tire catching between my bumper and my hood, stopping its slide over the edge.

Canty was now halfway out of the open side window, not four feet from my face, kicking at the steering wheel to propel him the rest of the way out before the car fell into the river.

His frenzy shifted the balance of the Buick, and it again began moving slowly over the edge. The Jeep began sliding with it, hooked by the Buick's rear wheel.

I jabbed hard at the brake, but it was no use. The Jeep was going over the edge, too.

I fumbled open the driver's door and pushed myself backward out of the Jeep. Fire shot up my left arm as first my shoulders, and then my back hit the planks. I dug my heels into the wood and scrabbled backward, kicking back from the carnage.

Herman Canty was still only halfway out when the car's trunk rose up to the sky. Gravity had trapped him, pulling him back into the car.

The Buick's front door disappeared over the side as its rear wheel, rising higher, gave a last tug at the Jeep's bumper and then broke free. The Buick's rear bumper vanished over the side of the bridge.

Canty screamed until the car crashed onto the rocks.

I lay on my back, frozen in the new, sudden stillness, afraid to move. The rain beat down on me as the river frothed high beneath the planks. At some point I reached to touch my left arm and found sticky wetness. I'd been shot. I'd not ducked down far enough. I laughed.

After a time I stood up and walked along the center of the bridge, careful to look only forward until I got safely to the solid ground on the other side. Even then, I walked another ten feet before I dared to turn around to look at the river below.

The Buick lay upside down, pinned between two boulders in the churning, swollen water. Its roof had been crushed by the fall.

I am told that I pulled off my belt and cinched it around my left arm above where the blood was the stickiest. I don't remember. Nor do I remember the man in the flatbed truck who slowed behind me as I wobbled down the middle of County M, by then a mile from the bridge. He saw the blood on my shirt and the vacancy in my eyes, and raced me to an emergency medical clinic in a town I'd never heard of.

SIXTY-FOUR

While I was being stitched up, an enterprising nurse thought to try the last numbers in the call memory of my phone. She got both Leo and Amanda. They drove up together and arrived at the clinic about the time the sedatives began to lift.

Amanda sat beside my bed and took my good hand. Leo sat in the corner, a blur of tropical colors.

'I don't know about your father,' I said to her – but I did, or at least I was afraid I did.

She didn't ask whether I was talking about Wendell's whereabouts or his complicity in Arthur Lamm's crimes. She merely sat for a moment, silently squeezing my hand like she was afraid of letting go. I told her to go find a sheriff's deputy, to see if they'd learned anything. I wanted to talk to Leo, because I was running out of time.

Agent Krantz materialized in the doorway before I could say a word. He must have been lurking in a side corridor, waiting for Amanda to step out.

'You got here fast,' I said.

'It is standard procedure to notify the sheriff about a gunshot wound. This particular sheriff remembered you'd stopped by, asking about Lamm and, more interestingly, your father-in-law.'

'Ex-father-in-law,' I corrected.

'The sheriff also remembered our own inquiry about Arthur Lamm's whereabouts, so he called me. I've filled him in with some particulars, but I've left my concerns about you vague. For the time being, he's agreed to let me be your only law enforcement contact.'

'Feds trump locals,' I offered.

'Every time.'

Leo got up from his chair and came to stand by the bed.

Krantz made a show of looking closely at Leo's clothes. Leo was wearing an outrageous medley, a shirt of pink parrots and lavender orchids on a yellow and black background, lime green trousers, and brown-and-white wingtip shoes with orange soles. 'You are?'

'Mr Elstrom's advisor,' Leo said.

'Advisor for what?'

'Haberdashery.' He fingered the hem of his shirt, having noticed Krantz's scrutiny of his duds, and then said, 'Along with everything else.'

'Does this seem eerily familiar?' I asked Leo.

Leo smiled, whitening the entire room with teeth. He, too, was remembering Sweetie Rose. 'Same state, different cop.' He turned to Krantz. 'We've done this before,' he said, signaling we had previous practice and were real sharpies at admitting nothing to law enforcement officers.

Krantz frowned and turned to me. 'He's quite odd,' he said as Leo went back to sit in the corner.

I shrugged as best I could using only my right arm, the left having been shot. 'I need him to speak for me because I've been sedated and can't be responsible for anything I say.'

'You're worried about vehicular manslaughter?'

'Nah.'

Krantz sat down in the chair Amanda had vacated. 'We have no body.'

I started to sit up, but the torn ligaments in my legs, and my shot left arm, tugged me back like I was on a leash. 'What the hell, Krantz?'

'We found a handgun and an aluminum case full of money, but no sign of Canty.'

'He was stuck half out of the driver's window when the car went over.'

'We don't yet know if it was Canty, Lamm or Phelps who was driving that Buick.'

'Why would I lie?'

'To protect Phelps.'

'Let's not talk until you find Canty's body.'

'Relax,' he said. 'I believe you. That river is running fast from the storm, and it might take a while to find him downriver, or in one of the lakes that feeds off it. But when they do, they'll compare his fingerprints to those on the gun they recovered. The bullet they took out of your arm also looks to match one found in a dead young man in Arthur Lamm's cabin, and together they will tie to the gun. You're in the clear, Elstrom, so tell me everything.'

'I went to Lamm's camp, looking for Wendell, and got clubbed going in the door,' I said. 'I woke up to hear someone firing a shot, but I was trussed and covered by a blanket. I couldn't see anything.'

'Why were you left alive, Elstrom? Why didn't Canty shoot you, too?'

I'd expected he'd ask that one. I couldn't admit it was because Canty needed to be certain I'd brought up the Carson cash, so I said, 'Charm,' because it was all I could think to say.

Only Leo laughed, from the corner.

Krantz pulled out his smart phone, selected a picture. 'This is the young man we found in Lamm's cabin.'

It looked like an Illinois driver's license photo. 'Delray Delmar,' I said.

'Richie Bales,' Krantz said. 'A small-time repo man out of Chicago Heights. He did collections and auto repossessions. Ring any other bells?'

It rang a big bell. 'He must have been the "R.B." on the calendar I gave you.'

'Phelps hired Small, and Small hired Bales,' he said. 'For what?'

'As I've told you, Wendell never told me who he hired, but I do believe it was for surveillance. Wendell's friends were dying. His goals were noble; he wanted to stop it.'

'Wendell Phelps killed Small, for what he found out.'

'There you go again, fencing with me about Wendell. Someone else killed Small, for what he found out.'

'Who?'

'Either Arthur Lamm, because Small discovered his scheme, or Canty, on Lamm's orders, or Richie Bales, to get Small out of the way so he could extort big money out of Lamm.'

Krantz reached for the little bronze-colored Thermos on my bed tray and poured coffee into the matching bronze cup.

'No coffee, thanks,' I said.

Krantz smirked and took a sip. 'Arthur Lamm's brokerage wrote insurance policies on the lives of Benno Barberi, Jim Whitman and Grant Carson, each in the amount of two million dollars. Remember who owns half of Lamm Enterprises?'

'You told me in Amanda Phelps's kitchen.'

'Your father-in-law, Wendell Phelps,' he said anyway.

'Ex-father-in-law,' I corrected anyway, adding, 'Wendell's the good guy in this, Krantz. I think he bought half of Lamm's brokerage to help out an old friend who had problems.'

'Money problems?'

'IRS problems.'

Undeterred, Krantz went on 'Each of those life insurance policies was from a different company, but they all named something called Second Securities as beneficiary. It's not listed as a business anywhere, but I'm thinking you've heard of it.'

Once Krantz got a whiff inside Second Securities, he'd open up the small Ford, see he had another murder on his hands, and come at me like a locomotive if he suspected I'd been there and hadn't admitted it. And come at Wendell, because of his half-share in Lamm's insurance agency, if Wendell was still alive. I needed to talk to Leo.

'I've heard of it, yes,' I said, feeding out some truth in case Krantz's agents had already questioned the glittered receptionist.

'Phelps told you about Second Securities?' he said, watching my face, still testing.

'I got the name from an insurance company contact.'

'Did you get an address?'

'I'll check my file.'

'Cut the crap, Elstrom. Second Securities is on Milwaukee Avenue in Chicago. They wired the Barberi and Whitman payouts to a bank on Grand Cayman. That money is gone. But the Carson check was converted to cash at an outfit laundry in Chicago.'

'An *outfit laundry*?' I asked, as though I'd never heard the term for a mob-controlled bank that converts checks into cash for people with connections.

'We're thinking that since Lamm's been hiding out, it was likely his partner Phelps who ran the check through the laundry.'

'You're trying to pin things on the wrong guy, Krantz.'

'If Phelps is so innocent, then where is he?'

'Maybe dead,' I said, thinking of the car at Second Securities. I really needed to talk to Leo.

A faint, smug smile had formed on his face. He might have had more against Wendell; he might have been bluffing. I wanted to smash that smugness with a hammer, but all I had were words.

'You put a brick on Lamm's passport?' I asked.

His smile broadened from smug to obnoxious. 'Some trouble with Homeland Security.'

'Bricking Lamm's passport was your way of preventing Lamm from going to Grand Cayman to get at the Barberi and Whitman payouts?'

'Four million, total. Damned shame,' he said.

'When did you put the brick on his passport?'

'First of this year.' He wanted to crow.

'Wait until Keller reports that you singlehandedly got Carson killed six weeks later. You made Lamm hang around to kill again – Carson this time – for new getaway cash. If you hadn't bricked Lamm's passport, he would have been long gone to Grand Cayman, and Grant Carson would still be alive.' I smiled. 'Details will be following.'

The maddening smile flickered, but not his self-righteous calm. His hand was steady as he poured himself more coffee. 'About that Carson cash . . . that money I said we found in Phelps's Buick?'

'A million.'

Leo shifted abruptly in his chair, Krantz's smile widened, and I knew, in an instant, that I'd slipped.

Krantz pounced. 'I never said how much was in that case.'

'I've been sedated,' I offered, too feebly and too late.

'I just told you the Carson payout was for two million, Elstrom. We found only half of that in the Buick. We're thinking that was Lamm's share, fifty per cent, which Canty got by killing Lamm. Question is: who's got the other million? Answer: Wendell Phelps.'

'Wendell doesn't need a new million. He's got hundreds of them already.'

'It was Phelps's car you pushed in the river.'

'That day you called Wendell, to set up an interview?' I asked.

'He blew me off.'

'How hard did you lean on him? Did you threaten him, tell him he would do time for Lamm's crimes?'

'I might have.' Still the bastard smirked.

'You set Phelps off like a live grenade, Krantz. He didn't simply skip his appointment with you. Most likely, he charged right up here to confront Lamm, a man who'd been his friend for years, for setting him up. Knowing Wendell just a little, he probably planned on throwing Lamm in his trunk and driving him back to Chicago to deliver to you.'

'Nice try, Elstrom. Phelps didn't leave until two days after we set up our appointment. Phelps came up here to collect his half of the Carson payout.'

'Then Richie Bales enticed Wendell to drive up to help his old friend. Remember, there was nothing on the news that Richie, the infamous Delray Delmar, was impersonating a Chicago police officer when Wendell took off from home. So far as Wendell knew, Delray Delmar was a real cop.'

'You're trying awfully hard to come up with excuses for your father-in-law.'

'Find Lamm. And find Wendell, if you can find him still alive.' I looked away.

'We're getting warrants to search Second Securities,' he said, to the back of my head.

'Enlightenment looms,' I managed, through teeth that surprisingly had not started chattering.

Amanda came into the room.

Krantz, the gentleman, stood up. 'Ms Phelps,' he said.

'Secret Agent,' she said.

Krantz turned to me. 'I'm going to think about what you've told me,' he said. 'Very carefully. I'll be back tomorrow.'

He nodded at Leo and Amanda and started to leave. But he stopped at the door. 'Any news about your father, Ms Phelps?' he asked.

She frowned. He left.

'There's a ski resort two miles outside of Bent Lake,' Amanda said. 'Plenty of rooms.'

'I heard it was closed,' I said.

'They were thinking about closing for the season, but changed their minds when I said we'd need lodging.'

Leo's eyebrows rose.

'Dek won't be staying there at all,' she said, mock-frowning at Leo, ever the romantic. She turned to me. 'Leo and I will stay there tonight. The doctor said you can leave tomorrow. Leo will drive you home and I'll stay on up here, until something is learned about my father.'

'I'm getting out of here now,' I said.

'You can't,' Amanda said.

'You're nuts,' Leo said.

'I'm ready,' I said, because now I had no choice.

SIXTY-FIVE

It was night, just past nine o'clock, before I got out of the clinic and then only with dire warnings of my likely demise from infection.

'I expected Amanda would be hauling you back to Rivertown horizontally, like truck-smacked venison,' Leo said, explaining the long Cadillac Escalade he'd rented for the drive up. Amanda had parked it behind the Jeep at the front of the clinic.

'I don't know if I trust you driving my Jeep back to Chicago,' I said.

'It's a wonder it still runs,' he said. 'Or why.'

I maneuvered myself up onto the Cadillac's passenger seat and handed him my crutches to toss in back. My wounds weren't much – a gunshot that missed bone in my left arm and ligaments torn in both legs from straining to throttle the Jeep into the Buick while trying to lie beneath Canty's gunfire. But working the Jeep's clutch and shifter was out of the question for a couple of weeks.

'You noted the extent of the Jeep's damage?' Leo asked, trying for light as I closed my eyes, waiting for the pain to go away. 'To restore it to its previous, uh, condition, you'll have to find a used fender in cracked, faded black plastic; a used front bumper, also faded black, but in rusted metal. You'll need a radiator cover and a hood in the same tarty red, if you can find one mottled with enough of the aforementioned rust to match the rest of your heap. The whole repair shouldn't set you back more than two hundred bucks.'

Amanda would be coming out at any moment. 'You forgot to take off the spare tire,' I said.

'Ah, yes, the spare.' He left me to hustle forward in the Escalade's headlamp beams.

Amanda came out of the clinic holding a big white envelope with my medical instructions and pills. She went up to Leo, who'd taken out a lug wrench and was removing the Jeep's spare tire. He shook his head and jerked a thumb back at me. She shrugged, gave him a hug, and came to slide in behind the wheel of the Cadillac.

'He won't tell me what he's doing,' she said.

'Putting my spare tire into the back of this thing for the night,' I said.

He came back and tossed the Jeep's spare in the back of the Escalade.

'Why?' she asked.

'The tire is out of air.'

'Is that supposed to make sense?' she asked.

'Must be the meds,' I said, patting my pockets like I was missing something. 'I think I left my phone in my room.'

'I'm not sure they should have released you,' she said, managing a laugh. She went back inside.

Leo shut the rear door and came around to the passenger side.

'You're clear on what to do when we get to the ski lodge?' I asked.

'Let me do it alone. It'll save me another round trip up here.'

'The less you know . . .'

'You're being irrational. It's Lamm in the trunk of that car at Second Securities.'

'Who knows what Canty and Delray were thinking? I have to be sure it's not Wendell, and if it is, I want him moved, away from such a link to Lamm.'

He gave it up. 'That nurse that called Amanda and me?'

'Yes?'

'She also called Jenny's cell number. Jenny called me from

California, and made noises about flying in. I said you'd had a
slight accident, nothing serious.'

'I'll call her when I'm done.'

'If we haven't been arrested.'

I held up my phone as Amanda came outside. 'Had it after all,'
I lied, by way of explanation.

'Meds,' she said, accepting, and we drove away.

Fifteen minutes later, she pulled to a stop under a stone-pillared
canopy. The resort was old, made of logs darkened by tens of
decades of winters and moss-covered, rough-hewn roof shingles.
She told me it had gently sloping halls, a restaurant with wide
booths, and firm leather couches that were easy to get out of. They
were used to people on crutches.

'I can bird dog the sheriff by myself,' she said, for the fifth
time.

And I agreed, for the fifth time, telling her I knew she was
perfectly capable of harassing the sheriff until he found her father.
Her worst fear, and my second-worst fear, was that Wendell was
lying dead somewhere in the surrounds of Bent Lake.

They walked, and I hobbled, to the registration desk. The lobby
was deserted.

'You said three rooms for tonight, then two for the next week?'
the desk clerk asked.

From old habit, Amanda hesitated. So did I. So did Leo.

'That's correct: three for tonight, then two,' she said.

'As I told you on the phone, I can only do coffee, cold cereal
and milk in the morning,' the desk clerk said. 'Our handyman
goes home at three. After that, I'm the only one here until the next
morning.' She smiled at me. 'You'll have the run of the place,'
she said to me, offering a joke about my crutches.

Amanda said we'd manage. She and Leo were given rooms
down the long hall, in the new wing. The desk clerk gave me a
room just four doors past the lobby, saying it had been fitted with
thick grab handles and wider doors should a wheelchair become
necessary, of which she had two, right on the premises.

The desk clerk handed us old-fashioned, square steel keys. I
walked, of a fashion, the few steps to my room. Leo went ahead,
as if to go into his room.

'You'll sleep?' Amanda asked.

'I've been well medicated,' I said, offering a yawn as proof. I unlocked my door and went in.

I waited a minute, then stuck my head out. The hall was empty. The door to the back parking lot was only a few feet away.

Leo had pulled the Jeep around to the back. He pushed open the passenger door; I put in my crutches and got in.

'*Que?*' he asked in Spanish. It is a language he does not know.

'*Pronto*,' I responded in kind, sounding every bit as fluent as him.

SIXTY-SIX

'I'm here merely to shift your gears; I get that,' he said after we'd driven a dozen miles in silence. 'You're sure you'll be able to drive the little Ford?'

'It's got an automatic transmission. No shifting.'

I repeated what I'd outlined quickly in front of the clinic while we waited for Amanda. 'Total turnaround time will be less than twelve hours, most of it in darkness.'

'Except the last few, when I cart you back to the ski resort in broad daylight.'

'We alibi each other. We went out to hunt up doughnuts.'

'What about cell tower pings? I saw on TV that cell phones can place people at a site of perpetration.'

'*Perpetration?*' I asked. 'That's a stretch of a word, even for you.'

'Don't obfuscate. You didn't think of that little detail, did you?'

'I've only got tonight to perpetrate.' I told him where I wanted to be picked up so we wouldn't have to use our phones and risk being identified as perpetrators. Still, he handed his over and I removed the batteries from both our phones.

He reached to rattle the key in the Jeep's ashtray. 'This time, remember to leave the key on the floor,' he said.

I took it out and put it in my pocket. 'I hope I'll feel it was a good thing I didn't, the last time,' I said.

'How did Canty get in after you'd been there?'

'Or Delray?'

'Or Delray,' he agreed.

'They must have used Lamm's key,' I think I mumbled, before I fell asleep.

Five hours later, Leo tapped my neck. Thanks to the lingering meds, I'd slept all the way down to Chicago. He'd stopped around the corner from Second Securities. I grabbed the yellow gloves from the back, planted my crutches on the asphalt, and slid out of the Jeep.

'Wondering about surveillance cameras?' he asked.

'I have to risk them,' I said, pulling my knit hat low and tugging up the collar on my pea coat. 'Krantz will probably have his search warrant later this morning.'

I slipped on the gloves and started down the short half-block to Milwaukee Avenue. I hobbled more than I walked, and scraped along more than I hobbled. Ligaments in both legs were torn, and it would be some time before I got the hang of the crutches.

The middle of the block was dark, and I kept my head down as I unlocked the door, but I didn't imagine Krantz would have any difficulty identifying me from surveillance photos, if any were being taken. Men on crutches aren't often out in the middle of the night.

The scent of the glitter girl's cheap perfume and spearmint gum had gone; the place now smelled only of the stench I'd set free when I'd cut through the dead man's plastic shroud. I locked the door behind me and dropped the key to the floor. I wouldn't be going out that way.

I went through the door I'd splintered and into the garage. The smell of death was so thick it stuck to the back of my throat like rotten paste. I pushed what was left of the door closed behind me.

I needed a fast, clear look. I switched on the overhead fluorescents. The car sat in the center of the garage, rank and dented, exactly as I'd left it. I switched off the lights, crutch-walked across the garage to the overhead door's power switch and raised the door. Moonlight flooded into the garage.

I hobbled back to the car, slipped in, twisted the key I'd left in the ignition and backed out into the alley.

I wanted badly to speed away; a corpse was rotting in ripped plastic just three feet from my head. But an open door would draw cops too soon, and I was clutching at the faint hope that time would dissipate the smell before Krantz showed up with his search warrants. I got out, reached in to push the door button, got back in the car and drove to the end of the alley.

Leo was waiting around the corner, as we'd agreed. He must have been crazed with worry as he followed me deeper into the city. I was driving the Carson kill car, with someone else's body in the trunk.

He stayed well back when I turned off and parked on a side street in a run-down neighborhood on Chicago's west side. It was the middle of the night but I knew there were a hundred eyes on me, and him. It couldn't be helped. What I was doing was done often enough, on those blocks. I shut off the engine and left the key in the ignition. Leo shot forward, I got in, and he drove us west to the tollway north to Wisconsin.

He told me to unzip my side curtain as he did the same. I'd brought the stink of the death in that small Ford with me. After a few minutes I started shivering, from the cold and from worry that I'd left some trace of my DNA behind.

'What's wrong with you?' he asked.

'My DNA.'

'I've always worried about that, too,' he said.

SIXTY-SEVEN

Amanda and I met for breakfast at ten the next morning. The dining room was empty except for us, a pitcher of milk, a Thermos of coffee, and several little boxes of barely sweetened, nutritious, thoroughly uninteresting cereal.

'My room is charmingly ancient,' I said, chattering light. 'Real porcelain handles on the pedestal sink, cast-iron bed stand and a scratched maple dresser. Still, this place is quiet as a tomb, optimal for sleeping.'

She poured us coffee. 'What time did you and Leo get in this morning?'

'How did you know?'

She shrugged, trying to grin. 'Your rusted muffler is quite distinctive. I heard it start up ten minutes after we checked in. At first I thought it might be Leo, moving it to park in back, but when I looked out, I couldn't see it anywhere. It wasn't hard to guess that he might have driven off, or who'd gone with him. The only question is why you didn't take the Escalade.'

'We were being clever, and worried you'd go out to the Cadillac for something. Seeing the Jeep gone, you'd simply assume Leo was off in search of doughnuts.'

'Why did you go back if there was no chance for a peek in the trunk?'

'Eliminate a link.'

She touched my wrist. She realized I'd gone to separate Wendell from Lamm, if only a little, if Wendell had even been there at all.

'The other scenario is no better.' I told her about the orange rowboat I'd seen, bailed out and bobbing high on the water at Lamm's camp.

'It's why I'm waiting up here. I'm expecting he could be in a lake,' she said, looking away.

Her eyes were clear; her chin was raised. In that instant, I could see the chief executive she was destined to be. 'My father drove Jim Whitman home,' she said.

'I take that as proof of his innocence. Your father is not stupid. As I told you before, he wouldn't have risked driving Whitman if he'd had any part in killing him.'

'You're sure?'

'As much as I'm sure Whitman's death shocked your father into hiring Eugene Small at the end of January.'

'Two weeks later, Carson got killed.'

'And Eugene Small was murdered two weeks after that. It made your father frantic.'

'Richie Bales killed Small?'

'I told Krantz it was either Bales, looking to get Small out of the way so he could extort money from Lamm; Lamm himself, because Small had learned too much; or Canty, on Lamm's orders. Each had motive.'

'Why did my father come up here?'

'I told Krantz that either Krantz's threat to prosecute him for

Lamm's crimes sent him into a rage, to come up and confront his false friend, or Richie Bales got to him, still posing as a cop, demanding your father come up on one pretext or another, perhaps to help Bales locate Lamm.

'There's no chance my father is still alive?'

The soft way she was asking sent my mind back to the small photos I'd seen in Wendell's study, of the little girl she'd been, clutching a small cluster of blue balloons. The balloons would have soon gone away; there was never any helping that. Just like there was no way of helping her much now.

She said she was anxious to drive back to Bent Lake, to track down the sheriff. It was more likely she wanted to be alone, to prepare herself for a call from the sheriff. As I hobbled to walk her to the lobby door, we heard the resort manager yelling from a private office. 'I don't care where the hell he is. You tell him to get out here now with glass and new locks.' A desk phone was then banged down in anger.

'Tell the sheriff about that bailed-out rowboat,' I said by the front door, 'though he's already searching the lakes for Canty.'

'What's worse, Dek? Finding my father in a car, or in a lake?'

I shook my head. There could never be an answer to that.

SIXTY-EIGHT

Leo found me at twelve-thirty in the lobby, eating unsweetened Cheerios, dry, and watching television. There had been no report of a corpse being discovered in a car in Chicago, nor on the websites I'd snagged on my cell phone. Then again, it had been that kind of neighborhood.

He curled a forefinger for me to stand up, and went to the front desk to check out. 'Excellent beds you have here; I can't remember the last time I slept a solid twelve hours,' he said, as though he hadn't just done a round trip to Chicago to partake in the felonious transport of a corpse.

'You hear anything last night?' the resort manager asked. It was the same question she'd asked me, after Amanda left.

'I was out cold for twelve hours,' he said again. 'What happened?'

'Damned kids, looking for booze. They broke in the kitchen door.'

'Did they get away with much?'

She shook her head. 'That's just it: I can't see where anything was taken, other than maybe a box of crackers and a jar of peanut butter. Damn, dumb bored kids, looking for a thrill.'

Outside, I said to Leo, 'Clever, you saying that about being asleep for the whole night. Twice.'

'Cleverness is one of my many middle names,' he said.

'Amanda heard us leave.'

'Let's hope the desk lady did not,' he said, cleverness draining from his face. Then, 'No news?'

'Nothing on television or on the Internet.'

'I checked the Internet, too, after I went out to the Escalade earlier. No word of a car being found, boosted and stripped, with a body in the trunk.'

We went outside. 'Don't blow a tire; you're driving with no spare,' I said, peering into the back as he climbed into the Jeep. He'd put the Jeep's spare in the back, and covered it with my yellow rain poncho.

'Caution is another of my middle names,' he said, and took off for Chicago.

I called Jenny from the terrace.

'Leo had implied your vocal chords were healthy enough to call before now,' she said.

'It's been hectic.'

'Yes, that story,' she said. 'Tell me.'

'It's unresolved, and potentially damaging.'

'You're worried about Amanda?' she asked.

'And her father.'

'Where are you exactly?'

'A ski resort in the piney woods of Wisconsin.'

'Alone?'

'Amanda's here. Leo just left.'

'I'm going to be so proud to not ask the next question.'

'Separate rooms,' I said.

'This is so like high school.'

'You rented rooms in high school?'

Jenny laughed before the newswoman, never far away, took over again. 'Give me something for the future.'

I told her all of it.

'The wires out of Chicago have barely scratched the surface of this,' she said when I was done.

'I need you to watch those wires.'

'For a stolen car found stripped, with a body in the trunk.'

'With luck, they'll find it today, and then we'll know.'

'Are we still talking about you coming to San Francisco sometime?'

'Seafood on the Wharf.'

'There could be that,' she said, hanging up and leaving me to wonder why I'd ever want to waste time going to the Wharf.

SIXTY-NINE

Amanda got back just before dark, red-eyed and hollow-cheeked. She'd been gone eight hours, but she said it seemed she'd been gone twenty. We sat at the bar in the deserted, dark lounge and had drinks – a whiskey and water for her, a med-friendly ginger ale for me – that the resort manager had come in to make for us.

Amanda had brought two bags. One was plastic, and contained a loaf of rye bread, a jar of Dijon mustard and an orange brick of Wisconsin's official sustenance, cheddar cheese. The other bag was paper, and well worn. She'd ducked into an antique store that displayed used books in the window, and bought a collection of poems by somebody I'd never heard of, a guide to making soups, and a history of World Wars One and Two condensed into one hundred pages. She tried a big smile as she took out the last book, an old British mystery novel that she said was written when sexual activity was described with vague movements of eyebrows and fluttering hands, though she promised to take that one away if it set my own eyebrows and hands to twitching.

'How rough was your day?' I asked.

'Too many lakes,' she said.

'Maybe moving the car was dumb.'

'No; it was risky, and daring, and I love you for it.' Then, likely realizing she'd said something she didn't mean to say, she added, 'I called my office every hour. I said only that my father was up here and might have gotten stranded on one of the small lakes. Of course, they've been watching the news . . .'

'Not unusual. Most people in Chicago are following the Confessors' Club story.'

'No one said anything, but it would be impossible for them not to assume my father's caught up in all of that.'

We tried making jokes about what I might learn from the books she'd bought but mostly we just made silence.

Agent Krantz found us at eight o'clock, lapsed into sitting stiffly at the bar like two strangers on a train. He had to perch on the other side of Amanda because I'd taken the stool at the end of the bar so I could lean against the wall. The manager came in and Krantz ordered a low-carb beer. It figured.

'I assumed you'd gone back to Chicago,' I said, by way of an enthusiastic greeting.

'I promised we'd talk again today, and I didn't want to disappoint,' he said, taking a pull at the beer and not grimacing. 'There have been developments.'

Amanda glanced sharply at him.

'No news about your father, I'm afraid,' Krantz said quickly.

'Herman Canty?' I asked.

'Nor him, either, though the sheriff's people did find a note that Canty's girlfriend, a Wanda something, taped to the door at the Loons' Rest. It said she was off on an adventure of some sort.'

'That's a development for sure,' I said, agreeably.

'Except Canty's truck was found parked on a side street.'

'In plain view?'

He nodded.

'Wow,' I said. 'There's been some ace sleuthing done.'

Undeterred, he said, 'One of those tool bin things is bolted inside the truck bed, behind the rear window. Want to guess what was in it?'

'Not tools,' I said, 'because people around here say Canty never did much.'

'There was a freshly packed duffel bag inside. Our Mr Canty was planning a trip.'

'With the lovely Wanda, as her note said?'

'Could be, or not could be. That is the question.'

I groaned, but said nothing to spoil the taste of his low-carb beer.

'There was a fresh set of tire tracks in the fire lane closest to Lamm's camp, made by tires almost bald of tread,' he said. 'Jeep tires, just like yours, Elstrom. And just a few feet away, we found evidence that someone had been digging at the base of a tree.'

'I told you I got trussed up in Lamm's cottage. The fire lane was where I parked. As for the digging, there are beavers and raccoons up here.'

'One of my men had a peek inside your Jeep earlier this morning.'

'I've been meaning to clean out all those hamburger wrappers.'

'Why is your spare tire inside, instead of mounted on the bracket on the back?'

'It's out of air,' I said.

'And why was the hood warm?'

Amanda inhaled sharply, but stared straight ahead.

'From the sun,' I said, patting the crutches I'd leaned against the wall. 'Obviously I can't drive.'

He leaned forward so he see could more directly past Amanda. 'My warrant came through to search Second Securities.'

'What did you find?' I leaned back so he'd either have to almost lie across the bar to maintain eye contact, or lean backward and risk tipping over. It was immature and felt appropriate.

He chose to lean back. 'Not much except the identity of a girl who worked there. She told an odd story. The front door is all glass, and has a mail slot in the metal at the very bottom. She hadn't been paid the wages she was owed, so she walked out, pushing the key inside the mail slot after locking up for the last time. Later, she realized she'd left behind a bottle of black nail polish. She went back to reach in for the key so she could retrieve the nail polish, but the key was gone.'

'Another employee opened up, and took the key?'

'She was the only employee. Here's the odd part, Elstrom: When my agents arrived there this morning, the key was lying inside the locked front door, right where the girl said she'd left it.'

'Obviously, the key was there all the time,' I offered reasonably. 'The girl just got confused.'

'Or an intruder showed up after the girl quit, snagged the key through the mail slot, used it to go in the front door, locked that, and left by the garage. Since there were no signs of forced entry, it's a plausible explanation, especially since . . .' He let the thought dangle, prompting.

'Yes?' I asked.

'There were signs of forced entry inside. Someone smashed the inner door to get in the garage. The girl said it hadn't been that way when she worked there, and that it was always locked.'

'What did you find in the garage? More tire treads?'

'Fresh ones, pulling out. And little rubber cuppy marks.'

'Little rubber *what*?'

'Concentric circles, three of them, totaling an inch and three-quarters in diameter.' He pointed to my crutches, leaning against the wall. 'Exactly the sort of marks made by the rubber caps they put on the tips of crutches, to prevent them from slipping.'

I could see Amanda had caught her breath. I wanted to hold my own, too, for fear Krantz was going to ask to see my crutches.

'Trouble is, almost every crutch manufacturer uses those same caps,' he said, looking straight at my eyes. 'That garage smells like something's been dead in there for quite some time.'

'What was it?'

'We found nothing . . . yet.' He took another maddeningly delighted pull on his beer. 'Still, you know what's even more bothersome than that?'

'Apparently not your low-carb beer,' I said.

He frowned, but only a little. Obviously they spent hours teaching self-control at IRS Agent school. 'It's the two-million-dollar cash payout on Grant Carson's life.'

'Why?'

'Only one million dollars was found in that case in the Buick.'

'You said that at the clinic.'

'A number which you confirmed at the time.'

'I was medicated and confused.'

'I was in the local tap in Bent Lake, having a brew with the locals—'

'Low carb?' I interrupted.

'They didn't have any—' He caught himself and stopped. Then, 'They remembered you, especially your wit. Seems you came in carrying a metal case that looks exactly like the one we recovered from the Buick. When they asked you what was in it, you cracked them up by saying you had two million dollars in there.'

'That's right.'

'That's right?' Krantz set down his beer.

'My wit did sparkle that evening,' I said.

Amanda laughed, just once, but continued to stare straight ahead at the glasses gathering dust above the bar.

'I could haul you down to Chicago, keep you for forty-eight hours.'

'I had my briefcase in the bar that night. Somebody stole it from my Jeep when I was in the clinic.'

Krantz looked at me, and looked at Amanda. He stood up, knocked back the last of his de-carbed beer and left, looking less happy than when he'd arrived.

'What's the deal with the second million he keeps asking about?' Amanda said.

I shook my head; I was paranoid about a sticky microphone Krantz might have left behind. We ate cheese and bread and talked about World Wars One and Two, and then we finished our drinks and went outside where there would be only cheese-fed, native Wisconsin insects and not bugs imported from Chicago, made of plastic, batteries and bits of metal.

She touched my hand, questioning. 'What happened to the other half of the two million we found at Second Securities?'

'I held that half back to bargain with, in case I got double-crossed about where your father was,' I said.

'And now?'

'Somebody's owed something out of this,' I said.

SEVENTY

T he meds couldn't put me to sleep that night. I eased onto my good side to read the bedside alarm clock. If it was close enough to dawn I'd quit struggling to sleep and get up to read about soups and wars and sleuthing Brits.

No red numerals shone from the top of the nightstand. The alarm clock had died.

I reached to switch on the lamp. The lamp didn't work. The power to my room was out.

I found my phone. It was four-fifteen.

A moment after I laid back, I heard something click faintly, one-two, in fast succession, out in the hall – followed, after a delay, by a third, softer sound, a thud. Perhaps someone was out there, checking on the power. Then I remembered that there was no staff in the resort, except for the manager, and she'd likely be asleep in her rooms. It was the middle of the night.

There were no other guests, either, except for Amanda, probably also sound asleep.

And me, sleepless, with jitters that would jump at anything.

One-two; another pair of clicks came, followed again by the third sound, the soft thud.

I grabbed my crutches from the other side of the bed, and levered myself to stand. Moving had set the stitched bullet wound in my left arm and the torn ligaments in my legs to throbbing. I waited until I'd steadied and hobbled to the window.

The resort was dark. The entire building had lost power. No one was awake to notice.

Except for me.

Click-click; the new sounds seemed slightly louder now. Again, they were followed by a strange soft thud. I started toward the door.

The fourth pair of fast clicks came when I was still only halfway across. Definitely louder, definitely closer.

By the time I got to the door and pressed my ear against it, I was sweating like a man standing under a hot August sun. Fifth and sixth sets of noises had come, increasingly louder. By now I'd recognized them for what they were: doors were being unlocked with one of the big, square-cut metal keys. The first click was the sound of the lock bolt retracting, the second the sound of the bolt snapping forward after the door was opened. The soft thud following each delay was the sound of the door being gently closed.

Rooms were being searched.

'Damned dumb, bored kids, looking for booze,' the resort manager had called the intruders who'd broken in.

Damned dumb, bored kids didn't search an empty resort, room by room, looking for booze.

I pressed my eye to the magnified peep-hole. A light flashed for an instant, out in the hall. Tiny prickles shot across my scalp as I understood. Someone was using a pencil beam flashlight to quickly scan the rooms.

A new pair of clicks came loud. And, after only a second, the thud.

He'd spotted my Jeep parked in the lot, broken in for food, and for sanctuary. Until everyone was asleep.

The next clicks came loudest of all. I could hear him through the wall. He'd opened the room next door. Too soon, the soft thud came. He'd closed the door.

I could hear him breathe, out in the hall.

I pressed against the wall, steadying, seeing the faint low shape of the bed – my unmade bed. In an instant's flash of his light, he'd know I was there.

Metal scratched on my door. He'd slipped the master key into my lock.

I leaned one crutch against the wall, pressed back to brace myself, and raised the other crutch like a bat.

First click; the bolt retracted.

Second click; the bolt sprung back out. The door was opening.

His breathing was heavy, labored, not two feet from my face.

The pencil beam of light moved unsteadily, low across the carpet toward the bed.

The beam halted. He sucked in air. His flashlight had found my shoes, next to the bed.

The floor creaked as he stepped softly into the room.

SEVENTY-ONE

I swung my crutch like I was swinging for the moon, aiming high where I hoped was a head. I hit him with such force that the impact knocked the crutch out of my hands and slammed me back against the wall.

He shrieked, dropping his flashlight, but he didn't go down. The black shape of him turned on me like a monster, stretching his arms out for me like giant bat wings. I pushed off from the wall and half charged, half fell onto him. We went down with me on top, beating at his face with my good right fist, once, twice, three times, until I connected with something small. It crunched. I'd caught his nose, shattered a bone.

Exhaling hard, whistling wet through his nose, he raised up his hands to flail at my head.

I had no strength; my body was on fire with pain. I had to get away. But his giant hands reached up and found my neck. I beat down at his smashed wet nose again. He pushed me off, rolled on to his side and then onto his belly, to get up, to kick at my head.

I clambered on his back, put a knee into the small of it, and grabbed the hair at the back of his head with my good right hand, to force him down on his chest.

He reared back to raise his knees to buck me off. I dropped my hands around him, down to the carpet to steady myself, and found aluminum with both hands. The crutch that had been knocked from my hands now lay perpendicular under his chest. Tugging at the crosswise crutch with both hands, I forced my knee deeper into his back. My gunshot arm and torn legs raged in pain. But to let up was to die.

He took in a great breath, raised his head and got his knees up, six, eight inches, contorting into the beginning of an arch, but it was no good. I had him pinned. He slammed down face flat on the carpet, except now the front of his neck lay on the crutch.

Pushing all my weight through my knee deep into the small of his back, I tugged the crutch hard up under his neck. Hot blood flooded down my left arm; my stitches had torn loose from my flesh.

His right hand fluttered up, weak, trying to loosen my grip.

'Die, you son of a bitch,' I heard myself scream to the body writhing beneath me. 'Die!'

Something snapped loudly, wonderfully. The hand that had been flailing up to find me fell limp. I did not let up. I let the blood run hot down my left arm; I let my torn legs rage in pain. I tugged on both sides of the crutch until I could tug no more. And then I counted to a hundred.

Finally, I had nothing left. I fell off him and began to crawl out of my room. I could hear nothing but the frantic gasping of my own breathing.

At some point I tried to rise, at least up to my knees, to head down the hall, to find Amanda. Surely he'd found her first. But I had no strength. I slumped back to the floor and sort of rolled, kicked and crawled the dozen yards to the lobby.

There was a fire extinguisher mounted on the wall. And a fire alarm. I reached up and managed to pull the red handle down on the alarm.

Horns on, battery back-ups sounded down both halls. White lights flashed like lightning strikes.

I fell back; I could do no more.

'Dek?' Amanda's voice sounded after a time, from far away. Her breath found my cheek, on the floor. 'He's here?'

She didn't ask who; the blood running out of my torn left arm had already told her.

'The Escalade,' I managed to whisper. 'Get us inside, lock the doors, drive us away.'

Surely the man could not be killed. Surely he was still alive.

She ran to get her keys, knelt to help me up, and half dragged me out the lobby door and across the parking lot to the Escalade.

'Just lock the doors,' I said, after I'd crawled up onto the seat. Bright white lights were flashing everywhere, under the eaves, on the walls, out through the windows from inside.

I passed out.

SEVENTY-TWO

I'd killed.

I'd snapped Canty's neck with my crutch; his back with my knee. With time, I'd feel something more about that. For now, all I felt was numb.

After being re-stitched and re-bedded for the rest of the night at the clinic, Amanda was allowed to return me to the ski resort the next afternoon. However clumsily I'd walk-hobbled before, I was now bound to a motorized wheelchair, since I could only use my right hand. The resort manager's niece had moved us into a nice, wheelchair-accessible two-bedroom suite, just off the lobby. No charge for the upgrade or the motorized wheelchair, the niece said, though I was sure she would have been happier if she'd been allowed to tow me to the top of the highest ski run and push me over the back edge. I'd brought horror to the log resort. After cutting the resort's power and telephone landlines, Canty had beaten her aunt senseless before taking her master key.

Amanda and I slept well enough, separately. I supposed she was as unsettled as I by our close proximity, and how easily some of the old mannerisms and rituals we'd shared in marriage wanted to return. But she had much bigger worries, waiting for word of her father. There had been no news, either from the local sheriff, or from the cops in Chicago reporting a body found stuffed in a stolen car.

And we slept safe. Sheriff's deputies from two surrounding counties, supplemented by a special detachment of two armed special agents from the IRS, were now staying at the resort. I quickly grew fond of the deputies; they brought doughnuts, freshly fried and often topped with sprinkles.

Krantz's special agents, though, were another matter. They were a grim-faced pair, dispatched ostensibly to be vigilant, but more likely sent for what they might overhear. Krantz's frustration with me was growing exponentially. He was certain I knew plenty, but without Wendell around to squeeze, and nothing otherwise to link me to Eugene Small, Arthur Lamm or the Carson payout, he'd resorted to posting the two agents to hang around the lodge and pretend they weren't listening.

I'd found their bugs right away, one stuck under my nightstand, another stuck under Amanda's. I was tempted to reposition them on either sides of the toilet, to offer a stereophonic listening experience, but I left them where I'd found them. Amanda and I made sure to never discuss anything of substance in our small suite, for I was certain Krantz had planted more bugs.

The waiting drove Leo nuts, too, back in Rivertown. He enlisted Endora, no stranger from her modeling days to changing her look, to rent a car and look down the street where I'd abandoned the small Ford, while he rode ducked down in back. He then called me from an unfamiliar number.

'Burner phone,' he whispered. 'Forty bucks at Walmart. I'll toss it after this call.'

'But you called me on my regular phone,' I said, wanting to laugh for the first time since Canty.

'The eagle has flown,' he murmured.

Meaning the small Ford was gone. I could only marvel that Chicago's car thieves were as strong-stomached as its gang murderers. They'd boosted the car, likely stripped it, and with luck, turned it into a recyclable steel cube, albeit one that was slightly leaking.

Amanda said nothing of it. Or much about anything else. She left early each of the next three mornings to check on the sheriff's search plans for the day. After that, I think she just drove, or stopped somewhere. I never asked, and she never offered. She expressed no rage at her father, or at the world, or at me. She ate next to nothing, and I think slept little. Her hands trembled almost continuously. It was like that, waiting.

Krantz took a room at the lodge. He visited my mouth, in the wheelchair, in the lobby, twice a day in hope the new meds I'd been given had relaxed it enough to offer up more of what he was sure I knew.

'Where's Phelps?' he asked right off on the first, second and third mornings and afternoons after I'd killed Canty.

'The television news says Lamm has left the country,' I said, each time.

'Did I tell you the receptionist at Second Securities remembers you?'

'The one who couldn't remember her nail polish, or where she'd left a key?'

'I'll be bringing her in to look at you through a mirror.'

'No need. I went there, but I didn't break in, Krantz. I walked in through the front door.'

'Spewing some cocked-up story about being an inspector. You didn't say anything about that when we first spoke at the clinic. Withholding information from a federal investigation is prosecutable.'

'Meds,' I said. 'They made me forgetful.'

And so it went for those three mornings and three nights. Then, very early on the fourth day, the sheriff called to give Amanda directions to a tiny lake.

We packed what little we had and went out to the Escalade. I got behind the wheel. The stitches in my arm were holding, and the new fissures in my torn leg ligaments were healing. It was not a day for Amanda to drive.

'The sheriff will let you leave, afterward?' she asked, after we'd gone a mile.

'He termed what I'd done to Herman Canty "justifiable." I might not even have to come up for the inquest.'

'And Krantz?'

'He said he'll arrest me in Chicago.'

'He was kidding?'

'Krantz has difficulty with humor.'

'That low-carb business,' she said, struggling, looking straight ahead. No one should ever be required to be strong enough to look at someone fished dead from a lake.

Parked on the dirt road leading to the water were two county cruisers, Krantz's black Crown Victoria, an ambulance and the county medical examiner's van. The sheriff walked over, opened my door and leaned in. 'Mr Elstrom can handle this, Ms Phelps.'

'Yes, but who has ever been able to handle Mr Elstrom?' Her voice was surprisingly calm, forcing the new joke. She remained seated.

The sheriff had a high-wheeled off-road vehicle brought up and a paramedic got in with us. It was a rough five-minute drive through tall weeds to the edge of a small lake.

'No one ever comes to this lake, because they can't get to it,' the sheriff said. 'It's more like a retention pond that fills when there's been a lot of rain, and only then does it connect with the lakes to the north.'

They helped me stand, and we walked, of a fashion, to the shore. By then I was sweating.

They had them face down; two bodies on two tarps dragged from the edge of the lake, covered with other tarps. The paramedic bent to pull back the one covering the corpse closest to me.

Wanda screamed back at me in silent rigor.

'Not that one, you idiot,' the sheriff yelled at the paramedic. Then, to me, 'She knew too much, and with a million dollars, Canty must have figured he could afford better.'

The paramedic moved to uncover the body lying past Wanda.

I'm not good with ruined corpses. To buy time for a few deep breaths, I focused on the watch on his wrist. A Rolex with that much gold cost more than ten thousand dollars, and it looked to still be keeping perfect time. I supposed that would be expected. Certainly it was water resistant to a depth far greater than the shallows at the raw end of the small lake, and the gentle lapping of the water through the rushes was more than enough to engage the self-winding mechanism. It was a gentleman's wristwatch, designed for a wealthy man, a man of nuance, a man who need make only subtle gestures, even in death.

He had dressed well, his last day. His gray gabardine trousers were of the finest wool, light for the warm temperatures. Looking for identification, they'd turned back the label on his white shirt. It was from Pink's, on Jermyn Street in London. The shoes, I knew from Amanda, were English, too: lace-up broughams of sturdy leather that would have once held a high polish.

The clothes and shoes, of course, had not fared as well as the wristwatch. The press had gone from the trousers, and here and there tiny bits of milky flesh protruded where the wool had been abraded by the barky texture of the water reeds. The shirt was now a putrid green, mossed and dirtied by the muck at the shore. And the leather of his shoes had puckered and blistered, for even the finest of leathers, no matter how well oiled, are not meant to withstand submersion.

They turned him over. That part of his face closest to the bullet hole was gone, nibbled away in tiny bites by the sunny fish and microscopic urchins that worked the shore of the small lake.

I nodded and the paramedic covered him again.

'They were both shot somewhere else, then dumped in this lake by someone in a boat.' Krantz had come up to join us.

'An orange rowboat, recently bailed out,' I said.

The sheriff looked at me and nodded. 'Canty, in Lamm's boat,' he said.

The medical examiner held out two spent bullets for the sheriff to see. 'We'll have them tested,' he said, 'but they're the same caliber as those we found in Bales, and in . . .' He gestured toward me, the meat that had also caught a bullet from Canty's gun.

'Canty, for sure,' the sheriff said.

'Can you identify time of death?' I asked the medical examiner, to be certain.

Krantz looked sharply at me.

'Actually, yes, for both,' the medical examiner said.

And then I turned on my crutches, and started the slow walk back down the pressed tracks we'd just made, alone. No one had thought to offer to help me back. And that was good. I needed to understand all I'd just heard. And all I now believed.

At the car, I slid my crutches in back, and got in behind the wheel.

Amanda said nothing, the gold flecks in her eyes impossible to see behind the tears.

'Time to go back to Chicago,' I said.

'Do not start the car,' she said.

SEVENTY-THREE

'Tell me what happened up here, all of it, right now,' Amanda said in a surprisingly strong voice. 'In this, his last place.'

I let my hand fall away from the ignition switch. 'He's dead. One bullet.'

'Who shot him?'

'Canty. Delray was never a killer,' I said, sure of that and most everything else, now.

'From the beginning at Second Securities then, as best you see it.'

'Canty must have driven Lamm down to Chicago to convert the Carson check to cash, and probably to help Lamm leave the country from there. Except Canty saw an opportunity to change his own life instead. He killed Lamm, stuffed him in the trunk of the Carson kill car along with the cash, and came back up here to erase the only other person who knew what he'd been up to.'

'Wanda.'

'Unfortunately for Canty, Richie Bales was up here by then, looking for Lamm. He surprised Canty, maybe as Canty was bailing the boat to take Wanda on her last ride, or maybe when Canty got back to the dock after disposing of her. Canty must have breathed a huge sigh of relief when Richie told him he wanted half the payout. Don't forget, Canty still thought Richie was a cop, and saw him as one who could be bought off.'

'So they drove down to Second Securities to split the money?'

'Where, surprise, surprise, Canty saw the splintered door and the trashed car and thought the money had gone forever, and with it his hopes for getting out of the country a rich man. Richie, though, took a broader view.'

'Meaning he saw how you could have learned through your insurance contracts that Second Securities was the Carson beneficiary, and gotten to the money ahead of them.'

'And he saw how he could use your father to get that money back.'

'All he had to do was lure my father up here to hold as hostage,' she said.

'I'll bet checking your father's phone records will show your father received a call from a burner phone just a few minutes before he left Lake Forest for work that Thursday morning. That would have been Richie, who your father still believed was a cop named Delray Delmar, telling him some of his and Arthur's legal problems might go away if he'd come up to Bent Lake to talk to him and Arthur.'

'Krantz had already frightened my father when he'd called for an appointment, threatening to prosecute him for Arthur's crimes because my father owned half of Lamm's agency.'

'Between Krantz and Richie, it was enough to induce sudden panic in your father. He shot up to Bent Lake with no hesitation.'

'When was my father killed?'

'As soon as he arrived up here, according to the medical examiner's timeline. They didn't need to keep your father alive to lure me up here with the money.'

She looked out the window. 'What could anyone have done?' she asked.

It was the question I knew she would ask, and the one I most feared. I took a breath. 'I wish I'd moved slower.'

She turned to look at me. 'That Tuesday, Confessors' Club day?'

'No. The day before, Monday, when I'd been in such a rush to call Keller.'

'You were in a panic; worried that Lamm would kill again the next night.'

'I didn't know Lamm was already dead, so I called Keller on Monday. On Tuesday morning, early, your father called me, furious. I got furious right back at him, saying he'd kept what he knew to himself for too long. He hung up on me before I could tell him that Delray Delmar was a fraud.'

'Because if he'd known Richie was no cop, he never would have come up here?'

'Yes.'

I waited for a moment and then for another, but there was nothing more to say. And so I started the engine and swung around to head back to Chicago.

Neither of us spoke the whole way down.

SEVENTY-FOUR

Debbie Goring came by a week after I'd gotten back from Wisconsin. It was eleven in the morning and I was on the bench by the river, watching Leo up in the purple ash. He was sawing off one of its main limbs. I'd come back from up north to find seven more leaves curled on the ground, but I fought the idea of cutting down the tree. There'd been too much death that spring.

She tossed a thick, letter-sized white envelope on the bench next to me and sat down. 'I was expecting to hear from you,' she rasped.

'I was vacationing, up in Wisconsin.'

'So I read in the newspapers. You got shot, pushed a killer off a bridge with your car and then snapped his neck and broke his back a few days later.'

'The vacation brochures are right: there's always plenty to do in Wisconsin.'

Debbie looked up at the ash. Leo, wearing an orange Sesame Street T-shirt, had begun hamming it up like a monkey, waving his bow saw at the front of the turret. Someone else had arrived.

'What's wrong with him?' she asked.

'His clothes, mostly.'

She turned back to me. 'Even though I received that anonymous cashier's check for a hundred grand—'

'Wendell Phelps sent you that check, though it need never be proved,' I interrupted.

'Then it's a shame, his death,' she said. 'Anyway, that check was a damned fine thing to receive, don't get me wrong, but I was still bummed thinking no one would ever be prosecuted for killing my father,' she said. 'Then I heard about your little foray into the woods. Now, at least, it might become obvious that my father was murdered.'

'It will never go to trial without Lamm. And Small and Richie Bales are dead.'

'Arthur Lamm has escaped, scot-free?'

'That's what everyone is saying.' Only Leo, Amanda and I knew that Arthur Lamm had escaped nothing. The Carson kill car had never been recovered, and by now I was daring to believe that it had been compressed to a small steel cube in a scrap yard friendly to car thieves, and that Lamm was on his way to becoming a doorknob spindle or perhaps part of a toaster.

She turned to look into my eyes. 'Everybody's saying also that Lamm escaped with a million dollars that's missing from Grant Carson's insurance.' She lit a Camel and blew smoke at the Willahock.

Up in the ash, Leo was smiling down. Amanda had come around the side of the turret followed by a thickset man in a black suit. Wendell's corporation had lost no time imposing a security detail on its new largest shareholder.

Amanda and I had not spoken one word since leaving Bent Lake, and when she dropped me at the turret, I was not sure she'd ever speak to me again.

'I told myself that I'd have to live with Lamm's permanent disappearance,' Debbie went on, 'but then, this morning, a messenger from a bonded delivery service brought me a box.'

Amanda glanced only briefly at me and went on talking up to Leo.

'Want to guess what was in the box I got?' Debbie asked behind a puff of smoke.

'Flowers?'

'Something that smells even better. Here, take a whiff.' She picked up the envelope, opened the flap, and fanned the contents inside with her thumb.

I made a sniffing noise, but kept my eyes on Amanda. She'd opened a small rectangular box and was holding up its contents to show Leo, whose face had turned serious.

I turned back to Debbie. I couldn't smell anything other than cigarette smoke.

'Smells like a tire, doesn't it?' Debbie said.

'Why would it smell like a tire?'

'Look closely, Mr Elstrom. They even have little bits of rubber dust on them, like from the inside of a tire.'

'Interesting,' I said.

'Got any idea why these might have been inside a tire?'

'Not a clue.' I pushed myself up to stand. I'd been off the crutches for three days, but that was more from temperament than prudence. I needed to walk, to take steps to get on with my life.

'Me, neither.' Debbie Goring flicked her cigarette butt in the river and stood up, too. 'Two million in insurance was what I had coming, but a million cash, even smelling like the inside of a tire, made me a damn sight happier than when I first woke up.' She reached for my wrist, slapped the thick white envelope into my hand and started to walk away.

'Wait,' I said. I looked closely into the envelope. There were eleven packets of currency inside. Fifty-five thousand dollars.

She came back. I extracted one packet – five thousand – and jammed it into my khakis. I held out the envelope to her.

She backed away. 'No, no, Elstrom. Our deal was five per cent. You earned that, off the cashier's check and the contents of this morning's delivery.'

'The papers mentioned an IRS agent named Krantz?'

She nodded.

'He'd planned on making a big, career-boosting arrest of Arthur Lamm for income tax evasion. He'll seize many of Lamm's assets, but Krantz will be criticized for letting four million dollars get sent to Grand Cayman, where it can never be seized by the IRS. Krantz did recover a million dollars from Wendell Phelps's Buick, but there's no proof that it was the Carson payout, so he'll never be able to seize that either.'

A huge grin lit up her face. 'The newspapers are saying Lamm used the other half of that insurance money to get away. You saying you can't always believe what you read in the papers?'

'Krantz will hunt for that missing million for the rest of his days because he doubts that Lamm got away. He thinks I know something about that, and he'll be watching me and my tax returns for years. If he finds me with money I can't explain, he'll redouble his efforts to nail me, along with anyone else he thinks might know something.'

'Meaning me?'

'Meaning anyone connected with the case that shows sudden signs of wealth.' I pressed the envelope into her hands. 'Be prudent, Debbie. Hide it all in a dozen places, trickle it out in small amounts over a lot of years, for clothes and tuition and a vacation every once in a while.'

'As my father would have wanted.'

'Yes.'

Her eyes got wet, and she stepped forward like she was going to kiss me. But reason took hold, and she turned. 'You're not half bad, Elstrom,' she called back, as she disappeared around the front of the turret.

I started towards the ash, un-crutched but wobbling. Amanda met me halfway.

'I noticed your spare tire is back on your Jeep,' she said.

'It just needed new air.'

'I'll bet. That happy woman was Debbie Goring?' she asked.

'She gave me five grand.'

'How much did she want to give you?'

I looked up the hill, past the turret. A black limousine was idling at the curb. No doubt the driver was armed, just like the bodyguard who'd followed her down the hill and now stood a few vigilant steps away. Her new life had begun.

When I didn't answer, she said, 'I checked my father's incoming calls. He got a call from a burner phone thirty minutes before he left for Bent Lake.'

'Delray Delmar, the fake cop,' I said. 'Your father was a good man.'

'You always find the good, don't you, Dek?'

'You're going to do fine as a tycoon,' I said.

'There will be bumps. The Pig Lady's lawyer called this morning, saying she's going to sue for all of it. Otherwise, he said, she's going to go hungry.'

'Send her lettuce and tomatoes. Properly frugal, she can have BLTs for years.'

Amanda laughed at that, a good, long, healing laugh. She handed me the small white box.

A great creak came from the tree. Leo had stopped sawing.

'How many leaves remain?' she asked.

'Six,' I said, 'per this morning's count.'

'You're cutting off only one limb?'

'It's a minor setback, nothing terminal.'

Leo kicked the limb. We watched it fall. The tree, now with only one limb, looked like the hands on a clock, set at ten to six.

She kissed me, maybe longer than she'd ever kissed me before.

I looked at the gold flecks in her eyes.

'I need to accept that I never knew my father,' she said.

'You know enough.'

I walked with her, and the bodyguard behind us, up the hill.

'That ash will survive, Dek?' she asked, at the limo.

'Perhaps stronger than before.'

The bodyguard opened the front passenger door.

'Aren't you going to open your gift?' she asked.

I did.

She got in front, next to the driver. The guard closed her door, and got in back. In time, she'd learn to ride in back.

Her car pulled away, and in a minute it had disappeared. I looked down at the sunny-colored, yellow bow tie, wondering if it was more of a declaration than a gift, and thinking of my other bow tie, the purple one hanging on a nail in my almost-finished closet.

I started back down to the river, to look some more at the water and at Leo up in a tree, moving as best I could, one step at a time.

Lightning Source UK Ltd.
Milton Keynes UK
UKOW04f0620110116

266139UK00001B/15/P